T0137845

Lecture Notes of the Institute for Computer Sciences, Social Informatics and Telecommunications Engineering 412

More information about this series at https://link.springer.com/bookseries/8197

Mulatu Liyew Berihun (Ed.)

Advances of Science and Technology

9th EAI International Conference, ICAST 2021
Hybrid Event, Bahir Dar, Ethiopia, August 27–29, 2021
Proceedings, Part II

 Springer

Editor
Mulatu Liyew Berihun
Bahir Dar Institute of Technology, Faculty of Civil
and Water Resource Engineering
Bahir Dar University
Bahir Dar, Ethiopia

ISSN 1867-8211   ISSN 1867-822X (electronic)
Lecture Notes of the Institute for Computer Sciences, Social Informatics
and Telecommunications Engineering
ISBN 978-3-030-93711-9   ISBN 978-3-030-93712-6 (eBook)
https://doi.org/10.1007/978-3-030-93712-6

This Springer imprint is published by the registered company Springer Nature Switzerland AG
The registered company address is: Gewerbestrasse 11, 6330 Cham, Switzerland

Preface

We are delighted to introduce the proceedings of the ninth edition of the EAI International Conference on Advancements of Science and Technology (EAI ICAST 2021). EAI ICAST 2021 is an annual conference that takes place at Bahir Dar Institute of Technology, Bahir Dar University, Bahir Dar, Ethiopia. The conference covers topical science and technology issues and has brought together researchers, engineers, developers, practitioners, scholars, scientists, and academicians from around the world.

The technical program of EAI ICAST 2021 consisted of seven main tracks: Track 1, Chemical, Food and Bioprocess Engineering; Track 2, Electrical and Electronics Engineering; Track 3, ICT, Software and Hardware Engineering; Track 4, Civil, Water Resources, and Environmental Engineering; Track 5, Mechanical and Industrial Engineering; Track 6, Material Science and Engineering; and Track 7, Energy Science, Engineering and Policy. A total of 202 full papers were submitted, from which 102 papers were accepted in a peer reviewed process. Each paper was reviewed by on average three reviewers who are experts in the area. After a thorough evaluation process, the technical program consisted of 80 high quality full research papers in oral presentation sessions in the seven main conference tracks. The technical program of EAI ICAST 2021 also featured one invited talk, three keynote speeches, and seven session keynote speeches along with exhibitions and 12 poster presentations. The three keynote speakers were Timnit Gebru, the cofounder of Black in AI from the USA; Girma Gebresenbet from the Swedish University of Agricultural Science, Sweden; and Yilma Sileshi from the Addis Ababa Institute of Technology, Addis Ababa University, Ethiopia.

We sincerely appreciate the work of the Steering Committee chair and members, the Organizing Committee chair, Kibret Mekuanint, the Organizing Committee co-chairs, Mekuanint Agegnehu and Elias Wagari, and the Technical Program Committee (TPC) chair, Mulatu Liyew Berihun, for their constant support and guidance which ensured the success of the conference. It was also a great pleasure to work with such an excellent Organizing Committee team, we note that their hard work in organizing and supporting the conference. We are grateful to the Technical Program Committee led by our TPC chair, Aynadis Molla (Track 1), Hailu Desalegn (Track 2), Mekonnen Wagaw (Track 3), Mitiku Damtie (Track 4), Betsha Tizazu (Track 5), Misganaw Alemu (Track 6), and Muluken Temsgen (Track 7). They followed and completed the peer-review process for the technical papers and designed a high-quality technical program. We are also grateful to the conference manager, Viltare Platzner, for her support, and all the authors who submitted their papers to the EAI ICAST 2021 conference.

We strongly believe that the EAI ICAST 2021 conference provided a good forum for all scientific communities and a scientific body of knowledge we could use to discuss all science and technology aspects relevant to each track. We also expect that future EAI ICAST conferences will be as successful and stimulating, as indicated by the contributions presented in this volume.

Mulatu Liyew Berihun

Conference Organization

Steering Committee

Imrich Chlamtac   Bruno Kessler Professor, University of Trento, Italy

Seifu Admassu Tilahun   Bahir Dar Institute of Technology, Bahir Dar University, Ethiopia

Organizing Committee

General Chair

Kibret Mequanint   University of Western Ontario, Canada

General Co-chairs

Mekuanmt Agegnehu Bitew   Bahir Dar Institute of Technology, Bahir Dar University, Ethiopia

Elias Wagari Gabisa   Bahir Dar Institute of Technology, Bahir Dar University, Ethiopia

Solomon Workineh   Bahir Dar Institute of Technology, Bahir Dar University, Ethiopia

Technical Program Committee Chair

Mulatu Liyew Benhun   Bahir Dar Institute of Technology, Bahir Dar University, Ethiopia

Technical Program Committee

Aynaddis Molla   Bahir Dar Institute of Technology, Bahir Dar University, Ethiopia

Misganaw Alemu   Department of Materials Science and Engineering, Bahir Dar University, Ethiopia

Mitiku Damtie   Bahir Dar Institute of Technology, Bahir Dar University, Ethiopia

Betsha Tizazu   Bahir Dar Institute of Technology, Bahir Dar University, Ethiopia

Mokonnen Wagaw   Bahir Dar Institute of Technology, Bahir Dar University, Ethiopia

| Muluken Temesgen | Bahir Dar Institute of Technology, Bahir Dar University, Ethiopia |
| Hailu Desalegn | Bahir Dar Institute of Technology, Bahir Dar University, Ethiopia |

Sponsorship and Exhibits Chair

| Bantelay Sintayehu | Bahir Dar Institute of Technology, Bahir Dar University, Ethiopia |

Local Chair

| Alganesh Ygzaw | Bahir Dar Institute of Technology, Bahir Dar University, Ethiopia |

Workshops Chair

| Bezawork Tilahun | Bahir Dar Institute of Technology, Bahir Dar University, Ethiopia |

Publicity and Social Media Chair

| Temesgen Getnet | Bahir Dar Institute of Technology, Bahir Dar University, Ethiopia |
| Bezawork Tilahun | Bahir Dar Institute of Technology, Bahir Dar University, Ethiopia |

Publications Chair

| Addisu Negash Ali | Bahir Dar Institute of Technology, Bahir Dar University, Ethiopia |

Web Chair

| Samuel Ashagirie | Bahir Dar Institute of Technology, Bahir Dar University, Ethiopia |

Posters and PhD Track Chair

| Fasikaw Atenaw | Bahir Dar Institute of Technology, Bahir Dar University, Ethiopia |

Panels Chair

| Dagnachew Aklog | Bahir Dar Institute of Technology, Bahir Dar University, Ethiopia |

Demos Chair

Melkamu Binle   Bahir Dar Institute of Technology, Bahir Dar
                                 University, Ethiopia

Tutorials Chairs

Abreham Debasu   Bahir Dar Institute of Technology, Bahir Dar
                                 University, Ethiopia

Co-Technical Program Committee

Elefelious Getachew   School of Information Technology and Scientific
                                 Computing, Addis Ababa Institute of
                                 Technology, Ethiopia
Mesfin Abebe   School of Electrical Engineering & Computing,
                                 Adama Science and Technology,Ethiopia
Abdulkadir Aman   Addis Ababa Institute of Technology (AAiT),
                                 Addis Ababa University, Ethiopia
Sisay Addis   Debre Markos University, Ethiopia
Tadele Mamo   Mettu University, Ethiopia
Wuletawu Abera   International Center for Tropical Agriculture
                                 (CIAT), Zambia
Wubshet Mekonnen   Department of Chemistry, Wollo University,
                                 Ethiopia
Mulugeta Atlabachew   Jimma University, Ethiopia

Contents – Part II

Mechanical and Industrial Engineering

Material Science and Engineering

Energy Science, Engineering and Policy

Contents – Part I

Electrical and Electronics Engineering

ICT, Software and Hardware Engineering

Civil, Water Resources, and Environmental Engineering

Investigation of Properties of Concrete Containing Recycled Concrete Coarse Aggregate and Waste Glass Powder

Habtamu Melaku Dessie[1]([✉]) and Denamo Addissie Nuramo[2]

[1] Bahir Dar Institute of Technology, Bahir Dar University, Bahir Dar, Ethiopia
[2] Ethiopian Institute of Architecture Building Construction and City Development (EiABC), Addis Ababa University, Addis Ababa, Ethiopia

Abstract. The construction industry in Ethiopia is booming with a resulting increase in requirement of cement concrete as an input. The industry faced with depletion of natural aggregate, increasing the scarcity of landfills, haulage and landfill costs. The environmental and economic concern is not limited to concrete wastes but it also includes non-degradable wastes originating from materials like waste glass. In this study, recycled concrete aggregate (RCA) produced from a demolished concrete structure and waste glass powder (WGP) sourced from end-life and broken glass containers and bottles are used. A detailed experimental analysis is conducted to assess the workability and compressive strength of recycled aggregate concrete (RAC) made with partial replacement of natural aggregate (NA) and cement by recycled concrete aggregate (RCA) and waste glass powder (WGP) respectively. A concrete mix prepared with 0%, 25%, 50%, and 75% replacement of NA by RCA and 0%, 10% and 20% partial replacement of cement by WGP in each RAC mixes. The result shows that the waste glass powder replaced recycled aggregate concrete shows better workability and compressive strength development than the recycled aggregate concrete mix without waste glass powder and comparable with the control mix. The waste glass powder (WGP) as a partial replacement of cement can overcome the limitations of recycled concrete aggregate and paving the way for its broadly used in recycled aggregate concrete (RAC) production. The outcomes of this research would assist the growing construction industry to be sustainable thereby reducing waste and conserving the natural resource.

Keywords: Recycled concrete aggregate (RCA) · Recycled aggregate concrete (RAC) · Waste glass powder (WGP) · Workability · Compressive strength

1 Introduction

The growth in industrialization and urbanization of a country could manifested by the level of construction activities including buildings, roadways, and bridges. The construction industry should continue to meet the demand of the growing population of

M. L. Berihun (Ed.): ICAST 2021, LNICST 412, pp. 3–14, 2022.
https://doi.org/10.1007/978-3-030-93712-6_1

one country, which as a result needs a huge amount of construction materials such as concrete. One of the most widely and extensively used construction materials in almost all conceivable construction activities is cement concrete.

Cement concrete is composed of Portland cement, fine aggregate, coarse aggregate, water, pozzolans, and admixture. It creates two major negative impacts on the environment within the Globe. On one hand, the production of concrete consumes large amounts of Natural Aggregate (NA). For instance, the concrete industry in the world demands more than 10 billion tons of natural aggregate (NA) every year, and this demand will doubled in the next 20 to 30 years [1]. On the other hand, concrete waste will be produce due to reconstruction, demolition, and renovation, which creates a large amount of C&D waste.

Currently, the concrete industry in the world not only have been making use of industrial wastes like fly ash, silica fume, and blast furnace slag as pozzolans but also waste glass powder is partially replacing cement [2]. Million tons of waste glass generated annually all over the world [3]. For example, the total global waste glass production was estimate 130 Mt, in which Europe, China, and the USA produced approximately 33 Mt, 32 Mt, and 20 Mt, respectively [3]. In Egypt, about 3.45 Mt of waste glass produced per annum and 84% of which is lifted to landfills [4].

Even in developing nations, these huge glass wastes given less attention to use for application purpose [5]. Current studies also show that most developing countries are facing a shortage of consumers' disposal waste site [5]. Considering the consumers' waste glass, there is no full effort to recover rather end up at disposal landfill or stockpiling in a huge mass. According to IGNIS [6] Joint project report, in Addis Ababa; the total annual glass waste is 5843t that covers 2.4% of the total waste, only 977t glass is recovered and the remaining thrown to landfill. Here, recovery and recycling mechanism in Ethiopia is minor.

Recycling of aggregate is not limited to new concrete production rather it also used as a raw material for pipe bedding, landscape materials, and as base course material for road construction [7]. Additionally, in recent studies using recycled concrete aggregate (RCA) for concrete production have shown that there could be a reduction of fuel consumption and dumping cost, as natural aggregate consumes a considerable amount of energy at each step of the production process [8]. Considering this precedent, the economic advantage of recycling in Ethiopia is to overcome a limited land for a wastage disposal site [9]. Here, the author does not show the improvement methods of RAC and usage of pozzolanic material like WGP. On the other way, different researchers tried to improve the quality of recycled concrete aggregates by using chemical treatment method, mechanical action and using pozzolans to increase the hardened properties of RAC [10].

According to F.Nosouhian and D.Mostofinejad [11], show the potential usage of Waste Glass Powder and the workability of recycled aggregate concrete is slightly increase with the addition of Waste Glass Powder. For fresh state of concrete Nasser [12], reveals that the workability increased by 9 mm when cement replaced by 20% with waste glass powder and natural aggregate replaced by 50% with RCA by weight. Waste glass powder with 20% by weight of cement results in good improvement of the structure of hydrated cement paste in RAC. On the contrary, the use of glass powder as cement replacement decreases concrete workability. Approximately, each 5.0% glass powder addition decreases the slump value by 10 mm in RAC [13]. This trend may be due to the increase of fine material content, which increases the cohesion of the concrete mix and thus decreases the concrete slump.

For harden properties of concrete, WGP have a positive effect on RAC, which undergo pozzolanic reactions with cement hydrates (adhered mortar), forming secondary calcium silicate hydrate (C–S–H) since it contains silicate compounds in a large amount [14]. The compressive strength of RAC containing 50% RA and 20% WGP as partial replacement of cement is comparable with conventional concrete [15]. Moreover, there is an improvement in concrete compressive strength is observed up to 10.0% glass powder cement replacement and 50% RCA content [13]. On the other contrary, a test conducted by R. Nassar and P. Soroushian [12], conclude that the 28-day compressive strength of RAC containing 20% waste glass powder and 50% recycled aggregate shows a decrease in strength.

The previous behavior of RAC concrete containing WGP is somehow contradict with different researchers' discussion and now the compressive strength and workability is observed too. The limits of practicing of WGP as a pozzolanic material in RAC is investigate in new concrete production and its contribution towards sustainable concrete production in the Ethiopian construction industry.

2 Materials and Methods

The research focuses on recycling demolition concrete wastes from demolished buildings, which exist in the city of Bahir Dar, Ethiopia. The sample taken is included only concrete wastes that were produce from a demolished concrete structure like column, beams, and slabs. In addition, the waste glass was source from the end-life and broken glass containers and bottles.

2.1 Material Preparation

Ordinary Portland cement (OPC) 42.5R grade, which is available in the local market, is used. This cement is equivalent to ASTM type I. Well-graded crushed basaltic stone collected in quarry sites located around Bahir Dar area were use in this study. The recycled concrete coarse aggregate were collect from existing demolition building structures that exist in Bahir Dar. After all, jaw crusher around Bahir Dar has crushed the collected demolition waste. Locally available river sand used as a fine aggregate for the investigation. For assuring requirements of aggregates, all aggregates tested based on different test methods of ASTM standards. Tables 1, 2 and 3 show the physical properties of recycled concrete coarse aggregate, natural coarse aggregate and river sand; respectively. In addition, Waste Glass used for this study is collected at Bahir Dar town. The waste glass collected from end-life and broken glass containers and bottles. WGP were produce after grinding waste glass with crasher and after all, it allowed passing in a 75-μm ASTM sieve. Figure 1 shows the preparation of waste glass powder.

(a) Waste Glass before crushing (b) Small sized Glass Culets (c) WGP after crushing

Fig. 1. Waste glass powder preparation

Table 1. Physical properties of recycled concrete coarse aggregate

Type of test	Test method	Test result	ASTM requirement
Unit weight	ASTM C29 [16]	1540 kg/m^3	1280 to 1920 kg/m^3
Specific gravity	ASTM C127 [17]	2.6	2.4 to 3.0
Absorption capacity	ASTM C127 [17]	3.3%	0.2% to 4%
Moisture content	ASTM C566 [18]	1.8%	–

Table 2. Physical properties of natural coarse aggregate

Type of test	Test method	Test result	ASTM requirement
Unit weight	ASTM C29 [16]	1640 kg/m^3	1280 to 1920 kg/m^3
Specific gravity	ASTM C127 [17]	2.7	2.4 to 3.0
Absorption capacity	ASTM C127 [17]	1.85%	0.2% to 4%
Moisture content	ASTM C566 [18]	1.01%	–

Table 3. Physical properties of fine aggregates (river sand)

Type of test	Test method	Test result	ASTM requirement
Fineness modules	ASTM C136 [19]	2.9	2.3 to 3.1
Unit weight	ASTM C29 [16]	1710 kg/m^3	1280 to 1920 kg/m^3
Specific gravity	ASTM C128 [20]	2.7	2.4 to 3.0
Absorption capacity	ASTM C128 [20]	2.5%	0.2% to 2.5%
Moisture content	ASTM C566 [18]	1.6%	–

2.2 Chemical Test

Before using Waste Glass Powder (WGP) for concrete application, determining the mineralogical composition of it was essential. The chemical analysis of WGP was determined using Analytical method. After all, the chemical composition test results checked that whether or not conforms to ASTM C618 chemical test requirement. The chemical properties of WGP shown in Table 4.

Table 4. The chemical analysis of waste glass powder and other reference pozzolans

Chemical composition	Results (mass %)	ASTM C 618 limits [21]		
		Class N	Class F	Class C
Silicon Oxide (SiO_2)	75.56	–	–	–
Aluminum oxide (Al_2O_3)	1.38	–	–	–
Iron Oxide (Fe_2O_3)	0.66	–	–	–
Sum of ($SiO_2 + Al_2O_3 + Fe_2O_3$)	77.6	70 min	70 min	50 min
Sulfur trioxide (SO3)	< 0.01	4 max	5 max	5 max
Calcium Oxide (CaO)	9.14	–	<10%	>10%
Magnesium Oxide (MgO)	0.48	–	–	–
Sodium Oxide (Na_2O)	12.06	–	–	–
Potassium Oxide (K_2O)	0.5	–	–	–
Moisture content (H_2O)	0.2	3 max	3 max	3 max
Loss on Ignition (LI)	0.52	10 max	6 max	6 max

2.3 Mix Proportion of Concrete Mixes

The mix design were performed for C-25 grade concrete with targeted workability of 25-50mm as per ACI 211.1. The RCA replacement in coarse NA and partial cement replacement with WGP were varied with 0–75% and 0–20%; respectively. For all mixture's w/c ratio was constant and it was 0.49. Mix proportioning of RAC is shown in Table 5.

2.4 Concrete Casting and Curing

All ingredients of concrete mixes measured by weight in accordance with their proportion and mixture series. Based on the mixture series; all ingredients are added to a mixer and dry mixture was applied. After dry mixing, water added gradually and the concrete mixed uniformly. Once the concrete mixed uniformly, the workability of concrete tested with a slump cone. After all, 15 × 15 × 15 cm cubical samples casted verywell. The samples immersed in a curing tank until the data recorded. All tests carried out according to the provision of relevant ASTM standards.

2.5 Compressive Strength Testing

The compressive strength of 15 * 15 * 15 cm cubes was done on 3rd, 7th, 28th & 56th days after casting depending on ASTM C 109. For compressive strength test, ELE test machine is used. After all, after removing the water on the surface of the concrete, the cubes were tested.

2.6 Data Analysis of Test Results

As an analysis tool for compressive strength test on hardened concrete, simple Microsoft Excel is used.

3 Results and Discussions

3.1 Workability of Concrete Mixes

Table 5 shows the workability of different recycled aggregate concrete mixes without and with waste glass powder having a constant w/c ratio of 0.49. With the same w/c ratio, as the replacement proportion of RCA with NA increases the workability decreases. This is due to the recycled concrete coarse aggregate has higher absorption capacity than natural one; since the recycled coarse concrete aggregate has clinging mortar at the surface. The decrease in workability of concrete containing RCA is attributed to the higher absorption capacity, the rougher surfaces and more irregular shapes of it [22].

Table 5. Mix proportion of different concrete mixes

Mix designation	% RCA	% WGP	Weight of material in Kg/m^3						Total (Kg/m^3)	Slump (mm)
			Cement	WGP	Water	NA	RCA	Sand		
[a] 0RA0WG	0	0	360	0	195.2	1090	0	800	2445	40
[b] 0RA10WG		10	324	36	195.1	1090	0	792.5	2438	45
[c] 0RA20WG		20	288	72	195	1090	0	787	2433	55
25RA0WG	25	0	360	0	196.3	817.5	258.8	806.3	2438	35
25RA10WG		10	324	36	196.3	817.5	258.8	798.8	2432	40
25RA20WG		20	288	72	196.3	817.5	258.8	793.5	2426.7	48
50RA0WG	50	0	360	0	198	545	517.5	812.5	2431.5	25
50RA10WG		10	324	36	197.5	545	517.5	805.3	2425.5	36
50RA20WG		20	288	72	197	545	517.5	800	2420	43
75RA0WG	75	0	360	0	199.5	272.5	776.3	818.8	2425	20

(*continued*)

Table 5. (*continued*)

Mix designation	% RCA	% WGP	Weight of material in Kg/m^3						Total (Kg/m^3)	Slump (mm)
			Cement	WGP	Water	NA	RCA	Sand		
75RA10WG		10	324	36	199	272.5	776.3	811.6	2419	30
75RA20WG		20	288	72	198.8	272.5	776.3	806.5	2414	40

[a]Control mix.
[b]Counterpart mix that used as a reference for all 10%WGP RAC mixes.
[c]Counterpart mix that used as a reference for all 20% WGP RAC mixes.

On the other hand, with the same w/c ratio and constant partial replacement of cement by waste glass powder, as the replacement proportion of natural coarse aggregate by recycled aggregate increases the workability decreases. However, RAC having WGP has greater workability than RAC without WGP incorporation. This is due to the lower water absorption capacity of WGP than cement. For instance, the workability of RAC mix of 25RA10WG having 10% WGP was greater than the RAC mix of 25RA0WG without waste glass powder by 5 mm slump. To support this argument, the effect was attributed to the relatively low moisture absorption of waste glass powder when compared with cement [12].

3.2 Compressive Strength

Figure 2 shows the compressive strength test results at different concrete ages with similar w/c ratio mixes produced with various percentage of RCA replacing NA, without waste glass powder.

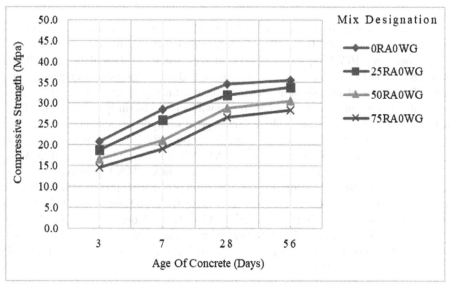

Fig. 2. Compressive Strength of RAC without WGP at Different Ages

Figures 3 and 4 depict that the compressive strength test results of the corresponding RAC mixes containing 10% and 20% partial cement replacement with WGP, respectively. From the RAC mixes without WGP and similar w/c ratio, the compressive strength depends on the proportion of RCA. Its strength decreases with an increased proportion of RCA. Strength development of RAC mixes containing 25% RCA is comparable with the control mix. However, the control mix (0RA0WG) strength development is significant than other RAC mixes. This is due to RCA contains the weak clinging mortar on its surface.

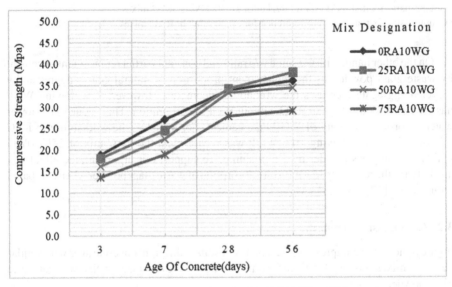

Fig. 3. Compressive Strength of RAC with 10% WGP at Different Ages

Among the RAC mixes containing 10% WGP (Fig. 5), the compressive strength of counterpart concrete mix (0RA10WG) is greater than those of the corresponding RAC mixes containing 10% WGP until 28th-days of ages. After 28th-days of the age of RAC, this trend was not continued due to the WGP benefited the compressive strength development. The statistical analysis of test results indicated the significant benefits of WGP as a partial replacement of cement in RAC mixes with an increase in age of concrete. Here, RAC made with incorporation of WGP show a good strength development as the curing age increases up to 56th-days; where at the 56th-day, 25RA10WG concrete mix is 6% and 7% higher than the counterpart mix (0RA10WG) and the control mix (0RA0WG), respectively. In addition, a 25RA10WG RAC concrete mix is 11% higher than the counterpart mixes of 25RA0WG. Similarly, the strength of the RAC mix of 50RA10WG is 3.3% and 2% lower than the counterpart mix (0RA10WG) and control mix (0RA0WG) at 56th-days, respectively. Furthermore, a 50RA10WG RAC mix increased the 28th-day strength by 14% from that of 50RA0WG RAC mix. This strength development is comparable with the control mix and shows an insignificant difference. This is why the WGP has a positive effect on RAC.

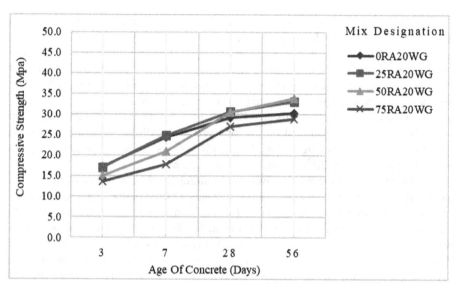

Fig. 4. Compressive Strength of RAC with 20% WGP at Different Ages

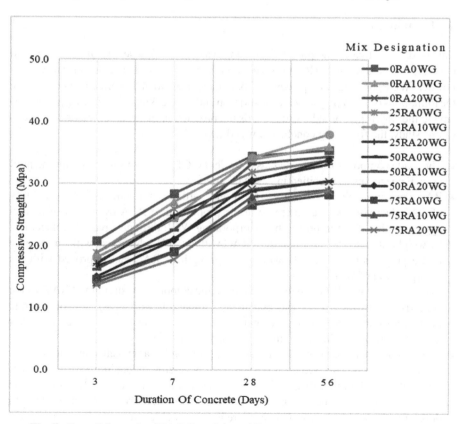

Fig. 5. Overall Strength of RAC Containing Different Percentages of WGP and Ages

The compressive strength test results for RAC mixes containing 20%WGP (Fig. 4) follows trends similar to those for RAC mixes containing 10%WGP. RCA concretes made with WGP replacement continue their strength development up to the 56th-day. The strength development of concrete mixes of 25RA20WG and 50RA20WG are significant at later ages of concrete curing. However, the increase in compressive strength is not significant like the strength of RAC mixes containing 10% WGP.

According to the result, the recycled aggregate concrete containing 25%RCA and 10%WG show a better marginal means for more than 28th-day strength. A recycled aggregate concrete containing 50%RCA and 10% WG also show comparable marginal means for more than the 28th-day strength development.

Therefore, the significant improvement in strength after 28th days of ages is an indirect measure of the pozzolanic reaction between adhered mortar at the RCA surface and the silicate compounds in the WGP. This reaction creates additional cement paste (secondary C-S-H: calcium hydrate silicate) which helps for strength development. This beneficial effect of WGP also observed by earlier researchers who studied the effects of WGP in RAC production [12]. Therefore, this reveals that WGP continues the strength development at a later day as long as there is a favourable amount of temperature and moisture.

4   Conclusion

This study investigated the potential of using waste glass powder (WGP) and recycled concrete coarse aggregate (RCA) in new concrete production. The use of waste glass powder (WGP) as a partial replacement for cement is estimated to effectively overcome the limitations of RCA (higher water absorption and the weakness due to clinging mortar) paving the way for its broadly use towards the production of RAC. Based on the results of this study, the following conclusion was drawn:

- The oxide composition of waste glass powder (WGP) conforms to the requirement of class F pozzolans as specified in ASTM C 618.
- RAC containing WGP have good fresh and hardened properties. The workability of RAC decreases with an increase in the proportion of RCA by weight of natural aggregates but it can improved by incorporating WGP through a partial replacement by weight of cement. The strength of RAC without WGP decreased with an increase in the proportion of RCA. However, the strength of RAC can improved with the incorporation of WGP.
- The replacement of WGP up to 10% enhance the compressive strength of RAC which comprises up to 50% RCA replacement and comparable with the strength of concrete made with natural aggregate and without waste glass powder. However, a further increase in RAC and WGP results a decreased in strength.
- The significant increases in later age strength of recycled aggregate concrete containing waste glass powder achieved through the conversion of calcium hydroxide (CH) into Calcium-Hydrate-Silicate (C-S-H) gel available in the adhered mortar to the surface of recycled concrete aggregate. Therefore, in RAC WGP continues strength development at a later age as long as there is a favourable amount of temperature and moisture.

References

1. Sonawane, T.R., Pimplikar, S.: Use of recycled aggregate in concrete. Int. J. Eng. Res. Technol. **2**, 1–9 (2013)
2. Jhala, A.S., Goliya, H.: Suitability of glass powder as partial replacement of cement in concrete. Int. J. Emerg. Trend. Eng. Dev. **1**, 93–104 (2015)
3. IEA. Tracking Industrial Energy Efficiency and CO2 Emissions (2007). https://doi.org/10. 1787/9789264030404-en
4. Bajad, M., Modhera, C.:Effect of glass on strength of concrete subjected to sulphate attack. Int. J. Civ. Eng. Res. Dev. **1**(2), 1–13 (2011). https://ssrn.com/abstract=3501397
5. Vasudevan, G., Pillay, K.: Performance of using waste glass powder in concrete as replacement of cement. Am. J. Eng. Res. **2**(12), 175–181 (2013). http://www.ajer.org/papers/v2(12)/U02 12175181.pdf
6. IGNIS. IGNIS Joint Project Background. [Online] Federal Ministry of Education and Research. Ethio-Germany Joint Project Report, Addis Ababa, Ethiopia (2014)
7. Radonjanin, V., Malesev, M.: Recycled aggregate concrete-composition, properties and application. **40**, 48–91 (2009)
8. Wilburn, D.R., Goonan, T.G.: Aggregate from Natural and Recycled Sources Economic Assessments for Construction Application: A Material Flow Analysis," pp. 1–40 (1998). https://doi.org/10.3133/cir1176
9. Yehualaw, M., Woldesenbet, A.: Economic Impact of Recycled Aggregate for Developing Nations: A Case Study in the Ethiopian Construction Industry, ASCE, pp. 250–259 (2016). https://doi.org/10.1061/9780784479827.026
10. Juan, M.S., Gutierrez, P.A.: Study on the influence of attached mortar content on the properties of recycled concrete aggregate. Constr. Build. Mater. **23**(2), 872–877 (2008). http://worldcat. org/issn/09500618
11. Nosouhian, F., Mostofinejad, D.: Influence of milled waste glass as partial cement replacement on durability of recycled aggregate concrete in sulphate environment. SMART (2013). https:// data.smar conferences.org/SMAR_2013_Proceedings/papers/258.pdf
12. Nasser, R., Soroushian, P.: Strength and durability of recycled aggregate concrete containing milled waste glass as partial replacement for cement. Constr. Build. Mater. **29**, 368–377 (2012). https://doi.org/10.1016/j.conbuildmat.2011.10.061
13. Akhtar, A., Sarmah, A.K.: Construction and demolition waste generation and properties of recycled aggregate concrete: a global perspective. J. Clean. Prod. **186**, 262–281 (2018). https:// doi.org/10.1016/j.jclepro.2018.03.085
14. Priscilla, M., Naik, P.A.: Strength and Durability Study on Recycled Aggregate Concrete Using Glass Powder, vol. 11 (2014). http://iranarze.ir/wp-content/uploads/2018/07/E8482-IranArze.pdf
15. Letelier, V., et al.: Mechanical properties of concrete with recycled aggregates and waste glass. Struct. Concr. **18**, 40–53 (2017). https://doi.org/10.1002/suco.201500143
16. ASTM C 29. Standard Test Method for Bulk Density ("Unit Weight") and Voids in Aggregate (2007)
17. ASTM C 127. Standard Test Method for Density, Relative Density (Specific Gravity), and Absorption of Coarse Aggregate (2007)
18. ASTM C 566. Standard Test Method for Total Evaporable Moisture Content of Aggregate by Drying (2004)
19. ASTM C 136. Standard Test Methods for Sieve Analysis of Fine and Coarse Aggregates (2005)
20. ASTM C 128. Standard Test Method for Density, Relative Density (Specific Gravity), and Absorption of Fine Aggregate (2007)

21. ASTM C 618. Standard Specification for Coal Fly Ash Raw or Calcined Natural Pozzolan for Use as a Mineral Admixture in Concrete (2000)
22. Verian, K.P., Ashraf, W., Cao, Y.: Properties of recycled concrete aggregate and their influence in concrete production. Resour. Conserv. Recycl. **133**, 30–49 (2018). https://doi.org/10.1016/j.resconrec.2018.02.005

Application of Potential Based Cohesive Model for Analysis of Concrete Fracture

Habtamu A. Tadesse[1(✉)], Temesgen Wondimu Aure[2],
and Alemayehu Golla Gualu[1]

[1] Faculty of Civil and Water Resources Engineering, Bahir Dar Institute
of Technology, Bahir Dar University, Bahir Dar, Ethiopia
[2] College of Architectural and Civil Engineering, Addis Ababa Science
and Technology University, Addis Ababa, Ethiopia
temesgen.wondimu@aastu.edu.et

Abstract. Concrete is the main construction material used for infrastructure construction around the globe. Since it is a brittle material, applied loads on concrete structures will result in sudden failure of the structure, and consequently the service of the structure will be affected. To prevent such failure, it is necessary to understand and predict the behavior and failure mechanics of concrete. Recently, the concept of the cohesive zone model has been widely applied to investigate various material failure phenomena. The potential-based model has advantages over the non-potential-based cohesive model in that their traction-separation relations are determined by taking the derivative of potential (cohesive interaction) concerning normal and tangential opening displacements. The purpose of this study is to evaluate the application of potential-based cohesive model for the study of concrete fracture by employing a user element in ABAQUS. The simulation is compared with reproduced experimental results and good agreement has been found between load-displacement curves.

Keywords: Cohesive model · Potential based model · Concrete fracture · Fracture mechanics

1 Introduction

Fracture of construction materials has been a problem since the construction of man-made structures has started. Nowadays the problem actually has become worse than in the previous centuries because of the spread of advanced and technologically complex construction. One of the most important aspects of fracture mechanics is to identify the potential dangers whenever the structural complexity is increased (Anderson et al. 1971).

The application of fracture mechanics into concrete has helped to achieve uniform safety margins and/or reliability. Fracture mechanics can help to understand the failure of high strength concrete structures and concrete structures of unusually large sizes. It has been discovered that many failures have been caused by pre-existing flaws in materials that initiate cracks that grow and finally lead to fracture.

© ICST Institute for Computer Sciences, Social Informatics and Telecommunications Engineering 2022
Published by Springer Nature Switzerland AG 2022. All Rights Reserved
M. L. Berihun (Ed.): ICAST 2021, LNICST 412, pp. 15–26, 2022.
https://doi.org/10.1007/978-3-030-93712-6_2

The collapse and failure of these infrastructures result in significant accidents, life loss, and damaging property and highly influence the local economy. To prevent such disasters, it is necessary to understand and predict the deformation and failure mechanisms of concrete (Park 2009).

Previous studies have indicated that a two-dimensional cohesive model was implemented in commercial software ABAQUS for different materials. However, the built-in traction separation relations for cohesive elements in commercial software have limitations since the tangent stiffness under the softening condition for the traction–separation relationship leads to non-physical responses. This limitation can be solved by providing a user element in ABAQUS. The user element (UEL) has been developed based on potential-based cohesive elements proposed by Park et al. (2009). However, the application of these elements for concrete fracture has not been examined.

The objective of this study is to implement a potential-based cohesive model for concrete fracture using UEL subroutine in commercial software ABAQUS. That means crack propagation phenomena is investigated through the potential based constitutive model in association with robust and efficient computational method.

More specifically, this study addresses with comparing analytical solutions and numerical simulation results by varying physical macroscopic fracture parameters, such as the shape of softening curve.

2 Methodology

The general purpose finite element software ABAQUS and analytical computations are used to investigate crack propagation phenomena of concrete through the user-defined element subroutine of ABAQUS. The user element subroutine of the ABAQUS code is written in FORTRAN. There are two approaches for inserting a cohesive element into the mesh. One way is either inserting the cohesive element along the pre-selected fracture path, by restricting the crack propagate where the user has specified or another way is by inserting it between all bulk elements in a region of mesh, allowing the fracture to propagate freely within that region (Daniel and Glaucio 2014).

The goals of this study will be achieved through the potential-based cohesive model first proposed by Park et al (PPR) (2009) in conjunction with robust and effective computational methods as the first step. The PPR model is a function of four basic independent parameters in the normal and shearing fracture modes, namely cohesive strength, fracture energy, the shape of softening curve, and the initial slope of the traction–separation relationship. The potential (for 3D in general), ψ, is given by (Park and Paulino 2012)

$$\Psi(\Delta n, \Delta t1, \Delta t2) = \min(\phi n, \phi t) + \left[\Gamma' n \left(1 - \frac{\Delta n}{\delta n} \right)^{\alpha} \left(\frac{m}{\alpha} + \frac{\Delta n}{\delta n} \right)^{m} + (\phi n - \phi t) \right]$$
$$* \left[\Gamma' t \left(1 - \frac{\sqrt{(\Delta t1)^2 + (\Delta t2)^2}}{\delta t} \right)^{\beta} \left(\frac{n}{\beta} + \frac{\sqrt{(\Delta t1)^2 + (\Delta t2)^2}}{\delta t} \right)^{n} + (\phi t - \phi n) \right] \tag{1}$$

Numerical simulation of mixed-mode fracture is implemented in commercial software ABAQUS with a user element subroutine. The rectangular plane stress element (Q4) is used for the bulk element, while the cohesive surface element is inserted along the crack path.

The rationale behind using this model is that the post peak behavior is captured well using different parameters with the most powerful function called *Potential Function*. A two dimensional simulations has been used by assuming a unit thickness to minimize the computation time.

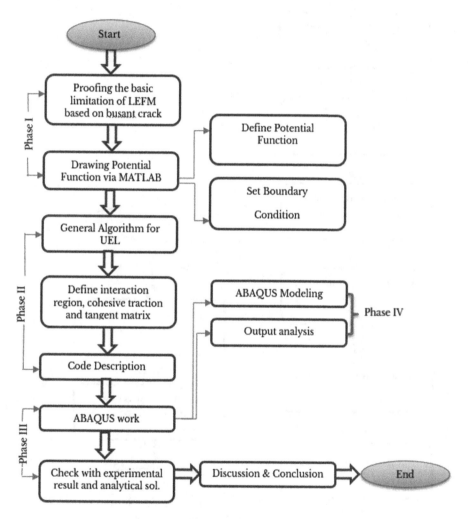

Fig. 1. Flow chart

The flow chart show in Fig. 1 illustrates the basic steps that have been followed to implement the user element. The procedure starts with receiving nine input data including thickness of a cohesive element. Those global coordinates are changed to local coordinates. Next, normal and tangential cohesive traction are computed. Finally, the cohesive interaction is defined in four chapters is Contact formulation, softening condition, unloading/Reloading condition, and complete failure (Fig. 2).

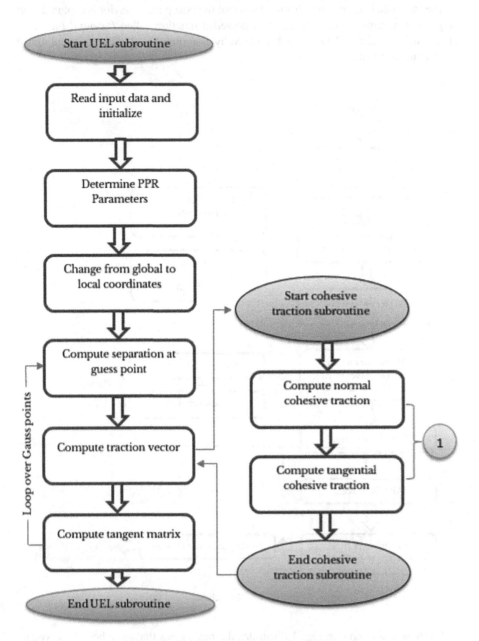

Fig. 2. General flow chart for UEL

2.1   PPR Implementation in ABAQUS

To alleviate any confusions between the code and this paper is the description in detail (Table 1 and Fig. 3):

Table 1. PPR UEL nomenclature and description

Paper	Fortran	Description
Bc	Bc	global displacement-separation relation matrix
$f coh$	Fc	internal force vector of a cohesive surface element
$Kcoh$	Sc	tangent matrix of a cohesive surface element
m, n	m, n	Non-dimensional exponents in the PPR model
N	ShapeN	shape functional matrix
Tc	T	cohesive traction vector
u	U	displacement field
U	U_l	nodal displacement vector in the local coordinates
α, β	alph, beta	shape parameters in the PPR model
$\Gamma n, \Gamma t$	Gam_n, Gam_t	energy constants in the PPR model
$\delta n, \delta t$	dn, dt	normal and tangential final crack opening widths
$\Delta nmax, \Delta tmax$	deln_max, delt_max	maximum normal and tangential separations in the loading history
$\lambda n, \lambda t$	ln, lt	initial slope indicators in the PPR model
Λ	R	coordinate transformation matrix
$\sigma max, \tau max$	Tn_m, Tt_m	normal and tangential cohesive strengths
$\varphi n, \varphi t$	Gn, Gt	normal and tangential fracture energies

3 Results and Discussion

3.1 Validation of the PPR Model

To validate the PPR model for quasi-brittle materials (like concrete), numerical simulation results are compared with reproduced experimental results from the three-point bending test of plain concrete (Roesler et al. 2007), shown in Fig. 4. The cohesive element size is taken to be 1 mm which is small enough to capture the local fracture process (Tables 2 and 3).

Table 2. Hardened properties of the concrete

Modulus of elasticity (GPa)	32
Compressive strength (MPa)	58.3
Poisson's ratio	0.2

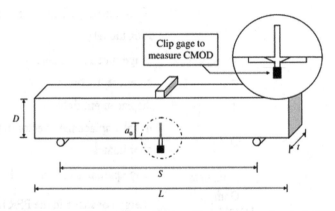

Fig. 3. Specimen dimensions and test configuration (Roesler et al. 2007)

Table 3. Specimen geometry of three-point test according to Roesler et al. (2007) experiment

	Specimen dimensions (mm)				
Beam Specimen ID	Length (L)	Depth (D)	Thickness (t)	Notch (a_o)	Span (S)
B150-80	700	150	80	50	600

It has an initial notch (ao) of 50 mm and a length of 700 mm. The simply supported beam mesh detail around the crack tip is shown in Fig. 4.

The finite element model of the beam is shown below which is created by the 2D planar option. The following beam has 150 mm depth and 700 mm length. The notch depth was taken to be 50 mm (Fig. 5).

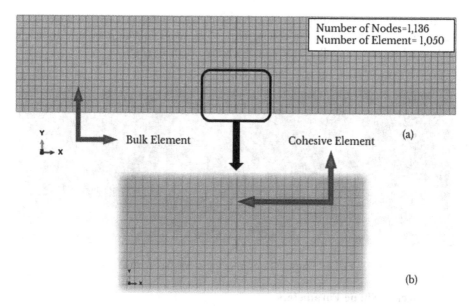

Fig. 4. 2D planar model mesh around the notch (b)

The following two-dimensional planar simply supported beams have been analyzed in ABAQUS UEL configuration. Since this research is concerned with mode I fracture, the crack is assumed to be propagated on a straight line in the vertical direction. As a result, ABAQUS ODB file indicated the following damage (Fig. 6) propagation for 10 stepwise increments with a 0.01 mm/s loading rate. The post peak behavior and the evolution of crack is independent of loading rate and thus taking this rate will be fair enough. The support assumed to carry vertical load only (roller support). The figure shows the stress distribution at the stated stage. Since the stress distribution shows maximum values at the loading points, which are expected locations to attract maximum effect at an early stage of loading, the numerical analysis result will be convenient.

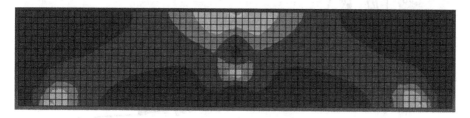

Fig. 5. Damage level from initial loading

At the final step of loading rate the cohesive element sweep in a vertical direction as shown in the figure below. The connectivity of elements has been assured by equal mesh size between the bulk element and cohesive element (Fig. 7).

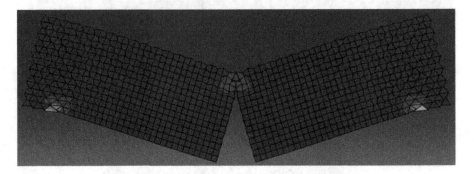

Fig. 6. Damage level from initial loading to final

3.2 Effect of Shape Parameters

The effect of shape values for numerical analysis has been investigated. The load-displacement relationship in Fig. 8 illustrates different α values under the same load control while other parameters were maintained. Initially, the load-displacement relationship of the analysis result has shown linear and similar behavior for different α values with slightly different behavior near to peak loads. However, in the post-peak region, the relationship of load-displacement for different α values has shown different behavior. As it can be seen from the graph, the experimental and the numerical analysis result has shown a good agreement when the value of α becomes greater than two.

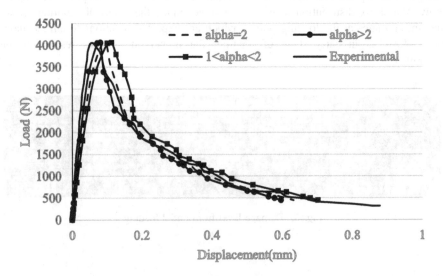

Fig. 7. Load vs displacement curve for different shape values (α = 1.5, 2, 5)

Based on the comparison between numerical and experimental values for peak load, the error has found to be 1.7%. Since the error is insignificant, this shows that the numerical simulation in ABAQUS UEL is acceptable.

3.3 Effect of Fracture Energy

The change in α value on potential function will also affect fracture energy. For each of the following cases, the fracture energy is calculated according to the PPR polynomial function. The area under the cohesive interactions corresponds to fracture energy:

$$\emptyset_n = \int_0^{\delta n} Tn(\Delta n, 0)d\Delta n \tag{2}$$

The following normal traction curve is generated from Matlab GUIDE which indicates the value of fracture energy at the atomistic level.

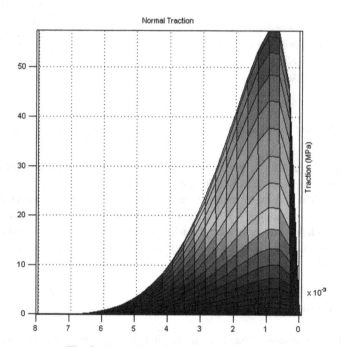

Fig. 8. Normal traction curve for alpha = 5

The normal traction Tn is expressed as:

$$T_n(\Delta n, \Delta t) = \frac{\Gamma n}{\delta n} \left[m\left(1 - \frac{\Delta n}{\delta n}\right)^{\alpha} \left(\frac{m}{\alpha} + \frac{\Delta n}{\delta n}\right)^{m-1} - \alpha \left(1 - \frac{\Delta n}{\delta n}\right)^{\alpha-1} \left(\frac{m}{\alpha} + \frac{\Delta n}{\delta n}\right)^{m} \right]$$

$$* \left[\Gamma t \left(1 - \frac{\Delta t}{\delta t}\right)^{\beta} \left(\frac{n}{\beta} + \frac{\Delta t}{\delta t}\right)^{n} + \langle \phi t - \phi n \rangle \right]$$

(3)

Although the two-dimensional potential model captures fracture behavior by changing the softening curve, the models do not have the same fracture energy in modes I and II (Fig. 9).

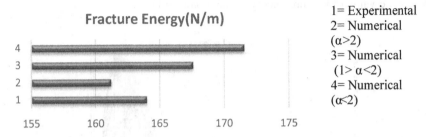

Fig. 9. Fracture energy comparison between numerical and experimental simulation

The above figure shows the fracture energy value of the experimental result and numerical analysis results with different alpha (α) values. When it has compared between numerical and experimental values of fracture energy with alpha equal to 5, the error has found to be 1.52%. This error is also insignificant like the load-displacement relationship error found with experiment and analysis results. This can have confirmed that ABAQUS can simulate the real post-peak behavior of concrete in the PPR model.

4 Conclusion

From the analysis results, it has been found that there is good agreement between the load-displacement curve obtained from the experiment and numerical simulation. And the shape factor is the most determinant factor in the PPR model. So far polynomial PPR function that represents the best fit for numerical simulation in softening curves is α = 5. Again the maximum load has also a good agreement between the two simulations. The good agreement between alpha value and compressive strength are not related directly or inversely.

For α greater than two, the cohesive traction separation relationship has a convex shape, which can be utilized for plain concrete.

It should be noted that one of the key contributions of this research is to link the experimental fracture properties with the numerical fracture properties with PPR and implement into finite element in UEL subroutine to predict crack propagation and behavior. In addition to this, the evolution of crack is related with critical stress of the crack tips. Whenever the stress at initial crack is critical, the micro crack will created by connecting another element which reached with critical stress.

References

Anderson, G.P., Ruggles, V.L., Stibor, G.S.: Use of finite element computer programs in fracture mechanics. Int. J. Fract. Mech. **7**(1), 63–76 (1971)

Anderson, T.L.: Fracture Mechanics: Fundamentals and Applications. CRC Press (1995)

Anderson, T.: Fracture Mechanics Fundamentals and Application. London (2005)

Andrew, J.: A Descriptive Analysis of Stadiums as Non-sporting Event Values (2017)

ASTM. Standard Test Method for Mixed Mode-I Mode II Interlaminar Fracture Toughness of Unidirectional Fiber Reinforced Polymer Matrix Composites. ASTM D 6671/D 6671M. ASTM International (2006)

Banks-Sills, L., Bortman, Y.: A mixed-mode fracture specimen: analysis and testing. Int. J. Fract. **30**(3), 181–201 (1986)

Barenblatt, G.I.: The formation of equilibrium cracks during brittle fracture. General ideas and hypotheses. Axially-symmetric cracks. J. Appl. Math. Mech. **23**(3), 622–636 (1959)

Barker, R.M., Puckett, J.A.: Design of Highway Bridges: An LRFD Approach, 2nd edn. Wiley, New York (2007)

Bazant, Z.: Fracture and Size Effect in Concrete and Other Quasi-Brittle Material. Madrid (1997)

Bažant, Z.P., Becq-Giraudon, E.: Statistical prediction of fracture parameters of concrete and implications for choice of testing standard. Cem. Concr. Res. **32**(4), 529–556 (2002)

Bažant, Z.P., Caner, F.C.: Microplane model M5 with kinematic and static constraints for concrete fracture and anelasticity. I: Theory. J. Eng. Mech. **131**(1), 31–40 (2005)

Bažant, Z.P., Caner, F.C., Carol, I., Adley, M.D., Akers, S.A.: Microplane model M4 for concrete. I: formulation with work-conjugate deviatoric stress. J. Eng. Mech. **126**(9), 944–953 (2000)

Bazant, Z.P., Planas, J.: Fracture and Size Effect in Concrete and Other Quasibrittle Materials. CRC Press (1998)

Beltz, G.E., Rice, J.R.: Dislocation nucleation versus cleavage decohesion. In: The Minerals, Metals & Materials Society (TMS), pp. 457–480 (1991)

Borsi. Advanced Mechanics of Material (2002)

CEO, A.: Getting Started with Abaqus_Standard Manual (2012)

Cornec, A., Scheider, I., Schwalbe, K.-H.: On the practical application of the cohesive model. Eng. Fract. Mech. **70**(14), 1963–1987 (2003)

Daniel, W.S., Glaucio, H.P.: A growing library of three dimensional cohesive elements for use in ABAQUS. Eng. Fract. Mech. (2014)

Falk, M., Needleman, A.: A Critical Evaluation of Cohesive Zone Models of Dynamic Fracture, vol. 11. Netherlands (2001)

Hillerborg, A., Modéer, M., Petersson, P.-E.: Analysis of crack formation and crack growth in concrete by means of fracture mechanics and finite elements. Cem. Concr. Res. **6**(6), 773–782 (1976)

Hutchinson, V.T.: The influence of plasticity on mixed mode interface toughness. J. Mech. Phys. Solids **41**(6), 1119–1135 (1993)

Ingraffea, A.R., Gerstk, W.H., Gergely, P., Saouma, V.: Fracture mechanics of bond in reinforced concrete. J. Struct.. Eng. **110**(4), 871–890 (1984)

Jorg, F.U., Stafen, E., Carsten, K.: Modelling of cohesive crack growth in concrete structures with extended finite element method. Comput. Method. Appl. Mech. Eng. (2007)

Needleman, A.: A continuum model for void nucleation by inclusion debonding. J. Appl. Mech. **54**(3), 525–531 (1987)

Needleman, A.: An analysis of tensile decohesion along an interface. J. Mech. Phys. Solids **38** (3), 289–324 (1990)

Needleman, A., Tvergaard, V.: An analysis of ductile rupture in notched bars. J. Mech. Phys. Solids **32**(6), 461–490 (1984)

Park, K.: Concrete Fracture Mechanics and Size Effect. Illinois (2003)

Park, K.: Potential Based Fracture Mechanics Using Cohesive Zone and Virtual Internal Bond Modeling. University of Illinois, Urbana, Illinois (2009)

Park, K., Paulino, G.H.: Computational implementation of the PPR potential-based cohesive model in ABAQUS: educational perspective. Eng. Fract. Mech. **93**, 239–262 (2012)

Park, K., Paulino, G.H., Roesler, J.R.: Determination of the kink point in the bilinear softening model for concrete. Eng. Fract. Mech. **75**(13), 3806–3818 (2008)

Park, K., Paulino, G.H., Roesler, J.R.: A unified potential-based cohesive model of mixed-mode fracture. J. Mech. Phys. Solids **57**(6), 891–908 (2009)

Park, K., Pereira, J.P., Duarte, C.A., Paulino, G.H.: Integration of singular enrichment functions in the generalized/extended finite element method for three dimensional problems. Int. J. Numeric. Method. Eng. **78**(10), 1220–1257 (2009)

Park, K., Paulino, G.H.: Cohesive Zone Model: A Critical Review of Traction-Separation Relationship Across Fracure Surfaces. Trans. ASME (2014)

Parks, M.L., Lehoucq, R.B., Plimpton, S.J., Silling, S.A.: Implementing peridynamics within a molecular dynamics code. Comput. Phys. Commun. **179**(11), 777–783 (2008)

Paulino, G.H., Menezes, I.F.M., Cavalcante Neto, J.B., Martha, L.F.: A methodology for adaptive finite element analysis: towards an integrated computational environment. Comput. Mech. **23**(5–6), 361–388 (1999)

Perez, N.: Fracture Mechanics. London (2004)

Roesler, J., Paulino, G.H., Park, K., Gaedicke, C.: Concrete fracture prediction using bilinear softening. Cem. Concr. Compos. **29**(4), 300–312 (2007)

Rosa, A.L., Yu, R.C., Ruiz, G., Saucedo, L., Sousa, J.L.: A loading rate dependent cohesive model for concrete fracture. Eng. Fract. Mech. (2011)

Uday, N.P.: Experimental determination of fracture energy by RILEM method. Int. J. Eng. Sci. **06**(03), 106–115 (2017)

Xu, X.-P., Needleman, A.: Void nucleation by inclusion debonding in a crystal matrix. Model. Simulat. Mater. Sci. Eng. **1**(2), 111–132 (1993)

Xu, X.-P., Needleman, A.: Numerical simulations of fast crack growth in brittle solids. J. Mech. Phys. Solids **42**(9), 1397–1434 (1994)

Evaluations of Shallow Groundwater Recharges and Water Use Practices at Robit Watershed

Dagnew Y. Takele[1]([✉]), Seifu A. Tilahun[2], Fasikaw A. Zimale[2], Petra Schmitter[3], Bayu G. Bihonegn[4], and Daniel G. Eshetie[5]

[1] Water Supply and Sanitation Core Process, Amhara Design and Supervision Works Enterprise, Bahir Dar, Ethiopia
[2] Faculty of Civil and Water Resource Engineering, Bahir Dar Institute of Technology, Bahir Dar University, Bahir Dar, Ethiopia
[3] International Water Management Institute, P.O. 11081, Yangon, Myanmar
[4] Department of Hydraulic and Water Resource Engineering, Kombolcha Institute of Technology, Wollo University, Dessie, Ethiopia
[5] Department of Hydraulic and Water Resource Engineering, Institute of Technology, University of Gondar, Gondar, Ethiopia

Abstract. Groundwater resources have a fundamental importance to satisfy the rapidly increasing agricultural, livestock and domesticwater requirements within the region especially in Robit watershed. Hence the quantification of this water resource is important for the efficient and sustainable water resource management. In this study spatial variability of irrigation water requirement, water use (abstractions) and groundwater recharge were estimated for Robit watershed within the eastern part of Lake Tana. Satellite image of Planet Scope on 2nd February 2017 was used to estimate area and type of crops cultivated in the watershed. CROPWAT model has been used to calculate the particular evapotranspiration and water requirement for irrigation using local climatic data. This was calculated for the dominant irrigated crops of Khat (Catha edulis Forsk), hop (Rhamnus prinoides), coffee, tomato and green pepper within the study area. Calibrated QSWAT model was applied to estimate net ground water recharges using local climatic data, soil map, crop management data and derived land use map from satellite image processing. The assessment showed that the entire amount of water applied for irrigation, domestic and livestock purposes was estimated as 1.35 Mm^3/year, 0.02 Mm^3/year and 0.03 Mm^3/year respectively. Net groundwater recharge was estimated as 3.18 Mm^3/year within the watershed. The estimation from the water abstraction survey showed that the total volume of water abstracted within the watershed was estimated as 1.40 Mm^3/year. From the assessment it can be clearly seen that only 44% of ground water resource is extracted annually within the area and there is some potential to expand irrigation areas and the current water usage for various purposes in the future.

Keywords: Water abstraction survey · PLANETSCOPE image · ERDAS IMAGINE · QSWAT · GW recharges · CROPWAT · SWATCUP

M. L. Berihun (Ed.): ICAST 2021, LNICST 412, pp. 27–48, 2022.
https://doi.org/10.1007/978-3-030-93712-6_3

1 Introduction

The spatial distribution of water resources determines the overall performance of any country in different aspects and particularly its economic development. even if it needs detailed researches, based on the present knowledge, water resources in the country are estimated as 30 billion cubic meter (BCM) groundwater, 70 BCM lake water and 124.4 BCM river water resources [1]. These resources are determined in the framework of the rising population and natural aspiration to become and be realized as a developing nation. With fast development and high demands of improved life expectations, Natural resources within the earth faces increasing pressure. Decisions in water management can have social, economic, physical and environmental impact which is wide spread and prevalent. It is essential to possess more appropriate information for having rational decisions for most of the people that leads to have the maximum amount of benefits. Therefore having of consistent and accurate information to the water resources will be an important for the systematic management of resources.

Classification of irrigation areas with best accuracy will help to have better information for the changes in water uses for different seasons. Having such information for the concerned bodies can help to have an improved information of the annual supply and abstractions of the water resource systems. Economic experts will also examine this data together with other socio-economic data to develop scientific knowledge of the aspects of agricultural lands.

Current information on the spatial distribution of irrigated crops in conjunction with temporal variations of the crops could help to have a strategic management of water resource systems [2], using of surveyors for the classification of irrigated land uses are not only time consuming but also tiresome [3] that leads to the problem of getting irrigated land use data with better quality and accuracy. Therefore using remote sensing technologies, that uses a reliable technology and low-priced user costs, to gather estimations for areas under irrigation across a ranges of scale [4]. The satellites of remotely sensed are monitoring the ground continuously, making them compatible for analyzing variations to different scales of irrigated crop lands and understanding water resource management [3]. Remote sensing data can also afford the power to detect the environmental and social influences that subsidizes to observed variations in the watershed.

Majority of models for crops including Cropwat and AquaCrop are point-scale models supported field or plot experimentations and are not consider spatial variations in such factors as irrigation scheduling and practices, crop types and soil characteristics. Therefore, unless such point scale estimates could be up-scaled to the spatial watershed scale, the complete impact of such plot scale investigations cannot be real. Geographic information system is often used to extend their implications to watershed and regional scales through close, embedded loose or close couplings [5]. Therefore, in this study CROPWAT model with GIS software and QSWAT Model have used to compute the effect of land managing practices in Robit watershed (A watershed defined by different crop types, different water resources and with different soil textures.), that can save both operating time and enabled estimates of the spatial pattern of irrigation water requirements and ground water recharges respectively.

2   Materials and Research Methods

2.1   Description of the Study Area

Robit watershed is an experimental watershed with an entire area of 1,412.29 ha located at the north of Amhara region, Bahirdar zuria woreda, Robit bata kebele administration near Lake Tana, the source of Blue Nile River. Robit bata Kebele has a total area coverage of 4,159.62 ha and located 12 km north of Bahir dar town, along the Bahir dar - Gondar asphalt road, it has a sub-tropical ("Woina Dega") climate with average yearly rainfall of 1500 mm, temperature ranges from 11.6 °C to 27.1 °C, and average sunshine hours of 8.0 h. It is a plain with a majority of the catchment area reaching an elevation of 1850 m above mean sea level.

Livelihood system relies on both crop and livestock production and it is one among the potential areas suitable for manual well drilling. Main rain-fed crops grown are finger millet, eragrostis tef, maize and other grains. the area has vast area coverage of the commercial crops like khat (Catha edulis Forsk), coffee, mango and Hop (Rhamnus prinoides) which are the most source of income and irrigated in the dry season and supplementary in the rainy season in cases of long dry spells using both surface and groundwater. Irrigation of those dry season crops are mainly practiced using ground water lifting technologies (i.e. mainly manual water lifting) and motor pumping of surface water when available. Because of the extensive irrigation practices and therefore the large surface water abstractions, Yegasho River dries up in the end of November up to the end of May depending on the rainy season occurrence (Formal interview with local people and Bahirdar zuria agricultural office).

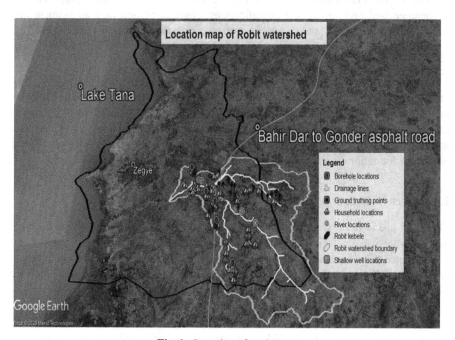

Fig. 1. Location of study area

Because of its close distance to Lake Tana, groundwater potential and experience in smallholder irrigation is comparatively high within the watershed. Shallow groundwater source is the main sources of irrigation water [6] (Fig. 1).

2.2 Remote Sensing Data Processing

The products of PlanetScope images are found in 3 different sources: 1B level PlanetScope image is an image with sensor having radiometric corrections, that is produced for the user with high quality of image processings. 3B level PlanetScope multispectral image is an orthorectified product which is produced to a cartographic projections. 3A Orth Tile PlanetScope image is orthorectified products and can achieve a high variations of uses that require exact geological locations and cartographic projections [7].

A cloudless 3B level PlanetScope multispectral image of Robit Bata watershed has been captured for the mid-season of the irrigated crops on 02/02/2017 in order to differentiate the land use classes accurately (Table 1).

Table 1. Remote sensing data used for LULC classification

ID	Image codes	Date	Spatial resolution
1	20170202_071408_0e2f_3B_AnalyticMS	2/2/2017	3 m

The LULC classification process was achieved following image preprocessing of unsupervised and supervised classifications, conducting accuracy assessment and compilation of Land use land cover and crop area classifications in the watershed.

2.3 River Discharge Data Collection

Stream flow data at Robit watershed outlet was measured from 2015–2018. The river flow at the outlet of Robit watershed from 2015 to 2018 was obtained from innovation Lab for Small-Scale irrigation (ILSSI) project with Bahir Dar University. These data were used in calibration and validation of SWAT model. The flow from 2015–2017 have been used for calibration and the flow for the year 2018 was used for validation.

2.4 Water Abstraction Survey

The water use in Robit watershed is largely defined by the land covers with in the area. The main land use with in the watershed is agriculture, which includes irrigated and non-irrigated crop farming like khat, hop (Rhamnus prinoides), coffee, tomato, green pepper and cultivated lands. Ground and surface water sources within the watershed are used for irrigation, livestock and domestic purposes. The water abstraction survey for the above purposes was surveyed from November 2016–September 2017 for one year which is used to determine the total water abstracted from the study area. For doing a water abstraction survey, a standard questioner was prepared for the collection of domestic, irrigation and livestock water uses in the watershed by the community. On the questioner information regarding to the owner's name, GPS coordinates of sources, actual abstraction assessment, planting and harvesting dates, and frequency of water used days per week. The GPS coordinates had taken directly at the point of abstraction. The water abstraction assessment was an important part of the survey; it was also the most difficult part of the survey. Because during the interview the farmers may increase the number of buckets by desiring awards from government or they may decrease the number of buckets they extract per day by misgiving Taxes.

The abstraction assessment was done by recording the number of buckets the farmers extract per day. Then this volume was multiplied by the time they extract per week. This volume multiplied by the total usage time per year gives the estimated abstracted volume of water per year. The data had been taken from 34 households through ILSSI project.

2.5 Determination of Crop Water and Irrigation Water Requirement

CROPWAT 8 Model has been used to calculate the irrigation water requirements of major crops grown in the watershed. A 10 year average climate data of Bahir dar meteorological station was used because of its proximity to Robit watershed. Although the water requirement of crops and evapotranspiration of crops (ETc) are seems to be the same, water requirement of crops is the quantity of water that needs to be delivered, while evapotranspiration of crops is defined as the quantity of water that must be lost via evapotranspiration. The model calculates (ETc) using Eq. (1). The values for Kc for each types of crops were adopted from [8]. The estimation of irrigation water required for the crops was determined after calculating the effective rainfall by USDA Soil Conservation Service Method [8]. When rainfall is insufficient, therefore in order to meet the water lost by evapotranspiration irrigation is required.

To determine the irrigation water requirement of crops, CROPWAT 8 estimates a daily water balance of the root zone using Eq. (2). To determine the total water requirement of crops at scheme level, the data for irrigated area of each crop type as input to the model should be incorporated that is found from crop map classification.

$$ET_c = K_c \times ET_o \tag{1}$$

ETc - crop actual evapotranspiration crops (mm/day)
Kc - dimensionless coefficient of crops
ETo - reference evapotranspiration of crops (mm/day)

$$IWR = (ET_c - ER) \tag{2}$$

Where, IWR - Irrigation Requirement of crops (mm)
ETc - actual Evapotranspiration of crops (mm)
ER - Effective Rainfall (mm)

2.6 Descriptions of QSWAT Model

The water balance components resulted from QSWAT model includes evapotranspiration, infiltration, precipitation, surface runoff, interception, percolation and lateral subsurface flow within the aquifer and the soil profile [9]. Surface runoff has been determined by a modified soil conservation Service (SCS) curve number method [10].

İn the model output the surplus available water after the occurrence of initial abstractions and runoff from surfaces infiltrates inside the soil layer. Within the soil layer Percolation is simulated for every layer. When there is exceeding of the soil water to field capacity, flow of water downwards the soil profile occurs and its flow rate is directed by saturated hydraulic conductivity of the soil. The flow at every soil profile is governed by employing the method of storage routing. Within the soil profile Lateral subsurface flow simultaneously with percolation can be estimated by a kinematic storage routing method using slope length, saturated hydraulic conductivity and slope. Similarly, the water uptake by plants and evaporation from the soil can be estimated by a depth distribution method. Amount of water that undergoes beneath the rock layer by percolation flows into vadose zone before becoming groundwater recharge. When the water in the soil layer exits, exponential decay weighting function can exploited to account the time delay in groundwater recharge. In QSWAT model Ground water is categorized in two: a shallow aquifer and a deep aquifer that water flows to streams within the watershed and outside the watershed respectively. Consequently, groundwater recharge can be divided into shallow aquifer recharge and deep aquifer recharge.

Land Use Map

Using a 3 m by 3 m high spatial resolution planetscope image, a land use map in the year 2017 was classified with best accuracy. Google Earth view of the watershed in 2017 fits correctly and represents all land use classes in the watershed. According to the supervised classification, the most important crops grown in Robit watershed are khat (Catha edulis Forsk), hop (Rhamnus prinoides), coffee, tomato, green pepper, and cultivated lands. Especially Khat, Coffee, and Hop are being cultivated in the watershed throughout the year. In recent years even if the Ethiopian government planned to avoid khat and replaced it with other crops, but more and more farmers are cultivating khat. Khat is a valuable product for local people and for export purposes. As a result, it is a basic source of income for local peoples in the area. Mango trees are also cultivated in the area and during the classification process; they were considered to be dense forests based on their reflectance values.

The plant characteristics of the crops khat and hop have been replaced by plant characteristics of coffee due to lack of known parameters in SWAT 2012 database.

Soil Map and Data

The soil map used in this research was Africa Soil Information Service (AFSIS) that is downloaded from https://www.isric.org/projects/soil-property-maps-africa-250-m-res olution. AFSIS soil summary with its database file and areal coverage is used for the definition of each HRUs in the watershed. Based on its spatial distribution there are nine different soil types in the watershed as shown in Fig. 2 (Table 2).

Weather Data

The daily weather data used in the model are minimum and maximum temperature, solar radiation, precipitation, relative humidity and wind speed data. Angstorm-Prescott equation was used to estimate solar radiation by using daily sunshine hour by relating short-wave radiation with other physical factors, as optical air mass, turbidity, and

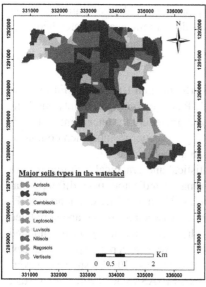

Fig. 2. Soil map of Robit watershed

Table 2. Percentage of major soil coverage in the watershed

FID	Major soils	Area	Percent coverage
1	Acrisols	0.67	0.05
2	Alisols	494.30	35.00
3	Cambisols	56.99	4.04
4	Ferralsols	40.02	2.83
5	Leptosols	10.79	0.76
6	Luvisols	335.70	23.77
7	Nitisols	320.52	22.70
8	Regosols	37.05	2.62
9	Vertisols	116.25	8.23
Total		**1412.29**	**100**

extraterrestrial radiation, water vapor content of the air and type and amount of cloud cover [12].

The daily metrological data from 1993–2018 were obtained from Bahir Dar meteorological service. Bahir Dar station weather data was used for this study as Robit watershed is located 12 km from the station and it has the same topographic and climatic characteristics. The WGEN uses average monthly meteorological data as aparameters for long period of yeras. The weathe generator data can also be prepared for QSWAT model using independent techniques such as dew.exe for dew point temperature and pcpSTAT for rainfall [13].

İn QSWAT weather generator model is incorporated to fill missing weather data during recordings. Missing weather data are left as it was in name.dbf format and a value of −99.00 inserted for missed values. QSWAT understands these values to generate weather data for that missed data at that day.

Model Sensitivity Analysis

The capability of the model to simulate water balance components sufficiently could be tested by using global sensitivity analysis, calibration and validation of the model [15].

For this study sensitivity analysis was performed in the model using the data from (1993–2018) and for the entire observed river flow data from (2015–2018).

Sensitive parameters were selected by studying previous calibration parameters and documents and from SWAT manual and researches done in the nearby watersheds e.g. [16–18].

SWAT Model Calibration

Automatic model calibration was done by SUFI-2 (Sequential Uncertainty Fitting version 2) which is a SWAT-CUP interface. SWAT-CUP is a separate uncertainty and calibration program established by [19] and SUFI-2 is a procedure for uncertainty and calibration analysis [20] as proposed by [21], SUFI-2 gives better results when compared with other programs even for small number of simulations.

To evaluate the performance of the model statistical and graphical techniques have been used. [14] recommended three model performance indicators from different statistical model evaluation methods. The dimensionless Nash-Sutcliffe efficiency (NSE) [22] measures normalized magnitude of the variances between measured and simulated flow. Values of NSE varies from −1 to 1. NSE of 1 shows the exact fit between simulated and observed flows. The value of NSE less than zero shows unacceptable performances.

The second performance indicator is PBIAS (percent bias). PBIAS shows the average variations between measured and simulated flows. PBIAS value of zero shows exact similarity; negative value shows overestimations and positive value shows underestimations of the model. R^2 (regression coefficient) describes the proportion of the total variance in the observed flow which could be clarified by the model. When the value of R^2 approaches to 1, there is high agreement between measured and simulated flows.

SWAT Model Validation

Validation of measured Yigashu River flows was done using an autonomous set of data without any adjustments of the calibrated parameters. The process continued till simulation of validation-period stream flows confirm that the model performs satisfactorily.

For this study, measured Stream flow data at the outlet of Yigashu River from 2017 to 2018 was used for the validation techniques to evaluate the model accuracy.

3   Results and Discussion

3.1   Land Use Map of the Study Area

Once the classification was completed, the land use land cover map of the study area was prepared and actual irrigated crop areas for Robit watershed was masked from this map as shown in Figs. 3 and 4.

The land use classes with their areal coverage is shown in Table 3 and this classification was used for HRU definition in SWAT modeling since overall accuracy and kappa coefficients are greater than 85%.

Table 3. Area of each land cover

FID	Class name	Area (ha)	Percent coverage
1	Khat (Catha edulis Forsk)	81.17	5.75
2	Hop (Rhamnus prinoides)	39.57	2.8
3	Coffee	2.56	0.18
4	Tomato	46.46	3.29
5	Green pepper	13.89	0.98
6	Cultivated land	1000.59	70.85
7	Dense forest	33.43	2.37
8	Eucalyptus trees	62.05	4.39
9	Farm village	45.37	3.21
10	Grazing land	63.47	4.49
11	Road	19.53	1.38
12	Shrub land	4.17	0.3
Total Area		**1412.29**	**100**

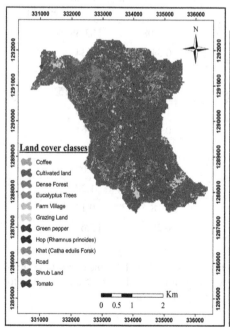

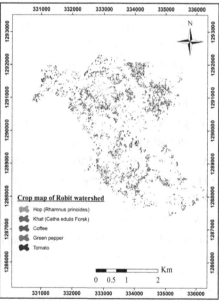

Fig. 3. Land use land cover map of Robit watershed

Fig. 4. Irrigated crop map of Robit watershed

3.2 Sensitivity Analysis

For sensitivity analysis twenty two flow parameters were tested by the default parameter values of upper and lower bounds. During the test analysis twelve of them have found to have higher effects on stream flow simulation. The selected parameters during sensitivity analysis were used for the process of calibration. A full clarifications of the parameters has been given in SWAT manual [14].

3.3 Calibration and Validation QSWAT Model

Model Calibration Results

The model was simulated for a 26 data years from 1993 to 2018 with three years of warm up periods (1993–1995). The measured stream flow data of the period from 2015 to 2017 were used for calibration and the data for these years were selected based on the measured data availability. Monthly observed data and simulated results comparison were used during the analysis calibration was simulated until the results for the performance indicators have reasonable values (Table 4).

Table 4. Calibrated values of flow parameters

Parameter name	Unit	SWAT default value	Fitted value	Calibrated parameter value
1:R__CN2.mgt	–	91	−0.08	83.53
2:V__GW_REVAP.gw	–	0.02	0.34	0.34
3:A__GW_DELAY.gw	days	31	−2.31	28.69
4:A__GWQMN.gw	Mm	1000	1704.15	2704.15
5:A__CANMX.hru	mm	0	1.06	1.06
6:V__ESCO.hru	–	0.95	0.61	0.61
7:V__CH_N2.rte	–	0.01	0.74	0.74
8:V__RCHRG_DP.gw	fraction	0.05	0.09	0.09
9:V__ALPHA_BF.gw	days	0.05	1.28	1.28
10:R__SOL_AWC.sol	mm/mm	0.12	0.18	0.14
11:R__SOL_K.sol	mm/h	2.08	0.29	2.68
12:A__REVAPMN.gw	Mm	750	153.12	903.12

Note: from the above Table 4, R (relative) stands for multiplying initial parameter by (1 + a given value). V stands for Replacement of initial parameter by calibrated value. A (absolute) stands for adding or subtracting calibrated parameter value to the original value.

Parameter Value Evaluations

Twelve flow parameters were processed during automatic calibration and their parameter values were iterated with permissible ranges until best agreements between simulated results and measured flow data was found.

It is significant to look for what extents the default parameter values established for the USA conditions were familiarized towards African conditions in the calibration process. Great attentions should be given for the calibrated parameters where unrealistic results may come from wrong parameter values. These parameters manage processes which result in a water loss from the system. The SCS curve number for moisture condition II (CN2) is related with permeability of the soil land use classes and antecedent soil water conditions. Groundwater "revap" coefficient (GW_REVAP) is the process of capillary rise, but somewhat the equation clarifies evapotranspiration from the shallow aquifer which is determined by the reference evapotranspiration. The volume of "revap" water is not passing to the soil surface, but it may lost from the system and should not be excessively high. Soil evaporation compensation factor (ESCO) is integrated to permit the user to adjust the depth distribution used to fulfill the soil evaporative request to account for the influences of capillary actions; it ranges from 0 to 1. When the value decreases, the model can extract more of evaporative demands from lower levels.

The fraction of Deep aquifer percolation (RCHRG DP) simulates the water that passes to deep aquifers that will not discharge towards the river. Such water losses to deep aquifer losses may be important in small catchments. Base flow alpha factor (ALPHA_BF) shows groundwater flow response to changes in recharge. Values changes from 0.9 to 1.0 for land with a fast response and values from 0.1 to 0.3 for lands with low responses to recharge. The time delay (GW_DELAY) can be defined as the required time for water escaping from the lower part of the root zone to enter the shallow aquifer and threshold depth of water in the shallow aquifer required for return flow to occur. (GWQMN) is a threshold depth in the shallow aquifer, and recharge will occur when the aquifer level goes outside GWQMN. As QSWAT model may start with an empty shallow aquifer, it may take many years before the GWQMN level is reached. In that situation, the model will start flow of water in the shallow aquifer whereby the rainfall will not matched with the output flows and losses.

GW_REVAP is a coefficient which determines revap flows. revap flow may not be occur, if GW_REVAP is null and revap will be potential evapotranspiration when its value is 1. GW_REVAP ranges from 0.02–0.20. Maximum canopy storage in mm of H_2o (CANMX) will exactly influence surface runoff infiltrations and evapotranspiration. As rain falling, the interception canopy reduces the erosive energy of droplets and apportion of rainfall is trapped within the canopy (Figs. 5 and 6 and Tables 5 and 6).

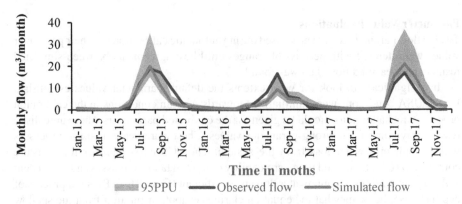

Fig. 5. Hydrograph of the observed and simulated monthly flows for the calibration period at the outlet of Robit watershed

Table 5. Calibration statistics for measured and simulated flows at Robit watershed

Calibration period	R^2	NSE	PBIAS	p-factor	r-factor
Jan 2015–Dec 2017	0.80	0.80	−5.4%	0.28	0.75

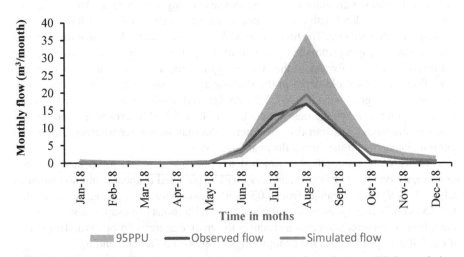

Fig. 6. Hydrograph of the observed and simulated monthly flows for the validation period

Table 6. Validation statistics for measured and simulated flows at Robit watershed

Validation period	R^2	NSE	PBIAS	p-factor	r-factor
Jan 2018–Dec 2018	0.96	0.95	−12.9	0.33	0.43

3.4   Spatial Variability of Irrigation Water Requirement

Net Crop water requirement and irrigation requirement has been estimated for the crop lands in the area for the 2016/2017 cropping season. The crop coefficients listed in CROPWAT model were used to estimate the water requirements of major crops at each growth stages. For the irrigated crops with in the watershed the result of the CROPWAT model is presented as shown in Table 7.

Table 7. Results of net and gross irrigation requirements of crops with-in the area

Crop	Area (ha)	NIR (mm/season)	NIR (Mm^3/season)	Irrigation efficiency (%)	GIR (Mm^3/season)
Khat	81.17	935.6	0.76	0.7	1.09
Hop	39.57	714.7	0.28	0.7	0.40
Coffee	2.56	806	0.02	0.7	0.04
Tomato	46.46	360.4	0.17	0.7	0.34
Green pepper	13.89	271.7	0.04	0.7	0.08
Total	183.65		1.27		1.95

The total irrigation water requirement for each crop types for the 2016/2017 cropping season was calculated as:

$$IR_{total} = IR_{khat} * \frac{A_{khat}}{A_{total}} + IR_{hop} * \frac{A_{hop}}{A_{hop}} + IR_{coffee} * \frac{A_{coffee}}{A_{total}} + IR_{tomato} * \frac{A_{tomato}}{A_{total}} + IR_{greenpepper} * \frac{A_{greenpepper}}{A_{total}}$$

3.5   Estimation of Water Used for Irrigation

From the water abstraction survey the volume of groundwater abstractions for irrigated crops was calculated for the whole irrigation season. The depth of irrigation water was calculated by dividing the total volume of water abstracted from a shallow well by the area of each crop type with in the watershed. The actual water that the farmer applied for each crop was compared to the theoretical value of CROPWAT results.

The information presented in the table below, show the actual quantity of irrigation water applied in terms of volume and depth of irrigation and irrigated area in Robit watershed and the CROPWAT result (Table 8).

Table 8. Comparison of applied irrigation and theoretical irrigation water requirements

Crop type	Area (ha)	Irrigation applied per season (mm)	Irrigation applied per season (Mm^3)
Khat	81.17	620.74	0.50
Hop	39.57	786.10	0.31
Coffee	2.56	344.69	0.01
Green pepper	13.89	961.97	0.13
Tomato	46.46	837.55	0.39
Sum	183.65		1.35

3.6 Estimation of Water Used for Livestock

Livestock production was found to be primarily dependent on groundwater for all or part of the watershed. Multiple numbers of livestock data was collected from Robit Kebele agriculture office. For these multiple animal types the water used per livestock per day was also collected by interviewing with model farmers in Robit kebele. Water used was calculated for each animal type by multiplying the average water used per livestock per day by the number of days used in the study year as indicated in Table 9. As the information obtained from the questioner, the farmer use hand dug wells for livestock for months starting from November to May, which counts 210 days. The total volume of water abstracted for livestock consumption was 25,840.29 m^3 per year at the watershed level. There are also unaccounted water (water loses) due to overflow of containers, illegal water usages, in accuracies in counting of the number of buckets used and over use of water for emergencies and ceremonies. As a result of these uncounted water uses 15% loss is adopted from [24]. Therefore the annual livestock water abstraction becomes 29,716.33 m^3. The total area of the watershed used for ground water storage was estimated as 1412.29 ha, and the annual equivalent depth for livestock consumption represents approximately 2.1 mm per year. The total water demand for livestock purposes based on single livestock demand specified in the ministry of water resources guideline is 47,737.31 m^3. So that as clearly seen from Table 9 the volume of water they abstracted for livestock consumption is less than the amount of water calculated based on [24].

Table 9. Water used and water demand computations for different animal types in the watershed

Livestock type	Number	Average water used/Live stock (L)	Total water used (m^3)	Water demand/ Livestock/day (L)	Total water demand (m^3)
Cow	998	30	6,287.40	50	10,479.00
Ox	1200	35	8,820.00	50	12,600.00

(*continued*)

Table 9. (*continued*)

Livestock type	Number	Average water used/Live stock (L)	Total water used (m³)	Water demand/ Livestock/day (L)	Total water demand (m³)
Bull	452	25	2,373.00	50	4,746.00
Heifer	564	25	2,961.00	50	5,922.00
Calf	474	10	995.4	10	995.4
Sheep	686	8	1,152.48	10	1,440.60
Goat	102	8	171.36	10	214.2
Donkey	476	30	2,998.80	50	4,998.00
Mule	11	35	80.85	50	115.5
Water loses	(15%)		3,876.04		6,226.61
Sum			**29,716.33**		**47,737.31**

3.7 Estimation of Water Used for Domestic Purposes

The population data at each village was collected from Robit Kebele agriculture office for the year 2017. The daily average domestic water consumption per person for a single person was estimated as 55 L for five households which corresponds to 11 L per capita per day. And the amount of water abstracted from ground water for domestic purpose in terms of volume was estimated as 13,546.61 m³ per year. There are also unaccounted water (water loses) due to overflow of containers, illegal water usages, in accuracies in counting of the number of buckets used and over use of water for emergencies and ceremonies. As a result of these uncounted water uses 15% loss is adopted from [24]. Therefore, the annual domestic water abstraction becomes 15,578.60 m³. The total area of the watershed used for ground water storage was estimated as 1412.29 ha, and the yearly equivalent depth of water for domestic use shows around 1.10 mm per year.

Table 10. Water used and water demand computations for domestic purposes in 2017

Sex	Number	Average percapita water consumption in liters	Domestic water used (m³)	per capita water consumption (L)	Domestic water demand (m³)
Male	1694	11	6,801.41	25	15,457.75
Female	1680	11	6,745.20	25	15,330
Water loses (15%)			2,031.99		4,618
Sum	**3374**		**15,578.60**		**35,405.91**

Generally as clearly seen from Table 10 the volume of water they abstracted for domestic use is less than the amount of water calculated based on [24].

3.8   Estimation of Total Water Abstractions for the Watershed

The total water abstraction is the sum of water abstracted for irrigation, livestock and domestic purposes with-in the watershed. The volume of water abstracted for irrigation, livestock and domestic uses is calculated as 1.40 Mm^3/year (1.35 Mm^3/year + 0.02 Mm^3/year + 0.03 Mm^3/year) (Fig. 7).

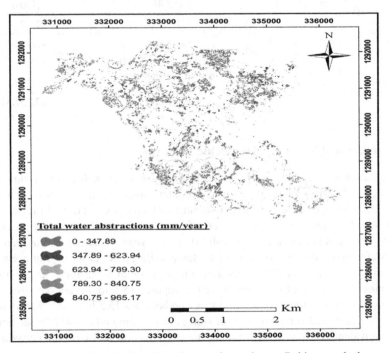

Fig. 7. Spatial variations of total water abstractions at Robit watershed

3.9   Base Flow (Return Flow)

Base flow (Return flow) is the quantity of stream flow come from groundwater. QSWAT segments groundwater into two systems of aquifers: a shallow unconfined aquifer, that create base flow to streams within the watershed, and a deep confined aquifer, that contributes base flow to streams outside the watershed. Water percolating beyond the bottom of the root zone separated into two parts each part becomes recharge for one of the aquifers. The return flow of water which arrives the main channel for Robit watershed is used for different purposes especially for irrigation purposes from November up to the end December and the spatial variability of base flow from QSWAT model is presented in Fig. 8. The average annual base flow obtained from the calibrated QSWAT model for the whole watershed area of 1412.29 ha was estimated to be approximately 1.37 Mm^3/year.

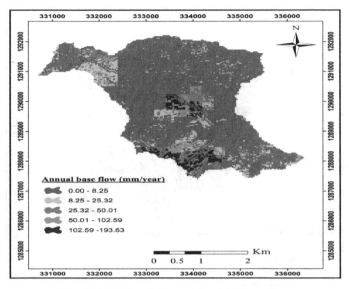

Fig. 8. Spatial variations of simulated base flow

3.10   Availability of Groundwater Recharge

A major determining factor of groundwater storage, groundwater table and thus ground-water resource estimation is the recharge. The groundwater recharge is essential in ascertaining the sustainability of withdrawals and for efficient management of ground-water resources. QSWAT model gave an indication of the spatial and temporal variation of this recharge, with respect to properties of the overlaying soil cover.

The average annual groundwater recharge obtained from the calibrated QSWAT model with in the watershed area of 1412.29 ha was estimated to be approximately 4.55 Mm^3/year. The detail recharge at each hydrologic response unit is presented in the appendices section. The spatial variations as shown in Fig. 9 shows a clear spatial pattern with a significant difference reflecting the great differences in land use and soil characteristics with in the watershed.

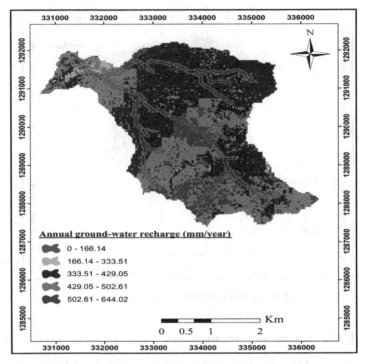

Fig. 9. Spatial variations of simulated groundwater recharges

3.11 The Interaction of Ground Water Use and Availability

See Table 11.

Table 11. General information about water use and availability of groundwater recharges within the watershed

Description	Amount
Watershed area (ha)	1,412.29
Area of irrigated crops (ha)	183.65
Percentage of irrigation area from total watershed area (%)	13
Water abstractions for irrigation purposes (Mm^3/yr)	1.35
Water abstractions for domestic purposes (Mm^3/yr)	0.02
Water abstractions for livestock purposes (Mm^3/yr)	0.03

(*continued*)

Table 11. (*continued*)

Description	Amount
Total Water abstractions for all purposes (Mm³/yr)	1.4
Water demand for domestic purposes (Mm³/yr)	0.04
Water demand for livestock purposes (Mm³/yr)	0.05
Irrigation requirements (Mm³/yr)	1.95
Total water demand for all purposes (Mm³/yr)	2.04
Total groundwater recharges (Mm³/yr)	4.55
Base flow (Mm³/yr)	1.37
Net groundwater recharges (Mm³/yr)	3.18
Percentage of total water abstractions from total recharge (%)	44
Percentage of total water demand from total recharge (%)	64.2
Level of groundwater exploitations	Underexploited

3.12 Discussions and Comparison of the Current Study with the Other Studies

Understandings on hydrological processes is the crucial element in water resource development and management programs. Watershed based hydrologic simulation models are used for the evaluations of the volume of water. QSWAT model was applied and was successfully evaluated through sensitivity analysis, model calibrations and model validations. Subsurface flow parameters were more sensitive to stream flows of the study area, showing the area has good recharge capacity.

QSWAT model has been found to obtain a reliable estimations of annual recharge for Robit watershed that was confirmed with different model performance measures. As a result, the calibrated parameters can be considered for further hydrologic analysis of the watershed. The QSWAT model can also considered as a potential model for the processing of the hydrology of ungauged watersheds in mountainous areas, which may have similar hydrological and meteorological characteristics with Robit watershed.

Model efficiency values were similar to those found by [25] using SWAT for monthly stream flow. In order to calibrate the water balance components of the watershed they used observed long-term stream flow data of the nearby watershed of Gumara river flow to calibrate the SWAT model. In their study Observed stream flow data from 1994–2016 of Gumara river was used for the calibration of SWAT model using Sequential Uncertainty Fitting program under the Uncertainty Procedures (SWAT-CUP) and found a Nash Sutcliff efficiency (NSE) of 0.80 and Percent Bias (PBIAS) of 5.4% which fits with the ongoing study. In this study the annual recharge varies spatially from 247 mm to 317 mm. this result has some variations with the ongoing study and this variations come from input data variations of SWAT model such as land use data soil database and stream flow data.

On the other hand, [26] estimated the annual recharges (interflow + base flow) by the Thornthwaite method and found 477 mm in 2014 and 344 mm in 2015. In their study when they only considers the part of the watershed with deep soils layers which is 52% of the watershed, the recharge to the aquifer was obtained as 933 mm/year in 2014 and 667 mm/year in 2015.

4 Conclusions

Water resources are the fundamental portions of life, therefore in order to upgrade their usage, wise planning, utilization and proper management is vital in the twenty-first century. In that case, the expansion of applications of GIS and remote sensing methods make the assessment and water resource modeling effective and easy for such purpose. QSWAT model that is an open access model for groundwater recharge estimation is based on hydro-meteorological and biophysical characteristics and it is essential to estimate long-term average yearly groundwater recharge in annual and seasonal basis for proper utilization, wise management and future planning of water resource systems.

In this study applying high resolution planetScope images for land use and crop area classification is simple and gives acceptable results with reasonable accuracy.

The model has been calibrated for the years of 2015–2017 and validated for year 2018. The value for NSE and R^2 for calibration (2015–2017) were 0.80 and 0.80 respectively. For validation (2018), NSE and R^2 are 0.95 and 0.96 respectively. These values show that model results are good and estimated net recharge values are reliable.

The assessment of the spatial variability of irrigation requirements in Robit watershed indicates that it increases spatially from 271.7 mm/year to 935.6 mm/year by considering an irrigation efficiency of groundwater as 70% at the watershed level.

The annual net recharge was estimated by subtracting the water abstraction surveyed in 2016–2017 from the total groundwater recharge and the annual average water abstraction was 44% of the annual average net recharge contribution during the study period and this result shows that there is high potential of groundwater recharges in the area.

Generally, the study indicates that there was enough water in the watershed even during the dry time and from the spatial map of the water abstraction survey the farmers apply less water than the crops require.

Finally this study provides evidence for the first time to link size of land parcels and the water use practices within the area and the available groundwater recharges.

Acknowledgements. First and for most we would like to acknowledge the enabling Environment created by the joint venture between the Ethiopian Road Authority and Bahir Dar university institute of technology and also we are grateful to Amhara Design and Supervision Works Enterprise for granting time to pursue this study and for all the help they have rendered to us.

We are also grateful to International Water Management Institute (IWMI) for financial support for this study and for providing data and facilitating the study needs.

References

1. Berhanu, B., Seleshi, Y., Melesse, A.M.: Surface water and groundwater resources of Ethiopia: potentials and challenges of water resources development. In: Nile River Basin, pp. 97–117. Springer (2014)
2. Ozdogan, M., Gutman, G.: A new methodology to map irrigated areas using multi-temporal MODIS and ancillary data: an application example in the continental US. Rem. Sens. Environ. **112**(9), 3520–3537 (2008)
3. Velpuri, N., et al.: Influence of resolution in irrigated area mapping and area estimation. Photogramm. Eng. Rem. Sens. **75**(12), 1383–1395 (2009)
4. Thenkabail, P.S., et al.: Sub-pixel area calculation methods for estimating irrigated areas. Sensors (Basel, Switzerland) **7**(11), 2519 (2007)
5. Li, J., et al.: Modeling crop water consumption and water productivity in the middle reaches of Heihe River Basin. Comput. Electron. Agric. **123**, 242–255 (2016)
6. Woldemeskel, H.M.: Production, Water Use and Development of Crop Coefficient for Napier Grass Underground Water Irrigation in Robit Kebele (2015)
7. Asrat, Z., et al.: Estimation of forest area and canopy cover based on visual interpretation of satellite images in Ethiopia. Land **7**(3), 92 (2018)
8. Liu, Y., Luo, Y.: A consolidated evaluation of the FAO-56 dual crop coefficient approach using the lysimeter data in the North China Plain. Agric. Water Manag. **97**(1), 31–40 (2010)
9. Neitsch, S.L., et al.: Soil and Water Assessment Tool Theoretical Documentation Version 2009. Texas Water Resources Institute (2011)
10. Slack, R., Welch, R.: Soil conservation service runoff curve number estimates from landsat data 1. J. Am. Water Resour. Assoc. **16**(5), 887–893 (1980)
11. Saeed, F.H., Al-Khafaji, M.: Assessing the Accuracy of Runoff Modelling with Different Spectral and Spatial Resolution Data Using SWAT Model. University of Technology (2016)
12. Revfeim, K.: On the relationship between radiation and mean daily sunshine. Agric. For. Meteorol. **86**(3–4), 183–191 (1997)
13. Liersch, S.: The Programs dew.exe and dew02.exe: User's Manual (2003)
14. Arnold, J., et al.: SWAT 2012 Input/Output Documentation. Texas Water Resources Institute (2013)
15. White, K.L., Chaubey, I.: Sensitivity analysis, calibration, and validations for a multisite and multivariable SWAT model 1. J. Am. Water Resour. Assoc. **41**(5), 1077–1089 (2005)
16. Shawul, A.A., Alamirew, T., Dinka, M.: Calibration and validation of SWAT model and estimation of water balance components of Shaya mountainous watershed, Southeastern Ethiopia. Hydrol. Earth Syst. Sci. Discuss. **10**(11), 13955–13978 (2013)
17. Mechal, A., Wagner, T., Birk, S.: Recharge variability and sensitivity to climate: the example of Gidabo River Basin, Main Ethiopian Rift. J. Hydrol. Region. Stud. **4**, 644–660 (2015)
18. Woldeyohannes, M.: Estimating Water Balance of Tegona Watershed in Southeastern Ethiopia, Using SWAT Model, Madda Walabu University (2016)
19. Abbaspour, K.C., et al.: Modelling hydrology and water quality in the pre-alpine/alpine Thur watershed using SWAT. J. Hydrol. **333**(2–4), 413–430 (2007)
20. Setegn, S.G., et al.: Spatial delineation of soil erosion vulnerability in the Lake Tana Basin, Ethiopia: climate change, land-cover dynamics and ecohydrology of the Nile River Bassin. Hydrol. Process. **23**(26), 3738–3750 (2009)
21. Zhou, B., et al.: The great 2008 Chinese ice storm: Its socioeconomic–ecological impact and sustainability lessons learned. Bull. Am. Meteor. Soc. **92**(1), 47–60 (2011)
22. Nash, J.E., Sutcliffe, J.V.: River flow forecasting through conceptual models part I—A discussion of principles. J. Hydrol. **10**(3), 282–290 (1970)

23. Moriasi, D.N., et al.: Hydrologic and water quality models: performance measures and evaluation criteria. Trans. ASABE **58**(6), 1763–1785 (2015)
24. Resources, T.F.D.R.o.E.M.o.W.: Urban Water Supply Design Criteria. Water Resources Administration Urban Water Supply and Sanitation Department, 31 Jan 2006
25. Worqlul, A.W., et al.: Water resource assessment, gaps, and constraints of vegetable production in Robit and Dangishta watersheds, Upper Blue Nile Basin. Ethiopia. Agricult. Water Manag. **226**, 105767 (2019)
26. Tilahun, S.A., et al.: Establishing irrigation potential of a hillside aquifer in the African highlands. Hydrol. Process. **34**(8), 1741–1753 (2020)

Experimental Study of Recycled Aggregate Concrete Produced from Recycled Fine Aggregate

Wallelign Mulugeta Nebiyu[1]([⊠]), Denamo Addissie Nuramo[2], and Abel Fantahun Ketema[1]

[1] Faculty of Civil and Water Resource Engineering,
Department of Civil Engineering,
Bahir Dar Institute of Technology, Bahir Dar University, Bahir Dar, Ethiopia
[2] Ethiopian Institute of Architecture Building Construction and City Development (EiABC), Addis Ababa University, Addis Ababa, Ethiopia

Abstract. Currently, in developing countries, the construction industry which uses a huge amount of concrete is booming at a faster growth rate due to an ever-increasing population and urbanization. To satisfy the high concrete demand natural resources like natural sand are depleting and river beds are eroded due to mining of natural sand. On the other hand, construction and demolition wastes disturb the environment due to different construction and demolition activities. Thus, in this study RCFA from concrete cubes at a laboratory was used to check the suitability of RCFA for concrete production as a partial replacement of natural sand. A mix of C - 25 concrete was prepared with 0%, 10%, 20%, 30%, 40%, 50%, and 100% replacement of natural sand by RCFA with and without admixture to check the compressive strength and workability of concrete. The workability of mixes without admixture increases as the replacement ratio of RCFA increases and vice versa for mixes with an admixture. The compressive strength of concrete decreases as the replacement ratio of RCFA increases. Even if there is a decrease in compressive strength as replacement ratio of RCFA increases, it is possible to replace NS up to 20% without an admixture and up to 50% with an admixture for the production of C-25 concrete without a significant compressive strength loss from the control mix.

Keywords: Recycled concrete fine aggregate (RCFA) · Recycled aggregate concrete (RAC) · Workability of concrete · Compressive strength of concrete

1 Introduction

The construction of infrastructures like buildings, bridges, roadways, and railways is increasing from time to time in the construction sector due to the ever-increasing population and urbanization. This demand has led to the construction of high-rise structures and demolishing existing old low-rise ones (Kisku et al. 2017). Newly constructed infrastructures mainly use concrete as the main input. Accordingly, the demand for concrete making ingredients like aggregates is increasing from time to time, since a huge amount of concrete is required in the construction industry for

M. L. Berihun (Ed.): ICAST 2021, LNICST 412, pp. 49–67, 2022.
https://doi.org/10.1007/978-3-030-93712-6_4

different infrastructures. Concrete's versatility, durability, sustainability, and economy have made it the world's most widely used construction material (Kosmatka et al. 2002). As Dixit et al. (2010), the construction industry is responsible for one of the largest impacts of all human activities 40% of raw stone, gravel and sand consumption, 25% of virgin wood, 40% of total energy and 16% of annual water consumption. The current annual consumption of concrete in the world is around 20 billion tons per year (Tosic et al. 2017).

Aggregates generally occupy 60% to 75% of the concrete volume (70% to 85% by mass) and strongly influence the concrete's fresh and hardened properties, mixture proportions, and economy (Kosmatka et al. 2002). From aggregates used in concrete production about 33–40% is a fine aggregate (Sonawane and Pimplikar, 2013). The consumption of natural sand in the world for concrete production is around 1000 million tons per year and making it scarce and limited (Ingalkar and Harle 2017). Accordingly, using this huge amount of fine aggregate in the construction industry depletes the natural environment; especially river beds that are the main sources of natural sand in the construction industry of Ethiopia.

On the other hand, nowadays, the volume of demolished concrete is increasing due to different reasons such as demolishing of structure for construction of new ones, destruction of structures due to natural disasters, crushing of cubes and blocks from different laboratories, destruction of buildings due to a new master plan, destruction of buildings due to the construction of new road, etc. Even if there is no exact recorded data on generation of C & D waste, more than 3 billion tonnes of construction and demolition waste are generated annually in the world (Akhtar and Sarmah 2018). The share of C&D in the total waste generation differs considerably between countries worldwide. According to Ulubeyli et al. (2017), the share is estimated as, Japan (16%), Germany (19%), USA (29%), EU (30%), China (30–40%), Hong Kong (38%), Australia (42%), the UK (50%), and Spain (70%). Per capita C&D waste generation in ton also shows large variations with low values in Norway (0.2), Poland (0.5), Spain (1), intermediate values in Germany and the UK (2), Hong Kong (3), France and Ireland (4), and high values in Luxembourg (15)". As Luangcharoenrat et al. (2019) pointed out, the proportion of construction debris (by weight) that is landfilled in each country shows between 13% and 60% compared with the total amount of waste.

Demolished concrete is available at various construction sites in huge quantity which are now posing a serious problem of disposal. Until now these materials are mostly used for landfilling works. But demolition and construction wastes have the potential to produce concrete by partially replacing natural aggregates. Thus, there are two problems in the construction industry i.e. depletion of natural resources and waste disposal problems. "To solve these two problems, People have started searching for suitable alternative materials that could be used either as an additive or as a partial replacement to the conventional ingredients of concrete so that the existing natural resources could be saved to the possible extent, and could be made available for the future generation" (Sirisala Chandrusha et al. 2017).

Since construction and demolition is booming, using recycled concrete for new concrete production very essential. Even if there is no sound literature on the amount of construction and demolition waste in the Ethiopian construction industry, annually around 204 tons of concrete waste produced from four Bahir Dar city material laboratory institutions (Yehualaw and Woldesenbet 2016). Using recycled concrete aggregate produced by crushing concrete waste reduces the consumption of natural aggregate (NS & NCA) as well as the amount of concrete waste that ends up in landfills which affect the environment negatively. Different researchers done a research and proposes the use of recycled aggregate for concrete production.

As Zega and Di Maio (2011) pointed out, it is possible to replace natural sand up to 30% by recycled concrete fine aggregate for concrete production having a similar mechanical and durable performance with 100% NS concrete using plasticizer admixture. The authors state that replacing natural sand up to 30% by RCFA is possible for structural concrete. On the other hand, Yaprak et al. (2011), state that the concrete produced by using the RCFA show lower strength by 4.3% for 10 RCFA, 5.9% for 20 RCFA, 9.8% for 30 RCFA, 12,7% for 40 RCFA, 18.6% for 50 RCFA and 35.4% for 100 RCFA. The authors state that RCFA can be used up to 10% ratio for producing C30 concrete, between 20% to 50% ratios for producing C 25 concrete.

Pereira et al. (2012), mention that using recycled fine aggregate as natural sand decreases the slump of concrete from 123 mm to 112 mm for mix without admixture, fixed constant 125 mm for regular super plasticizer and decreases from 130 mm (0% replacement) to 120 mm (100% replacement) for high range super plasticizer. The slump of concrete at 50% replacement and using regular super plasticizer increases from 125 mm to 130 mm. Similarly, Cartuxo et al. (2016), state that for the same slump value, the (w/c) increased up to 16.3% for mixes without admixture, the (w/c) decreased up to 15.7% for mixes using regular super plasticizer and, the (w/c) decreased up to 25.5% using high performance super plasticizer. The other researcher Khatib (2005), states that there is a systematic increase in slump of concrete as the content of recycled concrete fine aggregate in the mix increases, whereas there is a decrease in slump with the increase in recycled brick content. Similarly, Kou and Poon (2009), state that the slump of concrete increases as the replacement ratio of natural sand by recycled sand increases with a maximum increment of 5% at full replacement ratio.

Wang et al. (2019), uses both recycled fine and coarse aggregate for concrete production and the author concludes that there is a slight increase in the compressive strength of concrete mixes when NS was replaced with RCFA regardless of the coarse aggregate replacement level. The author observed that the mechanical properties of RCA decreased significantly when using 100% RCA with respective ranges of 8.7–14%, 18.9–23.6%, and 12.6–26.9% for compressive strength, modulus of elasticity and splitting testing strength test respectively. Similarly Kenai et al. (2002), investigated that the mechanical properties of concrete with recycled coarse and fine aggregates and found a reduction in compressive strength after 28 days in the order of 10% to 20% for concrete with recycled coarse aggregates, 10% to 30% for concrete with fine recycled aggregates and up to 35% for concrete with both coarse and fine aggregates. The other researchers Kou and Poon (2009), state that the compressive and tensile splitting strengths of the RA-SCC mixtures prepared without the addition of fly ash decreased with increasing fine recycled aggregate content.

Cartuxo et al. (2016), state that for concrete produced using fine recycled aggregate as natural sand, the compressive strength decreased up to 35% at 7 days, 29% at 28 days and 30% at 56 days for mixes without an admixture, increased up to 47% at

7 days, 35% at 28 days and 43% at 56 days for mixes with regular super plasticizer and, increased up to 82% at 7 days, 63% at 28 days and 59% at 56 days for mixes with high performance super plasticizer. On similar manner Pereira et al. (2012), pointed out that replacing natural sand by recycled concrete fine aggregate showed a decrease in compressive strength with figures of 4.8%, 15.4% and 3.3% for the without admixture, SP_1 and SP_2 families, respectively from the respective control mix at the age of 28 days.

Even if there are lots of researches studied by partially replacing natural sand by recycled concrete fine aggregate none of the researches are conducted by considering the whole water absorption capacity recycled concrete fine aggregate. Accordingly, this research undertaken to investigate the effect of replacement of natural fine aggregate with recycled concrete fine aggregate on properties of concrete by considering the whole absorption capacity of recycled concrete aggregate. The study was evaluated in terms of workability and compressive strength of concrete.

2   Materials and Experimental Design

2.1   Material Preparation and Properties

The recycled concrete fine aggregate used in this work were obtained from Bahir Dar university material laboratory crushed cubes. Then the cubes were crushed by jaw crusher at Zenzelima and the fine part were used as natural sand replacement. The crusher is primary crusher which is used for crushing stone for the production of aggregate. Dry mix were used on RCFA to reduce the amount of mortar on the surface of recycled concrete fine aggregate. When RCFA was dry mixed by mixer the attached mortar is separated (removed) from the fine aggregate. Additionally, RCFA becomes more smother. As compared from recycled concrete fine aggregate before dry mix to that of recycled concrete fine aggregate after dry mix, the mortar was separated from the aggregate after dry mix.

Locally available Lalibela natural sand and Meshenti coarse aggregate that satisfies ASTM requirement were used to conduct tests. Ordinary Portland cement 42.5 N made by Derba cement factory were used as a binding material. Tap water from Bahir Dar university and mega flow SP2 super plasticizer obtained from Addis Ababa with a dosage of 2% of cement were used for the production of concrete.

Physical Properties of Aggregates (Fine and Coarse Aggregate)
Gradation of Aggregate: The grading of aggregate is very essential for the production of good and suitable concrete. Well-graded aggregate decreases the porousness of concrete produced and also the cement consumption. The gradation of coarse aggregate, recycled concrete fine aggregate and natural fine aggregate satisfies ASTM standards as illustrated on the graph below. As shown on Figs. 1 and 2 the gradation of both fine and coarse aggregate is within the recommended limit of ASTM standard.

The rest physical properties of aggregates are tabulated in Table 1.

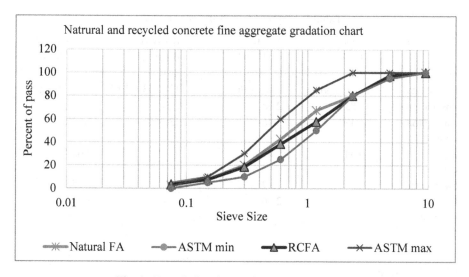

Fig. 1. Recycled and natural sand gradation chart

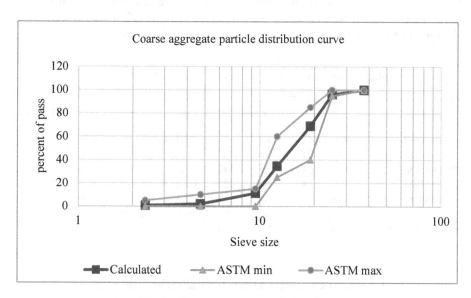

Fig. 2. Coarse aggregate gradation chart

Table 1. Physical test results of aggregates

Type of test	Coarse aggregate	Natural fine aggregate	Recycled concrete fine aggregate	
			Before dry mix	After dry mix
Unit weight	1707 kg/m^3	1619 kg/m^3	1386.33 kg/m^3	1523.70 kg/m^3
Specific gravity	2.83	2.68	2.34	2.42
Absorption capacity	1.43%	2.46	13.76%	10.4%
Moisture content	0.343	1.82	–	2.62%
Silt content	–	1.897	–	2.05%
Finesse modulus	–	2.86	–	3.04

2.2   Mix Design

After conducting the physical properties recycled concrete fine aggregate and natural fine and coarse aggregate mix design was performed by using ACI 211. The quantities of each concrete making ingredients are tabulated in Tables 2 and 3.

Table 2. Mix proportion by weight for mixes without admixture

Mix designation	Percent of RCFA	W/C ratio	Adjusted W/C	Weight of materials in Kg/m^3					Total weight of materials (Kg/m^3)
				Cement	RCFA	Sand	CA	Water	
0RCFA100NS	0%	0.49	0.54	365	–	786.0	1141.0	196.00	2488
10RCFA90NS	10%	0.49	0.55	365	74	707.4	1138.3	201.27	2486
20RCFA80NS	20%	0.49	0.57	365	148	628.8	1135.6	206.54	2484
30RCFA70NS	30%	0.49	0.58	365	222	550.2	1132.9	211.81	2482
40RCFA60NS	40%	0.49	0.59	365	296	471.6	1130.2	217.08	2480
50RCFA50NS	50%	0.49	0.61	365	370	393.0	1127.5	222.35	2478
100RCFA0NS	100%	0.49	0.68	365	740	–	1114.0	248.70	2468

Table 3. Mix proportion by weight for mixes with admixture

Mix Designation	Percent of RCFA	Percent of admixture	W/C ratio	Adjusted W/C	Weight of materials in Kg/m^3						Total weight of materials (Kg/m^3)
					Cement	RCFA	Sand	CA	Water	Admixture	
10RCFA90NS	10%	2% Cement	0.49	0.44	365	72.6	693	1138	161.20	7.3	2437
20RCFA80NS	20%	2% Cement	0.49	0.45	365	145.2	616	1136	165.30	7.3	2434
30RCFA70NS	30%	2% Cement	0.49	0.46	365	217.8	539	1133	169.40	7.3	2431
40RCFA60NS	40%	2% Cement	0.49	0.48	365	290.4	462	1130	173.47	7.3	2428
50RCFA50NS	50%	2% Cement	0.49	0.49	365	363.0	385	1128	177.60	7.3	2425
100RCFA0NS	100%	2% Cement	0.49	0.54	365	726.0	–	1114	198.08	7.3	2410

2.3   Test Methods for Materials

To check the suitability of concrete making ingredients different standards were adopted. The following are the test methods adopted for concrete making ingredients (Tables 4 and 5).

Table 4. Test methods for concrete making materials

Aggregate type and properties		Test methods
Gradation test	CA & FA	ASTM C 136 and ASTM C 33
Bulk density test	CA & FA	ASTM C 29
Water absorption test	CA	ASTM C127
	FA	ASTM C128
Specific gravity test	CA	ASTM C 127
	FA	ASTM C128
Silt content	FA	IS 2386
Organic impurity	FA	ASTM C 40
Moisture content	CA & FA	ASTM C 566

Table 5. Test methods for concrete

Concrete properties	Test method
Workability	ASTM C 143 M-08
Compressive strength	BS 1881-116

2.4   Experimental Design

This research focuses on replacing natural sand by recycled concrete fine aggregate for normal concrete production. Natural sand was replaced with recycled concrete fine aggregate partially and fully to analyze the effect of replacing natural sand by RCFA on concrete properties. To do the experimental work 0%, 10%, 20%, 30%, 40%, 50%, and 100% of natural sand is replaced by RCFA with and without admixture, and tests were conducted on hardened and fresh properties of concrete. 0% replacement is used as a control mix (reference mix). A total of 13 series of mixes and 117 cubes were prepared and tested for workability and compressive strength. Since recycled aggregate has high water absorption capacity three enhancement methods were used to compromise high water absorption capacity of recycled concrete fine aggregate. The methods were dry mix, using high range water reducing admixture and stage mix.

2.5   Mixing and Testing Methods for Concrete

Mix without Admixture: After all ingredients were prepared coarse aggregate, RCFA, and NS were added to the mixer and dry mix was conducted. Then cement was added to the mixer and dry mixed. Finally, water is added to the mix gradually and the concrete mixed uniformly. Once the concrete mixed uniformly, the workability of concrete was checked by a slump test. After the slump test, the concrete was cast in 15 cm * 15 cm * 15 cm cube molds. After one day cast cubes were demolded and cured into curing tanks at Bahir Dar Institute of Technology construction material laboratory. A total of 63 cubes were cast in this mix.

Mix with an Admixture: In this mixing procedure, after all ingredients were prepared RCFA, NS, and 67% mixing water were added to the mixer and mixed for 4 min. Then coarse aggregate was added to the mixer and mixed for 2 min. Finally, the remaining 33% mixing water, cement, and admixture were added to the mix and mixed for 4 min until the concrete was mixed uniformly. Once the concrete was mixed uniformly workability of concrete was checked by slump test. After testing the slump, the concrete was cast in 15 cm * 15 cm * 15 cm cube molds. After one-day cast cubes were demolded and cured into curing tanks at Bahir Dar Institute of Technology construction material laboratory. In this mixing method, the water reducing capacity of admixture was assumed to be 20% and the water content is reduced by 20%. This 20% was selected since high range water reducers can reduce the amount of mixing water by 12% to 30%. According to Cartuxo et al. (2016), high range water reducers can reduce the free mixing water up to 25.5% with the same slump to the control mix. In this mixing method, a total of 54 cubes were cast.

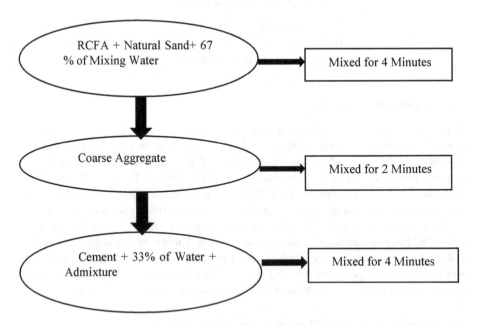

Fig. 3. Mixing procedure for mixes with an admixture adopted from Cartuxo et al. (2016)

Slump Test: The slump test of concrete was conducted after thoroughly mixing concrete by using ASTM C-143 M-08 standard.

Compressive Strength Test: Compressive strength test was carried out according to BS 1881-116 standard by using a hydraulic compression machine of capacity 2000 KN. The loading rate of the machine was 0.35 MPa/s. After casting concrete by 15 cm * 15 cm * 15 cm cubes and curing in curing tank, compressive strength test was conducted at 3rd, 7th and 28th day by using a compressive strength machine at Bahir Dar Institute of Technology.

3   Results and Discussions

In this section the results from slump test, compressive strength test and unit cost of concrete are discussed.

3.1   Workability of Concrete Produced from Recycled Concrete Aggregate

The slump test was performed to study the effects recycled fine aggregate concrete on workability according to ASTM C-143 M-08. The water to cement ratio varies due to the different water absorption capacity of each trial mix.

Workability of Concrete Mixes Without Admixture

Table 6. Workability of mixes without admixture

Mix designation	Percent of RCFA	W/C ratio	Adjusted W/C	Slump (mm)
0RCFA100NS	0%	0.49	0.54	40
10RCFA90NS	10%	0.49	0.55	42
20RCFA80NS	20%	0.49	0.57	45
30RCFA70NS	30%	0.49	0.58	47
40RCFA60NS	40%	0.49	0.59	50
50RCFA50NS	50%	0.49	0.61	55
100RCFA0NS	100%	0.49	0.68	71

W/C ratio = water to cement ratio for the production of C 25 concrete. Adjusted W/C ratio = water to cement ratio by considering absorption.

Concrete mixes without an admixture were done by considering all the absorption capacity of recycled concrete fine aggregate to the mix. As shown in Table 6 above the slump of concrete was increased as the replacement ratio of natural sand by RCFA was increased. This because the RCFA does not absorb all the water added to the mix by considering its water absorption capacity. "As Cartuxo et al. (2016) states, about 10 min are required for RCFA to absorb about 70% of its absorption capacity." Thus, if an adjustment is done on the mix design of concrete, the slump of concrete increases as the replacement of NS by RCFA increases. This result is also argued by (Kou and Poon

2009) and (Khatib 2005). The authors state that the workability of concrete increases as the replacement ratio increases at an early age and reduces substantially as time goes because of RCFA water absorption. The slump of concrete in mixes without an admixture was increased by 5%, 12.5%, 17.5%, 25%, 37.5%, and 77.5% from the control mix at 10%, 20%, 30%, 40%, 50%, and 100% replacement ratios respectively. Even if the slump of concrete increases as replacement ratio increases, the concrete was bleeding and segregated at higher replacement ratios.

Workability of Concrete Mixes with Admixture

Table 7. Workability of concrete for mixes with admixture

Mix designation	Percent of RCFA	Percent of admixture	W/C ratio	Adjusted W/C	Slump (mm)
10RCFA90NS	10%	2% Cement	0.49	0.44	45
20RCFA80NS	20%	2% Cement	0.49	0.45	40
30RCFA70NS	30%	2% Cement	0.49	0.46	37
40RCFA60NS	40%	2% Cement	0.49	0.48	35
50RCFA50NS	50%	2% Cement	0.49	0.49	32
100RCFA0NS	100%	2% Cement	0.49	0.54	27

Unlike concrete mixes mixed without an admixture, the slump of fresh concrete for mixes with an admixture and stage mixing was decreased as the percent of replacement of RCFA increases. This is because the stage mix gives time for RCFA to partially saturate and absorb more water. Besides, the effectiveness of high range water reducing admixtures decreases as the replacement ratio of RCFA increases (Pereira et al. 2012). Thus, the slump of the concrete mix was decreased as the replacement ratio of RCFA increases. This result is argued by test results found by (Solyman 2005), (Cartuxo et al. 2016) and (Pereira et al. 2012). Even if the slump of concrete decreases as the replacement ratio of RCFA increases, all concrete mixes mixed with an admixture have a suitable slump for concrete work (25 mm to 50 mm). As compared to the control mix, a maximum of 32.5% slump loss was observed at 100% replacement of natural sand by RCFA. To easily understand the difference, the slump results are shown in the graph below (Table 7).

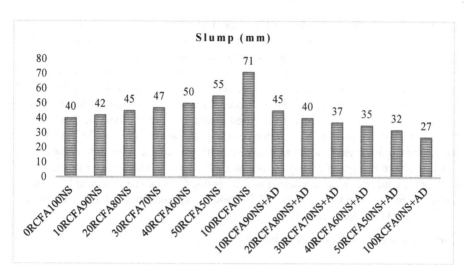

Fig. 4. Slump of concrete using RCFA at different replacement ratio

3.2   Compressive Strength Test

Compressive Strength Without Admixture

Table 8. Compressive strength without admixture

Mix designation	Percent of RCFA	W/C ratio	Adjusted W/C ratio	Average compressive strength		
				3 day	7 day	28 day
0RCFA100NS	Control (0)	0.49	0.54	21.41	29.87	36.54
10RCFA90NS	10	0.49	0.55	21.03	29.74	36.45
20RCFA80NS	20	0.49	0.57	19.84	28.13	34.75
30RCFA70NS	30	0.49	0.58	18.47	26.37	33.24
40RCFA60NS	40	0.49	0.59	17.77	25.14	31.58
50RCFA50NS	50	0.49	0.61	16.84	24.05	30.16
100RCFA0NS	100	0.49	0.68	12.40	19.68	25.42

Partially replacing NS by RCFA reduces the compressive strength of concrete as the replacement ratio of RCFA increases this is because the high absorption capacity of RCFA increases the water to cement ratio in the mixture. The 3rd day compressive strength of concrete reduced by 2%, 7%, 14%, 17%, 21%, and 42% from the control mix with 10%, 20%, 30%, 40%, 50%, and 100% replacement ratios respectively. Similarly, the compressive strength of concrete reduced from 0% to 34% at the 7th day, and from 0% to 30% at 28th day with replacement ratios ranging from 10% to 100%. This result is similar to the test result found by Cartuxo et al. (2016). The author found that full replacement of natural sand with RCFA reduces the compressive strength of concrete by 35%, and 29% at 7th, and 28th day respectively. Generally, the compressive strength of concrete reduces as the replacement ratio of natural sand by RCFA increases. When the age of concrete is increased the reduction in compressive strength of concrete from the control mix is decreased in all the concrete mixtures. This is due to the fact that the hydration of unhydrated cement paste on the surface of RCFA. At 20% replacement ratio, even if the compressive strength of concrete is lower than the control mix by 4.9% at the age of 28 days, it is slightly higher than the target mean strength of C 25 grade concrete. Thus, according to test results, C 25 can be produced by partially replacing natural sand with 20% RCFA and using locally available construction materials in Bahir Dar (Table 8).

Compressive Strength with Admixture

Table 9. Compressive strength with admixture

Mix designation	Percent of RCFA	W/C ratio	Adjusted W/C ratio	Average compressive strength		
				3 day	7 day	28 day
0RCFA100NS	0			21.41	29.87	36.54
10RCFA90NS+Ad	10	0.49	0.44	29.35	37.19	42.36
20RCFA80NS+Ad	20	0.49	0.45	28.91	36.34	40.26
30RCFA70NS+Ad	30	0.49	0.46	26.79	34.60	37.29
40RCFA60NS+Ad	40	0.49	0.48	25.13	32.89	35.41
50RCFA50NS+Ad	50	0.49	0.49	24.29	31.33	34.69
100RCFA0NS+Ad	100	0.49	0.54	19.86	26.03	29.72

As shown in Table 9 above, at 3rd day 37%, 35%, 25%, 17%, and 13% compressive strength increment were obtained from the control mix when 10%, 20%, 30%, 40%, and 50% of NS was replaced by RCFA respectively. But at the full replacement of NS by RCFA there is a loss of 7% compressive strength from the control mix. Similarly, at 7th day there is 24%, 22%, 16%, 10%, 5% compressive strength increment at 10%, 20%, 30%, 40%, and 50% replacement ratio of NS by RCFA respectively. But, at the full replacement of NS by RCFA there is a loss 13% compressive strength from the control mix. At the age of 28th day 16%, 10%, 2% compressive strength increment was obtained at 10%, 20%, and 30% replacement of NS by RCFA respectively. But at 40%, 50%, and 100% replacement of NS by RCFA there is a loss of 3%, 5%, and 19% compressive strength from the control mix respectively.

The compressive strength increment at an early age is higher for all mixes as compared to the control mix. This is due to the fact that the admixture used in the mix accelerates the strength gain of concrete. Since the admixture used was high range water reducing and accelerating admixture. From the test results obtained, RCFA can replace NS up to 50% by using water-reducing admixture for the production of C 25 concrete with a slight increment in compressive strength (3.5%) from the target mean strength. This finding is supported by (Ahmed 2014), the concrete containing RCFA contents up to 50% exhibited similar or slightly better at all ages from the control mix. From the test results, C 25 concrete can be produced by partially replacing NS with RCFA up to 50% by using different enhancement methods. Even if the compressive strength of concrete produced at 50% replacement is slightly lower than the control mix, it attains the target mean strength. To easily understand the difference in results, the results are shown in Fig. 5 below.

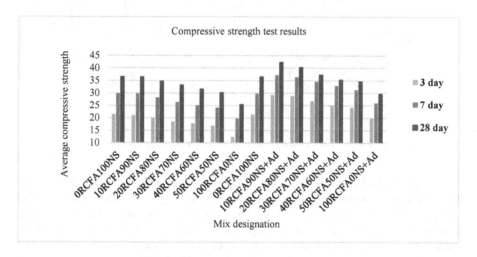

Fig. 5. Compressive strength test results

3.3 Cost Comparison

In this work, only material costs were considered to estimate the cost of concrete. The costs of the materials were collected from local material suppliers in Bahir Dar.

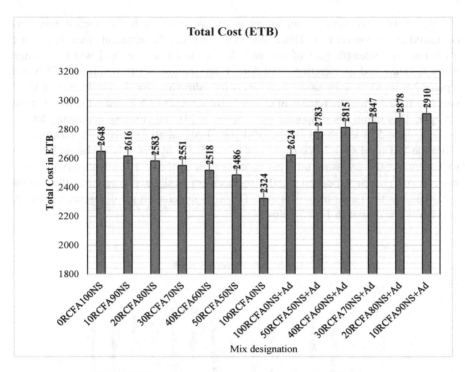

Fig. 6. Unit cost comparison for concrete using RCFA

Partially replacing natural sand by 10%, 20%, 30%, 40%, 50%, and 100% with RCFA without an admixture can save a material cost of 1.23%, 2.45%, 3.68%, 4.9%, 6.13%, and 12.25% respectively from the control mix. Though, the compressive strength of concrete reduces as the replacement ratio of NS by RCFA increases. Unlikely, as shown on Fig. 6 above using admixture in concrete incurs a material cost of 9.89%, 8.69%, 7.49%, 6.29% and 5.09% at 10%, 20%, 30%, 40%, and 50% replacement of natural sand by RCFA respectively. However, the full replacement of natural sand by RCFA with an admixture can save a material cost of 0.92% from the control mixture. Even if using an admixture in concrete incurs a cost, it increases the compressive strength of concrete. At the age of 28 days, the compressive strength of concrete can be increased by 16% at 10% replacement of natural sand with RCFA even if the mix is the costliest. Generally, the material cost of concrete decreases as the replacement ratio of natural sand by RCFA increases regardless of compressive strength loss.

According to the test results, replacing natural sand by RCFA up to 20% without an admixture and up to 50% with an admixture doesn't have a significant effect on the compressive strength of concrete. Thus, one can save a material cost of 2.45% by replacing NS with 20% RCFA. From this, a contractor can save approximately 6500 Birr from 100 m³ concrete by replacing 20% of natural sand with RCFA. For mixes with an admixture, one can replace natural sand by RCFA up to 50% without a significant compressive strength loss from the control mix. However, the material cost of concrete is increased by 5.09% from conventional concrete. Even if the cost of concrete produced using an admixture is costly, using an admixture with RCFA is very essential to solve waste disposal problems. By using an admixture, the optimum percent replacement of natural sand with RCFA is increased from 20% to 50%, and one can reduce 30% concrete waste by using admixture regardless of cost increment. Thus, when using RCFA as natural sand one can use up to 20% to save material cost and the other can use up to 50% with an admixture to solve waste disposal problems.

The construction industry is economical if it conserves natural resources, reduces energy consumption, solves waste disposal problems, and preserves the environment from degradation. Even if using water-reducing admixtures in concrete increases the material cost of concrete, the above-listed benefits are obtained when using recycled concrete fine aggregate as natural sand. Using recycled concrete fine aggregate saves waste transportation cost, saves landfill space, saves landfill charges, saves soil and groundwater contamination, reduces natural sand extraction, saves river beds from erosion, ensures sustainability, and improves the public image and environmental concern. Therefore, using construction and demolition waste for concrete production is very essential.

4 Conclusions

Finally, the following conclusions are drawn from the test results obtained from concrete produced by using RCFA as a partial replacement of natural sand.

1. Except for high water absorption and lower specific gravity, the physical properties of RCFA comply with the standards for good concrete production. Hence, RCFA can partially replace natural sand by using a dry mix, stage mix, and an admixture as an enhancement of RCFA.
2. The slump of concrete increases as replacement ratio RCFA increases for mixes without an admixture. This is because the concrete doesn't absorb all the water added to the concrete by considering the water absorption capacity of RCFA. When stage mix and an admixture were used, the slump of concrete was reduced as the replacement ratio NS by RCFA increases because the long mixing time gives the concrete to absorb the water added to the concrete by considering RCFA water absorption.
3. The compressive strength of concrete decreased as the replacement of RCFA increases since the amount of water added to the concrete was increased due to the high-water absorption capacity of RCFA. But, the compressive strength of concrete can be enhanced by using high range water reducing admixture and stage mixing. A maximum compressive strength increment of 16% is obtained at 28 days when 10% of sand is replaced by RCFA and using an admixture. Generally, the compressive strength of concrete reduces 5% to 30% for mixes without admixture and 3% to 19% for mixes with an admixture from the control mix at the age of 28 days.
4. From the test results, RCFA can replace NS up 20% by applying dry mix on RCFA and up to 50% by applying dry mix, stage mixing, and high range water reducing admixture without a significant compressive strength loss from the control mix.

5. From the cost comparison between conventional concrete and RCFA concrete, RCFA can save about 2.45% material cost than conventional concrete for a mix without an admixture at a 20% replacement ratio. Unlikely for mixes with an admixture the concrete incurs a material cost of 5.09% than conventional concrete at maximum replacement ratio of 50%.
6. Even if using RCFA incurs a cost, it should be used for concrete production to satisfy the NS demand, to reduce the waste released to the environment (waste disposal problem), to reduce energy consumption, and to reduce erosion of river beds for NS mining.

Generally, using RCFA for aggregate production is very essential for sustainability in the construction industry. Since sustainability is necessary and it isn't an option, using alternative construction materials like RCFA is economical to preserve the environment, to reduce natural resource extraction, to reduce energy consumption, and to solve waste disposal crises in the construction industry.

References

Agamuthu, P.: Challenges in Sustainable Management of Construction and Demolition Waste. SAGE, London (2008)

Ahmed, S.: Properties of concrete containing recycled fine aggregate and fly ash. J. Solid Waste Technol. Manag. **40**(1), 70–78 (2014)

Akhtar, A., Sarmah, A.K.: Construction and demolition waste generation and properties of recycled aggregate concrete: a global perspective. J. Clean. Prod. **186**, 262–281 (2018)

Anand Rangasamy, L.I.: (2019, October 31). https://www.quora.com/What-is-the-specific-gravity-of-sand

ASTM, A.: C128-07a Standard Test Method for Density, Relative Density (Specific Gravity), and Absorption of Fine Aggregate. ASTM International, West Conshohocken (2007)

ASTM, C.: 127 Standard Test Method for Density. Relative Density (Specific Gravity), and Absorption of Coarse Aggregate (2007)

ASTM, C.: 494/C 494 M. Standard Specification for Chemical Admixtures for Concrete. ASTM International (2005)

ASTM, C.: 125 Standard terminology relating to concrete and concrete aggregates. In: Annual Book of ASTM Standards, vol. 4 (2007)

ASTM, C.: 143 Standard test method for slump of hydraulic cement concrete. In: ASTM International (2007)

ASTM, C.: Standard test method for sieve analysis of fine and coarse aggregates (2006)

ASTM, C.: 33, 2008 "Standard Specification for Concrete Aggregates". West Conshohocken, USA (2008)

ASTM, C.: Standard test method for bulk density ("unit weight") and voids in aggregate. In: American Society for Testing and Materials. Annual Book, West Conshohocken (2009)

Begum, R.A., Siwar, C., Pereira, J.J., Jaafar, A.H.: A benefit–cost analysis on the economic feasibility of construction waste minimisation: the case of Malaysia. Resour. Conserv. Recycl. **48**(1), 86–98 (2006)

Behera, M., Bhattacharyya, S., Minocha, A., Deoliya, R., Maiti, S.: Recycled aggregate from C&D waste & its use in concrete–a breakthrough towards sustainability in construction sector: a review. Constr. Build. Mater. **68**, 501–516 (2014)

Ben Nakhi, A., Alhumoud, J.M.: Effects of recycled aggregate on concrete mix and exposure to chloride. Adv. Mater. Sci. Eng. (2019)

BMI. (2020, August 4). https://constructionreviewonline.com/2015/05/growth-of-ethiopia-construction-sector-to-surpass-that-of-regional-peers-bmi-says/

ASTM: 40/C40M11, Standard Test Methods for Organic Impurities in Fine Aggregates for Concrete. ASTM International, West Conshohocken (2011)

Cartuxo, F., de Brito, J., Evangelista, L., Jiménez, J., Ledesma, E.: Increased durability of concrete made with fine recycled concrete aggregates using superplasticizers. Materials 9(2), 98 (2016). https://doi.org/10.3390/ma9020098

Chandar, S.P., Thakur, N., Reddy, C.L.K., Babu, B.S., Reddy, T.S.P., Kosika, S.: Experimental investigation on partial replacement of fine aggregates by demolished concrete in the production of normal concrete. Int. J. Civ. Eng. Technol. 8(4), 386–393 (2017)

Chew, K.: Singapore's strategies towards sustainable construction. IES J. Part A: Civ. Struct. Eng. 3(3), 196–202 (2010)

ACI 211.1-91 Committee, A.: Standard Practice for Selecting Proportions for Normal, Heavyweight, and Mass Concrete, No. 9. Unites States, pp. 120–121 (2002)

Committee, A., Standardization, I.O.F.: Building Code Requirements for Structural Concrete (ACI 318-08) and Commentary (2008)

de Brito, J., Saikia, N.: Construction and demolition waste aggregates. In: de Brito, J., Saikia, N. (eds.) Recycled Aggregate in Concrete, pp. 81–113. Springer, London (2012). https://doi.org/10.1007/978-1-4471-4540-0_3

Deshmukh, M.: Replacement of fine aggregate by demolished waste. In: International Conference on Emanations in Modern Technology and Engineering (ICEMTE-2017), pp. 46–52 (2017)

Dixit, M.K., Fernández-Solís, J.L., Lavy, S., Culp, C.H.: Identification of parameters for embodied energy measurement: a literature review. Energy Build. 42(8), 1238–1247 (2010)

EPA: Construction and Demolition Debris Management in the United States. Office of Resource Conservation and Recovery, USA (2020)

Falcioni, R.: Ethiopians Construction Industry. A Market Insights Report by ITE Build & Interiors (2016)

Evangelista, L., De Brito, J.: Concrete with fine recycled aggregates: a review. Eur. J. Environ. Civ. Eng. 18(2), 129–172 (2014)

Fumoto, T., Yamada, M.: Influence of quality of recycled fine aggregate on properties of concrete. In: Memoirs of the Faculty of Engineering, Osaka City University, vol. 43, pp. 97–103 (2002)

Ghosh, S.K., Haldar, H., Chatterjee, S., Ghosh, P.: An optimization model on construction and demolition waste quantification from building. Procedia Environ. Sci. 35, 279–288 (2016)

Ingalkar, R.S., Harle, S.M.: Replacement of natural sand by crushed sand in the concrete. Landsc. Architect. Region. Plan. 2(1), 13–22 (2017)

Institutions, B.S.: Method for Determination of Compressive Strength of Concrete Cubes (BS 1881-116: 1983). London (2003)

Jin, R., Chen, Q.: Investigation of concrete recycling in the US construction industry. Procedia Eng. 118, 894–901 (2015)

Kenai, S., Debieb, F., Azzouz, L.: Mechanical properties and durability of concrete made with coarse and fine recycled concrete aggregates. Paper presented at the Challenges of Concrete Construction: Volume 5, Sustainable Concrete Construction: Proceedings of the International Conference held at the University of Dundee, Scotland, UK 9–11 Sept 2002 (2002)

Khatib, J.M.: Properties of concrete incorporating fine recycled aggregate. Cem. Concr. Res. 35(4), 763–769 (2005)

Kisku, N., Joshi, H., Ansari, M., Panda, S.K., Nayak, S., Dutta, S.C.: A critical review and assessment for usage of recycled aggregate as sustainable construction material. Constr. Build. Mater. **131**, 721–740 (2017). https://doi.org/10.1016/j.conbuildmat.2016.11.029

Kosmatka, S.H., Kerkhoff, B., Panarese, W.C.: Design and Control of Concrete Mixtures, vol. 5420. Portland Cement Association Skokie, IL (2002)

Kou, S., Poon, C.: Properties of self-compacting concrete prepared with coarse and fine recycled concrete aggregates. Cem. Concr. Compos. **31**(9), 622–627 (2009)

Luangcharoenrat, C., Intrachooto, S., Peansupap, V., Sutthinarakorn, W.: Factors influencing construction waste generation in building construction: Thailand's perspective. Sustainability **11**(13), 3638 (2019)

Macozoma, D.S.: Developing a Self-Sustaining Secondary Construction Materials Market in South Africa. University of the Witwatersrand (2006)

Massara, V.: The Brazilian legislation for the reuse of civil construction waste. MOJ Civ. Eng. **4** (5), 410–412 (2018)

Mohd, M., et al.: Utilization of demolished waste as fine aggregate in concrete. J. Acad. Indus. Res. **1**(7), 398–400 (2012)

Nagapan, S., Rahman, I.A., Asmi, A., Memon, A.H., Latif, I.: Issues on construction waste: The need for sustainable waste management. Paper presented at the 2012 IEEE Colloquium on Humanities, Science and Engineering (CHUSER) (2012)

Nelles, M., Gruenes, J., Morscheck, G.: Waste management in Germany–development to a sustainable circular economy. Procedia Environ. Sci. **35**(6), 14 (2016)

Paulo Roberto Lopes, L., Monica Batista, L.: Influence of CDW recycled aggregate on drying shrinkage of mortar. Open J. Civ. Eng. (2012)

Pereira, P., Evangelista, L., De Brito, J.: The effect of superplasticisers on the workability and compressive strength of concrete made with fine recycled concrete aggregates. Constr. Build. Mater. **28**(1), 722–729 (2012)

Polat, G., Damci, A., Turkoglu, H., Gurgun, A.P.: Identification of root causes of construction and demolition (C&D) waste: the case of Turkey. Procedia Eng. **196**, 948–955 (2017)

Rahdhika, K., Bramhini, A.: Construction and demolition waste as a replacement of fine aggregate in concrete. Int. J. Sci. Eng. Technol. Res. 1016–1021 (2017)

Solyman, M.: Classification of recycled sands and their applications as fine aggregates for concrete and bituminous mixtures (2005)

Sonawane, T.R., Pimplikar, S.S.: Use of recycled aggregate concrete. IOSR J. Mech. Civ. Eng. **52**, 59 (2013)

Surya, M., Vvl, K.R., Lakshmy, P.: Recycled aggregate concrete for transportation infrastructure. Procedia Soc. Behav. Sci. **104**, 1158–1167 (2013). https://doi.org/10.1016/j.sbspro.2013.11. 212

Taffese, W.Z.: Suitability investigation of recycled concrete aggregates for concrete production: an experimental case study. Adv. Civ. Eng. **2018**, 1–11 (2018). https://doi.org/10.1155/2018/8368351

Teychenne, D., Parrot, L., Pomeroy, C.: Building Research Establishment. Garston, 11 March (1978)

Tosic, N., Marinkovic, S., Stojanovic, A.: Sustainability of the concrete industry: current trends and future outlook. Tehnika **72**(1), 38–44 (2017). https://doi.org/10.5937/tehnika1701038T

Turkyilmaz, A., Guney, M., Karaca, F., Bagdatkyzy, Z., Sandybayeva, A., Sirenova, G.: A comprehensive construction and demolition waste management model using PESTEL and 3R for construction companies operating in Central Asia. Sustainability **11**(6), 1593 (2019). https://doi.org/10.3390/su11061593

Ulubeyli, S., Kazaz, A., Arslan, V.: Construction and demolition waste recycling plants revisited: management issues. Procedia Eng. **172**, 1190–1197 (2017). https://doi.org/10.1016/j.proeng. 2017.02.139

Vasoya, N.K., Varia, H.R.: Utilization of various waste materials in concrete a literature review. Int. J. Eng. Res. Technol. **4**(4), 1122–1126 (2015)

Wang, Y., Zhang, H., Geng, Y., Wang, Q., Zhang, S.: Prediction of the elastic modulus and the splitting tensile strength of concrete incorporating both fine and coarse recycled aggregate. Constr. Build. Mater. **215**, 332–346 (2019). https://doi.org/10.1016/j.conbuildmat.2019.04. 212

Winkler, G.: Recycling Construction & Demolition Waste: A LEED-Based Toolkit (Green-Source). McGraw Hill Professional (2010)

Xiao, J.: Recycled Aggregate Concrete Structures. Springer, Heidelberg (2018). https://doi.org/ 10.1007/978-3-662-53987-3

Yaprak, H., Aruntas, H.Y., Demir, I., Simsek, O., Durmus, G.: Effects of the fine recycled concrete aggregates on the concrete properties. Int. J. Phys. Sci. **6**(10), 2455–2461 (2011)

Yehualaw, M.D., Woldesenbet, A.K.: Economic impacts of recycled concrete aggregate for developing nations: a case study in the Ethiopian construction industry. Paper presented at the Construction Research Congress 2016 (2016)

Zega, C.J., Di Maio, A.A.: Use of recycled fine aggregate in concretes with durable requirements. Waste Manag. **31**(11), 2336–2340 (2011). https://doi.org/10.1016/j.wasman.2011.06.011

Prediction of Irrigation Water Supply Using Supervised Machine Learning Models in Koga Irrigation Scheme, Ethiopia

Menwagaw T. Damtie[1(✉)], Seifu A. Tilahun[2], Fasikaw A. Zimale[2], and Petra Schmitter[3]

[1] Department of Hydraulic and Water Resources Engineering, Debre Tabor University, 272 Debre Tabor, Ethiopia
[2] Faculty of Civil and Water Resources Engineering, Bahir Dar Institute of Technology, 26 Bahir Dar, Ethiopia
[3] International Water Management Institute (IWMI), Addis Ababa, Ethiopia

Abstract. Estimating water supply through irrigation canal distribution systems is a crucial process for better water management in the irrigation schemes. This study aimed to develop an approach to predict the discharge delivered to unregulated irrigation canals (such as quaternary canals) from geometric and hydraulic information of regulated section of the system (such as tertiary and others) using machine learning approaches. The prediction performance of four Caret-based Supervised Machine Learning Models, namely; Multivariate Adaptive Regression Splines (MARS), Artificial Neural Networks (ANN), Random Forest (RF), and Radial Basis Support Vector Machines (SVM), were developed in the R programming environment, followed by variability assessment among canal outlets at Koga irrigation Scheme. Water delivery performance at quaternary canals showed a significant flow variation among the canal outlets. The comparative study of model prediction results showed identified MARS as the optimal model, both at the training stage (RMSE = 0.074 & R^2 = 0.86 with normalized data) and testing stage (RMSE = 3.89 & R^2 = 0.85 with rescaled data). Furthermore, the model building process and output equations of MARS were relatively interpretable compared to neuro and tree-based models, such as Artificial Neural Network and Random Forest. Thus, the MARS model was recommended to estimate the water supply to ungated irrigation canals as a function of flow rate information at gated distributary canal and other field data at lower components of irrigation schemes.

Keywords: Canal outlet · Machine learning · R environment · MARS

1 Introduction

Most large-scale irrigation schemes developed in Africa have serious water management problems caused by the absence of flow controlling gates in canal distribution networks, infrequent maintenance of the systems' infrastructures and poor operation of the system relying on traditional basis, which all are greatly reducing the sustainability of irrigation schemes [1]. The study of Adhakari [4] also explained that many of the

© ICST Institute for Computer Sciences, Social Informatics and Telecommunications Engineering 2022
Published by Springer Nature Switzerland AG 2022. All Rights Reserved
M. L. Berihun (Ed.): ICAST 2021, LNICST 412, pp. 68–81, 2022.
https://doi.org/10.1007/978-3-030-93712-6_5

modern irrigation systems are equipped with water control gates only at the upper canal networks whereas, the irrigation water flow across low level canals is kept either at full supply level or at no flow condition for some days on a rotational basis. These low-level canals are mostly built with non-adjustable outlet structures, to provide proportional distribution of irrigation supply to the watercourses [5]. However, the assessment result of Tariq et al. [5] clearly indicates significant flow variability across canal outlets with head outlets are withdrawing more than planned discharge, while tail outlets suffer the most [5].

Koga irrigation project, one of the modern schemes in Ethiopia, currently faces water share disputes of users where flow is not adequately controlled and regulated [6]. Since flow controlling mechanisms are absent at quaternary canal levels of the scheme, quantifying the actual amount of irrigation water at these outlets is very difficult, which leads to inequitable, unreliable and inadequate supply of water to the irrigation fields within and across irrigation blocks [27].

Associating irrigation water supply at ungated irrigation canal outlets with available operational and field information is a crucial step towards improving scheme governance and efficiency.

Since irrigation water supply is reliant on field and operational conditions, machine learning models are required to predict the discharge response delivered to small irrigation water courses at data scarce environments.

Divya et al. [10] defined that machine learning is simply training a model with data and then using the model to predict any new data. After the training, the machine can perform automatically and can also learn to fine-tune. In the learning system, it comprises of four design choices; namely, choosing the training data, the target function, the representation and the learning algorithm [11, 12].

The study of Mohri et al. [13] classifies machine learning into three broad categories: namely; supervised learning, unsupervised learning and reinforcement learning. In supervised machine learning technique, the machine is fed with paired sets of inputs and outputs, which are called labeled datasets whereas, in case of unsupervised machine learning, the machine is given a dataset without the output sets [14].

The application of machine learning models is currently emerging to create new opportunities to understand data intensive processes in agricultural activities [15]. Prediction of various water resource problems were investigated by different scholars. Gu et al. [16] used neural network and genetic algorithm machine learning algorithms to develop the yield-irrigation water model for predicting the corn yield for different irrigation systems under subsurface drip irrigation. The hybrid model of these algorithms gave accurate predictions of the yield with the average error of 0.71%.

Parsaie et al. [17] had applied supervised machine leaning models such as, Multivariate Adaptive Regression Splines (MARS), Artificial Neural Network (ANN), and Support Vector Machine (SVM) for prediction of discharge coefficient (Cd) of lateral intakes, irrigation and drainage networks. The result of the study indicated that MARS model outperforms the ANN and SVM models. The tangent sigmoid and radial basic functions were found to be the most efficient transfer and kernel functions for ANN and SVM respectively.

It was found that the performance of MARS model was high compared with neuro based and fuzzy inference systems, for prediction of monthly stream flow in a mountainous basin [18]. It was also studied that the MARS and SVM-Radial Basis Function models generally performed better than gene expression programming (GEP) and SVM-Polynomial models in estimating monthly mean reference evapotranspiration [19]. A study of groundwater potential mapping was made using multivariate adaptive regression spline (MARS) and random forest (RF) with the aid of GIS tool [2]. The prediction performance of RF and MARS are relatively good in estimating groundwater spring potential, the later slightly performed higher from the two models [2].

In general, MARS was first presented by Friedman [20], and recently it is used in most fields of water resources engineering. It is a nonparametric statistical method which simply develops interpretable functional relationships between a set of input variables and the target dependent variables [21]. The nature of the MARS feature breaks the predictor into two groups and models the relationships between the predictor and the outcome in each group [22]. Among the many options, machine learning algorithms are chosen on the basis of the input data and the learning task.

R provides support for machine learning in input data processing and learning tasks [23]. It is a free open-source programming language that has several packages needed for machine learning [24]. Caret (short, for Classification and regression training) is a unified interface package available for download in Cran into R, to simplify the analysis and interpretation of black box machine learning models [24]. Caret includes several other packages and also have methods for pre-processing training data, model training, tuning, calculating variable importance, and model visualizations [24, 25].

In this study, the performance of four machine learning models (multivariate adaptive regression spline artificial neural network, support vector machine, and random forest) were compared for irrigation water supply prediction, to provide insights by applying such models in data scarce irrigation systems.

2 Materials and Methods

2.1 Description of the Study Area

Koga Irrigation scheme is found in the upper source of the Blue Nile, specifically located in Koga Watershed near Merawi town, West Gojjam Zone, Ethiopia [26]. The reservoir of Koga has a capacity to store about 83 mm^3 of water, which can irrigate 12 irrigation blocks covering a total of 7,000 ha reaching more than 10000 beneficiaries [26]. The canal network comprises of 19.7 km of lined main canal, 52 km of lined secondary canals, 156 km of tertiary canals, 905 km of unlined quaternary canals and 11 Night Storage Reservoirs [27]. The head of quaternary canals are built without controlling gates and quantifying the water delivered through these units is a difficult task. Canal flow through quaternary units is operated by group leaders so called "water fathers" in a rotational basis among farmers.

2.2   Field Investigation and Data Collection

This study was carried out at Koga Irrigation Scheme through the support of a collaborative partnership between the International Water Management Institute (IWMI) and Bahir Dar University in a FAO funded project entitled 'Closing the Water Productivity Gap' during 2018 and 2019 irrigation seasons. The field setup was appropriately planned at different reaches of the scheme, to observe the spatial and temporal variability of water supply through canal outlets. Six blocks out of twelve available irrigation blocks (two blocks from each head, middle and tail reaches of the scheme), six tertiary canals (one tertiary canal from each block), and 18 quaternary canal outlets (three outlets from each tertiary canal) were selected. Water level data were recorded in a weekly basis by using a standard thin plate 90^0-notch weir. This type of weir is used as temporal flow measuring device at minor irrigation canals [6]. According to Erikson [6] and Halefom et al. [7], a $90°$ v-notch thin-plate weir is often preferred because of its greater accuracy at low flows, and its lesser sensitivity to approach channel geometry and velocity distribution.

The weirs were installed at selected irrigation blocks just near to the exit of quaternary canals. The water level of quaternary canals was first recorded from the graded notches and then converted to discharge using an equation stated by USBR's water measurement manual [8] as follows,

$$Q = 1.38H^{2.5} \tag{1}$$

where, Q = discharge over the weir and H = water head above the weir notch. Alongside, water level data were collected at regulated tertiary canal heads. The existing rectangular concrete weirs at tertiary canal heads variable dimensions and hence a dimensionless number (h), the ratio of water level to weir width was used for further analysis. The data of dimensionless parameter (a = the ratio of irrigated area under a quaternary canal to tertiary canal), was collected from Koga Agricultural Bureau. The manning's coefficient for canal beds were used from design information and previous soil analysis results whereas, the distance of quaternary canal outlets from tertiary canal heads (l) were directly measured using GPS tracks. The diameter of canal outlet pipes (d) was measured using tapes, and the rank of operated outlets (r) was recorded during flow measuring events.

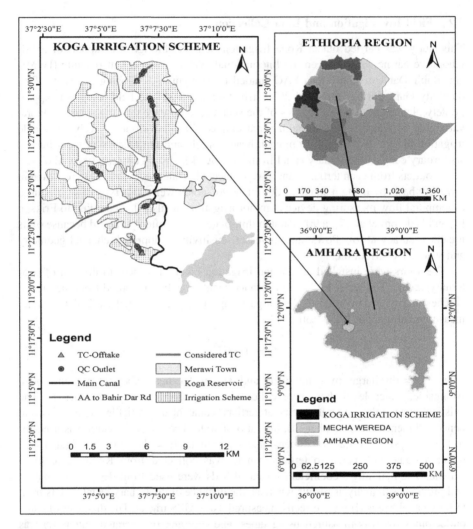

Fig. 1. Location of the study area

2.3   Developing Models

Model Inputs: The primary goal of this study was to develop a predictive model for estimating the irrigation water supply at a quaternary canal outlet, located at certain distance from the regulated distributary head canal. Several factors such as, geometric of the outlet structures, hydraulic characteristics, location, and operational management factors would affect the delivery performance of the outlets. Finally, six parameters were involved for estimating outlet discharge as follows;

$$Q \approx f(h, a, l, n, r, d) \tag{2}$$

where, Q = estimated outlet discharge at quaternary canal (l/s), h = water level per unit width at tertiary canal head weir($h = \frac{H}{B}$, dimension less), a = ratio of irrigated area (A) under quaternary canal outlet to total irrigated area(At) under tertiary canal weir ($a = \frac{A}{At}$, dimensionless), H = water level at tertiary canal off-taking weir (m), B = width of off-taking weir structure (m), l = distance of the outlet from the TC head (m), n = Manning roughness coefficient at tertiary canal (dimensionless), d = diameter of the outlet structure, and r = the ranking order of the operated outlets in ascending order along a tertiary canal (dimensionless) to describe the cumulative flow errors at the outlets u/s of the considered outlet. Table 1 shows number of pairs of observations and the statistical description of model input variables.

Table 1. Statistical summary of variables

Variable	Unit	Dataset	Minimum	Maximum	Mean	Std. Dev
Q	l/s	453	2.35	47.57	27.05	
h	–	453	0.41	0.98	0.71	0.13
a	–	453	0.07	0.20	0.15	0.03
l	m	453	20.00	1734.64	665.19	517.26
n	–	453	0.02	0.03	0.02	0.00
r	–	453	1.00	7.00	3.51	1.85
d	m	453	0.15	0.15	0.15	0.00

Data Preprocessing: The goal of transforming a set of data in machine learning is to facilitate faster learning of the algorithms. Unless the values of all variables have the same ranges, some machine learning algorithms such as, ANN would show syntax error to display the model performance criterion. A maximum- minimum normalization technique was used to transform data into the required format. Data partitioning into training and testing sets were performed many times in different ratios to get models best fit of the data.

Machine Learning Models: In this study, the motive behind applying machine learning models was their strong ability to map and learn the input data to predict the desired output where other methods such as multiple linear regression could not perform well. Several machine learning models were reviewed. The research was a multivariate supervised machine learning problem which required a quantitative modeling approach. The R environment has an immense number of packages for machine learning. Since selection of models from several individually named machine learning algorithms is difficult and time consuming, the Caret package was selected to train and compare many algorithms at a time, using a resampling technique. The initial selection of machine learning models was mostly literature based using recent water science studies with a similar scope.

Based on the research target, accessibility of algorithms, and the reviewed prediction performance, four classic machine learning models were selected [16, 17]. The models were; Multivariate Adaptive Regression Splines (MARS), Artificial Neural Networks (ANN), Support Vector Machines (SVM) with radial basis, and Random Forest (RF).

Model Development Process: The flow chart in Fig. 2 showed the procedures to develop the final model for predicting canal outlet discharge:

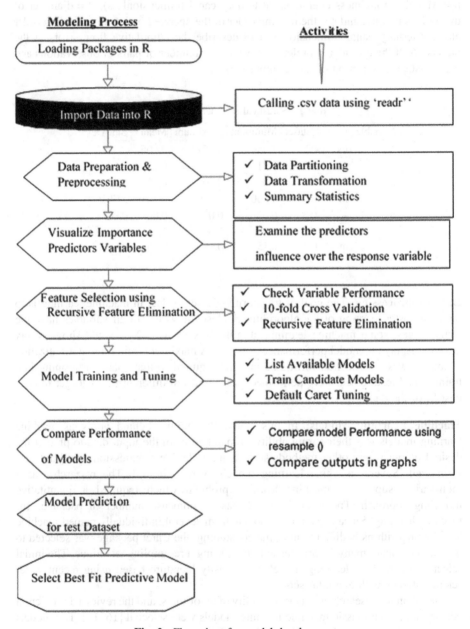

Fig. 2. Flow chart for model development

Model Evaluation Criteria: Evaluation of models refers to describing how well the trained model is performing to predict the targeted problem. The following regressive metrics were used in to evaluate the performance of models:

1. **Root Mean Square Error (RMSE)** is the standard deviation of the residuals (prediction errors). The residuals imply that how far the data points are from the regression line. The RMSE is calculated as,

$$RMSE = \sqrt{\frac{\sum (y_i - y_p)^2}{n - 1}} \tag{3}$$

2. **Coefficient of determination (R^2)** is interpreted as how much of the variability of the response variable is explained by the predictor variable. R^2 is an alternative measure of fit for the model over the RMSE, and is described as,

$$R^2 = 1 - \frac{\sum (y_i - y_p)^2}{\sum (y_{i-\bar{y}})^2} \tag{4}$$

3. **Mean Absolute Error (MAE)** is the average of the difference between the observed and predicted over the whole dataset, which is described as,

$$MAE = \frac{1}{n}\sum_{i=0}^{n} |y_i \bar{y}| \tag{5}$$

Where, y_i is the ith observed value, y_p is predicted value, and $\bar{y}$ is mean of observed values

3 Results and Discussion

3.1 Model Building and Variable Importance

The objective of this study was to develop an alternative approach to predict discharge in data scarce irrigation schemes. The observed discharge in ungated quaternary canals show significant flow rate variations both at spatial and temporal scales, compared with the planned flow rate per unit area at each quaternary canal. After several attempts of a randomized data splitting in boosting the best fit, a ratio of 70: 30% was used for model training and testing, respectively.

Six predictor variables, namely; water level per unit width (h), command area ratio (a), distance of outlets from tertiary canal head(l), Manning roughness coefficient of tertiary canals (n), rank of operated quaternary canal outlet along a tertiary canal (r), and modular outlet diameter were used to predict a response variable Q (outlet discharge).

Variable Importance: To examine how the predictors, influence the output discharge (Q), importance of variables was computed in R environment with caret for each model. The importance level of predictor variables was different for each model as shown at

Fig. 3. The canal outlet diameter (d) has the lowest importance level in developing all the models whereas, the area ratio(a) has the highest variable importance with ANN and MARS models.

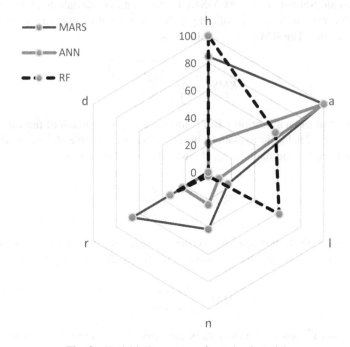

Fig. 3. Variable Importance for trained models

In Fig. 3, MARS is Multivariate Adaptive Regressive Spline, RF is Random Forest, and ANN is Artificial Neural Networks.

A recursive feature selection technique with 10-fold cross validation repeated three times, was used to analyze the resampling performance. The combination of top three model inputs variables h, a and l were selected as shown in Table 2.

Table 2. Recursive resampling performance over combination of inputs

Model inputs	RMSE	R^2	MAE
h	0.19	0.15	0.15
h, a	0.10	0.75	0.08
h, a, l	**0.08**	**0.85**	**0.06**
h, a, l, n	0.09	0.83	0.07
h, a, l, n, r	0.10	0.79	0.08
	0.08	0.84	0.07

The recursive feature selection using recursive feature elimination (rfe) method, agrees with the variable importance selection of RF model. However, selection of variables with the rfe technique and eliminating the least selected variables is not advisable as different models have different importance levels. Thus, training and default tuning of models was performed using a Caret package in the R environment.

During model training using resamples, there were no significant performance differences between the models. RF slightly outperformed (RMSE = 0.075, R^2 = 0.87 and MAE = 0.056) followed by MARS (RMSE = 0.075, R^2 = 0.86 and MAE = 0.058) and ANN (RMSE = 0.078, R^2 = 0.85 and MAE = 0.06). All the metric values are with normalized datasets, including the values displayed in Fig. 4.

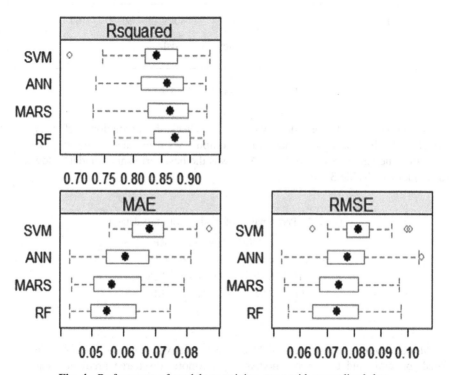

Fig. 4. Performance of models at training stage with normalized data

The learning speed of the models in the R environment for the training dataset was examined. MARS has taken the shortest duration (7.2 s) to train the model with 319 datasets and 6 predictors while, RF has taken the longest (60.1 s) in the normalized dataset (see Fig. 5).

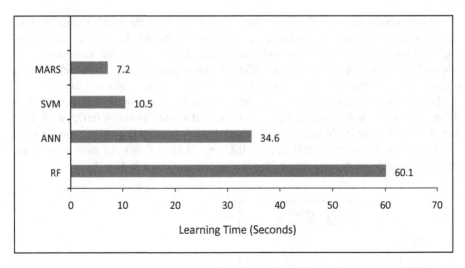

Fig. 5. Learning time of models

A randomized 30% test data was used to check the prediction performance of models with the normalized data and the outputs were rescaled to the original data structure. The results revealed that MARS was the best performing model followed by RF model (see Table 3).

Table 3. Performance of models with test dataset

	MARS	ANN	SVM	RF
R^2	**0.82**	0.76	0.76	0.78
RMSE	**3.89**	4.45	4.43	4.28
MAE	**2.91**	3.42	3.45	3.14

Model development process of MARS was relatively fast and interpretable compared to neuro and tree-based models. Furthermore, discharge prediction equation, which comprised of twelve basic functions and one intercept, was developed by this model. Three times repeated 10-fold cross validation of six variables were used to generate fifteen basic functions, out of which thirteen terms and five predictors were selected to develop the prediction equation. Figure 6 showed that the degree of prediction errors decreases as number of basic functions increase.

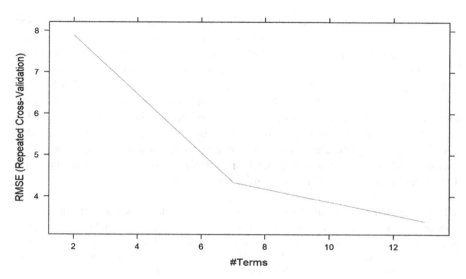

Fig. 6. Degree of errors with number of basic functions

The general Prediction equation developed by MARS was described as,

$$f(X) = 26.5 + \sum_{i=0}^{12} \beta i \mathrm{BFi}(X) \tag{6}$$

Where, BFi is the ith basic function, βi is the coefficient of basic functions and X is the predictor variable. Since all the basic functions generated by predictor variable (l), have zero multiplying coefficients, they were removed from Eq. 6. Using a combination of predictors, different equations were developed to predict canal outlet discharge, and the prediction performance is well described by Table 4.

Table 4. Discharge Prediction performance of MARS equations

Input variable	R^2	RMSE
a, h	0.38	5.40
h, n, r	0.60	6.34
a, h, r	0.71	5.66
a, h, r, n	0.80	4.27

The equation with all input variables, except canal outlet distance (l) has best prediction performance (RMSE = 4.27 m³/s, R^2 = 0.8).

4 Conclusions

Water delivery performance of quaternary canal outlets were assessed in Koga irrigation scheme during the irrigation season of 2019, and significant water supply variations were found at spatial and temporal scales. Discharge prediction equation at quaternary canal outlets was developed using six field parameters, using supervised machine learning algorithms in R environment. Four machine learning models were developed, and the optimal model both at the training stage (RMSE = 0.074 & R^2 = 0.86 with normalized data) and testing stage (RMSE = 3.89 m^3/s & R^2 = 0.85 with rescaled data) was Multivariate Adaptive Regressive Spline (MARS). The development process of MARS model was relatively interpretable compared to neuro and tree-based models. Furthermore, a prediction equation, which comprised of twelve basic functions and one intercept, from five predictors was developed by the Model. Since the distance parameter is eliminated due to its zero regression coefficients, the developed MARS equation was using four variables to predict discharge with prediction performance of RMSE = 4.27 m^3/s and R^2 = 0.80.

Acknowledgements. This study was made possible through the support of International Management Institute (IWMI) and Bahir Dar University Institute of Technology collaborative project entitled 'closing water productivity gaps' at Koga Irrigation Scheme, Ethiopia from 2017–2019. The sightings of this study are the full responsibilities of the Authors, and do not necessarily reflect the views of the above-mentioned organizations.

References

1. Agide, Z., et al.: Analysis of Water Delivery Performance of Smallholder Irrigation Schemes in Ethiopia: Diversity and Lessons Across Schemes, Typologies and Reaches (2016)
2. Zabihi, M., Pourghasemi, H.R., Pourtaghi, Z.S., Behzadfar, M.: GIS-based multivariate adaptive regression spline and random forest models for groundwater potential mapping in Iran. Environ. Earth Sci. **75**(8), 1–19 (2016). https://doi.org/10.1007/s12665-016-5424-9
3. Sanaee-Jahromi, S., Depeweg, H., Feyen, J.: Water delivery performance in the Doroodzan irrigation scheme Iran. Irrig. Drain. Syst. **14**(3), 207–222 (2000)
4. Adhakari, B.: Design of water distribution system: appropriateness of structured system in large irrigation projects in Nepal. Hydro Nepal J. Water Energy Environ. **19**, 25–30 (2016)
5. Tariq, J.A., Kakar, M.J.: Effect of variability of discharges on equity of water distribution among outlets. Sarhad J. Agric. **26**(1), 51–59 (2010)
6. Eriksson, S.: Water Quality in the Koga Irrigation Project, Ethiopia: A Snapshot of General Quality Parameters (2012)
7. Halefom, A., Sisay, E.: Performance assessment and diagnostic analysis of minor irrigation canal. Eng. Sci. Technol. Int. J. **7**, 10–17 (2017)
8. United States. Bureau of Reclamation: Water Measurement Manual. The Bureau (2001)
9. Chanson, H., Wang, H.: Unsteady discharge calibration of a large V-notch weir. Flow Meas. Instrum. **29**, 19–24 (2013)
10. Divya, K.S., Bhargavi, P., Jyothi, S.: Machine learning algorithms in big data analytics. Int. J. Comput. Sci. Eng. **6**(1), 64–70 (2018)
11. Weimer, M.: Machine Teaching–A Machine Learning Approach to Technology Enhanced Learning (Doctoral dissertation, Technische Universität) (2010)
12. Ciaburro, G., Venkateswaran, B.: Neural Networks with R: Smart Models Using CNN, RNN, Deep Learning, and Artificial Intelligence Principles. Packt Publishing Ltd. (2017)
13. Mohri, M., Rostamizadeh, A., Talwalkar, A.: Foundations of Machine Learning. (2012)
14. Ahmed, O.: Dataset Modification to Improve Machine Learning Algorithm Performance and Speed (Doctoral dissertation) (2014)

15. Liakos, K.G., Busato, P., Moshou, D., Pearson, S., Bochtis, D.: Machine learning in agriculture: a review. Sensors **18**(8), 2674 (2018)
16. Gu, J., Yin, G., Huang, P., Guo, J., Chen, L.: An improved back propagation neural network prediction model for subsurface drip irrigation system. Comput. Electr. Eng. **60**, 58–65 (2017)
17. Parsaie, A., Haghiabi, A., Shamsi, Z.: Intelligent modeling of discharge coefficient of lateral intakes. AUT J. Civil Eng. **2**(1), 3–10 (2018)
18. Adnan, R.M., Liang, Z., Parmar, K.S., Soni, K., Kisi, O.: Modeling monthly streamflow in mountainous basin by MARS, GMDH-NN and DENFIS using hydroclimatic data. Neural Comput. Appl. **33**(7), 2853–2871 (2020). https://doi.org/10.1007/s00521-020-05164-3
19. Mehdizadeh, S., Behmanesh, J., Khalili, K.: Using MARS, SVM, GEP and empirical equations for estimation of monthly mean reference evapotranspiration. Comput. Electron. Agric. **139**, 103–114 (2017)
20. Friedman, J.H.: Multivariate adaptive regression splines. In: The Annals of Statistics, pp. 1–67 (1991)
21. Rezaie-Balf, M.: Multivariate adaptive regression splines model for prediction of local scour depth downstream of an apron under 2D horizontal jets. Iranian J. Sci. Technol. Trans. Civil Eng. **43**(1), 103–115 (2019)
22. Kuhn, M., Johnson, K.: Measuring performance in classification models. In: Kuhn, M., Johnson, K. (eds.) Applied predictive modeling, pp. 247–273. Springer New York, New York, NY (2013). https://doi.org/10.1007/978-1-4614-6849-3_11
23. Probst, P., Bischl, B., Boulesteix, A.L.: Tunability: Importance of hyperparameters of machine learning algorithms. arXiv preprint arXiv:1802.09596 (2018)
24. Kuhn, M.: A short introduction to the caret package. R Found. Stat. Comput. **1**, 1–10 (2015)
25. Grün, B., Leisch, F.: FlexMix version 2: finite mixtures with concomitant variables and varying and constant parameters. J. Stat. Softw. **28**(4), 1–35 (2008). https://doi.org/10.18637/jss.v028.i04
26. Eguavoen, I., Tesfai, W.: Rebuilding Livelihoods After Dam-Induced Relocation in Koga, Blue Nile basin, Ethiopia (No. 83). ZEF Working Paper Series (2011)
27. Asres, S.B.: Evaluating and enhancing irrigation water management in the upper Blue Nile basin, Ethiopia: the case of Koga large scale irrigation scheme. Agric. Water Manag. **170**, 26–35 (2016)
28. Rochette, P., Desjardins, R.L., Pattey, E.: Spatial and temporal variability of soil respiration in agricultural fields. Can. J. Soil Sci. **71**(2), 189–196 (1991)

Numerical Investigation on the Effect of Reinforcement Shear Connectors in Load Bearing Capacity of Partially Encased Composite Beams

Tamirat Semu[1(✉)], Temesgen Wondimu[2], and Belay Worku[1]

[1] Bahir Dar University, Bahir Dar, Ethiopia
[2] Addis Abeba Science and Technology University, Addis Ababa, Ethiopia

Abstract. The efficient use and combination of the compressive strength of the concrete and the tensile strength of the structural steel create a high-quality solid composite material. However, the loose bond between the two materials has a huge negative effect by lowering the bending capacity unless connectors are introduced. Even if headed stud shear connectors are commonly used in the construction sector, the present study investigated the load-bearing capacity of partially encased composite beams through the replacement of the head studs with T shaped reinforcement shear connectors. Three-point loading with displacement control analysis had been performed numerically. The length of the flange, the height of the web and the location of the shear connections were considered key parameters. Among the parameters, the increased flange of the shear connector improved the tensile behavior of the concrete through the formation of adhesion. On the other hand, the intermediate web height showed a positive result to confine the concrete with the equivalent bond formation with the structural steel. For general composite beams, slip and concrete cracking increase away from the neutral axis which reduces the load-bearing capacity of the composite beams. Hence, lowering the shear connector's location to the bottom flange reduced the slip. As a result, the capacity of the composite beam was improved by creating an efficient anchorage with the shear connector, which increased the stiffness of the composite beam.

Keywords: Composite beam · Headed stud · Reinforcement shear connector · Load bearing capacity

1 Introduction

Since the effective combination of the two extreme structural elements, concrete and steel, create composite action, the new material is quite efficient in upgrading structural resistance as compared to their performance. The composite beam mostly consists of a steel girder and concrete slab with or without profiled steel sheet. Although the studs and the frictional interaction between the concrete and steel used to protect the shear, friction is a more imperative mechanism for the failure modes [1]. Most researches concentrate on improving either the quality or arrangement of the shear connectors,

© ICST Institute for Computer Sciences, Social Informatics and Telecommunications Engineering 2022
Published by Springer Nature Switzerland AG 2022. All Rights Reserved
M. L. Berihun (Ed.): ICAST 2021, LNICST 412, pp. 82–98, 2022.
https://doi.org/10.1007/978-3-030-93712-6_6

independently. In the contract, there is less interest in the investigation of both the concrete behaviour together with the shear connector.

The shear slip between the concrete and the structural steel components in a composite beam creates considerable deformation, which reduces rigidity resulting in a lower stiffness [2]. The slip, caused by the shear, requires an anchor to create a stable combination between the steel and concrete. In addition to the friction, the bondage between the structural steel and the concrete also plays a crucial role in the reduction of the slip [3]. Conversely, the absence of reinforcements and studs leads to a catastrophic failure without forming diagonal shear cracks in the concrete portion of the composite beam [4].

Even if the shear connectors play a role in protecting the longitudinal shear, their importance is more pronounced through placing them on the optimum location across the web of the structural steel [5]. Indeed, the alteration of the arrangement and location of the shear connectors affects the behaviour of the composite beam. Considering channel shear connectors, face to face welding showed positive result against the opposite welding mechanism [6]. Even though the stiffness impact was limited, the crack in the concrete of the back-to-back connection started at an early stage.

The stiffness of the composite beam is related to the spacing of the shear connectors including the behaviour of concrete and steel [5, 6]. Rigidity comes in action with narrowing the spacing of the shear connectors. However, deflection is linearly related to the flexural behaviour of the composite beam. But first, the profiled steel sheet fails before the failure of other parts.

Flexure or shear failure cannot be investigated individually, particularly in the case of the loading capacity of the composite beam. Yet, the introduction of the shear force can reduce the bending capacity of the composite beam. Hence, the effectiveness of the composite beam is more profound with the combination of moment and shear rather than individual impact [7].

The structural steel grade considered as one of the sensitive parameters altering the strength of the composite beam [8]. As the elastic module varies with the behaviour of the steel, the resistance depends directly on the elastic moduli of the composite beam. On the other hand, the Slip and degree of shear connection have an indirect relationship with the steel grade [9].

Even if span length is directly proportional to the shear resistance of the composite beam, the introduction of a hole in the steel web results in the stress increment on the slab [10]. Shear and pullout failure increase with the short span composite beams. Since openings can manage the formation of crack, they have a role in the increment of the ultimate loading capacity of the composite beam [11]. The higher the steel ratio, the more ductility will be and vice versa.

On the other hand, an upgrade on the shear capacity of the beam leads to an increment in the bearing capacity of the composite beam, itself [12]. If we achieve an efficient shear connection, upgrading the strength of the concrete will increase the bending capacity of the composite beam, itself. The upgrade on load and flexural capacity can also depend on shear protection with effective stress transfer [5].

All the above researches stated positive results of shear connectors. Since friction between concrete and steel alone is insufficient, studs introduced to enhance the slip resistance. Moreover, the research [5] showed the importance of tackling the slip in the composite beam by altering shear connector's location. However, studs are not capable of enhancing the behaviour of the concrete through the anchorage and composite bondage. Hence, this research is conducted to investigate the load capacity improvement on composite beam through introducing flange portion on the shear connectors with a variation on the web height which will have a role in altering the behaviour of the concrete. Crack can be decreased by increasing the flange length which will preserve the stiffness of the cross-section.

2   Methodology

The shear connector's dimensional variation on the flange length, web height including the arrangement studied primarily. Each parameter contained three variants where the web height of the connector is perpendicular to the web of structural steel. Since the clear spacing is 71.5 mm the maximum web height of 40 mm is quite considerable. On the other hand, the flange length of the shear connector is parallel to the longitudinal axis. Since the clear spacing between the connectors is 260 mm, 80 mm flange length is quite valid. For the loading sequence, displacement control three-point testing considered for the shear connector with a simple support condition of a 3 m long beam.

2.1   Numerical Modeling and Validation

The numerical Modeling was conducted using ABAQUS version 6.13 software through validating experimental research conducted in Brazil [5]. Figure 1 shown below is taken from the validation model of the original research. However, the cross-section of the original research for validation was not symmetrical across the neutral axis which later modified to account for the effect of friction in the concrete and utilize the structural steel effectively. On the other hand, the behavior of the concrete utilized for the validation is specified in Table 1 below.

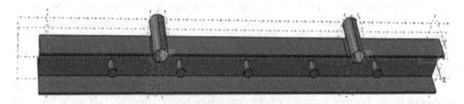

Fig. 1. Shear connector and loading arrangement for the validation

Table 1. Validation data for the concrete

Specification of the concrete	Assumed data
Elastic modulus	32500 Mpa
Compressive strength	35.5 Mpa
Tensile strength	2.7 Mpa
Maximum tensile strain	$\varepsilon_u = 16\varepsilon_{cr}$

All the other specifications are stated in Table 2 below.

2.2   Composite Beam Parametric Tests

Composite beam modelling required the combination of heterogeneous materials to form one structural element. Since three parameters were taken into consideration, their comparison was checked against each other and their preliminary validation was carried out against experimental research in composite beams [5].

Table 2. Validation and modelling specifications

Consideration	For the validation	For the research
Type of loading	2-point loading	1-point loading
Nonlinearity	Both material and geometric	Both material and geometric
Concrete data	From Table 1	From Table 1
Shear connector spacing calculation	From the experiment	11 according to ES EN 1994-1-1:2015 [13]

2.2.1   Flange Length Effect

The flange of the shear connector is a connector that is parallel to the longitudinal length of the composite beam. It was taken to have a variation of 20 mm, 50 mm and 80 mm where the web height kept constant of 40 mm over the structural steel's web. As shown in Fig. 2 below, the height of the web is set to 40 mm with a shear spacing of 260 mm. Concrete behavior was taken directly from previously performed research [5]. However, the structural steel was tested in the structural laboratory of Bahir Dar Institute of Technology with yield and ultimate strength of 292 Mpa and 390 Mpa, respectively. The following Fig. 2 shows a shear connector made of a reinforcement bar.

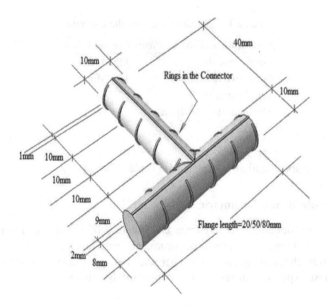

Fig. 2. Dimensional properties of a shear connector with fixed 40 mm web height

2.2.2   Location of Shear Connector

Three positions of shear connectors had been considered for the shear connector. It comprises straight welding on the structural steel web, staggered welding on the structural steel web and finally on the lower flange of the structural steel. Spacing was constant while the 20 mm, 50 mm and 80 mm flange length was considered for all three positions.

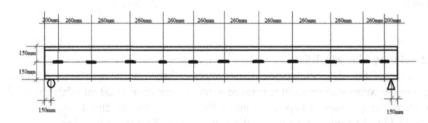

Fig. 3. Arrangement of shear connectors in a linear pattern

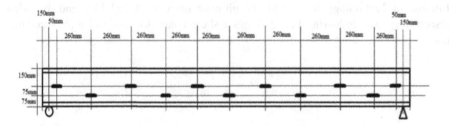

Fig. 4. Arrangement of shear connectors in a staggered pattern

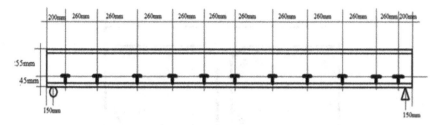

Fig. 5. Arrangement of shear connectors weld on the bottom flange of the structural steel

2.2.3   Web Height Effect

The web height is the length of the shear connector perpendicular to the structural steel web. It is considered with variations of 20 mm, 30 mm and 40 mm keeping the flange length constant at a dimension of 50 mm. Since the height of the web was a single parameter, it later combined with the modification on the placement of the three lengths as shown in Fig. 3, 4 and 5 above. Figure 6 below shows the picture of the 20 mm web height keeping the flange length at a constant length of 50 mm.

Fig. 6. 20 mm web height shear connector

2.3   Composite Beam Comparative Tests

The test done in the previous search [5] was modified with the reinforcement bar shear connector. The shear connector considered on the original test was a headed stud with a height of 75 mm and a diameter of 19 mm. However, the rebar shear connector introduced with a fixed height of 75 mm with a variable flange length from 0 to 35 mm and finally at 70 mm. All the other parameters kept the constant in the composite beam with just a 20 mm diameter shear connector made of reinforcement bar for the web.

Typically, the full composite beams test is considered with the one-point loading, except the comparative study. The loading performed with a displacement of 25 mm at the middle of the composite beam for the three-point testing while the comparative study aligned with the original laboratory test. The arrangement of the concrete and structural steel in the cross-section of the composite beam shown in the Fig. 7 below.

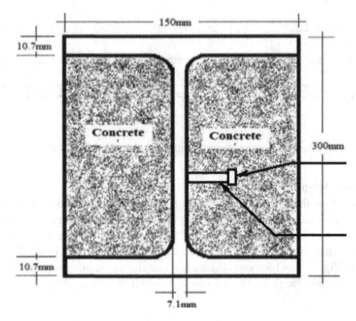

Fig. 7. Cross-section of the composite beam

Flange portion of the shear connector is parallel to the beam axis. Since the spacing is 260 mm, maximum of 80 mm length along the beam direction is quite efficient.

Web height of the shear connector is perpendicular to the web of the structural steel. With 71.5 mm clear spacing, a maximum of 40 mm web height is quite efficient.

3   Result and Discussions

3.1   Validation Results

The result for both the modelling and the experiment are plotted together as shown in Fig. 8 below. The maximum error between the two results was calculated to be 3.68%. This indicates that the numerical modelling technique used in this study could be extended to the more rigorous investigations presented in the subsequent sections.

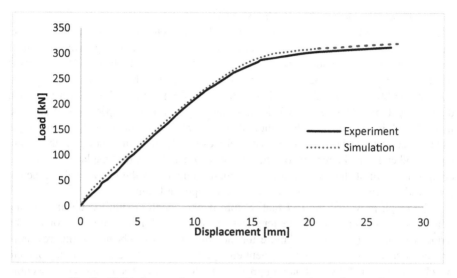

Fig. 8. Validation graph as compared to the experimental research

3.2 Parametric Modeling Results

3.2.1 Mesh Sensitivity Analysis

The control beam had a shear connector welded linearly on the web of the structural steel. It was modelled with 50 mm flange length and 40 mm web height, yet, mesh sensitivity analysis was required for the change in mesh size of shear connectors. Hence, 1.5 mm and 15 mm mesh sizes selected to compare the results. The output of the variation between the two mesh sizes is quite small. As a result, the 15 mm tetrahedral linear element selected as a mesh size for the shear connector regarding the analysis of the composite beam (Fig. 9).

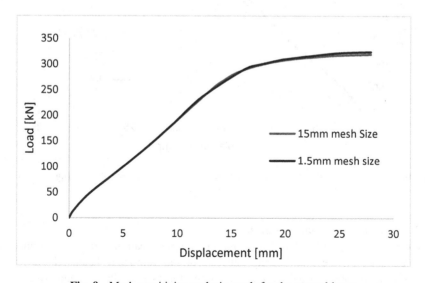

Fig. 9. Mesh sensitivity analysis result for the control beam

3.2.2   Flange Length of Shear Connectors

The flange length is considered as a section of the connector parallel to the longitudinal axis altered with uniform increments. As shown in Fig. 10 below, increasing the flange length enhanced the load-bearing capacity of the composite beam. The recorded loading for the composite beams having a shear connector with flange length of 20 mm, 50 mm and 80 mm were 311.909 kN, 316.873 kN and 326.272 kN with a mid-span displacement of 28.98 mm, 28.3611 mm and 27.0541 mm, respectively. Since the flange length is parallel to the longitudinal axis, it provides an anchor helping to delay a small percentage of the crack in the concrete, especially near the middle of the beam. On the other hand, increment on the flange length reduced the displacement of the composite beam at the mid-section. The small reduction in the crack of the concrete preserved the cross-sectional stiffness of the composite beam.

The graph prevailed the fact that 20 mm flange length couldn't coup up with the other connectors. Since the flange length is small, the crack in the concrete couldn't be reduced which is the mode of failure for the entire composite beams in this research. The other shear connectors are sufficient enough to withstand the crack in the concrete which accompanied by a small improvement in the stiffness in the cross-section. However, the shear connectors are located near the neutral axis where the slip is almost zero which reduces the contribution of the flange length variations. The composite beam with an 80 mm flange length shear connector possesses a 3.97% load increment with a 4.608% displacement reduction compared to the control beam.

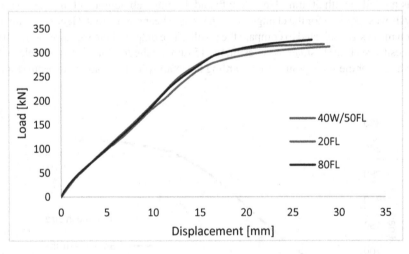

Fig. 10. Load versus mid-span displacement output for the variation of the flange length with linear welding

3.2.3   Location of Shear Connector

As shown in Fig. 11, 12 and 13 below, rearranging the location of the shear connectors had an impact on the load-bearing capacity of the composite beams. Figure 12 is plotted for a composite beam with a shear connector having a flange length of 50 mm.

The loading in the composite beams for linear, staggered and bottom welding was 316.272 kN, 320.065 kN and 326.6955 kN with mid-span displacement of 28.3611 mm, 27.8514 mm and 26.6955, receptively. On the other hand, Fig. 13 is plotted for an 80 mm flange length shear connector. The loading recorded in the composite beams for the same arrangement was 326.272 kN, 331.501 kN and 339.788 kN with mid-span displacement of 27.0541 mm, 26.4177 mm and 25.6984 mm.

The load-bearing capacity of all the three composite beams with bottom welding is better than the rest of the shear connectors' location because of slip reduction in the composite beam. Since slip increases down from the neutral axis, moving the shear connectors towards the bottom is an option. On the other hand, reducing the slip results in enhanced capacity for the composite beam. Hence, the mid-span displacement is smaller with improved stiffness on the composite beam. The composite beam having a 50 mm flange length shear connector, welded at the bottom flange of the structural steel, increased the load-bearing capacity by 3% and displacement reduction of 5.87% compared to the control beam. These values for the 80 mm flange length are 7.23% load increment with 9.388% displacement reduction, respectively.

On the other hand, variation of the shear connectors' location with 80 mm flange length brought positive impact on the composite beam compared to the shear con-nectors with 20 mm and 50 mm flange lengths. The gap between the plots for Fig. 11, 12 and 13 is huge with higher loading capacity, stiffness and lower displacements. This happens since the shear connector's flange length contributed to preserving the con-crete from cracking. Since crack in the concrete started from the bottom, providing better flange length contributed through anchoring concrete particles together which preserved the cross-sectional stiffness with lower displacement on the middle of the composite beam.

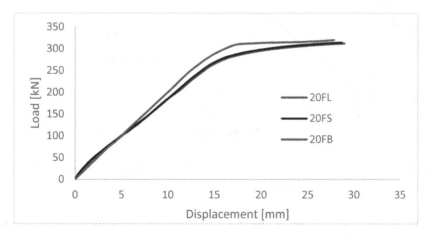

Fig. 11. Load versus mid-span displacement output for the change in location of the shear connector with 20 mm flange length

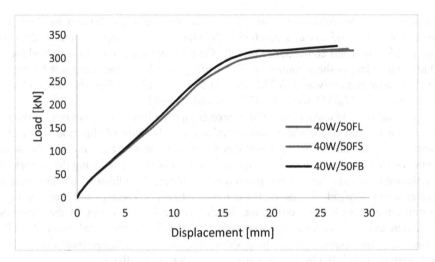

Fig. 12. Load versus mid-span displacement output for the change in location of the shear connector with 50 mm flange length

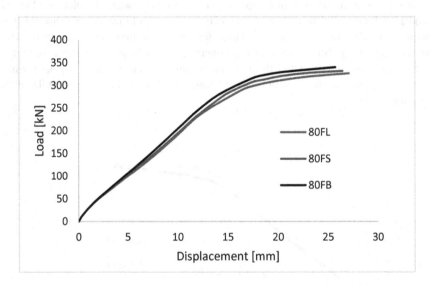

Fig. 13. Load versus mid-span displacement output for the change in location of the shear connector with 80 mm flange length

As shown in Fig. 17 below, the entire behavior and capacity of the composite beams altered with a variation on the flange length combined with location change in the shear connector. The highest capacity was recorded for the composite beam with 80 mm flange length shear connector welded at the bottom of structural steel and have the lowest displacement of all the other beams. On the other hand, the lowest loading capacity was recorded for a composite beam with a shear connector having 20 mm flange length and welded linearly on the web of the structural steel. Side with this, the displacement is highest of all. Hence, flange had an impact in preserving concrete through creating bondage while the location of the shear connector had an impact on the protection of the beam against slip failure.

3.2.4   Web Height Effect of the Shear Connectors

The effect of web height combined with the variation on the location of the shear connectors to visualize the ultimate effect. As shown in Fig. 14, 15 and 16 below, there is a visible small difference in the effect of change in web heights of the shear connector. Considering the linear welding as shown in Fig. 14 below, peak loading of composite beams with a shear connector having 20 mm, 30 mm and 40 mm web heights were 316.54 kN, 324.52 kN and 316.873 kN with mid-span displacement of 29.281 mm, 28.943 mm and 28.3611 mm, respectively.

The higher loading capacity of the middle connector comes due to the higher ductility of the 40 mm web height and the low confining capability of the 20 mm web height shear connector. The 40 mm web height shear connector bends higher than the other shear connectors which made it highly ductile with reduced mid-span displacement. On the other hand, the 20 mm web height is small to create a bond with the concrete which weakens the interaction in the composite beam. This, on the other hand, increased the deflection of the composite beam at the mid-span.

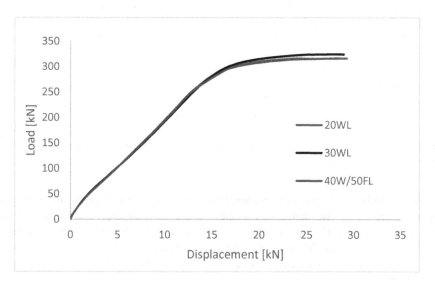

Fig. 14. Load versus mid-span displacement for the shear connector with a variation on the web height with linear welding

Figure 15 below is a graph of the shear connectors with staggered welding mode. The shear connector was moved lower as compared to the plotting of the above figure. The staggered mode by itself led to load capacity increment for all three web height changes. The peak loading recorded in the composite beams were 318.93 kN, 326.88

kN and 320.065 kN with mid-span displacement of 28.928 mm, 28.402 mm and 27.8514 mm for 20 mm, 30 mm and 40 mm web heights, respectively. Hence, the 30 mm web height brought a higher load as compared to the other shear connectors. However, the 20 mm web height deflected higher than the other due to its rigidity.

Since the cross-sectional slip increases away from the neutral axis, the lower connectors faced higher stress at the section. Some of the connectors faced higher slip due to their location which was much lower than the neutral axis. On the other hand, the 20 mm web height shear connector was not capable of delaying the crack in the concrete which resulted in lower capacity in the composite beam. Compared to the others, the 40 mm web height shear connector had the capacity of confining higher portion concrete. Hence it protected localized stress making the effective shear connection with reduced mid-span displacement.

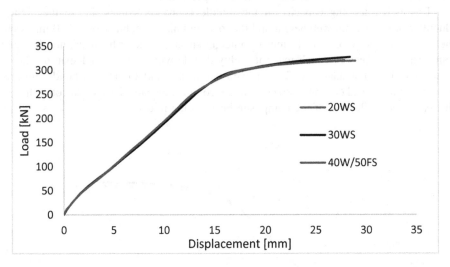

Fig. 15. Load versus mid-span displacement for the shear connector with a variation on the web height with staggered welding

Figure 16 below displays shear connectors when they are welded on the bottom of the structural steel. The flange of the shear connector was approaching the bottom portion of the concrete helping to increase loading capacity. The peak loading recorded for 20 mm, 30 mm and 40 mm web heights were 326.15 kN, 337.86 kN and 326.431 kN with a mid-span deflection of 27.773 mm, 27.316 mm and 26.6955 mm, respectively.

Without considering the variation on the web heights, the bottom welding brought tremendous positive results. Since the slip is higher at the bottom section the web of the connector contributed to the reduction of slip. It improved the loading capacity while the mid-span displacement was reduced. On the other hand, the flange of the 40 mm web height shear connector was far from the bottom of the concrete which couldn't protect the early crack in the concrete. Yet, the flange of 20 mm web height shear connector was almost at the bottom of the concrete. Since it was not longitudinal reinforcement, and the cross-sectional area of the concrete at the bottom decreased creating a low capacity of the composite beam. Hence the optimum web height at the bottom of the structural steel was recorded to be 30 mm.

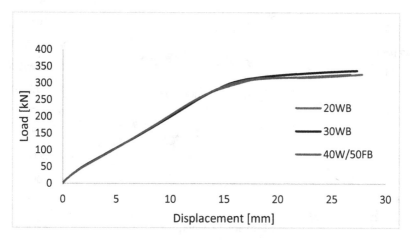

Fig. 16. Load versus mid-span displacement for the shear connector with a variation on the web height with bottom welding

30 mm web height shear connector is optimum where it balances the force due to slip and the concrete confinement. Due to the shortness of the web height for the 20 mm web height shear connector, it couldn't produce firm contact making it less important compared to the others. Finally, the 30 mm web height shear connector welded at the bottom possessed a 6.62% higher loading capacity with 3.68% deflection decrement at the mid-span compared to the control composite beam with a shear connector having 40 mm web height with 50 mm flange length linearly welded on the structural steel.

It is clear from the bottom Fig. 17 below that both the load-bearing capacity and displacement resistance enhanced with the lowering of the shear connectors. It is quite efficient in reducing slip at the critical location. Hence, the location of the shear connector is the most sensitive parameter while the web height is the least sensitive parameter of all.

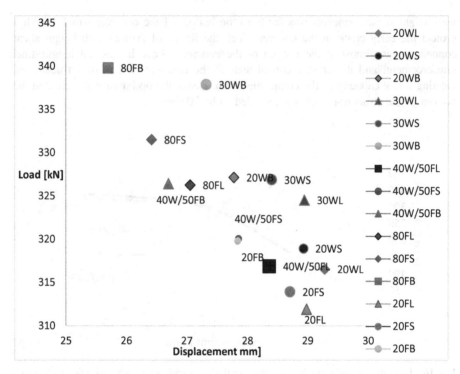

Fig. 17. Loading versus mid span displacement for the whole models in the ABAQUS

3.3   Replacement of Headed Stud Shear Connector

The headed stud replacement in the original research [5] had been made with an equivalent reinforcement shear connector so that the results could be investigated. It had been done through the increment of the shear connector flange length. The results are plotted in Fig. 18 below.

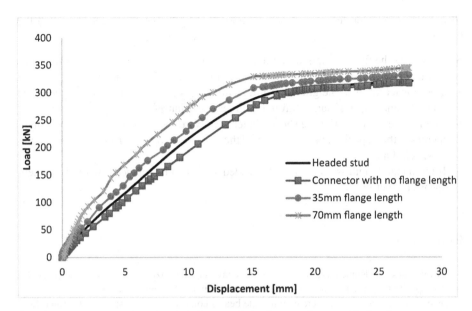

Fig. 18. Replacement of the headed shear studs in the experiment with the shear connectors made of reinforcement bars with a variation on the flange length

As shown in Fig. 18 above, the headed stud shear connector was replaced with the shear connector made of the reinforcement bar. The flange length varied from zero to 70 mm long with 35 mm as a medium flange length. Since the loading was 4-point, a larger area of the beam was subjected to deflection while the middle was more horizontal. The increment on the flange length helps in increasing the stiffness together with the loading capacity of the composite beam. Bonding between the concrete particles enhanced with the increment on the flange length resulting in better loading capacity. However, the negligence of the flange length brought phase slippage of the concrete reducing stiffness of the system succeeded later by a slight decrement in the loading capacity.

4   Conclusion

Parametric study on the dimensional variation of the shear connector's flange length, web height and its location had been studied in partially encased composite beams. The flange length is considered as the dimension of the shear connector parallel to the longitudinal direction of the composite beam. The increment on the flange length enhanced the load-carrying capacity of the composite beam by creating an interlock between the concrete particles. On the other hand, the web height is considered as the length of the shear connector which is perpendicular to the web of the structural steel. The results showed that lower web height couldn't confine the concrete while longer web height became too flexible. Hence, the optimum web height was required with a length of 30 mm. The shear connector's location was the most sensitive parameter of all the others. Slip protection was vitally improved by lowering the location with the flange considered as anchorage between the concrete particles.

- Increasing the flange length of the reinforcement shear connector enhances the load-bearing capacity of the composite beam through concrete bondage.
- The impact of web height is visible with only optimum dimension where the bondage and slip resistance through stiffness is balanced.
- Reducing the location of the shear connector toward the bottom of the flange length increases the capacity and deflection of the composite beam through the protection of slip failure.
- If the flange length is quite enough, headed studs can be replaced by reinforcement shear connectors.

References

1. Kuhlmann, U., Kürschner, K.: Structural behaviour of horizontally lying shear studs. In: Composite Construction in Steel and Concrete, Kruger National Park (2005)
2. Nie, J., Cai, C.S.: Steel-concrete composite beams considering shear slip effect. Struct. Eng. **129**(4), 495–506 (2003)
3. Dipaola, V., Prete, F., Prete, G.: The elasto-plastic behavior of encased composite beams for slim floors in multi-storey buildings. In: International Congress in-Fib, Naples (2006)
4. Hegger, J., Goralski, C.: Structural behavior of partially concrete encased composite sections with high strength concrete. In: Composite Construction in Steel and Concrete, Kruger National Park (2005)
5. De Nardin, S., Debs, A.L.H.C.E.: Study of partially encased composite beams with innovative of the stud bolts. Construct. Steel Res. **65**(2), 342–350 (2009)
6. Fanaie, N., Esfahani, F.G., Soroushnia, S.: Analytical study of composite beams with different arrangements of channel shear connectors. Steel Comp. Struct. **19**(2), 485–501 (2015)
7. Baskar, K., Shanmugam, N.E.: Steel–concrete composite plate girders subject to combined shear and bending. J. Construct. Steel Res. **59**(4), 531–557 (2003)
8. Ban, H., Bradford, M.A.: Flexural behavior of composite beam with high strength steel. Eng. Struct. **56**, 1130–1141 (2013)
9. Shamass, R., Cashell, K.: Behavior of composite beams made using high strength steel. Structures **12**, 88–101 (2017)
10. Roberts, T.M., Al-Amery, R.I.M.: Shear strength of composite plate girders with web cutouts. Struct. Eng. **117**, 1897–1910 (1991)
11. Adnan, M., Abou Saleh, Z., Ahmad, S.: Analytical and Experimental investigation on flexural behavior of partially encased composite beams. Alexand. Eng. **57** (2017)
12. Harish, M.L., Prabhakara, R., Vinay, N.: Experimental investigation in on flexural behavior of the steel-concrete beams. Int. Res. J. Eng. Technol. (IRJET), 1295–1301 (2015)
13. Ministry of Construction, ES EN 1994-1-1, Addis Ababa (2015)

Lake Level Fluctuation Impact on River Morphology Change

Sisay Mengistie Eshetie[1]([✉]) and Mengistie Abate Meshesha[2]

[1] School of Civil and Water Resources Engineering,
Woldia Institute of Technology, Woldia, Ethiopia
[2] Faculty Civil and Water Resources Engineering,
Bahir Dar Institute of Technology, Bahir Dar, Ethiopia

Abstract. In the recent time Ribb River is under immense morphological change due to various natural, planned and unplanned anthropogenic activities such as, lake level regulation for hydropower production, embanking, sand mining, and water extraction. In the present time, Lake Tana level is raised (kept fairly constant) after the Chara-Chara weir construction and Belese Hydropower operation. These will strongly alter both River regime water and sediment discharge to downstream reach and causing morphology adjustment. Hence, this study assessed Lake level fluctuation impact on River morphological change on Ribb River, Lake Tana Basin, Ethiopia for about 20 km. The objectives of this study were to assess lake level impact on river cross-sections of Ribb River and investigate back water extension length and its consequent for River training structures. Primary data (River cross-sections, dyke dimensions and grain sizes) were collected through, surveying using standard measuring equipment's (total station, GPS) and laboratory analysis. Secondary data (stream flow, Lake level, sediment, rainfall and climatic) were also collected from MoWRIE. For data preparation and analysis, Arc GIS and HEC-RAS were used. River bed change has been studied from 2005 to 2014 period and the result show that the reach exhibit both aggradation and degradation. The study reach is affected by back water for about 1.5 km length and this back water effect caused an average annual rate of 0.22 m deposition.

Keywords: Lake Tana · River morphology · Ribb River · HEC-RAS model

1 Introduction

Rivers play most important role in terrestrial and aquatic ecosystem (Kamboj et al. 2017). However, in the recent time alluvial rivers are under immense pressure change due to various kinds of natural, planned and unplanned anthropogenic disturbances (Kamboj et al. 2017). Alluvial rivers in nature adjust their slope, planform and pattern to recover its former equilibrium. Regime rivers are always change their dimensions to response sediment and discharge change due to human and natural influence (Hekal 2018).

Hence, understanding the current, past and future morphological trend and river dynamic is the key role to identify human induced factor and on-going climate changes on the function of rivers. Acquiring this knowledge is the first steps for unscientific

© ICST Institute for Computer Sciences, Social Informatics and Telecommunications Engineering 2022
Published by Springer Nature Switzerland AG 2022. All Rights Reserved
M. L. Berihun (Ed.): ICAST 2021, LNICST 412, pp. 99–111, 2022.
https://doi.org/10.1007/978-3-030-93712-6_7

human activity monitoring and undertake mitigation measures. Ribb River is one of the components of the Blue Nile River system that depict morph dynamic changes due to planned and unplanned human disturbances (SMEC 2008). For long time, the river has been subject to human disturbance like, water diversion, sand mining, trenching and irrigation water in dry season (Mulatu et al. 2018). In addition, back water effect from Lake, after Chara-Chara weir construction has main causes of morphology change and flooding problem in the recent time (Abate et al. 2015).

Flooding problem in lower reach caused loss of human lives, displaced from their homes, swept agricultural lands and adversely affect health centers, schools and hydraulic structure (SMEC 2008). In 2006 E.C. 43,140 people were faced flooding problem and 8,730 displaced from their living home due to channel shifting and flooding (Abera 2011). These damages are mainly caused due to Lake level increment at lake shore when flood coincide with high lake level, sediment supply from breach dyke and insufficient channel flood carrying capacity. Hence, the general objective of this study is to assess Lake level fluctuation impact on morphology change, analyze response of river sedimentation, and change of flow regime on Ribb River, Lake Tana basin.

2   Materials and Method

2.1   Description of Study Area

Ribb catchment is located within Lake Tana basin in Ethiopia (Fig. 1). The river rises from high Ethiopian plateau Guna Mountain and travels 130 km northwestern direction and debouches into Lake Tana at elevation of 1787 m amsl. The river catchment covers 1865 km^2 area and extends 4130 m altitude to 1784.5 m amsl. The average annual maximum temperature in the upper part of Ribb River basin is 27 $^\circ$C while the minimum falls below 0 °C in December. For long time the river influenced by (sand mining, irrigation, trenching, damming). However, back water extension length from Lake and its consequences along river were not investigated.

The river drains from the western slope of high mountainous area Town of Debre Tabor to very flat to Lake Tana (Abera 2011). In the lower reach of the river, especially near to Lake Tana channel have very flat slope and sediment loading discharge flows slowly that causes sediment deposition and bank over flow (SMEC 2008). The catchment is characterized broad and very flat flood plains, old bench forming terrace and low to high relief basaltic hills with steep to flat slopes (SMEC 2008). The upper catchment is characterized by mountainous wedge-shaped and steep-slope greater than (3.6%) and lower reach near to Lake is characterized by flat slope less than (1%) due to back water effect and channel deposition (Mulatu et al. 2018).

The Ribb catchment have high rainy season from June to September around 1300 mm mean annual rain fall at Adiss Zemen metrological station. In rainy months maximum temperature falls below (22 °C), wind speed (1.2 m/s), and sunshine hours (4.2 h) are low as compared to dry month and relative humidity is high reaching about 80% in the rainy months.

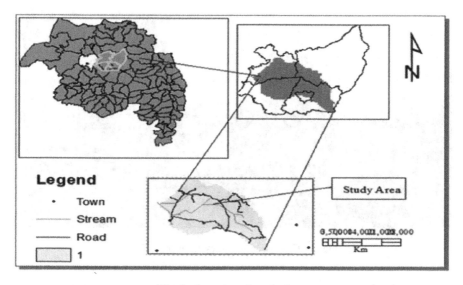

Fig. 1. Location of study Area

2.2 Data Formatting and Preparation

In the study reach more than 118 river cross-sections survey data were collected and laid out normal to the direction of flow at specified interval measured along the center line of the main channel. Mainly cross-section data were collected where, discharge, slope, shape, roughness, and where levees begin and end (Lumpur 2010). These survey data was collected as reference point on left side of the river and with increasing towards right looking down stream and an elevation of point in meter (Fig. 2). To assess water surface profile with and without dyke, 0.33 to 3.4 m height and 3 m set back distance dyke dimensions were collected. These dyke dimensions were fixed after 100-year return period design discharge computed (217 m^3/s). Even if representative samples of river bank material are difficult (van Rijn 1984), six representative river bank and bed samples has been implemented at Bahir Dar soil laboratory (Fig. 5). Other Secondary (stream flow, Lake level, sediment, and rainfall) data were also collected from MoWRIE Office (Table 1).

HEC-RAS has the capability of drawing the spatial plot for many hydraulic characteristics like; sediment transport either quasi-unsteady or unsteady flow, Water surface elevation, shear stress (U.S. Army Corps of Engineers 2016). Quasi-unsteady hydraulic analysis is only used to sediment computation by assumes approximate continuous hydrograph (histograms) with series of discrete steady flow profiles (U.S. Army Corps of Engineers 2016).

Sediment transport in quasi-unsteady flow type is non–linearity and irregular time step. It is desirable by approximating low flow for larger durations and high for relatively short durations (U.S. Army Corps of Engineers 2016). HEC-RAS includes several quasi-unsteady downstream boundary conditions, but only one upstream quasi-unsteady boundary. Therefore, 32-year selected annual record discharge is discretized

Fig. 2. Cross-section survey (January 2021)

Table 1. Summary of primary and secondary input data and their sources

Data Type	Data period	Sources	Purpose
River cross-section	April, 2020	From Field survey	Input for HEC-RAS model
Sediment data	January, 2021	From study reach	To understand bed gradation
Geological map	–	MoWRIE	Study area with soil, sand formation
DEM model	–	Office/institutions	For study area delineation
Streamflow (m³/s)	2005–2014	MoWRIE	Used for u/s boundary condition
Lake Tana level (m)	2005–2014	MoWRIE	Used for d/s boundary condition
Sediment flow data	1990–2010	MoWRIE	Input for quasi-Unsteady flow

in continues hydrograph with series discrete (histograms) in rectangular shaped for upstream boundary conditions.

From 32-year recorded stream flow data (2005–2014) maximum monthly flow data were used to upstream boundary condition for this study (Fig. 3). In the other hand, HEC-RAS includes three options for setting quasi-unsteady downstream boundary conditions such as, stage time series, rating curve, or normal depth. Since study deals about back water extension length and its effect stage time Series was selected for downstream boundary condition (Fig. 6).

Sediment transport is process interrelating erosion and deposition for natural stream channels. When the rate of upstream sediment supplies higher than stream's sediment transport capacity, stream bed will start to aggrade at the rate defined by the difference between the rate of sediment supply and sediment transport rate of the stream (Bekić et al. 2015). However, if a stream's sediment transport capacity exceeds the rate of sediment supply from upstream, the balance sediment load has to come from channel itself. These two condition causses morphological unbalance between aggradation and degradation along river reach (Hekal 2018). Sediment transport from given set of steady-state hydraulic parameters and sediment properties are predicted using sediment continuity Exner equation (Eq. 1). Erosion and deposition of sediment by Exner equation translates differencing between inflow and out flow load in to bed change, eroding (degradation) or deposition (aggradation) of channel. This equation written as shown below;

$$(1 - \lambda p)B * \frac{\partial \eta}{\partial t} = -\frac{\partial Qs}{\partial x} \tag{1}$$

where; B, channel width, η, channel bed elevation, x, distance of control volume, Qs, Transport sediment load, p, active layer porosity, T, Time. From Eq. (1) above, left hand side shows change in sediment volume and right hand shows the difference between inflow sediment and outflow sediment load. The equation used to calculate transport capacities for each cross section in downstream direction. If flow capacity greater than supply, the model satisfies its deficit by eroding from the bed and if supply exceeds than flow capacity the model can deposits surplus sediment (U.S. Army Corps of Engineers 2016).

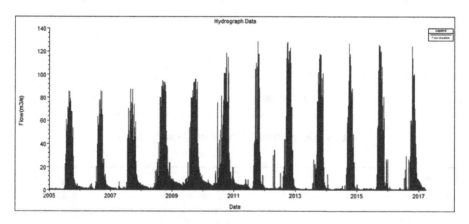

Fig. 3. Quasi-unsteady flow series for upstream boundary conditions (2005–2017).

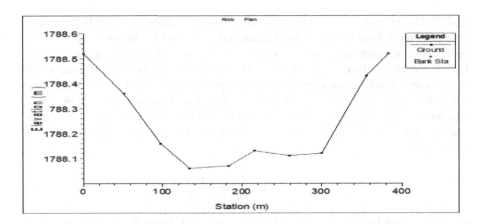

Fig. 4. Cross section. (Station - 35) without proposed dyke

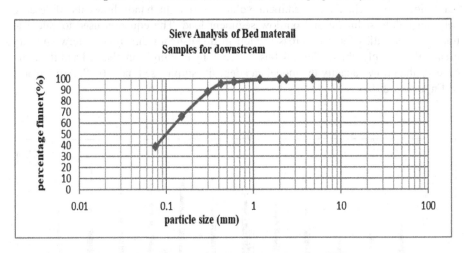

Fig. 5. The grain size distribution (January, 2021)

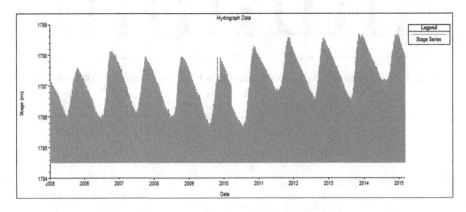

Fig. 6. Lake stage-time series data for downstream boundary conditions (2005–2015)

3   Results

3.1   One Dimensional Steady Flow Analysis

Water surface profile computation for different return period discharge is essential for flood plain management, flood insurance and channel modification studies (U.S Army Crop of Engineers 2016). In recent time in lower Ribb River reach close to Lake Tana crop yields and human lives are under risk every summer season. This is mainly caused by Lake back water due to lake level raising after artificial weir constructing and several human interventions. Hence, the study assessed back water extension length, channel carrying capacity, water surface increment and dyke carrying capacity for 100-year return period discharge using HEC-RAS model.

For one dimensional steady flow analysis the model was simulated with and without considering dyke dimension. From simulation result for 10, 50 and 100-year return period discharge, averagely the channel cannot convey for 100-year return period design discharge safely and flood raises about 1.5 m height above normal flood plain (Fig. 7). On contrary (Fig. 8) right bank side may accommodate forecasted flood with planned dyke dimensions, because terrain situated at relatively higher elevation on the right side of flood. Generally flooding problem in lower Ribb reach is mainly caused insufficient channel carrying capacity due to channel aggradation and degradation, because alluvial rivers are self-regulatory. They change their longitudinal bed slope, flow velocity and sediment settling velocity due to external human disturbances.

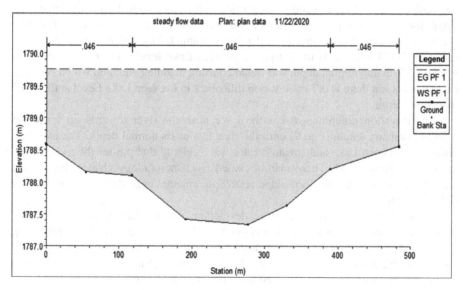

Fig. 7. Plot of inundate cross-section at river station-35 without proposed dyke.

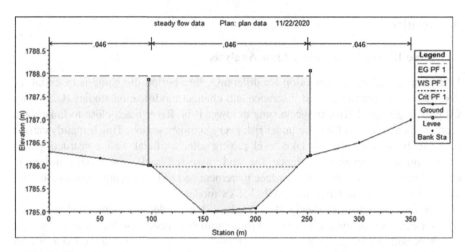

Fig. 8. Plot of inundate cross-section study reach at river station-35 with proposed dyke

3.2 Back Water Profile Computation

The term backwater expresses long water surface profile from obstructions like, Reservoirs, Lakes, Sea, Dams, weir and Flume. This phenomenon is occurred when the normal natural flow goes from mild to milder slope (Chow 1959). It is common in lower Ribb River reach mouth join to Lake Tana after lake level regulation that caused longitudinal slope reduction and settling velocity increment. The back water extension length for this study was assessed after some year Lake Level and channel normal flow depth computation. The average Lake depth was computed by deduct average Lake bed elevation (1784.5 m amsl) to 100-year computed Lake level flood (1788.2 m amsl) which is 3.7 m and normal depth was obtained using manning equation which is (3 m). From calculation there is 0.7 m elevation difference in between Lake Level and normal river flow depth.

This elevation difference makes the Lake push the river towards up for about 1.5 km extension length (Fig. 9) until the river attains its normal depth. The elevation difference between Lake and stream creates wave celerity that pushes the river toward up and additional flood. These mainly caused river morphology change, insufficient sediment carrying capacity, bed slope reduction, channel aggradation and increasing sediment settling velocity.

Sediment transport functions were developing under different conditions, wide range can be expected from one function to others (U.S Army Crop of Engineers 2016). Some functions computed suspended load, bed load and others computed total load. For the study, power-law equation (discharge versus suspended sediment data) was prepared using both discharge and sediment recorded data at gauge station. Sediment-rating curve is relation between sediment load and river discharges which used to compute total sediment load. Such relationship is usually established by regression analysis, and the curves are generally expressed in the form of power-law type

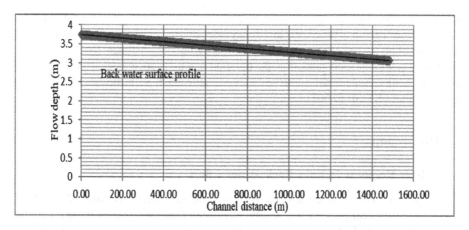

Fig. 9. Back water surface profiles near Ribb River mouth joining Lake Tana

Table 2. Maximum aggradation and degradation results

Sediment formulae	Study reach length	Simulation period (year)	Maximum aggradation (m)	Maximum degradation (m)
Engelund-Hansen	20	2005–2014	0.25	0.1
Yang	20	2005–2014	0.25	0.1
Wilcock-Crowe	20	2005–2014	0.21	0.1

equation. In sand-bed streams like, Ribb river with high transport rate, it is common for the suspended load to be orders of magnitude higher than in gravel-cobbled streams (Hekal 2018). Hence, from soil lab and power-law equation results (Engelund-Hansen, Yang and Wilcock-Crowe) transport formulae were appropriate with field as shown the result (Table 2).

Regarding to secondary and primary data results, the model was tested by three adopted sediment transport functions i.e., Engelund–Hansen, Yang and Wilcock-Crowe. The model runs for the existing conditions after calibration was achieved using 5-year recorded data from (2009–2014) and. From analysis the simulation result shows that the river reach exhibit both aggradations and degradation along study reach for three common transport functions (Table 2). The transport formulae were selected based on channel bed particle median size specification (D50) < 0.075 mm and total sediment load calculation. From (Table 2) Wilcock-Crowe transport shows maximum aggradation and degradation result than other functions. The main reason is that Wilcock-Crowe computes the influence of gravel and coble sand bed with hiding functions. However, Ribb River reach is not influenced by gravel and coble, rather it is dominated by fine sand and these results, high quantity degradation on some sections and aggradation on other sections resulting by Wilcock-Crowe equation. Generally, from three sediment transport result, the lower reach of the river is highly aggraded due to backwater effect and upstream sediment supply by dyke breaching that contribute additional sediment load for channel. For model calibration and validation, the optimum manning coefficient is 0.047 for main and river banks. Engelund-Hansen shows good agreement with measured documents with minimum RMSE (0.507).

4 Discussions

4.1 River Response to Lake Back Water Effect

The major observed bed change on river system was simulated from 2005–2014 channel avulsions for 20 km reach length in between Lake and main Bahir Dar-Gondar Bridge. The effect of lake level increment to the study reach was assessed using HEC-RAS model simulation and direct step iteration computation method. The contribution of Lake Tana level regulation is caused the River course variation and Lake rise from river mouth join to Lake for 100-year frequency analysis. The result indicates Lake propagates for about 1.5 km length until reach achieves its normal depth. This back water flow effect leads the river excess aggradation in some cross-section and degradation on other cross-section along the study reach.

These agradation and degrardation may cause many environmental problems such as, River course change, flooding and hydraulic structure damage. The simulated analysis shows that 0.7 m lake level increment have caused 0.25 m, 0.21 m and 0.33 m average River bed deosition for Engelund-Hansen, Yang and Wilcock-Crowe sediment

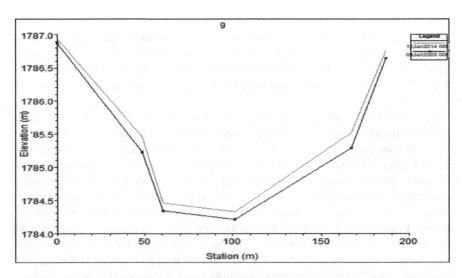

Fig. 10. Bed change plot for 10-year simulation period according to Engelund-Hansen

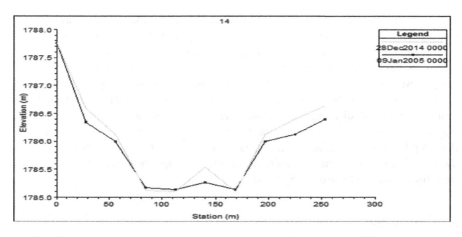

Fig. 11. Bed change plot for 10-year simulation period according to Wilcock-Crowe

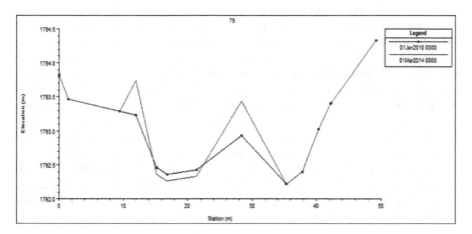

Fig. 12. Bed change plot for 10-year simulation period according to Yang

transport formulae respectively. This means that lake level regulation has direct contributed to the closure of the old channel which leads to channel shifting and severe flooding problem resulting by Wilcock-Crowe equation. Generally, from three sediment transport simulation result, lower reach the river is highly aggraded due to backwater effect and dyke breaching that contribute additional sediment load for channel. The optimum manning coefficient is 0.047 for both main channel and River banks. Engelund-Hansen shows good agreement with measured documents with minimum RMSE (0.507).

4.2   Effect of Dyke Construction on Channel Aggradation

The additional observed factor of river bed aggradation has been caused by upstream sediment supply and dyke failure in middle reach. In 2014, river training flood protection dyke was constructed more than 17 km between Lake and main bridge reach length with the aim of confining river water during high flood due to artificial Lake level rising (ADSWE 2019). However, due to design limitation, the dyke was failed before its design period. For study, one dimensional steady water surface profile analysis was simulated using HEC-RAS model for 10, 50 and 100-year return period discharge with and without planned dyke dimensions. From simulation results for 100-year return period discharge the channel cannot enough to convey without bank overflow for all cross-sections and the flood raises about 1.5 m height above normal flow depth for some stations. And extends more than 200 m both sides. Therefore, dyke height or set back distance increment is the main options to resist incoming flood from back water and surrounding flood.

5 Conclusion

This study investigates Lake level fluctuation impact on river morphology change of Ribb River. The main task is analyzing steady water surface profile, vertical bed level change and Lake back water extensions length determination using HEC-RAS model with and without considering planned dyke dimensions. From simulation result for 100-years return period discharge channel cannot convey without bank overflow and rises about 1.5 m height above normal flow depth, In addition the flood extended more than 200 m for 100-year return period discharge. This insufficient channel capacity is resulting due to Lake Level rising after artificial Chara-Chara weir construction and upstream sediment supply. The back water extendes for about 1.5Km length starting from river mouth join to the Lake until the river achieves its normal depth.. This extension length was computed using HEC-RAS model and direct step iteration method. Due to this back water effect, the reach exibits 0.22m depostion and 0.1m erosion in the lower and uper reach for 10-year simulation period for the study reach. These depostion and erosion mainly due to sediment migration from dyke slid, longitudinal bed slope reduction and sediment settling incensement.

Acknowledgments. I would like to thanks Amahara design work and supervision enterprise for total station equipment support for survey data collection, Ministry of Water, Irrigation and Electricity for supplying secondary data. Finally, would like to thanks international conference on advancements of science and technology (EAI ICAST, 2021) and springer publisher.

References

Abate, M., et al.: Morpho-logical changes of Gumara River channel over 50 years, upper Blue Nile basin, Ethiopia. J. Hydrol. **525**, 152–164 (2015)

Abera, Z.: Flood mapping and modeling on Fogera flood plain. Addiss Ababa (2011)

ADSWE: Feasibility study & detail design of lower Ribb river flood mitigation and community resilience project (dyke, suspension bridge and water control gates) (2019)

Bekić, D., Mikoš, M., Oskoruš, D.: To-wards practical guidance for sustainable sediment management using the Sava river basin as a showcase establishment of the sediment monitoring system for the Sava river basin (2015). (Issue November)

Chow: Poen channel hydraulic, in development of uniform flow and its formula, pp. 89–101. McGraw (1959)

Hekal, N.: Evaluation of the equilibrium of the River Nile morphological changes throughout "Assuit-Delta Barrages" reach. Water Sci. **32**(2), 230–240 (2018)

Kamboj, V., Kamboj, N., Sharma, S.: Environmental impact of river bed mining- a review. Int. J. Econ. Environ. **7**(1), 504–520 (2017)

Lumpur, K.: Ministry of natural resources and environment department of irrigation and drainage Malaysia (2010). (Issue August)

Mulatu, C.A., Crosato, A., Moges, M.M., Id, E.J.L., Mcclain, M.: Morpho dynamic trends of the Ribb river, Ethiopia, Prior to Dam Construction (2018)

Sewnet, A.: Water level fluctuations of lake Tana and its implication on local communities' livelihood, northwestern Ethiopia. J. River Basin Manage. **18**, 503–510 (2019)

Snowy Mountains Engineering Corporation (SMEC): Hydrological study of the tana-beles sub-basin: surface water investigation, January 2008

U.S Army Crop of Engineers: HEC-RAS river analysis system user's manual version 5.0 February 2016, institute of water resources engineering center. In Army Crop of Engineers, pp. 12–25 (2016)

Van Rijn, L.C.: Sediment transport, part III: bed forms. J. Hydraul. Eng. **110**(12), 1733–1754 (1984). In two companion papers (see Ref. [37])

Analyzing Seasonal Change of Water Quality Characteristics of Finote Selam Town Drinking Water Sources, Amhara, Ethiopia

Abayneh Agumass Amogne[1(✉)] and Fasikaw Atanaw Zimale[2]

[1] School of Civil and Water Resources Engineering, Debre Markos Institute of Technology, Debre Markos University, Debre Markos, Ethiopia
[2] Faculty of Civil and Water Resources Engineering, Bahir Dar Institute of Technology, Bahir Dar University, Bahir Dar, Ethiopia

Abstract. Water quality is used to demonstrate chemical, physical and biological characteristic of water. It has a significant impact on human's day to day activity. Even if it has such prominence, its quality is not constant with time and known as a media for disease transmission in the globe. In Ethiopia, there is a shortage of information in seasonal variation of water quality characteristics of drinking water sources. Thus, a cross-sectional study was undertaken to analyze water quality characteristics of drinking water sources in Finote Selam. A total of 32 water samples were collected from four drinking water sources and used to analyze turbidity, EC, TDS, NO_3, TC, FC, Ca, Mg, PO_4, PH, Fe, NH_3 and temperature. From a total of 16 water samples tested for water quality parameters in each season, some of the parameters were above the WHO standard in the dry and wet season. For turbidity 2 (12.5%), EC 16 (100%), TC 16 (100%), PO4 3 (18.75%) and FC 12 (75%) were above WHO standard in the dry season whereas for turbidity 11 (68.75%), EC 14 (87.5%), TC 16 (100%), PO4 6 (37.5%), Mg 2 (12.5%) and FC 16 (100%) were above WHO standard in the wet season. For PH 11 (68.75%) and 12 (75%) water samples were below WHO standard in the dry and wet season respectively. The research result indicated that the quality of water sources were not safe in dry and wet season since majority of the samples taken were not meet WHO standard. So, it is desirable to monitor and manage drinking water sources.

Keywords: Water quality · Water sources · Water quality characteristics · Finote selam town

1 Introduction

Water is most important and plentiful resource on earth. It is crucial for the survival of every organism [9]. Humans can survive more than weeks without food on the other hand only just few days without water. It has also an equivalent importance with the air we inhale in sustaining the vital processes of life. It is an important constituent for life and used for several purposes by man [2].

Water quality is the chemical, physical and biological characteristic of water. These characteristics are influenced by both natural processes and human activities. It changes

© ICST Institute for Computer Sciences, Social Informatics and Telecommunications Engineering 2022
Published by Springer Nature Switzerland AG 2022. All Rights Reserved
M. L. Berihun (Ed.): ICAST 2021, LNICST 412, pp. 112–127, 2022.
https://doi.org/10.1007/978-3-030-93712-6_8

from place to place with season, climate and the types of soil and rocks over which water moves [12]. A variety of human activities like industrial, mining, agriculture, urban expansion and recreation greatly transform the quality of natural water and alter the water use possibly [6]. All of these natural processes and human actions alter the quality and potentiality of the natural water [4].

Springs are unconstrained aquifers where flow of water is under gravity [13]. They occur where sloping ground and impermeable strata traverse with the ground water table. They became polluted as a result of poor site selection, protection and unhygienic management [14].

Groundwater is the world's biggest and most significant source of fresh potable water [11]. It is considered as safe source of drinking water. Nevertheless, ground water resources are susceptible to contamination. This is due to naturally occurring pollutants existing in the rocks and sediments [10]. Like surface water, its quality is different from place to place reliant on seasonal changes [5]. It is also altered based on the types of soils, rocks and surfaces over which it moves [12].

In addition, human activities can change natural composition of groundwater in spreading of chemicals and microbial matter on land surface and into soils through inoculation of wastes directly into groundwater. Industrial by products which are discharged from dissimilar factories in comprising various chemicals are the causes for the natural composition of groundwater alteration [3]. Agricultural and urban activities are other reasons for groundwater quality alteration [7]. Inappropriate supervision of both solid and liquid waste including disposal of waste can influence groundwater quality [1]. Urbanization is also gradually taking along the problems of contamination because of increased poor waste management and inadequate sanitation systems. Thus, influencing both the physical, chemical and microbial quality of water [10].

Water is a well-familiar transmission medium for communicable diseases all over the world. In Ethiopia, Seasonal change of water quality is not well understood and slight care is given. There is no study done concerning seasonal change of physicochemical and bacteriological quality of drinking water sources for Finote selam town. So, the current study is designed to evaluate the seasonal changes of physicochemical and bacteriological quality of drinking water sources in Finote selam town.

2 Materials and Methods

2.1 Study Area

The study was conducted in Finote selam town which is the capital city of West Gojam zone. It is located 387 km from Addis Ababa and 176 km from Bahir Dar. It has a longitude of 37° 16' E from the Greenwich meridian and 10° 42'N latitude from the equator with an elevation of 1917 m above mean sea level. According to the national population and housing census, the total population statistics of Finote selam town was 25,913. From this, 50.3% were men and 49.7% were women [8].

2.2 Study Design

A cross-sectional study design was conducted to evaluate the seasonal change of water quality parameters of drinking water sources in Finote selam town from January 2012 to October 2013. Membrane filtration and palintest photometer techniques were used for bacteriological and chemical water quality parameter analysis respectively.

2.3 Sample Size and Sample Collection

Four water sources were used for sample collection. They were designated as ws_1, ws_2, ws_3 and ws_4. A total of 32 water samples from these water sources were collected. That is, four water samples in the dry season and four water samples in the wet season.

Sample collection in dry season was carried out in January, February, March and April 2012. For wet season, samples were collected in June, July, August 2012 and September 2013. Water samples were collected using sterilized 2-L plastic containers. These containers were rinsed with sample at the sites of sample collection before samples were collected.

All samples were collected between 9:00 am to 12:00 am and transported to Finote selam town water supply and sewerage office laboratory in ice box and processed within 6 h after sample collection. The collected samples were analyzed for turbidity, electrical conductivity, temperature, PH, total dissolved solid, nitrate, ammonia, calcium, magnesium, phosphate, iron, total coli form and f-coli form.

2.4 Physicochemical Analysis

The study was carried out by analyzing some of the parameters on field and the others in the laboratory. The selected parameters analyzed in the field were temperature, pH, total dissolved solids, electrical conductivity and turbidity. These parameters were tested using the Palin test- multi-parameter and turbidity meter respectively (UK). The parameters analyzed in the laboratory were nitrate, ammonia, calcium, magnesium, phosphate and iron. These parameters were tested using the Palin test- photometer method (palintest-photometer 7500 Bluetoth, UK).

2.5 Microbiological Analysis

Total and faecal coliforms were analyzed by following palintest membrane filtration method. The media was prepared based on the manufacturer's instruction.Filtration unit was loosened and disinfected with methanol alcohol. A covered membrane filter was removed and transparent outer protection was peeled with forceps. The membrane filter was placed on the bronze filter support disc housed in the blue rubber base and then, filter funnel was locked firmly by pushing into the blue rubber base.Filter funnel base assembly was inserted into sampling cup and water sample was poured to the filter funnel up to 100 ml graduation. A hand vacuum pump was connected to filtration unit and pumping was begun. When all of the sample has been filtered, vacuum pump was detached and filter funnel was removed from blue rubber base. Petri dishes were placed on to the working - surface and sterilized with ethanol. After cooling, the absorbent pad was added by spinning. Then, media measuring device containing the liquid lorine sulphate broth media was shaked and then, the blue screw lid removed and placed lid-down on to the work-surface. Finally, the media was poured onto absorbent pad in petri dish. Sterilized forceps was used to lift membrane filter from the filtration in blue rubber base and was placed on top of the absorbent pad. Petri dish lid was replaced, labeled with sampling place and placed on to the petri dish rack. Then, petri dish was incubated at 37° for 18 h for total coliform and at 44 °C for 18 h for faecal coliform.

2.6 Data Analysis

The data obtained from field and in laboratory were analyzed using one way anova in SPSS software for windows version 21. One way anova was used to check whether there is a statistically significant difference or not among the water sources. The level of confidence interval was set as 95%.The results of the selected water quality parameters were compared with water quality standards set by [15].

3 Results and Discussion

In this research, a total of 32 water samples were collected from four water sources (two deep wells and two developed springs). Eight water samples were taken from each drinking water source.Water quality parameters of drinking water sources were compared with a global water quality standard [15].

Table 1. Analysis of variance for water quality parameters of water sources in dry season

Water quality parameters	Drinking water sources				P-value
	WS_1	WS_2	WS_3	WS_4	
Turb (NTU)	4.1 ± 0.6	5.9 ± 4.4	0.7 ± 0.1	3.0 ± 1.2	0.04
EC (μscm^{-1})	365.7 ± 59.2	637.7 ± 44.2	542.3 ± 43.2	540.2 ± 152.5	0.02
Temp (°C)	23.2 ± 0.83	25.9 ± 2	25.0 ± 0.6	22.9 ± 0.9	0.01
PH	5.4 ± 1.0	6.5 ± 0.6	6.06 ± 0.8	5.4 ± 1.0	0.24
TDS (mgL^{-1})	201.2 ± 37.6	350.7 ± 28.1	298.3 ± 27.4	297.1 ± 96.9	0.02
NO3 (mgL^{-1})	2.1 ± 0.1	1.6 ± 0.3	1.4 ± 0.2	3.1 ± 0.1	0.00
NH3 (mgL^{-1})	0.2 ± 0.0	0.2 ± 0.1	0.2 ± 0.0	0.2 ± 0.1	0.84
TC (CFU)	6.3 ± 4.2	3.5 ± 1.3	11.0 ± 5.4	10.00 ± 2.9	0.05
FC (CFU)	0.8 ± 1.0	0.5 ± 0.58	1.8 ± 0.1	3.0 ± 0.8	0.01
Ca (mgL^{-1})	8 ± 2.7	10.8± 3.8	17.0 ± 2.6	28.5 ± 5.2	0.00
Mg (mgL^{-1})	16 ± 2.7	21.3 ± 3	27.3 ± 3.0	27.8 ± 5.4	0.00
PO4 (mgL^{-1})	0.2 ± 0.0	0.4 ± 0.2	0.4 ± 0.1	0.6 ± 0.2	0.02
Fe (mgL^{-1})	0.1 ± 0.0	0.03 ± 0.01	0.1 ± 0.0	0.04 ± 0.0	0.00

Table 2. Analysis of variance for water quality parameters of water sources in wet season

Water quality parameters	Drinking water sources				P- value
	WS_1	WS_2	WS_3	WS_4	
Turb (NTU)	10.9 ± 5.4	7.7 ± 4.4	3.4 ± 0.9	15.2 ± 4.9	0.01
EC (μscm^{-1})	580.9 ± 177.6	502.6 ± 172.5	455.8 ± 141.2	616.3 ± 135.5	0.49
Temp (°C)	20.1 ± 1.6	21.0 ± 0.5	20.0 ± 2.1	20.7± 1.7	0.8
PH	6.5 ± 0.4	5.9 ± 0.7	5.4 ± 0.9	5.7 ± 0.9	0.21
TDS (mgL^{-1})	319.47 ± 97.7	276.4 ± 94.9	250.7± 77.6	338.9 ± 74.5	0.49
NO3 (mgL^{-1})	2.8 ± 0.4	2.09 ± 0.4	2.05 ± 0.2	3.2 ± 0.9	0.04
NH3 (mgL^{-1})	0.4 ± 0.2	0.3 ± 0.2	0.2 ± 0.1	0.1 ± 0.0	0.02
TC (CFU)	71.5 ± 37.3	36.3 ± 7.8	87.8 ± 33.6	115.3 ± 23.2	0.01
FC (CFU)	39.3 ± 11.2	16.0 ± 10.6	25.5 ± 10.1	57.0 ± 33.4	0.05
Ca (mgL^{-1})	11.8 ± 1.3	67.5 ± 7.2	20.0 ± 5.9	23.8 ± 9.5	0.13
Mg (mgL^{-1})	32.5 ± 7.2	32.0 ± 3.6	37.0 ± 9.3	52.0 ± 8.0	0.01
PO4 (mgL^{-1})	0.4 ± 0.2	0.4 ± 0.2	0.4 ± 0.1	0.7 ± 0.3	0.12
Fe (mgL^{-1})	0.2 ± 0.1	0.1 ± 0.0	0.1 ± 0.1	0.2 ± 0.1	0.68

Table 3. Compliance of drinking water sources in the dry season

Parameters		Ws_1		Ws_2		Ws_3		Ws_4		Total sample	
	WHO	N	P	N	P	N	P	N	P	N	P
Turb (NTU)	>5	0	0	2	50	0	0	0	0	2	12.5
	<5	4	100	2	50	4	100	4	100	12	87.5
EC (μscm^{-1})	>300	4	100	4	100	4	100	4	100	16	100
	<300	0	0	0	0	0	0	0	0	0	0
Temp (°C)	>15	4	100	4	100	4	100	4	100	16	100
	<15	0	0	0	0	0	0	0	0	0	0
PH	>8.5	0	0	0	0	0	0	0	0	0	0
	6.5–85	1	25	2	50	2	50	0	0	5	31.25
	<6.5	3	75	2	50	2	50	4	100	11	68.75
TDS (mgL^{-1})	>100	0	0	0	0	0	0	0	0	0	0
	<100	4	100	4	100	4	100	4	100	16	100
NO3 (mgL^{-1})	>50	0	0	0	0	0	0	0	0	0	0
	<50	4	100	4	100	4	100	4	100	16	100
NH3 (mgL^{-1})	>1.5	0	0	0	0	0	0	0	0	0	0
	<1.5	4	100	4	100	4	100	4	100	16	100
Ca (mgL^{-1})	>75	0	0	0	0	0	0	0	0	0	0
	<75	4	100	4	100	4	100	4	100	16	100
Mg (mgL^{-1})	>50	0	0	0	0	0	0	0	0	0	0
	<50	4	100	4	100	4	100	4	100	16	100
PO4 (mgL^{-1})	>0.50	0	0	1	25	0	0	2	50	3	18.75
	<0.50	4	100	3	75	4	100	2	50	13	81.25
Fe (mgL^{-1})	>0.30	0	0	0	0	0	0	0	0	0	0
	<0.30	4	100	4	100	4	100	4	100	16	100
TC (CFU)	>0	4	100	4	100	4	100	4	100	16	100
	<0	0	0	0	0	0	0	0	0	0	0
FC (CFU)	>0	2	50	2	50	4	10	4	10	12	75
	<0	2	50	2	50	0	0	0	0	4	25

Table 4. Compliance of drinking water sources in the wet season

Parameters		Ws_1		Ws_2		Ws_3		Ws_4		Total sample	
	WHO	N	P	N	P	N	P	N	P	N	P
Turb (NTU)	>5	4	100	3	75	0	0	4	100	11	68.75
	<5	0	0	1	25	4	100	0	0	5	31.25
EC (μscm^{-1})	>300	4	100	3	75	3	100	4	100	14	87.5
	<300	0	0	1	25	1	25	0	0	2	12.5
Temp (°C)	>15	4	100	4	100	4	100	4	100	16	100
	<15	0	0	0	0	0	0	0	0	0	0
PH	>8.5	0	0	0	0	0	0	0	0	0	0
	6.5–8.5	3	75	1	25	0	0	0	0	4	25
	<6.5	1	25	3	75	4	100	4	100	12	75
TDS (mgL^{-1})	>100	0	0	0	0	0	0	0	0	0	0
	<100	4	100	4	100	4	100	4	100	16	100
NO3 (mgL^{-1})	>50	0	0	0	0	0	0	0	0	0	0
	<50	4	100	4	100	4	100	4	100	16	100
NH3 (mgL^{-1})	>1.5	0	0	0	0	0	0	0	0	0	0
	< 1.5	4	100	4	100	4	100	4	100	16	100
Ca (mgL^{-1})	>75	0	0	0	0	0	0	0	0	0	0
	<75	4	100	4	100	4	100	4	100	16	87.5
Mg (mgL^{-1})	>50	0	0	0	0	0	0	2	50	2	12.5
	<50	4	100	4	100	4	100	2	50	14	87.5
PO4 (mgL^{-1})	>0.50	2	50	1	25	0	0	3	75	6	37.5
	<0.50	2	50	3	75	4	100	1	25	10	62.5
Fe (mgL^{-1})	>0.30	0	0	0	0	0	0	0	0	0	0
	<0.30	4	100	4	100	4	100	4	100	16	100
TC (CFU)	>0	4	100	4	100	4	100	4	100	16	100
	<0	0	0	0	0	0	0	0	0	0	0
FC (CFU)	>0	4	100	4	100	4	100	4	100	16	100
	<0	0	0	0	0	0	0	0	0	0	0

Key: N = number   of   sample = percent,   Turb = turbidity, temp = temperature, TC = total coliform, FC = feacal coliform

3.1 Physicochemical Quality of Drinking Water Sources

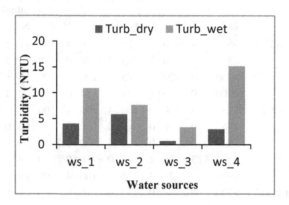

Fig. 1. Turbidity variation in season

Turbidity values ranged between 0.70 to 5.90 NTU in the dry season. A greater turbidity value of 5.90 NTU was noticed from ws_2. This was followed by ws_1 (4.07 NTU), ws_4 (2.98 NTU) and ws_3 with the lowest value of 0.70 NTU. In the wet season, results of turbidity fluctuated between 3.37 to 15.20 NTU. The values were gained in this decreasing order, ws_4 (15.20 NTU), ws_1 (10.94 NTU), ws_2 (7.69 NTU) and ws_3 (3.37 NTU). Turbidity values in this study were found higher in wet season than in the dry season across all the water sources (Fig. 1). This might be due to the entrance of run-off to the water sources that came from a nearby different anthropogenic activities. The reason for the greater difference between ws_3 and ws_4 was the variation in protection and geologic formation. A visible deviation between ws_1 and ws_2 is due to the difference in well characterstics.The result of one-way anova showed that there was a statistically significant difference in the mean turbidity values among the water sources in the dry and wet season (p $\leq$ 0.05). Among 16 drinking water samples collected in the dry season from four water sources tested for turbidity, 14 (87.5%) were below the upper limit of WHO guideline value for turbidity <5 NTU but 2 (12.5%) were above WHO guideline value for turbidity >5 NTU (Table 3).This low level of compliance was observed as of water samples collected from ws_2. In the wet season, 11 (68.75%) water samples were above the limit value of WHO standard whereas only 5 (31.25%) of the water samples were in accordance with the limit value of WHO standard (Table 4). The low level of compliance was observed from water samples collected from ws_2. The lowest compliance was observed as of water samples collected from ws_1 and ws_4. The lowest compliance was observed as of water samples collected from ws_1 and ws_4.

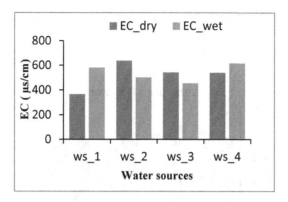

Fig. 2. EC variation in season

The electrical conductivity of the samples were found in the range of 365.72 μscm^{-1} to 637.66 μscm^{-1} in the dry season. Ws_2 was having the uppermost value of 637.66 μscm^{-1}. Next to it was ws_3 (542.32 μscm^{-1}), ws_4 (540.18 μscm^{-1}) and ws_1 (365.72 μscm^{-1}). The values varied between 455.29 μscm^{-1} to 616.25 μscm^{-1} in the wet season. Higher value of 616.25 μscm^{-1} was detected from ws_4. Subsequently, ws_1 (508.86 μscm^{-1}, ws_2 (502.61 μscm^{1}) and ws_3 (455.29 μscm^{-1}). Ws_4 and ws_1 showed higher EC values in the wet season and lower values in the dry season whereas Ws_2 and ws_3 revealed higher EC values in the dry season and lower values in the wet season (Fig. 2). The higher values of EC at ws_1 and ws_4 in wet season might be due to the entrance run-off which came from different human activities near the sources. The reasons for higher value of EC at ws_2 and ws_3 in the dry season might be due to the transformation of minerals to different ions from the rocks. As presented in Table 1, the results of one way anova showed that the spatial difference in EC was statistically significant in the dry season amongst the water sources. Contrary to this, there was no a significant difference in the means of EC amongst the water sources in the wet season (Table 2). For water samples tested from water sources in the dry and wet season, 16 (100%) and 14 (87.5%) were above the limit value of WHO standard (Table 3) while only none and 2 (12.5%) (Table 4) of the water samples were in accordance with the limit value of WHO standard respectively. The lowest compliance across all the water sources in the dry season might be due to the conversion of minerals to numerous ions from the host rocks.

The temperature of water samples analyzed altered between 22.93 °C to 25.85 °C in the dry season. Ws_2 recorded higher value of temperature 25.85 °C. This was followed by ws_3 with (24.95 °C), ws_1 (23.21 °C) and ws_4 with the lowermost value of (22.93 °C). In the wet season, the temperature readings ranged between (20.06 °C to 21.02 °C). Ws_2 was found to have the highest value of 21.02 °C, ws_4 (20.66 °C), ws_3 (20.08 °C) and ws_1 with lowest temperature of 20.06 °C. The values of temperature were found to be higher in the dry season across all the water sources. Based on one way anova carried out among the water sources in two different seasons, there was a significant difference among the means of all the water sources in the dry season (P $\leq$ 0.05).However, there was no a significant difference in the means of the water sources in the wet season (Table 4).

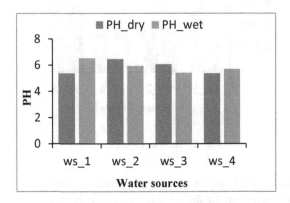

Fig. 3. PH variation in season

The values of pH found in this research ranged between 5.35 to 6.47 in the dry season. Upper pH values were recorded from ws_2 (6.47), ws_3 (6.06), ws_4 (5.37) and lower pH value in the dry season (5.35) was found from ws_1. During wet season, pH values varied between 5.40 to 6.54 with ws_1 having the highest value of 6.54, following it was ws_2 (5.94), ws_4 (5.70) and ws_3 with the lowest value of 5.40. Ws_1 and ws_4 indicated lower PH values in the dry season and higher PH values in the wet season.Ws_2 and ws_3 showed higher PH values in the dry season and lower values in the wet season (Fig. 3). The higher values from ws_1 and ws_4 in the wet season might be due to the infiltration of run-off from different human activities around the sources whereas the reasons for greater value in the dry season at ws_2 and ws_3 might be due to the release of different ions from the rocks. The spatial variation among the water sources in both the seasons remained insignificant (p $\geq$ 0.05). From a total of 16 water samples collected in the dry season from four water sources, 11 (68.75%) water samples were below the lower bound of WHO standard (Table 3). The lower level of compliance from ws_3 and ws_4 might be due to the activity of bacteria during the decomposition of dead wood and plant leaves that has been fallen. In the same way, water samples collected in the wet season from water sources, 12 (75%) of the water samples were below the lower bound of WHO standard (Table 4).

The results of TDS was gained in the range of 201.15 mgL^{-1} to 350.71 mgL^{-1} in the dry season. Ws_2 had the higher value of 350.71 mgL^{-1}. This was followed by ws_3 (298.28 mgL^{-1}), ws_4 (297.10 mgL^{-1}) and the lowest value of ws_1 (201.15 mgL^{-1}). The result ranged from 250.68 mgL^{-1} to 338.94 mgL^{-1} in the wet season. Ws_4 had the uppermost value of 338.94 mgL^{-1}. Subsequently, ws_1 (319.47 mgL^{-1}), ws_2 (276.44 mgL^{-1}) and ws_3 had the lowermost values of 250.68 mgL^{-1}. Ws_1 and ws_4 revealed higher values of TDS in the wet season and lower values in the dry season where ws_2 and ws_3 showed higher values of TDS in the dry season and lower values in the wet season. The result of one-way anova showed that there was statistically significant difference in the mean TDS values among the water sources in the dry season($p \leq 0.05$) while there was statistically insignificant difference in the mean TDS measurements among the water sources in the wet season (Table 2). From a total of 16 water samples tested for TDS from four water sources in the dry and the wet seasons, 16 (100%) had less than 1000 mgL^{-1} in each of the seasons Tables 3 and 4.

The results of nitrate fluctuated from 1.37 to 3.06 mgL^{-1} in the dry season. The uppermost value was occurred at ws_4 (3.06 mgL^{-1}).This was followed by ws_1 (2.10 mgL^{-1}), ws_2 (1.64 mgL^{-1}) and the lower values was detected from ws_3 (1.37 mgL^{-1}). In the wet season, the values of nitrate varied from 2.05 mgL^{-1} to 3.15 mgL^{-1}. Highest values were noticed from ws_4 (3.15 mgL^{-1}).The rest were found in order, ws_1 (2.82 mgL^{-1}), ws_2 (2.09 mgL^{-1}) and lowermost value of 2.05 mgL^{-1} from ws_3. Nitrate values in this study were found higher in the wet season than in the dry season across all the water sources. This might be due to the entrance of run off to the water sources that came from various anthropogenic activities. The results of nitrate among the water sources in the dry season revealed a significant variation since the p-value (0.00) is less than the significance level (0.05) (Table 1).In the same way, the results of nitrate in the means of the water sources was significant in the wet season because the p-value (0.04) is less than the significance level (0.05) (Table 2). All the water samples tested for nitrate from four water sources in both season, they were in the acceptable limit value (50 mgL^{-1}) of WHO standard Tables 3 and 4.

Results of ammonia varied between 0.20 mgL^{-1} to 0.24 mgL^{-1} in the dry season. Ws_3 had the higher value of 0.24 mgL^{-1}. This was followed by ws_1 (0.22 mgL^{-1}), ws_4 (0.21 mgL^{-1}) and the lowest value of ws_2 (0.20 mgL^{-1}). The result ranged from 0.07 mgL^{-1} to 0.36 mgL^{-1} in the wet season. Ws_1 had the uppermost value of 0.36 mgL^{-1}. This was followed by ws_2 (0.26 mgL^{-1}), ws_3 (0.16 mgL^{-1}) and ws_4 had the lower most value of 0.07 mgL^{-1}. Ws_1 and ws_2 had higher values in the wet season and lower values in the dry season whereas ws_3 and ws_4 had lower values in wet season and higher values in the dry season. The different value between the wet and dry season for ammonia is because of geological and physical factors. The result of one way anova indicated a statistically insignificant variation in water quality among the water sources in the dry season ($p \geq 0.05$).Nevertheless, there was a significant difference in water quality in terms of ammonia among the water sources in the wet season (Table 2). Comparing the total of thirty two water samples collected in the dry and wet season for ammonia with the water quality standards revealed that, all the water sources were found within the allowable limit of water quality standards of (1.50 mgL^{-1}) both in the dry and wet seasons(Tables 3 and 4).

The results of calcium was found in the range of 7.50 mgL^{-1} to 28.50 mgL^{-1} in the dry season. Ws_4 had the higher value of 28.50 mgL^{-1}. This was followed by ws_3 (17.00 mgL^{-1}), ws_2 (10.75 mgL^{-1}) and ws_1 (7.50 mgL^{-1}). The result ranged from 11.75 mgL^{-1} to 23.75 mgL^{-1} in the wet season. Ws_4 had the highest value of 23.75 mgL^{-1}, ws_3 (20.00 mgL^{-1}), ws_2 (17.50 mgL^{-1}) and ws_1 had the lowest value of 11.50 mgL^{-1}. Concentration of calcium was found to be higher in the wet season than in the dry season across all the sampling points with the exception of ws_4. The greater value of calcium in the wet season might be due to the dissolution from the rocks because of the natural occurrence of calcium in the earth crust. The result of one-way anova showed that there was statistically significant difference in the mean calcium measurements among the water sources in the dry season (Table 1) but the result of one way nova showed that there was no statistically significant difference among the mean values of calcium of the water sources in the wet season (Table 2). In a total of 32 water samples tested for calcium in both the dry and wet seasons, all calcium concentrations of water sources were acceptable by WHO standard.

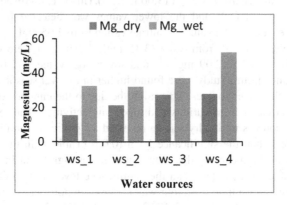

Fig. 4. Magnesium variation in season

The mean values of magnesium ranged from 15.50 to 27.75 mgL^{-1} in the dry season. The variation was found in this order ws_1 < ws_2 < ws_3 < ws_4. Ws_1 had the lowest value of 15.50 mgL^{-1} and ws_4 had the highest value of 27.75 mgL^{-1}. During wet season, the concentration of magnesium ranged from 32.00 to 52.00 mgL^{-1} in the order ws_2 < ws_1 < ws_3 < ws_4. Ws_4 had the highest value of 52.00 mgL^{-1} and ws_2 had the lowest value of 32.00 mgL^{-1}. The mean values of magnesium were higher in the wet season than in the dry season (Fig. 4). The reasons for such greater value of magnesium in the wet season across all the water sources might be due to washing of magnesium from the rocks containing a large number of minerals which held magnesium. According to the results of one way anova, there was a significant difference amongst the means of the water sources in both the two seasons (Tables 1 and 2). In analysis of the chemical quality of water samples for magnesium in the wet season, 2 (12.5%) water samples were greater than the recommended limit of WHO standard. Only 14 (87.5%) of water samples were found to be met the WHO standard acceptable limit (Table 3). From a total of 16 water samples collected from the water sources in the dry season for magnesium, all magnesium concentrations of water sources were acceptable by WHO standard (Table 4).

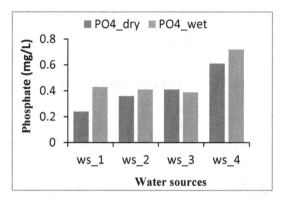

Fig. 5. Phosphate variation in season

The results of phosphate ranged from 0.24 to 0.61 mgL^{-1} in the dry season. Ws_4 had the highest value of 0.61 mgL^{-1}. Next to it was ws_3 (0.41 mgL^{-1}), ws_2 (0.36 mgL^{-1}) and ws_1 with the lowest value of 0.24 mgL^{-1}. In the wet season, the values of phosphate ranged from 0.39 to 0.72 mgL^{-1}. Ws_4 had the highest value of 0.72 mgL^{-1}, followed by ws_1 (0.43 mgL^{-1}), ws_2 (0.41 mgL^{-1}) and ws_3 with the lowest value of 0.39 mgL^{-1}. Values of phosphate from ws_1, 2 and 4 were higher in the wet season than the dry season whereas ws_3 was lower in the wet season than the dry season (Fig. 5). The mean values of phosphate among the water sources showed a significant difference in the dry season but did not revealed a significant variation in the wet season (Tables 1 and 2). Among 16 drinking water samples collected in the dry season from four water sources tested for phosphate, 13 (81.25%) were below the upper limit of WHO guideline value for phosphate <0.5 mgL^{-1} but 3 (18.75%) were above WHO guideline value for phosphate >0.5 mgL^{-1} (Table 3). The low level of compliance was occurred as ws_2 and the lower level of compliance was noticed from ws_4. In the wet season, water samples tested for phosphate from the water sources, 6 (37.5%) were above the limit value of WHO standard whereas only 10 (75.5%) of the water samples were in accordance with the limit value of WHO standard (Table 4). The low level of compliance was detected from ws_2.The lower level of compliance was occurred at ws_1 and the lowest level of compliance was shown from ws_4. The lower compliance of phosphate as ws_4 might be due to the entrance of agricultural run off as well as owing to run off from open grass land above the spring.

Iron values varied between 0.03 to 0.12 mgL^{-1} in the dry season. A higher iron value of 0.12 mgL^{-1} was detected from ws_1. This was followed by ws_3 (0.11 mgL^{-1}), ws_4 (0.04 mgL^{-1}) and ws_2 with the lowest value of 0.03 mgL^{-1}. In the wet season, the values of iron ranged between 0.11 mgL^{-1} to 0.17 mgL^{-1}. The values were obtained in this order ws_4 (0.17 mgL^{-1}), ws_1 (0.16 mgL^{-1}), ws_3 (0.12 mgL^{-1}) and ws_2 with the lowest value of 0.11 mgL^{-1}. Iron values in this research were found higher in the wet season than in the dry season across all the sampling points. The result of one-way anova showed that there was statistically significant difference in the mean iron values ($p \leq 0.05$) among the water sources in the dry season. However, there was no a statistically significant difference in the mean iron amounts ($p \geq 0.05$)

among the water sources in the wet season. In a total of 32 water samples tested for iron in both the dry and wet seasons, all iron concentrations of water sources were acceptable by WHO standard value of 0.3 mgL^{-1} (Tables 3 and 4).

3.2   Bacteriological Quality of Drinking Water Sources

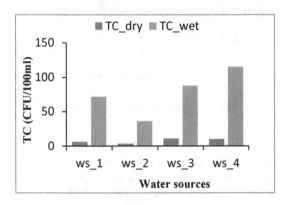

Fig. 6. Total coliform variation in season

Total coliforms ranged from 3.50 to 11.00 CFU in the dry season. Ws_3 recorded higher number of coliforms 11.00 CFU, ws_4 (10.00 CFU), ws_1 (6.25 CFU) and ws_2 recorded 3.50 CFU. In the wet season, the number of coliforms observed varied from 36.25 to 115.25 CFU with ws_4 having the highest number of coliforms 115.25 CFU, ws_3 (87.75 CFU), ws_1 (71.50) and ws_2 with the lowest number of coliforms 36.25 CFU. The total coliform counts were higher in the wet season than in the dry seasons across all the water sources (Fig. 6). The reasons for such greater values of total coliform in the wet season might be caused by the movement of organic matter from various human activities through run off. According to one way anova test, there was significant variation among the means of the water sources in the dry season (Table 1). Similarly, there was a significant difference among the water sources in the wet season since p-value (0.01) is less than the significance level (Table 2). From a total of 16 water samples tested for total coliform count from four water sources in the dry season, 16 (100%) were above the limit value of WHO standard (Table 3). Low compliance was observed from water samples collected from all the water sources in the dry season. Among 16 water samples collected and tested for total coliform in the wet season, 16 (100%) were above the upper limit of WHO guideline value but zero percent was in line with WHO guideline value across all the water sources (Table 4). The higher value of total coliform from ws_1 and ws_2 might be due to human, animal contact and storm run-off that came from poor sanitation system of both legally and illegally expanded urbanization around the sources. The highest total coliform from ws_4 might be due to human and animal contact.

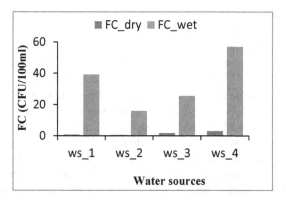

Fig. 7. Feacal coliform variation in season

Faecal coliform count values were found in the range of 0.50 to 3.00 CFU in the dry season with ws_4 having the highest value of 3.00 CFU and ws_3 (1.75 CFU), ws_1 (0.75 CFU) and ws_2 having the lowest value of 0.50 CFU. In the wet season, the value of faecal coliform ranged from (16.00 CFU to 57.00 CFU).The highest value of faecal coliform was observed from ws_4 (57.00 CFU).This was followed by ws_1 (39.25 CFU). Next to it was ws_3 (25.50 CFU) and the lowest value of 16.00 CFU was observed from ws_2. Values of faecal coliforms were found higher in the wet season than in the dry season across all the water sources (Fig. 7). The reasons for such greater value of faecal coliform in the wet season might be due to the transport and entrance of various human and animal feces to the water sources through run off which came from polluted surfaces. The result of one way nova showed that there was a statistically significant difference among the mean counts of faecal coliform (p 0.05) of the water sources in both the dry season (p = 0.01) and in the wet season (p = 0.05) (Tables 1 and 2).12 (75%) water samples in the dry season were unacceptable by WHO standard while 4 (25%) of the water samples were acceptable by WHO standard (Table 3). Low compliance was observed from water samples collected as ws_1 and ws_2 water sources. The lowest level of compliance was observed from water samples collected from ws_3 and ws_4. Among 16 water samples collected from four water sources tested for feacal coliform in the wet season, 16 (100%) water samples were above the upper limit of WHO guideline value but zero percent was in line with WHO guideline value (Table 4). The higher faecal coliform at ws_1 and ws_2 might be due to human and animal contact. The numerous feacal coliform from ws_4 might be due to feces of animals and humans that released from the above open grass land and open defecation of the rural residents above the grass land.

4   Conclusion

This study analyzed the drinking water sources quality variation and compliance in the dry and wet season based on thirteen water quality characteristics (total coliform, nitrate, electrical conductivity, turbidity, total dissolved solid, faecal coliform, calcium, magnesium, phosphate, iron, PH, temperature and ammonia) in Finote Selam town. Most parameters recorded greater values in the wet season and others were at their higher values in the dry season. The average values of turbidity (9.30 NTU), electrical conductivity (538.88 μscm^{-1}), total dissolved solid (296.38 mgL^{-1}), nitrate (2.39 mgL^{-1}), total coliform (77.69 cfu/100 ml), faecal coliform (34.44 cfu/100 ml), calcium (18.25 mgL^{-1}), magnesium (38.38 mgL^{-1}), phosphate (0.49 mgL^{-1}), iron (0.14 mgL^{-1}) and PH (5.90) were found higher in the wet season than in the dry season. Those of temperature (24.23 °C) and ammonia (0.22 mgL^{-1}) were found higher in the dry season than in the wet season. According to the analysis of the result, it may conclude that, the quality of water varies with the season. Turbidity, electrical conductivity, temperature, total dissolved solid, nitrate, total coliform, calcium, phosphate and iron showed a significant difference in the dry season while insignificant variation in the wet season. However, Faecal coliform and magnesium showed a significant variation both in the dry and wet season but ammonia revealed significant variation in the wet season and insignificant difference in the dry season. PH signified insignificant variation in both the dry and wet season. Based on anova, there is water quality variation among the water sources both in the dry and wet season. For turbidity 2 (12.5%),for phosphate 3 (18.75%), for electrical conductivity 16 (100%), for total coliform 16 (100%) and faecal coliform 12 (75%) were above WHO standard in the dry season whereas for turbidity 11 (68.75%), for electrical conductivity 14 (87.5%),for phosphate 6 (37.5), for total coliform 16 (100%), for magnesium 2(12.5%) and faecal coliform 16 (100%) were above WHO standard in the wet season. For PH 11 (68.75%) and 12 (75%) of the water samples collected were below the lower bound of WHO standard both in the dry and wet season respectively. The result showed that the drinking water sources are not safe since most of the water samples taken were not fulfilled WHO standard in the dry and wet season.

References

1. Bello, O.O., Osho, A., Bankole, S.A., Bello, T.K.: Bacteriological and physicochemical analyses of borehole and well water sources in Ijebu-Ode Southwestern Nigeria. IOSR J. Pharm. Biol. Sci. **8**, 18–25 (2013)
2. Egbai, J.C., Adaikpoh, E.O., Aigbogun, C.O.: Water quality assessment of groundwater in Okwuagbe community of delta state Nigeria. Tech. J. Eng. Appl. Sci. **3**, 2347 (2013)
3. Govindarajan, M., Senthilnathan, T.: Groundwater quality and its health impact analysis in an industrial area. Int. J. Curr. Microbiol. App. Sci. **3**, 1028–1034 (2014)
4. Idris, S.: Assessment of seasonal changes of some physicochemical parameters of drinking water in Dutsinma city Katsina state. Int. J. Sci. Res. Sci. Tech. **4**, 68–75 (2018)
5. Ir, A., Ce, O., Ka, K., Ahmed, I., Cc, E.: Physicochemical properties bacteriological quality and antimicrobial resistance profile of isolates from groundwater sources in ile-ife Suburbs, Southwest Nigeria. Environ. Taxicol. **13**, 58–65 (2019)
6. Longe, E.O., Balogun, M.R.: Groundwater quality assessment near a municipal landfill, Lagos, Nigeria. Res. J. Appl. Sci. Eng. Technol. **2**, 39–44 (2010)
7. Moyo, N.A.G.: An analysis of the chemical and microbiological quality of ground water from boreholes and shallow wells in Zimbabwe. Phys. Chem. Earth Parts A/B/C **66**, 27–32 (2013)

8. E.O. of the Population, H.C. Commission, Summary and statistical report of the: Population and Housing Census: population size by age and sex, p. 2008. Federal Democratic Republic of Ethiopia, Population Census Commission (2007)

9. Onilude, A.A., Adesina, F.C., Oluboyede, O.A., Adeyemi, B.I.: Microbiological quality of sachet packaged water vended in three local governments of Oyo State, Nigeria, African. J. Food Sci. Technol. **4**, 195–200 (2013)

10. Palamuleni, L., Akoth, M.: Physico-chemical and microbial analysis of selected borehole water in Mahikeng, South Africa. Int. J. Environ. Res. Public Health. **12**, 8619–8630 (2015)

11. B. Quality, O.F. Selected, ISSN : 1119-1104 PHYSICOCHEMICAL AND BACTERIO-LOGICAL QUALITY OF SELECTED WELL ISSN : 1119-1104, (2016)

12. Seth, O.N., Tagbor, T.A., Bernard, O.: Assessment of chemical quality of groundwater over some rock types in Ashanti region, Ghana. Am. J. Sci. Ind. Res. **5**, 1–6 (2014)

13. Singh, S., Negi, R.S., Dhanai, R.: A study of physico-chemical parameters of springs around Srinagar Garhwal valley, Uttarakhand. Int. J. Eng. Dev. Res. **2**, 2321–9939 (2014)

14. Szewzyk, U., Szewzyk, R., Manz, W., Schleifer, K.-H.: Microbiological safety of drinking water. Annu. Rev. Microbiol. **54**, 81–127 (2000)

15. WHO, Guidelines for Drinking-water Quality (2011)

Impact of Land Use Land Cover Dynamics on Stream Flow: A Case of Borkena Watershed, Awash Basin, Ethiopia

Metafet Asmare Abebe[1], Temesgen Enku[2(✉)],
and Seid Endris Ahmed[1,2]

[1] Wollo University, Komolcha Institute of Technology, Kombolcha, Ethiopia
[2] Faculty of Civil and Water Resources Engineering, Bahir Dar Institute
of Technology Bahir Dar University, Bahir Dar, Ethiopia

Abstract. In the recent decade, the change in land use and land cover have
changed the ecosystem services more rapidly than the previous similar periods.
Land use land cover (LULC) change is the major factor that affect the watershed
response. The main objective of this study was to assess the impact of land use
and land cover change on the response of the Borkena watershed. The LULC
change analysis was evaluated using supervised classification in ENVI software.
The SWAT model was used to assess the impact of LULC change on streamflow for the period from 1996 to 2016. The study result revealed that the
Borkena watershed experienced significant LULC changes from 1986 to 2016.
Most of the grass land, cultivated land, and shrub land were changed to build-up
and bare Land. The LULC map showed an increase of buildup area and bare
land by 3.6% and 5.9%, respectively. There was a good agreement between
simulated flow and observed data with a coefficient of determination (R^2) and
Nash-Sutcliff Efficiency (NSE) values of 0.81 and 0.79 in calibration, and 0.75
and 0.74 in validation periods, respectively. The evaluation of the SWAT
hydrologic response due to the change in LULC showed that monthly streamflow was increased by 5.4 m^3/s in the wet season and decreased by 0.5 m^3/s in
the dry season, and there was a significant effect ($p < 0.05$) of LULC change on
watershed response. The changes in land use have resulted in changes in
streamflow, due to the expansion of urbanization and land degradation.

Keywords: Land use land cover · StreamFlow · SWAT model · Awash basin ·
Ethiopia

1 Introduction

The Land use and land cover change in the recent decade, have changed the ecosystem
services more rapidly than the previous similar periods [1]. This is due to the increased
agricultural activity the cost of forest cover for food production, increased urbanization,
overgrazing, and increased demand for ecosystem services. In addition, the change in
climate has also contributed for the rapid changes in land use land cover. These all-
dynamic activities had led to environmental changes and degradation of the ecosystem
services [3]. Water resource management studies are related with the hydrological

© ICST Institute for Computer Sciences, Social Informatics and Telecommunications Engineering 2022
Published by Springer Nature Switzerland AG 2022. All Rights Reserved
M. L. Berihun (Ed.): ICAST 2021, LNICST 412, pp. 128–143, 2022.
https://doi.org/10.1007/978-3-030-93712-6_9

processes in all watershed scales [2]. These processes are affected by several factors: including anthropogenic activities and natural factors [4]. The land use/land cover (LULC) dynamics has significant effect on the watershed response: the surface runoff pattern, baseflow volume, groundwater recharge, and soil moisture content [5].

The impact of LULC dynamics on the watershed response can be analyzed using Soil & Water Assessment Tool (SWAT) model using remote sensing data and geographical information system (GIS). Because there is a strong relationship between watershed properties and watershed processes [6]. Due to the rapid growth of population, urbanization, and industrialization activities, the Borkena watershed is one of the most fragile natural systems in the upper Awash basin [7]. However, there is limited study in the upper Awash basin, where LULC, climate change, and climate variability have significant impacts on the hydrology of the watershed. Therefore, understanding the effect of the LULC change on watershed hydrology is crucial. Rapid LULC change alters the environment and has a pronounced impact on the water balance of a watershed [8]. Therefore, understanding of how LULC change affects watershed hydrology is vital for sustainable natural resources management. The objective of this study was to assess the impact of land use and land cover change on the response of the Borkena watershed.

2 Methodology

2.1 Description of the Study Area

The Borkena watershed is located in the Amhara national regional state, South Wollo zone, and including the and partly in the Oromia special Zone (Fig. 1). The Borkena watershed contributes a lot to Awash River basin. It drains from the mountainous chains and escarpments found in the northern plateau which is adjacent to the Afar rift down to the southeastern direction and after joining the Jara River, it finally drains the Awash River.

Borkena watershed covers about 1677 km². The gauging station of the watershed is found near to Kemsie town at 10°38′ N latitude and 39°56′ E longitude. The topography of the watershed is very undulating and the elevation ranges from 1378 m to 3499 m above mean sea level, therefore it is grouped under the "Woina Dega Agroecology" Ethiopian climate classification system.

The climate of the Borkena watershed varies from sub-humid to subtropical and the main annual rainfall over the catchment is 1028 mm and most of which is concentrated in the main rainy months that lasts from July to September and contributes about 84% of the annual rainfall [7]. The soil in the study area includes predominantly chromic cambisols, lithosols, regosols, rock surface, and chromic vertisols where the chromic cambisols dominates the north part of the study area as shown in Fig. 2.

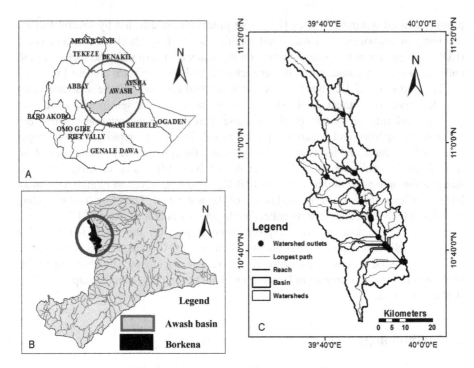

Fig. 1. Location map of Borkena watershed

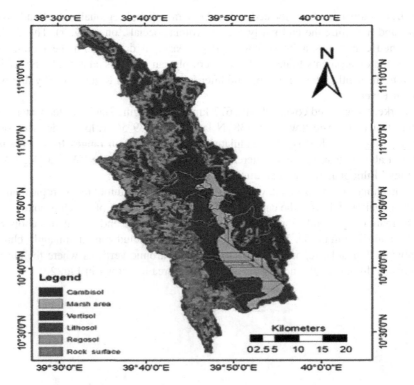

Fig. 2. Soil Classification map of the study area

Traditional grazing on communal lands has also been practiced for years with little or no modification. In addition to the long years of agricultural activities in the area, the present size of human and livestock population pressure has led to the overutilization of land resources where people are faced to turn mountain slopes into farmlands. The Land-use the land cover of the study area which was classified by the Ministry of Water Resource, Irrigation, and Energy in 1987 [9] is shown in Fig. 3.

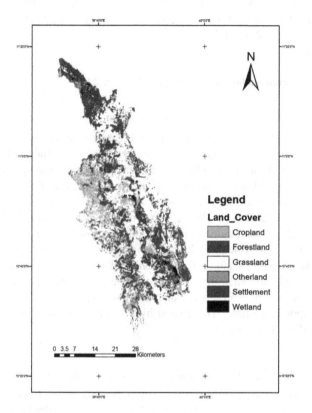

Fig. 3. The Land use land cover of the study area, which was classified by the Ministry of Water Resource, Irrigation and Energy in 1987

2.2   Method and Material

Sources and Types of Data. To achieve the objectives of this study, primary and secondary data including satellite imagery data were collected. The data included remote sesig spatial data, hydrological data, and meteorological data.

Satellite Image and GIS Data Collection. Time series LandSat images of 1986, 1996, 2006, and 2016 were used to analyze the LULC dynamics of the Borkena watershed. Satellite images were downloaded from USGS-GLOVIS (www.glovis.usgs.gov). All images used in this study were 30 m spatial resolution and below 10% cloud cover (Table 1).

Table 1. Summary of spatial data sets

Dataset type	Acquisition Date	Pixel Resolution (m)/Scale	Path/Row	Producer
Satellite data				
Landsat TM	1986-02-13/25	30 m	168/052 & 53	USGS
Landsat TM	1996-01-23/25	30 m	168/052 & 053	USGS
Landsat ETM +	2006-02-12/19	30 m	168/052 & 053	USGS
Landsat OLI/TIRS	2016-02-02 & 2016-01-24	30 m	168/052 & 053	USGS
Ancillary data				
Field data				
GPS point for each land-use class: May, 2019 - June, 2019				

Meteorological and Hydrological Data. The meteorological data were obtained from the National Meteorological Agency of Ethiopia (NMA) at Bahir Dar branch for Kombolcha, Dessie, Kemisie, Cheffa, and Majetie meteorological stations which are located in the watershed and some of them are in the outside of the watershed. The daily streamflow data from the year 1996 to 2016 was obtained from the Ministry of Water, Irrigation and Energy (MoWIE). These data were used in the SWAT model to do sensitivity analysis, calibration, and validation purposes. In this study, the missed meteorological data were calculated by using Arithmetic and Normal ratio methods by observing the surrounding stations. The normal annual ratio method was selected to fill some of the missed data when the difference of the normal annual precipitations and 10% of normal annual data are greater than other stations normal annual precipitation with the correspondence time. The missed hydrological data were filled by an arithmetic method (Fig. 4) (Table 2).

Table 2. Availability and classes of meteorological data

Station name	Precipitation	Temperature	Relative humidity	Solar radiation	Wind speed	Stationclass	Station coverage area (Km²)	Recording periods
Dessie	x	x	–	–	–	III	169	1996–2016
Kemisie	x	x	–	–	–	III	423.5	1996–2016
Cheffa	x	x	x	x	x	I	607.5	1996–2016
Kombolcha	x	x	x	x	x	I	320	1996–2016
Majetie	x	x	x	x	x	I	316.4	1996–2016

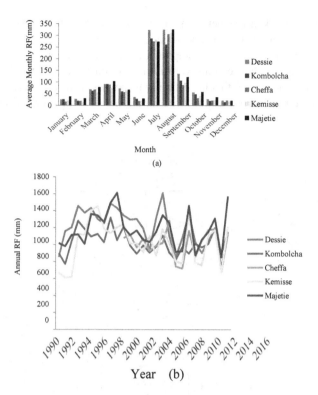

Fig. 4. Average rainfalls pattern of the stations at (a) Monthly and (b) annual scale

2.3 Data Processing and Analysis

Image Pre-processing. The Geometric and Radiometric corrections and image enhancement were conducted by ENVI before the image classification. Geometric correction involves the conversion of data to ground coordinates for example to Universal Transverse Mercator by the removing the distortions from sensor geometry, Radiometric correction, on the other hand, involves correcting unwanted sensor due to atmospheric noise and correcting the data for sensor irregularities [10]. The satellite images used in this study were projected to UTM projection, Zone 37N and datum of WGS84.

Land Use Land Cover Classification. Image classification involves categorizing raw remotely sensed satellite images into a fewer number of individual LU/LC classes, based on the reflectance values. Image enhancement and classification for this study were performed using ENVI. ENVI was also used for the preparation of land use land cover data for SWAT input. The Landsat data image of the catchment which shows the land use land cover for four different years of 1986, 1996, 2006, and 2016 were downloaded and used for ENVI for further image enhancement, processing, and re-classification. The supervised classification routine of ENVI were used for the classification of images take from satellite.

A signature level taken was between 15 and 20 for each of the land cover classes as ground truth/verifi- cation. The main technique for accuracy assessment is using change maps for evaluating each class and computing the expected accuracy by error matrix's [5]. Post-classification enhancements were used to diminish the classification errors from base fields, cities, and classes that have similar responses with crop areas and wetlands. Accordingly, an error matrix was produced for all images in this study (Fig. 5).

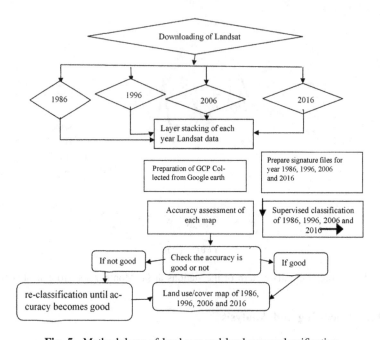

Fig. 5. Methodology of land use and land cover classification

Land Use and Land Cover Change Detection Analysis. Comparison of the classified images was used to determine the extent of land cover changes over the period of 1986 and 2016. The rate of change of the different land covers was estimated based on the following formulas [11].

$$\%coverchange = \frac{area_i year_x - area_i year_{x+1}}{\sum_{i=1}^{n} area_i year_x} * 100$$

where,
$area_i year_x$ is the area cover I on the first date;
$area_i year_{x+1}$ is the area of cover I on the next date;
$\sum_{i=1}^{n} area_i year_x$ is the total area at the first date.

2.4   SWAT Model Set-Up and Simulation

SWAT and SWAT-CUP Model Description. SWAT model (i.e. ArcSWAT) is an extension of ArcGIS, developed by the United States Department of Agricultural Research Service (ARS). The globally widely used SWAT model is a semi-distributed physically based hydrological model. The model is able to simulate runoff, sediment, nutrients, and pesticide transport from agricultural watersheds [1]. Hydrological response units (HRU's) are utilized to consider spatial heterogeneity within a watershed. Using the water balance approach of the model, it simulates the hydrological parameters as shown in the equation below [6].

$$SW_t = SW_o + \sum_{i=1}^{t} (R_{day} - Q_{surf} - E_a - W_{seep} - Q_{gw})$$

where,

SW_t- is the final water content (mm)

SW_o- is the initial water content (mm)

$R_{day}-$ is the amount of Precipitation on day i (mm).

$t-$ is the time (day)

$Q_{surf}-$ is the surface runoff on day i (mm)

E_a- is the evaporation on day i (mm)

$W_{seep}-$ is the amount of water entering the vadose zone day i (mm), and

$Q_{gw}-$ is the return flow on day i (mm)

The SWAT built in sensitivity analysis tool was used to do the sensitivity analysis of the parameters. The sensitivity analysis tool is helpful to model users in identifying parameters that are most influential in governing streamflow response. The calibrated parameters were used to run SWAT model with the input data including digital elevation model, soil map, land use map, rainfall, and observed streamflow. Details of model sensitivity analysis, calibration, and validation concepts are discussed in the next sections.

Sensitivity Analysis. In a SWAT simulation, it is common to have a discrepancy between the simulated results and the observed data [12]. Determining the parameters which affects the results most is important to minimize this discrepancy. The sensitivity is used to estimate the rate of change of model outputs concerning the change of model inputs. To determine the influential parameters in the model, for a better understanding of how the Borkena hydrologic system behaves, and further evaluation of the model performance, sensitivity analysis was conducted. Identifying the location of the sub-basin where observation data was collected is important to ease comparison of the simulated result and observed data. For the sensitivity analysis, the 27 parameters selected with the default lower and upper bounds were used [6]. Finally, the parameters mean relative sensitivity values were used to rank the parameters and their category of classification. The sensitivity category was defined based on the classification as shown in Table 3 [13].

Table 3. The sensitivity category

Class	MRS sensitivity	Category
I	$0.00 \leq MRS < 0.05$	Small to negligible
II	$0.05 \leq MRS < 0.2$	Medium
III	$0.2 \leq MRS < 1$	High
IV	$MRS > 1$	Very high

Model Calibration. The time series of river flow data at the outlet of the watershed which found near to Kemsie town at 10°38′N latitude and 39°56′E longitude was used for calibration and validation of the model, 13 years of observed data (from 1996 to 2008) was used to calibrate the model, and the most sensitive parameters that affect most the watershed response were identified and ranked according to their sensitivity ranks. These parameters were automatically calibrated by using SWAT CUP for the first 13 years until the model simulation result becomes acceptable as per the model performance measures (Fig. 6).

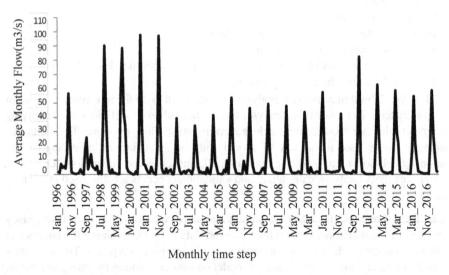

Monthly time step

Fig. 6. Average monthly streamflow data of Borkena River

Model Validation. For validation, the performance of the model was tested with an independent 8 years (from 2009 to 2016) set of observed data. The model predictive capacity will be determined in both calibration and validation phases, when the objective functions are met. Based on the performance the model, it will be used for future predictions under different scenarios.

To evaluate the goodness-of-fit of model coefficient of determination (R2), and the Nash Sutcliff Efficiency (NSE) were applied. R2 ranges from 0 that indicates poor model performance to 1 that indicates the best model performance, generally higher values indicating less error variances.

2.5 Evaluation of Streamflow Variability Due to LULC Change

The watershed streamflow is the amount of water leaving the watershed outlet in the stream channel. The quantity of watershed response is affected by watershed characteristics (including land use) and weather (increase during rainy periods and decrease during dry periods). The impact of LULC on the variability of streamflow was evaluated for the year 1996 to 2016. In the three independent periods, SWAT model was run on a monthly time step for the years 1996, 2006, and 2016 LULC, keeping other input parameters unchanged. Finally, seasonal streamflow variability due to LULC change was assessed based on the simulation outputs. A one-way analysis of variance (ANOVA) for one factor (land use land cover change) at 5% significance level was conducted (Fig. 7).

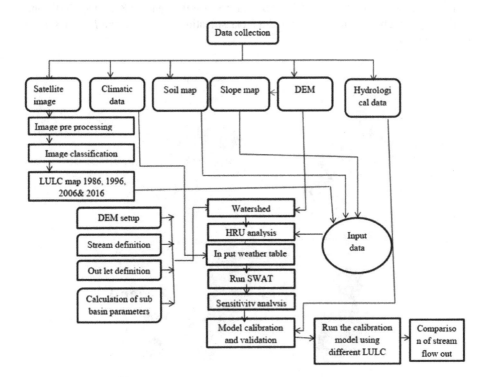

Fig. 7. The conceptual Methodology framework of the study

3 Results and Discussion

3.1 Land Use Land Cover Change Analysis

For the land cover detection, maps having eight classes of land use/cover were created: Cultivation land (CL), Grass land (GL), Shrub land (SL), Forest land (FL), Bare lands (BL), Waterbody (WB), Marsh land (ML), and Built-up area (BA) in the years 1986, 1996, 2006 and 2016.

According to the maximum likelihood classification of the 1986 Landsat satellite image; the land cover classes (Fig. 8) showed dominantly covered with cultivated land with 53% coverage, followed by Shrub Land, Grass land, and Forest land with 19.9%, 11.3%, and 11.2% coverage respectively. Marsh land, Bare land, Built-up area, and Water Body covers small percentages: 2.7%, 0.95%, 0.82%, and 0.08%, respectively.

The maximum likelihood classification results of the 2016 Landsat satellite image; the land cover classes (Fig. 8) were also dominated by cultivated land with 54.3%. Other land cover classes also cover the remaining 45.7%, with shrub land 21.3%, grass land 7.0%, bare land 6.9%, built-up area 4.5%, forest 5.1%, and marsh land 0.84%, and water body 0.06%. The Kappa coefficient for each land use land cover was also computed as: K value of 0.86, 0.87, 0.85, and 0.87 for the years 1986, 1996, 2006, and 2016, respectively. The result indicated the classification is better as the K values are it is more than 0.8.

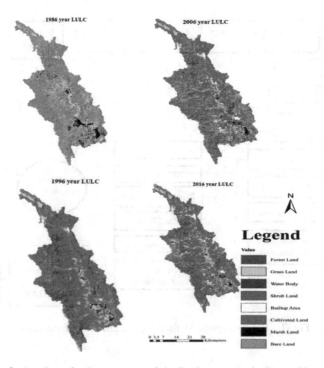

Fig. 8. Land use land cover map of the Borkena watershed over 30 years

These results remarked, there was a Bare Land and Built-up area expansion during the periods 1996–2006, with a rapid increase of Bare Land by 5.05% and rapid increase of Built-up area by 1.17% on one hand and a decrease of grass land, cultivated land, water body and shrub Land by 1.74%, 2.0%, 0.02%, and 1.76%, respectively. These reveals that the changes in one or more land use/ cover resulted in a change on the other land cover types.

The land use and land cover change detection were done by ENVI and GIS. Figure 9 shown that the increasing and decreasing of land use land cover type from one year to another year. Generally, there was an increment of bare land, built up, and decrement of forest land, grass land, shrub land, and cultivated land.

It can be observed that there was an increase in built-up area and bare lands in both periods. On the other hand, forest lands were decreased. This change is due to the demand for urban expansion. According to Kebrom Tekle and Lars Hedlund [7], urban expansion has a great impact on the hydrology of the area.

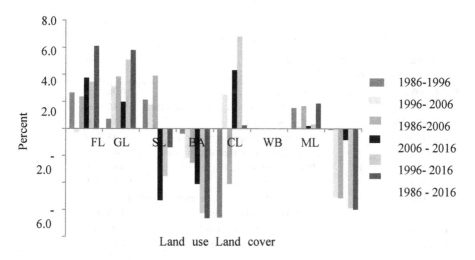

Fig. 9. The land use/cover change in percentage area of Borkena catchment

3.2 Streamflow Modeling

Sensitivity Analysis of Simulated Streamflow. For the SWAT model calibration of this study, out of 24 potential parameters, only 11 flow parameters have a significant effect on the streamflow of the watershed (Tables 4 and 5).

Table 4. List of parameters with fitted values after calibration using SUFI-2 for average monthly stream- flow

Parameter name	Description	Range		Fitted_Value
		Min_ value	Max_ value	
R CH_COV1.rte	Channel cover factor	−0.109	0.299	0.123
R SOL_AWC (..).sol	Available water capacity of the soil layer	−0.224	−0.20	−0.212
A GW_DELAY.gw	Groundwater delay (days)	6.791	8.908	8.886
A EPCO.hru	Plant uptake compensation factor	1.957	5.342	1.936
V ESCO.hru	Soil evaporation compensation factor	0.171	0.224	0.184
V RCHRG_DP.gw	Deep aquifer percolation fraction	0.449	1.338	0.881
V TLAPS.sub	Temperature lapse rate	29.209	30.312	29.551
V CH_N2.rte	Manning's "n" value for the main channel	1.281	1.858	1.299
V CH_EROD(..).rte	Channel erodibility factor	−1.278	−0.421	−1.012
V BIOMIX.mgt	Biological mixing efficient	0.565	0.578	0.576
R CN2.mgt	SCS runoff curve number	0	100	18.786

Table 5. Sensitive parameter

Parameter name	Sensitivity Rank	Description	-Stat	P-value
R CH_COV1.rte	1	Channel cover factor	−0.08	0.93
R SOL_AWC(..).sol	2	Available water capacity of the soil layer	−0.15	0.88
A GW_DELAY.gw	3	Groundwater delay	0.22	0.83
A EPCO.hru	4	Plant uptake compensation factor	−0.45	0.65
V ESCO.hru	5	Soil evaporation compensation factor	0.66	0.51
V RCHRG_DP.gw	6	Deep aquifer percolation fraction	−0.92	0.36
V TLAPS.sub	7	Temperature lapse rate	0.94	0.35
V CH_N2.rte	8	Manning's "n" value for the main channel	1.22	0.23
V CH_EROD(..).rte	9	Channel erodibility factor	−1.99	0.05
V BIOMIX.mgt	10	Biological mixing efficient	−2.08	0.04
R CN2.mgt	11	SCS runoff curve number	−15.8	0.01

Stream Flow Calibration and Validation Analysis. Calibration was done for the most sensitive parameters of the SWAT model inputs using observed streamflow. The Calibration result showed that the coefficient of determination (R^2) and the Nash Sutcliffe Efficiency (NSE) are 0.81 and 0.79, respectively. Additionally, the validation result showed that the coefficient of determinations (R^2) and the Nash Sutcliffe Efficiency (NSE) are 0.75 and 0.74, respectively. In general, the model performance indicated a good agreement between the simulated and measured flows in the monthly time step (Fig. 10).

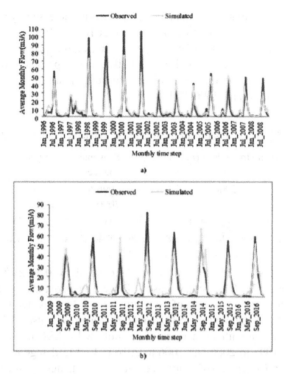

Fig. 10. Average monthly observed and simulated flow a) Calibration (1996–2008) and b) Validation (2009–2016) period

3.3   Evaluation of Streamflow Due to Land Use Land Covers Change

In this study the impact of LULC change on streamflow in the Borkena watershed was assessed. Seasonal variability of streamflow was also evaluated on wet (July, August, and September) and dry (January, February, and March) months.

Table 6. Streamflow simulations on Mean annual streamflow and change for 1996, 2006, and 2016 LULC

Mean annual streamflow (m³/s)				Mean annual flow change due to LULC change of					
Period	LULC map			1996 to 2006		2006 to 2016		1996 to 2016	
	1996	2006	2016	m³/s	%	m³/s	%	m³/s	%
1996–2016	11.53	12.6	13.3	1.07	9.3	0.70	5.56	1.77	15.35

The result indicates that mean annual streamflow was increased by 9.3%, 5.6%, and 15.4% in the LULC change 1996 to 2006, 2006 to 2016, and 1996 to 2016 respectively (Table 6). As a result, a high runoff was generated during this period; this increases the streamflow of 2006 as compared to 1996 and 2016 as compared to 2006 in the study periods. This stream changes due to an increase of built-up area and bare lands for both periods i.e. 1996–2006, and 2006–2016.

Table 7. Wet and dry seasons streamflow simulation and variabilities.

Period	Seasonal streamflow (m3/s)						Seasonal streamflow changes LULC change					
	1996		2006		2016		1996 to 2006		2006 to 2016		1996 to 2016	
	Dry	Wet	Dry	Wet	Dry	Wet	Dry	Wet	Dry	Wet	Dry	Wet
1996–2016	2.34	31.52	1.94	0.36	1.8	36.96	−0.40	3.84	−0.14	1.6	−0.54	5.44

The amount of seasonal streamflow was decreased by 0.54 m³/s due to LULC change from 1996 to 2016 in the dry season. There was also a change in stream flows in the wet season with an increase of streamflow by 5.44 m³/s due to LULC change from 1996 to 2016 in the study period (Table 7). There was also a change in stream flows in the wet season with an increase of streamflow by 3.84 m³/s and 1.6 m³/s due to LULC change 1996 to 2006 and 2006 to 2016 in LULC change respectively. There was a significant effect ($p < 0.05$) land use land cover change on stream flow.

4   Conclusion

From this study, it can be concluded that the Borkena watershed has practiced a substantial change in land use and land cover over the past 31 years. It can be recognized that deforestation and increase of built-up area and bare lands were exhibited by a rapid increase of the human population which changes the whole Borkena watershed in general and sub watersheds. The scope of this study would be limited to evaluate the impact of land use/land cover change effect on streamflow in the Borkena watershed. The study was not considered the impact of climate change and soil erosion on the water and land resources of the watershed.

The dynamics in land use land cover have caused in changes in streamflow. The increase of urban area and bare lands increases surface runoff. This change (increase or decrease) in streamflow was due to LULC change over some time. Therefore, this study results can be used to encourage different users and policymakers for planning and management of water resources and the adoption of suitable adaptation measures in the Borkena watershed and other similar regions of Ethiopia.

Acknowledgments. The authors of this paper are thankful to the Ministry of Water and Energy, National Meteorological Agency, and Ministry of Agriculture of Ethiopia for providing necessary data. The authors acknowledge the anonymous reviewers, whose comments were valuable to improve the paper.

Author Contributions. MAA. Comprehended developed the research framework, MAA and TDM did the data processing and analysis. MAA and SEA wrote and revised the manuscript. TE supervision and revised the manuscript. All authors have read and agreed to the published version of the manuscript.

Conflicts of Interest. The author declares no conflict of interest.

References

1. Nigusie, A., Dananto, M.: Impact of land use/land cover change on hydrologic processes in Dijo watershed, central rift valley, Ethiopia. Int. J. Water Resour. Environ. Eng. **13**(1), 37–48 (2021)
2. Samuel Kassa Beyene, M.P., Kemal, A., Murlidhar, S.: Impact of land use/land cover change on watershed hydrology: a case study of upper awash basin. EJWST **1**, March 2018 (2019)
3. Shiferaw, A.: Evaluating the land use and land cover dynamics in Borena Woreda South Wollo Highlands, Ethiopia. Ethiop. J. Bus. Econ. **2**(1), 87–107 (2011)
4. Dibaba, W.T., Demissie, T.A., Miegel, K.: Watershed hydrological response to combined land use/land cover and climate change in Highland. Water **12**, 1801 (2020)
5. Muhlestein, K.N.: Land use land cover change analysis of Maverick county Texas along the US Mexico Border (2008)
6. Neitsch, S., Arnold, J., Kiniry, J., Williams, J.: Soil & water assessment tool theoretical documentation version 2009. Texas Water Resour. Inst. 1–647 (2011)
7. K. T. and L. Hedlund, "Land cover changes between 1958 and 1986 in Kalu District, Southern Wello, Ethiopia," Int. Mt. Soc., vol. 20, no. 1, pp. 42–51, 2000
8. D. Phiri and J. Morgenroth, "Developments in Landsat land cover classification methods: A review," Remote Sens., vol. 9, no. 9, 2017
9. MoWRIE: Ministry of water resource, irrigation, and energy. Annual report (1987)
10. Melese, S.M.: Effect of land use land cover changes on the forest resources of Ethiopia Solomon. Int. J. Nat. Resour. Ecol. Manage. **1**(2), 102 (2016)
11. Guzha, A.C., Rufino, M.C., Okoth, S., Jacobs, S., Nóbrega, R.L.B.: Impacts of land use and land cover change on surface runoff, discharge and low flows: evidence from East Africa. J. Hydrol. Reg. Stud. **15**, 49–67 (2018). https://doi.org/10.1016/j.ejrh.2017.11.005
12. Shehata, A., Metwally, A.: Landuse Landcover Changes in Delta Province of Egypt: 1984–2000–2016. ATTRA Publication no. P280. NCAT (2018)
13. El-Sayed, M.E.M., Zumwalt, K.W.: Comparison of two different approaches for making design sensitivity analysis an integrated part of finite element analysis. Struct. Optim. **3**(3), 149–156 (1991)

Application of *in Situ* Thermal Imaging to Estimate Crop Water Stress and Crop Water Requirements for Wheat in Koga Irrigation Scheme, Ethiopia

Tewodrose D. Meselaw[1]([✉]), Fasikaw A. Zimale[2], Seifu A. Tilahun[2], and Petra Schmitter[3]

[1] Kombolcha Institute of Technology, Wollo University, Kombolcha, Ethiopia
[2] Faculty of Civil and Water Resources Engineering, Bahir Dar Institute of Technology, Bahir Dar University, Bahir Dar, Ethiopia
[3] International Water Management Institute (IWMI), Colombo, Sri Lanka

Abstract. Enhancing performance of irrigation schemes requires an improvement in the timing and amount of irrigation application from head to tail of irrigation infrastructures. This can be achieved using non-invasive techniques using thermal imaging to assess soil moisture regimes and plant water status. An infrared thermometry with hand held thermal camera attached to a tablet was used to measure the temperature of wheat canopy under three irrigation treatments in Koga irrigation scheme: wetting front detector (WFD), chameleon and control reflecting farmers' practices. The experiment followed a randomized complete block design (RCBD) in two irrigation blocks (Adibera and Chihona) with three treatments and three replications. The temperature of the canopy was measured before and after irrigation. The calculated Crop Water Stress Index (CWSI) using canopy temperature was significantly different in the WFD treatment during the development stage given the larger irrigation intervals observed ($p > 0.05$). Overall, both irrigation technologies show potential in improving water management close to the overall estimated gross irrigation requirement with some further improvement in the mid development stage. The study showed the potential of using thermal imaging to not only identify CWSI and assess the effect of agronomic field trials using in-situ thermal camera's but also the potential of using canopy temperatures in estimating actual ET and therefore gross irrigation requirements. This would provide a new opportunity for agricultural extension agents to advice smallholder farmers in irrigation schemes and beyond on when and how much to apply without the need for WFD or chameleon sensors. Further research is needed to calibrate and validate the irrigation predictions based on different soil and crop types.

Keywords: Crop water stress index · Gross irrigation water requirements · Irrigation water productivity · Thermography

© ICST Institute for Computer Sciences, Social Informatics and Telecommunications Engineering 2022
Published by Springer Nature Switzerland AG 2022. All Rights Reserved
M. L. Berihun (Ed.): ICAST 2021, LNICST 412, pp. 144–159, 2022.
https://doi.org/10.1007/978-3-030-93712-6_10

1 Introduction

In Ethiopian, the majority of agricultural land is under low input- low output rainfed agriculture and highly susceptible to rainfall variability both in magnitude as well as occurrence [1]. Ethiopia has great irrigation potential, which is estimated as 5.3 million hectares of land of which 3.7 million hectares can be developed using surface water sources and 1.6 million hectares using groundwater and rainwater management [2].

While the human population and demands for freshwater resources are increasing, drought and regular water scarcity can put global food security at risk by severely disrupting agricultural production. The challenge is to meet rising productivity demands by improving methods of crop management which requires a deeper understanding of plant response to abiotic stresses [3]. Water stress detection based on canopy temperature measurements is probably the most widely used plant-based approach for remote sensing that applies to irrigation scheduling of several crops. As plants absorb solar radiation, canopy temperature increases, but is cooled when that energy is used for evapotranspiration [4].

Canopy temperature measured with infrared thermometers or other remote infrared sensors is an important tool for detecting crop water stress [5]. The crop water stress index (CWSI) is the most often used index which is based on canopy temperature to detect crop water stress [6]. Detection of crop water stress and ET enhances decision making on irrigation timing and application amounts, which might increase crop water productivity, cut back percolation and nutrient losses below the root zone, and cut back irrigation associated labor.

In Northern Ethiopia highland, Bahir Dar Institute of Technology with International water management institute (IWMI) has worked with farmers to enhance water productivity by using water management tools such as the wetting front detector (WFD) and the chameleon sensor (https://via.farm/). Those instruments provide information on the soil moisture status, enhancing irrigation decision making [7]. Scholars have shown the positive effect of using WFDor chameleon sensors on crop yields and a reduction on irrigation water applied and nutrients leached [8]. However, little is known whether the plants are stressed at any given plant development stage and despite the positive effects on crop yields being recorded.

The crop water stress index (CWSI) has been used to characterize plant water stress and schedule irrigation. Romero et al. [9] showed that CWSI can successfully detect crop water stress of African eggplant under full and deficit irrigation treatment in the early development, vegetative and maturity stage. The study measured CWSI using individual eggplant leaves. However, wheat leaves are small and hence accurate CWSI might be challenging using mobile phone based thermal imaging. Therefore, this research evaluated the application of in situ thermal imaging of wheat canopy to detection of crop water stress and estimate actual ET requirement to further enhance irrigation performance and crop water productivity.

The main objective of this study was therefore to assess whether in situ thermal imaging can be used to estimate gross irrigation water requirements for wheat under different crop water stress levels. Firstly the study looked at whether crop water stress differed among different irrigation treatments of wheat. Secondly, the study assessed whether there was a relationship between CWSI, soil moisture and stomata conductance and developed an equation to estimate gross irrigation requirements.

2 Methodology

2.1 Description of the Study Area

The data in this study were collected in Koga Irrigation scheme which is situated adjacent to the town of Merawi in the Mecha Woreda, West Gojam Zone in Amhara Regional State, Ethiopia (Fig. 1). In the Koga irrigation scheme, there are 11-night storages, which are used to irrigate 12 blocks. The catchment is situated between 11°10′ to 11°32′N and 37°04′ to 37°17′E. The catchment area contributing to the dam is 170.9 km^2 and extends to an altitude of 3,200 m.a.s.l. From 12 blocks the FAO water productivity projects introduced on-farm water management technologies in six blocks: Kudmi, Teleta, Tagel, Andinet, Adibera, and Chihona blocks. For this study fields using WFD and Chameleon sensors as well as control plots (i.e. farmers' practice) in Chihona and Adibera were selected. The storage capacity of the reservoir is 83.1 Mm^3 with an altitude of 1998 masl. The command area has a total population of 57,155.

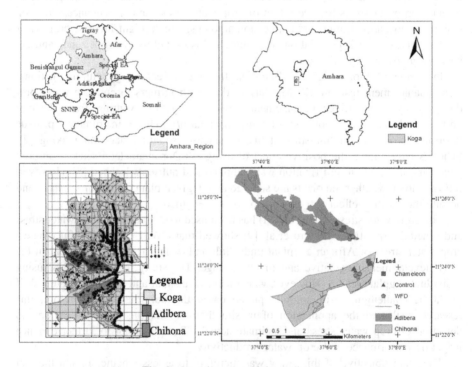

Fig. 1. Location map of the study area

The annual precipitation ranges from 800 to 2200 mm, with a mean of 1,420 mm [10] and an average day time temperature of 24 °C. The soil for all experimental plots are classified as clay loam with an average field capacity of 34.4% and permanent wilting point of 23.69%. The major crops irrigated are wheat, onion, potatoes, and tomatoes. As > 70% of the area irrigated is cultivated for wheat, wheat farmers were chosen.

2.2   Description of Irrigation Scheduling Tools

Bahir Dar Institute of Technology with International Water Management Institute introduced two low cost tools, the Chameleon soil moisture sensor and the Full Stop wetting front detector (https://via.farm/via_tools/) in Koga irrigation scheme. The chameleon reader measure soil water status at any given time and is connected to three gypsum blocks, each installed at different depths. Each depth is represented by a light, and each light can be blue (wet soil), green (moist soil) or red (dry soil). The lights give a picture of soil water conditions from the top to the bottom of the root zone. The wetting front detector records the depth of infiltration of the irrigation water and pops up an indicator when irrigation water has reached the WFD at the installed depth. These tools form the basis of an experimental learning system for small-scale irrigators. The study found that farmers quickly learned from the tools and changed their management within a short time. The cost of implementing a learning system would be a small fraction of that of building or revitalizing irrigation schemes.

2.3   Experimental Design and Treatment Setting

In Koga, two irrigation blocks, Adibera, and Chihona, were selected as the experimental site and the experimental design was a Randomized Complete Block Design (RCBD) with three replications for each irrigation treatment. In each block, nine farmers participated in the study: 3 farmers were using WFDs (WFD treatment), 3 were using chameleon sensors (chameleon treatment) and 3 were applying their own irrigation practice (control treatment). The proposed plot was selected based on the following criteria: a) all experiment plots have the same type of soil, b) all farmers use the same type and rate of fertilizer and c) all farmers follow the treatment recommendation. An overview of the experimental layout per block is given in Fig. 2. In each farmer field, 4 sub-plots (0.5 m * 0.5 m) were marked within one field (i.e. P1, P2, P3 and P4 in Fig. 2).

Farmers in the experimental field plowed each plot with traditional Marsha plow pulled by oxen for proper seed germination. Wheat (Kekeba genotype) was planted in December 2018 and irrigated using furrows with an average length of 30 m and a width of 25 cm. The furrow length for one farm was the same for all farmers to ensure that irrigation timing and quantity is as uniform as possible among farmers within one treatment group. A pair of wetting front detectors (shallow and deep WFD) was installed in the second or third and subsequent furrows from the border of the field. The WFD was installed at 75% of the furrow inlet where the shallow detector (yellow flag) was placed at 20 cm depth and the deep detector (red flag) at 40 cm depth details can be found in Stirzaker [11]. Chameleon was installed at 75% of the furrow inlet

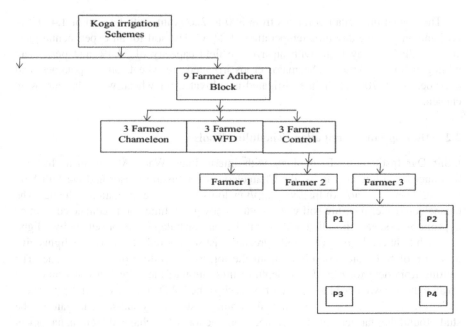

Fig. 2. General layout of the experimental plot for two blocks in Koga irrigation scheme

where the shallow detector was placed at 20 cm depth, amid detector was placed at 40 cm and the deep detector was placed at 60 cm.

2.4   Data Collection

Climatic Data. Daily meteorological data containing maximum and minimum temperature (°C), wind speed (m/s), solar radiation (MJ/ m²/day), relative humidity (%) and the daily rainfall (mm/day) were collected from Ethiopia Meteorological Agency, Bahir Dar branch.

Thermal Image. In this study, a ground-based, handheld FLIR camera (model E30, FLIR Systems, Inc., Wilsonville, Oregon, USA) was used to take canopy thermal images. The thermal image was taken at four experimental sub-plots which have (0.50 m × 0.50 m) size within one farmer's field (see Fig. 2). Two sub-plots were located ¾ of the furrow length from the inlet or ¼ of the length from the outlet and two plots were located at the top corner of the field in order to check the water distribution efficiency of the field. The vertical distance between wheat and the camera remained approximately equal for all measurements and the image was taken before and after irrigation. According to other studies, midday canopy temperature is the best indicator to detect crop water stress [4, 8, 13]. Therefore, measurements were taken between 12:00 am to 13:30 am during clear sky conditions throughout the season. At each measurement, three images were taken: (i) canopy temperature (T_{canopy}), (ii) some leaves were used as T_{wet} reference (i.e. no water stress) by spraying water on both sides

[14] and (iii) 1 or 2 leaves were used as T_{dry} reference by covering both sides with petroleum jelly (vaseline) to prevent transpiration (i.e. extreme water stress).

Soil Moisture Measurements. Soil moisture readings using a calibrated Time Domain Reflector meter (TDR) were taken within the sub-plots at 10 cm depth in each field before and after irrigation based on the irrigation interval. Measurements were taken in each treatment and used to explore a relationship between soil moisture status and CWSI.

Irrigation Depth Applied and Wheat Performance. The amount of irrigation water applied by the farmer was determined by measuring the flow rate using a 90° v-notch weir (triangular weir) at the field inlet and multiplying this by the irrigation duration for each field. The following equation was used to determine the discharge through a 90° v-noch weir:

$$Q = 1.38H^{5/2} \tag{1}$$

where Q = discharge (m^3/sec) and H = head (m) flowing over the vertex of the v-notch. Wheat yield was measured for all farmers by weighing the amount of the wheat bags and counting the number of wheat bags harvested per field. The collected yield converted to kg ha^{-1} using the harvested area.

2.5   Data Analysis

Thermal Image Processing and Canopy Temperature Calculation. ThermalCAM Researcher Pro 2.8 SR-1 (FLIR Systems, Inc., Boston, MA) software was used to convert the thermal JPEG format images to FLIR Public file (.fpf) format. The software calculates the average canopy temperature taking into account numerous canopy pixel points from the plant material in the image. As wheat has small leaf it needs, background pixels needed to be ignored. Hence, the spot meters' tool was used to only measures visible (RGB) or NIR from selected pixels to determine temperature of the leaves. The reference canopy temperature (T_{canopy}) was calculated by averaging the sample leaf temperature. Then finally the canopy temperature of the farm was taken by averaging the plot temperature from the 4 sub-plots in each field. The dry leaf temperatures (T_{dry}) were taken from the spot measurements for the leaves under Vaseline treatment. The wet leaf temperature (T_{wet}) was taken from the spot measurements for the leaves which were sprayed with water.

Crop Water Stress Index (CWSI). Crop water stress index measures the plant water status. The value of CWSI varies between 0 and 1, where 1 represents full stress (i.e. actual evapotranspiration is zero), and 0 represents the absence of stress (i.e. potential evapotranspiration) as plants transpire at a maximum rate. CWSI was calculated for each sub-plot according to Jones developed by Idso [13] as follows:

$$CWSI = \left(T_{canopy} - T_{wet}\right)/\left(T_{dry} - T_{wet}\right) \tag{2}$$

where, T_{canopy} is the mean canopy temperature of the plot (the average of 10 spot measurements from the thermal image), T_{wet} and T_{dry} are the temperatures of the leaves when stomata are opened and stomata are closed, respectively.

According to Jones developed by Idso [13], stomatal conductance (gl) can be calculated as follows:

$$gl = \left(T_{dry} - T_{canopy}\right)/\left(T_{canopy} - T_{wet}\right) \tag{3}$$

Estimating Actual Crop Evapotranspiration. The actual canopy evapotranspiration can be directly calculated using the energy balance model from the measured canopy temperature. In this approach, canopy temperature measurements provide the real-time feedback aspect. The ET_c at a given time can be estimated using the following equation developed by Jackson [4]:

$$ET_c = ET_0(1 - CWSI)k_c \tag{4}$$

where CWSI is the crop water stress index, kc is the crop coefficient and ET0 the potential evapotranspiration. CWSI was calculated for each irrigation event by considering the stress index before and after irrigation and the crop coefficient value was taken from FAO following the respective growth stages.

The ET_c per irrigation event was estimated as the average of the ET_c after and before irrigation. The average ET_c was multiplied with the number of days between these two irrigation events and summed to obtain the total ET_c throughout the season.

Net and Gross Irrigation Requirements Under Different Irrigation Treatments:
The net irrigation requirement (I_{net}) was calculated by subtracting the effective rainfall (P_e) from the estimated ET_c:

$$I_{net} = ET_c - P_e \tag{5}$$

Gross irrigation requirement (I_{gross}) are equal to net irrigation requirement divided by application efficiency (E_a).

$$I_{gross} = I_{net}/E_a \tag{6}$$

An application efficiency of 0.65 was used for furrow [15].

2.6   Statistical Analysis

The collected data were analyzed using R software. For each block, the significance of a treatment was assessed using a two-way analysis of variance (ANOVA) at a 5% significance level. Before analysis, the quality of the data was checked by the Q-Q normality test and by frequency distribution graph.

3   Results and Discussion

3.1   Irrigation Depth Applied Under Different Irrigation Treatments

The average seasonal total irrigation depth for each treatment is presented in Fig. 3. As expected, farmers applied the most water in the control treatment (675 mm from Adibera block and 689 mm from Chihona block) followed by the chameleon and the WFD. The depth of irrigation applied per season in the chameleon and WFD treatments were significantly lower ($p < 0.05$) and on average 71% and 58% of those applied in the control treatment, respectively.

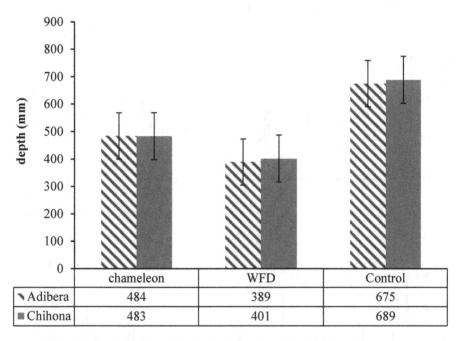

	chameleon	WFD	Control
＼ Adibera	484	389	675
■ Chihona	483	401	689

Fig. 3.   Seasonal total irrigation depth for each irrigation treatment

3.2   Variation in CWSI Between Irrigation Treatments

Before irrigation, the maximum CWSI were observed in the WFD treatment (0.45 to 0.6), followed by the chameleon treatment (0.40 to 0.56) and the control (0.42 to 0.52) (Fig. 4). Comparison of the CWSI values before irrigation showed a significant difference between the WFD and other two treatments (i.e. control and chameleon) during the development stage, indicating that the larger irrigation interval for WFD has resulted in a significantly higher CWSI ($p < 0.05$). There were no significant differences observed in CWSI between the different phenological changes for the same treatment or between treatments for the other crop growth stages.

Across the two irrigation blocks, the CWSI after irrigation varied between 0.10 and 0.22, 0.11 and 0.23, 0.11 and 0.22 for chameleon sensor, WFD, and control treatment respectively. According to the Attahi [16] adopted threshold, little or no water stress regimes were found in the 3 treatments (p > 0.05) (Fig. 4). This means that for all irrigation treatments the crop water demand was satisfied.

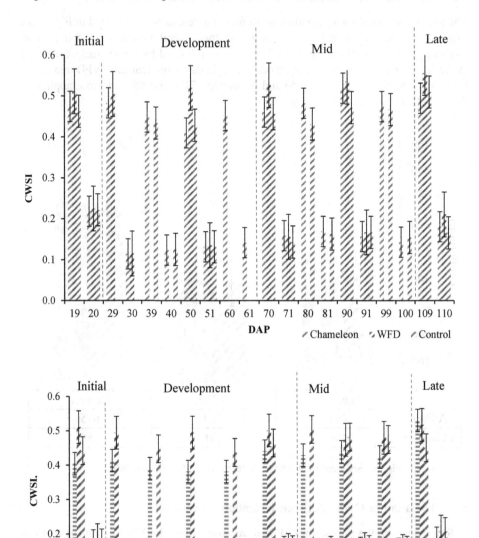

Fig. 4. The variation of the average CWSI both after and before irrigation conditions at different stage in Adibera (top) and Chihona block (bottom).

3.3   Relationship Between CWSI, Soil Water Status and Stomatal Conductance

A linear relationship was found between CWSI and the soil water content measured at 10 cm depth for all treatments (Fig. 5). A unit decrease in soil moisture resulted in a larger increase in CWSI in the control group (−0.53) compared to the WFD (−0.41) and chameleon (−0.41).

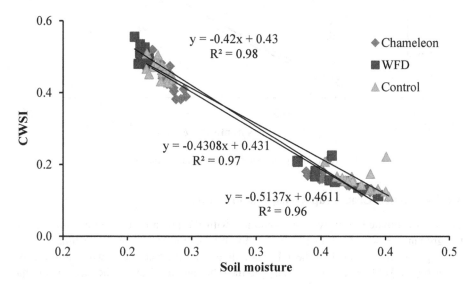

Fig. 5. The relationship of CWSI and soil moisture in all treatment

The relationship between CWSI and stomatal conductance is well established. The study investigated the relationship between the soil moisture and the estimated stomatal conductance. A linear relationship confirmed that the higher soil moisture values corresponded to a higher stomatal conductance and therefore a lower CWSI. of stomata conductance with soil water content in all treatment. A unit decline in soil moisture resulted in a stronger decline in the stomatal conductance of wheat in the WFD fields (Fig. 6). in chameleon treatment for average soil moisture at 10cm depth with stomata conductance.

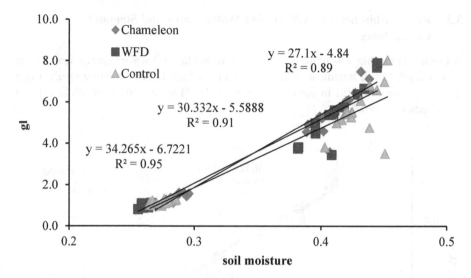

Fig. 6. The relationship of stomatal conductance and soil moisture

3.4   Estimated Crop Evapotranspiration (ET$_c$)

The total estimated crop evapotranspiration with the potential evapotranspiration for the growing season are shown in Fig. 7. In all irrigation treatments the estimated ET$_c$ was significantly lower than the ET$_0$. In Adibera the estimated ET$_c$ was significantly lower for the WFD treatment compared to the other two treatments whereas in Chihona no difference.

3.5   Irrigation Water Productivity

The average yield for the WFD treatment was 2.7 t/ha, 2.4 t/ha for the chameleon and 2.2 t/ha for the control. This resulted in a 20.7% (WFD) and 11.2% (chameleon) yield increase compared to the control. A positive reduction in irrigation depth and increase in yield resulted in an increase in irrigation water productivity. Average irrigation productivity for WFD treatment was 0.72 kg/m^3 and 0.64 kg/m^3 in Adibera and Chihona block respectively and significantly higher than those obtained in the control field (0.34 kg/m^3 and 0.32 kg/m^3). The difference was significant at a 5% significance level at both blocks between the technology user (both chameleon and WFD) and control farmer. However, there was no significant difference between WFD and Chameleon treatment in both blocks (Table 1).

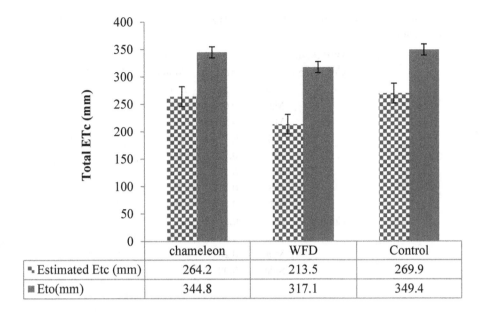

	chameleon	WFD	Control
▪ Estimated Etc (mm)	264.2	213.5	269.9
▪ Eto(mm)	344.8	317.1	349.4

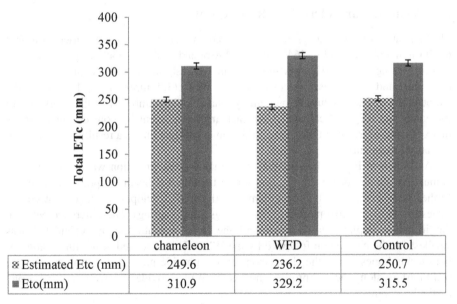

	chameleon	WFD	Control
▨ Estimated Etc (mm)	249.6	236.2	250.7
▪ Eto(mm)	310.9	329.2	315.5

Fig. 7. The total estimated crop evapotranspiration (ETc) and potential evapotranspiration (ETo) of each irrigation treatment in Adibera (top) and Chihona block (bottom)

Table 1. Irrigation water productivity (kg/m^3) measured in both blocks across the three irrigation treatments.

IWP (kg/m^3)			
Chameleon		**Adibera**	**Chihona**
	Average	0.53[a]	0.44[a]
	Max.	0.66	0.49
	Min.	0.37	0.36
	Stdev	0.15	0.07
WFD	Aveage	0.72[a]	0.64[a]
	Max.	0.75	0.69
	Min.	0.71	0.57
	Stdev	0.02	0.06
Control	Aveage	0.34[b]	0.32[b]
	Max.	0.41	0.35
	Min.	0.28	0.29
	Stdev	0.08	0.03

3.6   Estimated Gross Irrigation Requirement

The estimated total average gross irrigation requirement in the system varied from 308 to 395 mm and from 344 to 364 mm for Adibera and Chihona block, respectively. The highest average gross irrigation requirement was estimated in the control treatment (395 mm) and the lowest was estimated in WFD (308 mm) irrigated fields in the Adibera block. This is could be potentially related to the number of irrigation events. In this study the ET$_c$ was calculated for each irrigation event by considering its stress index so control treatment had more irrigation event than others a result of the different irrigation treatments.

As shown in Fig. 8, the cumulative estimated gross irrigation was lower than the cumulative applied depth of irrigation for all treatment indicating a potential room for further improvement. All three treatments, the mid development stage showed the largest room for improvement (i.e. 50–70 days after planting). The difference between the irrigation application recorded and the gross irrigation depth calculated was smallest for the chameleon followed by the WFD. This is related to the functioning of both technologies where the chameleon sensors provide more gradual information on soil moisture along the soil profile whereas the WFD provides the wetting front at one particular depth.

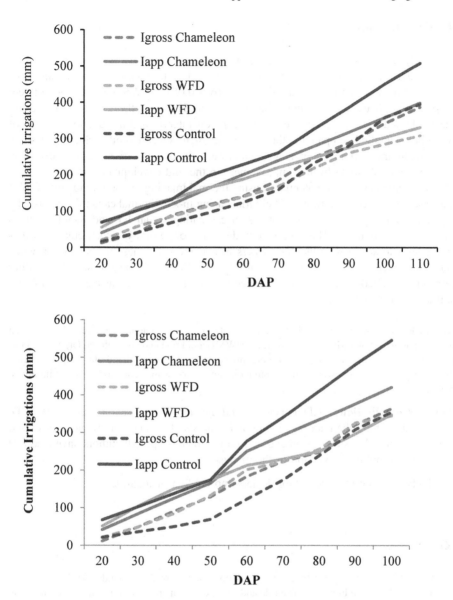

Fig. 8. Cumulative depth of irrigation application (Iapp) and Cumulative estimated gross irrigation application (I_{gross}) in Adibera (top) and Chihona block (bottom)

4 Conclusions

The study showed that the use of wetting front detector (WFD) and chameleon sensors could reduce irrigation amounts without significantly introducing crop water stress. At farm level there was no significant difference ($p > 0.05$) in CWSI between the different crop phenological stages within the same treatment. However, the CWSI was highest in the WFD and was related to the larger irrigation interval and a reduction in 42% of water being applied compared to the control treatment. Overall, both technologies show potential in improving water management close to the overall estimated gross irrigation requirement with some further improvement in the mid development stage.

The study showed the potential of using thermal imaging to not only identify CWSI and assess the effect of agronomic field trials using in-situ thermal camera's but also the potential of using canopy temperatures in estimating actual ET and therefore gross irrigation requirements. This would provide a new opportunity for agricultural extension agents to advice smallholder farmers in irrigation schemes and beyond on when and how much to apply without the need for WFD or chameleon sensors. Further research is needed to calibrate and validate the irrigation predictions based on different soil and crop types.

Acknowledgments. The research was implemented under a collaborative partnership between the International Water Management Institute (IWMI) and Food and Agricultural Organization so the authors would like to thank to those organizations for the financial and other support during this work. We also acknowledge the anonymous reviewers, whose comments greatly improved the paper.

Author Contributions: T.D. conceived and developed the research framework. T.D. and F.A undertook the data processing and analysis. T.D. and S.T. wrote and revised the manuscript. P.S. supervision and revised the manuscript. All authors have read and agreed to the published version of the manuscript.

Conflicts of Interest: The author declares no conflict of interest.

References

1. Haile, G.G., Kassa, A.K.: Irrigation in Ethiopia : a review. J. Dry lands (2015)
2. Tesgera, W.D., Guluma, W.: The role and significance of small scale irrigation in improving household income in Ethiopia. Int. J. Res. Bus. Stud. Manage. **7**(3), 20–35 (2020)
3. Padhi, J., Misra, R.K., Payero, J.O.: Estimation of soil water deficit in an irrigated cotton field with infrared thermography. F. Crop. Res. **126**, 45–55 (2012)
4. Jackson, R.D., Reginato, R.J., Idso, S.B.: Wheat canopy temperature: a practical tool for evaluating water requirements. Water Resour. Res. **13**(3), 651–656 (1977)
5. Möller, M., et al.: Use of thermal and visible imagery for estimating crop water status of irrigated grapevine. J. Exp. Bot. **58**(4), 827–838 (2006)
6. Jones, H.G., Serraj, R., Loveys, B.R., Xiong, L., Wheaton, A., Price, A.H.: Thermal infrared imaging of crop canopies for the remote diagnosis and quantification of plant responses to water stress in the field. Funct. Plant Biol. **36**(11), 978–989 (2009)

7. Stirzaker, R., Mbakwe, I., Mziray, N.R.: A soil water and solute learning system for small-scale irrigators in Africa. Int. J. Water Resour. Dev. **33**(5), 788–803 (2017)
8. Mdemu, M., et al.: The role of soil water monitoring tools and agricultural innovation platforms in improving food security and income of farmers in smallholder irrigation schemes in Tanzania. Int. J. Water Resour. Dev. **36**(1), 1–23 (2020)
9. Romero-Trigueros, C., Bayona Gambín, J.M., Nortes Tortosa, P.A., Alarcón Cabañero, J.J., Nicolás, E.N.: Determination of crop water stress index by infrared thermometry in grapefruit trees irrigated with saline reclaimed water combined with deficit irrigation. Remote Sens. **11**(7), 1–23 (2019)
10. Ministry of Water Resources and the National Meteorological Services Agency: Initial national communication of Ethiopia to the united nations framework convention on climate change, pp. 1–113, June 2001
11. Stirzaker, R., Car, N., Christen, E.: A traffic light soil water sensor for resource poor farmers: proof of concept. Final Project report. Australian Centre for International Agricultural Research (ACIAR), Canberra. http//aciar.gov.au/files/aciar_traffic_light_final_report_sept_14_2_2. pdf (2014). Accessed 9 May 2017
12. Anteneh: Application of thermal imaging for the assessment of irrigation water stress in tomato plant. MSc thesis (2018)
13. Jackson, R.D., Idso, S.B., Reginato, R.J., Pinter, P.J.: Canopy temperature as a crop water stress indicator. Water Resour. Res. 17, 1133–1138 (1981)
14. Zia, S., Wenyong, D., Spreer, W., Spohrer, K., Xiongkui, H., Müller, J.: Assessing crop water stress of winter wheat by thermography under different irrigation regimes in North China plain. J. Exp. Bot. **5**(3), 24–34 2014
15. Holzapfel, E.A., Leiva, C., Mariño, M.A., Paredes, J., Arumí, J.L., Billib, M.: Furrow irrigation management and design criteria using efficiency parameters and simulation models. Chil. J. Agric. Res. **70**, 287–296 (2010)
16. Attahi, F., Abazadeh, K.B., Ajafi, N., Edghi, P.S.: Scheduling maize irrigation based on crop water stress index (CWSI). Appl. Ecol. Environ. Res. **16**(6), 7535–7549 (2018)

Effect of Glass Fiber on Fracture Energy of Plain Concrete

Samuel Demeke Shiferaw[1($\boxtimes$)], Temesgen Wondimu Aure[2], and Alemayehu Golla Gualu[1]

[1] Bahir Dar University-Bahir Dar Institute of Technology, Bahir Dar, Ethiopia
[2] Addis Ababa Science and Technology University, Addis Ababa, Ethiopia
temesgen.wondimu@aastu.edu.et

Abstract. Concrete has a very low fracture energy and due to this, it cracks at very low load in brittle mode. The main objective of this study was to determine the effect of the addition of glass fiber on the fracture energy of plain concrete of grade C20/25 and C25/30. The percentage of glass fiber added ranges from 0% to 0.6% by volume with a constant increasing interval of 0.2%. The glass fiber are placed in three layers with equal amount placed at uniform interval. The test is performed according to RILEM TC 50 FMC recommendation following the Work of Fracture Method (WFM). It has been observed that addition of glass fiber increases the fracture energy of plain concrete very significantly and change the failure mode from brittle to ductile.

Keywords: Fracture energy · Glass fiber · Plain concrete

1 Introduction

Concrete is a composite material made up of fine and/or coarse aggregates, cementitious materials and water combined together to give artificial hardened material. Due to this nature of concrete, it usually fails in a brittle manner, which is undesirable characteristics in the use of concrete as a structural element. It cracks at a very small tensile load compared to its compressive capacity. During this early formation of crack, there will be a release of energy from the concrete. This release of energy from cracked surface is expressed in terms of the fracture energy of the material.

Fracture energy is defined as the amount of energy necessary to create a unit area of crack. The area of a crack is defined as the projected area on a plane parallel to the main crack direction. (RILEM TC 50- FMC Fracture Mechanics of Concrete 1985) It is found to increase around the crack tip, and is generally a function of displacement and not strain. It plays a significant role in determining the amount of ductility a structure exhibits.

Fiber is a natural or synthetic material that has significant length compared to its thickness. Glass fiber is a material consisting of numerous extremely fine fibers of glass, which has very high tensile strength (3000–5000 MPa) and compressive strength (1000–1600 MPa).

Fiber reinforced concrete is defined as concrete made with hydraulic cement, containing fine or fine and coarse aggregate and discontinuous discrete fibers. The

M. L. Berihun (Ed.): ICAST 2021, LNICST 412, pp. 160–174, 2022.
https://doi.org/10.1007/978-3-030-93712-6_11

fibers can be made from natural materials (e.g., asbestos, sisal, cellulose) or from manufactured products such as glass, steel, carbon, and polymer (e.g. polypropylenes, Kevlar). (ACI committee 544 2002).

The purpose of reinforcing the cement based matrix with fibers is to increase the tensile strength by delaying the growth of cracks, and to increase the toughness by transmitting stress across a cracked section so that much larger deformation is possible beyond the peak stress than without fiber reinforcement. Fiber reinforcement is observed to improve the impact and fatigue strength, and reduce shrinkage. (A.M. Nevile 2010).

The orientation of the fiber relative to the plane of a crack in concrete influence the reinforcing capacity of the fiber. The maximum benefit occurs when the fiber is uni-directional and parallel to the applied tensile stress, and the fibers are of less benefit when randomly oriented in three dimensions (A.M. Nevile 2010).

Fracture energy was significantly enhanced by using basalt fiber. As the basalt fiber content increased, the concrete showed higher ultimate loads, larger deflections before failure and higher fracture energy values. (Kabay 2013) A slight increase in fracture energy was observed for basalt and glass fiber reinforced concrete at the dosage of 0.25%. However, significant increase was observed beyond this dosage, fracture energy increased by more than 50% at 1.0% fiber inclusion for both basalt and glass fibers. (Ahmet B. Kizilkanat 2015) Basalt and glass fiber addition increase the fracture energy of ordinary concrete almost by 35%, this indicates the increase in ductility and energy dissipation capacity of ordinary concrete. (Arslan 2016).

The main objective of this study is to show the combined effect of plain concrete with glass fiber added in the tensile region in layers on the improvement of fracture energy of plain concrete grades with C20/25 and C25/30.

The most direct way of determining fracture energy is by means of a uniaxial tensile test, where the complete stress-deformation curve is measured. The test has to be stable, which means the deformation is increased slowly, without any sudden jumps.

Unfortunately, it is difficult to perform stable tensile tests. However, it is much easier to perform stable bending tests on notched specimens. The simplest test of this type is the three-point bend test on a notched beam. Therefore, this test has been chosen for the proposed RILEM recommendations.

The specimens shall be beams with a central notch according to Fig. 1. The depth of the beam as tested shall be horizontal during casting and the size of the beam shall depends on the maximum size of the aggregate, Dmax, according to Table 1. The notch shall always have a depth, which is equal to half of beam depth $\pm$ 5 mm, and the notch width at the tip should be less than 10 mm.

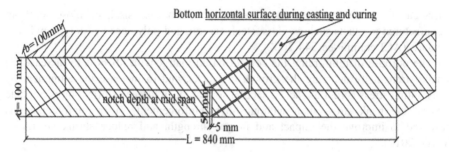

Fig. 1. The geometry of the beam to be used for the test. (RILEM TC 50- FMC Fracture Mechanics of Concrete 1985)

Table 1. Recommended sizes of test beams. (RILEM TC 50- FMC Fracture Mechanics of Concrete 1985)

D_{max} (mm)	Depth d (mm)	Width b (mm)	Length L (mm)	Span l (mm)
1–16	100 ± 5	100 ± 5	840 ± 10	800 ± 5
16.1–32	200 ± 5	100 ± 5	1,190 ± 10	1,130 ± 5
32.1–48	300 ± 5	150 ± 5	1,450 ± 10	1,385 ± 5
48.1–64	400 ± 5	200 ± 5	1,640 ± 10	1,600 ± 5

The supports and loading arrangements shall be such that the force acting on the beam are statically determinate, as shown in Fig. 2.

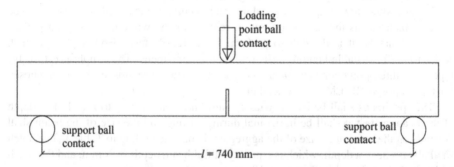

Fig. 2. Support and loading arrangement for the test. (RILEM TC 50- FMC Fracture Mechanics of Concrete 1985)

The deformation of the center of the beam shall be determined with regard to a line between two points on the beam above the supports. The deformation shall be measured with an accuracy of at least 0.01 mm.

The load-deformation curve is corrected for eventual non-linearities at low loads. The energy W_o, represented by the area under the curve is measured as well as the deformation δ_o at final Fracture.

The fracture energy is calculated from the equation:

$$G_f = (W_o + mg\delta_o)/A_{lig} \ [N/m] \tag{1}$$

Where: W_o = area according to Fig. 3. [N.m]

$$m = m_1 + 2m_2$$

m_1 = weight of the beam between the supports, calculated as the beam weight multiplied by l/L [Kg].m_2 = weight of the part of the loading arrangement which is not attached to the machine, but follows the beam until failure [Kg].

$$g = \text{acceleration due to gravity, } 9.81 \text{ m/s}^2$$

$$\delta = \text{deformation at the final failure of the beam (m);}$$

A_{lig} = area of the ligament, defined as the projection of the fracture zone on a plane perpendicular to the beam axis [m^2].

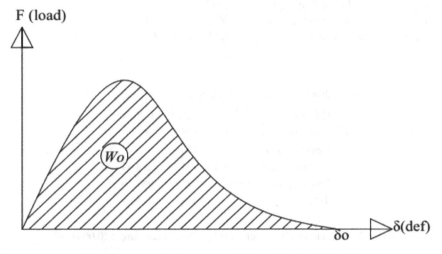

Fig. 3. Load vs beam's center deflection curve. (RILEM TC 50- FMC Fracture Mechanics of Concrete 1985)

2 Methodology

2.1 Materials

The following materials were used to conduct the experiments on this study:

- Glass Fiber- fiber type E-glass with tensile strength of 3445 Mpa and Density 2580 kg/m^3.
- Cement (Dangote PPC)

- Fine and coarse aggregates
- Water
- Different types of Molds
- Metal plate to create Notch beam
- Mixer
- Universal testing machine

2.2   Procedures

First, the appropriate mix-designs are prepared and the amount of glass fibers to be added is determined.

Mix-design for C20/25 and C25/30 grade concrete based on ACI method (ACI).

Material Properties:

- Specified compressive strength = 25 Mpa and 30 Mpa respectively
- Ordinary Portland cement specific gravity = 3.15
- Maximum aggregate size = 9.5 mm
- Dry unit weight of aggregate = 1373.73 kg/m^3
- Moisture content of aggregate = 1.336%
- Fineness modulus of fine aggregate = 2.97
- Unit weight of fine aggregate = 1675.76 kg/m^3
- Density of glass fiber = 2580 kg/m^3 (Tables 2 and 3)

Table 2. Mix design results per 1 m^3 of concrete

Components	C20/25	C25/30
Water (kg/m^3)	205	205
Cement (kg/m^3)	420	488
Coarse Aggregate (kg/m^3)	604.44	604.44
Fine Aggregate (kg/m^3)	1055.56	987.56
Total	2285	2285

Table 3. Amount of glass fiber added per one beam sample (0.0084 m^3)

Glass fiber (% by volume)	Per 0.0084 m^3 (one test sample volume)
0.20%	43.9 gm (14.4 gm per layer)
0.40%	86.6 gm (28.8 gm per layer)
0.60%	130.0 gm (43.3 gm per layer)

Then, the test samples were prepared for each test parameters combination as shown below in table of parameters combination. Test samples without glass fiber were casted and tested for reference purpose.

There are six parameters combination used for this study, each with three samples. Therefore, there are eighteen test beam samples (Tables 4 and 5).

Table 4. Parameter combinations for three point bending test

Test parameters	Levels	Parameters combination applied for 3 point bending tests					
		1	2	3	4	5	6
Concrete grades	1	x	x	x			
	2				x	x	x
% of glass fiber	1	x			x		
	2		x			x	
	3			x			x
Fiber layer	1	x	x	x	x	x	x

Table 5. Legends

Legend		
Test parameters	Levels	Description
Concrete grades	1	C20/25[a]
	2	C25/30[b]
% of glass fiber	1	0.20% by total volume of the sample
	2	0.40% by total volume of the sample
	3	0.60% by total volume of the sample
Fiber layers	1	3 layers at uniform interval starting from the end of notched depth

[a] C20/25 – refers to a concrete with 20 Mpa cylindrical and 25 Mpa cubic compressive strength.
[b] C25/30 – refers to a concrete with 25 Mpa cylindrical and 30 Mpa cubic compressive strength.

Three Point Bending Test

This test is performed to determine the fracture energy of concrete by using notched beams test specimens. This test are performed according to RILEM TC 50-FMC Recommendation (Work of Fracture Method).

The following procedures are followed:

- Prepare $100 \times 100 \times 840$ mm^3 beam sample with notch at the middle of the beam

Glass fibers are added in three layer after the concrete is mixed separately in the mixer and casted in the beam mold with the given dimensions. The number of glass fiber layer is constant for all samples, but the amount in each layer is different for different samples based on the percentage of glass fiber used.

First, place 15 mm of concrete then place the first layer of glass fiber, then place the next 15 mm of concrete then place the second layer of glass fiber, then place the next 15 mm of concrete then place the third layer of glass fiber. After the third layer of glass fiber is placed, fill the rest of the sample beam with concrete by placing the notch making plate at the middle (Fig. 4).

Fig. 4. Glass fiber in layer, casted beam with notch plate & notch plate removed

- Cure the sample for 28 days

The test samples are cured in open water tanker after they are removed from the mold until 3–4 h to test (Fig. 5).

Fig. 5. Sample curing for 28 days.

- Perform 3-point bending test using universal testing machine

The test is performed with an approximately constant rate of deformation, which is chosen so that the maximum load is reached within about 30–60 s after the start of the test. The testing machine records the deformation of the center of the beam and the corresponding load until the beam is completely separated into two halves.

The load shall be measured with an accuracy of at least 2% of the maximum value in the test. The area of the ligament, A_{lig}, shall be measured.

The length L of the beam as well as the span l during the test shall be measured with an accuracy of at least 1 mm.

- Record the load vs deflection results (Table 6)

Table 6. Test result format for 3- point bending test

Type of test	Test samples	Test results for 3 point bending test parameters combination					
		1	2	3	4	5	6
3–point bending test	1	x	x	x	x	x	x
	2	x	x	x	x	x	x
	3	x	x	x	x	x	x

3 Results and Discussion

The fracture energy of concrete is calculate using the RILEM TC 50-FMC Recommendation (Work of Fracture Method). As it has shown in the literature review, to calculate the fracture energy first the load vs displacement curve from the three point bending test must be drawn and the area under the curve must be calculated. Then using the given analytical formula from the RILEM TC 50-FMC Recommendation, the fracture energy is calculated.[1,2]

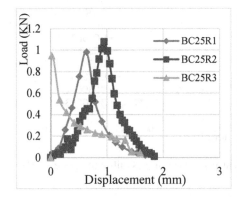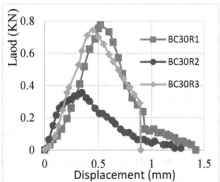

Fig. 6. Load vs Displacement curves for 0% glass fiber for grade C20/25 & C25/30 design concrete respectively.

Figure 6 shows that plain concrete of grade of C20/25 and C25/30 with no addition of glass fiber respectively. It shows very brittle failure with a maximum

---

[1] BC25R1, 2, 3 – refers to beam sample with 25 Mpa cubic compressive strength cast without addition of glass fiber as reference test sample 1, 2 & 3.

[2] BC30R1, 2, 3 - refers to beam sample with 30 Mpa cubic compressive strength cast without addition of glass fiber as reference test sample 1, 2 & 3.

displacement less than 2 mm at the central notched section of the beam (Fig. 7).[3,4]

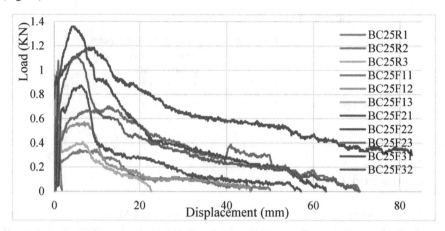

Fig. 7. Load vs Displacement curves for different percentage of glass fiber for grade C20/25 design concrete.

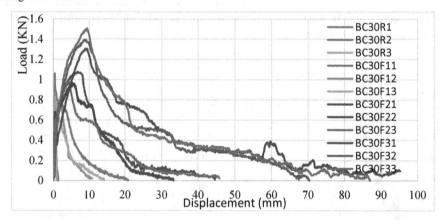

Fig. 8. Load vs Displacement curves for different percentage of glass fiber for grade C25/30 design concrete.

---

[3] BC25F11, 2, 3 – refers to beam with 25 Mpa cubic compressive strength cast with 0.2% by volume addition of glass fiber as test sample 1, 2 & 3.
   BC25F21, 2, 3 – refers to beam with 25 Mpa cubic compressive strength cast with 0.4% by volume addi-tion of glass fiber as test sample 1, 2 & 3.
   BC25F31, 2 – refers to beam with 25 Mpa cubic compressive strength cast with 0.6% by volume addition of glass fiber as test sample 1 & 2.
[4] BC30F11, 2, 3 – refers to beam with 30 Mpa cubic compressive strength cast with 0.2% by volume addition of glass fiber as test sample 1, 2 & 3.
   BC30F21, 2, 3 – refers to beam with 30 Mpa cubic compressive strength cast with 0.4% by volume addi-tion of glass fiber as test sample 1, 2 & 3.
   BC30F31, 2, 3 – refers to beam with 30 Mpa cubic compressive strength cast with 0.6% by volume addi-tion of glass fiber as test sample 1, 2 & 3.

Figures 7 and 8 shows that the maximum displacement of the notched beam for C20/25 & C25/30 grade concrete respectively. It shows the maximum displacement increase significantly with the addition of glass fiber, which change the failure mode from very brittle (0% glass fiber) to very ductile (0.6% glass fiber addition by volume). The figure also shows there is an increase in the maximum load carried by the beam as the percentage of glass fiber addition increases.

The effects of the addition of glass fiber on fracture energy of plain concrete is presented in table format below.

Table 7. Experimental results for fracture energy by three point bending test

No.	Sample code	Mass (Kg)	ml (l/L) Kg	Area of ligament (m²)	Final disp. (m)	Area under load vs Disp. curve (N.m)	Fracture energy (N/m)	Average fracture energy (N/m)	Max. load (KN)	Avg. Max. Load (KN)	Avg. Max. Disp. (m)
1	BC30R1	19.3	17.13	0.0048	0.00142	0.416	136.381	111.08	0.776	0.625	0.00120
2	BC30R2	19.3	17.13	0.00474	0.00128	0.2	87.611		0.355		
3	BC30R3	19.4	17.26	0.00499	0.0009	0.393	109.252		0.743		
4	BC30F11	18.8	16.73	0.00479	0.02085	5.713	1,905.321	1,413.49	1.056	0.890	0.01532
5	BC30F12	18.7	16.60	0.00459	0.01089	3.355	1,117.242		0.786		
6	BC30F13	19.2	17.06	0.0047	0.01421	3.3457	1,217.892		0.829		
7	BC30F21	19.3	17.15	0.00469	0.04452	16.297	5,069.761	4,363.01	1.077	1.009	0.04121
8	BC30F22	19	16.86	0.0049	0.03329	12.876	3,751.700		0.969		
9	BC30F23	19	16.90	0.00504	0.04581	13.912	4,267.570		0.980		
10	BC30F31	19.1	16.99	0.0052	0.09537	39.19	10,593.884	10,205.8	1.303	1.400	0.08424
11	BC30F32	19.1	16.95	0.00515	0.07037	33.902	8,863.931		1.390		
12	BC30F33	18.8	16.73	0.0047	0.08699	38.176	11,159.464		1.508		
13	BC25R1	19.1	16.92	0.0047	0.00168	0.5154	168.996	172.885	0.980	1.002	0.00170
14	BC25R2	18.9	16.79	0.0047	0.00184	0.635	199.596		1.077		
15	BC25R3	19.2	17.08	0.00475	0.00159	0.446	150.063		0.948		
16	BC25F11	17.5	15.57	0.00489	0.05004	7.214	3,039.464	2,746.31	0.345	0.499	0.03941
17	BC25F12	17.3	15.37	0.0049	0.04549	9.614	3,362.124		0.571		
18	BC25F13	18.2	16.15	0.0048	0.0227	5.222	1,837.344		0.582		
19	BC25F21	18.8	16.71	0.0048	0.05718	14.169	4,904.184	8,586.60	0.873	0.919	0.07024
20	BC25F22	18.7	16.62	0.005	0.08278	52.909	13,280.688		1.185		
21	BC25F23	18.7	16.55	0.00485	0.07075	25.257	7,574.915		0.700		
22	BC25F31	19.3	17.16	0.00475	0.06293	29.707	8,479.261	8,148.08	1.357	1.239	0.06669
23	BC25F32	19.3	17.13	0.00475	0.07045	25.313	7,816.892		1.120		

Table 8. Comparison of fracture energy test results between C20/25 & C25/30 grade concretes for different percentage of glass fiber addition by volume ratio.

Concrete Grades	Fracture energy for different percentage of Glass fiber by volume (N/m)			
	0%	0.20%	0.40%	0.60%
C20/25	172.885	2,746.310	8,586.596	8,148.076
C25/30	111.081	1,413.485	4,363.010	10,205.760

Table 9. Comparison of maximum load carried test results between C20/25 & C25/30 grade concretes for different percentage of glass fiber addition by volume ratio.

Concrete Grades	Maximum load for different percentage of Glass fiber by volume (KN)			
	0%	0.20%	0.40%	0.60%
C20/25	1.002	0.499	0.919	1.239
C25/30	0.625	0.890	1.009	1.400

Table 10. Comparison of maximum displacement recorded results between C20/25 & C25/30 grade concretes for different percentage of glass fiber addition by volume ratio.

Concrete Grades	Maximum displacement for different percentage of glass fiber by volume (mm)			
	0%	0.20%	0.40%	0.60%
C20/25	1.703	39.410	70.237	66.690
C25/30	1.200	15.317	41.207	84.243

As it is shown in Tables 7, 8, 9 and 10 the fracture energy of pain concrete increases with the addition of glass fiber and this effect is greater for C20/25 design grade concrete than C25/30 design grade concrete. The above results shows that C20/25 design grade concrete have higher fracture energy due to the larger center of beam displacement than C25/30 design grade concrete. However, the C25/30 design grade concrete have better maximum load carrying capacity as the content of glass fiber increase.

3.1   Effects Observed During the Experimental Periods

During the conduct of tests, the following effects were observed due to the addition of glass fiber:-

For C25/30, grade concrete:

- With 0% glass fiber (Reference), the samples breaks instantly in brittle manner without showing any crack pattern.
- With 0.2% glass fiber by volume, the samples break in brittle manner, but there are visible crack patterns lines and crack width and the crack growth very fast to the upper end of the beam breaks suddenly.

Fig. 9. Crack patterns at 0.2% glass fiber addition for C25/30 design grade concrete just before failure.

- With 0.4% glass fiber by volume, the samples shows ductile behavior before failure after a very noticeable crack patterns lines and crack width and finally breaks into two halves (Fig. 10).

Fig. 10. Crack patterns at 0.4% glass fiber addition for C25/30 design grade concrete just before failure.

- With 0.6% glass fiber by volume, sample shows very ductile behavior and the samples do not breaks into two halves (Fig, 11).

Fig. 11. Crack patterns at 0.6% glass fiber addition for C25/30 design grade concrete.

For C20/25, grade concrete:

- With 0% glass fiber (Reference), the samples breaks instantly in brittle manner without showing any crack pattern.
- With 0.2% glass fiber by volume, the sample shows little ductile behavior and noticeable crack patterns and crack width and this crack patterns are similar to the 0.4% by volume of glass fiber for C25/30 grade concrete samples, and the sample breaks into two halves (Fig. 12).

Fig. 12. Crack patterns at 0.2% glass fiber addition for C20/25 design grade concrete just before failure.

- With 0.4% glass fiber by volume, the sample shows very ductile behavior and very noticeable crack patterns and crack width and this crack patterns are similar to the 0.6% glass fiber by volume for C25/30 grade concrete samples, and the sample breaks into two halves (Fig. 13).

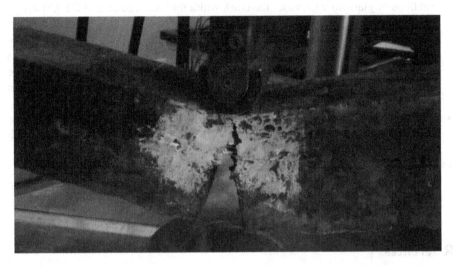

Fig. 13. Crack patterns at 0.4% glass fiber addition for C20/25 design grade concrete just before failure.

- With 0.6% glass fiber by volume, the sample shows very ductile behavior with very noticeable crack patterns and crack width (Fig. 14).

Fig. 14. Crack patterns at 0.6% glass fiber addition for C20/25 design grade concrete just before failure.

4 Conclusions

- Addition of glass fiber increases the fracture energy of plain concrete for both C20/25 and C25/30 design grade concrete, and it has more effect for C20/25 design grade concrete than C25/30 design grade concrete.
- Addition of glass fiber increases the crack width for both C20/25 and C25/30 design grade concretes.
- The fracture energy increases for both C20/25 and C25/30 design grade concretes with the increases of glass fiber content. But after 0.4% by volume addition of glass fiber, it shows that the glass fiber layer slips on one other, so for higher percentage of glass fiber the fiber must be distributed in thin layers to create strong contact bond with the concrete.
- The maximum displacement of the center of the beam increases with the increases of glass fiber content and the increase for C20/25 design grade concrete is more than the C25/30 design grade concrete.
- Addition of glass fiber increase the maximum load carried by the test beam and its effect for C25/30 design grade concrete is greater than for C20/25 design grade concrete.

References

Nevile, A.M., Books, J.J.: Concrete Technology, 2 (ed.). Pearson Education Limited, Harlow (2010)

ACI. (n.d.).: ACI standard practice for selecting proportions for normal, heavyweight and mass concrete (ACI 211.1–81)

ACI committee 544: Report on fiber reinforced concrete (2002)

Kizilkanat, A.B., Kabay, N.: Mechanical properties and fracture behavior of basalt and glass fiber reinforced concrete: an experimental study. Constr. Build. Mater. **100**, 218–224 (2015)

Arslan, M.E.: Effects of basalt and glass fibers addition on fracture energy and mechanical properties of ordinary concrete: CMOD measurement. Constr. Build. Mater. **114**, 383–391 (2016)

Kabay, N.: Abrasion resistance and fracture energy of concrete with basalt fiber. Constr. Build. Mater. **50**, 95–101 (2013)

RILEM TC 50- FMC Fracture Mechanics of Concrete: Determination on the fracture energy of mortar and concrete by means of three-point bend test on notched beams. Mater. Struct. **18** (106), 285–290 (1985)

Assessment of Flood Hazard Areas Using Remote Sensing and Spatial Information System in Bilate River Basin, Ethiopia

Teshale Tadesse Danbara[1]([⊠]), Mulugeta Dadi Belete[1], and Ayele Getachew Tasew[2]

[1] Department of Water Resources and Irrigation Engineering, Institute of Technology, Hawassa University, Hawassa, Ethiopia
teshaletadesse@hu.edu.et
[2] Department of Hydraulic and Water Resources Engineering, Institute of Technology, Hawassa University, Hawassa, Ethiopia

Abstract. Floods are considered as harmful and the most dangerous natural disaster affecting annually millions of people. This study aimed to present a geospatial information system based multi-criteria evaluation techniques (MCE) methodology for flood hazard areas mapping. The distance from drainage network, slope, recurrent heavy rainfall, curve number, normalized difference vegetation index (NDVI), and the population density are the six factors considered as relevant to the flood hazard areas mapping of the basin. The final flood hazard areas map of the basin shows a satisfactory agreement between the spatial distribution of historical floods that happened in the basin for the past years and the flood hazard zones. The flood hazard map showed that Bilate-Humbo area at the very entry of Bilate River to Lake Abaya, Shashego area at Boyo Lake resulting from Guder River, and Shashego area at Boyo Lake resulting from Metenchiso River are the areas of very high flood hazard. These areas are categorized by low NDVI, gentle slope, high rainfall, high curve number and close to the drainage network. The proposed methodology of assessing flood hazard areas using spatial information system delivers a good basis for developing a system of flood risk management in a river basin.

Keywords: Flood hazard · Weighted overlay · Bilate River basin · GIS · AHP

1 Introduction

Population around the world is vulnerable to natural disasters. Floods are considered as harmful and the most dangerous natural disaster producing many environmental and socio-economic consequences (Aronica et al. 2009; Dawod et al. 2012; Douben 2006; Duan et al. 2012; Forkuo 2011; Foudi et al. 2015; Heidari 2014; Marchand et al. 2009; Pradhan and Youssef 2011; Taylor et al. 2011; Tsakiris 2014; Vorogushyn et al. 2012; Yahaya et al. 2010) affecting annually 170 million people (Kowalzig 2008). The occurrence of such type disasters are with increased frequency as a consequence of land-use and socio-economic developments, and due to increased climate variability (Bajabaa et al. 2014). Hazard is a possibly harmful physical phenomenon that may

© ICST Institute for Computer Sciences, Social Informatics and Telecommunications Engineering 2022
Published by Springer Nature Switzerland AG 2022. All Rights Reserved
M. L. Berihun (Ed.): ICAST 2021, LNICST 412, pp. 175–194, 2022.
https://doi.org/10.1007/978-3-030-93712-6_12

cause the loss of life, damage of properties, degradation of environment, and economic and social distraction. Hazards can comprise latent conditions that may represent future threats and can have natural or induced by human processes origins. According to their origin and effects hazards can be categorized as single, sequential or combined. The characterization of each hazard is based on by its location, intensity, and probability. Therefore, the assessment of hazard is to detect the specific hazard's occurrence probability, in a specific future time, and its intensity and area of impact.

Mapping the flood hazard areas define the area at risk of flooding and should be useful for the programs to reduce all damage caused by flood and to take subsequent actions. Flood hazard maps at river basin level are one of the main outputs of the flood risk management plans. Many studies were conducted in mapping flood hazard zones using multi-criteria evaluation (De Sherbinin et al. 2012; Fernández and Lutz 2010; Kazakis et al. 2015; Kourgialas and Karatzas 2011; Tehrany et al. 2013; Tehrany et al. 2014; Wang et al. 2011) they came up with a good result. The aim of mapping flood hazard areas is to increase the awareness of people of the areas at risk of flooding, to provide reliable information of areas at risk of flooding by identifying flood risk zones to give feedback to spatial planning and assist the processes of prioritizing, justifying and targeting investments as to manage and decrease the risk to people, property and the environment.

The Bilate River basin is among major sub-basins in rift valley lakes basin of Ethiopia and it flows into Abaya Lake. The areas of the Bilate River basin are extensively under agriculture and densely populated. In spite of the water stress the Bilate River basin is susceptible to flooding and it is considered as a flood prone. Therefore, the main aim of this study is, to assess those areas which have frequently been attacked by floods and to map the flood hazard areas by using different geospatial parameters such as distance from drainage network, slope, the recurrent heavy rainfall, curve number (CN), NDVI, and the population density.

2 Materials and Methods

2.1 Description of Study Area

Bilate River Basin is the sub-basin located in the main Ethiopian rift valley lakes basin. It is formed after Boyo swampy lake which has two main sources Guder and Weira Rivers and it drains at Abaya Lake. It covers an area of about 5686.86 km^2. The rainfall pattern of the Bilate River basin is bimodal (Negash 2014) and its climatic conditions are humid and semi-arid. The average annual rainfall variability is linearly correlated to the altitude in the watershed. As stated by Negash (2014) and approved by the satellite image classification in this study, the vegetation cover in the basin is decreasing due to deforestation for agricultural land expansion and energy purposes. The deep gullies and barren land in the basin make the basin vulnerable to erosion hazard (Negash 2014).

The altitude of the Basin ranges from 1116 m to 3358 m (Fig. 1). This implies the high variation in the topography which ranges from lowland plain areas to high land mountainous areas. The effect of this difference in elevation makes the morphology of the basin quite complex. As it has been shown in Fig. 1 the north, northwest, and southwest areas are characterized by steep slopes. The central and the southern parts of the basin areas are characterized by gentle slopes.

The land use maps of the basin show that the cultivated land increased by 12.41% from 1986 to 2018 and the forest area is decreased by 13.32% from 1986 to 2018. The decrease in vegetation cover and increase in cultivated land aggravates the runoff and increase the vulnerability of the basin area to be flooded. The land use maps were prepared from Landsat satellite imageries (Landsat-5 for 1986 land use, Landsat-7 for 2000 land use and Landsat-8 for 2018 land use) of the basin and the land use land cover changes of the basin are shown in Table 1.

Table 1. The land use land cover change of Bilate River Basin for 1986, 2000 and 2018 years.

Land use	Area (km^2)	Percentage (%)	Area (km^2)	Percentage (%)	Area (km^2)	Percentage (%)
Year	1986		2000		2018	
Barren land	109	1.93	321.88	5.71	122.33	2.17
Cultivated land and built up	2173.81	38.56	2757.24	48.92	2872.41	50.96
Forest	1539.35	27.31	471.97	8.37	788.31	13.99
Marsh land	73.25	1.30	141.15	2.50	165.73	2.94
Shrub land	428.77	7.61	336.33	5.97	460.20	8.16
Water body	177.91	3.16	227.87	4.04	54.34	0.964
Wooden + Agroforestry	1134.86	20.13	1380.31	24.49	1173.42	20.82

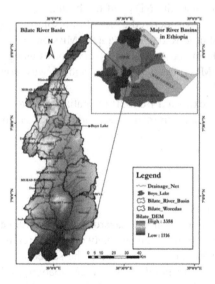

Fig. 1. The study area with the stream network and DEM

2.2   Source of Data Used

Long-term daily rainfall data is available for ten meteorological stations in the river basin. The precipitation data was collected from the Ethiopian Metrological Agency (EMA). The daily rainfall data of 30 years of each station were collected and the point rainfall is converted into areal rainfall for the stations by using the Thiessen polygon method.

Hydrologic soil group a key factor to estimate the curve number (CN) which is directly related with runoff. The soil data was obtained from Ethiopian Ministry of Water, Irrigation and Energy (MoWIE) and Digital Soil Map of the World, Harmonized world soil database (HWSD). The field observation and measurement were taken place to verify the collected soil data. Land use land cover data with hydrologic soil group helps to calculate the CN of the area. The land use land cover data was acquired from the supervised satellite image classification. For this section the Landsat-8 satellite images of the year 2018 were used for the classification. The freely available 30 m spatial resolution Landsat-8 satellite images of the basin (Path/Row 169/55, 169/54 and 168/55) were downloaded from the respective website (http://glovis.usgs.gov/ or http://earthexplorer.usgs.gov/) and classified to different land use land cover classes using ERDAS IMAGINE 2014 and ArcGIS-10.2.

Normalized Difference Vegetation Index (NDVI) is an index shows the variation of vegetation cover in the study are and was calculated from Landsat-8 satellite images. The 4th (RED band) and 5th (NEAR INFRARED band) bands of Landsat-8 satellite images were used to calculate the NDVI of the basin.

The slope of the basin was derived using 30m resolution Digital Elevation Model (DEM) data from the Shuttle Radar Topography Mission (SRTM) and the percentage slope of the basin is determined on a pixel-by-pixel basis using ArcGIS. The SRTM's, a 30 m resolution DEM is freely available and it was downloaded from http://earthexplorer.usgs.gov/.

Drainage network is extracted from 30 m spatial resolution DEM using Archydro tool in ArcGIS. The distance from drainage network is calculated using Euclidean distance tool in ArcGIS.

2.3   Methodology

Flood Hazard Parameters

In this study, identification of flood hazard areas was done by characterizing 6 parameters namely: distance from drainage network, topography (slope), CN, recurrent heavy rainfall, NDVI, and population density. The selection of these parameters was based on their significance to flood hazards areas mapping (Haan et al. 1994). The thematic maps of these six factors were visualized and the data was processed in a GIS environment. Indubitably, approaches against floods' effect at basin level need the description of prone zones (Tehrany et al. 2013) to give early-warning, enable fast feedback and reduce the effect of possible flood events (Kia et al. 2011).

The slope of the basin is calculated from DEM which is one of the prime factors controlling floods (Ullah and Zhang 2020; Das 2019). Lowland areas may get flooded faster as water flows from high altitude to low altitude. Low land areas usually have a higher probability of flooding compared to areas located at a higher elevation (Das 2018; Liuzzo et al. 2019). The slope map was prepared from SRTM DEM of 30 m spatial resolution using the surface tool in ArcGIS 10.2. In hydrological studies, slope plays an important role in regulating surface water flow (Khosravi et al. 2016; Das 2018) and controlling the surface runoff and the intensity of water flow that provokes erosion of soil and vertical percolation (Jahangir et al. 2019). The study has showed that the area having a lower slope is more exposed to flooding (Liuzzo et al. 2019).

The drainage network was extracted from SRTM DEM and distance from drainage network was developed by applying Euclidian distance in spatial analyst ArcGIS 10.2. Distance to drainage network is highly related with flooding. A higher likelihood of flooding is directly linked to the area near to the drainage network.

The Soil Conservation Service-Curve Number (SCS-CN) method is uncomplicated, predictable and stable conceptual method to estimate a direct runoff depth based on storm rainfall depth and its applicability to estimate Runoff Potential in GISEnvironment is studied by Ahmad et al. (2016). The curve number grid of the study basin was created from land use land cover classes and hydrologic soil group type, in combination with runoff CNs. The CNs for different combination of land use land cover and hydrologic soil group was obtained from the SCS-CN table. The HEC-GeoHMS which is an ArcGIS extension was used to create the curve number grid. HEC-GeoHMS used the merged feature class of the basin land use land cover and hydrologic soil group and the lookup table to generate the CN grid. The higher the CN value indicates the higher the runoff potential and the lower the CN value indicates the lower the runoff potential of the area.

The NDVI is a normalized form of the NIR to RED reflectance ratio, developed to standardize Vegetation Index (VI) values to between −1 and +1 (Didan et al. 2015). It is usually denoted as:

$$NDVI = \frac{NIR - RED}{NIR + RED} \tag{1}$$

In this study the Landsat-8 images covering the study basin were downloaded from the USGS website and the NDVI of the basin was calculated using Eq. 1.

The population data of the basin was obtained from central statistical agency (CSA) of Ethiopia and projected to the study period. The census CSA of (2007) was used to project the population and the population density of the basin was extracted.

Reliable information on magnitude and frequency of flood-flow is required for the economic design of flood-control structures and for floodplain management. Their underestimation may result in disruption of facility, costly maintenance, may even cause loss of life, while overestimates may result in excessive construction costs. The Gumbel method of frequency analysis, which is based on extreme value distribution and uses frequency factors, was used to estimate the design rainfall. The method utilizes general equation given for hydrologic frequency analysis which is shortened as below (Eq. 2). The most commonly used flood-flow statistics in flood-related projects include the flood flows expected every 25, 50, 75, and 100 years. In our case, 50 years return is selected following the recommendation by MoWR (2002) guideline.

The indicators used to assess flood hazard areas are shown in Fig. 2.

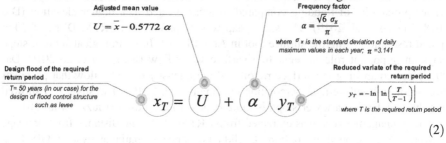

$$x_T = U + \alpha\, y_T \tag{2}$$

Normalization Technique

The procedure to calculate the flood hazard areas is by transforming each locally identified parameter into a normalized (from 0 to 1) dimensionless number using actual, minimum and maximum values from the spatial elements under consideration. The following equation (Eq. 3) used for the normalization processes.

$$Normalized\ value = \frac{Actual\ value - minimum\ value}{Maximum\ value - minimum\ value} \tag{3}$$

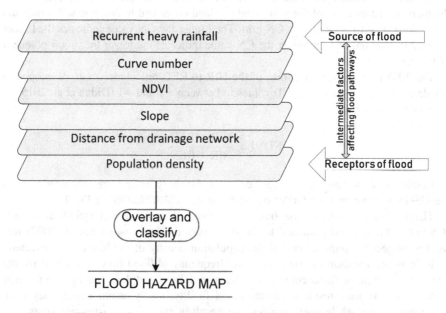

Fig. 2. Indicators used for identification of flood hazard areas

The final results were presented by means of a standardized number, ranging from 0 to 1 (Table 2), which symbolizes comparatively low or high flood risk areas between the various spatial scales.

Table 2. Flood risk interpretation (Balica 2012)

Index value	Description
< 0.01	Very small risk of flood
0.01 to 0.25	Small risk of flood
0.25 to 0.5	Risky to floods
0.5 to 0.75	High risk of flood
0.75 to 1	Very high risk of flood

Weight of the Parameters

The Analytical Hierarchy Process (AHP) of Saaty (1990a, 1990b) was used to define the weight of each parameter. The weights of the parameters are defined after they are ranked based on their relative significance to flood hazard areas mapping. Thus, once all parameters are sorted according to their hierarchical manner, a pairwise comparison matrix for each parameter is formed to enable a significance comparison. The relative importance between the parameters is assessed from 1 to 9 indicating less significant to high significant parameters, respectively (Saaty 1977). Though the pairwise comparisons method by AHP is subjective, it is widely implemented in many applications (Valle Junior et al. 2014; Oikonomidis et al. 2015; Worqlul et al. 2015; Rediet et al. 2020) and is suggested to be adapted for regional studies (Ayalew and Yamagishi 2005; Worqlul et al. 2015).

Table 3. Pair-wise comparison scale and definition

Intensity of importance	Definition	Explanation
1	Equal importance	Two factors contribute equally to the objective
3	Somewhat more important	Experience and judgment slightly favor one over the other
5	Much more important	Experience and judgment strongly favor one over the other
7	Very much more important	Experience and judgment very strongly favor one over the other. Its importance is demonstrated in practice
9	Absolutely more important	The evidence favoring one over the other is of the highest possible validity
2, 4, 6, 8	Intermediate values	When compromise is needed

This study uses 6 × 6 matrix, where the six factors are listed in columns and rows; hence the row factors were compared with the columns factors for their importance to the flood hazard areas mapping. In Table 4 the weight of the parameters are sorted in a hierarchical manner, for the study basin. The values of each row describe the significance between two parameters. The first row of the Table 4 shows the significance of the first parameter in regard to the other parameters which are placed in the columns. The value assigned for each parameter describes the significance of the parameter in relation to the other parameters. The intensity of importance and the explanation of the values are given in Table 3.

Table 4. The weights of the parameters using AHP

Factors	Distance from drainage network	Slope	CN	Recurrent heavy rainfall	NDVI	Population density
Distance from drainage network	1	3	3	3	3	5
Slope	1/3	1	2	3	3	3
CN	1/3	1/2	1	2	3	3
Recurrent heavy rainfall	1/3	1/3	1/2	1	3	7
NDVI	1/3	1/3	1/3	1/3	1	3
Population density	1/5	1/3	1/3	1/7	1/3	1

To calculate the weight, a normalized comparison matrix was formed by dividing each value in the matrix by the sum of its column. Then the mean of each row of the normalized matrix was determined to get the weights of the individual factors (Table 5).

Table 5. Normalized comparison matrix of the parameters

Factors	Distance from drainage network	Slope	CN	Recurrent heavy rainfall	NDVI	Population density	Parameter's weight (%)
Distance from drainage network	0.39	0.55	0.42	0.32	0.23	0.23	35
Slope	0.13	0.18	0.28	0.32	0.23	0.14	21
CN	0.13	0.09	0.14	0.21	0.23	0.14	16
Recurrent heavy rainfall	0.13	0.06	0.07	0.11	0.23	0.32	15
NDVI	0.13	0.06	0.05	0.04	0.08	0.14	8
Population density	0.08	0.06	0.05	0.02	0.03	0.05	5

The results of pair-wise comparison in Table 4 show that the parameter distance from drainage network is the most significant parameter followed by the slope. The list significant parameter in considering the flood hazard areas mapping is population density followed by the NDVI.

In the application of the AHP method it is important to check the consistency of the weights derived from a pairwise comparison matrix and the weights need to be consistent. Therefore, a statistically reliable estimate of the consistency of the resulting weights was made and it's value is less than 0.1. Saaty (1977) indicated that a consistency ratio of 0.10 or less shows a reasonable level of consistency whereas if the consistency ratio is greater than 0.1, the comparison matrix should be revised.

3   Results and Discussion

3.1   Design Rainfall of 50 Years Return Period

Figure 3(a) presents the design rainfall of 50 years return period all over the basin. As shown in Fig. 3, occurrence probability of heavy rainfall increasing while moving from upstream to down to the outlet. The magnitude of these rainfall events is inconsistent with the usual report of flood occurrences at the downstream such as Boyo Lake and at convergence site of Bilate River and Lake Abaya. The relative spatial flood hazard map based on 24-h rainfall of 50 years return period is presented in Fig. 3(b).

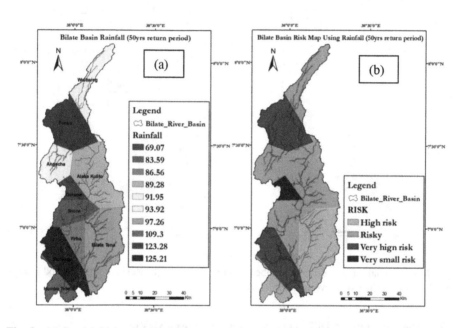

Fig. 3. (a) Spatial 24-h rainfall of 50 years return period of the basin and (b) Relative spatial flood hazard map based on 24-h rainfall of 50 years return period

3.2   Curve Number (CN)

Curve number is a conceptual parameter, ranging from 1 to 100, introduced by the Soil Conservation Service (SCS 1972). The CN value depends on land use land cover and hydrologic soil group conditions. The higher the CN value indicates the higher the volume of direct surface runoff.

As shown in Fig. 4(a), high flood potential appears to be on the downstream part of the basin. The coincidence of high rainfall (indicator 1) and high curve number (which implies low permeability and sparse land cover) promotes the occurrence of high flood risk on these places. After normalizing these CN values, the relative spatial flood hazard map has been produced. Figure 4(b) shows that, the Boyo Lake and the downstream areas of the basin are categorized as a very high risk area of being flooded.

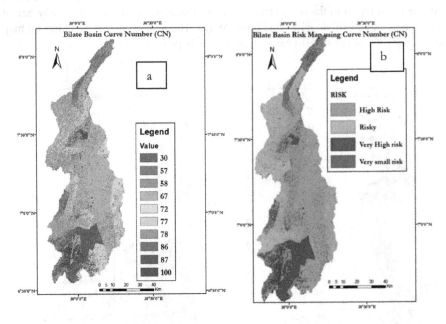

Fig. 4. (a) Spatial values of curve number (CN) in the basin (b) Relative spatial flood hazard map based on values of curve number (CN)

3.3   The Normalized Difference Vegetation Index (NDVI)

The NDVI is one of the most commonly used vegetation indices and its value implies the vegetation cover and the greenness of the study area. Very low values of NDVI which is less than 0.1 correspond to barren land of rock and sand. Moderate values of the NDVI, which are in between 0.2 and 0.3, represent shrubs and grasslands. Whereas, high values of NDVI, which are in between 0.6 and 0.8, indicate dense forests. This NDVI is inversely related to flood risk and treated accordingly. As shown in Fig. 5(a), degree of vegetation greenness tend to decrease downstream supporting the previous two indicators (rainfall and soil permeability + land cover combined as curve number). The Boyo Lake area also shows the small values of NDVI which depicts the less vegetation coverage and the water body.

The normalized NDVI values of the basin are categorized according to their response to the flood and the spatial flood hazard map of the basin based on NDVI values is presented in Fig. 5(b). According to the flood hazard map based on NDVI the Boyo lake area as well as the downstream area of the basin are fall under a category of flood risky area.

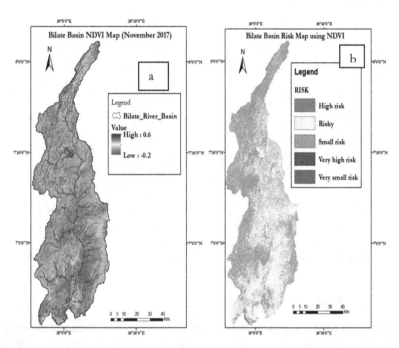

Fig. 5. (a) Spatial values of NDVI in the basin and (b) Relative spatial flood hazard areas based on NDVI

3.4 Topography (Slope)

From the perspective of flood hydrology, steep areas generate more flood as compared to flatter areas. On the other hand, from the perspective of 'flood receptor', flat areas specially locating at the downstream of flood generating uplands are more susceptible. The latter condition appears to occur in Bilate basin where many places with flatter set-up are found to be frequently flood. Figure 6(a) also supports these cases. The spatial flood hazard map of the basin based on slope is presented in Fig. 6(b), and the majority of the basin's areas fall under a category of high risk area to be flooded.

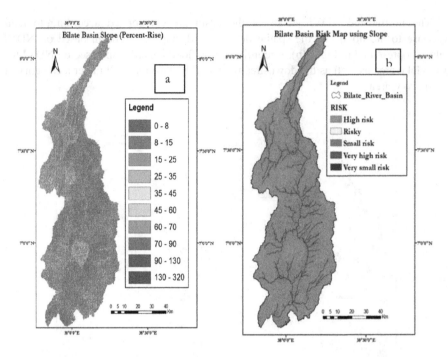

Fig. 6. (a) Spatial distribution of slope in the basin and (b) Relative spatial flood hazard map based on slope

3.5 Distance from Drainage Network

This indicator is meant to portray the degree of exposure of the area and population to be affected by overflows from the drainage network. The distance map from the stream network is shown in Fig. 7(a). It is obvious that the nearest area to the drainage network is more susceptible to flood than the farthest area. Figure 7(b) shows the flood hazard areas map of the basin based on its proximity to the drainage network.

3.6 Population Density (Inhabitants/km^2)

This parameter is meant to represent the vulnerability component of flood risk. For mapping purpose, the Kebele shape file has been updated with population data from census CSA (2007) to extract the spatial density of population. Gross population density calculation method is used to calculate the number of person per square kilometers per kebele. Figure 8(a) shows the population density map of the basin per kebele. As depicted by Fig. 8(b) below, more flood risked areas are less populated. This situation will offer an opportunity for flood risk management through non-structural measures such as re-locating some of the community members away from flood plains. Personal communications with Woreda and Kebele early warning personnel revealed that significant number of the community is encroaching to flood-plains due to population pressure. Such situation may complicate the non-structural measure of flood risk management.

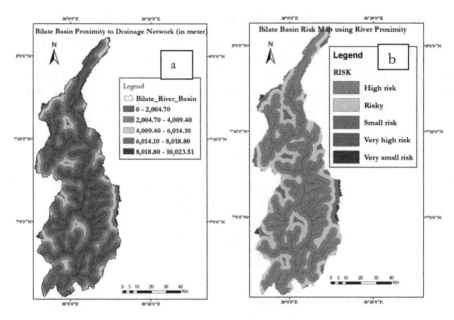

Fig. 7. (a) Proximity to the drainage network of the basin and (b) Relative spatial flood hazard map based on proximity of land surfaces to drainage networks

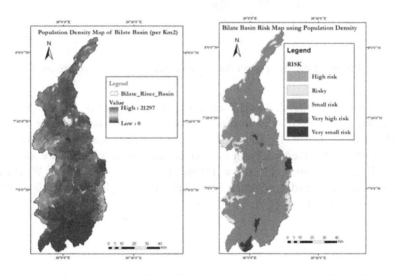

Fig. 8. (a) Population density map of the Bilate basin and (b) Relative spatial flood hazard map based on population density

3.7   Result of Weighted Overlay Analysis

The overlay analysis of the individual flood hazard parameters has been carried out by assigning their weight presented in Table 5. Figure 9 shows the susceptibility of the basin area to be flooded in percent. The higher percentage value depicts the high risk of the area to be flooded. According to this map the areas near Boyo Lake and the downstream area are highly susceptible to the flood.

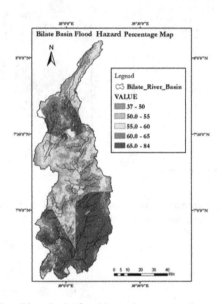

Fig. 9. Bilate River basin flood hazard areas map in percentage risk

After defining the threshold value of which the percentage of risk to flood greater than 70, the flood hazard areas map of the basin for each corresponding Woreda is created and shown in Fig. 10. The flood hazard areas in hectares and percentage of the areas to be flooded in the river basin for each corresponding Woredas are presented in Table 6. Boricha, Siraro, Loka Abaya, Deguna Fanigo, Humbo, Damot Woyide, and Shashogo are the Woredas in which from their areas ranging from 30% to 5% are vulnerable to be flooded.

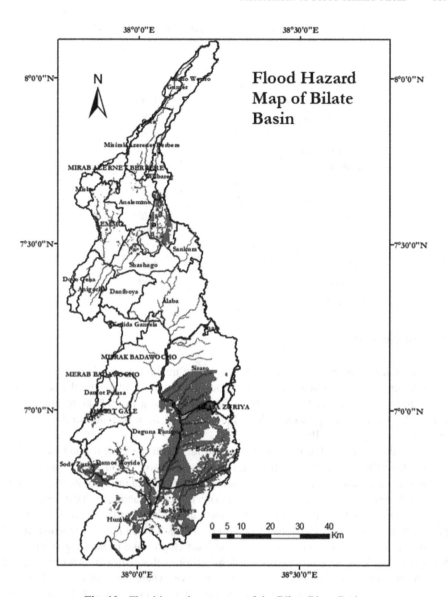

Fig. 10. Flood hazard areas map of the Bilate River Basin

Table 6. Flood hazard areas of each Woreda in the basin

Woreda name	Flood hazard area (ha)	Percentage (%)
Siraro	21279.33	22.39
Boricha	29074.65	30.59
Hawassa Zuriya	1015.01	1.068
Loka Abaya	13446.53	14.15
Humbo	6442.19	6.78
Damot Woyide	5799.99	6.1
Sodo Zuriya	1107.82	1.17
Deguna Fanigo	9670.58	10.2
Damot Gale	764.68	0.8
Damot Pulasa	214.44	0.23
Shashogo	4761.05	5.01
Lemmo	738.73	0.78
Analemmo	256.64	0.27
Wulbareg	466.6	0.49

4 Conclusion

The spatial information based flood risk assessment method shown that there are some areas which are more vulnerable for the flood. Accordingly Bilate-Humbo area at the very entry of Bilate River to Lake Abaya, Shashego area at Boyo Lake resulting from Guder River and Shashego area at Boyo Lake resulting from Metenchiso River are the three critical areas (Fig. 10).

The indicator-based hazard risk assessment identified the critical flood susceptible areas holistically. In order to validate the spatial information system based flood hazard assessment result and grasp further understanding, formal and informal interviews with regional bureau, zonal departments, wereda offices, kebele and very local level informants were conducted. As a result, it was recognized that significant portion of flood problems in the basin is originated from river overflow. This situation gets worse at and around Lake Boyo where this river overflow joins Boyo Lake in Shashego wereda of Hadiya Zone. This area is characterized by all-time flooded area. Another critical location is at the very downstream part of Bilate River where the river travelled long in gorgy channel (upstream) and eventually become flood plain at about 8–10 kms before joining Lake Abaya.

Oriented by the local condition, the following options are likely applicable (to be further analyzed during the actual project implementation) based on the possible purpose of implementing organization:

1. Increasing the river capacity so as to safely drain the design discharge by construction levees along the river reaches → (managing the source)

2. Protecting the flood prone areas from overflow by construction dykes (structural measures) → (managing the source) and/or relevant non-structural measures → (managing the receptor)
3. Reducing and/or controlling the peak discharge itself by constructing detention dams → (managing the pathway)
4. Preventing the inland flood by constructing cut-off drains → (managing both the receptors and pathways).

Acknowledgment. We would like to acknowledge the Southern Nation Nationalities People Regional State Water and Irrigation Development Bureau Irrigation Construction and Scheme Administration Agency for funding this study. Our deepest thanks go to the staff members of Hawassa University, Institute of Technology, Department of Water Resources and Irrigation Engineering for their valuable comments and suggestion.

References

Aronica, G.T., Brigandí, G., Morey, N.: Flash floods and debris flow in the city area of Messina, north-east part of Sicily, Italy in October 2009: the case of the giampilieri catchment. Nat. Hazards Earth Syst. **12**, 1295–1309 (2012)

Ayalew, L., Yamagishi, H.: The application of GIS-based logistic regression for landslide susceptibility mapping in the Kakuda-Yahiko Mountains, Central Japan. Geomorphology **65**, 15–31 (2005). https://doi.org/10.1016/j.geomorph.2004.06.010(ISSN0169555X)

Ahmad, I., Verma, M.K.: Surface runoff estimation using remote sensing & GIS-based curve number method. Int. J. Adv. Eng. Res. and Sci. **3**(2), 73–78 (2016)

Bajabaa, S., Masoud, M., Al-Amri, N.: Flash flood hazard mapping based on quantitative hydrology, geomorphology and GIS techniques (case study of Wadi Al Lith, Saudi Arabia). Arab. J. Geosci. **7**(6), 2469–2481 (2013). https://doi.org/10.1007/s12517-013-0941-2

Baky, A.A., Zaman, A.M., Khan, A.U.: Managing flood flows for crop production risk management with hydraulic and GIS modeling: case study of agricultural areas in Shariatpur. APCBEE Proc. **1**, 318–324 (2012)

Balica, S.F., Wright, N.G., van der Meulen, F.: A flood vulnerability index for coastal cities and its use in assessing climate change impacts, Nat. Hazards **64**(1), 73–105 (2012)

Brunner, G., Bonner, V.: HEC River Analysis System (HEC-RAS). US Army Corps of Engineers Institude for Water Resources Hydrologic Engineering Center, Davis (2010)

Carson, E.C.: Hydrologic modeling of flood conveyance and impacts of historic overbank sedimentation on west fork black's fork, Uinta mountains, northeastern Utah, USA. Geomorphology **75**(3–4), 368–383 (2006)

Das, S.: Geospatial mapping of flood susceptibility and hydro-geomorphic response to the floods in Ulhas basin, India (2019). Remote Sens. Appl. Soc. Environ. **14**, 60–74 (2019). https://doi.org/10.1016/j.rsase.2019.02.006

Das, S.: Geographic information system and AHP-based flood hazard zonation of Vaitarna basin, Maharashtra, India. Arab. J. Geosci. **11**(19), 1–13 (2018). https://doi.org/10.1007/s12517-018-3933-4

Dawod, G.M., Mirza, M.N., Al-Ghamdi, K.A.: GIS-based estimation of flood hazard impacts on road network in Makkah city. Saudi Arabia Environ. Earth Sci. **67**, 2205–2215 (2012)

De Sherbinin, A., et al.: Migration and risk: net migration in marginal ecosystems and hazardous areas. Environ. Res. Lett. **7**(4), 045602 (2012)

Didan, K., Munoz, A.B., Solano, R., Huete, A.: MODIS vegetation index user's guide (MOD13 series). University of Arizona: Vegetation Index and Phenology Lab (2015).

Douben, N.: Characteristics of river floods and flooding: a global overview, 1985–2003, Irrig. Drainage **55**, S9–S21 (2006)

Duan, W., et al.: Anomalous atmospheric events leading to Kyushu's flash floods, 11–14 July 2012. Nat. Hazards **73**, 1255–1267 2014

Fan, C., Ko, C.-H., Wang, W.-S.: An innovative modeling approach using Qual2K and HEC-RAS integration to assess the impact of tidal effect on River Water quality simulation. J. Environ. Manage. **90**(5), 1824–1832 (2009)

Fernández, D.S., Lutz, M.A.: Urban flood hazard zoning in Tucumán province, Argentina, using GIS and multi-criteria decision analysis. Eng. Geol. **111**, 90–98 (2010). https://doi.org/10. 1016/j.enggeo.2009.12.006(ISSN00137952)

Forkuo, E.K.: Flood hazard mapping using aster image data with GIS. Int. J. Geomat. Geosci. **1**, 19 (2011)

Foudi, S., Oses-Eraso, N., Tamayo, I.: Integrated spatial flood risk assessment: the case of Zaragoza. Land Use Policy **42**(278), 292 (2015)

Giudice, G.D., Padulano, R., Rasulo, G.: Factors affecting the runoff coefficient .Hydrol. Earth Syst. Sci. Discuss. **9**, 4919–4941 (2012)

Haan, C.T., Barfield, B.J., Hayes, J.C.: Design Hydrology and Sedimentology for Small Catchments. Elsevier, Amsterdam (1994)

Heidari, A.: Flood vulnerability of the Karun river system and short-term mitigation measures. Flood Risk Manage. **7**, 65–80 (2014)

Jahangir, M.H., Mousavi Reineh, S.M., Abolghasemi, M.: Spatial predication of flood zonation mapping in Kan River basin, Iran, using artificial neural network algorithm. Weather Clim. Extrem. **25**, 100215 (2019). https://doi.org/10.1016/j.wace.2019.100215

Kazakis, N., Kougias, I., Patsialis, T.: Assessment of flood hazard areas at a regional scale using an index-based approach and analytical hierarchy process: application in Rhodope-Evros region, Greece. Sci. Total Environ. **538**, 555–563 (2015)

Khosravi, K., Pourghasemi, H.R., Chapi, K., Bahri, M.: Flash flood susceptibility analysis and its mapping using different bivariate models in Iran: a comparison between Shannon's entropy, statistical index, and weighting factor models. Environ. Monit. Assess. **188**(12), 1–21 (2016). https://doi.org/10.1007/s10661-016-5665-9

Kia, M.B., et al.: An artificial neural network model for flood simulation using GIS: Johor River basin Malaysia. Environ. Earth Sci. **67**, 251–264 (2011). https://doi.org/10.1007/s12665-011-1504-z(ISSN1866-6280)

Kourgialas, N.N., Karatzas, G.P.: Flood management and a GIS modeling method to assess flood-hazard areas: a case study. Hydrol. Sci. J. **56**(2), 212–225 (2011). https://doi.org/10. 1080/02626667.2011.555836(ISSN0262-6667)

Kowalzig, J.: Climate, poverty, and justice: what the Poznań UN climate conference needs to deliver for a fair and effective global deal. Oxfam Policy Prac. Clim. Change Resilience **4**(3), 117–148 (2008)

Liuzzo, L., Sammartano, V., Freni, G.: Comparison between different distributed methods for flood susceptibility mapping. Water Resour. Manage. **33**(9), 3155–3173 (2019). https://doi. org/10.1007/s11269-019-02293-w

Marchand, M., Buurman, J., Pribadi, A., Kurniawan, A.: Damage and casualties modeling as part of a vulnerability assessment for tsunami hazards: a case study from Aceh. Indonesia. Flood Risk Manage. **2**, 120–131 (2009)

Melton, M.A.: An analysis of the relations among elements of climate, surface properties, and geomorphology. DTIC document (1957)

Ministry of Water Resources (MoWR): Water sector development progamme 2002–2016, Main Report, vol. 2. Ministry of Water Resources, Federal Democratic Republic of Ethiopia, Addis Ababa, October 2002

Negash Wagesho Catchment dynamics and its impact on runoff generation: Coupling watershed modelling and statistical analysis to detect catchment responses. International Journal of Water Resources and Environmental Engineering Vol. **6**(2), 73–87 (2014)

Nyarko, B.K.: Application of a rational model in GIS for flood risk assessment in Accra . J. Spatial Hydrol. **2**(1), 1–14 (2002)

Oikonomidis, D., Dimogianni, S., Kazakis, N., Voudouris, K.: A GIS/remote sensing based methodology for groundwater potentiality assessment in Tirnavos area. Greece. J. Hydrol. **525**, 197–208 (2015)

Pappenberger, F., Beven, K., Horritt, M., Blazkova, S.: Uncertainty in the calibration of effective roughness parameters in HEC-RAS using inundation and downstream level observations. J. Hydrol. **302**(1–4), 46–69 (2005)

Pradhan, B., Youssef, A.: A 100-year maximum flood susceptibility mapping using integrated hydrological and hydrodynamic models: Kelantan River Corridor Malaysia. Flood Risk Manage. **4**, 189–202 (2011)

Girma, R., Gebre, E., Tadesse, T.: Land suitability evaluation for surface irrigation using spatial information technology in Omo-Gibe river basin, Southern Ethiopia. Irrig. Drainage Sys. Eng. **9**, 245 (2020). https://doi.org/10.37421/IDSE.2020.9.245

Saaty, T.L.: A scaling method for priorities in hierarchical structures. J. Math. Psychol. **15**, 234–281 (1977)

Saaty, T.L.: How to make a decision: the analytic hierarchy process (1990). (ISSN 03772217)

Saaty, T.L.: An exposition of the AHP in reply to the paper remarks on the analytic hierarchy process. Manage. Sci. **36**(3), 259–268 (1990)

Soil Conservation Service (SCS): Section 4: hydrology, US National Engineering Handbook, US Department of Agriculture, Washington (1972)

Taylor, J., Davies, M., Clifton, D., Ridley, I., Biddulph, P.: Flood management: prediction of microbial contamination in largescale floods in urban environments. Environ Int. **37**, 1019–1029 (2011)

Tehrany, M.S., Pradhan, B., Jebur, M.N.: Spatial prediction of flood susceptible areas using rule based decision tree (DT) and a novel ensemble bivariate and multivariate statistical models in GIS. J. Hydrol. **504**, 69–79 (2013). https://doi.org/10.1016/j.jhydrol.2013.09.034 (ISSN00221694)

Tehrany, M.S., Pradhan, B., Jebur, M.N.: Flood susceptibility mapping using a novel ensemble weights-of-evidence and support vector machine models in GIS. J. Hydrol. **512**, 332–343 (2014). https://doi.org/10.1016/j.jhydrol.2014.03.008(ISSN00221694)

Tenalem Ayenew (1998). The hydrogeological system of the Lake district basin, Ethiopia, Unpub. Ph.D. Thesis, ITC, Enschede, The Netherlands, 259p.

Tsakiris, G. Flood risk assessment: Concepts, modelling, applications. Nat. Hazards Earth Syst. **14**, 1361–1369 (2014)

Ullah, K., Zhang, J.: GIS-based flood hazard mapping using relative frequency ratio method: a case study of Panjkora river basin, eastern Hindu Kush, Pakistan. Plos one **15**(3), e0229153 (2020)

Valle Junior, R.F., Varandas, S.G.P., Sanches Fernandes, L.F., Pacheco, F.A.L.: Environmental land use conflicts: a threat to soil conservation. Land Use Policy **41**, 172–185 (2014)

Vorogushyn, S., Lindenschmidt, K.E., Kreibich, H., Apel, H., Merz, B.: Analysis of a detention basin impact on dike failure probabilities and flood risk for a channeldikefloodplain system along the river Elbe Germany. J. Hydrol. **436**, 120–131 (2012)

Wang, Y., Li, Z., Tang, Z., Zeng, G.: A GIS-based spatial multi-criteria approach for flood risk assessment in the Dongting lake region, Hunan Central China. Water Resour. Manage. **25** (13), 3465–3484 (2011). https://doi.org/10.1007/s11269-011-9866-2(ISSN09204741)

Worqlul, A.W., Collick, A.S., Rossiter, D.G., Langan, S., Steenhuis, T.S.: Assessment of surface water irrigation potential in the Ethiopian highlands: the Lake Tana Basin. CATENA **129**, 76–85 (2015)

Yahaya, S., Ahmad, N., Abdalla, R.F.: Multi-criteria analysis for flood vulnerable areas in Hadejia Jama'are River basin Nigeria. Eur. J. Sci. Res. **42**, 71–83 (2010)

Torsional Behavior of Steel Fiber Reinforced Concrete: A Review

Esmael A. Asfaw[1(✉)], Temesgen W. Aure[2],
and Alemayehu G. Gualu[3]

[1] School of Civil and Water Resources Engineering, Woldia Institute
of Technology, Woldia University, Woldia, Ethiopia
[2] College of Architecture and Civil Engineering, Addis Ababa Science
and Technology University, Addis Ababa, Ethiopia
[3] Faculty of Civil and Water Resources Engineering, Bahir Dar Institute
of Technology, Bahir Dar University, Bahir Dar, Ethiopia

Abstract. Steel fiber improves the strength, ductility (post-peak ductility), and energy absorption capacity of concrete. Despite of its numerous advantages, application of steel fiber in structural members like beam, column and elevated slabs is still in its early stage. In a structural member where complexity of loading is prevailed due to many reasons, torsional or twisting load avail itself either with other loads like shear and flexure or dominantly by itself called pure torsion. Failure of torsion of concrete on the post cracking stage can be predicted by the skew bending or space truss analogy and it is reliant on the tensile strength of the concrete and its ductility which in turn concrete is lack of. Therefore, with the advancement of technology addition of fiber (i.e. that is well known by its crack arresting behavior) in concrete gives an advantage on concretes inability. The improvement degree of steel fiber in concrete is also affected by concrete strength, fiber type, volumetric ratio, and fiber aspect ratio. Thus, this paper provides a summary of the properties of steel fiber reinforced concrete subjected to a twisting loading and gives a recommendation on areas that yet need further investigation.

Keywords: Torsion · Steel fiber · Matrix strength · Aspect ratio · Volumetric ratio · Reinforcement · Failure

1 Introduction

Torsion or twisting or torque is a moment acting about the longitudinal axis of a member caused predominantly by eccentric loading (i.e. equilibrium torsion or statically determinate torsion) and deformation compatibility due to continuity (i.e. compatibility torsion or statically indeterminate torsion) in a structural member like beams Wight and MacGregor [1].

Torsional load does not attract the consideration of most designers like its associated axial, shear, and flexural properties unless this particular property comes up with dominant effect. Eventually in the current design codes of concrete structures a strict consideration of torsion effect is followed [2]. The main reason for that is probably its

© ICST Institute for Computer Sciences, Social Informatics and Telecommunications Engineering 2022
Published by Springer Nature Switzerland AG 2022. All Rights Reserved
M. L. Berihun (Ed.): ICAST 2021, LNICST 412, pp. 195–208, 2022.
https://doi.org/10.1007/978-3-030-93712-6_13

complex nature that the effect it could make when it combines with axial, shear and flexure effect and also the arrangement of structural system.

Torsional load seldom act alone (i.e. pure torsion) and are almost always simultaneous with bending moments, transverse shear [1] and sometimes with axial force in column even if the pure torsion effect that is categorized under equilibrium torsion is the apprehension of this review. Twisting moment can occur in curved bridge girder, spandrel beams, spiral stairways, balcony girders, asymmetrical structure subjected to earthquakes and shells.

1.1   Material and Its Effect on Concrete Structures

From the point that concretes wide applicability in the construction industry, researchers devote to avoid its salient weakness (i.e. tensile strength and ductility). With this objective in mind utilization of fibers in general was seen as one alternative. By far steel fiber is the most widely used type in the fiber application and in research areas that devoted for triggering fibers in the structural application [1, 3, 4]. The reason for that is probably its recognized compatibility with the concrete matrix and its attributed intrinsic properties that support its reinforcing effectiveness such as tensile strength, durability, and elongation [5] other than the opposing fiber types (synthetic, natural and glass fibers).

Steel fibers in the current construction industry are performance oriented than that of its late 1970s uniform and straight steel fiber type that is produced mainly by cutting a wire or by cutting thin low strength sheet materials. The current steel fibers produced from either wire, sheet, or bulk raw materials incorporating surface deformation like surface roughening, surface indentation and crimping other than straight fiber profile to improve pullout resistance, and enhanced anchorage effect by hook or enlargement of fiber ends [5].

Bentur and Mindess [6] stipulate due to the fact fibers are short, discontinuous, and randomly distributed through the matrix, they are not sufficient to endure the tensile stress alone. However, their closeness in distribution over the concrete matrix than the conventional reinforced bars make them better at arresting cracking which is mainly by transmitting force between cracks. Accordingly, the conventional reinforcement bar is thus used for the improvement of the load-bearing capacity of the concrete section while the fibers are more effective at controlling crack.

Though, in the case of High-performance fiber reinforced concrete (HPFRC) having a strain hardening behavior owing to the high percentage of fiber volume, fibers may reasonably improve ductility, energy absorption, impact resistance, fatigue and abrasion resistance with a significant additional enhancement in strength. In HPFRC, the cracking strength of the composites and the post cracking strength are a key parameter that determines its hardening behavior. Whereas the cracking strength is mostly dependent on the strength of the matrix, the post cracking strength is reliant on the fiber reinforcement and the fiber to matrix interaction or interface bond [7].

Conventional FRC provides post cracking ductility, they are a strain-softening material with a significant improvement in tensile strength of plain concrete matrix that is dependent on matrix strength, volume fraction, aspect ratio, the tensile strength of fiber, fiber modulus, fiber surface bonding and aggregate size [8].

Fiber dosage and length or aspect ratio in general in a particular mix is dependent on fiber type and target performance. However, practical consideration aimed at the application of steel fibers for satisfactory workability intended for consolidation, effortlessness of placement and finishing without much effort providing uniform distribution of fiber (avoiding balling or bundling effect) without segregation and bleeding limit the range of volume of fraction of steel fiber in structural application to be 1.5% [1, 8]. The usual diameter and length range of steel fiber is 0.25 to 1 mm and 12 mm to 70 mm respectively (see ACI Committee 544 [8]).

Despite of the fact that fibers are not introduced in national building standard codes, their application in the construction industry mostly with the conventional concrete reinforcement (reinforcing bars and prestressing tendons) mainly in Europe and United States of America is promising. Because of their flexibility in the method of fabrication, economy, random distribution over the mix, discreteness or smallness in size and their improved strength character, makes them viable for any application. For example, in slabs on grade, mining, tunneling, and excavation support applications, steel and synthetic fiber reinforced concrete and shotcrete are the lists of application [8].

1.2   Research Significance

Steel fiber addition in a concrete matrix improves the mechanical behavior of the member including principal enrichment in ductility, durability, improved energy absorption and reduction of crack width. In addition, the steel fibers delay the formation of crack by controlling the crack opening process in which that leads to a distributed crack pattern that is characterized by a closely spaced crack. The literature reviewed in this study expected to add insight about the increase of resistance of concrete to torsional stress with the addition of different percentages of steel fibers. Consequently, the significance, besides moves further to the practical world (working sites) by revealing the main behavior of the addition of steel fiber for torsion prone member (beams, helical stair, spandrel, slabs, and shell) in the structural application.

2   Failure and Analysis Highlight

To idealize failure pattern and or for designing of concrete member under torsion the "skew bending theory" and the "thin-walled tube or plastic space truss model" approaches are widely known in most design codes. However, the latter that is easy for visualization and simpler in calculation procedure than the skew bending theory is used in the current European design code (EC-2) and American concrete design code (ACI-318) [1, 9].

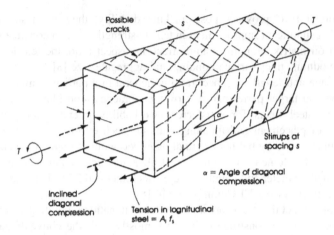

Fig. 1. Failure in space truss analogy [10].

The space truss model analysis is based on an equivalent tubular member, since test data confirms after the torsional crack occurs in a member, the central cross-sectional region of a member has no significant effect on torsional strength [1]. Thus, shear stressed (i.e. shear flow) in this case is assumed to be constant over a tubular thickness and resist the applied torsion. The analysis procedure is clearly depicted in Wight and MacGregor [1], McCormac and Brown [2], Hassoun and Al-Manaseer [10] and others (see Fig. 1).

The approach of the skew bending theory is that failure of member assumed to by bending accompanied with torsion on a skew surface (plane) that is 45° inclined and crack spiral around the sides of the member (see Fig. 2) [1, 10]. Failure or angle of failure for steel fiber is confirmed similar to that of the concrete as explained herein in a skew axis parallel to the long face of beam [11] except the modified skew bending analysis proposed in Mansur and Paramasivam [4] work overestimate the torsional capacity. The failure modes in this case are [9];

- The mode I (dominant positive flexural moment) failure; has a compression zone at the top face and failure is case by yielding of bottom longitudinal reinforcement and transverse reinforcement along the three remaining faces.
- The mode II (dominant torsional shear) failure; has a compression zone along a side face and failure is caused by yielding of the longitudinal reinforcement on the opposite side face and in the transverse reinforcement along the three face in tension.
- The mode III (dominant negative flexural moment); has a compression zone along the bottom side and failure is opposite of mode I failure type.

Combined action (torsion, bending, and shear) phenomenon with the pure torsion of hooked steel fiber shows a skewed bending failure (i.e. failure mode 1 and 2), where a spiral crack along the three faces of the beam is noticed [12].

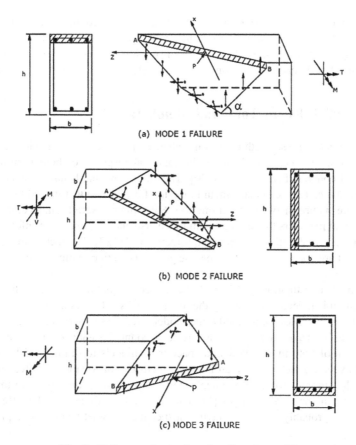

(a) MODE 1 FAILURE

(b) MODE 2 FAILURE

(c) MODE 3 FAILURE

Fig. 2. Failure modes in skew bending theory [9].

Laboratory investigation on capturing the elastic stage or pre-cracking stage up to the first cracking where reinforcement steel has a negligible effect on torsional response and the post cracking behavior is examined by Chalioris [13] through utilization of two analysis techniques for the pre and post cracking stages namely by smeared cracking approach [14, 15] and the softened truss model [16, 17] respectively. The analysis result shows a good agreement with the tested 15 reinforced concrete beams in initial torsional stiffness, ultimate torsional strength, and cracking torque moment. This is significant because it highlights that the softened truss model can capture the post cracking stages where a structure's ultimate carrying capacity is established.

It is similarly described (space truss model) can be used for the case of SFRC under pure torsion [18] which surprisingly confirmed in the earlier analytical and experimental study of Mansur, Nagataki [19] by considering a simplified tensile stress-strain relationship of steel fiber on Hsu and Mo [16] softened truss model of concrete.

3   Effect of SFRC in Torsional Members

The increase in tensile strength or overall enhanced post cracking behavior of concrete due to addition of steel fiber benefits the torsional response of both reinforced and unreinforced concrete beams [11, 18–20]. The crack arresting behavior as boldly said before contributes for the enhancement in torsion for concrete that is well known by its brittle failure nature in twisting actions too. Steel fibers overall enhancement begins from adding in members that contain both transverse and longitudinal reinforcement up to replacing especially the transverse reinforcement [21, 22]. The factors that affect the enhancement are concrete grade or type, the geometry of fiber, volume fraction of fiber, aspect ratio, and cross section type [22].

Analytical investigation of SFRC beam under torsion was studied affirming torsional strength is indeed enhanced by the inclusion of steel fibers in concrete beams [4, 12, 18, 19, 23, 24]. Most importantly, the models were based upon modification of the tensile strength characteristics of concrete to account the enhancement gained from fiber addition of both in the skew and space truss models recommended for concrete beams. However, a lack of standardized test methods for torsion of SFRC gives different results among several experiments starting from no enhancement up to a 100% improvement in torsional strength [6]. The reason for this as stated in Bentur and Mindess [6] is probably the difference in test specimen geometry and testing procedure.

3.1   Concrete or Matrix Strength

The concrete grade that determines the matrix strength, stiffness and most importantly, the fiber-matrix bondage also assessed in different literature for torsional behavior. Rao and Seshu [11] exploit four different grades of concrete (20, 30, 40 and 50 MPa) with fiber contents that stretch up to 1.2% (i.e. F4) at a 0.3% increasing interval. Though, the grades of concrete are under the class of normal strength concrete (NSC) a significant difference in the improvement of both strength and ductility was noticed as shown in the Fig. 3. In their study, the higher concrete grade that is 50 MPa shows a higher improvement in ultimate torque, ductility (twist angle), initial torsional stiffness and torsional toughness (i.e. from the area of torque twist curve).

Lightweight concrete and normal weight concrete effect was studied by Yap, Khaw [25] considering three fiber aspect ratios (55, 65 and 80) with an identical steel fiber volume ratio of 0.5%. Compared to the normal weight concrete matrix, light weight concrete shows more significant enhancement due to the addition of steel fiber in torsional ductility and torsional toughness (see Fig. 4). The cracking torque, ultimate torque, ultimate twist, twist at failure and torsional toughness of lightweight steel fiber reinforced concrete increased by 56%, 56%, 54%, 25% and 125% respectively when it is compared to the control lightweight concrete specimen.

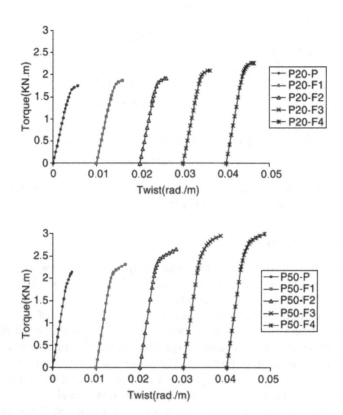

Fig. 3. Torque Twist response of 20 MPa and 50 MPa plain concrete beam series [11].

In other study by Fehling and Ismail [26], Fehling, Ismail [27] ultra-high performance concrete having a cylindrical compressive strength of 200 MPa shows an effective load carrying mechanism at a lower fiber volume ratio (0.9%) unlike the NSC. A similar study by Yang, Joh [28] that utilizes an ultra-high performance concrete (i.e. compressive strength greater than 150 MPa) confirms an improvement is noticed as fiber volume fraction increases. This is may be due to the fact that the increase in brittle nature of the concrete as the concrete grade hereto called matrix strength increases.

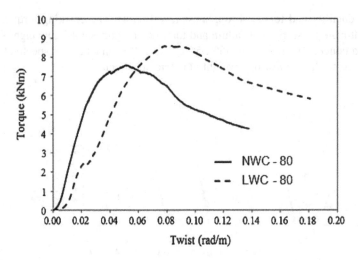

Fig. 4. Comparison between Normal strength concrete (NSC) and Light weight concrete (LWC) containing 80 aspect ratio steel fiber [25]

3.2 Fiber Aspect Ratio

Steel fiber length which is dominantly known by the aspect ratio (fiber length to diameter ratio) has a direct relation with strength of FRC as it symbolizes the pull-out characteristic of a fiber from the matrix. In a torsion induced beam the aspect ratio has a crucial part to perform like its pull-out behavior under a tensile load.

An investigation has been made on this respect by considering small fiber length (30 mm length and 0.5 mm diameter), large fiber length (50 mm length and 0.5 mm diameter), and combination of both [20]. The investigation detected that a small fiber length is not able to surpass both large length fiber and the combination of small and large length fiber in ultimate torque capacity and rotational capability.

Most importantly Mansur and Paramasivam [4] confirmed the reason of the increase in torsional strength as the fiber aspect ratio increase is due to the fact that longer fiber can develop an interfacial bond stress. As the length increase friction is enhanced between the matrix and the fiber, the bond is therefore increased and finally a good strength improvement is handy. But tests on this regard unlike fiber content are still limited. The fundamental cause possibly is as the aspect ratio and volume fraction increases the workability become uncertain for the FRC mix.

3.3 Fiber Volume Ratio

The volume fraction addition clearly shows an effect on the behavior of a steel fiber reinforced concrete. In the analytical study of Ju, Kim [23] the experiment undertaken for 1.5% and 2.0% volume fraction of steel fiber creates 54% and 81% increase in torsional strength. On another study [11] having a fiber volume fraction of 0.3, 0.6, 0.9 and 1.2% with a beam dimension of $100 \times 200 \times 2000$ mm an improvement in torsional strength that is led from an increased tensile strength, ultimate torque, torsional toughness and torsional stiffness is confirmed.

However, the question that should be raised here is how much percentage does it needs to promote a significant enhancement in the overall twisting behavior of a beam. ACI Committee 544 [29] emphasizes 1.2% by volume of fiber cannot show a multi-tracking behavior. But the paper underlines (i.e. ACI Committee 544) improvements in ductility were possible at a dosage of 0.9% where sudden brittle separation of beam is avoided. This argument is also supported by Rao and Seshu [11] even though around 88% increase in angle of twist for the 50 MPa concrete grade (that is the maximum concrete grade of all the examined) with a 0.6% of fiber is noticed where a matrix strength illustrates its effect on the decision of the fiber dosage (see Fig. 3).

For the case of multitracking behavior contrasting ACI Committee report current research [18] on reinforced concrete with and without fiber proves the possibility to see a small crack localization at a percentage of steel fiber of 30 kg/m^3 (i.e. around 0.4% volume fraction) that is below 1.2% (see Fig. 5). This is worth noting as it clarifies even at a considerably lower amount of dosage improvements can be able to captured in the structural performance of the beam.

In another similar study by Facconi, Minelli [30], a longitudinally reinforced beam sample with a volume fraction of 25 kg/m^3 (i.e. 0.32%) and a fiber aspect ratio of 86 (i.e. having a length of 30 mm and diameter of 0.35) shows an increase in torsional strength of 10% with an improved torsional toughness. In addition, the experiment unravels improved ductility that shows a stable fracture process characterized by a post peak softening in such a lower fiber volume fraction when it is compared to the sample without SF.

As a concluding remark, it is understood improvements are prevailed especially in ductility with a relatively lower fiber volume fraction in torsion. However, torsional strength improvement is not easily prevailed as the volume fraction reduces. The limiting fiber volume ratio for overall torsional behavior is not much advanced and needs further investigations. But from the standing point of workability or in general rheological properties of fiber reinforced concrete [31] this limitation may be taken. The usual limiting fiber content except the case of higher fiber dosage of SIFCON or SIMCON is in between 1.5% and 2.0% (see [8, 31] perhaps the later might need a small sized coarse aggregate or no coarse aggregate options to a high super plasticizing admixture to make a slurry of flowing concrete.

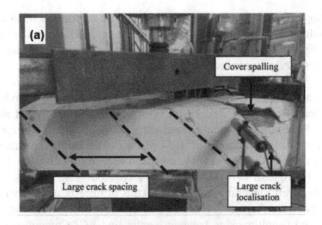

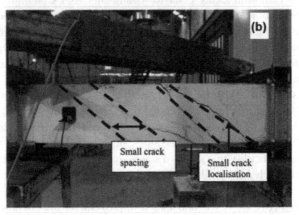

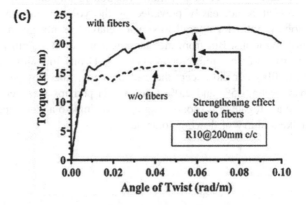

Fig. 5. Failure mechanism of beam diameter 10@200 mm under pure torsion a) without fiber b) with 30 kg/m^3 fiber c) test result [18].

3.4   Steel Fiber as a Reinforcement Option

The proximate uniform distribution of steel fiber gives rise to several advantages over replacing or use in partial replacing with conventional reinforcement known as a hybrid system. The random distribution that is assumed to be uniform in the member at a closer spacing than the smaller diameter conventional reinforcing bar which cannot able to control smaller cracks that rise to a larger crack leads to reinforcement yielding, the fibers capability of increasing first cracking tensile strength and ultimate tensile strength of the member and shear friction strength is increased due to pull out behavior and crack bridging effect are the leading reasons that makes it viable [8].

In torsional load similar to other load type steel fibers effect begins to sought after the matrix crack commencement and thus the usual reinforcing effect starts at this stage [13]. Chalioris and Karayannis [22] investigated steel fiber as the alternative to replace shear torsional reinforcement considering 1% and 3% volumetric ratio of steel fiber. A comparison of the behavior of non-fibrous reinforced concrete having both longitudinal bar and stirrups with that of SFRC with longitudinal reinforcement of rectangular beam is described in Fig. 6. Under this investigation flanged and rectangular beam cross sections are used and the replacement of stirrup by fiber shows for rectangular beam (with torsional transverse reinforcement ratio of 0.63%) was efficient (see Fig. 6) than the flange beams.

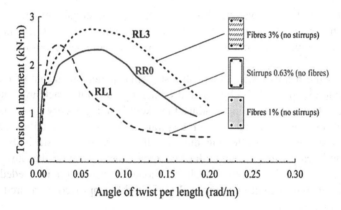

Fig. 6. Steel fiber as shear torsional reinforcement (stirrups) [22].

In another similar investigation both partial and full replacement of stirrups and longitudinal reinforcements are investigated by Narayanan and Kareem-Palanjian [21]. In this investigation the reinforcement ratio of longitudinal or transverse reinforcement (stirrups) is totally and partially replaced by the fiber volume fraction. A significance gain in ultimate strength is found in both the partial and full replacement of transverse reinforcement. Unlike the partial replacement of transverse reinforcement, the replacement of longitudinal reinforcement is not substantial since ductility is reduced [21].

In both of studies [21, 22] NSC is used for the investigations. However in another study [26, 27] ultra-high performance (UHPC) concrete matrix with 0.5 and 0.9% volume fraction is used to see the alternative of reinforcement replacement. This investigation disregards the ideology of the impossibility of longitudinal reinforcement replacement. But as a concluding remark usage of both transverse and longitudinal reinforcement with an appropriate volume percentage yields an outstanding performance in both of the pre and post cracking stages of twisting force.

Even though the experimental work of [21, 22] come up with a positive result a refined investigation and additional tests are needed to conclude its possibility. As that of shear reinforcement replacement discussed before [32] in the torsional stirrup case full replacement is not convenient because of fibers which fails mainly by pull out cannot bring the required ductility that can be provided by the conventional reinforcement stirrups were a great plastic deformation failure could appear [22]. Regarding the ductility behavior of fiber and stirrups, the area is still open for investigation in addition to the limited database of strength behavior.

4 Conclusion

Based on the findings of literatures discussed in the subsequent sections the following conclusions with a recommendation are drawn;

- Steel fiber reinforced concrete shows an improved torsional strength and ductility even if the pre-cracking stage effect of steel fiber reinforced concrete is negligible in a relatively lower percentage volume of fiber (i.e. volumetric ratio less than 2 or 3%).
- Failure of the beams tested shows almost similar pattern with that of normal concrete beam except in fiber addition multi cracking due to its crack arresting attribute was seen. In torsion-bending loading the skew bending theory holds and in pure torsional member the usual 45-degree spiral crack controls the failure pattern.
- Matrix strength is also affecting the overall performance of steel fiber and it is dominant in case when the strength of concrete matrix increases because brittleness increases. In addition, even though additional investigation is needed torsional response of light weight concrete (LWC) is highly improved compared to normal weight concrete (NWC).
- The possibility of fibers replacing concrete is promising except the steel cross sectional area, yield strength and combination of with high strength reinforcement needs further investigation.
- Furthermore, SFRC particularly SIFCON, SIMCON and ECC should be investigated for torsion to see if their strain hardening and ductility behavior can manifest.

References

1. Wight, J.K., MacGregor, J.G.: Reinforced Concrete: Mechanics and Design, 6th edn. Pearson Education Inc., Upper Saddle River (2012)
2. McCormac, J.C., Brown, R.H.: Design of Reinforced Concrete, 9th edn. Wiley, Hoboken (2014)
3. Löfgren, I.: Fibre-reinforced concrete for industrial construction - a fracture mechanics approach to material testing and structural analysis, Ph.D. Dissertation in Civil and Environmental Engineering (Structural Engineering), Chalmers University of Technology, Göteborg, Sweden (2005)
4. Mansur, M.A., Paramasivam, P.: Steel fibre reinforced concrete beams in pure torsion. Int. J. Cem. Compos. Lightweight Concrete 4(1), 39–45 (1982)
5. Johnston, C.D.: Fiber-reinforced cements and concretes. In: Malhotra, V.M. (ed.) Advances in Concrete Technology, vol. 3. Taylor & Francis, Madison Ave, New York (2010)
6. Bentur, A., Mindess, S.: Fibre Reinforced Cementitious Composites, 2nd edn. Taylor & Francis, Wiltshire (2007)
7. Naaman, A.E.: Fiber reinforcement for concrete: looking back, looking ahead. In: Fifth International RILEM Symposium on Fibre-Reinforced Concrete (FRC). RILEM Publications SARL (2000)
8. ACI Committee 544: Report on fiber reinforced concrete, in ACI 544.1R-96, American Concrete Institute, Farmington Hills, MI. (2009)
9. ACI Committee 445: Report on torsion in structural concrete, in Joint ACI-ASCE Committee 445 (ACI 445.1R-12), American Concrete Institute, Farmington Hills, MI (2013)
10. Hassoun, M.N., Al-Manaseer, A.: Structural Concrete: Theory and Design, 4th edn. Wiley, Hoboken (2008)
11. Rao, T.D.G., Seshu, D.R.: Torsion of steel fiber reinforced concrete members. Cem. Concr. Res. 33, 1783–1788 (2003)
12. Mansur, M.A., Paramasivam, P.: Fiber reinforced concrete beams in torsion, bending, and shear. ACI J. 82(2), 33–39 (1985)
13. Chalioris, C.E.: Behaviour model and experimental study for the torsion of reinforced concrete members. In: 3rd International Conference on High Performance Structures and Materials (HPSM 2006). WIT Press, Ostend, Belgium (2006)
14. Karayannis, C.G.: Smeared crack analysis for plain concrete in torsion. J. Struct. Eng. ASCE 126(6), 638–645 (2000)
15. Karayannis, C.G., Chalioris, C.E.: Experimental validation of smeared analysis for plain concrete in torsion. J. Struct. Eng. ASCE 126(6), 646–653 (2000)
16. Hsu, T.T.C., Mo, Y.L.: Softening of concrete in torsional members – theory and tests. ACI J. 82(3), 290–303 (1985)
17. Hsu, T.T.C.: Toward a unified nomenclature for reinforced-concrete theory. J. Struct. Eng. ASCE 122(3), 275–283 (1996)
18. Amin, A., Bentz, E. C.: Strength of steel fiber reinforced concrete beams in pure torsion. Struct. Concr. 19(3), 684–694 (2018)
19. Mansur, M.A., Nagataki, S., Lee, S.H., Oosumimoto, Y.: Torsional response of reinforced fibrous concrete beams. ACI Struct. J. 86(1), 36–44 (1989)
20. Craig, R.J., Parr, J.A., Germain, E., Mosquera, V., Kamilares, S.: Fiber reinforced beams in torsion. ACI J. 83(6), 934–942 (1986)
21. Narayanan, R., Kareem-Palanjian, A.S.: Torsion in beams reinforced with bars and fibers. J. Struct. Eng. 112(1), 53–66 (1986)

22. Chalioris, C.E., Karayannis, C.G.: Effectiveness of the use of steel fibres on the torsional behaviour of flanged concrete beams. Cement Concr. Compos. **31**, 331–341 (2009)
23. Ju, H., Kim, K.S., Lee, D.H., Hwang, J.-H., Choi, S.-H., Oh, Y.-H.: Torsional responses of steel fiber-reinforced concrete members. Compos. Struct. **129**, 143–156 (2015)
24. Ju, H., Lee, D.H., Hwang, J.-H., Kang, J.-W., Kim, K.S., Oh, Y.-H.: Torsional behavior model of steel-fiber-reinforced concrete members modifying fixed-angle softened-truss model. Compos. Part B, **45**, 215–231 (2013)
25. Yap, S.P., Khaw, K.R., Alengaram, U.J., Jumaat, M.Z.: Effect of fibre aspect ratio on the torsional behaviour of steel fibre-reinforced normal weight concrete and lightweight concrete. Eng. Struct. **101**, 24–33 (2015)
26. Fehling, E., Ismail, M.: Experimental investigations on UHPC structural elements subject to pure torsion. In: Ultra-high Performance Concrete and Nanotechnology in Construction, Kassel University Press, Kassel, Germany (2012)
27. Fehling, E., Ismail, M., Leutbecher, T.: Experimental tests and analytical modeling of UHPC beams subjected to torsion. In: Zingoni, A. (ed.) The Fifth International Conference on Structural Engineering, Mechanics and Computation, pp. 1673–1678. Taylor & Francis Group, Cape Town, South Africa (2013)
28. Yang, I.-H., Joh, C., Lee, J.W., Kim, B.-S.: Torsional behavior of ultra-high performance concrete squared beams. Eng. Struct. **56**, 372–383 (2013)
29. ACI Committee 544: Report on measuring mechanical properties of hardened fiber-reinforced concrete, in ACI 544.9R-17. American Concrete Institute, Farmington Hills, MI (2017)
30. Facconi, L., Minelli, F., Plizzari, G.A., Ceresa, P.: Experimental study on steel fiber reinforced concrete beams in pure torsion. In: FIB Symposium 2019 "Concrete - Innovations in Materials, Design and Structures", Krakow, Poland (2019)
31. ACI Committee 544: Guide for specifying, proportioning, and production of fiber-reinforced concrete, in ACI 544.3R-08, American Concrete Institute, Farmington Hills, MI (2008)
32. Cucchiara, C., Mendola, L.L., Papia, M.: Effectiveness of stirrups and steel fibres as shear reinforcement. Cement Concr. Compos. **26**, 777–786 (2004)

Mechanical and Industrial Engineering

Performance Analysis of Cotton Seed Biodiesel in Diesel Vehicle on Chassis Dynamometer

Marta Zeleke[1]([⊠]) and Ramesh Babu Nallamothu[2]

[1] Mechanical Engineering Department, University of Gondar, Gondar, Ethiopia
marta.zeleke@uog.edu.et
[2] Mechanical Systems and Vehicle Engineering Department,
Adama Science and Technology University, Adama, Ethiopia
ramesh.babu@astu.edu.et

Abstract. There is a need to identify alternative fuels suitable for running diesel engine as a replacement of diesel to address the problems like depletion of fossil fuel reserves and environmental pollution. The fuels derived from bio-resources found to be good alternatives for conventional petro-fuels in solving such issues. The impact of cotton seed oil biodiesel blend on vehicle performance with four stroke four cylinder diesel engine was investigated. Emission test was performed on six cylinder engine vehicle using 100% diesel of petroleum origin (fossil diesel), and B10, B20, B30 of cottonseed oil methyl ester. Analysis was carried out on major performance parameters P_b, T_b, bsfc & emissions such as NOx, CO, CO_2, O_2 and HC. It is observed that Blends of biodiesel B10, B20 & B30 reduced brake torque by 5%, 7% & 12%, also reduced brake power by 6%, 8% & 11% and increased in fuel consumption by 4%, 8% & 20% respectively. However, the emissions of the CI engine running on three biodiesel blends were reduced, CO by up to 16%, CO_2 by 17% and HC by 12% & increase NOx by 14% & O_2 by 18% as compared to diesel fuel. It is concluded that blend of 20% cotton seed biodiesel can be used in an unmodified diesel engine.

Keywords: Biodiesel · Blends · Performance and emission · Transesterification

1 Introduction

The issue of extinction of fossil fuel reserves due to higher rate of usage in daily life became a focal attention of most of the people in the world who are very much dependent on fossil fuels to meet their daily energy needs. Air pollution thereby health problems and global warming issues which are caused by continuous burning of fossil fuels is another issue attracting the attention of the engineers and scientists. The harmful emissions from the vehicles of the transportation sector, which are contributing much of the environmental pollution, must be controlled [1]. The available reserves of fossil fuels in the world are observed to be unsustainable and declining day by day. For solving these problems, it became a priority issue for automotive industries and researchers to explore the ways of replacing or minimizing the usage of fossil fuels by identifying the fuels which are ecofriendly, economical, sustainable and renewable [2]. Biodiesels which are derived from bio origin (vegetable oils, fat) are observed to be better

© ICST Institute for Computer Sciences, Social Informatics and Telecommunications Engineering 2022
Published by Springer Nature Switzerland AG 2022. All Rights Reserved
M. L. Berihun (Ed.): ICAST 2021, LNICST 412, pp. 211–225, 2022.
https://doi.org/10.1007/978-3-030-93712-6_14

alternative fuels, which can be used in CI engines without much modification to the engine. Biodiesels can be better replacement alternative fuels for conventional petroleum fossil fuels and reduce the dependency on fossil fuels. Biodiesels are nonpolluting, biodegradable, nonpoisonous, renewable and can be used in CI engines at any proportion by blending with conventional diesel [3]. Biodiesel is a mono-alkyl ester which is produced from long chain fatty acids present in animal fats and vegetable oils. Any type of vegetable oils like cotton, sunflower, jatropha etc. can be used for biodiesel production [4]. The problems of using vegetable oil as fuel in CI engines can be reduced by blending with diesel and engine life can be extended [5, 6]. The viscosity of the biodiesel is almost close to petro diesel. There is a inbuilt oxygen in biodiesels which is about 10–11% by weight. So the combustion of biodiesel in CI engine is better than conventional diesel which is hydrocarbon based [7].The methods like transesterification, blending, emulsification can be used for reducing the viscosity of vegetable oils [8]. Conversion of triglycerides to biodiesel is normally done by transesterification process which is a well-established procedure. In this process, mono alkyl ester is produced by allowing the reaction between light alcohol and triglycerides of vegetable oils in the presence of suitable catalyst. Potassium and Sodium hydroxides are found to be better catalysts for this purpose [9, 10]. But alkali catalysts are very much sensitive to free fatty acids and water, which is a limitation of this process [11]. Transesterification is generally carried out at 60 °C which is closer to the boiling point temperature of methanol. Alcohol to oil molar ratio of 5:1 is normally recommended [12].

2 Methodology

2.1 Materials

Table 1 shows the list of materials for biodiesel production.

Table 1. Materials used for biodiesel production.

No.	List of materials
1	Methanol
2	KOH
3	Cotton seed
4	Crude cotton seed oil
5	Distilled water

Crude cotton seed oil was extracted from expeller, Addis modjo edible oil complex company (i.e. screw pressed cottonseed oil) by mechanical pressing. Methanol and potassium hydroxide were obtained from an Agent of Yeshadam Chemicals trading plc in Addis Ababa. The laboratory facility available at Chemistry department of ASTU was used for chemical reaction process and blending process. Chassis dynamometer test rig available at automotive laboratory, ASTU and the facilities available at Maj General Mulugeta Buli technical college were used for conducting performance test.

Diesel fuel was purchased from fuel station, Adama. Here, it worth to note that measurements were taken at two different place because measuring instruments like chassis dynamometer and exhaust gas analyzer could not be found at a place.

2.2   Biodiesel Production

The following Fig. 1 shows the working flow for biodiesel production.

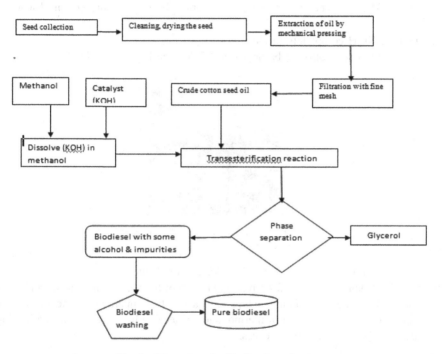

Fig. 1. Flow chart for biodiesel production

2.2.1   Transesterification of Cotton Seed Oil

The chemical reaction involves the reaction of triglycerides of cotton seed oil with methanol in the help of alkali catalyst KOH, producing ester and glycerol. In this process 5 g of potassium hydroxide was dissolved in 100 ml of methanol. The mixing ratio was taken as (the catalyst and alcohol quantity are 1% and 20% of oil respectively). Which is full dissolved for each sample of 500 ml of crude cotton seed oil.

1. Crude cotton seed oil (500 ml) was measured and poured in a flask per each sample.
2. For each sample, 100 ml of methanol and 5 gms of KOH were taken (see Fig. 2).

Fig. 2. Measuring the crude oil sample, measuring KOH and dissolving in methanol

3. Dissolve KOH completely in methanol.
4. Crude cotton seed oil is to be heated to 65 °C (see Fig. 3)

Fig. 3. Heating the crude oil

5. Methanol and KOH mixture is to be added to the heated oil.
6. Heat the dissolved mixture for 1 h at fixed temp of 65 °C, heating and stirring takes place at the same time continuously, and measure the temperature of the reactant for every 10 min with the help of thermometer. After one hour, switch off the heating mantel to stop the reaction process.

The products were kept for 24 h in separating funnel after transesterification process. There was a formation of two phases with different densities (Fig. 4).

Fig. 4. Two layers of oil formed.

In the two layers, glycerin exists in the lower layer and biodiesel, soap and alcohol exist in the upper layer. Soap may be formed due to side reactions. Glycerin is to be removed from the bottom of the funnel. The glycerin can be used to make soap (see Fig. 5).

Fig. 5. Biodiesel (left side), and glycerin and fatty acid (right side).

7. The ester is to be washed with warm water (at 55 °C) for removing the alcohol and catalyst (Fig. 6).
8. Repeat washing process six times until water is mostly clears (Fig. 7).

Fig. 6. Soap and impurities during washing process.

Fig. 7. Final washing step, water becomes clear and Biodiesel after washing process.

The biodiesel was dried by heating at a temperature of 100 °C for one hour using hot plate (Fig. 8).

Fig. 8. Heating, drying the biodiesel and collected biodiesel.

2.2.2   Characterization of Cotton Seed Biodiesel

Characterization is the process of determining physicochemical properties of petroleum products and non-petroleum products like biodiesel blends. Before testing the performance & emission of blend fuels it's very important to check physicochemical properties. The properties of the fuel include flash point, kinematic viscosity, cloud point, density, acid number, distillation range.

Fuel blends prepared for characterization are B 10, B 20, B 30 and B 100. To prepare B 10 blend fuel, 50 ml of cotton seed biodiesel mixed with 450 ml of diesel fuel to produce B 20, 100 ml of biodiesel & 400 ml diesel fuel mixed & for B 30 150 ml of biodiesel blend with 350 ml of diesel fuel. Properties of biodiesel was measured in ASTU, (UV spectroscopy & PH) in chemistry department) & other physical properties mentioned below are measured in Ethiopian petroleum supply enterprise (quality control laboratory).

2.2.3   Experimental Facilities for the Test

The experimental measurement of gaseous emissions was carried out on Maj. General Mulugetabuli technical college using a FGA- 4100 emission analyzer and on the Mercedes Benz truck vehicle at selected five engine speed (500, 1000, 1500, 2000, 2500 rpm). The performance measurements were carried out in the work shop of ASTU. The test was performed on 3 L Toyota vehicle using Sunroad–a-matic XII chassis dynamometer. On both cases the fuels used were diesel (no 2). This is used as a reference fuel and a blend of B10, B20, and B30. Baseline data was collected by running the engine with pure diesel. Then engine was run with blends of biodiesel and the data obtained was compared with the data of the pure diesel. After comparison better blend was identified.

Table 2 shows the vehicle specification for exhaust gas measurement, and Table 3 shows the vehicle specification for performance measurement.

Table 2. Vehicle specification for exhaust gas measurement

No.	Descriptions	Font size and style
1	Vehicle model	Mercedes Benz truck
2	Strokes	4
3	Cylinders	6
4	Transmission	Manual
5	Fuel	Diesel
6	Chassis	WDB 380013-15-339123
7	Engine number	3621880102
8	Cooling system	Water cooled

Table 3. Vehicle specification for performance measurement

No.	Description	Specifications
1	Engine	Toyota 3L-4122571
2	Strokes	4
3	Cylinders	4
4	Transmission	Manual
5	Fuel	Diesel
6	Chassis	LN 106-0136567

Figure 9 shows the chassis dynamometer and vehicle for performance test.

Fig. 9. Chassis dynamometer and vehicle for performance test.

2.2.4   Emission and Performance Test Procedure in Diesel Vehicle

The Emission gases test was performed on truck vehicle running the engine with no load conditions at different engine rpm connect the emission analyzer and keep it to warm up for 15 min then displays emission gases with respect to engine rpm. The performance test was performed by driving the vehicle with chassis dynamometer (sun Road-a-Matic XII) starting from 15 km/hr upto 75 km/hr in a interval of 10 km/hr. The parameters measured are wheel power (kW), tractive force (kN) and wheel power (kW). All four gears (1st, 2nd, 3rd and 4th) were used for test. The fuel consumption was measured by recording the time for the consumption of ten grams of fuel. By measuring the fuel consumption, torque and power at different speeds, the performance of the engine was evaluated. Experiments were conducted for pure diesel, and B 10, B 20 and B 30 biodiesel blend.

3   Result and Discussion

3.1   Oil Content from Extraction

Mechanical pressing was used to extract the crude oil from cotton seed. From 40 kg of cotton seed the yield of oil was 7 L which is 17.5% (v/wt.). Oil extraction by mechanical pressing is economical and time saving method.

3.2   Production of Biodiesel

From 7L of cotton seed oil biodiesel production yield was 5L which is 71.5% by performing transesterification process. The activities like glycerin separation, washing about six times with distilled water and drying by heating up to 100 °C for 1 h were performed.

Table 4 shows the transesterification process, and Table 5 shows the characterization of blended fuels.

Table 4. Transesterification process.

Amount of cottonseed oil (ml)	Molar ratio of alcohol	Catalyst (KOH) %	Alcohol (Methanol) in (ml)	KOH in (gm)	Reaction time in (minute)	Reaction temperature in (°C)	Settling time in (hr)
500	1:5	1.0	100	5.0	60	65	24

Table 5. Characterization of blended fuels.

No.	Property	B100	B10	B20	B30	ASTM method	ASTM 6751 standard
1	Density@15 °C, (g/cm³)	0.8911	0.8574	0.8611	0.8641	D4052	0.86–0.9
	Density@20 °C, (g/cm³)	0.8877	0.8539	0.8576	0.8613	D4052	
2	Cloud point, °C	+4	+1	+1	+1	D2500	As report
3	Flash point, °C	178	86	89	90	D93	Min 130
4	Distillation	–	–	–	–	D86	
	IBP, °C	320.0	193.5	196.5	165.5		
	10% volume, recovered °C	331.5	229.0	233.5	240.5		–
	40% volume, recovered °C	334.5	287.5	293.5	302.5		–
	50% volume, recovered °C	335.5	299.5	306.0	315.0		–
	90% volume, recovered °C	361.0	354.0	355.0	358.0		282–362 °C
	95% volume, recovered °C	363.0	367.0	358.0	368.0		–
	FBP, °C	363.0	369.0	363.0	369.0		Max 390 °C
5	Acid value (mg of KOH/gm)	0.06	0.02	0.04	0.05	D974	0.8 mg of KOH/gm
6	Kinematic viscosity@40 °C	5.9	–	–	–	D445	1.9–6 mm²/s
7	Cetane index	45.3	50.7	50.5	50.5	D976	Min 40 °C
8	UV spectrum (nm)	229	256	256	257		220–300
9	PH	6.85	7.00	6.99	6.99	6.85	Approx. to (neutral)

3.3   Results from Emission Test

Analyzed emissions in the present investigation are CO, NOx, O_2, CO_2 and HC. Figure 10 shows the influent of engine speed on CO emission.

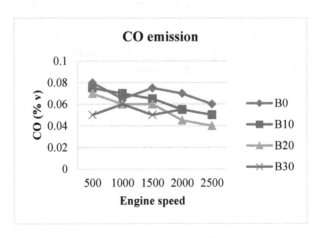

Fig. 10. Variation of CO

Figure 10 shows, CO emissions in the blends of the biodiesel is lower than that of the diesel due to the less carbon content in to the biodiesel blends. B10, B20 and B30 reduce CO emission by 7%, 13% and 16% compared with B0 fuel, respectively.

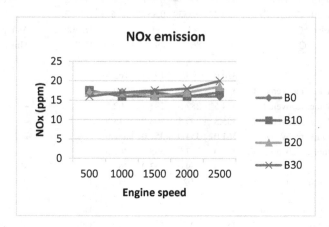

Fig. 11. NOx emission.

With increasing engine speed NOx observed to be increasing (Fig. 11). Three blend fuels increase NOx emission by 5%, 8%, 11% respectively. This can be due to higher oxygen content which lead to increased combustion temperature.

3.4   Vehicle Performance Test

The performance of diesel vehicle was tested using chassis dynamometer. The performance parameters like tractive force in (kN) and wheel power in (kW) were measured.

BrakePower(P_b) is an engine performance parameter. Brake power (Pb) is given by, $Pb = \frac{2\pi NT}{60}$ Where, T is torque in N-m and N is the speed in revolutions per minute & also we can express brake power as the following.

$$Pb = \frac{Pw}{\eta t} \tag{1}$$

Where; Pb is brake power, Pw is wheel power, and ηt is gear box efficiency (Fig. 12).

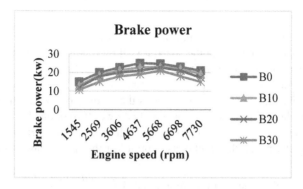

Fig. 12. Variation of brake power.

It can be seen that from the graph the biodiesel blend fuels produced lower Pb than diesel fuel. As the engine speed increasing brake power increasing until 5668 rpm and then starts to decrease. Biodiesel blend fuels B 10, B 20 and B 30 decreased Pb by 6%, 8% and 11% compared with diesel. It might be because of lower calorific value of biodiesel. Also, fuel consumption of blended fuels is more due to lower density of biodiesel.

Brake Torque (Tb) is the torque available at the 'output shaft' of the engine or at the 'Flywheel'.

$$Pb = \frac{2\pi NT}{60} \tag{2}$$

$$Tb = \frac{Pb}{\omega} = \frac{60 \times Pb}{2\pi N} \tag{3}$$

$$Tb = \frac{60 \times Pb \times 1000}{2\pi N}, Pb \text{ in kW}; N \text{ in rpm, and } Tb \text{ in Nm.}$$

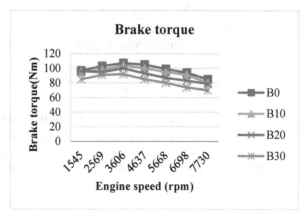

Fig. 13. Variation of brake torque.

Up to engine speed of 3606 rpm, brake torque observed to be increasing and then starts decreasing with increase in the speed for all fuels (Fig. 13). Diesel fuel produced more torque than the blends. It might be due to lower calorific value of the biodiesel. There is a reduction of 5%, 7% and 12%, respectively.

Brake specific fuel consumption (bsfc): is the amount of fuel consumed by engine in 'kilogram per hour (kg/h)' to develop a brake Power (Pb) of one kilowatt (kW) while running at a constant engine speed (N) in 'rpm'. It is an engine performance parameter which mainly determines, the 'fuel consumption' or the 'fuel economy' of the engine.

$$\text{Specific fuel consumption (sfc)} = \frac{mass\,flow\,rate}{Power} \tag{4}$$

$$Brake\,specific\,fuel\,consumption\,(bsfc) = \frac{\text{mass flow rate}}{Brake\,power} \tag{5}$$

The bsfc is given by the Eq. 6.

$$\text{bsfc}\left(\frac{gm}{kwhr}\right) = \frac{mf\left(\frac{gm}{se}\right) * 3600}{Pb} \tag{6}$$

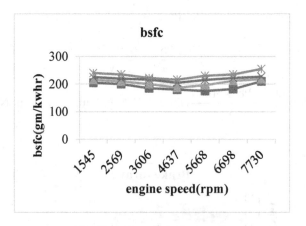

Fig. 14. bsfc with engine speed.

Figure 14 shows that diesel fuel had the lowest BSFC, but the BSFC increases as biodiesel increases in the blends. It is due to its higher viscosity, lower density may reduce fuel atomization and then due to this require large mass of fuel flow. The increased fuel consumptions for blend fuels are 4%, 8%, 20% respectively.

3.5   Engine Performance Curves for Diesel and Biodiesel Blend

Figures 15, 16, 17 and 18 shows the engine performance curve for B0, B10, B20 and B30, respectively.

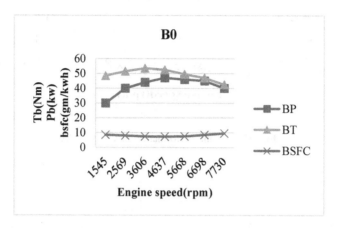

Fig. 15. Engine performance for B0.

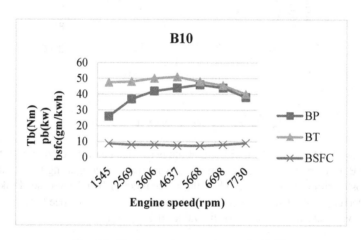

Fig. 16. Engine performance curve for B 10.

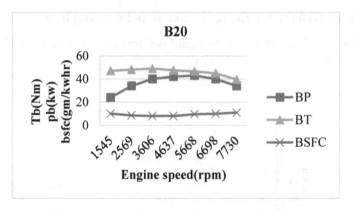

Fig. 17. Engine performance curve for B 20.

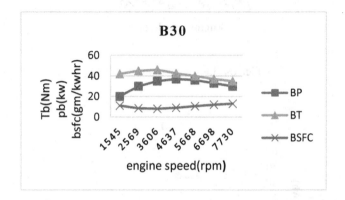

Fig. 18. Engine performance curve for B 30.

Figures 15, 16, 17 and 18 indicate that the performance of the engine with B0, B10, B20 and B30, respectively. The comparison was made by comparing the brake power, Tb and bsfc with engine speed. When the percentage of blend increases brake torque and Pb decreases and bsfc increases with the increase in engine speed. This is because of higher viscosity and lower calorific value of biodiesel.

4   Conclusions

Various experiments were conducted in this research work with the aim of testing performance and emission of cotton biodiesel in diesel vehicles. Pure biodiesel was not used because it is found that the viscosity of cotton biodiesel is higher than petro diesel. So, blends of biodiesel B10, B20 and B30 were used for testing. From the results, it is observed that performance of the engine when fueled with biodiesel blends is comparable to that when fueled with diesel. The bsfc when fueled with the biodiesel blend is observed to be higher than when fueled with petroleum diesel. The conclusions are summarized as follows.

1. Properties of cotton seed biodiesel and its blends conform to ASTM D6751 standards.
2. Torque and power performance gets reduced and fuel consumption increased as percentage of biodiesel in blends increase. It happens because of lower calorific value of the biodiesel compared to diesel.
3. The biodiesel blends producing lower emission with drop in CO, CO_2 and HC emission while NOx and O_2. Emissions are show a little increment compared to the conventional diesel. This is due to that biodiesel is a green fuel and contain less carbon molecules.
4. The results obtained in this work suggest that cotton seed biodiesel blend can be used in an unmodified diesel engine since their performance and emission characteristics were very close to that of diesel and it is environmental friendly with reduced emissions.

References

1. Rao, Y.V.H., Voleti, R.S., Raju, A.V.S., Reddy, P.N.: The effect of cottonseed oil methyl ester on the performance and exhaust emissions of a diesel Engine. Int. J. Ambient Energy **31**(4), 203–210 (2010)
2. Putrasaria, Y., Nura, A., Muharama, A.: Performance and emission characteristic on a two cylinder DI diesel engine fuelled with ethanol-diesel blends. Energy Procedia **32**, 21–30 (2013)
3. Atabani, A.E., et al.: Non-ediblevegetable oils: a critical evaluation of oil extraction, fatty acid compositions, biodiesel production, characteristics, engine performance and emissions production. Renew. Sustain Energy Rev. J. **18**, 211–245 (2013)
4. Kumbhar, S.R., Dange, H.M.: Performance analysis of single cylinder diesel engine, using diesel blended with Thumba oil. Int. J. Soft Comput. Eng. (IJSCE), **4**, 2231–2307 (2014)
5. Bartholomew, D.: Vegetable oil fuel. J. Am. Oil Chem. **58**, 286A–288A (1981)
6. Barsic, N.J., Humke, A.L.: Vegetable oils: diesel fuel supplements. Automotive Eng. **89**, 37–41 (2009)
7. Gopinath, A., Pushan, S., Nagarajan, G.: Effect of unsaturated fatty acid esters of biodiesel fuels on combustion, performance and emission characteristics of a DI diesel engine. Int. J. Energy Environ. **1**, 411–430 (2010)
8. Liu, L., Cheng, S.Y., Li, J.B., Huang, Y.F.: Mitigating environmental pollution and impacts from fossil fuels. Energy Sour. Part A Recov. Utilization Environ. Effects **29**(12), 1069–1080 (2007)
9. Pushparaj, T., Ramabalan, S.: Green fuel design for diesel engine, combustion, performance and emission analysis. In: International Conference on Design and Manufacturing IConDM (2013)
10. Moser, B.R.: Biodiesel production, properties, and feedstocks (2009)
11. Kombe, G.G., Temu, A.K., Rajabu, H.M., Mrema, G.D.: High free fatty acid (FFA) feedstock pre-treatment method for biodiesel production. In: Second International Conference on Advances in Engineering and Technology (2012)
12. Dilip Kumar, K., Ravindra Kumar, P.: Experimental investigation of cotton seed oil and neem Methyl esters as biodiesel on CI engine. Int. J. Modern Eng. Res. (IJMER) **2**(4), 1741–1746, 2012

Computational Fluid Dynamics Modeling of the Spray Process of Resin Over a Laid Up Fiber Stack for the Purpose of Fiber Impregnation and Composite Materials Manufacturing

Amare Demelie Zegeye[1(✉)], Mulugeta Ademasu Delele[2], and Aart Willem Van Vuure[1,2]

[1] Faculty of Mechanical and Industrial Engineering, Bahir Dar Technology Institute, Bahir Dar University, Bahir Dar, Ethiopia
aartwillem.vanvuure@kuleuven.be
[2] KU Leuven University, Leuven, Belgium

Abstract. Composite materials are group of engineering materials which are combinations of more than one material type with the intention of getting specific material properties. The components of the composite may be metals, ceramics, plastic or other materials. The manufacturing methods of composite materials especially fiber reinforced plastics requires combining two or more materials in defined orientation. Among the different fiber reinforced plastic composites manufacturing methods hand layup method comprises 22% and exclusively implemented in developing countries. Other advanced manufacturing methods such as resin transfer molding, compression molding and auto calve require high capital and technical expertise. It is possible to say all the manufacturing methods have their own limitations. Resin spray over a laid up fiber stack is first phase of a new manufacturing setup which will be followed by pressure compaction. In this paper the spray process is modeled using computational fluid dynamics in 3D spray region of size $30 \times 30 \times 60$. In the modeling spray characteristics of the fairly viscous unsaturated polyester resin using different nozzle types have been analyzed. The result shows only few types of nozzles are capable of spraying the 0.3 kg/m-s viscosity liquid with fairly good area and distance of coverage. In the case of pressure swirls atomizer about 30 cm distance from the atomizer results a fairly uniform distribution.

Keywords: Composite materials · Spray · CFD modelling · Manufacturing

1 Introduction

Composite materials are group of engineering materials which are combinations of more than one material type with the intention of getting specific material properties. Fiber reinforced plastics are groups of composite materials with a reinforcing element, fiber, and a compatible resin binder (matrix) to obtain specific and unique characteristics and properties [3–8]. Composites materials receive much attention not only

© ICST Institute for Computer Sciences, Social Informatics and Telecommunications Engineering 2022
Published by Springer Nature Switzerland AG 2022. All Rights Reserved
M. L. Berihun (Ed.): ICAST 2021, LNICST 412, pp. 226–232, 2022.
https://doi.org/10.1007/978-3-030-93712-6_15

because they are on the cutting edge of active material research fields but also due to appearance of many new types of composites, e.g., nano-composites and bio-medical composites. Composite materials have great deals of promise for its potential applications in various industries ranging from aerospace to construction due to its various outstanding properties. While metals and plastics are currently the dominant materials in product development applications, composite materials with superior physical performance characteristics are increasingly used to replace traditional metal and plastic material in engineered products [2]. Most widely used composite material groups are fiber reinforced plastics (FRP) with components of glass fibers, carbon fibers, Kevlar fibers, etc. and thermoses matrixes such as polyester, epoxy and vinyl ester. The composite materials technology is emerging; many new classes of materials have been developed to satisfy various new applications, a ceramic matrix composite that incorporates a metal phase to increase the toughness of the brittle ceramic matrix is one of them [1]. It is possible to say pure metals and metallic alloys will be replaced by the most versatile material generations, composite materials. The main advantage behind these composite materials is attaining material properties that could not be attained by pure materials, for instance in carbon epoxy composite, the material gets the strength from the carbon fiber and the toughness from the epoxy.

The manufacturing technology with composite materials is one of top research areas. Combining materials with different properties to a single product is not as straight forward as single component metals or plastic manufacturing. The main manufacturing technique implemented are Hand layup/open mold processes, Resin transfer molding, Compression molding, Autoclave and other continuous processes with increasing in development of new and modified processes [9]. All types of processes have their own strength and weakness. Hand layup manufacturing method comprising 22% share is easy to implement and requires low investment with compromise of quality, productivity and exposure of toxic chemicals [9]. Resin transfer molding with different varieties being developed requires relatively higher investment than hand layup and it has pressure related issues. Autoclave is implemented for high performance products with low productivity and very high investment. Compression and injection moldings with high level of productivity applied only for low performance products. Other continuous processes mainly have limitation of shape complexity. This paper is part of a PhD research work of full composite manufacturing set up (Fig. 1). The system incorporates a spray and a compaction stage. The resin will be sprayed over the laid fiber stack. The sprayed mist of resin will infiltrate through thickness by capillary effect of fiber and compaction pressure applied by the pressure plate backed by a pushing balloon enlarged by compressor pressure. In this setup resin infusion is mainly towards the thickness which is unique, in most other processes the resin infusion is along the width and length or simply areal.

2   Material and Methods

The specific geometry of fiber stack selected is flat shape of dimension 30 cm × 30 cm in a vertical position with intention of studying the most difficult position in composite materials manufacturing practice. The composite components modeled are unsaturated polyester resin of viscosity 0.3 kg/m-s and E glass fiber chopped strand mat. The former being a liquid phase to be sprayed over the laid up stack of fiber.

2.1 General Model Setup

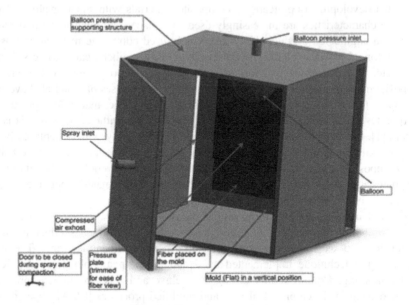

Fig. 1. General process setup

The model setup (Fig. 1), shows the whole set up of spray and compaction phases of the flat geometry of product selected 30 cm × 30 cm size in vertical position. The fiber stack of dimension 30 cm × 30 cm, density 450 g per meter square (gsm) and 3 number of layer stack is placed in the mold (flat) in vertically position. The frame door will be closed and resin to be sprayed through the spray inlet to the fiber stack. After the spray phase completed, the process will get in to the next stage of the process i.e. the compaction phase which is not addressed in this paper.

2.2 CFD Modeling Setup up for the Spray

The spray phase modeling is performed with a 3D geometry of size 30 cm × 30 cm × 60 cm flow region (Fig. 2), where the 30 cm × 30 cm is the sample size and the 60 cm length is the variable distance between the nozzle tip and the laid fiber. (0, 0, 0) is the coordinate for atomizer position. Flow rate of 0.02 kg/s or 20 g/s is expected for 10 s to spray about 0.2 kg resin which results a composite product of 35% to 65% fiber to resin ratio.

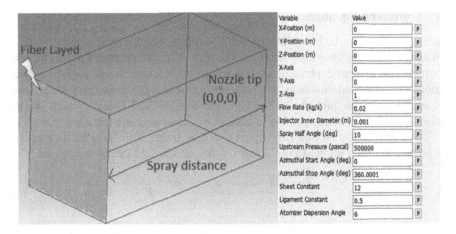

Variable	Value	
X-Position (m)	0	P
Y-Position (m)	0	P
Z-Position (m)	0	P
X-Axis	0	P
Y-Axis	0	P
Z-Axis	1	P
Flow Rate (kg/s)	0.02	P
Injector Inner Diameter (m)	0.001	P
Spray Half Angle (deg)	10	P
Upstream Pressure (pascal)	500000	P
Azimuthal Start Angle (deg)	0	P
Azimuthal Stop Angle (deg)	360.0001	P
Sheet Constant	12	P
Ligament Constant	0.5	P
Atomizer Dispersion Angle	6	P

Fig. 2. CFD spray setup

2.3 Mesh Generation and Analysis Mesh Generation and Analysis

3D mesh is generated with hex dominant method of element size 0.0375 m. The mesh/grid of the model is shown in Fig. 3. The mesh was generated based on medium relevance center and has 1377 nods and 1024 elements. The grid was refined to confirm mesh independence. When the percentage different between the two successive meshes is negligible, it is possible to say there is mesh independency. To identify mesh independency, the simulation was proceeded from coarse to medium mesh and the variation of the desired simulation out was checked. It is also possible to have mesh independent solution by using a very fine uniform mesh. However, analysis time will be too much.

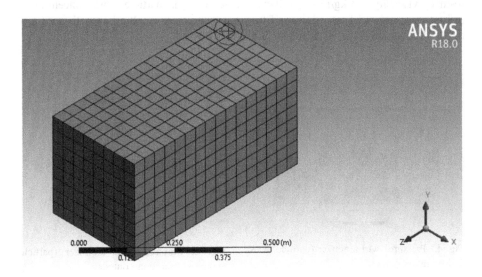

Fig. 3. Mesh generated

2.4   Governing Equations

Multi-phase Eulerian-Lagrangian approach is implemented for solving the flow problem and for tracking the path of droplets. The phases are air, continues phase and resin droplets. The dispersed phase/droplet is solved by tracking large number droplets through the calculated flow field. The dispersed phase can exchange momentum, mass, and energy with the fluid phase. The CFD package ANSYS Fluent predicts the trajectory of a discrete phase particle or droplet by integrating the force balance on the particle, which is written in a Lagrangian reference frame. This force balance equates the particle inertia with the forces acting on the particle, and can be written as:

$$\frac{d\vec{u}p}{dt} = \frac{\vec{u} - \vec{u}p}{\tau r} + \frac{\vec{g}(\rho p - \rho)}{\rho p} + \vec{F} \tag{1}$$

Where $\vec{F}$ is an additional acceleration (force/unit particle mass) term, $\frac{\vec{u} - \vec{u}p}{\tau r}$ is the drag force per unit particle mass and τr is the particle relaxation factor, $\vec{u}$ is the air velocity $\vec{u}p$ is the particle velocity, μ is the molecular viscosity of the fluid, ρ is the fluid density, ρp is the density of the particle.

3   Results and Discussion

Air atomizing spray nozzles are preferable for viscous liquids rather than hydraulic nozzles for a better dispersion and angle of coverage. Among the various types of atomizers modeled in this study: simple cone atomizer, Flat fan atomizer, plane orifice atomizer pressure swirl atomizer, Air blast atomizer, effervescent atomizer only few of them are capable of atomizing and spraying the viscous liquid unsaturated polyester resin of viscosity 0.3 kg/m-s. As it can be seen in the particle mass concentration contour pressure swirl atomizer and Effervescent atomizer result a better distance and angel of coverage (Figs. 4, 5, 6 and 7) .

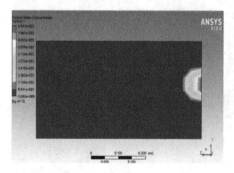

Fig. 4. Pressure swirl atomizer (particle mass concentration contour)

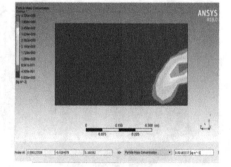

Fig. 5. Pressure swirl atomizer (particle mass concentration contour)

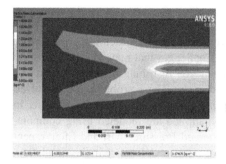
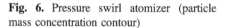

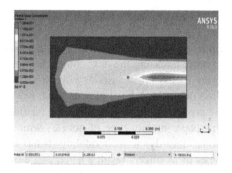

Fig. 6. Pressure swirl atomizer (particle mass concentration contour)

Fig. 7. Effervescent atomizer (particle mass concentration contour)

In the cross sectional view of the spray distribution, it can be possible to see the concentration coverage at different distances from the nozzle in the case of pressure swirl atomizer. It is possible to see that at distances 10 to 20 cm far from the nozzle tip have low concentration and with short distances less than 10 cm the angle of coverage is small. So, it requires balancing between the two (Fig. 8).

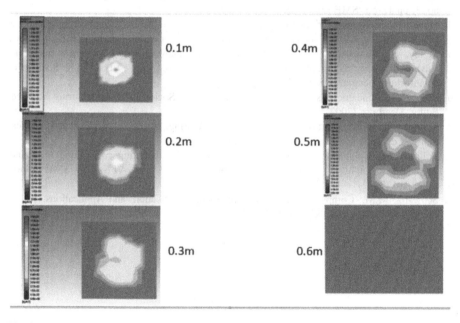

Fig. 8. Cross-sectional *view: resin distribution at different distances for pressure swirl atomizer*

4 Conclusion and Recommendation

Spraying and uniformly distributing a resin over a laid up fiber stack is a critical work in order to easing the next compaction process. Challenges that may happen during the spray of the fairly viscous polyester resin are uneven distribution, accumulation and drop down, high level of resin mist, wastage and others. These problems can be solved by properly selecting nozzle type, setting appropriate parameters such as pressure. In this paper mainly type of nozzles which can be applied are modeled using computational fluid dynamics modeling. It has been observed Pressure swirl and Effervescent types of atomizers result a better angle of coverage/area and distance in the simulation. In the case of pressure swirls atomizer about 30 cm distances from the atomizer tip results a wider and relatively uniform distribution.

References

1. Lo, C., Flinn, B., Zok, F.W., Evans, A.: "Fracture resistance characteristics of a metal toughened Cceramics. J. Am. Ceram. Soc. **7**, 369–75 (1993)
2. Mazundar, S.K.: Composites Manufacturing: Materials, Products, and Process Engineering. CRC Press, New York (2002)
3. Bullen, N.G.: Unified Composite Structures. Manufacturing engineering magazine, vol. 144, no. 3, pp.47–55. SME Editor, Dearborn (2010)
4. Morey, B.: Innovation Drives Composite Production. Manufacturing engineering magazine, vol. 142, no.3, pp.49–60, Society of manufacturing engineer editor, Dearborn, MI, USA 2009
5. Morey, B.: Composites Challenge Cutting Tools. Manufacturing engineering magazine, Advanced technology supplement 2007, vol. 138, no.4, pp. AT6–AT11. Society of manufacturing engineer editor, Dearborn (2007)
6. Rufe, P.D.: Fundamentals of Manufacturing, 2 (edn.). Society of Manufacturing Engineer Editor, Dearborn (2002)
7. Strong, A.B.: Fundamentals of Composite Manufacturing. Materials, Methods and Applications, 2 (edn.) SME Editor, Dearborn (2008)
8. Tolinski, M.: Composites Challenge Cutting Tools. Manufacturing engineering magazine, Advanced technology supplement 2007, vol. 138, no.4, pp. AT1–AT5. SME Editor, Dearborn, (2007)
9. Schwartz, M.M.: Composite Materials - Processing, Fabrication, and Applications, vol. 2. Prentice Hall PTR, Hoboken (1997)

Performance Evaluation of Locally Fabricated Public Water Cooler

Atrsaw Jejaw$^{(\boxtimes)}$ and Aschale Getnet

Faculty of Mechanical and Industrial Engineering, Bahir Dar Institute
of Technology, Bahir Dar University, Bahir Dar, Ethiopia

Abstract. This study aims to supply sufficient drinking water for hot land regions in Ethiopia, specifically higher institutions such as ASTU, Dilla, Semera, Derie dawa, Gambiela and Assosa Universities. The investigation focuses on evaluating the performance of locally manufactured public water coolers developed using the VCRS system.

The predestined parameters are inlet temperature of water (44 °C), the estimated time, the volume of water, surrounding temperature of the air (28 °C), and heating load of evaporates (12847.87 kJ). Two models are designed in the present investigation, the first one for experimental and the second for numerical analysis and for compare with experimental analysis and previse investigation. After design and select the component the model developed and simulated using EXCEL. R134a is selected as a refrigerant because it has less global warming potential, zero ozone depletion potential value, inexpensive and easily available. Aluminum sheet, R134a, spray foam, thermostat, and VCRs components are materials used to fabricate the coolers. The walls of the storage tank is wounded by the evaporator coil. Due to high performance of cooler, the storage type of water cooler is selected. The theoretical results have been validated with experimental results and the present study compares with the literature. As per this investigation, the cop of the cooler is recorded 3.17 and 3.89 for experimental and theoretical results respectively. This result variation is detected due to ideal assumption of VCRs process.

Keywords: VCRs · Storage tank · Locally manufactured · COP · Public water cooler

Nomenclature

VCRs	= Vapour compression refrigeration system
ASTU	= Adama Science and technology University
Cop	= Coefficient of performance

1 Introduction

This study is focus on storage type water cooler using VCRs. Human being consume two-litter water per day [1]. However, in hot region of Ethiopia challenges to supply cooled water to their society for higher institutions, social service organizations and industries. Specifically in higher institutions such that ASTU, Asosa, Semera, and Dilla university directly use hot water for drinking purpose. The society buy mineral waters daily. Locally fabricated public water cooler seems the solution for this challenge and unexpected expenses. A storage type water cooler is developed to produce cold water and to preserve water temperature between 7 °C and 13 °C by reduce the temperature of hot water from 44 °C [2].

In nature heat is always transfer from high-temperature to low-temperature object without requiring any devices. However, the reverse process cannot occur by itself. Therefore, refrigerators device require transferring heat from a low-temperature to a high-temperature region. Water cooler is one of refrigerator device to cools water by removing heat from it, using VCRs or absorption refrigeration cycle [3]. This paper use VCRs using four basic components. In VCRs, the refrigerant compressed in compressor then condense in constant pressure in condenser them routed in capillary tube to decrease the temperature of refrigerant for evaporation in evaporator coil [4] (Fig. 1).

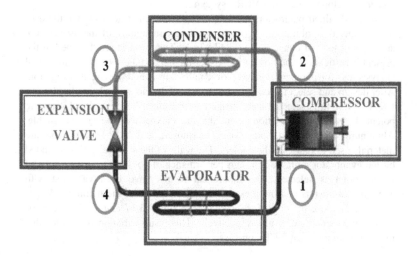

Fig. 1. Simple VCRC schematic diagram

2 Methods and Materials

The fabricated cooler design is based on knowledge from previse investigation and Numerical analysis. Theoretical and experimental approaches used as a methodology in this study. The numerical (theoretical) approach use governing equation in each analysis of components. The experimental approach used in this study is to test and validation with numerically developed model results at the same working condition. Therefore, in order to achieve the required objective, this study will use both numerical and experimental method.

In this paper aluminum sheet, evaporator coil, compressor, condenser coil, dryer, expansion valve, the refrigerant and thermostat are used as raw materials. Due to its higher thermal conductivity to absorbed heat easily through the wall of the tanker from the hot water aluminum is chosen material for the tanker. Insulation material used to prevent heat transfer from surrounding to tanker. In addition, aluminum less expensive than stainless steel and it is the second most common food grade materials. The materials and individual components of refrigeration system that are used to fabricate public water cooler are easily available in the market so, it is necessary to fabricate water cooler locally (Figs. 2 and 3).

Fig. 2. Fabrication process of box of cooler

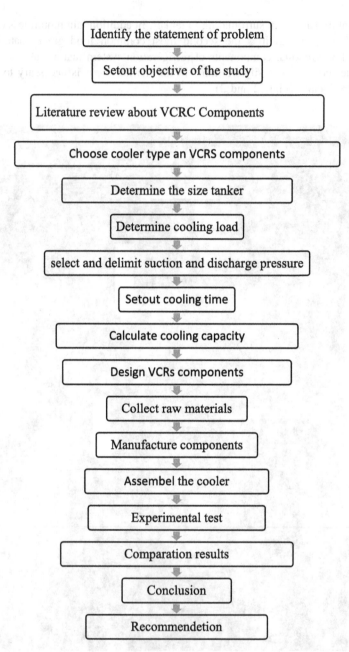

Fig. 3. Design methodology of cooler

Measured and Assumption Variables

T_{in} inlet temperature (°C)

T_{out} exit temperature (°C)

V Size of tanks (L)

C_p Specific heat $(J/kg°C)$.

ρ_i Water Density $\left(\frac{kg}{m^3}\right)$

T Time to cool (s)

k *Thermal conductivity* $\left(^W\!/m * {}^\circ C\right)$

D_{co}, D_e D_{ca} *Diameter of condenser, evaporater and expansion valve (mm)*

Calculated Variables

Cooling load

$$Q_L = \rho_i(kg/m^3) * C_p(J/kg^\circ C) * (T_{in} - T_{out})(^\circ C) \tag{1}$$

Cooling capacity

$$Q_C = \frac{Q_L}{time(min)} \tag{2}$$

Pressure ratio

$$r_p = \frac{P_c}{P_e} \tag{3}$$

Mass flow rate $\left(^{kg}\!/_s\right)$

$$\dot{m} = \frac{\text{Cooling capacity } (Q_c)}{(h_1 - h_4)} \tag{4}$$

Input power (Fig. 4) (Table 1)

$$(\dot{W}_c) = \Delta h_c * \dot{m} \tag{5}$$

Table 1. Refrigeration cycle and components of cooler

Components	Choose for the investigation
Refrigeration cycle	VCRs
Water cooler	Storage
Compressor	Centrifugal
Condenser	Air cooled
Thermostat	Cold thermostat
Expansion valve	Coiled
Filter	Dispose type
Evaporator	Tube type
Insulation	Spray foam
Refrigerant	R-134a

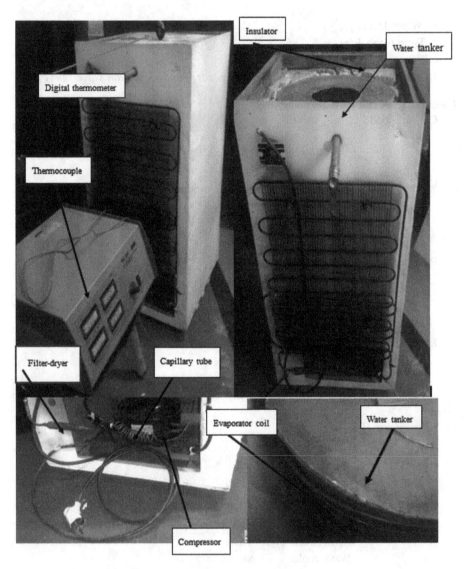

Fig. 4. Experimental set-up of water cooler

COP

$$COP = \frac{h_1 - h_4}{h_2 - h_1} \tag{6}$$

$$insulation \ R_c = \frac{K}{h_o} \tag{7}$$

3   Result and Discussion

Fabricated cooler use for develop experiment using evaporating condensing temperatures (−4 °C), condensing temperatures (46.3 °C), flow rates of refrigerant and ambient temperature of air (28 °C), volume of water-cooled (0.083 m^3) reduce to 10 °C from of 44 °C in 30 min. Condensing temperatures, the evaporating temperature, flow rates of refrigerant and ambient temperature, are operational parameters that affect overall performance of system. Tests with the experimental cooler was planned for the evaluations of their effects on COP and various operational conditions (Fig. 5).

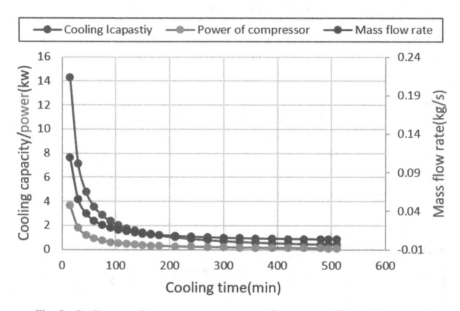

Fig. 5. Cooling capacity, compressor power and flow rate at different time to cool

3.1   Comparisons of Theoretical and Experimental Results

Due to frictional pressure drops in connecting lines, heat loss and lack of perfect insulation the results is slight variation between two results occurs as shown in Table 2.

As show in the above COP of experimental result is less than that of theoretical result because of heat transfer in non-forced convection only. Figure 6 shows the comparison between the numerical and experimental performance of the cooler.

To control the temperature of water cold thermostat require to open or close the compressor when temperature of water around 10 °C. When water temperature increase due to heat transfer from environment the cold thermostat open the motor until Tw = 10 °C.

Table 2. Experimental results and theoretical results comparison

No	Name of parameters	Results				Unit
		Theoretical		Experimental	Percentage error (%)	
t		30 min	300 min	300 min		
1	Pe	252.71	252.71	2571	1.701	kPa
2	Pc	1200	1200	1252.92	4.21	kPa
3	mr	0.0553	0.00553	–	–	Kg/s
4	Pr	4.752	4.752	4.881	2.721	–
5	Win	2.45	0.25	0.25	1.23	hp
6	COP	3.892	3.892	3.173	18.53	–
7	Le	50.88	14.9	15.24	2.24	m
8	Lc	15.32	6.34	6.75	6.72	m
9	Lct	3.81	3.14	3.62	13.93	m

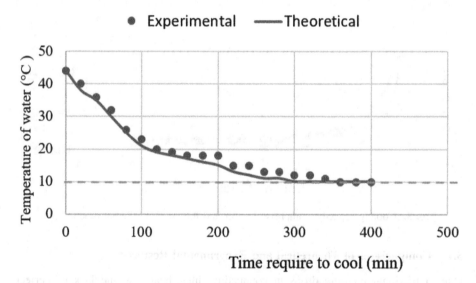

Fig. 6. Numerical and experimental water temperature versus time

In the above figure temperature of water with time require cooling, experimental and theoretical result are almost the same but some variation shows due to heat leakage occurs and materials properties assumed to be constant but change with temperature.

3.2 Comparison of Previse Investigation with the New Study

Table 3. New study with Previse investigation comparison

Parameters	Chow et al. [6]	Heydari [7]	Phelan et al [9]	Seyfettin [8]	Present Study		
					Theoretical		Experimental
					Time to cool		
					30 min	300 min	300 min
Heat load(w)	32	–	100–300	45	7137.70	713.77	713.77
T_e(°C)	12	20	5	0	−4	−4	−3.5
T_c(°C)	–	60	55	50	46.31	46.31	48.2
$P_e(kpa)$	443	571	349.85	292.8	252.7	252.7	257
$P_c(kpa)$	–	1681.8	1495.6	1317.7	1200	1200	1252.9
$T_{amb}(°C)$	45	36	33	30	28	28	28
Flow rate (g/s)	16.3	–	0.8–2.5	0.35	54.78	5.48	–
Refrigerant	R134a	R134a	R134a	R134a	R134a	R134a	R134a
COP	3.34	3.0	3.0	3.89	3.90	3.90	3.17
Compressor type	Centrifugal	Piston	Scroll	Piston	Hermetic sealed	Hermetic sealed	Hermetic sealed

As shown in the above, in this paper, the COP for theoretical 3.90 and for experimental is 3.17 and in previously investigated findings shows COP for Chow et al. [6] is 3.34, Heydari [7] is 3.0, Phelan et al. [9] 3.0 and Seyfettin [8] is 3.89. Therefore, this paper has higher COP than previse investigation for both numerical and experimental aspect (Fig. 7) (Table 3).

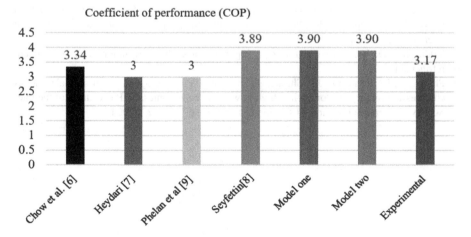

Fig. 7. Charts of comparisons between present study and literature in COP values

4   Conclusion

The experimental model is designed considering basic components of VCRs and parameters like T_{cond}, T_{eva} and $\dot{m}$. And, cooling load is 12847.87 kJ plus 10%. Currently, two cases are investigated. The first model realized a model designed by taking a 30 min to cool down from 44 °C to 10 °C, with 7.14 KW cooling capacity and the second one takes 300 min with 0.71 KW cooling capacity. Besides, compressor power requires for a first is 2.46 hp and second models is 0.245 hp. And for both model R134a is used to conduct the experimental set up. In addition, the perceived COP variation as some assumptions shows experimental results (3.17) and the theoretical results (3.89).

In the end, this study shows the public water cooler improved performance in comparisons of the previous investigation.

References

1. https://www.pmengineer.com/articles/88298-online-news-halsey-taylor-appoints-new-sales-reps-for-water-cooler-drinking-fountain-line
2. Mukund, Y., Pande, A.P.: Comparative study of different passages over dimpled plate evaporator for a small water cooler. Int. J. Res. Sci. Eng. **3**(2), 2394–8280 (2017)
3. Venkatarathnam, G., Shrinivasa Murthy, S.: Refrigerants for vapour compression refrigeration system. Int. J. Therm. Sci. **43**, 3467–3478 (2010)
4. Ashrae: ASHRAE Handbook Fundamentals, American Society of Heating, Refrigerating and Air Conditioning Engineers, 5th (edn.), Atlanta (1993). ISBN 1–883413–54–0
5. http://www.essay.uk.com/essays/engineering/manufacturing-and-analysis-of-water-cooler-cum-refrigeration-system/
6. Chow, L.C., et al.: Design and analysis of a meso-scale refrigerator. In: Proceedings of the ASME International Mechcanical Engineering Congress and Exposition, ASME, pp. 1–8 (1999)
7. Heydari, A.: Miniature vapor compression refrigeration systems for active cooling of high performance computers. In: Proceedings of the Inter Society Conference on Thermal Phenomena, IEEE, pp. 371–378 (2002)
8. Yildiz, S.: "Design and simulation of a vapor compression refrigeration cycle for a micro refrigerator (2010)
9. Phelan, P.E., Swanson, J., Chiriac, F., Chiriac, V.: "Designing a meso-scale vapor-compression refrigerator for cooling high-power microelectronics. In: Proceedings of the Inter Society Conference on Thermal Phenomena, IEEE, pp. 218–223 (2004)

Recycled Polymer for FDM 3D Printing Filament Material: Circular Economy for Sustainability of Additive Manufacturing

Menberu Zeleke Shiferaw[1]([✉]) and Hailu Shimels Gebremedhen[2]

[1] Faculty of Mechanical and Industrial Engineering, Bahir Dar Institute
of Technology, Bahir Dar University, Bahir Dar, Ethiopia
[2] College of Electrical and Mechanical Engineering, Addis Ababa Science
and Technology University, Addis Ababa, Ethiopia

Abstract. Plastics have become the most popular and ubiquitous material in our daily lives and global plastic production has increased significantly. A large portion of the plastic is used to produce disposable packaging items, which are discarded and accumulated as post-consumer wastes both on the land and oceans. Distributive recycling of waste plastics through additive manufacturing became the most effective solution to overcome environmental pollution and reduce the use of fossil oils and gases. With the rise of additive manufacturing, the demand for polymers has increased exponentially and many scholars are concerned about how 3D printing filaments should be reproduced from recycled plastics. This review aimed to study the potentials of using recycled plastic for 3D printing filament to minimize environmental pollution and preserve material sustainability. The study revealed promising results for the use of recycled post-consumer plastic as a more sustainable and environmentally friendly 3D printing filament material. The impact of plastic degradation on their mechanical and thermal properties due to subsequent extrusion and contamination of plastics by impurities was also studied. Besides, the additive materials used to enhance mechanical properties and increase the molecular weight of recycled material are discussed. Finally, a conclusion is drawn and future research opportunities are also addressed.

Keywords: Additive manufacturing · 3D printing filament · Plastic waste · Plastic recycling

1 Introduction

Plastic has become the most popular material for humans after the production of phenol-formaldehyde resin through the polycondensation process from phenol and formaldehyde monomer units in 1909 [1]. In recent years, plastics become the most widely used material in several industrial sectors such as packaging, bags and containers, construction, furniture, transportation, automobiles, micro-devices, and biomedical components. This is due to their lightweight, durability, versatility, and low cost as compared to other materials [2–6]. Plastic production is increasing around the world due to its ability to replace metal, paper, wood, and glass in many engineering applications [4, 7–10].

© ICST Institute for Computer Sciences, Social Informatics and Telecommunications Engineering 2022
Published by Springer Nature Switzerland AG 2022. All Rights Reserved
M. L. Berihun (Ed.): ICAST 2021, LNICST 412, pp. 243–261, 2022.
https://doi.org/10.1007/978-3-030-93712-6_17

The world's annual plastic production was 1.5 million tons in 1950. It has increased significantly to 322 million tons in 2015, raised by over 500% in the last three decades, and is forecast to reach 850 million tons by the year 2050. The plastics industry is almost entirely dependent on nonrenewable oil and gas resources, which is not a sustainable option since these scarce resources will eventually run out. Plastic feedstock accounts for around 4% of global fossil oil and gas production, with another 3–4% used to provide energy for their production [4, 10–18].

Packaging and textile fibers account for the largest demand for plastics, accounting for approximately 80% of all synthetic polymers consumption [19]. Most plastics are non-biodegradable and poisonous to burn, so their widespread production and mismanaged use have a severe environmental effect and contaminate both the land and water. Landfilling and incineration, the most popular methods of disposing of plastic waste, both have the potential to damage the environment. Plastic incineration releases harmful substances into the atmosphere such as carbon dioxide, sulfur oxides, ashes, and dioxin. On the other hand, landfilling of plastic wastes occupy a lot of space and requires a long time to decompose because they are not often non-biodegradable. As a result, the linear economy paradigm (based on the "take–make–dispose of" model) has devastating effects on the environment, including depletion of natural resources, environmental pollution, and non-sustainable development [5, 6, 10, 12, 14, 18, 20–23].

To tackle environmental pollution, the circular economy (CE) concept overcomes environmental problems and ensures sustainability by addressing the contamination caused by plastic waste. Recycling is the best option in the circular economy for handling post-consumer plastics since it reduces the severe environmental impact of waste plastics and the use of petrochemical resources. The collection and transportation of low-density plastic waste to collection and reclamation centers, however, requires a significant amount of energy in traditional recycling. Separation and reconstruction require a substantial amount of labor and can have a significant impact on the environment. Distributed plastic recycling in which consumers recycle their waste saves energy for transportation and can reduce energy demand as compared to traditional recycling [12, 24–26].

One method of recycling is distributed recycling of plastics waste for additive manufacturing [26]. Additive manufacturing (AM), which is also known as 3D printing, is a process to make a 3D solid object from a 3D model through additive processes of successive layers of material under computer control [27–29]. 3D printing technology has progressed significantly in the processing of polymers in a variety of fields, including aerospace, unmanned aerial vehicles (UAVs), agriculture, biomedical, civil engineering, bioprinting, membrane technology, metal matrix composites, and food production [18].

The most popular 3D printing technology, fused deposition modeling (FDM), melts and extrudes thermoplastic filament via a temperature-controlled nozzle. The most commonly used filament materials acrylonitrile butadiene styrene (ABS) and polylactic acid (PLA). With the rise of additive manufacturing technology, many scholars concern about how the filament material can be manufactured from recyclable plastic, which offers a viable solution and made it more environmentally friendly and sustainable [30, 31]. Different scholars investigate the possibility of utilizing recycled waste plastics as source material for 3d printing filament. For example, HDPE and ABS plastic wastes [21], PET bottles [9, 14, 32], polypropylene [5], PLA [23], and ABS [33] has been examined for 3D printing filaments material.

This study aimed to review the potentials of using recycled plastic wastes for 3D printing filament to minimize environmental pollution by waste plastics and preserve material sustainability in additive manufacturing. The study concerns the recycling potential of plastic wastes for 3D printing filament and it revealed that recycled plastic wastes can be utilized as a more sustainable and environmentally friendly material for 3D printing filament. This review also examines the degradation of the plastics during subsequent extrusions and contamination of the material by impurities can affect the mechanical properties of recycled polymer material. Besides, the additive materials used to enhance mechanical properties and increase the molecular weight of recycled material are discussed. This study is organized as follows: Plastic solid waste, its environmental effects, and management techniques are discussed in Sect. 2. Section 3 addresses additive manufacturing, the most commonly used thermoplastics for 3D printing filament material, and recycled polymers for 3D printing filament. Polymer degradation during subsequent extrusion and additives used to strengthen recycled polymer are also discussed. Also discussed. Section 4 addressed the conclusions and future research opportunities.

2 Plastic Solid Wastes and Its Management Techniques

2.1 Plastic Solid Wastes

Plastic is a synthetic organic chemical compound produced by polymerization of several monomers or repeating units. The majority of monomers used in plastic manufacturing are hydrocarbons extracted from fossil fuels such as coal and petroleum. Plastics' plasticity allows them to be formed, extruded and cast into different shapes and forms. Plastics are highly versatile materials that are used almost everywhere due to their lightweight, solid, durable, and flexible properties [1, 4, 34–37].

The high demand for plastic products, intense production, and unsustainable use and disposal results in the accumulation deposition of waste plastics in the environment. In recent years, the production of plastics has increased significantly. Packaging plastics are the most popular polymers, accounting for the majority of MSW. Post-consumer and industrial plastics, such as polyethylene terephthalate (PET), high-density polyethylene (HDPE), polypropylene (PP), polystyrene (PS), low-density polyethylene (LDPE), polycarbonate (PC), polyvinyl chloride (PVC), and others are the most common plastic solid wastes. The versatility and durability of plastics for diverse applications were anticipated, but the problems associated with the disposal of plastic debris were not [38–40].

2.2 Plastic Waste Environmental Pollution

The majority of plastic additives are poisonous chemicals that can cause environmental pollution and results in public health risks. Ingestion, inhalation, and skin touch are indeed the main ways that people are subjected to these additives. Indiscriminate plastic waste disposal results in environmental pollution, entanglement, and death of marine life, and clogging of drainage systems in towns and cities, etc. [37].

Land Pollution - Plastic waste pollutes the terrestrial environment before making its way into the aquatic environment. Because of the deterioration of the plastics and the leaching of hazardous plastic additives into different environmental compartments, dumping plastics on the land leads to environmental pollution. Chlorinated plastics can leach harmful chemicals into the soil, which can then seep into groundwater or the natural marine ecosystems, thereby contaminating the environment [37].

Water Pollution - Plastic makes up about 80% of the debris found in the oceans. In 2012, it was reported that there were about 165 million tons of waste plastic in the oceans. Around 8 million tons of waste plastic is dumped into the ocean per year. After several years of decay in the ocean, harmful chemicals such as nonylphenol, dichlorodiphenyldichloroethylene (DDE), phenanthrene polystyrene, and bisphenol a (BPA) are released into the water, causing water pollution [37].

Plastic debris ingestion and entanglement of animals in waste plastics are frequently occurring events in the ocean. Plastics in the ocean break down into microplastics, which then find their way into food chains after being consumed by a variety of freshwater and marine organisms. Most aquatic species, such as microorganisms, sea turtles, seabirds, fish, and invertebrates, confuse plastic waste dumped into the ocean for food, ingesting it and reducing the animals' digestive capacity, resulting in hunger, malnutrition, and death. Entanglement with plastic products such as nets also hurt, injure, or even kill marine animals [37].

Air Pollution - It is one of the most serious environmental risks to public health, causing over 6 million deaths. When landfilled waste plastics decompose, carbon dioxide and methane are released into the atmosphere and contaminating it. Carbon dioxide is also emitted into the air when plastic products are burned, and this $CO2$ can absorb radiant heat and prevent it from leaving the earth, resulting in global warming. When plastics products are burned directly, contaminants such as dioxins, heavy metals, and furans are released into the air, posing health risks, especially respiratory problems [37].

2.3 Plastic Waste Management

Plastic waste management is critical for reducing the adverse effects of waste plastic on the environment. PSW management can, in general, reduce the accumulation of PSW in the environment and avoid environmental hazards. Improved plastic waste collection, processing, and disposal are needed to reduce global plastic debris and marine pollution. The most popular methods for managing plastic waste are disposal in a landfill, incineration, and recycling [37, 39, 41].

Landfilling - It is the conventional method of disposing of waste plastic in many countries; but, because most plastics take a long time to degrade, the discarded wastes have occupied the land for several years, and space for landfilling is becoming a major issue. Owing to the insufficient supply of oxygen in landfills, plastic waste on land can continue for several years. From a sustainability standpoint, one of the main disadvantages of landfills is that none of the material resources used to manufacture the plastic are recovered. Plastic waste in landfills also serves as a source of secondary contaminants such as benzenes, xylenes, benzene, toluene, ethyl, and trimethyl benzenes. Because of the types and amounts of hazardous chemicals present in landfills, and their potential for leaching, there is an increasing environmental and public health issue about the impact of landfills. If landfills are properly handled, environmental contamination and public health risks can be minimized [4, 37, 41].

Incineration - Plastic incineration is another method for disposing of waste plastics that avoids some of the disadvantages of landfilling in that it does not require a large amount of space and even allowing recovery of energy in the form of heat. Plastic incineration emits hazardous gases including halogenated chemicals and polyvinyl chloride, as well as furans, dioxins, and polychlorinated biphenyls (PCBs) to the environment. The air pollution produced by the noxious gases emitted into the atmosphere is a downside of the combustion of plastics. Plastics permanently damage the combustion heater of flue systems during incineration of plastic, and the chemicals released are harmful to both human health and the environment. Low molecular weight compounds can combust immediately into the air, polluting the environment [37, 41].

Recycling - Considering the extreme environmental consequences of landfilling and incineration, the preferred method of waste disposal is recycling. It eliminates the major environmental drawbacks of both incineration and landfill disposal of plastic. Recycling conserves money and energy, decreases pollutant emissions, decreases landfill consumption, creates jobs, and boosts local economies [24, 42]. Plastics recycling is a vital part of the global initiative to reduce the 8 million tons of waste plastic that enters the ocean each year. Regardless, from 1950 to 2015, roughly 9.5% of all plastic generated was recycled, while 12.5% was incinerated, and the remaining 78% was dumped in landfills [4, 37, 39, 41] as shown in the Fig. 1.

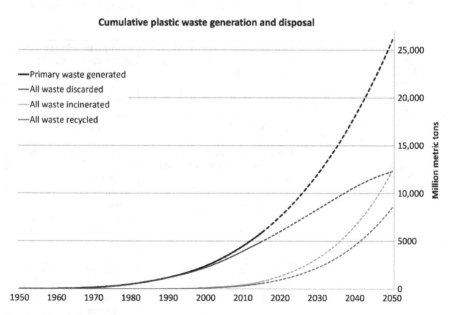

Fig. 1. Cumulative global plastic waste generation and disposal (in million metric tons). Solid lines show historical data from 1950 to 2015; dashed lines show projections of historical trends to 2050 [44].

Plastic recycling can be categorized into four: primary, secondary, tertiary, and quaternary recycling. Primary recycling is the mechanical reprocessing of plastics into the extrusion cycle to create a new product of the same material with similar properties. Secondary recycling is the mechanical recycling of plastics to create new items that replace virgin plastic or a portion of virgin plastic. As a result of this process, plastic degradation occurs, and the addition of various additives enhances the properties of the plastic and makes it suitable for new applications. Tertiary recycling, also known as chemical recycling, breaks down polymer chains into smaller molecules that can be used to make oils, new polymers, or other chemicals. Plastic waste is incinerated in quaternary recycling, and energy is recovered through the generation of heat and/or electricity. The most environmentally sustainable and cost-effective treatment approach tends to be primary recycling. However, since this process needs non-degraded, clean, and homogeneous plastic waste, it is limited. As a result, the majority of life cycle assessment studies are focused on secondary recycling, which is the second-best

Table 1. Plastic types, resin identification, their properties, and common uses [37].

Recycling Symbols	Plastics types	Properties	Common uses
PETE	PET	Clear, tough, solvent resistant, a barrier to gas and moisture, softens at 80 °C.	Soft drink and water bottles, containers, salad dressing, biscuit trays, and salad domes.
HDPE	HDPE	Hard to semi-flexible, resistant to chemicals and moisture, easily colored, processed, and formed	Shopping and freezer bags, buckets, detergent, shampoo, milk and juice bottles, etc.
PVC	PVC	Strong, tough, softens at 80 °C, Flexible, clear, elastic, can be solvent welded.	Fittings, plumbing pipes, blister packs, wall cladding, roof sheeting, garden hose,
LDPE	LDPE	Soft flexible, waxy surface, translucent, softens at 70 °C, scratches easily.	Refuse bags, mulch film, cling wrap, garbage bags, squeeze bottles.
PP	PP	Hard and translucent, soften at 140 °C, translucent, withstand solvents, versatile.	Microwave dishes, lunch boxes, packaging tape, garden furniture, and ice cream tubs
PS	PS	Clear, glassy rigid, opaque, semi-tough, affected by fat, acids, and solvents, but resistant to alkalis, salt solutions, low water absorption	Plastic cutlery, imitation glassware, toys, protective packaging, building, and food insulation
OTHER	Other like PC, ABS	Includes all resins and multi-materials (e.g. laminates) properties dependent on plastic or a combination of plastics.	Automotive and appliance components, computers, electronics, cooler bottles, packaging.

environmental solution and is favored over other management procedures in terms of reducing total energy consumption and greenhouse gas emissions [43].

Table 1 Summarizes the various forms of plastics, as well as their properties, resin identification codes, and common uses.

3 Polymers for FDM Additive Manufacturing

Additive manufacturing (AM), also known as 3D printing, is the process of making three-dimensional (3D) solid objects by laying down successive layers of material under computer control. It is distinguished from traditional machining techniques, which rely on material removal by milling, grinding, boring, cutting, and other methods [27, 45]. One of the fastest-growing industries is 3D printing. In comparison to 2016, the market is expected to rise by over 23% by 2021, reaching over 10 million USD. In recent years, 3D printing has gained a lot of popularity across a wide range of industries, with the aerospace, military, automotive, medical, and construction industries [24, 46].

There are now a large number of AM techniques available. Some techniques, such as selective laser sintering (SLS), selective laser melting (SLM), and fused deposition modeling (FDM), melt the material to make the layers, while others cure liquid materials using, such as stereolithography (SLA) [27, 47].

Among the various AM techniques, the FDM is a less expensive and simpler method that only involves a basic design and readily available raw materials. In FDM, a molten thermoplastic material is extruded from a temperature-controlled nozzle to create the layers of an object with a high degree of precision. The thermoplastics feedstock materials are suitable for functional prototypes, durable manufacturing equipment, and low-volume manufacturing components. Filaments for 3D printing are most commonly made in the extrusion process, which involves feeding a pellet or polymer powder into an extruder, where it is converted into a homogeneous material in the shape of a line with given parameters under the influence of temperature. Filaments made from recycled PLA or ABS are becoming more widely available.

3.1 Commonly Used Polymers for FDM Additive Manufacturing

Different materials may be used in FDM 3D printing technology depending on the working conditions. Thermoplastics, such as acrylonitrile butadiene styrene (ABS), polylactic acid (PLA), polycarbonate (PC), polyamides (nylon), polystyrene (PS), polyvinyl alcohol (PVA), high-impact polystyrene (HIPS), and various forms of polyethylene (PE), such as low-density polyethylene (LDPE), polyethylene terephthalate (PET) are used for 3D printing filament. Among these, the most commonly used filament materials are ABS and PLA [24, 30, 48].

Acrylonitrile-Butadiene-Styrene (ABS) - ABS is a carbon chain copolymer made up of polymerized acrylonitrile, butadiene, and styrene monomer units that are joined together to form a single polymer as shown in the figure below. These monomers contribute to the high impact strength and mechanical strength of this thermoplastic polymer, which makes it an opaque and strong thermoplastic appropriate for tough consumer goods. It has a wide range of processing properties, including the ability to be solid and stable at low temperatures while still being heat and chemical-resistant [8, 16, 32, 49].

Polylactic Acid (PLA) - PLA is a biodegradable thermoplastic made from sustainable (renewable) materials including cornstarch, sugar cane, tapioca roots, and potato starch. PLA is currently the most common 3D printing filament in the 3D printing world. It is more environmentally friendly as compared to other plastic materials. PLA is increasingly preferred over ABS due to its low toxicity, resistance to warping, and availability in glow-in-the-dark and translucent colors. The temperature range for printing is approximately 180 °C to 230 °C [8, 16, 32, 49].

3.2 Mechanical Recycling of Waste Plastic for 3D Printing Filament

The recent developments of open-source 3D material extrusion printers and extruders provide a new approach to plastic recycling with higher potential value-added products. In the conventional recycling process, the waste must be delivered to a recycling processing facility and then to a reclamation plant. After being recycled, the plastic is distributed a third time to the producers, who will use it to make new goods. Distributive recycling allows materials to be processed and used directly by the consumers. Since the distributive manufacturing case can be used and recycled locally, there is little to no need for shipping, allowing for substantial energy and cost savings [24, 50].

3D printing using recycled polymeric materials is a novel, rapidly emerging technology with the greatest degree of future viability. The mechanical recycling approach involved reprocessing post-consumer plastic products to produce new, similar, or different products. It is regarded as the easiest and most straightforward recycling process. The various activities involved are collecting, separating, and sorting, shredding, washing, and cleaning, drying, pelletizing, and extruding [8, 49, 51–53] as shown in Fig. 2.

Plastic waste collection involves collecting all types of plastics in one place for further treatment. After the materials have been collected in one place, the separation process begins, in which the plastic is sorted and separated using resin identification codes established by the Society of the Plastic Industry (SPI) as shown in Table 1. Since the sorting process affects the resin quality in part, the plastic must be sorted efficiently to prevent various plastic mixtures along the way [8, 49, 51, 54].

After sorting and separating, the plastic is normally washed with water, surfactants (detergents), and a sodium hydroxide (NaOH) solution to eliminate contaminants such as dust, grease, stickers, oil, and other pollutants. Depending on the post-processing conditions and level of contamination, the washing could be performed before or after the plastics are shredded and transformed into flakes. The shredding of the plastic involves grinding the sorted and gathered plastic into smaller-sized flakes. After shredding, the material is dried with enough heat in a drying machine to remove all moisture at the material's prescribed drying temperature.

The plastic flakes are extruded into pellets and then extruded in a filament extruder machine to produce 3D printing filament. The filament extrusion process is a continuous procedure in which shredded plastic flakes or pellets are fed into the heated barrel

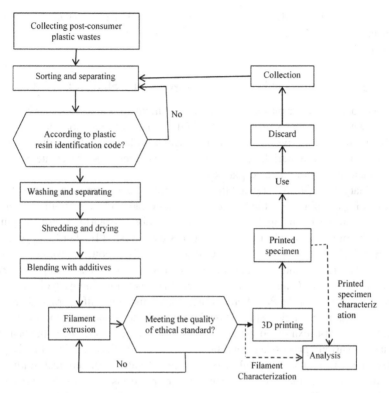

Fig. 2. Manufacture of recycled filament from postconsumer plastic waste materials.

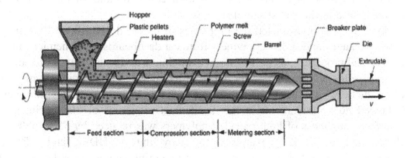

Fig. 3. Single screw plastic extruder [49].

of the extruder via a hopper as shown in Fig. 3. The material is carried through the barrel by a screw that rotates with a high torque motor. The pellets are heated, mixed, and compressed in the barrel before being squeezed out as a wire-shaped filament material through the die /nozzle. After that, the extruded filament is fully cooled and cut to the desired length before being rolled over the spool [8, 49, 55–58].

Plastic additives and virgin materials are mixed with recycled material and then extruded to modify its properties and avoid plastic degradation during extrusion.

Finally, using an FDM 3D printer, the prepared recycled filament is used to print a specimen. Finally, Mechanical, rheological, and thermal analysis are on the printed element [24].

3.3   Recycled Plastics for FDM Filament Material – State of the Art

Recycling post-consumer plastics for 3D printing filament will address the global issue of plastic waste while also making the manufacturing process more environmentally friendly. To resolve the problem of environmental pollution and to reduce the use of petroleum for plastic material, several attempts have been made to create 3D printing filament materials from recycled plastics.

Choudhary et al. [9] investigated the environmental and economic impacts from the recycling of PET plastic bottle waste with renewable and conventional sources of electricity in India by using three different scenarios. Scenario A uses virgin PET pellets with conventional electricity, scenario B uses waste PET bottle recycling with conventional electricity, and scenario C uses waste PET bottle recycling with solar electricity. The results indicate that scenario B has the greatest environmental effects, followed by scenarios C and A and it showed that renewable energy (solar electricity) should be used to recycle PET bottle waste for filament manufacturing. The study's drawback is that it is a region-specific environmental and economic impact experiment.

Ferrari et al. [14] examined the recycling of PET bottles collected at the beach. The influence of various processing conditions on the crystalline structure of 3D printed samples made from the extruded wire was investigated. Rheological studies were carried out to see whether there was any change in the viscosity of PET after several processing cycles. The degradation temperature decreased as the number of processing cycles increased, indicating a reduction in thermal stability. Tensile testing revealed a difference in mechanical properties due to high concentrations of the crystalline or amorphous phase in the tested sample.

Pinho et al. [18] investigated the properties of recycled 3D printed PLA polymer from food packages and ABS copolymers from car dashboards. The chemical, thermal, and mechanical properties, as well as surface roughness and wettability, were compared to characterize the 3D printing performance of the recycled and virgin polymers. PLA showed reductions in both tensile stress and flexural strength by 33% while recycled ABS showed no improvements in the mechanical properties of the specimens. The mean surface roughness of both recycled polymers was reduced by 55 to 65%.

Mohammed et al. [21] examined the recycling of HDPE and ABS plastic wastes into FDM 3D printing filaments to refine print parameters and create a range of demonstration models. The results show that the proposed supply chain can produce highly repeatable ABS and HDPE filaments with diameters of 1.74 ± 0.1 mm for ABS and 1.65 ± 0.1 mm for HDPE materials. Finally, producing usable filaments from waste plastics could be a feasible option for reducing the burden of increased landfill and use.

Lanzotti et al. [23] studied the 'mechanical properties of specimens printed with virgin and recycled PLA', as well as performing short-beam mechanical tests. One-time recycled (106.8 ± 9.0 MPa) and twice recycled (108.5 ± 9.9 MPa)) specimens had comparable short-beam strength to that of the virgin specimens (119.1 ± 6.6 MPa).

Leonard et al. [32] investigated recycled PET specification and extrusion parameters. Mechanical and thermal property test of recycled PET printed dog bone showed a melt flow index (2.85 g/10min), tensile strength (35.7 MPa), Young's modulus (2457 MPa), melting temperature (250 °C), and extruding temperature (250–260 °C) of recycled PET. These properties are comparable to commercial filaments within an appropriate range, allowing recycled PET to be used for 3D printing filament, and the results provide recycling parameters.

Herianto et al. [5] used the Taguchi and ANOVA methods to investigate the production of recycled Polypropylene filaments to optimize extrusion processing parameters. The results showed that an average filament diameter of 1.6 mm is produced at an extrusion speed of 40 rpm, a spooler speed of 4 rpm, and an extrusion temperature of 2000 C. However, since recycled PP 3D printing filaments have a rough and easily curved surface, further research is needed.

For a single recycling cycle, Mohammed et al. [33] investigate the feasibility of using 100% recycled ABS for FDM 3D printing filament material and characterize the resulting improvements in printing quality and mechanical properties. According to the result, ABS can be recycled into consistent 3D printing filaments without the use of virgin material. The findings showed that waste ABS can be recycled and reprinted using 3D printing technology, which could open up new possibilities for long-term sustainability.

Table 2 summarizes various works of literature review on recycled post-consumer polymers for FDM 3D printing filament material.

Table 2. Recycled Filaments from plastic solid waste.

Material	Origin	Reference
PP	From household appliances, post-consumer electric devices, and automotive parts	[5]
ABS	Terluran GP-35 ABS, My 3D Media, Australia	[6]
HDPE	Detergent containers, Shampoo bottles, milk jars, cleaning agent bottles	[8]
HDPE	Post-consumer milk jug	[10]
ABS	Post-consumer ABS	[12]
PET	PET bottles from seaside	[14]
PLA	PLA type 4043D (Nature Works)	[17]
PLA, ABS	From food packages and car dashboards, respectively	[18]
PP	CIRCO® recycled PP	[59]
PLA	4032D type PLA (Nature Works)	[20]
ABS, HDPE	Waste milk cartons (HDPE) and failed/waste 3D prints (ABS)	[21]
PLA	Virgin and recycled PLA	[23]
PLA	Virgin and recycled PLA	[48]
HDPE	Fortum CIRCO® HDPE	[49]
PET	PET water bottles	[32]

(continued)

Table 2. (*continued*)

Material	Origin	Reference
HDPE	HDPE scraps	[52]
ABS	Failed 3D prints and support material	[33]
PET	Soda bottles water bottles, and salad containers	[60]
HDPE	HDPE bottles	[61]
PET	Water bottles	[62]
PET	Carbonated drink bottle and water bottles	[63]
PC	Clear PC regrind provided by McDonnough Plastics, Fenton, MI	[64]
HDPE	Milk bottles, shampoo bottles, detergent containers, and household bottles	[51]
PS	Polystyrene foam collected from an electrical appliance store	[65]
PS, ABS, PVC	Provided by Etelä-Karjalan Jätehuolto Oy and Destaclean Oy companies	[66]
HDPE	Filament purchased from Filaments.ca	[67]

3.4   Additives for Recycled Filament Manufacturing

The introduction of one or more additive materials significantly improves the properties of recycled materials Additives, such as polymer chain extensions and peroxide-based additives, have been extensively researched to increase the recycled polymer's molecular weight and boost its mechanical properties.

The effect of biopolymer lignin additive on the mechanical and thermal parameters of recycled PLA during the FDM process was investigated by Gkartzou et al. [68]. Ground PLA is combined with lignin in various weight ratios and extruded at temperatures ranging from 180 to 190 °C. In contrast to pure PLA samples, the addition of biopolymer lignin increases melting properties while decreasing tensile strength (18%) and Young's modulus (6%).

Tian et al. [69] investigated how 3D printed continuous carbon fiber reinforced (CFR) PLA composites could be recycled and remanufactured. The bending ability of remanufactured CFR thermoplastic composites specimens was 25% higher than that of original specimens. It was possible to achieve a material recovery rate of 100% for continuous carbon fiber and 73% for PLA matrix. Total energy consumption of 67.7 MJ/kg for recycling and 66 MJ/kg for remanufacturing processes was discovered and compared to traditional methods.

The mechanical and thermal efficiency of Biochar and recycled PET composite was investigated by Idrees et al. [70]. The addition of biochar (below 100 m) strengthened the composite's mechanical, thermal, and dynamic properties. In comparison to pure PET, a 0.5 wt% biochar infusion in the recycled PET increases the tensile strength (32%), and a polymer composite with a 5 wt% loading increases the tensile modulus (60%).

The effect of micronized rubber powder and styrene-ethylene-butadiene-styrene (SEBS) elastomer additives on the mechanical properties of recycled PET polymers was studied by Zander and Boelter [71]. In comparison with the pure recycled PET, the addition of 350% SEBS, 5wt% rubber, and over 550% maleic anhydride functionalized SEBS increased toughness (85%), however, there was no significant variance in tensile strength.

Pan et al. [72] investigated the physical and mechanical properties of recycled PP/HDPE plastics feedstock for filament extrusion after incorporating nanocrystalline powders of iron (Fe), chromium (Cr), silicon (Si), and aluminum (Al). As compared to the initial recycled filaments, the addition of a 1% mix of Fe–Si–Cr or Fe–Si–Al powder resulted in improved thermal stability, yield strength (375), and Young modulus (17%). This is due to improved interfacial adhesion between the polymer and the nano-metal powders which results in less crack formation.

Singh et al. [73] investigated the impact of adding SiC/Al2O3 reinforcement to recycled HDPE plastic waste base matrix with paraffin wax binding agent. To ensure uniform dispersion, a twin-screw extruder was used to prepare HDPE, SiC, and Al2O3 in various proportions. The results showed that the additives significantly increased the materials' mechanical strength while having a minor impact on the material's thermal properties.

Stoof and Pickering [74] investigated the impact of varying harakeke, hemp fiber, or recycled gypsum contents (0–50 wt%) in pre-consumer recycled polypropylene (PP) composite filaments. When compared to plain PP filament, the results showed that harakeke fiber (30 wt%), the most effective filament, improved tensile strength (74%) and Young's modulus (214%). In comparison to plain PP, 30 wt% harakeke filament had the least shrinkage of 0.34%, resulting in a net reduction of 84%.

3.5   Degradation of Polymers

Degradation of polymer is an irreversible process that causes a drastic change in the filament material's structure, resulting in the loss of properties. It's crucial to figure out how recycling affects the properties of polymers used in 3D printing. High temperatures present during the plastic recycling, and any shear stress, temperature, or oxygen present during extrusion degrade polymers. Multiple extrusion of polymeric materials has a significant impact on their properties, such as change of viscosity, a decrease of molecular weight, and mechanical property deterioration. The change of the polymer's physical properties has a major impact on the production of high-quality filament materials [16, 24].

Cruz et al. [17] studied the mechanical, rheological, and molecular properties of a recycled PLA filament material throughout five full recycling cycles. After 5 cycles, the mechanical experiment revealed a reduction in the strain at break (10.63%) and a decrease in molecular weights 26.73% and 46.91% after 3 and 5 extrusions cycles respectively. The material viscosity was also reduced from 2729.21 Pa.s during extrusion 1 to 219.85 Pa.s in extrusion 5. In comparison to the virgin value, the melt flow index was increased by around 6.05 times after 5 recycling cycles.

Mohammed et al. [6] investigate the changes in mechanical properties of ABS as it is manufactured using FDM 3D printing at various stages of recycling. As compared to virgin polymer, the recycled polymer had lower tensile and compressive strengths. The ultimate tensile strength of one-time recycled ABS was reduced by 26 to 32%, while two-time recycled ABS was reduced by 16 to 52%. The result also revealed several property changes of the polymer, including decreased melt flow, higher glass transition temperatures, and the production of carbonyl groups due to the thermal-oxidative degradation of both the SAN and butadiene ingredients of ABS.

The properties of filament material are degraded by the introduction of impurities into the material during recycling. During injection molding, Torres et al. [75] investigated thermomechanical degradation of post-consumer PET bottles versus virgin PET. In comparison to virgin PET, contaminants and residual moisture promote crystallization of the recycled PET. The intrinsic viscosity and molecular weight are reduced as a result of this. Due to differences in crystallinity, impurities in recycled PET, and the virgin and recycled materials' thermal and mechanical backgrounds, Virgin PET bottles were ductile (>200% elongation at break), while post-consumer PET bottles were brittle (less than 10% elongation at break).

4   Conclusion and Future Outlook

Plastics have become extremely common in recent years owing to low production costs, lightweight, durable, and high strength. Due to the high demand for plastics and its intensive production, the amount of waste plastic disposal is increasing which needs environmentally friendly plastic waste valorization methods. Plastics are not vulnerable to biodegradation and the decomposition of plastic wastes after several years results in environmental pollution. The most common methods for plastic waste disposal are incineration and landfilling which result in severe environmental impact. In the circular economy concept, distributed recycling of plastic waste is an effective method to treat post-consumer plastics to overcome environmental pollution and create a plastic waste-free environmental sustainability. One method of distributed recycling of plastic is to recycling of plastic waste for 3D printing filament.

In this review, the potential of using recycled post-consumer plastics for 3D printing filament material was discussed. The study shows promising results for the use of post-consumer recycled polymers as source materials for 3D printing filament material. Using recycled plastic wastes for FDM feedstock reduces CO_2 emission, energy consumption, and material costs.

Many researchers have explored the possibility of using recycled polymers to make 3D printing filaments, but there is a lack of performance testing for these filaments in the literature, so further research on the mechanical property range and limitations of recycled filament is needed. The effect of FDM process parameters on recycled polymer-based products and the bonding between printed recycled polymer layers should be also further investigated. These activities would almost certainly expand the use of recycled filament and the applications for which it can be used.

In comparison to commercial 3D printing filaments, recycled 3D printing filaments will have lower mechanical properties. With each subsequent recycling phase, the mechanical properties of plastics deteriorate. To improve the mechanical properties of the recycled plastic material, recycled plastics must be blended with virgin material and additives (plasticizers, chain extenders, etc.). Further research is required to determine which materials can be mixed and which materials need additives to be used in material extrusion AM applications. More research on blends of virgin and recycled materials, as well as additives, is required to allow for several more processing cycles of post-consumer plastics without degradation of properties.

References

1. Chen, S., Liu, Z., Jiang, S., Hou, H.: Carbonization: a feasible route for reutilization of plastic wastes. Sci. Total Environ. **710**, 136250 (2020). https://doi.org/10.1016/j.scitotenv. 2019.136250
2. Al-Salem, S.M., Lettieri, P., Baeyens, J.: Recycling and recovery routes of plastic solid waste (PSW): a review. Waste Manag. **29**(10), 2625–2643 (2009). https://doi.org/10.1016/j. wasman.2009.06.004
3. Hahladakis, J.N., Iacovidou, E.: Closing the loop on plastic packaging materials: what is quality and how does it affect their circularity? Sci. Total Environ. **630**, 1394–1400 (2018). https://doi.org/10.1016/j.scitotenv.2018.02.330
4. Hopewell, J., Dvorak, R., Kosior, E.: Plastics recycling: challenges and opportunities. Philos. Trans. R. Soc. B Biol. Sci. **364**(1526), 2115–2126 (2009). https://doi.org/10.1098/ rstb.2008.0311
5. Atsani, S.I., Mastrisiswadi, H.: Recycled polypropylene filament for 3D printer: extrusion process parameter optimization. In: IOP Conference Series: Materials Science and Engineering, vol. 722, no. 1 (2020). https://doi.org/10.1088/1757-899X/722/1/012022
6. Mohammed, M.I., Wilson, D., Gomez-Kervin, E., Tang, B., Wang, J.: Investigation of closed-loop manufacturing with acrylonitrile butadiene styrene over multiple generations using additive manufacturing. ACS Sustain. Chem. Eng. **7**(16), 13955–13969 (2019). https://doi.org/10.1021/acssuschemeng.9b02368
7. Arena, U., Mastellone, M.L., Perugini, F.: Life cycle assessment of a plastic packaging recycling system. Int. J. Life Cycle Assess. **8**(2), 92–98 (2003). https://doi.org/10.1007/ BF02978432
8. Hamod, H.: Suitability of recycled HDPE for 3D printing filament: plastics technology (December 2014)
9. Choudhary, K., Sangwan, K.S., Goyal, D.: Environment and economic impacts assessment of PET waste recycling with conventional and renewable sources of energy. Procedia CIRP **80**, 422–427 (2019). https://doi.org/10.1016/j.procir.2019.01.096
10. Kreiger, M.A., Mulder, M.L., Glover, A.G., Pearce, J.M.: Life cycle analysis of distributed recycling of post-consumer high density polyethylene for 3-D printing filament. J. Clean. Prod. **70**, 90–96 (2014). https://doi.org/10.1016/j.jclepro.2014.02.009
11. Lebreton, L.C., Greer, S.D., Borrero, J.C.: Numerical modelling of floating debris in the world's oceans. Mar. Pollut. Bull. **64**(3), 653–661 (2012). https://doi.org/10.1016/j. marpolbul.2011.10.027
12. Zhong, S., Pearce, J.M.: Tightening the loop on the circular economy: coupled distributed recycling and manufacturing with recyclebot and RepRap 3-D printing. Resour. Conserv. Recycl. **128**, 48–58 (2018). https://doi.org/10.1016/j.resconrec.2017.09.023
13. Thompson, R.C., Moore, C.J., Saal, F.S.V., Swan, S.H.: Plastics, the environment and human health: current consensus and future trends. Philos. Trans. R. Soc. B Biol. Sci. **364** (1526), 2153–2166 (2009). https://doi.org/10.1098/rstb.2009.0053
14. Ferrari, F., Corcione, C.E., Montagna, F., Maffezzoli, A.: 3D printing of polymer waste for improving people's awareness about marine litter. Polymers (Basel) **12**(8), 1738 (2020). https://doi.org/10.3390/POLYM12081738

15. World Plastics Production 1950–2015. https://committee.iso.org/files/live/sites/tc61/files/ThePlasticIndustryBerlinAug2016-Copy.pdf. Accessed 23 Dec 2020
16. Pakkanen, J., Manfredi, D., Minetola, P., Iuliano, L.: About the use of recycled or biodegradable filaments for sustainability of 3D printing: state of the art and research opportunities. Smart Innov. Syst. Technol. **68**, 776–785 (2017). https://doi.org/10.1007/978-3-319-57078-5_73
17. Cruz, F., Lanza, S., Boudaoud, H., Hoppe, S., Camargo, M.: Polymer recycling and additive manufacturing in an open source context: optimization of processes and methods. In: Proceedings - 26th Annual International Solid Freeform Fabrication Symposium - An Additive Manufacturing Conference, SFF 2015, pp. 1591–1600 (2020)
18. Pinho, A.C., Amaro, A.M., Piedade, A.P.: 3D printing goes greener: study of the properties of post-consumer recycled polymers for the manufacturing of engineering components. Waste Manag. **118**, 426–434 (2020). https://doi.org/10.1016/j.wasman.2020.09.003
19. Snowdon, M.R., Abdelwahab, M., Mohanty, A.K., Misra, M.: Mechanical optimization of virgin and recycled poly (ethylene terephthalate) biocomposites with sustainable biocarbon through a factorial design. Results Mater. **5**, 100060 (2020). https://doi.org/10.1016/j.rinma.2020.100060
20. Zhao, P., Rao, C., Gu, F., Sharmin, N., Fu, J.: Close-looped recycling of polylactic acid used in 3D printing: an experimental investigation and life cycle assessment. J. Clean. Prod. **197**, 1046–1055 (2018). https://doi.org/10.1016/j.jclepro.2018.06.275
21. Mohammed, M.I., Mohan, M., Das, A., Gibson, I.: A low carbon footprint approach to the reconstitution of plastics into 3D-printer filament for enhanced waste reduction, pp. 234–241 (2017). https://doi.org/10.18502/keg.v2i2.621
22. Dontsov, Y.V., Panin, S.V., Buslovich, D.G., Berto, F.: Taguchi optimization of parameters for feedstock fabrication and FDM manufacturing of wear-resistant UHMWPE-based composites. Materials (Basel) **13**(12), 1–26 (2020). https://doi.org/10.3390/ma13122718
23. Lanzotti, A., Martorelli, M., Maietta, S., Gerbino, S., Penta, F., Gloria, A.: A comparison between mechanical properties of specimens 3D printed with virgin and recycled PLA. Procedia CIRP **79**, 143–146 (2019). https://doi.org/10.1016/j.procir.2019.02.030
24. Mikula, K., et al.: 3D printing filament as a second life of waste plastics—a review. Environ. Sci. Pollut. Res. **28**(10), 12321–12333 (2020). https://doi.org/10.1007/s11356-020-10657-8
25. Cruz Sanchez, F.A., Boudaoud, H., Camargo, M., Pearce, J.M.: Plastic recycling in additive manufacturing: a systematic literature review and opportunities for the circular economy. J. Clean. Prod. **264**, 121602 (2020). https://doi.org/10.1016/j.jclepro.2020.121602
26. Woern, A.L., McCaslin, J.R., Pringle, A.M., Pearce, J.M.: RepRapable Recyclebot: open source 3-D printable extruder for converting plastic to 3-D printing filament. HardwareX **4**, e00026 (2018). https://doi.org/10.1016/j.ohx.2018.e00026
27. Gokhare, V.G.: A review paper on 3D-printing aspects and various processes used in the 3D-printing. Int. J. Eng. Res. Technol. **6**(06), 953–958 (2017)
28. Nale, S., Kalbande, A.G.: A review on 3D printing technology. Int. J. Innov. Emerg. Res. Eng. **5**(7), 2001–2004 (2020)
29. Saiyam Jain, U.S.: 3D printing. Int. J. Eng. Res. Technol. **578**, 1–14 (2020). http://www.globalview.gr/2016/06/30/62949/
30. Sai, P.C., Yeole, S.: Fused deposition modeling – insights. In: Proceedings of the International Conference on Advances in Design and Manufacturing (December 2014). https://doi.org/10.1201/9780203910795.ch8
31. Osswald, T.A., Puentes, J., Kattinger, J.: Fused filament fabrication melting model. Addit. Manuf. **22**, 51–59 (2018). https://doi.org/10.1016/j.addma.2018.04.030

32. Leonard Mutiva, B., Byiringiro, J.B., Eng, R., Peter Muchiri, S.N.: A study on suitability of recycled polyethylene terephthalate for 3D printing filament. IOSR J. Mech. Civ. Eng. **15**(2), 4–9 (2017). https://doi.org/10.9790/1684-1502030409

33. Mohammed, M.I., Das, A., Gomez-Kervin, E., Wilson, D., Gibson, I.: Ecoprinting: investigating the use of 100% recycled acrylonitrile butadiene styrene (ABS) for additive manufacturing. In: 28th Annual International Solid Freeform Fabrication Symposium – An Additive Manufacturing Conference, SFF 2017, pp. 532–542 (2020)

34. Whitacre, D.M.: Reviews of Environmental Contamination and Toxicology. Springer, Heidelberg (2012). https://doi.org/10.1007/978-1-4614-3137-4

35. Thompson, R.C., Swan, S.H., Moore, C.J., Vom Saal, F.S.: Our plastic age. Philos. Trans. R. Soc. B Biol. Sci. **364**(1526), 1973–1976 (2009). https://doi.org/10.1098/rstb.2009.0054

36. Proshad, R., Kormoker, T., Islam, M.S., Haque, M.A., Rahman, M.M., Mithu, M.M.R.: Toxic effects of plastic on human health and environment: a consequences of health risk assessment in Bangladesh. Int. J. Heal. **6**(1), 1 (2017). https://doi.org/10.14419/ijh.v6i1.8655

37. Alabi, O.A., Ologbonjaye, K.I., Awosolu, O., Alalade, O.E.: Public and environmental health effects of plastic wastes disposal: a review. J. Toxicol. Risk Assess.**5**(2), 1–13 (2019). https://doi.org/10.23937/2572-4061.1510021

38. Ghosh, S.K.: Plastics in municipal solid waste: what, where, how and when? Waste Manag. Res. **37**(11), 1061–1062 (2019). https://doi.org/10.1177/0734242X19880656

39. Antelava, A., et al.: Plastic solid waste (PSW) in the context of life cycle assessment (LCA) and sustainable management. Environ. Manag. **64**(2), 230–244 (2019). https://doi.org/10.1007/s00267-019-01178-3

40. Ismail, B., Sc, F.B., Yassin, E.E.: Management of PET plastic bottles waste through recycling in Khartoum State. Sudan Academy of Science. Engineering, Research and Industrial Council, p. 90 (2010). https://inis.iaea.org/collection/NCLCollectionStore/_Public/44/007/44007611.pdf

41. Webb, H.K., Arnott, J., Crawford, R.J., Ivanova, E.P.: Plastic degradation and its environmental implications with special reference to poly(ethylene terephthalate). Polymers (Basel) **5**(1), 1–18 (2013). https://doi.org/10.3390/polym5010001

42. Prata, J.C., et al.: Solutions and integrated strategies for the control and mitigation of plastic and microplastic pollution. Int. J. Environ. Res. Public Health **16**(13), 1–19 (2019). https://doi.org/10.3390/ijerph16132411

43. Maris, J., Bourdon, S., Brossard, J., Cauret, L.: Mechanical recycling: compatibilization of mixed thermoplastic wastes. Polym. Degrad. Stab. **147**, 245–266 (2017). https://doi.org/10.1016/j.polymdegradstab.2017.11.001

44. Geyer, R., Jambeck, J.R., Law, K.L.: Production, use, and fate of all plastics ever made, pp. 25–29 (2017)

45. Gopinathan, J., Noh, I.: Recent trends in bioinks for 3D printing. Biomater. Res. **22**(1), 4–7 (2018). https://doi.org/10.1186/s40824-018-0122-1

46. Shah, J., Snider, B., Clarke, T., Kozutsky, S., Lacki, M., Hosseini, A.: Large-scale 3D printers for additive manufacturing: design considerations and challenges. Int. J. Adv. Manuf. Technol. **104**(9–12), 3679–3693 (2019). https://doi.org/10.1007/s00170-019-04074-6

47. Sciaky: Additive manufacturing (2014)

48. Anderson, I.: Mechanical properties of specimens 3D printed with virgin and recycled polylactic acid. 3D Print. Addit. Manuf. **4**(2), 110–115 (2017). https://doi.org/10.1089/3dp.2016.0054

49. Angatkina, K.: Recycling of HDPE from MSW waste to 3D printing filaments (2018)

50. Zander, N.E.: Recycled polymer feedstocks for material extrusion additive manufacturing. In: Polymer-Based Additive Manufacturing: Recent Developments, Part 3 - Recycled Polymer Feedstocks for Material Extrusion Additive Manufacturing (2019). https://doi.org/10.1021/bk-2019-1315.ch003

51. Chong, S., Pan, G.-T., Khalid, M., Yang, T.-K., Hung, S.-T., Huang, C.-M.: Physical characterization and pre-assessment of recycled high-density polyethylene as 3D printing material. J. Polym. Environ. **25**(2), 136–145 (2016). https://doi.org/10.1007/s10924-016-0793-4

52. Baechler, C., Devuono, M., Pearce, J.M.: Distributed recycling of waste polymer into RepRap feedstock. Rapid Prototyp. J. **19**(2), 118–125 (2013). https://doi.org/10.1108/13552541311302978

53. Braanker, G.B., Flohil, J.J., Tokaya, G.E.: Developing a plastics recycling add-on for the RepRap 3D printer. Delft Univ. Technol. **42**, 8–20 (2010)

54. Gu, F., Guo, J., Zhang, W., Summers, P.A., Hall, P.: From waste plastics to industrial raw materials: a life cycle assessment of mechanical plastic recycling practice based on a real-world case study. Sci. Total Environ. **601–602**, 1192–1207 (2017). https://doi.org/10.1016/j.scitotenv.2017.05.278

55. Albi, E., Kozel, K., Ventoza, D., Wilmoth, R.: AKABOT: 3D printing filament extruder (2014)

56. Wankhade, M.H., Bahaley, S.G.: Design and development of plastic filament extruder for 3D printing. IRA-Int. J. Technol. Eng. **10**(03), 23–40 (2018)

57. Nassar, M.A., Elfarahaty, M., Ibrahim, S., Hassan, Y.: Design of 3D filament extruder for Fused Deposition Modeling (FDM) additive manufacturing. Int. Des. J. **9**(4), 55–62 (2019)

58. Raza, S.M., Singh, D.: Experimental investigation on filament extrusion using recycled materials (2020)

59. Iunolainen, E.: Suitability of recycled PP for 3D PRINTING FILAMENT, p. 48 (2017)

60. Zander, N.E., Gillan, M., Lambeth, R.H.: Recycled polyethylene terephthalate as a new FFF feedstock material. Addit. Manuf. **21**, 174–182 (2018). https://doi.org/10.1016/j.addma.2018.03.007

61. Arendra, A., Akhmad, S., Hidayat, K., Prasnowo, M.A.: Development of low cost recycled HDPE filament extruder for 3D printing filament, pp. 2–8 (2019). https://doi.org/10.4108/eai.18-7-2019.2288536

62. Little, H.A., Tanikella, N.G., Reich, M.J., Fiedler, M.J., Snabes, S.L., Pearce, J.M.: Towards distributed recycling with additive manufacturing of PET flake feedstocks. Materials (Basel) **13**, 4273 (2020)

63. Nwogu, C., Anthony, O.C.: Characterization of recycled polyethylene terephthalate powder for 3D printing feedstock. Int. J. Adv. Sci. Eng. Technol. **6**, 8844 (2019)

64. Bhadeshia, H.K.D.H.: Mechanical properties and applications of recycled polycarbonate particle material extrusion-based additive manufacturing. Mater. Sci. Technol. (U. K.) **32**(7), 615–616 (2016). https://doi.org/10.1080/02670836.2016.1197523

65. You, A., Be, M.A.Y., In, I.: Preparation and characterisation of 3D printer filament from post-used Styrofoam. In: AIP Conference Proceedings, vol. 2233, p. 020022 (May 2020)

66. Turku, I., Kasala, S., Kärki, T.: Characterization of polystyrene wastes as potential extruded feedstock filament for 3D printing. Recycling **3**(4), 57 (2018). https://doi.org/10.3390/recycling3040057

67. Wampol, C.: Additive Manufacturing with High Density Polyethylene : Mechanical Properties Evaluation. South Dakota State Univ. Open PRAIRIE Open Public Res. Access Institutional Repository and Information Exchange (2018)

68. Gkartzou, E., Koumoulos, E.P., Charitidis, C.A.: Production and 3D printing processing of bio-based thermoplastic filament. Manuf. Rev. **4**, 1 (2017). https://doi.org/10.1051/mfreview/2016020

69. Tian, X., Liu, T., Wang, Q., Dilmurat, A., Li, D., Ziegmann, G.: Recycling and remanufacturing of 3D printed continuous carbon fiber reinforced PLA composites. J. Clean. Prod. **142**, 1609–1618 (2017). https://doi.org/10.1016/j.jclepro.2016.11.139

70. Idrees, M., Jeelani, S., Rangari, V.: Three-dimensional-printed sustainable biochar-recycled PET composites. ACS Sustain. Chem. Eng. **6**(11), 13940–13948 (2018). https://doi.org/10.1021/acssuschemeng.8b02283

71. Zander, N.E.: Rubber toughened recycled polyethylene terephthalate for material extrusion additive manufacturing (2020). https://doi.org/10.1002/pi.6079

72. Pan, G.T., Chong, S., Tsai, H.J., Lu, W.H., Yang, T.C.K.: The effects of iron, silicon, chromium, and aluminium additions on the physical and mechanical properties of recycled 3D printing filaments. Adv. Polym. Technol. **37**(4), 1176–1184 (2018). https://doi.org/10.1002/adv.21777

73. Singh, N., Singh, R., Ahuja, I.P.S.: Recycling of polymer waste with SiC/Al2O3 reinforcement for rapid tooling applications. Mater. Today Commun. **15**, 124–127 (2018). https://doi.org/10.1016/j.mtcomm.2018.02.008

74. Stoof, D., Pickering, K.: Sustainable composite fused deposition modelling filament using recycled pre-consumer polypropylene. Compos. Part B **135**, 110–118 (2018). https://doi.org/10.1016/j.compositesb.2017.10.005

75. Torres, N., Robin, J.J., Boutevin, B.: Study of thermal and mechanical properties of virgin and recycled poly (ethylene terephthalate) before and after injection molding. Eur. Polym. J. **36**, 2075–2080 (2000)

Integrating Sustainability Measures and Practices in the Ethiopian Industrial Parks: From Review to Conceptual Model

Fitsum Getachew Bayu[1(✉)], Frank Ebinger[2], and Eshetie Berhan[1]

[1] School of Mechanical and Industrial Engineering, Addis Ababa Institute
of Technology, Addis Ababa University, Addis Ababa, Ethiopia
fitsum.getachew@aait.edu.et

[2] Department of Sustainability-Oriented Innovations and Transformation
Management, Nuremberg Campus of Technology (NCT),
Technische Hochschule Nuremberg, Nuremberg, Germany

Abstract. Sustainable performance demands to show a sustained competitive advantage that lasts a long period. "Industrial Parks" is now the gateway to sustainable development, especially in the least developing countries like Ethiopia, for example. The industrial parks are highly attracting foreign direct investment and working for the inclusive development of the country. Though this is a good start, the capability is at an initial stage and needs support in terms of their performance towards creating a sustainable operation. Based on the evidence of both theoretical and empirical literature findings, this study paper conducted a review and identified the sustainability measures and practices from which it tries to filter the key capability measures and practices for the Ethiopian industrial parks. For integrating the identified practices and measures, as a methodological approach, the theory of dynamic capability process is considered, encompassing sensing, learning, and transforming the cyclic loop. Practices and measures are incorporated in each process of dynamic capability pillars. A conceptual model was developed as the final output showing the holistic map of the integrated sustainability measures and practices. The measures and practices identified will fully support the sustainable growth and decision process of the industrial park operation. It also adds value to the body of knowledge in industrial sustainability in special economic zones.

Keywords: Sustainability measures · Sustainability practices · Ethiopian industrial parks · Dynamic capability

1 Introduction

Industrial parks or zones are set of business within a specific geographical area which shares resources and thereby increase profitability, reduce environmental impact, and improve social performance. The concept of industrial parks emerged during the 1990s and 2000s with so-called special economic zones. Industrial parks (IP) are an agglomeration of different firms operating in a given demarcated area following a sustainable business model. IP business models aim for a significant impact on the

© ICST Institute for Computer Sciences, Social Informatics and Telecommunications Engineering 2022
Published by Springer Nature Switzerland AG 2022. All Rights Reserved
M. L. Berihun (Ed.): ICAST 2021, LNICST 412, pp. 262–276, 2022.
https://doi.org/10.1007/978-3-030-93712-6_18

environment and society through changes in the way firms create and capture value (change their value prepositions) [1]. The business model goes beyond the economic value and addresses the other triple bottom line dimensions (environment and social).

In the current economy, countries in the least developing countries like Ethiopia are considering industrial parks as a policy instrument for economic growth. Ethiopia introduced the concept of "Industrial Parks" lately, 2012/13, and showing now a progressive change to the country's economic development. The government of Ethiopia targeted industrial parks as a major policy tool for the success of the Growth and Transformation Plan (GTPII), which runs to 2025 to transform Ethiopia into a global manufacturing hub.

According to recent literature, the current global economy pushes firms to think beyond their profit and consider the planet and people in the operation process [2]. This situation is important and sensitive to special economic zones and the Ethiopian industrial parks to sustain the development and performance and gain sustainable outcomes. Therefore, park operation management requires a holistic, customized system comprising the sustainability measures and practices, which the Ethiopian industrial parks lack in their current situation [3]. This has also still being a challenge in other countries of least developing countries, due to lack of awareness, lack of involvement of sustainability metrics, and organization structuring problems are some to mention [4].

Integrating sustainability measures and practices require customizing the generic indicator variables of sustainability measures and practices according to the operation process of Ethiopian industrial parks [5]. This is because literature developed several indicator variables and practices for sustainability in economic, social, and environmental pillars, but incorporating these variables at the firm's level requires customizing according to the firm characteristics and operation [6]. Therefore, this study paper conducts a review and identifies the sustainability measures and practices from which it tries to filter the key capability measures and practices of sustainability (economic, environmental and social) for the Ethiopian industrial park case. Moreover, the study develops a holistic framework showing how the practices and measures are integrated as a system.

2 Literature Review

2.1 Sustainability and Its Measures

Sustainability as a group of actions taken to meet the needs of the present moment without committing to future capacity [7]. Sustainability is the ability to maintain profits as expected by shareholders, manufacture without damaging the environment, and improve the quality of lives of stakeholders [8]. Several works of literature in the recent era of research are focusing on integrating sustainability indicators. Sustainability in the manufacturing industries has been an important aspect; several methods have been developed to assess sustainability at the firm level. However, most of the methods do not consider the holistic dimension of economic, social, and environmental indicators. Previous thoughts on creating long-term success with only focusing on financial aspects now widened by considering environmental and societal issues. These areas are now studied in the pillar of sustainability, incorporating people, planet, and profit. Jaehn [9]

Definitions regarding operation sustainability where a system is called sustainable if the environment influences the system so that it can exist permanently. The "permanent existence" of a system is not to be understood in a strict sense but instead in the sense of a very long time horizon. Kleindorfer [10] articulated that organization management is connected to sustainability, and it is now focusing on both operational drivers of profitability and their relationship to people and the planet. As cited by Gimenez [11] sustainable operation is defined as the set of skills and leverages that allow a company to structure its business process to achieve lasting performance [12].

Performance dimensions encompass the social aspect, mainly employees in this study, economic aspects of business indicators, and the environment. Sustainable operation management (SOM) includes the strategies, techniques, and practices to support these triple bottom sustainable dimensions [13]. Sustainable operations can also be seen as a system for aligned business activities throughout the product lifecycle to create value to stakeholders, commercial success, people's well-being, and the environment [14]. For achieving sustainable operations, Firms have to contemplate the three dimensions of TBL. However, the challenge is to define the relevant indicators for each dimension and understand how they connect to achieve a sustainable process. Table 1 shows the sustainability indicators in the literature.

Table 1. Sustainability measures; Source [15]

Area of performance	Category	Core indicators	Authors
Economic	Cost management	Return on investment	[16–20]
		Environment investment	
		Export sales	
	Operation efficiency	Productivity	
		Products quality and services	
		Lean manufacturing wastes	
	Suppliers	Number of suppliers	
		Just in time	
		Standards for suppliers	
	Customers	Number of complaints	
Environmental	Environmental management	Policy/standards; compliance cost; certification	[21–24]
	Environmental aspect	Suppliers with environment	
		Company image with environmental	
	Responsibility consumptions	Treatment/disposal of waste	
		Consumption of water, energy	
Social	Economic	Salary and benefits	[19, 25–28]
	Satisfaction level	Level of employee satisfaction; Absenteeism; turnover; health programs and safety employees; ergonomics	
	Human resource	Availability of skilled labor	
		Recruitment; performance evaluation	
	Health and safety	Accidents	
		Injuries	
		Personal protective equipment	

2.2   Sustainable Practices: Lean and Green

Sustaining competitiveness in the market demands to overcome external and internal pressures such as; regulations and fulfilling standard requirements, the need for the customer, supplier relationship, employee management, etc. [29]. These mentioned concerns ultimately influence firms and shake their sustainability in the global business. Therefore, focusing on sustainability, incorporating the operational, social, and environmental factors is taken as their primary goal beyond their operational gain. Integrating sustainability at the firm level and creating a balance within the operational production performance is challenging. The main reason because it demands to create a simultaneous outcome that balances the gain in profit, environment, and human capital development.

To compromise the above challenges and build sustainable operation capability resulting in a balanced outcome in all the three aspects of sustainable dimensions, academic authors and practitioners are giving attention to utilizing sustainable manufacturing philosophies. The lean and green philosophes are exemplary and most researched themes. The strong commonality that the two have to address sustainability paved the way for researchers to utilize them as balancing mechanisms for sustainable manufacturing. These philosophies compromise different practices both at technical and soft levels. The technical or hard practices are used to achieve process-level performances such as production cost, delivery, quality, and flexibility [30]. At the same time, the soft practices are oriented to people and organizations aiming to capitalize on the employee, customer, supplier, and management [31]. Lean and green practices have been spreading widely both in service and manufacturing industries, both targeting operational and environmental performance [32, 33]. Today, the techniques are applied beyond the manufacturing aspect and taken as management or thinking approaches in various organizations [34].

Table 2. Critical Lean-Green practices for sustainable performance

Practice bundles	Sub-variables	Authors
Soft practices	Environmental and social investments	[30, 35, 36]
	Eco-design and certifications	
	Green branding and promotion	
	Standardized and flexible working system	
	Employee engagement and participation	
	Sustainability awareness programs and leadership	
	Sustainability oriented training and job empowerment	
	Customer and supplier network	
	Communication platforms/channels	
Technical/hard practices	Lean tools (5S, TPM,VSM,QMS/ISO9001/)	[37–40]
	Green tools (Green VSM, Green purchasing, ISO1400, OHS/ISO45001)	

3 Methodological Approach and Theory Building

3.1 Methodological Approach

Building sustainable capabilities and performance requires integrating sustainable measures and practices. The integration requires a systematic approach. In this paper study, both theoretical literature and empirical review and investigation were conducted. The theoretical review was done to identify core sustainable measures and practices. Moreover, as a theoretical approach, the concept and dimensions of dynamic capabilities were also reviewed accordingly. With the support of theoretical knowledge, an empirical review was conducted to understand and identify the interference variables involved in sustainability measures and practices of Ethiopian industrial parks. As a supporting method, the review findings were further triangulated through interviewing operation managers, stakeholders, and foreign investors in the park.

Moreover, secondary research reports in the park performances were also used for better substance the outputs from the qualitative results. Basing both theoretical and empirical outputs, a conceptual model that helps assimilate sustainable practices through the use of the dynamic capability approach and build sustainable performance of industrial parks has been forwarded. This conceptual model creates a platform where dynamic capabilities are assimilated and help managers visualize the critical measures and practices for sustaining the park's performances. Understanding these variables aid in better decision-making and opens for early learning of dynamic situations. The conceptual model developed for EIP, aiming to reconfigure the existing static operational capabilities, takes the base of [41] theory. The theory of dynamic capabilities and their routines has taken as a base to influence the existing operational capabilities of the industrial park where the park operational influencing variables in social, economic, and environmental, and resources are taken as moderating variables. Operational capabilities reconfigured in such a way finally influence the sustainable performance of the parks (Fig. 1).

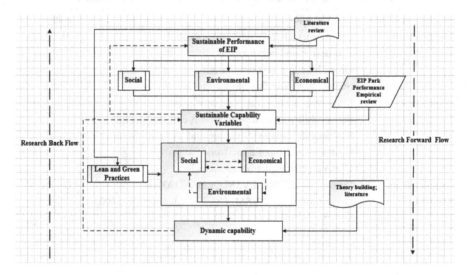

Fig. 1. Research framework

3.2   Theory Building: Dynamic Capabilities

Dynamic capabilities view originates in spirit from Schumpeter [42] innovation-based competition where competitive advantage is based on the creative destruction of existing resources and novel recombination into new operational capabilities. These ideas were further developed in the literature, such as architectural innovation [43], configuration competence [44], and combinative capabilities [45]. Extending these studies, [46] developed the notion of dynamic capabilities, and their seminal paper is considered the most influential source on dynamic capabilities, together with a current framework of dynamic capabilities [47]. The dynamic capabilities view follows the resource-based view (RBV). In contrast, RBV emphasizes resource picking (selecting resource combinations), dynamic capabilities stress resource renewal (reconfiguring resources into new combinations of operational capabilities). The DC theory suggests competitive advantage comes through leveraging a firm's managerial and organizational processes and developed through the integration of intangible assets and capabilities with a dynamic environment. This theory has become one of the most influential theoretical lenses in the firm's strategic management in today's changing global market. The term "dynamic" translate as the capacity to renew competencies so as to achieve congruence with the changing business environment. Dynamic capability concept originally defined as the "firm's ability to integrate, build, and reconfigure internal and external competencies to address rapidly changing environments" [48]. Competency reflects the managerial and organizational process or patter of practices and learnings. Eisenhardt [49] also subsequently defined dynamic capabilities as "the firm's process that uses resources to match and create market change". The authors also outlined examples of dynamic process such as product development routines, resource allocation routines, knowledge transfer routines. Another evolution of dynamic capability is focused on organizational learning, where it is considered as a source of dynamic capability. In this context, Zollo [50] defined it as "a learned and stable pattern of collective activity through which the organization systematically generates and modifies its operating routines in pursuit of improved effectiveness".

Therefore, this paper takes the dynamic capability view theory to integrate sustainability measures and practices.

4   Sustainability Measures and the Existing Situation in EIP

Based on the international framework for Eco-industrial parks, the performance requirements of industrial parks are categorized into four key categories: park management performance, environmental performance, social performance, and economic performance [51]. In general, park management related to infrastructures, organizing services, standards, and marketing and promotion of the park is the key activities. Environmental aspect dimensions are related to the effective management of resources, including water, wastewater, and climate change issues. The economic aspect of the industrial park focus on maximizing possible returns for business through revenue generation, job creation and competitiveness. The social aspect dimensions address the need of employees and the community around. Worker's management, safety and health and appreciating social incentives and infrastructures are some indicators. These performance requirements increase park management performance and improve the sustainability performance of the industrial parks. The following section summarizes the measures and gives a highlight summary of the existing situation of the version of the park in social, environmental, and economic aspects based on the empirical review and reports of [3, 52, 53]. To understand the existing sustainability of the park, cause and effect analysis is considered. Data required to identify the park's critical causes for limited performance is collected through both primary and secondary approaches. Observation, interview of managements, focus group discussion used as primary data and reports and documents utilized as secondary data.

4.1   Environmental Measures

Environmental sustainability focuses on tasks that will protect vital environmental functions for the future generation. It focuses on product lifecycle, operation process, and integration of supply chains [54]. Key indicators in industrial parks or special economic operations focus on the consumption level of energy, material use, emission. Energy efficiency strategies should be in place for the park management infrastructure and major energy-consuming park operators. Moreover, platforms for the exchange of energy and heat networks should be established in the park. Water-saving and reuse plans are also other essential to reduce total water consumption. System building in place to increase water saving and reuse. The same platform, low carbon technologies, and energy efficiency measures, and waste heat to reduce GHG emissions are essential for the high carbon emission manufacturing sector. On top of all the management and monitoring is critical for the sustainable operation, industry park has an appropriate, functioning environment and energy management system such as ISO14001 and ISO50001 respectively in place and achieves targets.

Based on evaluating the above objective of environmental sustainability, the EIP performance is at the initial stage. The authors' performance reports outlined and preliminary investigation shows that there is low awareness in adopting environmental management practices, capacity concerning knowledge of skills in utilizing and managing green technologies such as zero-liquid discharge. The adoption of regulation and international standards and certification is also at the low stage and is supported by international donors and experts. The below summary in Fig. 2 shows the environmental performance analysis with the EIP's primary root causes and effects.

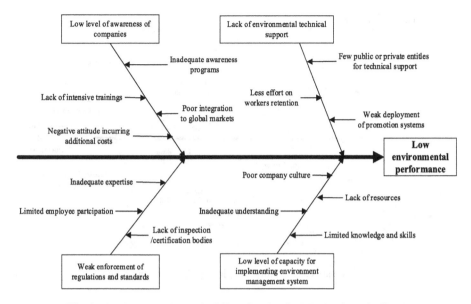

Fig. 2. Environmental sustainability situation in EIP (Authors findings)

4.2 Social Measures

Social sustainability aims to address the social aspects related to the human factor. Variables such as health and safety, salary and benefits, work satisfaction are considered as social sustainability indicators. Indicators focus on social aspects by creating job satisfaction, reducing absenteeism, improving the company image and productivity. Moreover, the absence of building awareness and delivering motivational training, employee recognitions are the core causes of high turnover and low productivity performance. Social management systems, including functioning systems, should be in place to ensure social infrastructure operational and performance and collect, monitor, and manage social innovations and impacts relevant to the industrial park. Implementing, OH&S management system in place based on ISO18001 standard, keep record rate of injury, occupational disease, absenteeism. Grievance management mechanisms should be in place, such as help desks, complaint boxes inside the industrial parks.

Furthermore, the social infrastructure focusing on primary infrastructures such as women's employment encouragement, public toilets, drinking water fountain, cafeteria, recreation areas, and childcare programs. Industrial park security including closed-circuit televisions (CCTV), centralized security, and night transportation provisioning. Capacity-building programs for skills training and development by employee category should be in place. Examples like training and skills development programs and women entrepreneurship development programs.

The social aspect comprises essential measures, and for EIP working in light industries focusing on the labor-intensive sector is crucial. Regarding social sustainability issues, the EIP is facing many challenges and is still in the process of managing the challenges. Key issues raised in the social aspects are; absenteeism, communication and cultural gap, salary and benefits, turnover rates, and worker's safety. Below the summary, Fig. 3 shows the social performance analysis with the EIP's major root causes and effects.

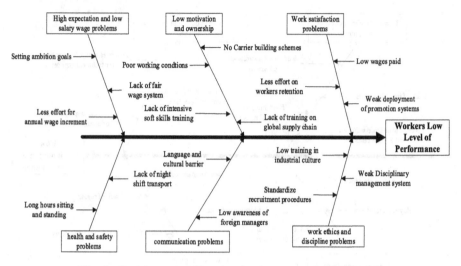

Fig. 3. Social sustainability situation in EIP (Authors findings)

4.3 Economic Measures

Economic sustainability performance is linked to the profitability of the firms. The decision-making in this aspect focuses on the investment ratio and its return according to the investor's expectation. Economic indicators contribute to managing the economic characteristics of the industrial parks and the effectiveness of actions for sustainability [55]. However, the integration requires sub-variables linked to the cost factors. In the case of industrial parks, employment generation is a core target in building local employment opportunities in countries like Ethiopia.

Moreover, longer-term employment to employees is one requirement for sustainable economic performance. Efforts in supporting local business and small and micro enterprises promotion through integrating local suppliers and local investors partnered with the multinational companies. This provides an increase in the growth of local business opportunities. Besides, economic value creation through making investment ready and essential infrastructure service should be offered, including access to water, energy, road, and logistics service.

The above existing situation of social and environmental challenges of the EIP impacted the economic value of the park. It has negatively impacted the factory efficiency and productivity level. On top of this situation, the administration and infrastructure process is at low-level needs encompassing the social and environmental aspects. Issues in aligning the business model in the Ethiopian industry culture are also another challenge faced by foreign investors. The local sourcing process of suppliers is at low capacity in terms of delivery and quality of the product, influencing the production and economic sustainability.

Below the summary, Fig. 4 shows the social performance analysis with the EIP's major root causes and effects.

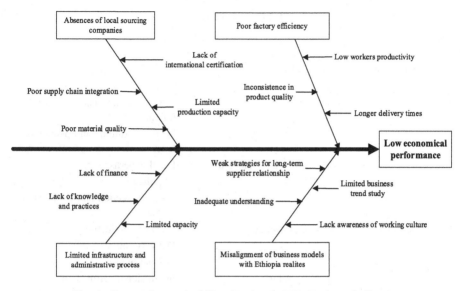

Fig. 4. Economic sustainability situation in EIP (Authors findings)

Basing the above sustainability measures and the existing situation of the EIP, a summary of the key sustainable capability measures is shown in Table 3.

Table 3. Customized sustainability measures for EIP

Capability bundles	Core influencing variables EIP level	Sub influencing-variables
Social aspect (employee)	Job satisfaction	Salary, incentives, and allowance
		Workers retention/attrition
		Absenteeism
	Motivation and commitment	Carrier building schemes
		Working conditions
		Hard and soft skills training
	Health and safety	Night transport availability
		Sitting and standing hours
		Sick leaves
	Communications	Language
		Communication channels
		Information standardization
	Work ethics and discipline	Workers discipline
		Workers industrial ethics and culture

(continued)

Table 3. (*continued*)

Capability bundles	Core influencing variables EIP level	Sub influencing-variables
Environment aspects	Technical supports	Public/private consulting entities
	Environmental awareness	Awareness programs
		Environmental management training
		Workers Attitude and perceptions level
	Regulations and standard	Local expertise
		IP policy
		Local Inspection and certification bodies
Economic aspects	Factory efficiency	Workers productivity
		Delivery times
		Product quality
	Local sourcing	International certifications
		Local suppliers product quality
		Local supplier producing capacity

5 Proposed Conceptual Model

Incorporating identified sustainability measures and practices from the theoretical and empirical review, a conceptual model is developed, shown in Fig. 5. The model follows a continuous loop starting with the inside and goes outside and has three loops. The first and the core center process is the dynamic capability of the EIP, which is sensing, learning, and transforming ability. The sensing embraces the lean-green practices (Table 2) that lead to more opportunity; the learning containing the practices that support the capability building; and the final the transforming considers lean-green tools that transform the sustainable knowledge and practices into the routine level. The second loops are critical capability variables in EIP in social, economic, and environmental levels summarized in Table 3. This second loop is impacted by the first loop of lean-green practice in the DC process. The practices in the DC process contribute to the capacity-building process in all the triple bottom dimensions accordingly. In the final stage, the second loop of the capability variables impacts the final loop of the sustainability performance measures (Table 1).

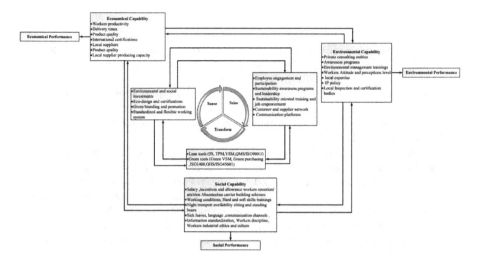

Fig. 5. Integrated sustainability measures and practices in dynamic capability process for EIP: a conceptual model

6 Conclusion and Recommendations

As a latecomer to industrialization, Ethiopia is now pushing forward to leapfrog and integrate into the global value chain. Industrial parks have been selected as the best policy options leading to sustainable development. The development process of industrial parks in different regions of the country is in a rapid process. Though the development speed is in progress, the operation management process is still at the initial stage and needs a lot of support for the sustainable performance of the parks. For this to happen, the literature suggests that incorporating sustainability measures and practices has been taken as a core area in the industrial sustainability of firms. Therefore, learning from literature findings on sustainability measures and practices, this study paper outlined the key measures (Table 1) and practices (Table 2) of sustainability in social, economic, and environmental dimensions. Basing the identified measures, an empirical review was conducted from secondary reports and primary data gathering of Ethiopian industrial parks, resulting in social, economic, and environmental aspects (Fig. 2, 3 and 4). Using a cause and effect diagram, the existing situation is illustrated following the empirical review findings, a comprehensive and summarized sustainability capability variables drawn (Table 3). Taking the dynamic capability view theory as a methodological approach to integrate the identified sustainability measures and practices, a holistic conceptual model was developed (Fig. 5).

As a general recommendation, Ethiopian industrial parks operation should be framed as a system incorporating sustainability measures and practices. Incorporating sustainability variables ultimately allows for the operation to achieve sustainable development in all the triple bottom lines. For this to happen, the different actors and functional units involved should contribute to this goal. Moreover, the EIP management system should initiate programs that contribute to social, environmental, and economic awareness and knowledge within the stakeholders and employees.

References

1. Pal, R.: Sustainable design and business models in textile and fashion industry. In: Muthu, S. S. (ed.) Sustainability in the Textile Industry. TSCT, pp. 109–138. Springer, Singapore (2017). https://doi.org/10.1007/978-981-10-2639-3_6
2. Fang, Y., Côté, R.P., Qin, R.: Industrial sustainability in China: practice and prospects for eco-industrial development. J. Environ. Manage. **83**(3), 315–328 (2007)
3. Azmach, E.W.: Regulating industrial parks development in Ethiopia: a critical analysis. Beijing Law Rev. **10**(1), 23–60 (2019)
4. Cherrafi, A., Elfezazi, S., Chiarini, A., Mokhlis, A., Benhida, K.: The integration of lean manufacturing, Six Sigma and sustainability: a literature review and future research directions for developing a specific model. J. Clean. Prod. **139**, 828–846 (2016)
5. Neri, A., Cagno, E., Di Sebastiano, G., Trianni, A.: Industrial sustainability: modelling drivers and mechanisms with barriers. J. Clean. Prod. **194**, 452–472 (2018)
6. Iranmanesh, M., Zailani, S., Hyun, S.S., Ali, M.H., Kim, K.: Impact of lean manufacturing practices on firms' sustainable performance: lean culture as a moderator. Sustainability **11**(4), 1112 (2019)
7. Clancy, G., Fröling, M., Svanström, M.: Changing from petroleum to wood-based materials: critical review of how product sustainability characteristics can be assessed and compared. J. Clean. Prod. **39**, 372–385 (2013)
8. Faulkner, W., Badurdeen, F.: Sustainable Value Stream Mapping (Sus-VSM): methodology to visualize and assess manufacturing sustainability performance. J. Clean. Prod. **85**, 8–18 (2014)
9. Jaehn, F.: Sustainable operations. Eur. J. Oper. Res. **253**(2), 243–264 (2016)
10. Kleindorfer, P.R., Singhal, K., Wassenhove, L.N.: Sustainable operations management. Prod. Oper. Manage. **14**(4), 482–492 (2009)
11. Gimenez, C., Sierra, V., Rodon, J.: Sustainable operations: their impact on the triple bottom line. Int. J. Prod. Econ. **140**(1), 149–159 (2012)
12. Kleindorfer, P.R., Singhal, K., Van Wassenhove, L.N.: Sustainable operations management [electronic version]. Prod. Oper. Manage. **14**(4), 482–492 (2005)
13. Machado, C.G., Pinheiro de Lima, E., Gouvea da Costa, S.E., Angelis, J.J., Mattioda, R.A.: Framing maturity based on sustainable operations management principles. Int. J. Prod. Econ. **190**, 3–21 (2017)
14. Wong, W.P., Wong, K.Y.: Synergizing an ecosphere of lean for sustainable operations. J. Clean. Prod. **85**, 51–66 (2014)
15. Helleno, A.L., de Moraes, A.J.I., Simon, A.T.: Integrating sustainability indicators and Lean Manufacturing to assess manufacturing processes: application case studies in Brazilian industry. J. Clean. Prod. **153**, 405–416 (2017)
16. Aguado, S., Alvarez, R., Domingo, R.: Model of efficient and sustainable improvements in a lean production system through processes of environmental innovation. J. Clean. Prod. **47**, 141–148 (2013)
17. Hallgren, M., Olhager, J.: Lean and agile manufacturing: external and internal drivers and performance outcomes. Int. J. Oper. Prod. Manage. **29**(10), 976–999 (2009)
18. Cagno, E., Neri, A., Howard, M., Brenna, G., Trianni, A.: Industrial sustainability performance measurement systems: a novel framework. J. Clean. Prod. **230**, 1354–1375 (2019)
19. Harik, R., El Hachem, W., Medini, K., Bernard, A.: Towards a holistic sustainability index for measuring sustainability of manufacturing companies. Int. J. Prod. Res. **53**(13), 4117–4139 (2015)

20. Sala, S., Ciuffo, B., Nijkamp, P.: A systemic framework for sustainability assessment. Ecol. Econ. **119**, 314–325 (2015)
21. Pampanelli, A.B., Found, P., Bernardes, A.M.: A Lean & Green Model for a production cell. J. Clean. Prod. **85**, 19–30 (2014)
22. Cherrafi, A., Garza-Reyes, J.A., Kumar, V., Mishra, N., Ghobadian, A., Elfezazi, S.: Lean, green practices and process innovation: a model for green supply chain performance. Int. J. Prod. Econ. **206**, 79–92 (2018)
23. Dieste, M., Panizzolo, R., Garza-Reyes, J.A., Anosike, A.: The relationship between Lean and environmental performance: practices and measures. J. Clean. Prod. **224**, 120–131 (2019)
24. Alves, A., Moreira, F., Abreu, F., Colombo, C.: Sustainability, lean and eco-efficiency symbioses. In: Peris-Ortiz, M., Farinha, L., Ferreira, J.J., Fernandes, N.O. (eds.) Multiple Helix Ecosystems for Sustainable Competitiveness. ITKM, pp. 91–112. Springer, Cham (2016). https://doi.org/10.1007/978-3-319-29677-7_7
25. Garbie, I.H.: Fundamental requirements for sustainability practices and implementation: an analytical modelling and empirical investigation. Int. J. Sustain. Manuf. **3**(4), 333–362 (2015)
26. Hubbard, G.: Measuring organizational performance: beyond the triple bottom line. Bus. Strateg. Environ. **18**(3), 177–191 (2009)
27. Amrina, E., Yusof, S.M.: Interpretive structural model of key performance indicators for sustainable manufacturing evaluation in automotive companies. In: IEEE International Conference on Industrial Engineering and Engineering Management, pp. 656–660 (2012)
28. Garbie, I.H.: An analytical technique to model and assess sustainable development index in manufacturing enterprises. Int. J. Prod. Res. **52**(16), 4876–4915 (2014)
29. Li, D., Eden, L., Hitt, M.A., Ireland, R.D.: Does product market competition foster CSR. Acad. Manage. J. **51**(2), 315–334 (2008)
30. Bhasin, S.: Performance of Lean in large organisations. J. Manuf. Syst. **31**(3), 349–357 (2012)
31. Ahuja, J., Panda, T.K., Luthra, S., Kumar, A., Choudhary, S., Garza-Reyes, J.A.: Do human critical success factors matter in adoption of sustainable manufacturing practices? An influential mapping analysis of multi-company perspective. J. Clean. Prod. **239**, 117981 (2019)
32. Banawi, A., Bilec, M.M.: A framework to improve construction processes: integrating Lean, Green and Six Sigma. Int. J. Constr. Manage. **14**(1), 45–55 (2014)
33. Inman, R.A., Green, K.W.: Lean and green combine to impact environmental and operational performance. Int. J. Prod. Res. **56**(14), 4802–4818 (2018)
34. Zokaei, K., Lovins, H., Wood, Y., Hines, P.: Lean and Green business process management techniques for improving profits and sustainability. In: Creating a Lean and Green Business System, pp. 65–100. Productivity Press (2013)
35. Bortolotti, T., Boscari, S., Danese, P.: Successful lean implementation: organizational culture and soft lean practices. Int. J. Prod. Econ. **160**, 182–201 (2015)
36. Costa, F., Lispi, L., Staudacher, A.P., Rossini, M., Kundu, K., Cifone, F.D.: How to foster Sustainable Continuous Improvement: a cause-effect relations map of Lean soft practices. Oper. Res. Perspect. **6**, 100091 (2019)
37. Souza Farias, L.M., Henrique da Silva Amorim, M., Gohr, C.F., Carvalho de Oliveira, L., Santos, L.C.: Criteria and practices for lean and green performance assessment: systematic review and conceptual framework. J. Clean. Prod. **218**, 746–762 (2019)
38. Verrier, B., Rose, B., Caillaud, E.: Lean and Green strategy: the Lean and Green House and maturity deployment model. J. Clean. Prod. **116**, 150–156 (2016)

39. Thanki, S., Govindan, K., Thakkar, J.: An investigation on lean-green implementation practices in Indian SMEs using analytical hierarchy process (AHP) approach. J. Clean. Prod. **135**, 284–298 (2016)
40. Chaplin, L., O'Rourke, S.T.J.: Could lean and green be the driver to integrate business improvement throughout the organisation? Int. J. Product. Perform. Manage. **67**(1), 207–219 (2018)
41. Pavlou, P.A., El Sawy, O.A.: Understanding the elusive black box of dynamic capabilities. Decis. Sci. **42**(1), 239–273 (2011)
42. Schumpeter, J.: Theory of Economic Development (2017)
43. Abernathy, W.J., Clark, K.B.: Innovation: mapping the winds of creative destruction. Res. Policy **14**, 3–22 (1985)
44. Henderson, R., Cockburn, I.: Measuring competence? Exploring firm effects in pharmaceutical research. Strateg. Manage. J. **15**(S1), 63–84 (1994)
45. Kogut, B., Zander, U.: Knowledge of the firm, combinative capabilities, and the replication of technology. Organ. Sci. **3**(3), 383–397 (1992)
46. Teece, D., Pisano, G., Shuen, A.: Dynamic capabilities and strategic management. Strateg. Manage. J. **18**(7), 509–533 (1997)
47. Helfat, C.E., et al.: Dynamic capabilities and organizational process (2007)
48. Teece, D.J.: Dynamic capabilities and strategic management. Strateg. Manage. J. **18**(7), 509–533 (2009)
49. Eisenhardt, K.M., Martin, J.A.: Dynamic capabilities: what are they? Strateg. Manage. J. **21** (10–11), 1105–1121 (2000)
50. Zollo, M., Winter, S.G.: Deliberate learning and the evolution of dynamic capabilities. Organ. Sci. **13**(3), 339–351 (2002)
51. The World Bank Group: An International Framework for Eco-Industrial Parks (2017)
52. Abebe, G., Assefa Gebrehiwot, B., Weldesilassie, A.B., Gebreeyesus, M.: A Study on industrial park development: issues, practices and lessons for Ethiopia, no. February (2017)
53. Park, I.: Assessment of workers' satisfaction and HR structure of factories in the Hawassa Industrial Park. Final Report, no. October (2017)
54. Hueting, R.: Why environmental sustainability can most probably not be attained with growing production. J. Clean. Prod. **18**(6), 525–530 (2010)
55. Roufechaei, K.M., Abu Bakar, A.H., Tabassi, A.A.: Energy-efficient design for sustainable housing development. J. Clean. Prod. **65**, 380–388 (2014)

Reducing Long-Run Average Planned Maintenance Cost Using Markov Decision Modelling Based on Shifting Paradigm and Penalty Model

Gedefaye Achamu Meretie[1]([✉]), Eshetie Berhan Atanew[2],
and Sisay Geremaw Gebeyehu[1]

[1] Bahir Dar Institute of Technology, Bahir Dar, Ethiopia
[2] Addis Ababa Institute of Technology, Addis Ababa, Ethiopia

Abstract. This paper aims at developing a model for the planned maintenance program and long-run average cost. Markov process decision approach in its discrete version used to model the problem. Penalty cost model due to shifting paradigm as approach applied for textile boiler maintenance program by taking three components of the boiler. Whereas, a three-step policy iteration algorithm, initialization, value determination and policy improvement, for numerical experimentation based on component current age and the schedule maintenance time for the planned maintenance program considered. Relative values (RV), which are not only immediate value from an action taken from planned activity but also are guaranteed values that would be resulted from the accomplishment of the maintenance action specified on the maintenance policy proposed. More importantly, unless a trade-off is made, RVs instead are costs in the long run and this is what the average cost-policy compromise and the policy iteration assures while, as time gets advance the deterioration rate of the components expected to increase, shifting forward will bear an extra cost is the underlying. With this proposed approach, for validation purpose, relative values (RV), based on the two shifting strategies, Forward (FW) and Backward (BW) shifting compared with that of on-schedule (OSC) maintenance, stationary policy based on the long-run average cost obtained to be 2053Birr for the specified case.

Keywords: Maintenance shifting · Markov decision process · Optimal cost · Long run average cost · Deterioration

1 Introduction

Maintenance concept encompasses the area of philosophies, maintenance support levels, work forces, and time required for maintenance. Establishing basis for both maintainability and total maintenance support requirement are the root purpose of the maintenance concept, which could possibly addressed with a proper maintenance analysis. Based on this analysis-anticipated frequency of failures, crew skill levels, spare parts, the tools and the facilities required can be worked out in advance. In general, the objective of maintenance falls to four basic considerations a) ensuring

© ICST Institute for Computer Sciences, Social Informatics and Telecommunications Engineering 2022
Published by Springer Nature Switzerland AG 2022. All Rights Reserved
M. L. Berihun (Ed.): ICAST 2021, LNICST 412, pp. 277–294, 2022.
https://doi.org/10.1007/978-3-030-93712-6_19

system function (availability, efficiency and product quality); b) ensuring system life (asset management), c) ensuring safety and d) ensuring human well-being [1]. Maintenance concept is a prior task for equipment design to meet the design function and the overall maintenance concept. One can then reach in conclusion to understand maintenance concept development is about the requirements, maintainability and facility provision, which in turn show the needs of the system design engineer and the requirement of logistic support planner. The objective behind deploying complex and sophisticated machine (automation) is to achieve higher productivity to have a good return in business (profit). However, this objective is dependent on the functionality and wellbeing of such machines. The measures taken by the industry to keep machine and operating system in trouble free condition are collectively termed maintenance engineering [2]. The reason behind to the out date of "run to failure" is the high cost of the machines than the maintenance cost incurred to make them available. Maintenance is a function to keep the equipment/machine in a working condition by replacing/repairing [3] some of the component of the machine. According to the British Standard (BS 3811-1984) maintenance is: the combination of all technical and associated administrative actions intended to retain an item in or restore it to a state in which it can perform its required function "stated condition". On its, evolution, Fig. 1, maintenance activity comes across different stages starting from run to failure operation until 1950s, proactive maintenance: Condition Based Maintenance (CBM), and Time Based maintenance and to the contemporary Reliability Cantered Maintenance (RCM) and Total Productive Maintenance (TPM). The type of the failure, the time that will failure occur, the condition for failure to happen, the priority to the failure effect and the all-inclusive are the frame work of these evolutions of maintenance. With regard to this maintenance progress and considerable match of the maintenance, type different maintenance policies have been formulated. Preventive maintenance (PM), Predictive maintenance (PdM), Reactive maintenance (RM), proactive maintenance (PrM), condition based maintenance (CBM) and time based maintenance (TBM) policies has found under the two main maintenance categories See [4, pp. 3–3] "planned and Unplanned maintenance programs". Nevertheless, the problem especially in planned maintenance is the accuracy in performing the maintenance activities with the equipment failure condition and time. Since preventive maintenance (PM) which also known as scheduled maintenance is eliminating the future drastic treatment in future [3] (preserving asset, preventing failure and deleting incipient faults preserving asset, preventing failure and deleting incipient faults.

In its usual nature of PM, preventive planned maintenance is the utilization of planned and coordinated routine maintenance activities such as inspection, adjustment, repair and replacement which minimize the interruption of the system with high cost whereas maintenance planning for deteriorating facilities seems to be hard because of their random aspects. For [5] machine in its service of production faces to fates: sudden failure or gradual deterioration which the latter potentially be characterized with frequent repair that lead to higher maintenance cost, however, at decreasing productivity.

Developing model that is insightful in describing aging phenomenon of technical components and that give option for action to cope with anticipated problem is question of recent research interest [1]. While with such distributed random protocol, Markov Decision process (MDP), helps to combine both deterministic and probabilistic nature of the problem domain [6] - an approach that has been mentioned to bridge the gap between analytic model and practice [1].

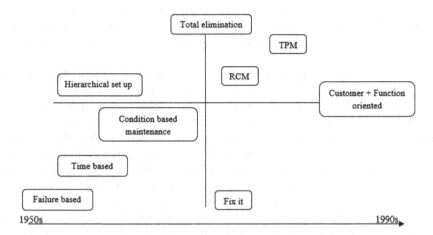

Fig. 1. Evolution of maintenance concept

Then it is the main purpose of this paper to integrate the planned maintenance program with the stochastic nature of the equipment failure and remaining are: Sect. 2 is about recent literature while methods and material presented in Sect. 3 and followed by Case description and it is modelling in Sect. 4. Section 5 provides experimentation and model validation with results and discussion in Sect. 6. Finally, conclusion and forwards presented in Sect. 7.

2 Recent Literatures

For their discrete time Markov (DTM) model, [3] considered the dynamic nature of system that has to be reviewed at equidistant of time for a possible set of state I that demand action appropriate to it. Since each state $s_i \in I$ and related action $a_i \in A$ are finite, understanding economical consequent through cost at each decision epoch is practical. As an alternative to current state of art of policy for corrective action [7] deployed Markov decision process (MDP) to evaluate corrective maintenance scheduling policies for offshore wind farms using production loss duet distinct policies. On the other hand, [8] proposed a generalized condition based maintenance (CBM) model using Markov decision process for cost effective decision making process. They start by introducing traditional maintenance practice- corrective maintenance (CM) and preventive maintenance (PM) which they specially emphases to one, which is prominent for PM-time, based maintenance (TBM) by arguing with the assumption behind, i.e. two component with similar age will never have similar failure rate which the opposite also holds true. Moreover, if defined well failure rate rather is a function of time than deterministic propagation as observed in time based models [8].

As is evidenced from their review report age of component takes share of failure rate from 15%–20% which the remaining 80%–85% is due to random effect (See also [8]).

Emphasizing to civil infrastructure sector, which unlike mechanical component, deterioration is slow and failure does not show direct economic consequence [1]. Random failure and failure due to deterioration considered by [9] and using policy iteration algorithm an optimum maintenance policy determined for proposed Markove decision model.

Recent work of [10] propose a preventive maintenance schedule for healthcare using Markov chain and were successful both in reducing use of resource and optimizing periodicity of routine maintenance cost. They classified the state of healthcare into nine state of nature (1 = excellent, 9 = unacceptable) and follow a statistical study for determining of probabilistic transition of such identified states. One which is similar to our setup content wise is the work of [11] propose decision model, which help to determine optimal time between periodic inspection. They provide a cost function based on two scenarios-one is for detecting failure without inspection, and the other is for detecting failure only through inspection. A review of probabilistic maintenance model by [12] mad clearly a distinction between deterioration model and decision model with the priori is to estimate the uncertain time to failure while the latter is to optimize the time maintenance activity using result of priori. Consequently, they deployed Markov process to model the uncertain deterioration of an object at concept of Markov Chain (MC). They considered three potential states for number of condition of state set $S = \{0, 1, \ldots m\}$ an item could attain; state $S = 0$ implies the newness state and $S = m$ indicates state of failure. The three potential state are based on the thresholds for preventive maintenance (r) and corrective maintenance (s) and includes for current state stat of itemcs, (i) functional state $cs < r$ (ii) is marginal state $r \leq cs < s$ and (iii) failed state $s \leq cs$ and for pictorial visualization of these state readers are referred to [11, p. 250]. By marginal state, an item is still functional but ready for an action weather it is preventive or replacement [13].

In general, the work of Kallen and van Noortwijk is motivational but one important contribution of our work is the issue of the paradigm of maintenance shifting (see Sect. 4.3) from principle of joint replacement [14, 15] with the underlying of relative value achieved through shifting the maintenance schedule. Both policy iteration and value iteration of Bellman methods from dynamic programing that are prominent solving method for Markov decision process (MDP) or Semi-Markov decision process (SMDP) [16].

3 Materials and Methods

The main objective of this paper is to formulate a planned maintenance policy by using discrete Markov chain decision process, modelling of the decision process making about the interval of the inspection and modelling the maintenance decision. Figure 2 presents research design that starts with case description of the problem domain and constructing deterioration model for problem to supply state of nature with their probabilistic occurrence to decision model constructed using discrete Markov decision chain (MDC) more preferably Markov Decision Process (MDP) as described in [1].

As contribution to this paper, shifting paradigm is to account relative values and we prefer rather the long-run average cost criteria than the total cost. Cost for various states identified, probabilistic value of each potential state described in [11] determined accordingly by normalizing each statistically. Since in its natural understanding, deterioration model is bas on continuous Markov chain uniformazation is followed approach followed to extract probabilities to each discrete state.

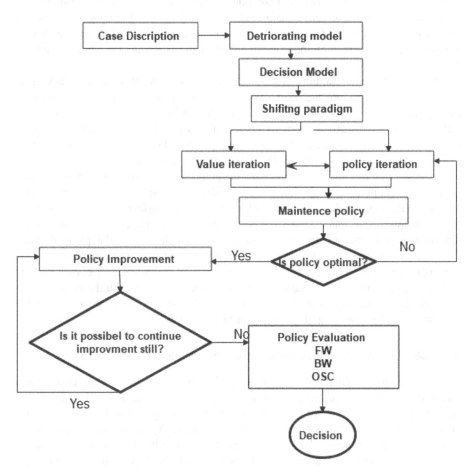

Fig. 2. Research design

4   Cause Description and Modeling

In textile industry, various utilities are utilized for the complete operation of the textile process. A steam or heated water is the most crucial one and can be generated from boiler. A boiler is a system at which water is heated under a pressure. The steam or heated fluid is expected to be circulated out of the boiler for the use of various applications such as sizing, drying, cooling, washing, and so one. It is a closed system and made up of various components. In this paper, the mainly considered components are safety valves, heaters, and temperature sensors. The failure occurs on one of each component causes the failure of the whole system of the boiler. As the function of each of the components and the exposing condition for them is distinct, it enforces the maintenance crew to a distinct time epoch of both preventive and corrective maintenance program. Keeping the routine preventive action as oiling, inspecting and checking as common these different components has different preventive action of time zone and subsequent corrective maintenance epoch. Not only the condition at which each component operate, it is the age of the components which deteriorates with time advance the failure rate of the components in particular and the whole system in general.

Among the various failures modes, overheating, rupture, leaking and cracking or crazing failure modes are the most frequently to occur and are need to be seriously managed. An assumption is made here, though may not it be important, about the failure rate and the planned maintenance activities for each component for the boiler. Each component is assumed to have relativity the same failure rate and repair rate for the same state of conditions. However, the effect related to this failure rate is not to be the same and that is why it is assumed that the planned maintenance activities are made from. The main purpose of this paper is to develop a cost effective maintenance policy via the application of the Discrete Markov chain and considering trade-off between taking separate maintenance action and combined action with respect to the set up cost. Considering only the set up cost is not the deriving factor for the planned boiler maintenance program, it is also to prevent the frequent stoppage of boiler due to each component preventive and corrective action. Each of the considered component are assumed to has similar deterioration model developed in model with the consideration of deterioration and maintenance (Sect. 4.1) which could transient such state of the equipment to the other state the equipment has to follow.

4.1 Discrete Markov Chain as Stochastic Modelling

While modelling a maintenance system using Markov chain defining concept of system and state transition are of basic important. Letting system state as X_n, $n = 0, 1, \ldots$ as time index is to mean that we have knowledge about the system at $X_0, X_1 \ldots X_{n-1}, X_n$. However, as far as X_{n+1} is concerned all states before X_n seems redundant, i.e., no memory is needed which is the Markov property. It is claimed that the system state X_n is a stochastic process and the time homogenous discreet Markov chain is assumed here as given in Eq. (1).

$$P(X_{n+1} = j | X_n = i) = P(X_1 = j | X_0 = i) \tag{1}$$

From Eq. (2), we can infer that whatever the value of $X_0, X_1 \ldots X_{n-1}, X_{n-1}$ the left side conditional probability is same. This is to mean that for a given present state of the system (X_n) the future state of the discrete time Markov chain (DTMC) (X_{n+1}) is independent of its past $(X_0, X_1 \ldots X_{n-1})$. Quantity P is called a one-step transition probability of the DTMC at time n. and since, Eq. (2) is a time homogeneous DTMCs, the one-step transition probability depending on i and j but is the same at all times n.

Therefore, throughout this paper it is to mean that a homogeneous time process when there is an expression of DTMC. Consequently, with the shorthand notation for the one-step transition probability P_{ij}, to convey that given the system is in state i at time t, it will be in a state j at time $(t + 1)$:

$$P_{ij} = P(X_{n+1} = j | X_n = i) \, for \, i, j = 1, 2, \ldots N \tag{2}$$

The transition probabilities are commonly expressed as an $N \times N$ matrix called the transition probability matrix (or transition matrix) P:

$$\boldsymbol{P} = \begin{bmatrix} p_{11} & p_{12} & \cdots & p_{1N} \\ p_{21} & p_{22} & \cdots & p_{2N} \\ \cdots & \cdots & \cdots & \cdots \\ p_{N1} & p_{N2} & \cdots & p_{NN} \end{bmatrix} \tag{3}$$

$$\sum\nolimits_{j=1}^{n} p_{ij} = 1 \, for \, i, j = 1, 2, \ldots, N \tag{4}$$

Based on the Chapman-Kolmogorov equation, the probability of the system moving from state i and state j after n periods (n transitions), that is, the n-step transition probability matrix, $\boldsymbol{P}^{(n)}$ can be obtained by multiplying the matrix P by itself n times Eq. (5). Thus, Eq. (5.) implies that the application of the Markov chain processes to the development of a deterioration model for a system. Alternatively, an equipment, once a reliable transition probability matrix for the system/equipment is identified, the expected condition of the system/equipment in the future or the expected years that the system will be in a degraded condition can be easily obtained.

$$P^{(n)} = P^n \tag{5}$$

The left side of Eq. (1) of course is general form of Discrete Time Markov Chain, DTMC, and taken as a one-step transition probability P_{ij} of state i and j that must be summed to unity. The model is then tries to integrate the planned maintenance with the characteristics and application of Markov chain by incorporate such three important concerns: Deterioration model, Decision model, cost model and Paradigm of Shifting in each of the respective section next.

4.2 Deterioration Model

Equipment pertains to a units' position in a state space with greater probability of failure than a former position. It can be modelled using general path model, random process model Markovian stochastic process model and time series model. Individual randomness and dynamic environment always cases for temporal uncertainty and is difficult to apply both general path and random process rather the Markovian stochastic process as it is flexible to such practical deterioration indicators. For the given deterioration, X_n in discrete time n and all possible of it contained in state space S can shift to each other according to the transient matrix with special state X_f called absorbing state representing the failure state of the asset. Equipment deterioration multi factor dependent and of these the way they are treated, preventive maintenance and inspection, takes the higher share. In Fig. 3 (b) N is nominal operation state and D_i is deterioration state or marginal before being state malfunctioning F. Since, Fig. 3(a) and Fig. 3(b) that respectively portrayed model of three state and general equipment models of deterioration are based on continuous Markov chain (CMC), uniformization based on Eq. (6) for uniform transition rate γ deployed. Dividing the original transitions by γ therefore gives probability value for each discrete state of Markov chain. By assuming the instant state after the maintenance is performed as a new state, the transition probability can be constructed using Eq. (7).

$$\gamma = \lambda_1 + \lambda_2 + \lambda_3 + \ldots + \mu_1\mu_2\mu_3 \tag{6}$$

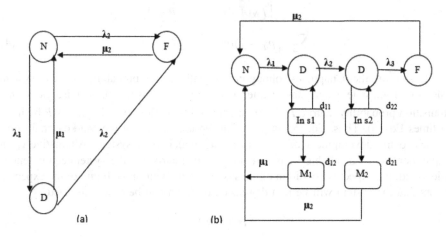

Fig. 3. Three state and general equipment model

$$P = \begin{bmatrix} NN & ND_1 & ND_2 & NF \\ D_1N & D_1D_1 & D_1D_2 & D_1F \\ D_2N & D_2D_1 & D_2D_2 & D_2F \\ FN & FD_1 & FD_2 & FF \end{bmatrix} = \begin{bmatrix} 1-\lambda_1/\gamma & \lambda_1/\gamma & 0 & 0 \\ \mu_1/\gamma & 1-\lambda_2/\gamma & \lambda_2/\gamma & 0 \\ \mu_2/\gamma & 0 & 1-\lambda_3/\gamma & \lambda_3/\gamma \\ \mu_3/\gamma & 0 & 0 & \mu_3/\gamma \end{bmatrix} \tag{7}$$

4.3   Decision Model

The equipment at the beginning of each day found to be in one of the working condition $S_i = 1, 2, \ldots, N$ and is obvious that working condition i is better than working condition $S_j = S_{i+1}$. Given the current condition i with no repair, probability of equipment to be on working condition j is $q_{s_i s_j}$ and is zero for $S_i > S_j$. An enforced repair action elapsed with m days has to take for $S_i = N$ while if the equipment is found between $1 < S_i < N$ there is a possibility to take or not to take a maintenance action. Hence, for the maintenance action Eq. (7) gives an alternative action. A repaired system has a working condition $S_i = 1$ and the cost of enforced repair is C_f and Cp_{s_i} is a pre-emptive repair cost. This problem can be put in the framework of a discrete-time Markov decision model and cost criterion from the maintenance point of view has been articulated as long-run average cost, total cost, marginal cost, or discount cost. Time horizon in the caused problem for maintenance action is assumed infinite hence; the long-run average cost is preferred rather than total cost criterion. Since an enforced repair takes m, days and the state of the system has to be defined at the beginning of each day, there should be an auxiliary state for the situation in which an enforced repair is in progress already for y days. Thus, the set of possible states of the system is chosen as $S = \{1, 2 \dots N, N + y\}$. State S_i with $1 \le S_i \le N$ corresponds to the situation in which an inspection reveals working condition i, while state $N + 1$ corresponds to the situation in which an enforced repair is in progress already for y day. Hence, if, a_i action it can be stated as Eq. (8).

$$a_i = \begin{cases} 0, \text{if no repair is done} & 1 \le j < N \\ 1 \text{ if preventive action is done} & 1 < j < N \\ 2 \text{ enforced repair done} \end{cases} \tag{8}$$

With repair time of $y < m$, the one-step transition probabilities $p_{ij}(a)$ are given:

- $p_{s_i, s_j}(0) = q_{s_i s_j}$ for $1 \le s_i < N$
- $p_{s_i, 1}(1) = 1$ for $1 < s_i < N$
- $p_{N, N+y}(2) = p_{N+y, 1}(2) = 1$

And it is institutive that for $p_{ij}(a) = 0$, $C_{si}(0) = 0$, $C_{si}(1) = Cp_{si}$, $C_N(2) = C_f$ and $C_{N+y}(2) = 0$.

4.4   The Paradigm of Shifting

A machine as a system, if m_i is the maximum life time of the component i, the possible state of the component are $m_i + 1$ and the state space is a result of the sum product of the number of product n and $m_i + 1$ equivalent to the $\prod_{i=1}^{n} mi + 1$. Each of the component limited to the control limit h_i^* (age) for replacement analogize to age of preventive action for the planned maintenance activity especially for time based preventive maintenance. In planned maintenance activity, different component may have different lifetime or have being exposed for different operational condition with different deterioration (limitation of planned maintenance). For the control limit age h* of the component, the expected age for the preventive maintenance, plays an important role to draw an argument about the long run average cost of preventive action and breakdown maintenance. The long-term average cost $g_i(h)$ in the control limit h_i^* of component i will have a relative value of V_i^j

that cane linearly formulated as given in Eq. (9) and a normalization equation $v_s = 0$ as a unique solution.

$$V^j{}_i = \min_a \{ C^j{}_i(a) + \sum_{k \in S} P_i^{jk}(a) v_s{}^k(h^*) \} - g_i^* \tag{9}$$

Where a and $C_i^j(\alpha) C^j{}_i(a)$ are action and cost due to this action for component i and $P_i^j(\alpha) C^j{}_i(a) P_i^{jk}(a)$ is the probability of transition of component i from state j to state k when action a is chosen. It is clear that different relative value can be inferred at each transition state as given by Eq. (10). It is stated that earlier that the objective in this paper is to make a trade-off between separate and combined maintenance activity under shifting paradigm.

$$V_i^j = \begin{cases} P_i^j V_i^j + q_i^j V_i^j - g_i & \text{for } j = 0..h^* - 1 \\ Cp_i + V_i^0 & \text{for } j = h^* m_i \\ b_i + Cp_i + V_i^0 & \text{for } j = m_i + 1 \end{cases} \tag{10}$$

Where Cp_i and b_i are cost of preventive and break down action for component respectively. While $V^0{}_i$ is value paid to bring component i to state zero. If we denote the average, set up cost by Δc the possibility to have cost effective action via taking combined preventive maintenance activities is given as $\Delta c + V^n{}_i > Cp_i + V^0{}_i$ and V_i^n indicates the value that would be paid if the preventive action on component iii were taken. Our trade-off to the combined action, however, has another challenge: penalty cost due to shifting, which can be forward (FW) or backward (BW) as given in Eq. (11). If the pre-planned preventative scheduling time, called epoch time is t_i, the three scenarios expected are: (1) if the component fail at its due date but prevention action is shifted forward (positive shifting), (2) if shift is backward (negative shifting) (3) if no shift.

$$shifting = \begin{cases} Postive, \text{ for } t > t_i, \Delta t = t - t_i, \Delta t > 0 \\ none & \text{for } t = t_i, \Delta t = 0 \\ negative, & \text{for } t < t_i, \Delta t < 0 \end{cases} \tag{11}$$

Equation (11) confirms that for no shifting of prevention action, component i gets immediate response as per the schedule and only the cost for planned activity incurs. On the other hand, there exist an expected cost of penalty costs due to postponing ($\Delta t > 0$) or due to early action ($\Delta t < 0$) and can be valued relatively. For control limit h^* and some constant number n of (Δt ($\Delta t = n$), if the component is not failed before $t_i + 1$ the next prevention action then is at epoch $t_i + n$ but at probability of $p_i^{h^*}$, otherwise malfunction with probability $q_i^{h^*}$, i.e., $1 - p_i^{h^*} = q_i^{h^*}$. A state space $j = j + 1$ and $j = m_i + 1$ are respectively operating and failed state and the average cost g_i^* for one period transition can be saved probabilistically. For a preventive action with probability $p_i^h \cdot p_i^{h+1}$, the relative value is $V_i^{h+2} - g_i^*$, otherwise a failure tends to occur with probability $q_i^h \cdot q_i^{h+1}$ and relative value is $V_i^{m+1} - g_i^*$ if response of corrective maintenance action taken. However, if these all not happen, state $j = n$ is valued as V_i^h

and a penalty cost $p_i(n)$ entertained and generalized using Eq. (12). Arranging along with the stationary policy for the Markov chain to Eq. (13) and cost for shifting preventive action is given Eq. (14) for shifting time Δt.

$$
\begin{aligned}
P_i(n) = {} & p_i^h \left(V_i^{h+1} - V_i^{h+1} - g_i^* \right) + q_i^h \left(V_i^{m+1} V_i^h - g_i^* \right) \\
& + p_i^h q_i^{h+1} \left(V_i^{m+1} V_i^{h+1} g_i^* \right) + p_i^h q_i^{h+1} \left(V_i^{m+1} - V_i^{h+1} - g_i^* \right)
\end{aligned}
\tag{12}
$$

$$
P_i(n) = \left(q_i^h b_i - g_i^* \right) + + p_i^h \left(q_i^h b_i - g_i^* \right)
\tag{13}
$$

$$
p_i(\Delta t) =
\begin{cases}
\displaystyle\sum_{j=h_i}^{h_i + \Delta t - 1} \left(q_i^j b_i - g^* \right) \sum_{l=h_i}^{j-l} p_i^l & \text{if } \Delta t > 0 \\
\displaystyle\sum_{j=h_i + \Delta t}^{h_i - 1} \left(g^* - q_i^j b_i \right) \sum_{l=h_i + \Delta t}^{j-l} p_i^l & \text{if } \Delta t < 0
\end{cases}
\tag{14}
$$

4.5   Maintenance Policy

An optimal maintenance activity and a stationary policy is a convenient one for average-cost Markov decision model with finite state space and finite action set. A stationary policy R is a policy that assigns a fixed action $a = R_j$ to each state j and always used whenever the system is in state j. By acknowledging the effort made, this section is based on the work of [15] with given state $j = n$ for $n = 0, 1, ..$ to define the state of the system X_n at the nth decision epoch, the markov chain is defined as $P\{X_{n+1} = k | X_n = j\} = p_{jk}(R_j)$ regardless of the past history of the system up to time n. The stochastic process $\{X_n\}$ is a discrete-time markov chain with one-step transition probability $p_{jk}(R_j)$ with incurred cost $c_i(R_j)$ each time the system visits state j and the long –run average cost per time unit under a given stationary policy could be invoked. Finding the optimal policy for average cost is NP hard for each stationary in separate and needs an effective algorithm to have an optimal average cost policy. Policy iteration and value iteration are the most widely used algorithms to compute an average cost optimal policy. Policy iteration arises from the unchain assumptions of Markov chain and works on a policy space and generate a sequence of improved policies whereas value iteration approximates the minimal average cost through a sequence value function. The relative values associated with a given policy R provide a tool for constructing a new policy $\overline{R}$ whose average cost is no more than that of the current policy R. In order to improve a given policy R whose average cost $g(R))$ and relative values $V_j(R), j \in S$ have been computed from the terms $g = g(R)$ and $V_j = V_j(R)$.

$$
C_j(\overline{R}_j) - g(R) + \sum_{k \in S} p_{jk}(\overline{R}_j) V_k \le V_j
\tag{15}
$$

By constructing a new policy $\overline{R}$ for each state $j \in S$, the cost based on the improved policy is as given by Eq. (14) for $g(\overline{R}) \le g(R)$ and for $a_j = R_j, a_j \in A$, the three step in policy iteration algorithm is as follow:

- Step 0 (initialization)

$$R^1 = R_j = a_j = \begin{cases} 0 \text{ if no repair is done } 1 < j < N \\ 1 \text{ if preventive action is done, } 1 < j < N \\ 2 \text{ enforced repair is done } j = N \end{cases} \quad (16)$$

Where, $N \in S$

- Step 1 (value determination):

The current unique solution $g(R)$, $V_j(R)$ for the given stationary point is computed for an arbitrary chosen state s with value of $v_s = 0$ and Eq. (17) used to determine the value V_j for $j = 1, 2, \ldots N$ and for $j = N + 1$, $V_j = v_s$ and known as normalizing value.

$$V_j(a, R) = C_j(a = R) - g(R) + \sum_{k \in S} p_{jk} V_j(R) \quad (17)$$

- Step 2 (Policy improvement):

At this step the possible minimum action a_j is to be taken for a minimum and guaranteed using testing Eq. (18) and current policy Eq. (19) while Eq. (20) for selecting an action with minimum $T_j(a, R)$.

$$T_j(a_j, R) = C_j(a) - g(R) + \sum_{k \in S} p_{jk} V_j(R) \quad (18)$$

$$T_j(a_j, R) = V_j(R) \quad (19)$$

$$\min_{a \in A(j)} C_j(a) - g(R) + \sum_{k \in S} p_{jk}(a_j) V_k(R) \quad (20)$$

These all then give an optimal to Eq. (21) of the relative value for component i and the new policy $\overline{R}_j = a_j$ for $j = 1, 2, \ldots N$.

$$V_i^j = \min_a \{ C_i^j(a) + \sum_k p_i^{jk}(a) V_i^k - g_i^* \} \quad (21)$$

- Step 3 (convergence test):

Now it is possible to compare the action for the optimum cost with old policy R and if $\overline{R} = R$, the algorithm is stopped otherwise go to step1 with new policy $\overline{R}$.

5   Experimentation and Verification

5.1   Input Data

Based on these arguments and the data synthesized, the following failure rate and maintenance rate both in months are: $\lambda 1 = 4$, $\lambda 2 = 3$, $\lambda 3 = 2$ and $\mu 1 = 0.133$, $\mu 2 = 0.1233$, $\mu 3 = 0.33$. By using equation, 3.1 and the deterioration model based on equation could be as given in Table 1. The time table for the planned maintenance to the boiler is seated as per the time horizon to take either the preventive or the corrective action. However, the corrective action depends on the decision taken upon the inspection time, which is different for the different components. As it is mentioned earlier for the components, $i = 1, 2, 3...n$. Table 2 is then the time schedules for the preventive maintenance actions. Again, it is understood that the age also is the other factor for the deterioration should be taken in to account and each components will have different life span and deterioration rate then when we assume the preventive action at time t_i the age is hi.

Table 1. The deterioration of the component (q_{ij})

State (i)	Overheating	Rupturing	Leaking	Cracking
Overheating	0.6	0.4	0	0
Rupturing	0.01	0.69	0.3	0
Leaking	0.01	0	0.79	0.2
Cracking	0.03	0.08	0.1	0.79

Table 2. Control limits of the components for maintenance action (hi)

Components	Current age	Ti	t = 5, 6, 8		
Safety valve	3	6	−1	0	2
Heaters	5	8	−3	−1	0
Temperature sensors	2	5	0	−1	−3

5.2   Model Verification

Using Eq. (13)–(21) the possible action that would be taken is iterated to come with the average cost to have a stationary policy R. The states that the component will found are four $N = 4$ and the possible action would be taken in response of the component conditions are given in Eq. (8). In the stationary policy rule, $R_i = a_i$ while the following simultaneous equation demonstrates the first iteration of the solution.

- Step-1: value determination

1. Policy initiation: the first policy $R_i^{(1)}$ initiated as to have the policy of $R_i^{(1)} = (0,0,1,2,2)$.)
2. Relative value of the policy: Based on Eq. (17) the following linear equations give both the relative value and the average cost for the given policy.

$$V_1 = 0 - g + 0.6V_1 + 0.4V_2$$

$$V_2 = 0 - g + 0.01V_1 + 0.69V_2 + 0.3V_3$$

$$V_3 = 1500 - g + 0.01V_1 + 0.79V_3 + 0.2V_4$$

$$V_4 = 2500 - g + 0.03V_1 + 0.97V_4$$

$$V_5 = 0 - g + 1V_1$$

Using $V_j = V_5$ for $j = N + 1 = 5$ known as normalization equation with the value of $V_5 = 0$ and gives $V_1 = g$.

Consequently, $V_1 R_i^{(1)} = 2038.1, V_2 R_i^{(1)} = 7,133.5, \quad V_3 R_i^{(1)} = 14,0833, \quad V_4 R_i^{(1)} = 17,446.3$ and hence, $g R_i^{(1)} = 2038$.

- Step 2: Policy improvement

Using Eq. (18) and Eq. (19) respectively for testing and current policy i.e.:
$T_j(a, R) = C_j(a) - g(R) + \sum_{k \in s} P_{jk} V_j(R)$ And $T_j(a, R) = V_j(R)$ for $a = R$ and take $j = 2$ for instance,

$$T_2(a_i, R) = C_2(a = 0) - g\left(R^{(1)}\right) + p_{21}v_1 + p_{22}v_2 + p_{23}v_3 + p_{24}v_4$$

$T_2(a_i, R) = 600 - 2038.1 + 0.01 * 2038.1 + 0.69 * 7,133.5$
$+ 0.3 * 14,083.3 = \mathbf{7,729.4}$ and continuing as if, consequently gives:

$$T_2(a_i, R) = C_2(a = 0) = 7,729.4, T_2(a_i, R) = C_2(a = 1) = 600$$

$$T_3(a_i, R) = C_2(a = 0) = 12.587.3, T_3(a_i, R) = C_2(a = 1) = 1,500$$

$$T_4(a_i, R) = C_2(a = 0) = 14,946, T_4(a_i, R) = C_2(a = 1) = 2500$$

Then, new improve solution based on Eq. (20) i.e. $\min(T_2(a = 0, a = 1), R_i^{(1)}))$ gives $R_i^{(2)} = (0,1,1,1,2)$. Using $R_i^{(2)}$ and continuing iteration II in similar fashion and the result gives then the policy of $R(^4) = (1, 1, 1, 2)$ Which is equivalent to the R $(^{3r}) = (1, 1, 1, 2)$ But the average cost $g^*(R)$ for $R(^3)$ is 2085 whereas for R^4 $g^*(R) = 2053$ and different relative values. The reason and the best policy will be discussed in the result and discussions part.

6   Results and Discussion

The calculation result obtained in the determination of the long run average cost of the maintenance action indicates that the cost is a function of different circumstance.

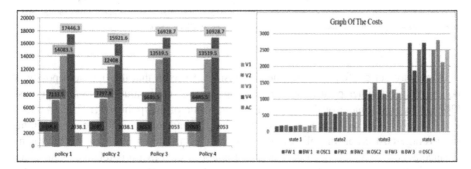

Fig. 4. Graphs of the relative values (left) and average costs for the different state of components (right)

Especially it is dependent on the period at which the age of the component taken, as the point of the action and it is the type of the response for the system or system's components current condition. Based on the formulated model for the long-run average cost of the maintenance action the discrete Markov chin results enables as to take trade-off about taking of the various maintenance action response towards the inspected and observed condition of the system or the component. As it is clearly, shown different relative values and an average cost could be obtaining through the iterative application of the policy iterations. Graphs in Fig. 4 depict the relative values of the maintenance action at the different state of the system. From the graph one an inferred that by applying the various maintenance policies which are relatively sufficient enough, it is possible to increase the relative values that could be obtained in return of performing of such policy. The relative value designated by the v1 is the immediate value that is obtained with respect to the current condition of the components. On the other hand, the other relative values (v2, v3 v4) are not the immediate values rather they are the guaranteed values resulted from the accomplishment of the maintenance action specified on the maintenance policy. Table 3 shows that penalty vs. scheduled cost at different state of the components. It is not the immediate result that to be taken for the maintenance action rather the long run values to be considered. Policy 1 $R_i^{(1)} = (0, 0, 1, 2, 2)$ state the application of no action at the first and second state of the components $(a = 0)$ and preventive action when the system is found at state three $(a = 1)$ and a corrective action at stat four and five if it will exist still. Whereas, with regard to the policy 2 of the model $R^2 = (0, 1, 1, 1, 2)$ the preventive action is expected at the second, third and fourth state and the system is to be kept as it's in its first state whatever its condition is and a corrective action is at the fifth state. According to the policy improvement iterations and the test results the stationary policy $R^2 = (0, 1, 1, 1, 2)$ and $R^3 = (0, 1, 1, 1, 2)$ are the same. However, if policy R^3 is improved to $R^{3'} = (1, 1, 1, 1, 2)$ which is equivalent to R^4 and the average cost will become 2,053.

Table 3. Penalty vs scheduled costs at different state of the components

	State 1				State 2				State 3				State 4			
	RV	FW	BW	OSC	RV	FW	BW	OSC	RV	FW	BW	OSC	RV	FW	BW	OSC
1	2053	1642	1843	200	66855	5683	5883	600	13519.5	12844	11492	1500	16928.7	2708	1862.2	2500
2	2053	1683	1852	200	66855	5405	59952	600	13519	12756	11511	1500	16928.7	2711	1634.7	2500
3	2053	1548	1861	200	66855	5702	5802	600	13519	12902	1170.7	1500	16928.7	2800	21213	2500
Total	6159	4873	5561	600	200565	1679	71637	1800	40557.5	38502	3471	4500	50786.1	8219	5618.2	7500

Note: RV = Relative value, FW = Forward shifting, BW = Backward shifting, OSC = on schedule

One may get confusion about the conclusion of giving that the optimum policy is policy relay on either policy three or four due to the small value of the average cost (2038) that would incur or the long run relative value of this policy (7,133.5, 14,083.3 and 1746.3) would be secured at each state. It is this mysterious which makes the long run average cost criterion policy is the best for the infinite time horizon of the maintenance action. What to mean here is that it is not to men that this relatives values are simply to be obtained they also are costs unless the trade-off is made. This is what the average cost-policy compromise and the policy iteration assures. The lose that would resulted in failing apply policy1 is then higher than to the other polices (immediate value = 0, and a maximum of the long run lose is 15407). Then policy 1 is not a feasible solution and as the average cost of operation is relatively higher for policy 2 than of policy 3 and the long run values that would be fail-safe is comparatively less and is not viable so. The last and not the least consideration that could be made, if needed, is to see the difference between policy 3 and policy 4. These policies only has a difference of whether to take the preventive action at the first inspection result of the components and this depends on the components exposure and the maintenance cost and effect on the production. However, as much as average cost is concerned policy 3 is an optimum maintenance policy. As it is depicted in the graph, observed from Table 3, both the forward and backward shifting penalty costs are smaller than the scheduled cost especially in state one, and state two of the component conditions. However, as the time gets advance the deterioration rate of the components expected to increase, shifting forward will bear an extra cost, and this is shown clearly on the graph above. For instance the penalty cost due to forward shifting for components 1, 2, 3, respectively in state 1 is 164.2, 168.3 and 154.8 whereas the backward shifting penalty costs are 184.8, 185.2 and 186.1. These figures convinced us about the importance of the forward shifting up to the extent of the component's condition, which is assumed to be not severs. However, it is the backward shifting that is to be used for the components found at the condition of beyond the moderately sever. Based on our model the state of conditions of the components are taken four on which the first state is assumed to have less effects and possibly to or not to take any maintenance response equipment will let to continue even with the knowledge of some sort of failure symptoms. The second and the third state conditions are the most and the valuable states depending to the response for them. It is here at which the critical decision plays an important role, it is the knowledge, and understanding as well as the experience of the maintenance manager and the crews under it to imitate and interpret the conditions occurred. Nevertheless, as the graph depicts it is recommended to take the backward shifting at such state of components. Hence the on-scheduled response action is then preferable than that of the forward shifting it is not only it is cost advantage but also to prevent the components from further deterioration and stoppage of the production for long time. With regard to the domain dimension of the system especially for machines having different components with different design function and exposure condition, the alignment, the preventive actions, the operative performance speed, and the loading factors have an essential influence. These and other circumstance then makes the planned maintenance program a decision under uncertainty and regret will develop in each of the programs schedule.

7 Conclusion

This paper aims to articulates the basics of the maintenance engineering and rooted from the basics and philosophy of the maintenance action as well as tried to explore the evolution of them maintenance as an introduction. It is the long-run average cost criterion, which is used in this paper as the criterion to develop the decision model about the actions. On the other hand, the decision about the response action for the various equipment condition needs other rules. Stationary policy is then the other considered idea in this paper to set the actions for the different state of the equipment or the systems at various conditions. Therefore, the decision model developed based on the long run average cost criterion and guided by the stationary policy. In the model for the average cost determination, the policy iteration algorithm is used to improve the policies to get an optimum policy that could be used as a maintenance program under the consideration of both the aging and deterioration factors. In this paper, not only developing of model for the maintenance considered, but also the paper tried to compromise the inefficiency of planned maintenance by the strategy of the application of the shifting of the maintenance schedule. Both the Discrete Markov Chain model for the long run average cost and the penalty cost model for the shifting strategy are test with a numerical case study for the textile boiler maintenance program by considering three components of the boiler with their current age and the schedule maintenance time for the planned maintenance program. Based on the analysis made and the result discussed the maintenance long run average cost will be attained if the stationary policy is based on the decision policy of R (i) = (0, 1, 1, 1, 2) with the long run average cost of 2053birr.

In general, in this paper the application of the Discrete Markov Chain is used to develop a maintenance model, which gives a long run average cost of maintenance cost under the consideration of the infinite time horizon of the maintenance action. Again, the paper introduces and proofs the importance of the shifting strategy of the maintenance action scheduled in the planned maintenance program.

References

1. Dekker, R., Nicolai, R.P., Kallenberg, L.C.M.: Maintenance and Markov decision models. In: Encyclopedia of Statistics in Quality and Reliability. American Cancer Society (2008). https://doi.org/10.1002/9780470061572.eqr085
2. Mishra, R.C., Pathak, K.: Maintenance Engineering and Management. Prentice-Hall of India Pvt. Ltd, New Delhi (2012)
3. Aisha, H.-S., Abubakar, U.Y.: Markov decision model for maintenance problem of deteriorating equipment with policy iteration. IPSR J. MAtmathic 12(1), 18–23 (2016)
4. CIBSE: Maintenance Engineering and Management. Chartered Institution of Building Services Engineers, London (2008)
5. Alam, M., Sarma, V.V.S.: Optimal maintenance and replacement via a semi-Markov decision model. Int. J. Syst. Sci. 6(9), 809–818 (1975). https://doi.org/10.1080/00207727508 941866
6. Hahn, E.M., Han, T., Kwiatkowska, M.: Model repair for Markov decision processes, p. 8 (2013)
7. Seyr, H., Muskulus, M.: Use of Markov decision processes in the evaluation of corrective maintenance scheduling policies for offshore wind farms. Energies 12(15), 2993 (2019). https://doi.org/10.3390/en12152993
8. Amari, S.V., McLaughlin, L., Pham, H.: Cost-effective condition-based maintenance using Markov decision processes. In: RAMS '06. Annual Reliability and Maintainability Symposium, 2006, Newport Beach, CA, USA, pp. 464–469 (2006). https://doi.org/10. 1109/RAMS.2006.1677417
9. Chan, G.K., Asgarpoor, S.: Optimum maintenance policy with Markov processes. Electr. Power Syst. Res. 76(6–7), 452–456 (2006). https://doi.org/10.1016/j.epsr.2005.09.010
10. González-Domínguez, J., Sánchez-Barroso, G., Sanz-Calcedo, J.: Scheduling of preventive maintenance in healthcare buildings using Markov chain. Appl. Sci. 10, 5263 (2020). https://doi.org/10.3390/app10155263
11. Kallen, M.J., van Noortwijk, J.M.: Optimal periodic inspection of a deterioration process with sequential condition states. Int. J. Press. Vessels Pip. 83(4), 249–255 (2006). https://doi.org/10.1016/j.ijpvp.2006.02.007
12. Frangopol, D.M., Kallen, M.-J., van Noortwijk, J.M.: Probabilistic models for life-cycle performance of deteriorating structures: review and future directions. Prog. Struct. Eng. Mater. 6(4), 197–212 (2004). https://doi.org/10.1002/pse.180
13. Flehinger, B.J.: A Markovian model for the analysis of the effects of marginal testing on system reliability. Ann. Math. Stat. 33(2), 754–766 (1962). https://doi.org/10.1214/aoms/1177704595
14. Dekker, R., Wildeman, R.E., van Egmond, R.: Joint replacement in an operational planning phase. Eur. J. Oper. Res. 91(1), 74–88 (1996). https://doi.org/10.1016/0377-2217(94)00363-7
15. Dekker, R., Wildeman, R.: Joint preventive replacement in an operational planning phase. In: Operations Research Proceedings 1993, pp. 522–522. Springer, Heidelberg (1994). https://doi.org/10.1007/978-3-642-78910-6_175
16. Gosavi, A.: Reinforcement learning for long-run average cost. Eur. J. Oper. Res. 155(3), 654–674 (2004). https://doi.org/10.1016/S0377-2217(02)00874-3

Development and Performance Testing of Rice Thresher for Fogera Hub Farmers in Ethiopia

Fetene Teshome Teferi[1(✉)] [iD], Eyob Messele Sefene[1],
Sisay Geremew Gebeyehu[1] [iD], and Kishor Purushottam Kolhe[2] [iD]

[1] Faculty of Mechanical and Industrial Engineering, Bahir Dar Institute
of Technology, Bahir Dar University, P.O. Box 26, Bahir Dar, Ethiopia
[2] College of Engineering, and Technology, Bule Hora University,
Bule Hora, Ethiopia

Abstract. Traditional paddy threshing is still carried out by man-power, and animal trampling in the rural village of Fogera district in the Amhara region of north-west Ethiopia. This paper was aimed to reduce paddy losses, minimize drudgery activities, and avail the technology in this area. The developed rice thresher also protects the paddy from mud mixing for further prevention of fast wearing and damaging of rubber roll during rice milling. The 3D modeling and working drawing are prepared by using CATIA software for fabrication and testing purposes. The paddy thresher is designed to separate paddy from panicles without damaging the stalk of rice. The research seeks to develop a power-operated rice thresher that can be manufactured by local manufacturers, and accessed by all small-holder rice producing farmers in Ethiopia. Components of the thresher were designed, fabricated, and assembled from the available materials in the local market. The experimental test in this study indicated that the threshing capacity of the designed paddy thresher is approximately 128 kg/h using two labor participation. Considering the unthreshed loss, drum loss, and broken grains, the average efficiency of the machine noted 96.6%.

Keywords: Prototype development · Rice thresher · Threshing capacity · Threshing efficiency · Threshing loss

Nomenclature

DL   Drum loss
SL   Separation loss
TE   Threshing efficiency
TC   Threshing capacity

1 Introduction

Rice (Oryza Sativa Linu) is the major food for 70% of the world's population, and it is consumed by 3.5 billion people or more [1]. Rice was initially announced in Ethiopia in the 1970s at a place of Fogera district, which has a wetland of south Gonder [2]. It is

© ICST Institute for Computer Sciences, Social Informatics and Telecommunications Engineering 2022
Published by Springer Nature Switzerland AG 2022. All Rights Reserved
M. L. Berihun (Ed.): ICAST 2021, LNICST 412, pp. 295–308, 2022.
https://doi.org/10.1007/978-3-030-93712-6_20

also a productive crop next to maize in the country [2] and is considered as the major cereal which is expected to contribute to food security in Ethiopia [3]. Rice is now suitably cultivated in different parts of the country. The predominant potential areas are West central high lands of Amhara region (Fogera, Gonder Zuria, Dembia, Takusa, and Achefer), North West low land areas of Amhara, and Benshangul Regions (Jawi, Pawi, Metema, and Dangur), Gambella regional state (Abobo, and Etang Woredas), South, and south-west low lands of SNNPR (Berklee, Weyito, Omorate, Gura Ferda, and Menit), Somali Region (Gode), and South Western high lands of Oromia Region (Illuababora, East and West Wellega, and Jimma Zones) [4]. 58% of the regional rice production and 28% of the national rice production is found in Fogera district, Ethiopia. About 72% of the households produced rice and about 50% of the farmers benefited from rice by using it as a cash crop [5]. This indicates that rice has both food and economic importance for small household farmers in the area [5]. According to CSA 2015 report, in the Amhara region, there are 79,683 small household farmers with a total area of 38,322 hectares of land covered by rice with a production volume of 1.13 million quintals that is 85.6% of that national production [6]. Since 1998 the first rice variety was released in the country, and till that time around 20 improved varieties are released. Among those varieties, only Gumara, Kokit, Tigabe, Andasa, Nercia 4, and Ediget are popularized in Fogera plain. Other than these the most popular and productive local varieties in Fogera are X-Jigna [6]. Investigators' efforts concentrated on the testing or introduction of highland varieties. Research data indicated that most farmers have used the X-Jigna variety to grow rice into the highland system, probably because of better yield potential, especially at times, and locations when/where water availability was not scarce [7]. However rice productivity is encouraging in the Fogera district, post-harvesting processes like harvesting and threshing are performed traditionally and cause undesirable loss of paddy.

Threshing is commonly accomplished by trampling several oxen, cows, and sometimes donkeys, some-times; beating panicles on the ground by using human power. In Fogera rice hub, threshing is done on the small fields prepared with a straw without using tarpaulins, plastic, or canvasses which intern is causing a mixture of sand, rocks, and other dirt. Threshing is followed by winnowing, cleaning, and destoning in the same field. Cleaning threshed paddy rice by tossing it into the air blowing off most of the light chaffs, and other impurities. However, this doesn't separate stones, soil, and weeds mixed in the paddy, and it is also a tedious time taking process. The major causes of rice losses during traditional threshing are grain remains in the bundles, and require repeated threshing, grain scattering, grain sticking to mud, wasting grains by birds, and domestic fowls. The panicles of rice should be well organized in the bundle to reduce losses during threshing with beaters. When threshing might be late, the harvested paddy stalk bundles also wait in a dry and shady place, which facilitates the air circulation, and prevents excessive heating. The undesirable loss of paddy during the threshing process can be predicted using the formula [8]:

$$\text{Threshing losses} = [\text{Weight of leftover grains}/\text{Total weight of collected grains}] \times 100\% \tag{1}$$

The maximum loss of rice is observed during threshing, and milling, this indicates that it needs interventions by using appropriate post-harvesting technology [9]. The rate of losses of rice starting from harvesting to milling process is depicted below in Fig. 1.

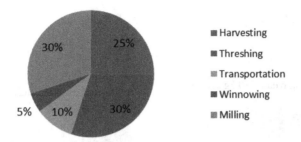

Fig. 1. Stages where post-harvest losses occur (adapted from Tilahun et al. 2012).

The appropriate wetness of rice before harvesting can be checked using a resistance-type moisture meter with small samples. The costly capacitive moisture meter is also important for a more sample but is more precise than resistance type units [9]. The preferred wetness of rice for threshing operation should be 20 to 25% for mechanical threshing and should be less than 20% for hand threshing [9]. The main impacts because of the inappropriateness of moisture content are incomplete threshing, grain damage, and cracking/breakage [9].

2 Materials and Methods

2.1 Materials

Fabrication Materials. The designed rice thresher was fabricated from the available materials in the local market of Bahir Dar city, Ethiopia. Different types of structural steel are used for the fabrication of different parts of the rice thresher; such materials are square hollow steel, black sheet iron, low carbon steel round bar, and aluminum pulley. The fabrication process was performed by applying cutting, bending, welding, and machining operations in the workshop of mechanical and industrial engineering faculty at Bahir Dar Institute of Technology.

Standard Items. The main standard accessories used for the fabrication of rice threshers in this study are the electric motor, v-belt, bearings, and hexagonal bolts and nuts. A single-phase electric motor, which has a 3 KW power rate, is selected. It is used to drive the threshing drum with the assembly of the pulley, and v-belt. The tension of the belt is adjusted by sliding the electric motor on its stand slot to get the appropriate rotation of the threshing drum. The bearings, which are used for the developed thresher machine, are identified by a number P206. It means that it has a 30 mm inner diameter to support the shaft at two ends. Bolts and nuts are used to assemble parts of the body of the machine for easy maintenance and transportation purpose.

Testing Instruments and Tools. The following testing instruments shown in Fig. 2 are used to conduct a basic experimental study for the performance evaluation of the newly developed rice thresher.

2a. Analog balance (0.5g sensitivity)

2b. Digital grain moisture meter

2c. Contact type Digital tachometer

2d. Sensitive digital Weighing Scale
(Sensitivity: 0.1 g)

Fig. 2. Testing instruments and tools used for the experimental study (2a–2d).

The main testing tools used in this study shown above in Fig. 2 are described shortly as follows.

Analog Balance. 0.5 g sensitivity analog balance is used to measure the weight of samples of un-threshed rice straw and threshed rice during the experimental test.

Digital Grain Moisture Meter. A digital grain moisture meter is used to determine the moisture content of rice grain before the threshing operation. The average of three trials is taken for checking of moisture content of rice paddy was found to be 11.23%. This data indicated that the rice is much more dried compare to the allowed moisture content of 20%.

Tachometer. The digital tachometer was used to measure the speed of the threshing drum, and other driven components with or without load expressed in RPM.

Weighing Scale. The sensitive digital weighing scale (sensitivity: 0.1 g) is used to measure the weight of samples of clean paddy grain, and loss amounts to determine the production capacity and efficiency of the machine during testing.

Canva Sheet. It is used to hold the threshed paddy grains temporarily during threshing, and sample measurements. It also prevents impurities and scattering losses of paddy grain.

Timer (Stopwatch). It is used to control the required operation time for threshing activities. The conditions of the crop, such as grain-straw ratio, and moisture content of the grain to be used in each test trial shall be taken using representative samples, which represent the different conditions of the test lot. This can be done by taking samples, each at the top, middle, and bottom of the pile. Samples representing the materials for each test trial shall be placed in appropriate containers for laboratory analysis.

Paddy Rice. Many varieties of rice are grown in Fogera farming lands which are developed in Woreta rice research center, Ethiopia. Among those varieties, X-Jigna, Gumara, Kokit, Tigabe, Andasa, Ediget, and NERICA are popularized in Fogera plain. Most of the names of the varieties of rice are given by the research center considering their cultivation area. X-Jigna variety was used in this study to evaluate the performance of developed rice threshers.

Grain-Straw Ratio (R). It is the ratio of the weight of the grains present in the panicles, to the total weight of the grain, and straw in the same sample [10].

$$\text{Grain - straw ratio}(R) = Wg/Ws \tag{2}$$

Where: Wg is the weight of grain, gram, and Ws is the weight of the sample (grain, and straw), gram. Harvested rice was collected from the test lot, to determine the grain-straw ratio, moisture content of the grain, straw length, and grain quality as the basic characteristics of the paddy are measured and presented in Table 1.

Table 1. Sample characteristics of threshed paddy

No.	Characteristics	Measured value
	Variety: Locally cultivated in Fogera (X-jigna)	
1	Average Grain moisture content	11.23%
2	Average Straw length	800 mm
3	Grain – Straw Ratio	0.546

2.2   Methods

To conduct this study, the major procedures and techniques are applied to design, develop, and evaluate the performance of rice threshers for satisfying the demand of Fogera hub farmers. The detailed methodologies followed for this investigation are carried out on these approaches are given below.

Gap Identification. In Fogera hub, threshing is commonly performed by integrating animal, and manpower on the around small field called "Awudima". In this scenario, the paddy will be mixed with stone, and mud during threshing which will result in the fast wearing of an expensive rubber roller mill during de-husking. This traditional threshing process also makes the final white and brown rice less competitive in the market because of its dirt, and breakage. As per our observation in the Fogera district, there was no experience of rice threshing with technology, except some testing from researchers. This indicates the high available demand for different types of threshers in the sector. While there are attempts in different parts of the country to adapt the threshing technology, the operation is practically seen dominated by the traditional methods in Fogera Hub. Hence, the authors were highly motivated to design, and develop an appropriate rice thresher that has a wire loop beater to separate the paddy from its panicles without breakage.

Literature Review. Selected scientific research works are assessed, and reviewed from journals, conference papers, bulletins, and books. There is an intermediate technology for rice threshing. This involves the use of mechanical; semi motorized, and completely motorized rice threshers. There is also the technology of threshing, which uses a pedal thresher. The pedals are attached to an overhead drum that is perforated to create fingers. As the machine is pedaled, and the straw placed on the drum the resulting centripetal forces loosens the grain from the straw. However, the thresher is also very laborious, has limited output, and is suited for only small farms. Crop moisture content and shattering ability influenced the threshing efficiency, threshing capacity, grain loss, broken grain, fuel, and physical energy requirement at rice threshing. The imported, as well as the modified rice threshers, were demonstrated for farmers in the area are not affordable in cost. Therefore, an affordable and convenient rice thresher should be designed, and fabricated for further application.

Design of Paddy Thresher. The paddy thresher is designed for Fogera farmers by considering important factors such as affordability within the capacity of the local farmers, the ergonomic, and safety requirements, ease of operation, the drudgery activities involved in the traditional methods of threshing, the cost to make the machine, the choice of materials, and manufacturing methods for the development of the machine, threshing capacity, and also threshing efficiency. The 3D drawing of the paddy thresher after conceptual design work is shown below in Fig. 3.

Fig. 3. 3D drawing of designed paddy thresher.

Design Analysis. The principal parameters of the threshing drum are the drum length, the drum diameter, the number of beaters on the drum, and the drum speed (http://www.knowledgebank.irri.org/). The drum length was obtained from the following equation [11].

$$f = f_p \times L \times n \tag{3}$$

Where: L = Drum length (m), f = Feed rate of thresher (kg/s), f_p = Permissible feed rate (kg/s), and n = Number of (rows of) beaters. Therefore, considering this equation, the drum length of the thresher is estimated at 700 mm, and the number of staggered wire loop beater is arranged 12 rows by 6 peripheral columns. The velocity of the threshing drum (V) is determined by using the following equation [12].

$$V = (\pi \times D \times N)/60 \tag{4}$$

Where: V = Velocity of threshing drum, D = Diameter of threshing drum, N = drum RPM. The speed of the driving motor and threshing drum can be correlated and computed using the equation below [13].

$$N_1 \times D_1 = N_2 \times D_2 \tag{5}$$

Where: N_1 speed of the driving pulley (rpm), D_1 diameter of a driving pulley (mm), N_2 speed of driven pulley (rpm), D_2 diameter of the driven pulley (mm). The nominal pitch length of the v-belt was calculated using Eq. (6) below to know the actual belt length required to transfer the speed from the electric motor to the threshing drum [14].

$$L = [(2 \times C) + (\pi/2 \times (D_1 + D_2)) + (D_2 - D_1) \times 2]/2 \times C \tag{6}$$

Where: D_1 and D_2 are the diameters of the driving, and driven pulley, respectively (mm), C is the distance between the centers of the driving, and driven pulley (mm). Generally, the major physical dimensions of a designed paddy thresher that was calculated for the better performance of the paddy thresher are presented in Table 2.

Working Principles. Hold on paddy threshers consist of a semi-closed rotating drum with a wire loop beater that can separate the paddy from its panicles. The designed paddy thresher machine can be worked using a single-phase electric motor or gasoline (petrol) engine. Initially, the power switch of the paddy thresher should be turned on to run the threshing drum. The operator grips the bundle of rice and holds the straw against the drum to be threshed by supporting it with the feeder table. The overall separation of the paddy is controlled by the operator by observing the situation there. When the wire loop beater hits the panicles the paddy and small size of dust will try to drop on the bottom tray. Two persons are enough to accomplish the tasks to get clean paddy without a winnowing process. The paddy thresher didn't damage the straw of the rice. Hence the farmers are using this straw for roof coverage, construction works, and animal feeds safely without significant wastes.

Fabrication of Paddy Thresher. The paddy thresher is manufactured from locally available structural steels and some standard items as it was presented under fabrication materials. The basic material used to fabricate the paddy thresher is square hollow steel, black sheet iron, electrode, bearing, pulley, belt, and motor. The basic parts of the paddy thresher machine are shortly described below.

Table 2. Physical dimensions of power-driven double loop beater paddy thresher.

No.	Item description	Manufacturer specifications
1	Overall dimensions of paddy thresher (L * W * H), mm	1300 * 600 * 1650
2	Stand height, mm	1000
3	Feeding table size (mm), L * W	845 * 240
4	Drum cover size (semicircular), mm	R = 380, L = 670
5	Overall weight without Engine, Kg	34
6	Threshing drum diameter, mm	D = 400
7	Threshing drum Length, mm	700
8	Threshing Drum shaft Diameter, mm	30
9	Threshing drum pulley diameter, mm	D = 290, W = 40
10	Double Wire loop beater size, mm	H = 65, W = 60
11	Number of a wire loop	63
12	Distance between wire loops beaters	120
13	Threshing Drum speed, RPM	370
14	Electric motor power rate	3 KW, 220 V
15	Motor pulley diameter, mm	75
16	Motor RPM	1400 RPM
17	Belt type, and size for the motor to drum drive	A56
18	Center to center distance (motor, and drum shaft), mm	502

Stand. The stand of the paddy thresher is fabricated from SHS (30 × 30 × 1.5) mm pipe and black sheet iron which has 1 mm thickness. The stand is mainly used to support the threshing drum and powerful engine. It is also collecting the separated paddy at the bottom of the tray and slides through the paddy outlet. The feeding table is used to support the bundle of rice and creates a conducive situation for threshing.

Threshing Drum. The drum of the paddy thresher is fabricated from a flat iron, black sheet iron, and wire loop which have a 6 mm diameter, spoke, and hub. The drum is assembled with the rotating shaft, and supported by a pair of bearing designated by P206 at two ends of a shaft. The wire loop is welded on the rolled sheet metal with a staggered arrangement for better threshing performance.

Assembled Paddy Thresher. The assembling of parts of the paddy thresher is performed by using welding, and temporary fasteners like bolts, and screws. The top cover of the thresher is used to protect the losses of scattering paddy. The cover is assembled with a door hinge, and it can be open, and close on the specified position to feed the bundles of rice safely.

Performance Testing and Evaluation. Tests were conducted on the paddy thresher machine to ascertain its performance. The most efficient mode of threshing is the use of a motorized rice thresher. To determine the effect of drum speed of the designed machine, moisture content for threshing, the capacity of the thresher, and efficiency, there is the need to carry out field testing of paddy thresher. The fabricated paddy thresher machine was tested at the Woreta rice research center laboratory in the Fogera district by preparing the required experimental setup as shown in Fig. 4.

4a. a weight measurement of sample rice

4b. samples of measured rice for testing

4c. Drum speed measurement using tachometer

4d. Threshing process during testing

4e. Collected threshed paddy grain

4f. Sample weight measurement of cleaned grain for performance analysis

Fig. 4. Experimental setup for paddy thresher testing

The following criteria are used to evaluate the performance of the paddy thresher: Threshing capacity (TC), threshing efficiency (TE), and Separation efficiency (SE).

Threshing Capacity. The weight of grains (whole and damaged) threshed, and received per hour at the main grain outlet is called capacity. At the end of each test, the total threshed grain was collected from the main grain outlet. The capacity was calculated from the following expression [15, 16].

$$TC(kg/h) = (WG(kg)/duration\ of\ test\ run) * 60\ min \qquad (7)$$

Where: TC, Threshing capacity (kg/h), WG, the weight of total output at the main outlet (kg).

Drum Loss. After threshing, the whole grain still attached to the straw of the rice stalk is called drum loss. The percent of cylinder loss was calculated as:

$$DL(\%) = [WDL(kg)/WG + WSL + WDL(kg)] \times 100 \qquad (8)$$

Where: DL, Drum loss (%), WDL, Weight of drum loss grain (kg), WSL, Weight of separating loss grain (kg).

Separating Loss. The loose grain was collected from threshed straw. It is the ratio of the weight of grains that remained in the panicles of the plants fed into the threshing chamber, to the weight of total grain input of the thresher, expressed in percent. The percentage of separating loss was calculated as follows:

$$SL(\%) = [WSL(kg)/WG + WSL + WDL(kg)] \times 100 \qquad (9)$$

Threshing Efficiency. The net threshed grain received at the main outlet concerning total grain input was expressed as percent by weight was termed as threshing efficiency. The threshing efficiency was calculated from the following expression:

$$TE(\%) = 100 - [\text{un - threshed grains at main outlet per unit time (kg)/total grain input}] \times 100$$

$$(10)$$

3   Result and Discussion

The designed paddy thresher is used to separate the paddy from its panicles by removing the dust, and fine straws without significant damage to the stalk of the rice, and paddy. The developed prototype of rice thresher is shown in Fig. 5.

Fig. 5. Developed prototype at Bahir Dar Institute of Technology-Bahir Dar University (photo captured in BiT-BDU, June 2020)

The developed rice thresher has a threshing cylinder wherein wires of the same arc and size are attached on the periphery of the cylinder in tandem arrangement with the threshing drum cover to protect scattering of grains and operators from accidents.

Testing Result. The developed prototype of rice thresher was tested following PNS/PAES 205:2015 agriculture machinery testing standards. The experimental tests were conducted by applying three trials. During each test trial, samples were collected from the outlet of the rice thresher to evaluate the losses and grain quality. For testing purposes, scattered grains were gathered since these grains are part of the total grain input. A spread canvas sheet was placed around the threshing floor area to catch these grains after each test trial. The collected scattered grains were labeled in appropriate containers for further analysis. Provisions had provided for the collection of scattered grains with a maximum distance of 1 m away from the base of the machine. The threshing losses were affected directly by different operating parameters such as feed rate, threshing drum speed, paddy moisture content, and others. The production capacity, efficiency of the machine, and other threshing testing parameters are summarized in the following Table 3.

Table 3. The performance evaluation result of thresher (Sample of un-threshed rice 2 kg).

No.	Parameters	Test result			
		Trial 1	Trial 2	Trial 3	Average
1	Threshing drum speed (RPM)	370	370	370	370
2	Net Threshed grains (g)	1070	964	1130	1054.67
3	Threshing time (min)	1:48	1:15	1:33	1:32
4	Unthreshed loss (g)	22	15	21	19.33
5	Drum loss (g)	16	17	15	16
6	Broken grains (g/100 g sample)	2	1.8	2.2	2

The experimental data shown in Table 3 is also depicted graphically in Fig. 6, and 7 as shown below.

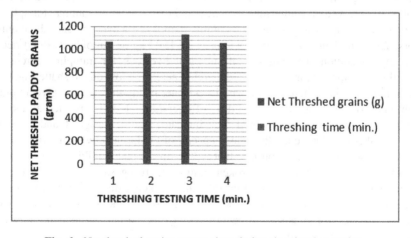

Fig. 6. Net threshed grains versus time during rice thresher testing.

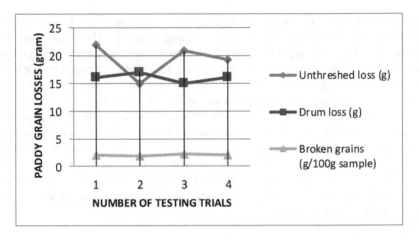

Fig. 7. Rice grain losses versus time during rice thresher testing.

During sample testing, the minimum, and maximum threshing capacity is presented on the second and third trials as shown in Fig. 7. The average net threshed grains in three trials were approximately 1.055 kg per 1:32 min using a 2 kg unthreshed rice sample with the one-person operation. Besides, the major grain losses which were observed in the test are graphically shown below in Fig. 7.

The main grain losses observed during testing of rice threshers are unthreshed grain loss, drum grain loss, and broken grain loss. The maximum unthreshed grain loss is depicted on the test as is shown in Fig. 7. The causes of unthreshed losses may be operators handling skills, and arrangement of wire loop beater. The broken grain losses are low because of the good profiles of wire beater, drum speed, and moisture content. According to the test result, the average actual threshing capacity of the machine is calculated at approximately 128 kg/h using two labor interventions. Hence, there is a possibility to get 1024 kg net paddy grain output at an eight-hour operation of a day. As it was observed, the threshing practice in Fogera Woreda, animal trampling is widely used on large scale in this area. Animal trampling on average takes three human labors, and more than 5 oxen for 10 h to produce 1500 kg output of fairly dried rice for three days operation. The absence of sufficient livestock for trampling forces also resulted in a prolonged threshing period thereby increasing loss due to shattering, pests, and rotting of grains. Therefore the wire loop beater paddy thresher can give an output paddy grain of 3072 kg within three days of operation which is operated at a similar time by the animal trampling method. This indicates that the designed, and developed paddy thresher can double the threshing capacity of the farmers by saving time, saving labor cost, and also avoids impurities that will harm the paddy milling process. In this experimental test, the weight of broken grains per 100-g sample is averagely 2%. Considering the unthreshed loss, drum loss, and broken grains, the performance efficiency of the machine is evaluated to be 96.6%. Therefore, the performance evaluation indicated that the rice thresher will benefit the targeted farmers by reducing unwanted losses, and drudgery activities.

4 Conclusion and Future Work

In time threshing is essential to reduce post-harvest losses, and to spare power sources for carrying out other farm operations. Threshing is time taking, drudgeries operation, so that suitable technology is required to reduce postharvest losses, and to increase the quality of paddy in the Fogera rice farm area. Government and other private sectors should consider spending on appropriate threshers to improve productivity, quality, and facilitate national self-sufficiency in rice production by Fogera marginal farmers. From the above development, and experimental study of rice thresher, the following conclusions are drawn:

- The paddy thresher is designed to be operated by exchanging either an electric motor or petrol engine as per its requirement. It is used to separate the paddy from panicles without feeding the overall stalk of rice. It means that the operator feeds the panicles part to the threshing drum to separate the paddy by hitting with wire loop beater. The machine is designed to reduce scattering loss and to increase the quality of paddy by preventing mud mixing during animal trampling.
- However, the moisture content of the sample is 11.23% and is below the recommended level, the breakage loss is an averagely of 2%. This indicates that the selected wire loop beater for the thresher design gives the advantage to reduce breakage loss.
- The developed paddy thresher can give an output paddy grain of 1024 kg per eight hours operation with three labor engagements. This experimental test and analysis show that the machine can save working time by a minimum of 50% compared to the animal trampling method. It also increases quality by avoiding mixture paddy with mud, and unwanted soil.
- The experimental test on the developed paddy thresher showed that the threshing capacity of the machine is about 128 kg/h using three labor engagements, and considering the unthreshed loss, drum loss, and broken grains. The performance efficiency of the machine is evaluated at approximately 96.6%. Also, the selling price of the paddy thresher is estimated at approximately 31170.50 ETB (954 dollars). This cost can be affordable by associated farmers in Fogera hub for their peer purposes. Generally, the paddy thresher is designed as simple to operate, and affordable for small-hold farmers for better improvement of productivity, and quality of paddy for Fogera hub farmers in Ethiopia.
- This research was focused on the development of affordable rice thresher to reduce drudgery activities for Fogera hub farmers in Ethiopia. In future research works, the rice thresher should include a modified blower to get clean paddy, and also have a sieve or grader of paddy to make the farmers competitive in the global market in this area.

References

1. Sreepada Hegde, V.H.: Assessment of global rice production and export opportunity for economic development in Ethiopia. Int. J. Sci. Res. (IJSR) **2**(6), 257–260 (2013)
2. Asmelash, Y.: Determinants of adoption of upland rice varieties in Fogera district, South Gondar, Ethiopia. J. Agric. Extension Rural Dev. **6**(10), 332–338 (2014)
3. Central Statistical Agency (CSA): Agricultural sample survey 2012/2113, volume III, Report on area, and production, Addis Ababa, Ethiopia (2013)
4. Hagos, H.: Production of upland rice and constraints faced by the farmers in Tselemti District, Northern Ethiopia. J. Poverty Invest. Dev. Int. Peer-Rev. J. **19**, 2422–2846 (2015)
5. Dawit, A.: Rice in Ethiopia: progress in production increase, and success factors. In: 6th CARD General Meeting (2015)
6. Gebremedhin, B., Hoekstra, D.: Cereal marketing and household market participation in Ethiopia: the case of TEFF, wheat, and rice. In: AAAE Conference Proceeding. International Livestock Research Institute (ILIR), Addis Ababa (2007)
7. AgroBIG: Rice value chain analysis programme for agribusiness induced growth in the Amhara region (2016)
8. Tilahun, G., Kahsay, B., Dirk, H., Alemu, B.: Rice Value Chain Development in Fogera woreda Based on the IPMS Experience. ILRI, Nairobi (2012)
9. Appiah, F., Guisse, R., Dartey, P.K.A.: Post-harvest losses of rice from harvesting to milling in Ghana. J. Stored Prod. Postharvest Res. **4**, 64–71 (2011)
10. Philippine National Standard: Agricultural machinery mechanical rice thresher method of test, PNS/PAES 204:2015, ICS 65.060.50 (2015)
11. Soja, J.J., Kallah, M.A., Sanbauna, S.A., Kutt, M.T.: Design and prototype development of a motorized rice thresher. NJERD **1**, 213–217 (2004)
12. Resnikov, A.: Fundamentals of Designing and Calculating Farm Machinery, 8th edn. Agroprom Publishers, Moscow (1991)
13. Singh, K.P., Pardeshi, I.L., Kumar, M., Srinivas, K., Srivastva, A.K.: Optimization of machine parameters of a pedal-operated paddy thresher using RSM. Biosyst. Eng **100**, 591–600 (2008)
14. Olugboji, O.A.: Development of a rice threshing machine. AUJ Technol. **8**, 75–80 (2004)
15. Behera, B.K., Swain, S.: Design, and development of a black, and green gram thresher. J. Agric. Eng. Today **2**, 30–34 (2007)
16. Teka, T., Tamiru, D.: Evaluation of existing threshers for threshing triticale crop. J. Multidiscip. Eng. Sci. Technol. (JMEST) **2** (2015). ISSN: 3159-0040

Metal Injection Molding (MIM) Process and Potential Remedies for Its Defects: A Review

Fetene Teshome Teferi[✉] and Assefa Asmare Tsegaw

Faculty of Mechanical and Industrial Engineering, Bahir Dar Institute
of Technology, Bahir Dar University, P.O. Box: 26, Bahir Dar, Ethiopia

Abstract. This review paper focuses on the metal injection molding process and undesirable defects that occur during part manufacturing. In this paper, common types of metals for injection molding, process parameters, and MIM applications are deeply reviewed from recent research works. MIM process merges the high capability of plastic injection molding technology to produce intricate molds with the advantages of a powder route to process metallic, ceramic, or composites materials. The drawbacks of the MIM process come from diverse technical steps involved in the production of the part (feedstock production, injection, debinding, and sintering). The product quality of MIM is depending on feedstock preparation, mold design, process parameters like temperature and pressure, debinding technique, sintering process, etc. However, the advancement of MIM has proven that can produce very small size and large volume production with low cost when we compare to another manufacturing process. Generally, this study has been presented MIM process parameters, existed defects in MIM and possible remedial solutions, and also future research scope.

Keywords: Metal injection molding · Feedstock · Debinder · Sintering · MIM defects

Nomenclature

MIM   Metal injection molding
PIM   Powder injection molding
SEM   Scanning electron microscopy

1 Introduction

1.1 Rationale

Currently, the Metal injection molding method is not yet implemented in developing countries widely, unlike plastic injection molding. However, the MIM process has many advantages over other traditional metal manufacturing processes, it has also drawbacks that need careful analysis and monitoring during operation to manufacture

M. L. Berihun (Ed.): ICAST 2021, LNICST 412, pp. 309–325, 2022.
https://doi.org/10.1007/978-3-030-93712-6_21

defect-free parts. This led the review paper to be more focused on introducing the technology process, equipment, and materials, application, process parameters, and also defect minimizing techniques. The metal injection molding method is a relatively complex process and time taking but the welfares will exceed by applying optimized process parameters. Moreover, the purpose of this review is to create awareness about the production method of MIM in Ethiopia for future implementation to replace expensive manufacturing methods. Generally, the main objective of this review paper is to provide a detailed understanding of the metal injection molding process and its major defect sources. Throughout the review, the emphasis will be directed on MIM process improvements as well as identifying research scopes for further investigation.

1.2   Method

The approach to review this paper is performed primarily through surveys and summarizes of previously published studies of the subject on metal injection molding (MIM). It includes journals, peer-reviewed articles, books, dissertations, and proceedings.

2   Metal Injection Molding (MIM) Process

MIM is the recent newly developed manufacturing method by merging the process parameters of polymer injection molding and powder metallurgy process. Powder injection molding (PIM) is currently replaced the major advantages of powder metallurgy in the production of intricate and near-net-mold parts [1]. This technique combines the advantages of plastic injection molding and the versatility of the conventional powder metallurgy technique. The drawbacks of powder metallurgy now the day overcomes by using powder metal injection. Some of the limitation areas in powder metallurgy are powder compaction, the cost of machining, the productivity limits of isostatic pressing and slip casting, and the defect and tolerance limitations of conventional casting [1, 2]. The assembling cycle of metal injection molding (MIM) is more unpredictable than that of polymer infusion shaping, which emerges from the need to dispose of the folio and to densify and reinforce the part [1]. MIM is compelling as a creation cycle when four primary contemplations are fulfilled. These are minimal expense versus serious manufacture courses, superior with cutthroat properties, high mold intricacy in a more modest segment, and huge creation quantities [1, 2]. The Metal powder infusion forming is prepared by infusing powdered metals and debinders with high pressing factors instead of the ordinary gravity-took care cycles. The powder metal infusion measure has various mixes of powders like covers, shaping strategies, debinding courses, and sintering heaters. Notwithstanding, all varieties share three interaction streams: feed-stock (powders, debinders, blending) readiness, forming (rheology, device configuration, machine drama on), and warm handling (debinding, sintering, and heat treatment) [2].

The MIM cycle is made out of four principal reformist strides as demonstrated in Fig. 1. These are blending of the powder and natural folio, infusion shaping, debinding where all covers are taken out and sintering [1–3].

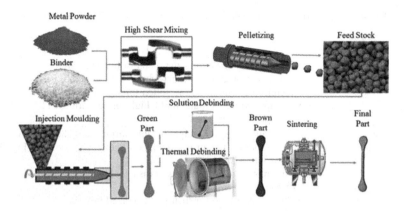

Fig. 1. Process flow of Metal Injection Molding (MIM) [3]

2.1   Steps of the Metal Injection Molding Process

2.1.1   Feedstock Preparation

Making a powder combination of metal and polymer for MIM is the essential action. The size of the metal particles utilized here is ordinarily under 20 μm than those utilized in acclimated powder metallurgy measures. Hot thermoplastic debinders are blended in with the better particles metals and afterward granulated into a uniform feedstock as pellets. The regular proportion of metal particles and polymer in the feedstock is ordinarily 60% and 40% by volume separately [1]. The fine metal particles are completely blended in with different waxes, thermoplastics, and different fixings, and the mix is granulated to frame a feedstock. The feedstock is then taken care of into a normally utilized polymer infusion shaping machine, with trim temperatures, for the most part, going from (149 °C–260 °C). When the feedstock has qualities of a toothpaste-like consistency, it tends to shoot up into openings to mold precise segments. The feedstock is the crude material of MIM that includes the accompanying two fundamental constituents [1, 2, 4].

a. Powders. The MIM powders have a state of little, round if not circular, and deagglomerated. Presently, MIM has utilized more than 1000 assorted combinations, yet a couple is ahead like 17-4 PH treated steel (AISI 630), 316L hardened steel, and a few other spotless sheets of steel, cobalt-chromium, copper, and titanium structures [4]. To get an ideal pressing thickness, circular metal particles are picked, and stream highlights of MIM feedstock; nonetheless, some benefit fit as fiddle retention has been seen with to some degree lopsided formed particles [4].

MIM powder fabrication techniques. Powder grouping for particles size and size conveyance is a significant advance in the creation of powders for MIM since numerous MIM powders are taken from a bigger parcel of powders that have diverse particles estimates and should be painstakingly taken out to guarantee that the MIM powders are consistent on a great deal to-part premise [10, p. 50]. The procedures utilized for the creation of MIM powder comprise gas atomization, water atomization, warm deterioration, and synthetic decrease (Table 1).

Table 1. Common MIM powder fabrication techniques [4, 5, 10, pp. 50–61].

No.	Fabrication techniques	Characteristics	Sample image
1.	Gas atomization	• Produced by liquefying the metal or amalgam by enlistment or another technique for warming and therefore constraining the soften through a spout • It is applied for its round mold, high surface virtue, and high pressing thickness	See Fig. 2
2.	Water atomization	• Typically somewhat unpredictably formed and show more noteworthy surface oxidation than gas atomization particles • The creation rate utilizing water is a lot higher than that of gas • Powder cost is lower than gas atomized powder	See Fig. 3
3.	Thermal decomposition	• This strategy produces powders that have purity greater than 99% and particle sizes in the 0.2–20 μm range • The metal of interest is responded with carbon monoxide at high pressing factor and temperature to deliver a metal carbonyl. This metal carbonyl fluid is purged, cooled, and consequently warmed within the sight of an impetus, which brings about fume deterioration into a powder	See Fig. 4
4.	Chemical reduction	• The measure uses a cleaned oxide which is therefore diminished utilizing a decreasing specialist like carbon to frame carbon monoxide or carbon dioxide • Particle size can be decreased utilizing a lower response temperature; in any case, the response energy is moderate	See Fig. 5

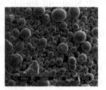

Fig. 2. A gas atomized stainless steel powder imaged by SEM.

Fig. 3. Water atomized stainless steel powder imaged by SEM.

b. Binders. The principal reason for covers in the MIM interaction is to allow the development of the particles into the form kick the bucket cavity, the fastener should wet the metal particles surface, to help to join together and shaping, so a few synthetic wonders that change wetting conduct are broadly utilized. The three significant pieces

Fig. 4. A thermally decomposed iron carbonyl powder imaged by SEM.

Fig. 5. A chemically reduced tungsten powder imaged by SEM.

of covers are polymers that offer strength, a filler stage that is effortlessly eliminated in the main period of debinding, and a surfactant to the connection between the folio and powder [4, 5]. As of now, there are numerous potential outcomes to pick the folio, yet no cover is great. Two fundamental prerequisites are needed for the folio: the first is to give a simple progression of the particles into the kick the bucket hole during trim, wax polymers which by and large have low thickness well satisfy this need; the subsequent one is to limit the detachment of the metal particles during the readiness of feedstock and forming, and new waxes are not satisfactory with this detail [1, 4, 5].

2.1.2 Injection Molding

The result of MIM can be formed utilizing similar hardware and tooling that are utilized in plastic infusion shaping. Nonetheless, the mold openings are planned about 20% higher to represent the segment constriction during sintering. In the MIM cycle, the feedstock is warmed, liquefied, and infused into the form opening, where it cools and solidifies into the state of the segment. The formed green part is projected out and afterward cleaned to eliminate all undesirable highlights [1, 4, 7] (Fig. 6).

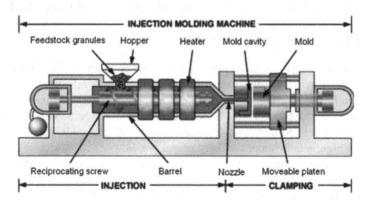

Fig. 6. Principle sketch of the injection molding equipment [7]

2.1.3   Debinding

The debinding phase of the MIM interaction dispenses with the polymer cover from the powder metal by warming it to roughly 400 °C. The outcome is known as the earthy colored part that holds its unique mathematical mold and size [1, 4, 5, 7]. The metal particles are fortified together by the remaining polymer before sintering. MIM utilizes a few variable folio evacuation strategies like warm, solvent, and synergist debinding. A bit by bit high temperature is needed in warm debinding cycles to eliminate the cover. Debinders can be additionally eliminated from the green part utilizing the solvent debinding method by dissolving it in synthetic substances or water.

The recently created debinding technique (synergist strategy) produces leaves behind the incredible mold and great dimensional control because the cycle stays beneath the conditioning point of the folio. The reactant debinding technique is tentatively demonstrated that can dispose of debinders from green parts five to multiple times faster than acclimated warm debinding measures. The temperatures needed for reactant debinding are gone from 120 to 130 °C [4, 5, 8].

2.1.4   Sintering

The last advance is to sinter the brown part in a high-temperature heater (up to 1371 °C) to little space to roughly 1–5%, bringing about a high thickness (95–99%) metal part [4, 8]. The inactive gases for the heater can be gotten from the environment and accomplish temperatures near 85% of the metal's dissolving point. Be that as it may, this withdrawal of the segment happens homogeneously and can be precisely anticipated. The sintered part saves the first formed mold with high resistances yet is present of a lot more prominent thickness. The warming temperature of the earthy-colored part is roughly 85% of the material's dissolving point during sintering, permitting densification and compression of the metal particles with the disposal of the pores [4, 5]. A net mold or close net-mold metal segment found at the last stage is comparative in properties to that of bar stock or billet. Toward the finish of the MIM cycle stage, the segments are warmed with a gum-based paint and climate profile explicit to the composite being prepared. The lingering cover is taken out at the lower temperatures of the sintering cycle (300 to 400 °C). At the point when the temperature expands, particles meld, pore volume therapists, and grain limits structure at particle contacts. The grain size and part thickness rely upon sintering time and temperature [4, 5].

2.2   Materials and Applications of MIM

The regular metal infusion-molded items are little and complex. In the MIM technique, a superior precise item is feasible to accomplish. Powder metal infusion shaping lessens the constraint forced by ordinary powder metallurgy strategies for example the sidewall ought to be equal. MIM has ready to deliver multi-practical parts with slim dividers, sharp corners, and undermines, cross openings, screw strings, molds, gear portions, and comparative highlights without auxiliary operations [4, 6–8].

The principal advantage of the MIM interaction is the creation of high-volume creation of little metal parts. The math of numerous parts made by MIM might be perplexing and have meager dividers and fine subtleties. The use of metal powders empowers a wide assortment of ferrous and nonferrous amalgams to be utilized and for the material properties (strength, hardness, wear opposition, and so forth) to be near those of created metals. The MIM measures don't need the softening of powder metal since high-temperature amalgams can be utilized with no adverse consequence on instrument life. The significant kinds of metals prepared by MIM are incorporate low composite prepares, treated steel, high velocity prepares, irons, cobalt combinations, copper amalgams, nickel compounds, tungsten alloys, titanium alloys, and so forth in various businesses, the results of MIM from metal parts are found like aviation, auto, buyer items, clinical/dental, and broadcast communications. The principal items made by metal powder infusion forming are found in PDAs, power devices, careful instruments, and different electronic and optical gadgets [4, 6, 8].

3 MIM Defects and Remedies

3.1 Problem of Feedstock Preparation

The crude powders utilized for MIM are normally very fine, generally under 20 µm, and subsequently, agglomeration could be not kidding. The solid hard constructions shaping during high-shear-rate manipulating, are remembered for the feedstock, the last sintered item could then contain inhomogeneous miniature designs [9, p. 236]. In the working interaction, a homogenous development is consistently a worry. The metal powders won't be consistently circulated if the manipulating time and shear rate are not satisfactory. Bothersome pockets of natural covers may likewise exist and cause rankling during the resulting warm debinding measure [3, 4, 9]. At the point when the powder diminishes and turns out to be consistent, the feedstock is prepared and ought to contain consistently appropriated powders and debinders. For this situation, a pycnometer thickness meter or a slender rheometer can affirm the uniform dispersion and parcel to-part consistency [4, 9].

Recycled feedstock. The decrease of the production cost of MIM items can be accomplished by reusing the entryway, sprinter, sprue, and faulty green parts. The received strategies by the MIM ventures are available [9]. The primary strategy is to add 30% to half reused feedstock to new materials, while the other is to utilize 100% reused materials. Sadly, these feedstocks debilitate the quantity of reusing emphases increments. Oxidation of the cover segments, especially on account of paraffin wax, brought about by the change of the C–C chain to the C=O chain causes the crumbling of feed-stock [4, 5, 9]. Significantly more breaks and twists of creation parts may result during dissolvable debinding with an additional emphasis on reusing because of more vulnerable holding among powders and debinders [9].

3.2 Molding Defects

MIM forming surrenders are generally equivalent to the ones experienced in conventional plastic infusion shaping. The utilization of ill-advised boundaries like temperature, pressing factor, and shot size are altogether regular reasons for issues in conventional infusion trim and they apply to MIM too. The forming apparatus itself can cause surrenders by comprising of complex math or lacking sufficient air channels. A most minor imperfection can be settled by modifying the temperature-time-pressure connection transport [5, 10, pp. 129–238] (Table 2).

Table 2. Common defects in metal injection molding [10, p. 242, 11, 12].

No.	Defects	Possible causes	Remedies
1	Flash	• Blazes happen when the feedstock is constrained into the clearances between mold parts under high embellishment pressures • Too high a pressing factor inside the die, the helpless evenness of form surface along the splitting line, venting channel excessively enormous • Insufficient clamping force • Viscosity issue	• Utilize a huge weight machine, appropriate instrument making, utilize a lower infusion speed and trim pressing factor, improve the switch point • Minimize infusion pressure in addition to press pressure • Expanding feedstock strong stacking to improve dissolve consistency, acquaint high sub-atomic weight polymers with improving the thickness of the soften
2	Weld lines	• Cold feedstock in the die • Weld lines form when two cold fronts meet each other	• Speed up injection time, mold temperature, and feedstock temperature, expand gate opening, add venting channels or flood wells close to weld line areas, move entryway area, update parts to stay away from stream segment
3	Flow mark	• Cold feedstock in the die • Flow marks occur when the feedstock temperature is too low	• Speed up, form temperature, and feedstock temperature, grow gate opening, change entryway area
4	Incomplete fill	• Misalignment of the splitting line, tooling issue, inadequate of liquid feedstock into the mold cavity • Material feeding problem • The gate gets hardened before the cavity is filled or that the shot size is essentially excessively little	• Ensuring tooling is appropriately positioned and clamped • Increment pack pressure, infusion speed, dissolve temperature, mold temperature, and shoot size • Decrease back pressure and size of the feedstock
5	Gate mark	• With a high shear rate at the gate, powder/folio separation happens and fastener-rich entryway marks structure	• If the first entryway has a narrow column opening and is situated at a flimsy segment, it very well may be augmented and moved to a thick area. Therefore, the degree of powder partition

(*continued*)

Table 2. (*continued*)

No.	Defects	Possible causes	Remedies
			will be decreased and the stream checks and weld lines will be limited
6	Sticking in cavity	• Too high a trim pressure, insufficient warm shrinkage, early launch, ill-advised form plan or making	• Use a lower infusion speed, forming/holding pressing factor, and mold temperature, increment cooling time, take out undercut and increment the draft point, change discharge region and area, rede-sign the fastener
7	Sink mark	• Thermal shrinkage, low density • Uneven shrinkage during cooling	• Increment forming/holding pressing factor and infusion speed, decline mold temperature, increment gate territory, add venting channels, de-wrinkle speed when passing thick areas
8	Voids	• Trapped gas, absorbed moisture	• Increase holding pressure, decline infusion speed, increment form temperature, increment entryway territory, move the gate to thick sections
9	Burn marks	• Overly heated binders	• Lessening infusion speed and feedstock temperature, increment gate region, change entryway area
10	Shrinkage and/or warpage	• Parts distort during ejection • Pressure gradient in component	• Reduction mold temperature and increment cool time; use im-demonstrated cooling instruments and means • Decrease holds pressure
11	Crack	• Part cracking during ejection	• Lessening pack pressing factor and liquefy temperature, increment form temperature

3.3 Debinding Defects

The stress which is existed during the removal of the binder may cause the product defect. During debinding, gravity and the decreasing amount of binder are not the only defects vulnerable for components. The debinding methods by themselves cause stress inside the parts. The irregular thermal expansion, harsh energy-rich atmosphere accommodates and other problems are the most common debinding defects like cracking and distortion [1, p. 210, 12, pp. 243–244].

3.3.1 Thermal Debinding

The main source for warm debinding imperfection is simply too fast warming. The cycle should be exceptionally delayed to keep away from surrenders, even a few days in length debinding times aren't extraordinary. Warm debinding works by debasement of cover parts into gas. If the gas development is large and legitimate pore channels haven't molded at this point pressure inside the parts will make pressure. The main defects like cracks and blisters are built up by the high pressure of molding. The gas build-up problem will not be solved rapidly by decreasing the heating rate. If the components find themselves distorted or bent the answer is probably going to be an equivalent. The reduction of distortions occurs by utilizing some sort of ceramic support for the parts. The removal of formed gas will be also accelerated by good airflow around the parts and thereby reducing the pressure inside [5, 10, pp. 245–248, 11].

3.3.2 Solvent Debinding

The defect of items in MIM that is helped by dissolvable debinding isn't straightfor-wardly corresponded to the debinding boundaries. The transcendent reason for abandons in MIM items is feedstock body electorate and trim methods. The elements of folio segments may not be flawlessly appropriate with one another in the dissolvable. The MIM segment can miss its underlying honesty if some folio part gets uncover at an evil fitting time. The inadmissible mix of spine polymer and the dissolvable is additionally a reason for deserts. Entering dissolvable in the fastener causes the polymer to grow, the bigger the development the more noteworthy the pressure. Drooping and breaking are the most regularly experienced deformities in dissolvable debinding. The change of cycle boundaries probably decreases abandons that can't be altered by folio science or high embellishment pressure. Guidelines to the embellishment cycle or exchanging feedstock/dissolvable will tackle these issues [5, p. 211, 10, pp. 244–245, 249].

3.3.3 Catalytic Debinding

The further developed and gentler strategy than warm or dissolvable debinding has a higher capacity to bear the boundaries and is more averse to create surrenders. The reactant strategy is created by consolidating the warm and dissolvable debinding strategies. The synergist strategy makes gas from the surface inwards, which means caught gas won't an issue as opposed to warm debinding [10, p. 244] (Table 3).

Table 3. Common defects found in debinding of MIM [9, p. 249, 11, 12].

No.	Defects	Possible causes	Remedies
1	Cracks (solvent debinding)	• Swelling of binder components, poor bonding between binder and powder, low strength of the backbone binder, too high a molding pressure, large differences in section thicknesses	• Change the type and composition of solvent or binder, use a lower injection speed and molding pressure, redesign parts with smaller differences in section

(*continued*)

Table 3. (*continued*)

No.	Defects	Possible causes	Remedies
			thicknesses, use lower debinding temperatures
2	Bending/distortion (solvent debinding)	• Residual stress from molding, lack of support for overhanging sections, entrapped air	• Bake between 50 and 908 °C, use fixtures, adjust molding parameters
3	Corrosion/stain (solvent debinding)	• The high acidity of solvent, humid environment	• Replenish solvents or use new ones, leave parts in a dry atmosphere
4	Cracks/blistering (thermal debinding)	• Overly fast heating absorbed water in feedstock, insufficient binder removal for solvent debinding, poor binder distribution, low solid content	• Use slow heating rates, extend solvent debinding time, use longer kneading time and adjust binder components, keep feedstock dry, use higher gas sweeping rate, and shorter flow path
5	Bending/distortion (thermal debinding)	• Overly fast heating, insufficient binder removal for solvent debinding, lack of support for overhanging sections, insufficient interparticle friction, too much binder	• Use slow heating rates, extend solvent debinding time, use fixtures or sands for the support, use higher gas sweeping rate, use more irregular powders, increase solids loading
6	Exfoliation (thermal debinding)	• Wax separation to the surface, overly high heating rate	• Extend solvent debinding time, use slower heating rate, and bake below 100 °C

3.4   Sintering Defect

Since this is the last cycle there are additionally minor deformities presented during past measures that will appear. The densification and shrinkage will be overseen under the sintering working guideline. Appropriately, the most well-known sintering deformities will likewise be identified with dimensional control. The natural climate is another unmistakable reason for sintering issues. For fruitful sintering, environment control is fundamental. Furthermore, the grouping of the gas chemistry needs to be adjusted. Notwithstanding dimensional and environment-related imperfections, the familiar forming and debinding absconds are breaking, twisting and rankles, and so forth are on the whole regular during sintered also [5, pp. 249–250]. The components' thickness will be expanded by observing dad parameters of sintering. The sintered segment will have great strength when its thickness is higher and compacted. On the off chance that the fastest-warming rate in the sintering cycle may cause the imperfections like breaking and twisting. If the pinnacle temperature isn't sufficiently high the metal particles won't intertwine as expected regardless of how long the sintering continues, leaving the thickness too low bringing about poor properties [10, p. 159]. Over sintering is an imperfection brought about by grain development in the microstructure. The enormous grain size getting in MIM segments causes a decrease in mechanical properties. The refinement of the grain size shows an ideal strength of the part as the thickness to be pretty much as high as could be expected (Table 4).

Table 4. Common defects found in sintering of MIM [9, 11, 12].

No.	Defects	Possible causes	Remedies
1	Dimensional defects	• Tool design error • Uneven heat exposure • Non-uniform shrinkage	• The size can be changed to some degree by expanding or lessening the sintering temperature • Increasing the sintering time can also be a cure
2	Atmosphere related defects	• Improper chemical reactions between the metal parts and the atmosphere • Oxygen leaking in the sintering furnace	• Using a surplus of carbon of decreasing the oxygen in the atmosphere
3	Low density	• Uneven heating of the furnace • Insufficient heating temperature	• Adjusting the heating rate can alter the densification
4	Low properties	• Incomplete densification • Grain segregation during cooling	• Increasing the sintering temperature • Adjustments to the cooling parameters
5	Large pores	• Feedstock mixing problem or over sintering	• Reducing the heating rate should ease grain growth
6	Cracking	• Too rapid heating	• By diminishing the warming rate at early sintering the segments will have the opportunity to develop fortitude before they get exposed to incredible pressure
7	Distortion	• Gravity and the component support • Uneven heating	• Support that follows the part mold grantees' support for the whole part • The temperature should be uniform as possible thermal gradients are less likely

The excluded abandons which come in metal infusion formed segments ought to be checked to stay away from revamps and cost increases. MIM is a net-mold cycle to deliver generally little metal parts with profoundly complex calculations, especially fit large scale manufacturing as portrayed in Fig. 7 [13]. On account of mold's multifaceted design, added substance fabricating is the lone regular method.

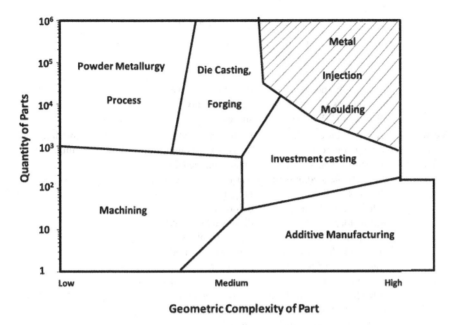

Geometric Complexity of Part

Fig. 7. Suitability of different manufacturing processes as a function of geometric complexity and quantity [13].

MIM items are different and range from buyer items, office gear, clinical instruments, and car segments to mechanical preparing hardware. In light of this wide application and its novel advantages, numerous analysts were included to research the ideal preparing boundaries. A portion of the exploration yields is introduced in Table 5 underneath.

Table 5. Recent research works on metal injection molding (MIM) [14–18]

Authors and years	Methods and materials	Results	Gaps/limitations
Wolff et al. (2016)	•Mg-alloys •Using a novel natural polymer cover, to be specific PPcoPE, material properties coordinating with those of human cortical bone tissue •Polymer content was varied between 5 and 35 m. % of the binder	•The first implant demonstrator parts could be successfully produced by the MIM technique •Dog bone molds tensile test specimens, Young's modulus test specimens, and more complex demonstrator parts, and biomedical implant screw	•Long sintering time •Sublimation of Mg-vapor on the surfaces of specimens holding the lowest temperature

(continued)

Table 5. (*continued*)

Authors and years	Methods and materials	Results	Gaps/limitations
	system. The powder loading was 64 vol. % for all feedstock batches	demonstrators were produced very successfully	
Veeresh et al. (2018)	•A nickel-based self-fluxing composite NiCrSiB (70% Wt.) was precisely blended in with Cr_3C_2-NiCr (30% Wt.) utilizing a high-energy ball factory •The powder (thickness of 4140 kg/m^3) with a volume part of 56% is blended in with polyethylene glycol (10% wt. Stake), Low-thickness polyethylene (35%wt. LDPE), paraffin wax (52%wt. PW), and stearic corrosive (3%wt. SA) by utilizing sigma Z cutting edge blender •The Feedstock was characterized using Differential Scanning Calorimetry (DSC) •The rheological behavior of the feedstock was determined using a Rotational Viscometer •The microstructure analysis and stage investigations of the ragged surfaces were done utilizing SEM, X-beam diffraction spectrometer (XRD)	•A nickel-based feedstock accomplished great homogeneity, warm and rheological properties, and deformity-free dissolvable debinding was done at 48 °C •The nickel-based composite was effectively evolved and created with various syntheses utilizing the MIM procedure	•Long debinding and sintering time
Askari et al. (2019)	•AISI 4605 MIM feedstock •Paraffin wax (PW) utilized as a filler to improve the rheological property of feedstock,	•The worth of thickness diminished with each additional expulsion step, while expanded the four times expulsion because of the	•If the cooling obliges a quick expansion inconsistency, the outcome might be shaping deformities

(*continued*)

Table 5. (*continued*)

Authors and years	Methods and materials	Results	Gaps/limitations
	Polypropylene (PP) and Polyethylene (PE) are spine polymers to keep the green part fit as a fiddle during the debinding and stearic corrosive (SA) utilized as a surfactant to improve the wettability of powder particles with the fastener framework	debasement of folio segments •By increasing the mixing time, powder particles are more distributed between the binder systems	like distortion and breaking in parts
Lin et al. (2020)	•MIM mold flow simulations with the Taguchi method	•The consistency of the powder particles fixation circulation can be improved by utilizing a more limited occupying time, a higher liquefy temperature, a lower pressing factor, a lower mold temperature, and a more modest gate size	•Formation of black lines •Lack of optimal MIM processing parameters

In general, many researchers have made significant studies on the MIM process by applying experiments and optimization techniques to reduce part defects and also product costs. However, MIM has a unique advantage over another manufacturing process, it is not yet implemented in developing countries like Ethiopia because of a lack of knowledge on the process application. Hence, the reviewer recommends that investors should emphasize their business in this area in the developing countries since it is untapped manufacturing technology for the production of high volume with lower cost.

4 Future Works

MIM is an effective manufacturing method for smaller size, massive in volume, and intricate mold of components from metallic powders. Thus, the debinding method and sintering process further demands scientific guidelines to obtain quality and cost-effective parts. Also, the process parameters need detailed analysis and optimization for valuable outputs using computer simulations and advanced optimization techniques. Moreover, the invention of a new type of feedstock enhances the versatility of product mixes in a specific industry. Researchers should also think about the integration of MIM with 3D printing and other suitable processes to improve the appropriateness of variable material powders.

5   Conclusion

With MIM processing technique micro parts, as well as biomaterial, can be success-fully processed/fabricated. The five primary steps required for Metal Injection Molding (MIM) are tooling, mixing, molding, stripping, and sintering. Conventional secondary operations could be added if required. The cost of MIM products becomes higher because of the long time sintering process. The compositions of binders are designed to separate sequentially, without disturbing part geometry. Generally, from this review the following conclusions and suggestions are drawn:

- The drawbacks of the MIM process are commonly observed in molding, debinding, and sintering that require improving through advanced research works, however, it is well suited to the high-volume production of complex mold parts and offers a freedom of design equivalent to that of injection-molded plastic parts or investment castings.
- Removal of debinders is a long cycle that subjects the formed parts to high inward pressure. The decrease of imperfections and chopping down measure term would be the primary focal point of optimization. There is a hostile event while streamlining any debinding strategy is the contention between limiting interaction term as opposed to limiting deformities. During the time spent time reduction, the initial step is to remove any abundance run-time, and the subsequent advance is to increment debinding power and accordingly cutting personal time significantly further. An increment in power will make more noteworthy pressure bringing about an expanded danger of imperfections like breaking, contortion, and others.
- The imperfections of bending become much more genuine when fluid stage sin-tering or weighty metals, for example, tungsten amalgams are utilized in the sin-tering interaction. The bending imperfection can be reduced by utilizing high solids stacking and more unpredictable powders. The necessity of installations in the sintering interaction is regularly to forestall twisting, and faker extensions, which are taken out by mechanical techniques after sintering, are frequently planned into the part to forestall opening of the long spaces during sintering.
- The feedstock is what makes the MIM process possible. Hence development and characterization of alternative feedstock are highly demanded and searched.
- Scientific guidelines for molding, debinding, and sintering should be researched. Specifically, computer simulation and parameter optimization techniques are looked into further for process and product improvement.

References

1. German, R.M., Bose, A.: Injection Molding of Metals and Ceramics. MPIF (1997)
2. Gülsoy, H.Ö., German, R.M.: Production of micro-porous austenitic stainless steel by powder injection molding. Scripta Mater. 58(4), 295–298 (2008)
3. Kafkas, F., Ebel, T.: Metallurgical and mechanical properties of Ti-24Nb-4Zr-8Sn alloy fabricated by metal injection molding. J. Alloys Compd. 617, 359–366 (2014)
4. Smith Metal Products: A design guide from metal injection molding (MIM) (2012)

5. German, R.M., Bose, A.: Injection Molding of Metals and Ceramics. Princeton, New Jersey (1997)
6. Kearns, M.: Alloy Metal Powders for Dental Applications. Sandvik Osprey Ltd., Neath (2007)
7. Dutilly, M., Ghouati, O., Gelin, J.C.: Finite-element analysis of the debinding and densification phenomena in the process of metal injection molding. J. Mater. Process. Technol. **83**(1–3), 170–175 (1998)
8. Song, J., Barriere, T., Gelin, J.C., Liu, B.: Powder injection molding of metallic and ceramic hip implants. Int. J. Powder Metall. **45**(3), 25–34 (2009)
9. Hwang, K.S.: Handbook of Metal Injection Molding, pp. 235–240. Woodhead Publishing Limited, Taiwan (2012)
10. Heaney, D.F.: Handbook of Metal Injection Molding. Woodhead Publishing Limited, Cambridge (2012)
11. German, R.M.: Metal Powder Injection Molding (MIM): key trends and markets. In: Handbook of Metal Injection Molding (2012). A volume in Woodhead Publishing Series in Metals and Surface
12. Shahbudin, S.N.A.: A review of metal injection molding- process, optimization, defects and microwave sintering on WC-Co cemented carbide. In: IOP Conference (2017)
13. Levy, G.N., Schindel, R., Kruth, J.-P.: Rapid manufacturing and rapid tooling with layer manufacturing (LM) technologies, state of the art and future perspectives. CIRP Ann.-Manuf. Technol. **52**, 589–609 (2003)
14. Dehghan-Manshadi, A., Yub, P., Dargusch, M., StJohna, D., Qian, M.: Metal injection molding of surgical tools, biomaterials, and medical devices: a review. Powder Technol. **364**, 189–204 (2020)
15. Martin, W., et al.: Metal Injection Molding (MIM) of magnesium and its alloys, MDPI. Metals **6**, 118 (2016). https://doi.org/10.3390/met6050118
16. Chinnathaypgal, V.N., Rangarasaiah, R.M., Desai, V., Samanta, S.K.: Evaluation of wear behaviour of metal injection moulded nickel based metal matrix composite. Silicon **11**(1), 175–185 (2018). https://doi.org/10.1007/s12633-018-9843-y
17. Askari, A., Alaei, M.H., Mehdipoor Omrani, A., Nekouee, K., Park, S.J.: Rheological and thermal characterization of AISI 4605 low-alloy steel feedstock for metal injection molding process. Met. Mater. Int. **26**(12), 1820–1829 (2019). https://doi.org/10.1007/s12540-019-00442-9
18. Lin, C.M., Wu, J.J., Tan, C.M.: Processing optimization for metal injection molding of orthodontic braces considering powder concentration distribution of feedstock. Polymers **12**, 2635 (2020). https://doi.org/10.3390/polym12112635

The Advancement of Aluminum Metal Matrix Composite Reinforced with Silicon Carbide Particles (Al-6061/SiCp): A Review

Fetene Teshome Teferi[1]([⊠]) [iD], Kishor Purushottam Kolhe[2] [iD],
Assefa Asmare Tsegaw[1], Tafesse G. Borena[3], and Muralidhar Avvari[4]

[1] Faculty of Mechanical and Industrial Engineering, Bahir Dar Institute
of Technology, Bahir Dar University, P.O. Box 26, Bahir Dar, Ethiopia
[2] College of Engineering, and Technology, Bule Hora University,
Bule Hora, Ethiopia
[3] Saint Mary's University, Winona, MN, USA
[4] Faculty of Mechanical and Industrial Engineering,
Arba Minch Uni, Arba Minch, Ethiopia

Abstract. It is true that advancement in engineering and technology directly depends on the advancement of modified or new engineering materials. Now a day's Composite materials are receiving remarkable attention by enhancing the desirable properties of monolithic materials. Some product design requires a material that has a combination of two or more desirable properties in one, such as strength, hardness, wear-resistant, corrosion-resistant, good thermal and electrical conductivity, castability, machinability, etc. Metal matrix composites can satisfy the functional requirements of a specific product by varying the weight ratio of the selected metal matrix, and reinforced particles. Currently, aluminum matrix composite has a wide application in the production of enhanced automotive, aerospace, medical, and other machinery spare parts. This review paper mainly focused on the aluminum metal matrix composite which contains silicon carbide particles as reinforcement. In this review paper, different properties like mechanical, chemical, and physical properties (thermal and electrical conductivity) of the aluminum matrix composite are discussed, besides various types of manufacturing techniques, process parameters, applications, and future research gaps were studied in detail. This review paper specifically studies the effect of silicon carbide particles (SiCp) reinforcement in the aluminum metal matrix and their related phenomenon.

Keywords: Metal matrix composite · Silicon carbide particles · Aluminum matrix composite

Nomenclature

AMMC	Aluminum Metal Matrix Composite
MMC	Metal Matrix Composite
SiCp	Silicon Carbide Particles

M. L. Berihun (Ed.): ICAST 2021, LNICST 412, pp. 326–336, 2022.
https://doi.org/10.1007/978-3-030-93712-6_22

1   Introduction

1.1   Objectives of the Review

Currently, metal matrix composites synthesized from aluminum are widely used by industries for different applications. Because of its easiness to tailor to the desired functional requirements compare to other metal matrix composites. Hence, this review paper is studied to provide a detailed understanding of the advancement of composites of Al-6061 alloy with specific silicon carbide reinforcement and their major drawbacks in experimental research works. Throughout the review, the emphasis will be directed on Al-6061/SiCp composites of alternative manufacturing techniques, constraints of fabrication, the weight ratio of reinforcements, physical properties, mechanical properties, as well as identifying research scopes for further investigation.

1.2   Basics of Composite Materials

In the modern age, the development of large varieties of materials enables designers to be as creative as possible for new technology innovation based on a wide range of material properties [1]. With the recent advancement in the science and technology research areas, the property of the material can be enhanced and refined by using some reinforcing material is known as composite materials. It consists of a matrix and reinforcement in its composition. Matrix materials transfer the external exerted force to the reinforcement material which shields and maintain the shape of the matrix material. The reinforcement segment is the second segment of the composite material. The high stiffness and high strength of the composite material is accounted for by its reinforcement. The modern utilization of composites as engineering materials is evidenced by the real availability in the market from 1600 engineering materials more than 200 are composites [2]. Now a day's composite materials are emerging with a distinct technology that makes inspiration for the synthesis of new and stronger materials. The engineering materials of the composite are generally developed by mish-mashing of the selected group of materials that yield better properties than monolithic materials used alone. The physical and chemical characteristics of the matrix are the major factors to classify composite materials. These are metal-matrix, polymer matrix, and ceramic composites. A metal matrix composite (MMCs) offers better performance when it is compared to other classes of composite materials.

By combining the desirable attributes of metals and reinforcements, there is a possibility to have well-designed metal matrix composites for specific applications. The mechanical properties of newly developed composite materials are intermediate between the matrix alloy and the reinforcement when high strength and high modulus refractory particles are added [3]. The required physical and mechanical properties of the matrix should be considered for selection purposes. Commonly, Al, Ti, Mg, Ni, Cu,

Pb, Fe, Ag, Zn, and Sn are used as the matrix material, but Al, Ti, Mg are used widely for the development of AMMC [4]. Similarly, discontinuous fiber compounds such as SiC, Al_2O_3, and B_4C can be dispersed effectively in molten aluminum.

1.3   Aluminum Matrix

AMMCs have distinctive properties such as high strength to weight ratio, good mechanical properties, and better durability. Hence, the demand for this material is highly increased in many manufacturing industries from time to time. Aluminum matrix composites are the most researched MMC which are commonly applied in automotive construction, aerospace, and other industries. AMMCs are widely used due to their high specific modulus, strength, and wear [2]. In particular, it has been reported that by increasing the weight ratio of reinforcement particles, AMMCs possess improved wear resistance and lower friction coefficient when it is equated to monolithic aluminum alloys.

1.4   Reinforcements

Reinforced material is that the main member of the composite family which bears the load over the matrix material. Reinforcement materials enhance the specified mechanical properties within the material during a discriminatory direction like strength, stiffness, hardness, etc. There are many sorts of reinforced particle which are selected depends on the specified property of the aluminum matrix composite materials. Particularly, reinforcements utilized in AMMCs are considered as continuous fibers, short fibers, whiskers, and equiaxed particles. The diameter of reinforcements also can vary widely from about 0.01 μm to 100 nm. If the ratio of length to the diameter of fibers lies above 100, they will be utilized in applications where higher specific strength and specific modulus are required. In particulate composites, the ratio of length to diameter approaches one [5]. Particle-reinforced MMCs differ from normal dispersion-hardened materials during which the particle size varies between 0.001 to 1 μm. The possible interparticle gap for MMCs is smaller than 5 μm, and therefore the weight ratio of the particulate is additionally less than 0.10 [5].

The weight percent of reinforcement highly affects the mechanical and physical characteristics of developed composites [6]. Numerous investigators have assessed that the quantity fraction of reinforced particles is below 30% is going to be used for structural and machining uses [7, 8]. Table 1 presents the common selection of mishmashes of aluminum metal matrix alloy and therefore the fiber dispersoids that are wont to produce cast MMCs, especially for the car industries.

Table 1. The possible AMMC and dispersoid combinations [9].

Matrix	Dispersoid	Size (μm)	Amount
	Graphite flake	20–60	0.9–0.815%
	Graphite granular	15–500	1–8%
	Shell char	125	15%
	Al_2O_3 particles	3–200	3–30%
	Al_2O_3 discontinuous	3–6 mm long, 15–25 μm dia	0–23 vol%
	SiC particles	9–12	3–60%
	SiC whiskers	5–10	10%, 0–0.5 vol%
	Mica	40–180	3–10%
	SiO_2	5–53	5%
	Zircon	40	0–30%
	Sand	75–120	36 vol%
	TiC particles	46	15%
	Boron nitride particle	46	8%
	Si_3N_4 particle	40	10%
	ZrO_2	5–80	4%
	TiO_2	5–80	4%
	TiB_2	2–10	3–9 wt%
	C_{SF}	3–5 mm %	1–3 volume

In AMMCs, the second phase like fibers, whiskers, and particulates are incorporated in aluminum alloys to realize properties that aren't obtainable in conventional monolithic materials. The main properties enhanced in MMCs are mentioned as a specific strength, specific modulus, toughness, fatigue, creep, electrical, thermal properties, and wear resistance. These are often achieved by selecting logically the reinforcement materials, their size, shape, and weight ratio. Among many dispersoids, silicon carbide particles are the foremost common reinforcement in AMMC due to their easy availability and manufacturability. AMMCs reinforced with silicon carbide can possess wear and thermal shock resistance, good mechanical properties, and also high working temperatures. When embedded in metal matrix composites, SiC certainly improves the general strength of the composite together with corrosion and wear resistance. The addition of SiC particles in aluminum MMCs increases 20% improvement within the commonest mechanical properties of materials [9]. Most properties of aluminum metal matrix and carbide reinforcements are summarized in Table 2.

Table 2. Summary of properties of candidate materials [9–11].

No.	Properties	Al-6061 T6	SiC
1	Density (Kg/m^3)	2700	2900
2	Melting temperature (°C)	660	2830
3	Thermal conductivity (W/m.K)	180	120–170
4	Coefficient of thermal expansion (ppm/K)	23	4.9
5	Electrical conductivity (% lACS)	43	3
6	Tensile Strength (MPa)	300	470
7	Compressive strength (MPa)	260	896
8	Hardness (BHN)	75	140
9	Tensile failure strain (%)	10	<0.1
10	Modulus of elasticity (GPa)	60	520
11	Machinability ratings	1.9	–

1.5   Manufacturing Techniques of Aluminum Metal Matrix Composites

The liquid state process of producing methods of the AMMCs are talking about as stir casting, compo casting, squeeze casting, spray casting, and in place (reactive) processing, ultrasonic-assisted casting. Alternatively, the Solid-state manufacturing process comprises powder metallurgy, high-energy ball milling, friction stir process, diffusion bonding, and vapor deposition techniques (Table 3).

Table 3. Comparative study of different fabrication processes to AMMCs [12, 13].

No.	Process	Shape	Size	Volume fraction	Reinforcement condition	Cost
1	Stir casting	Wide range of shape	Larger size up to 500 kg	Up to 0.3	No damage	Least expensive
2	Squeeze casting	Limited by performing shape	Up to 2 cm height	Up to 0.5	Severe damage	Moderate expensive
3	Spray casting	Limited shape	Large size	Up to 0.7	Reinforcement damage	Expensive
4	Powder metallurgy	Wide range	Restricted size		Reinforcement fracture	Expensive

Stir casting technology is being considered for future research because of its lower cost compared to the available manufacturing techniques of AMCs [14]. The commercial widespread of the composite material stir casting route is most suitable to achieve a good quality of composite materials. It is also accepted commercially due to the low cost of processing in comparison with other processing methods, and its flexibility. A good dispersion of reinforcement particles without damaging the reinforcement can be realized by controlling the stir casting parameters.

The aluminum matrix hybrid composite materials are preferably used for many automobile and aerospace spare parts such as driveshaft, engine block, engine liners, gearbox components, rotors, brake components, etc. Apart from these, many researchers have found several difficulties in fabricating the composite material. The most commons are poor chemical reaction between the reinforcement and matrix alloy, lack of wettability between reinforcements and matrix, sponginess in the cast MMCs, and problem in achieving a uniform distribution of the reinforcement material. However, MMCs can allow researchers to have optimal desirable properties as per the functional requirement of the product however there should be management and monitoring of process variable parameters to get the required output.

2   Materials and Methods

Generally, because of a large demand for advanced engineering materials to meet the design requirements of a product, many scholars and researchers were involved in the synthesis and characterization of metal matrix composites from ancient to recent. It means that scientific pieces of evidence and references can be accessed now a time for further investigation in this area. Especially aluminum metal was the most common metal matrix material because of its abundancy and suitable engineering properties for the most required functional requirements. Hence, the methodology to review this paper is performed primarily through surveys and summaries of previously published studies of the subject in aluminum metal matrix composites (AMMCs) from consistent websites. It comprises journals, peer-reviewed articles, books, dissertations, and conference proceedings.

3   Previous Research Works on Al-6061/SiC$_p$ Composites

Many research works were conducted by many scholars and researchers on aluminum matrix composites for a long time. Some of them are presented below (Table 4).

Table 4. Summary of previous research works in Al-6061/SiC$_P$ composites

No.	Authors (year)	Materials and methods	Results	Ref.
1	Chen et al. (2009)	• Al-6061 + 5% SiC + 5%Gr • Stir casting	• At 300 °C, the developed composite has higher thermal conductivity (163 W/m.K) than P20 steel (42 W/m.K). It can be an improved mold tooling for plastic materials	[12]
2	Prabu et al. (2006)	• High silicon content aluminum alloy • Silicon carbide metal matrix composite material, with 10%SiC • Brinell hardness test • SEM	• The particle clustering becomes lower when the stirring speed and time increased, and vice-versa was true during microstructure analysis • In addition, at a stirring speed of 600 rpm, uniform hardness was seen and it degraded beyond this speed	[15]
3	Veeresh Kumar et al. (2010)	• Al-6061-SiC • Liquid metallurgy	• Hardness, strength, density, and wear resistance increased	[16]

(*continued*)

Table 4. (*continued*)

No.	Authors (year)	Materials and methods	Results	Ref.
4	Mazahery and Shabani (2013)	• The experimental specimens were prepared from the average size of 15, 20, and 50 μm SiC and a weight ratio of 5%, 10%, and 15% to determine microstructure and wear characteristics • Management of stir casting factors like temperature of pouring, speed, time, and pre-heating temperature of particulate fibers • Composting method	• Rolling operation after stir casting can reduce porosity defects of composite • The hardness of tested materials increases with the increase of SiC particles amount • No more plastic deformation was seen on the worn-out surface of this composite material	[17]
5	Nair and Joshi (2015)	• Al-6061 as the matrix and silicon carbide (10%) was used • Stir casting • SEM	• SiC particles were dispersed nicely while it is analyzed using SEM • Minimization of porosity and improvement of wettability can be obtained by adding magnesium powder	[18]
6	Mishra and Srivastava (2016)	• Aluminum Al-6061 matrix and a mesh size of 150 and 600 SiC particles • The weight ratio of SiC in a specimen seriously varies as 5, 10, 15, 20, 25, 30, 35, and 40% • Stir casting method	• Regardless of mesh size, the wear resistance increases with an increasing volume fraction of particles • An optimal result has been obtained at a 35% weight fraction • At 600 mesh size of SiC particle, wear rate and coefficient of friction were decreased more relative to 150 mesh size	[19]
7	Natrayan et al. (2018)	• Alloy aluminum as matrix and SiC particles as fiber, • Leaf ashes used as the reinforcement • Bottom pouring stir casting method	• The addition of leaf ashes minimizes the wear rate of base metal • The hardness of the Al-6061 with the SiC reinforcement has been increased	[20]
8	Murugan et al. (2018)	• Al-6061 alloy • SiC 20-micron size and weight ratio (5, 10, and 15%) • Stirring speed (300, 350 & 400 rpm) • Fly ash (3%) • stir casting • Design of experiment (DOE) method • Taguchi method for predicting the better parameters	• Stir casting parameters such as time (2, 4 & 6 min), speed (300, 350 & 400 rpm) were wide-ranging to cast the vital specimens • The tensile strength value increases with the increase in wt. % of SiC and stirring time • Tensile strength decrease with the decrease in stirring speed	[21]
9	Dwivedi and Sahu (2018)	• Aluminum (Al-6061) based metal matrix composite successfully developed using SiC as reinforcement • Electromagnetic stir casting route • Three parameters (preheat temperature, size, weight percent) of SiC were selected	• The corrosion rate decreases by enlarging the preheat temperature of SiC • Increasing the particle size and weight percent of SiC, the corrosion rate also increases • Uniform distribution of composite was observed at optimum SiC particle parameters	[22]

(*continued*)

Table 4. (*continued*)

No.	Authors (year)	Materials and methods	Results	Ref.
10	Kumar et al. (2019)	• Al-6061 and SiC are used as a composition of specimens (i.e. weight ratio of 5%, 10%, and 15%) • EDM machining was used to test surface roughness	• An improved surface finish was found at a composition of aluminum 6061 with a SiC 10% weight ratio	[23]
11	Kumar Maurya et al. (2019)	• Determination of the influence of the composition of SiC on aluminum alloy Al- 6061 • The weight percent of SiC content was varied (0, 1, 2, 3, and 5%) • stir casting method	• By varying weight percent up to 5 wt% of SiC particles, the physical and mechanical characteristics like density, tensile strength, and hardness of composites were significantly improved	[24]
12	Bhat and Kakandikar (2019)	• Al-6061 and 5% SiC (50 μm size) were used for ingredients • The stir casting method is used for specimen fabrication • A Pin on disc tribometer with a load range of 5N-200N and RPM varying from 200 to 1500 was used for wear characteristics studying	• At a limited RPM, Wear-resistant decreases fastly when RPM increases in case of Al-6061 testing than Al-6061/SiC • Reinforced Al-6061 with SiC particles has better mechanical characteristics than an unreinforced alloy	[25]
13	Soltani et al. (2017)	• Aluminum ingot with 99.8 in wt. % commercial purity and weight ratio 3% SiC composites were used as constitutes to fabricate composites at two casting temperatures (680 and 850 °C) • The stir casting method and stirring times (2 and 6 min) were applied • SEM and HRTEM were used to test porosity, ceramic incorporation, and agglomeration of the particles	• An optimal stirring time is controlled to realize the desired metal and ceramic bonding at the interface • Improved ceramic incorporation was also found at higher stirring temperature (850 °C) • In addition, uninvited defects like shrinkage, porosity, and intensive formation of Al_4C_3 at the metal and particles interface were observed • A better Al/SiC bonding at 680 °C was caused by the formation of Al_4C_3	[26]
14	Pandiyan and Prabaharan (2020)	• Al-6061 T6 matrix and SiC (0, 5, 10, and 15 wt. %) were varied in the experiment works • Mechanical characteristics like density, tensile, compression, hardness, and impact strength were tested and evaluated • A dry sliding wear test was applied to determine the tribological behavior of the composites • Taguchi-based L'27 orthogonal array with input parameters such as SiC (wt. %), Sliding Distance (m), and load were considered to measure tribological behavior • SEM and energy dispersive X-ray analysis (EDX) were used to determine the dispersion of SiC in the Al-6061 T6 matrix	• When SiC constituents were increased in the Al-6061 T6 matrix, the physical properties like density values were increased • When SiC was added at 15 wt. % to Al-6061 T6, maximum tensile strength, compression strength, impact strength, and hardness values were evaluated • The existence of SiC particles in the composite counterattacked the wear of the material. When SiC was added at 15 wt. % there was enriched wear resistance • The sliding distance was the dominant factor that was ensured by ANOVA during tribological studies	[27]

By and large, a nonstop requirement for upgrades in AMMCs properties across a wide scope of uses is extremely high in numerous spaces like transportation, aviation, military designing, and so forth. A particular prerequisite is the advancement of lightweight high strength materials with improved mechanical properties. This can be accomplished by fostering another class of materials to meet the difficult issues presented inside engineering applications. The ideal redid mechanical properties can be conferred in metal framework composites. The choice of the creation technique for making the composite impacts the material conduct. The assembling strategies of AMMCs have an impact not just on the support circulation, homogeneity, bunching/agglomeration, wettability, hardness dispersion, and thickness dissemination, and so forth yet additionally on the mechanical conduct of the integrated material.

4   Recommendation and Future Works

The major selected research necessities in aluminum metal matrix composites while different manufacturing techniques applied are mentioned below:

- In stir casting, Prevention of agglomeration and clustering of micro and nano-sized reinforcements are important in aluminum metal matrix composites.
- The growing interface is also required to achieve uniform distribution of reinforcements in the matrix with good bonding, and involving engulfment of reinforcements.
- In situ reinforcements, using low-cost reinforcements and low-cost processing are recommended to reduce the cost of components.
- Machining difficulty has been observed in cast aluminum metal matrix components; hence further research is required to get optimal machining parameters.
- Developing a guiding principle to recycle aluminum metal matrix components at completed its usage life is also another research area.
- Agricultural and industrial waste like fly ash as fillers should be used to develop cheaper stir cast components with low exemplified energy.
- Developing manufacturing capability and user base for smart metal matrix castings including self-healing, self-lubricating, and shape recovering aluminum matrix composites are timely required.
- Improvement manufacturing methods of Al-6061 nanocomposites through stir casting should be one of the focus areas of future studies.

5   Conclusion

The quick development of designing and innovation straightforwardly relies upon the development of current materials. Aluminum metal matrix composites (AMMCs) have acquired huge consideration lately. The significant justification for its more popularity is a direct result of its lightweight, low coefficient of warm development, great machinability, and improved mechanical properties, for example, yield pressure, extreme elastic pressure, and hardness. Inferable from these benefits, they are utilized in aviation parts, automobiles, electronic segments, and other industrial machine components. Mix projecting (vortex strategy) is by and large acknowledged monetarily as a minimal expense technique for the manufacturing of AMMCs. Its motivations rely upon its simplicity, manageability, and relevance to large-scale manufacturing. The vortex strategy is less expensive than the existed methods for AMMCs creation, and it permits huge measured parts to be manufactured. Consequently, this audit paper stresses the investigation of aluminum matrix composite that would accomplish ideal consolidated attractive properties, for example, wear-safe, thermal conductivity and electric conductive, and great machinability for various applications. Due to the requirement for lighter-weight, wear-resistant, and higher thermal conductive segments, the interest for MMCs will keep on developing. Significant boundaries to the development of cast AMMCs incorporate significant expense, absence of plan information, and trouble in machining, setting up huge volume assembling, and reusing. Aluminum matrix composites cast to date incorporate aluminum-silicon carbide, aluminum alumina, aluminum graphite, and aluminum fly debris. A few projecting strategies including sand, speculation, lasting mold, crush projecting, radiating projecting, and removal projecting have been utilized to project metal matrix composite parts. Notwithstanding miniature composites, late work has been directed to create aluminum metal framework nanocomposites, syntactic froths, self-greasing up, and self-healing castings.

References

1. Ashby, M.F.: Materials Selection in Mechanical Design, 2nd edn., p. 502. Butterworth Heinemann, Oxford (1999)
2. Kumar, A., Kumar, S., Garg, R.: A review paper on stir casting of reinforced aluminum metal matrix composite. Int. J. Adv. Res. Sci. Eng. 4(1), 2319–8354 (2015)
3. Bhanot, V.K., Singh, D.: Research work on composite epoxy matrix & EP polyester reinforced material. Int. J. Eng. Res. Technol. 2(1), 1–20 (2013). ISSN: 2278-0181
4. Haghshenas, M.: Metal Matrix Composites. University of Waterloo, Waterloo, ON, Canada. Elsevier Inc. (2015). https://doi.org/10.1016/B978-0-12-803581-8.03950-3
5. Rohatgi, P.: Cast metal matrix composites: past, present, and future. In: Transactions of the American Foundry Society and the One Hundred Fifth Annual Castings Congress, pp. 1–25 (2001)
6. David Raja, S.J., Robinson Smart, D.S., Dinaharan, I.: Microstructure and some mechanical properties of fly ash particulate reinforced AA6061 aluminium alloy composite prepared by compo casting. Mater. Sci. 49, 28–34 (2013)
7. Ozben, T., Kilickap, E., Cakır, O.: Investigation of mechanical and machinability properties of SiC particle reinforced Al-MMC. J. Mater. Process. Technol. 198, 220–225 (2008)
8. Devi, N.C., Mahesh, V., Selvaraj, N.: Mechanical characterization of aluminium silicon carbide composite. Int. J. Appl. Eng. Res. 1(4), 793 (2010). ISSN: 09764259
9. Ajay Kumar, P., Rohatgi, P., Weiss, D.: 50 years of foundry-produced metal matrix composites and future opportunities. Int. J. Metalcast. 14(2), 291–317 (2019). https://doi.org/10.1007/s40962-019-00375-4
10. Copper Development Association Inc.: Copper Casting Alloys. New York (1994)

11. Goela, J.S., Brese, N.E., Burns, L.E., Pickering, M.A.: High-thermal-conductivity SiC and applications. In: Shindé, S.L., Goela, J.S. (eds.) High Thermal Conductivity Materials, pp. 8–12. Springer, New York (2006). https://doi.org/10.1007/0-387-25100-6_6

12. Chen, N.A., Zhang, H., Gu, M., Jin, Y.: Effect of thermal cycles on the expansion behavior of Al/SiC composite. J. Mater. Process. Technol. 209(3), 1471–1476 (2009)

13. Srivastava, A., Gaarg, P., Kumar, A., Krishna, Y.: A review of fabrication and characterization of hybrid aluminum metal matrix composite. Int. J. Adv. Res. Innov. 2(1), 242–246 (2014)

14. Mavhungu, S.T., Akinlabi, E.T., Onitiri, M.A., Varachia, F.M.: Aluminum matrix composites for industrial use: advances and trends. Procedia Manuf. 7, 178–182 (2017). International Conference on Sustainable Materials Processing and Manufacturing, 23–25 January 2017, Kruger National Park

15. Prabu, S.B., Karunamoorthy, L., Kathiresan, S., Mohan, B.: Influence of stirring speed and stirring time on the distribution of particles in cast metal matrix composite. J. Mater. Process. Technol. 171, 268–273 (2006)

16. Veeresh KumarG, B., Rao, C.S.P., Selvaraj, N., Bhagyashekar, M.S.: Studies on Al6061-SiC and Al7075-Al2O3 metal matrix composites. J. Miner. Mater. Charact. Eng. 9(1), 43–55 (2010)

17. Mazahery, A., Shabani, M.O.: Microstructural and abrasive wear properties of SiC reinforced aluminum-based composite produced by composting. Trans. Nonferrous Met. Soc. China 23, 1905–1914 (2013)

18. Nair, S., Joshi, N.: preparation of al 6061/SiC metal matrix composite (MMC) using stir casting technique. IJARIIE 1(3), 2395–4396 (2015)

19. Mishra, A.K., Srivastava, R.K.: Wear behaviour of Al-6061/SiC metal matrix composites. J. Inst. Eng. India Ser. C. 98, 97–103 (2016). https://doi.org/10.1007/s40032-016-0284-3

20. Natrayan, L., Gokulkrishnan, K.A., Bharath, S., Vikash, R., Kumar, M.S.: Investigation on microstructure and mechanical the behavior of AA6061 reinforced SiC and various leaf ashes using stir casting technique. IJIRST – Int. J. Innov. Res. Sci. Technol. 4(10), 107–112 (2018). ISSN: 2349-6010

21. Murugan, S., Velmurugan, M., Jegan, V.: Parameter optimization and the effect of parameters on mechanical properties of hybrid composite. Int. J. Mod. Stud. Mech. Eng. (IJMSME) 4(1), 1–10 (2018). https://doi.org/10.20431/2454-9711.0401001

22. Dwivedi, S.P., Sahu, R.: Effects of SiC particles parameters on the corrosion protection of aluminum-based metal matrix composites using response surface methodology. Jordan J. Mech. Ind. Eng. 12(4), 313–321. ISSN: 1995-6665

23. Bharani Kumar, S., Arul, S., Murugan, C., Sethuramalingam, P., Mayandi, K.: Experimental examination of metal matrix composite using EDM. Int. J. Innov. Technol. Explor. Eng. (IJITEE) 9(2S2), 535–538 (2019). ISSN: 2278-3075

24. Kumar, M.N., Maurya, M., Kumar, S.A., Prakash, D.S., Kumar, A., Chauhan, S.: Investigation of mechanical properties of Al 6061/SiC composite prepared through stir casting technique. Mater. Today: Proc. 25(2020), 755–758 (2019). https://doi.org/10.1016/j.matpr.2019.09.00

25. Bhat, A., Kakandikar, G.: Manufacture of silicon carbide reinforced aluminum 6061 metal matrix composites for enhanced sliding wear properties. Manuf. Rev. 6, 24 (2019)

26. Soltani, S., Azari, K.R., Mousavian, R.T., Jiang, Z., Fadavi, B.A., Brabazon, D.: Stir casting process for the manufacture of Al–SiC composites. Rare Met. 36(7), 581–590 (2017)

27. Pandiyan, G.K., Prabaharan, T.: Mechanical and tribological characterization of stir cast AA6061 T6 – SiC composite. Silicon 13, 1–8 (2020). https://doi.org/10.1007/s12633-020-00781-y

Material Science and Engineering

Modeling and Numerical Simulation of Ballistic Impact on Sandwich Composite Materials

Tibebu Merde Zelelew[1], Ermias Gebrekidan Koricho[2(✉)], and Addisu Negashe Ali[1]

[1] Faculty of Mechanical and Industrial Engineering, Bahir Dar University, Bahir Dar, Ethiopia
[2] Department of Mechanical Engineering, Georgia Southern University, Statesboro, GA, USA

Abstract. The objective of this work is to investigate the ballistic affect energy absorption behavior manufactured from Kevlar and jute-epoxy fiber sandwich composite materials by using finite element analysis and simulation techniques for impact protective helmet applications. Energy consumed and bullet speeds for these composites are examined analytically and using finite element analysis (FEA). Finite element analysis of Kevlar (KM2) plates is carried out at distinctive thicknesses (12 mm, 14 mm, and 24 mm). The analytical results of KM2 and KM2 with JE sandwich plates agree well with the results obtained from FE analysis with a maximum error of 1.14 m/s. The study on the KM2 composite plate uncovers that thickness has a noteworthy impact on the energy absorption properties. The energy absorption of the KM2 sandwich is 78.167% greater than the KM2 plates.

Keywords: Ballistic impact · Energy absorption · Sandwich composite

1 Introduction

The high-speed impact shot defensive shields comprised of mud, concrete, wood, and metals, and so forth have been utilized in old times to ensure humanity [1]. Those bullet-proof armors are made relying on different degrees of protection. Components to be considered are the heaviness of the slug and armor, sort of projectile, the speed of the shot, and solace. At the point when a projectile hits the shield, the energy of the slug is scattered onto the protective layer by disfiguring the shot. The shape of the deformed slug is called mushroom-molded. The inflexible reinforcement as a plate is embedded into the pockets of the vest [2]. The dynamic energy of the shot when affected by the objective is dispersed and consumed in different manners by the objective [3]. Personal armors ordinarily are exposed to high-speed projectile effect, so while planning the personal protective layers energy engrossing limit of the plate is essential to know. The energy-retaining limit of composites relies upon numerous elements like fiber properties, matrix properties, interfacial strength, thickness; fiber direction, and so forth [4–7]. The ballistic effect is the examination of that conduct of material disappointment

M. L. Berihun (Ed.): ICAST 2021, LNICST 412, pp. 339–349, 2022.
https://doi.org/10.1007/978-3-030-93712-6_23

brought about by the effect of shot/projectiles. This is especially essential to ensure people are just as apparatus in atomic and military applications. The effect conduct of composites relies upon the size, shape, mass, impact speed, and material of projectile [8, 9].

Analytical models for ballistic effect dependent on various speculations, for example, hydrodynamic and wave hypotheses are created to consider the conduct of the composites [10–13]. Mathematical investigation utilizing finite element analysis (FEA) is likewise investigated [14, 15] for the ballistic investigation of composites. through approval, FEA strategies have been found to foresee the conduct, very realistically [16–18]. The energy dissemination systems of jute texture composite were examined by checking electron microscopy and discovered to be the burst of the weak epoxy lattice just as the connection of the jute strands with the post-sway fragments [19]. The aftereffects of their examination demonstrated that thicker targets are more productive ballistically particularly against gruff projectiles [20].

One of the limitations of most previous researches is the absence of detailing in the modeling and impact analysis of the shot. Since the state of the shot assumes a crucial part in the disappointment system it is essential to create mathematical models with sensible calculations and materials. The material conduct of the shot likewise impacts the failure mechanism hence the usage of reliable material parameters for the analysis main consequence [21]. The fundamental utilization of bulletproof material isn't just to hinder high-velocity projectiles, yet in addition to guard the client against mounted guns shells, mortars, explosives, and other separating contraptions. As far as aviation applications, ballistic materials shield the body of the rocket from outside objects when it is flying at a high speed. Tactical armor carriers and protective caps or any ballistic-safe materials are known to contain high-strength [22].

In this paper, the current work is to examine neat Kevlar (KM2) texture, and Kevlar (KM2) – jute-epoxy sandwiches under the high-speed effect of the shot. Investigation of the ballistic exhibition of those composite materials has been completed utilizing scientific and FEM approaches. The examination has been done for one speed and four distinct thicknesses of the objective plate. To assess assimilated energy absorption, perforation velocity, and residual velocity with various layers on the mathematical investigation of 7.62×51 mm APM2 projectile penetration through composite material.

2 Methodology

Composite plate and sandwich made of unadulterated Kevlar and jute-epoxy focus are proposed for energy maintenance under ballistic impact whose configuration is showed up in Fig. 1(a) for wonderful Kevlar and Fig. 1(b) for Kevlar (KM2)- JE sandwich. The unrefined materials used are woven Kevlar surfaces. The holding/interfacing state of texture layers impacts the wave proliferation of the cross over the way and subsequently the energy ingestion system of the texture reinforcement [23].

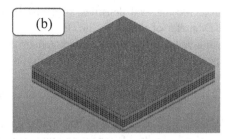

Fig. 1. (a) Schematic model of pure Kevlar and (b) for Kevlar (KM2) - JE sandwich

2.1 Analysis of Composite for Ballistic Effect

A created analytical model to compute the decrease in kinetic energy and leftover speed of shot infiltrating targets made out of diverse planer woven textures of Kevlar and natural fiber. The primary point of the analytical model is to predict the left speed of the shot when the board has been infiltrated. The shot infiltration closes when either the speed of the shot becomes zero or the last layer of texture in the numerous layered board's fizzles. The sensible model created for finding the remaining rate (Vr) of a plate presented to customary impact by a rigid shot is tended to by Eq. (1) [17, 24].

$$V_r = \frac{1}{1 + \Omega(D/d)^2 \left(\frac{T}{L}\right)} \left(V^2 - V_{xn}^2\right) \tag{1}$$

Where V = velocity of impact (m/s)
V_{xn} = minimum perforation velocity (m/s)

$$V_{xn} = \frac{4\Omega T^2 \psi \eta}{Ld\left\{1 + \left[\frac{L+\Omega T}{\Omega T}\left(1 + \frac{d}{\rho_s T \eta \psi}\right)\right]^{0.5}\right\}}$$

and

$$\psi = \frac{\rho_p C_P + \rho_s C_s}{\rho_p C_P \rho_s C_s}$$

$$C = \left[\frac{k}{\rho}\right]^{0.5}$$

$$k = \frac{E}{3(1 - 2v)}$$

$$\eta = 0.5\sigma_u$$

Where, C_p and C_s – sonic velocity within the project and plate (m/s), ρ_p and ρ_s the density of project and plate (kg/m^3), T-thickness of the plate (m). Ω = ratio of plate and projectile material densities, (dimensionless), D-plug diameter of plate = 0.00762 m, d-Diameter of the projectile (Pa), $\sigma_u = 82 \times 10^6$ Pa. k- bulk modulus (Pa) computed using values from Table 1 characteristic of composite target plates. From the remaining speed, energy consumed by the material can be determined utilizing Eq. (2) [25, 26].

$$E_{ab} = 0.5m_p\left(V_i^2 - V_r^2\right) \tag{2}$$

Where, E_{ab} = energy absorbed by the specimen(J), m_p = mass of the projectile(kg), V_i= Velocity of impact or input or initial velocity(m/s) V_r= the residual velocity (m/s). residual velocity and energy assimilated are used processed Eqs. (1) and (2) for composite objective plates.

2.2 Finite Element Examination of Composites for Ballistic Impact

FE examination finished for composite plates is created utilizing a composite plate (unadulterated Kevlar (KM2), and JE) of 100 mm × 100 mm with different thicknesses is considered for FE assessment. The FE model of the composite plates is made using the business FE programming model LS-DYNA. The composite target plate is considered as deformable, however, the shot of 7.62 mm broadness, the weight of 5 g is considered for the examination to address the slug/fired of self-stacking rifle (Fig. 2). For a high-energy 7.62 mm diameter of shot, multi-layered protection systems, additionally called composite defensive layers are generally favored [27–29]. The shot and target plate estimations are made, discretized, following which material properties are appointed. Concurred shot and target plate with limit conditions are fixed in each layer in all directions. FE examination of the composite is finished at different thicknesses 12 mm, 14 mm, and 24 mm at the speed of the shot is 350 m/s the mass of the bullet 5 g for neat kevlar plate and Kevlar sandwich with JE center of 8 mm plate.

Fig. 2. (a) FE analysis of Kevlar (KM2) (b) Kevlar (KM2)-jute sandwich composite with under impact conditions

Table 1. Material properties of target plates [30–33]

Sample	Properties	Values
Steel Bullet Projectile	Young's modulus Poisson's ratio Density	E = 210 GPa V = 0.3 P = 7.85 g/cm^3
Kevlar (Km2) Fabric	Young's modulus Poisson's ratio	E_1 = 1.34 Gpa, E_2 = 84.62 Gpa, G_{13} = 24.4 Gpa V_{31} = 0.6, V_{12} = 0.24 P = 1.44 g/Cm^3
Jute–Epoxy	Young's modulus Poisson's ration Density	17.57 GPa 0.3395 Density 1.3375 g/cm^3

3 Result and Discussion

Residual velocity and energy assimilation are processed from both analytical and FE models for Kevlar (KM2) plates of the thickness of 12 mm, 14 mm, and 24 mm as shown in Table 2. The sandwich plate thickness of 14 mm is a better result than other sandwich and pure Kevlar plates with analytical and FE analysis. The Kevlar (KM2) plate with greater thickness of 24 mm shows lower residual velocity and higher energy retention, and higher energy absorption. The consequence of FE examination is nearness with insightful estimations of remaining speed and energy assimilated. The most extreme mistake in remaining speed is about a similar thickness of 1.14 m/s and then, the FE model is viewed as approved for Kevlar (KM2) composites. The Kevlar (KM2) plates of various thicknesses to assess the ballistic properties. An expansion in energy absorption from 12 mm to 14 mm thick plate of Kevlar (KM2) jute-epoxy sandwich plate could be utilized for bulletproofing. The after-effects of Kevlar (KM2)-jute sandwich and Kevlar (KM2) plate of the equivalent thickness of 14 mm. FEA aftereffects of Kevlar (KM2)- jute sandwich plate energy retention is more prominent than Kevlar (KM2) plate about the thickness 78.167%. Figure 3 shows that the energy assimilation of three distinct plates is varied the result upon the platelayers, thickness, and material synthesis. The sandwich plate exhibited significantly higher energy absorption and lower residual velocities. At the thickness of 14 mm for a sandwich, the plate is to show higher energy assimilation and block of the bullet up to least effect load-incited, at that point after getting back to the way to deal with the first situation to show the Fig. 3 for red color, while unadulterated Kevlar (KM2) plates of 14 mm thickness within a similar speed for 350 m/s effectively penetrate and lower energy assimilation limit. Figure 3 shows the sandwich plate for the FE and the analytical analysis result is approach values obtained. In Fig. 3 the kinetic energy of the three plates is different based on different parameters considered to affect the results. The higher kinetic energy absorption of the sandwich plate in 14 mm thickness. Figure 4 shows that the energy absorption of three different plates is different depending on the platelayers, thickness, and material composition. At the thickness of 14 mm for a sandwich, the plate is to show higher energy absorption and resistance of the bullet up to minimum impact load-induced, then after return to approach to the original position

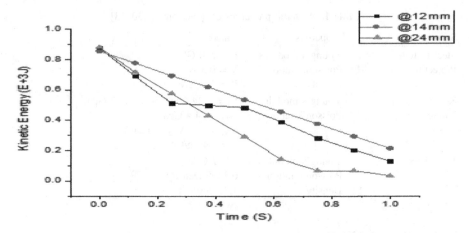

Fig. 3. Kinetic Energy of sandwich (12 mm and 14 mm) and neat Kevlar (24 mm) plate (Color figure online)

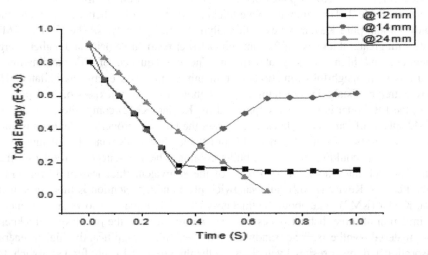

Fig. 4. Energy absorption of sandwich (12 mm) and neat Kevlar fabrics (14 mm) plate (Color figure online)

to show the in-Fig. 4. for red color, while pure Kevlar (KM2) plates of 24 mm thickness with in the same speed for 350 m/s easily penetrate and lower energy absorption capacity. The dynamic energy of the three plates is diverse dependent on various boundaries considered to influence the outcome. The energy absorption of the sandwich plate for distinctive thickness shows improvement compared to the pure plates.

Form Fig. 5 shows the residual velocity of the unadulterated Kevlar (KM2) and sandwich plate developed various outcomes. In the sandwich plate, the residual velocities are higher than pure (KM2) plates for FE analysis and analytical analysis

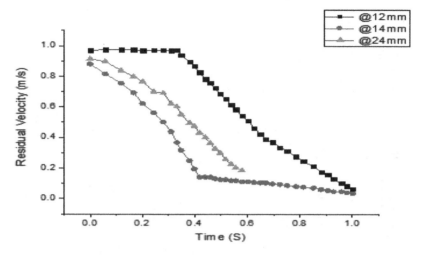

Fig. 5. Residual Velocity of sandwich (12 mm and 14 mm) and pure-Kevlar (24 mm) (Color figure online)

results. Residual velocity and energy absorption are calculated from both analytical and FE models for Kevlar (KM2) plates of the thickness of 14 mm and 24 mm are done in Table 2. The Kevlar (KM2) plate of the higher thickness exhibit lower residual velocity and higher, energy absorption. The result of FE analysis is proximity with analytical values of residual velocity and energy absorbed. The maximum error in residual velocity is about the same thickness of 1.14 m/s and thus the FE model is considered to be validated for Kevlar (KM2) composites. The Kevlar (KM2) plates of different thicknesses to evaluate the ballistic properties. An increase in energy absorption from 12 mm to 14 mm thick plate of Kevlar (KM2) jute-epoxy sandwich plate could be used for bulletproofing. The results of Kevlar (KM2)-jute sandwich and Kevlar (KM2) plate of equal thickness of 14 mm. FEA results of Kevlar (KM2)-jute sandwich plate energy absorption is greater than Kevlar (KM2) plate about the thickness 78.167%. This behavior could be analyzed from different thickness values simulated in FE for the sandwich plate and untreated Kevlar plate.

Table 2 shows analytical and FE approaches the perforation velocity increases the energy absorption capacity of the target plate increase absorption, whereas the residual velocity will decrease both analytical and FE approaches. The sandwich plate improves energy absorption capacity based on the influence of layer, thickness, and material composition. The residual velocity of the target plates are different results, but the maximum error of the analytical and finite element analysis of residual velocity result is 1.14 m/s in the thickness of 24 mm of pure Kevlar (KM2) plates. The perforation velocity of pure-Kevlar (KM2) and sandwich plates are different results. The highest perforation velocity was attained in the sandwich plate at the thickness of 14mm the perforation velocity of 21.36 m/s. the sandwich material will be a great role to improve perforation velocity results and energy absorption capacity. The energy absorption output of different target plates shows different results. When different thicknesses and

Table 2. Residual velocity and energy absorption of pure-Kevlar and Kevlar- jute-epoxy sandwich obtained by analytical and FE approaches

Sample	Thickness	No. layers	Initial velocity (m/s)	Analytical			FE		
				Perforation velocity (m/s)	Residual velocity (m/s)	Energy absorption	Residual velocity (m/s)	Energy absorption	Energy absorption (J)
Sandwich plate	12 mm	6 Layers and 8 mm core	350	13.26	340.48	16.4299	339.56	17.98
Sandwich plate	14 mm	10 Layer and 8 mm core	350	21.36	338.13	20.4074	337.03	22.27
Neat Kevlar (KM2) fabric	24 mm	22	350	18.67	334.46	26.5872	333.32	28.49

constant initial velocity are used the result of sandwich plates shows greater energy absorption than pure Kevlar (KM2).

Figure 6 illustrate the impact surface of the plate with different thicknesses of the plate with the same velocity and different surface damages. The damage of the target plate in the 12 mm sandwich target is a greater damage surface for the front face but does not penetrate the back face of the target plate. For the damaged surface of pure Kevlar (KM2) materials thickness of 14 mm easily penetrate and lower the damaged surface. The total energy absorption of the target plate indicates thickness and material compositions. The stress distribution of the plate within different plates due to the energy absorption effect is different results in Fig. 6. The greater energy absorption of the target plates it occurs greater stress results.

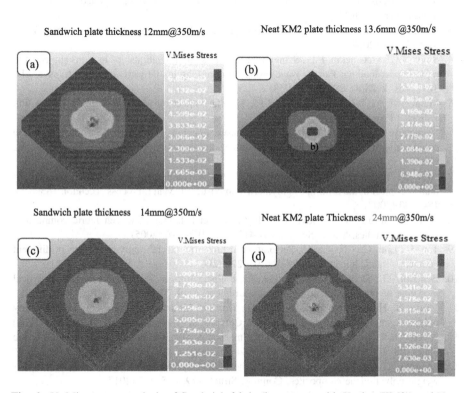

Fig. 6. V. Mises stress analysis of Sandwich fabric (jute epoxy with Kevlar (KM2)) and Neat Kevlar (KM2)

4 Conclusion

The results obtained indicate that sandwich materials can improve the ballistic impact energy retention properties significantly. FE investigation leads to conclude that Kevlar (KM2) plates which involve easy expansion on the material thickness, enhances its energy absorption capacity. The penetration velocity of the impact was higher which improves the energy absorption of the target plate. For the sandwich plate thickness of 14 mm, the energy retention was expanded by 78.167%. The energy absorption properties of the sandwich plate were increased compared to the unadulterated Kevlar (KM2) plates. The Kevlar (KM2) - jute-epoxy sandwich plate could be promising materials for a helmet design applicable for bulletproofing.

References

1. Abrate, S.: Impact Engineering of Composite Structures. Springer, Cham (2011). https://doi.org/10.1007/978-3-7091-0523-8
2. Dwarakanath Varun Kumar, A., Ramalingam, K.: A Comparative study on impact analysis of a projectile on a body armor. In: Trends in Engineering, Applied Science and Management, 19th May 2018
3. Naik, N., Shrirao, P.: Composite structures under the ballistic impact. Compos. Struct. **66**(1–4), 579–590 (2004)
4. Smith, J.C., McCrackin, F.L., Schiefer, H.F.: Stress-strain relationships in yarns subjected to rapid impact loading: Part V: wave propagation in long textile yarns impacted transversely. Text. Res. J. **28**(4), 288–302 (1958)
5. Mamivand, M., Light, G.: A model for ballistic impact on multi-layer fabric targets. Int. J. Impact Eng. **37**(7), 806–812 (2010)
6. Singletary, J., Davis, H., Song, Y., Ramasubramanian, M., Knoff, W.: The transverse compression of PPTA fibers Part II Fiber transverse structure. J. Mater. Sci. **35**(3), 583–592 (2000)
7. Arul, S., Vijayaraghavan, L., Malhotra, S.: Online monitoring of acoustic emission for quality control in the drilling of polymeric composites. J. Mater. Process. Technol. **185**(1–3), 184–190 (2007)
8. Naik, N., Shrirao, P., Reddy, B.: Ballistic impact behavior of woven fabric composites: parametric studies. Mater. Sci. Eng. A **412**(1–2), 104–116 (2005)
9. Tan, V., Lim, C., Cheong, C.: Perforation of high-strength fabric by projectiles of different geometry. Int. J. Impact Eng. **28**(2), 207–222 (2003)
10. Ben-Dor, G., Dubinsky, A., Elperin, T.: Ballistic impact: recent advances in analytical modeling of plate penetration dynamics–a review. Appl. Mech. Rev. **58**(6), 355 (2005)
11. Morye, S., Hine, P., Duckett, R., Carr, D., Ward, I.: Modelling of the energy absorption by polymer composites upon ballistic impact. Compos. Sci. Technol. **60**(14), 2631–2642 (2000)
12. Awerbuch, J., Bodner, S.: Analysis of the mechanics of perforation of projectiles in metallic plates. Int. J. Solids Struct. **10**(6), 671–684 (1974)
13. Langston, T.: An analytical model for the ballistic performance of ultra-high molecular weight polyethylene composites. Compos. Struct. **179**, 245–257 (2017)
14. Sikarwar, R., Velmurugan, R., Gupta, N.: Ballistic performance of Kevlar/epoxy composite laminates. Proc. Indian Natl. Sci. Acad. **79**, 789–799 (2013)
15. Sikarwar, R.S., Velmurugan, R.: Ballistic impact on glass/epoxy composite laminates. Def. Sci. J. **64**(4), 393–399 (2014)
16. Ramadhan, A., Talib, A.A., Rafie, A.M., Zahari, R.: High-velocity impact response of Kevlar-29/epoxy and 6061–T6 aluminum laminated panels. Mater. Des. **43**, 307–321 (2013)
17. Iqbal, M., Diwakar, A., Rajput, A., Gupta, N.: Influence of projectile shape and incidence angle on the ballistic limit and failure mechanism of thick steel plates. Theoret. Appl. Fract. Mech. **62**, 40–53 (2012)

18. Gupta, K.K., Kumar, A., Barnat-Hunek, D., Andrzejuk, W.: Dynamic response with the mass variation of laminated composite twisted plates. J. Mech. Sci. Technol. **32**(9), 4145–4152 (2018)
19. da Luz, F.S., Lima Jr. E.P., Louro, L.H.L., Monteiro, S.N.: Ballistic test of multilayered armor with intermediate epoxy composite reinforced with jute fabric. Mater. Res. **18**, 170–177 (2015)
20. Gellert, E., Cimpoeru, S., Woodward, R.: A study of the effect of target thickness on the ballistic perforation of glass-fiber-reinforced plastic composites. Int. J. Impact Eng. **24**(5), 445–456 (2000)
21. Horsfall, I., Ehsan, N., Bishop, W.: A comparison of the performance of various light armor-piercing ammunition. J. Battlefield Technol. **3**(3) (2000)
22. Azmi, A., Sultan, M., Jawaid, M., Nor, A.: A newly developed bulletproof vest using kenaf-X-ray film hybrid composites. In: Mechanical and Physical Testing of Biocomposites, Fibre-Reinforced Composites, and Hybrid Composites, pp. 157–169. Elsevier (2019)
23. Barauskas, R.: Combining mezzo-and macro-mechanical approaches in a computational model of a ballistic impact upon textile targets. In: Proceedings of the Fifth WSEAS International Conference on Simulation, Modeling, and Optimization, pp. 427–432. Citeseer (2005)
24. Recht, R., Ipson, T.: Ballistic perforation dynamics. J. Appl. Mech. **30**(3), 384–390 (1963)
25. Ahmad, M.R., Ahmad, W.Y.W., Salleh, J., Samsuri, A.: Performance of natural rubber-coated fabrics under the ballistic impact. Malays. Polymer J. **2**(1), 39–51 (2007)
26. Ramadhan, A., Talib, A.A., Mohd, A., Rafie, R.Z.: Experimental and numerical simulation of energy absorption on composite kevlar29/polyester under high-velocity impact. J. Adv. **2**, 52–67 (2012)
27. de Oliveira Braga, F., Lima Jr, É.P., de Sousa Lima, E., Monteiro, S.N.: The effect of thickness on aramid fabric laminates subjected to 7.62 mm ammunition ballistic impact. Mater. Res. **20**, 676–680 (2017)
28. Monteiro, S.N., Lima, É.P., Louro, L.H.L., Da Silva, L.C., Drelich, J.W.: Unlocking function of aramid fibers in multilayered ballistic armor. Metall. Mater. Trans. A. **46**(1), 37–40 (2015)
29. Monteiro, S.N., et al.: Novel ballistic ramie fabric composite competing with Kevlar™ fabric in multilayered armor. Mater. Des. **96**, 263–269 (2016)
30. Das, S., Jagan, S., Shaw, A., Pal, A.: Determination of inter-yarn friction and its effect on the ballistic response of para-aramid woven fabric under the low-velocity impact. Compos. Struct. **120**, 129–140 (2015)
31. Ramadhan, A., Talib, A.A., Mohd, A., Zahari, R.: Experimental and numerical simulation of energy absorption on composite Kevlar29/Polyester under high-velocity impact. J. Adv. **2**, 52–67 (2012)
32. Ahmed, K.S., Vijayarangan, S.: Elastic property evaluation of jute-glass fiber hybrid composite using experimental and CLT approach (2006)
33. Sangamesh, R., Kumar, N., Ravishankar, K., Kulkarni, S.: Mechanical characterization and finite element analysis of jute-epoxy composite. In: MATEC Web of Conferences 2018, vol. 144, p. 02014. EDP Sciences (2018)

Investigate the Effects of Fiber Surface Chemical Treatment on the Mechanical Properties of Bamboo Fiber Reinforced Polyester Resin Composites

Sewale Yasabu Enyew[1,2] and Addisu Negash Ali[1($\boxtimes$)] (iD)

[1] Faculty of Mechanical and Industrial Engineering, Bahir Dar Institute of Technology, Bahir Dar University, P.O. Box 26, Bahir Dar, Ethiopia
Addisu.Negash@bdu.edu.et

[2] School of Mechanical and Automotive Engineering, College of Engineering and Technology, Dilla University, P.O. Box 419, Dilla, Ethiopia

Abstract. The main objective of this study is to investigate the effects of the fiber surface treatment on the mechanical properties of bamboo fiber reinforced polyester resin composite materials for different applications. To investigate the mechanical properties of the materials different chemical treatments and experimental testing setups have been used. Four different types of testing samples were prepared from bamboo fiber reinforced polyester resin composites using untreated bamboo fiber, 10 Vol% NaOH treated bamboo fiber (10TBF), 20 Vol% NaOH treated bamboo fiber (20TBF), and 10 Vol% NaOH plus corn starch soaked for 30 min treated bamboo fiber. To characterize the mechanical properties of the fabricated composite materials, the WAW 1000D hydraulic universal tensile testing machine with ASTM ISO-6892 standard, ABAQUS CAE finite element analysis, and GOM Correlate Software integrated digital image correlation (DIC) analysis were used. The results obtained indicate that the use of higher volume percentage of NaOH treatment chemical leads to uniform distribution of stress fields on the surface of materials. In addition to that, the use of 10 Vol% NaOH plus corn starch soaking of bamboo fiber gives improved elastic and elongation properties.

Keywords: Bamboo fiber · Tensile test · Mechanical properties · NaOH · Corn starch · DIC tensile test · Finite element analysis

1 Introductions

A composite material commonly consists of two or more materials constituents in which one of the constituent materials is the reinforcing phase which can be in the form of fibers, sheets, or particles embedded or segregated in the matrix phase. The constituents of composite materials have different physical and chemical properties with separate and distinct individual properties. The primary phase of composite material is termed as a matrix having a continuous character and acts as a binder and holds the

M. L. Berihun (Ed.): ICAST 2021, LNICST 412, pp. 350–364, 2022.
https://doi.org/10.1007/978-3-030-93712-6_24

fibers in the desired position thereby transferring the external load to the reinforcing phase [1].

Most modern industrial components such as wind turbine blades, aircraft, ships and automotive parts are manufactured from a massive number of synthetic fibers composites. Modern composite materials consisted of a significant proportion of the engineered materials market ranging from everyday products to sophisticated comfortable applications such as in the field of mining and metallurgy, in hydraulic components and water tanks, in the cryogenics fuel tank, for a helmet and in transparent roofs. It is also known that composite materials have proved their usefulness as weight-saving materials. Composite materials have taken a large share of the manufacturing sector as a source material to produce different parts and the most commonly used synthetic fibers are glass, carbon, basalt, aramid fibers and others. However, these synthetic fibers have many drawbacks from the fact that their non-degradable behavior incurred disposal challenges, recycling problems and environmental impact which leads to enormous pollution to the surrounding environment. In response to this challenge, researchers are working on sustainable and recyclable materials to replace synthetic materials with natural and zero-waste economy materials. Currently, attention has been given to materials such as natural fibers including bamboo, jute, sisal, and other agricultural byproducts for engineering applications to control environmental degradation and to minimize materials cost [2]. Natural fibers which are mostly composed of cellulose such as hemp, sisal, kenaf and bamboo are used as a replacement for glass fibers (or synthetic fibers) in polyester-based composite due to the low cost of raw materials, low density, availability and environmental friendly [3].

Bamboo fiber is characterized as a highly energy-efficient, renewable and biodegradable natural resource with great potential to replace synthetic fiber. The strength-to-weight ratio of bamboo fiber is comparatively higher than conventional metallic fibers. Bamboo fibers are often known as natural glass fibers due to their high strength to their weight derives from fibers longitudinally aligned in their body [4]. Lignin, cellulose and hemicellulose are the important components in bamboo and these components constitute 90% of the total weight of bamboo [5]. Ethiopia has about 1 million hectares of highland and lowland bamboos. Thus, 67% of African bamboo resources and more than 7% of the world's total area are found in Ethiopia [6].

Currently, studies have generally trying to address the treatment of fibers to improve the performance of natural fiber composites and expand their industrial applications. One of the most effective methods used for improving the properties of natural fiber composites is applying a chemical treatment of fiber surface to enhance a matrix to fiber interface bonding and uniform distribution of matrix and fiber mixture to achieve optimum properties [7].

Bamboo fiber has several advantages over other natural fibers such as high growth rate, strength, and fixing the carbon dioxide. Also, it can be compared with glass fiber because of its lightweight, biodegradability, and low cost. Therefore, there is a great interest in using bamboo fiber as reinforced composite material in different applications. Several methods and adhesions have been used to improve the mechanical properties of bamboo fibers as reinforced composite. This can help to comprehend that bamboo fiber and bamboo fiber-reinforced composite can be used in more applications. In this study, NaOH chemical fiber treatment and corn starch soaking have been considered to improve the bamboo fiber surface roughness and other elastoplastic properties [8].

2   Materials and Methods

The bamboo fiber was extracted manually and the densities of bamboo fiber were tested using a pycnometer. The NaOH treated bamboo fiber reinforced composites were manufactured by hand-layup and compression techniques in a random orientation with fiber to polyester resin matrix ratio of 30:70 [9]. In this composite sample fabrications, the compression pressure at the time of curing was 0.027 MPa and the composite sample specimen were cured for 24 h at room temperatures [10]. The mechanical properties of the polyester resin reinforced with sodium hydroxide (NaOH) treated bamboo fiber composite materials were investigated. The samples of bamboo fiber composite materials with pure bamboo fiber, 10 Vol% NaOH (10TBF), 20 Vol% NaOH (20TBF), and 10 Vol% NaOH treated plus soaked with corn starch chemicals (STBF) for 30 min were used for the characterization of mechanical properties. The bamboo culm was collected from highland areas around Injibara city, in the North-Western part of Ethiopia as a green form. The sodium hydroxide (NaOH) and corn starch chemicals were purchased from the local market in Bahir Dar. And also, polyester resin and its hardener were taken from the poly fiber private manufacturing company in Bahir Dar.

The bamboo culm was peeled to obtain the strips and bundles of strips were soaked in water for three days, subsequently, the wetted strips were beaten and scraped with a sharp-edged knife and combed. It is commonly known that the physical process of scraping had a strong effect on the fiber quality and breakage which needs the careful scraping process [8, 12]. As shown in Fig. 1, the retting extraction method was used to extract fiber from the scraps which is one of the methods of many forms of mechanical extraction methods such as the steam explosion method, crushing, grinding, rolling in a mill, and retting. Mechanical extraction methods are used for the extraction of bamboo fiber for various applications in industries for making bamboo fiber-reinforced composites [8, 12]. The fibers extracted using a grinding method and crushing method are mostly used for particle composite fabrication [5]. Bamboo fibers can be used to reinforce both thermosetting and thermoplastic matrices. Thermosetting resins such as epoxy, polyester, polyurethane, phenolic are commonly used matrix materials in composites for higher performance applications [13, 14]. In this study, polyester resin, sodium hydroxide (NaOH), corn starch, treated and untreated bamboo fibers materials were used to fabricated bamboo fiber reinforced polyester resin matrix composite.

2.1   Treatment Methods

In this study, both sodium hydroxide (NaOH) and corn starch chemical treatments have been used to see the effects of bamboo fiber surface modification on the mechanical properties enhanced by the fiber-matrix interface bonding variations. Different treatment methods can be used to modify the bamboo fiber surface including alkali, acetyl, saline, enzymatic and other coupling agents. Alkali treatment method is one of the

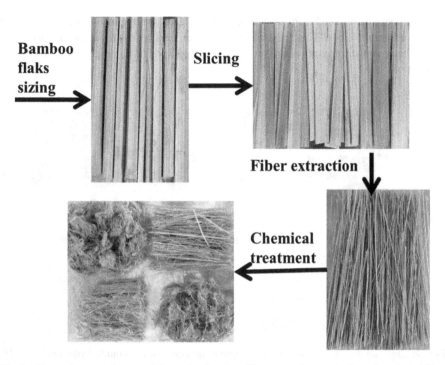

Fig. 1. General process layout of the retting bamboo fiber extraction method used to extract fiber for further chemical treatment applications.

simplest and most effective bamboo fiber treatment methods which can easily remove lignin. The most widely used chemical in the alkaline treatment process is sodium hydroxide (NaOH) solution [10, 16]. In addition to that, corn starch was used to further enhance the roughness and hardness of the fiber surfaces [17].

2.1.1 NaOH Treatment of Bamboo Fiber

Alkali treatment can make the fiber surface clean and rough by removing waxes, hemicellulose, pectin and parts of lignin. The removal of these fatty-like components from the bamboo fiber can lead the fiber to have low moisture absorption properties, reduce fiber weight, improve fiber roughness and its adhesive property at the fiber-matrix interface, and also improve fiber rigidity and stiffness [18, 19]. Before the process of alkali treatment, the bamboo fibers need to be washed thoroughly with tap water to remove any debris, dirt, and undesired particles and then, dried at room temperatures for more than seven days [20].

The bamboo fibers were treated with sodium hydroxide (NaOH) solution at 10%, and 20% volume (Vol%) of concentration in water as shown in Fig. 2. The bamboo fibers were soaked in NaOH solutions for 72 h at room temperature. In addition to that bundles of the bamboo fibers were treated with 10 Vol% of NaOH solutions for 72 h and soaked in corn starch chemicals for 30 min. The bamboo fibers were then washed with cold water and distilled water to remove absorbed alkali from the fiber. The washed fibers were dried at room temperature for four weeks to remove the moisture from the bamboo fiber. The dried fibers were stored in a sealed plastic bag to avoid atmospheric moisture contaminations before the composite manufacturing process or fabrications.

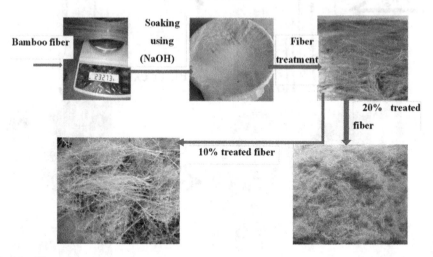

Fig. 2. Illustrations of bamboo fiber treatment process using sodium hydroxide (NaOH) chemical solution

2.1.2   NaOH (10 Vol%) Plus Corn Starch Soaking Treatment of Bamboo Fiber

During the corn starch chemical treatment process, the bamboo fiber was treated with 10 Vol% NaOH for 72 h, dried for one month at room temperature, and then, the bamboo fiber was further treated with corn starch chemical. The corn starch chemical to water ratio was determined based on the Bahir Dar Textile Share Company manual guide. The manual guide states that for 50 kg corn starch flour, 600-L water is needed. Based on this information, 0.5 g corn starch flour was used and the amount of water needed for 0.5 g corn starch flour was calculated. The amount of water needed for the given fiber composite materials and corn starch flour was 6 L. The corn starch treatment process considers boiled water at (100 °C) using a digital stove water boiler, subsequently, the bamboo fiber and corn starch flour were inserted into the beaker and cooked for 30 min and also stirred continuously for the uniform cooking of the bamboo fiber. After finishing the cooking process the bamboo fiber was dried at room temperature and made ready for a composite manufacturing process, as shown in Fig. 3.

Fig. 3. NaOH (10 Vol%) and corn starch soaking treated bamboo fiber.

2.2   Experimental Setup for Tensile Test

As shown in Fig. 4, a WAW 1000D hydraulic universal tensile testing machine was used with an overhead displacement of 0.1 mm/min. The ASTM ISO-6892 standard dimensions of three samples were taken for the tensile test of each type of sample specimen.

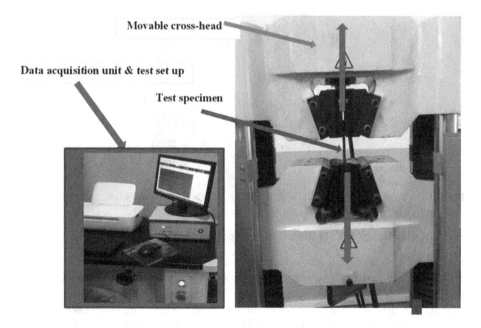

Fig. 4. Graphical illustration for the experimental tensile test setup.

2.3   Finite Element (FE) Analysis Using ABAQUS CAE

The tensile test sample specimens with ASTM standard dimensions were modeled using finite element analysis ABAQUS CAE Software. By considering the random fiber orientations and the complexity of length variations, the composite materials were taken as an anisotropic material during FE modeling. As indicated in Table 1, all the basic mechanical properties of each type of material were taken from the tensile test experimental results to fill in the ABAQUS CAE material property options. The number of elements was determined based on the mesh convergence analysis of each type of specimen and the hexagonal mesh 3D solid element type was considered for modeling each composite sample material. In this case, the number of elements for the tensile test model is 160. The convergence test was done with different mesh densities and the least percent of error of maximum stresses was selected to generate the FE analysis results. The convergence test percent error for pure bamboo fiber (PBF), 10 Vol% treated bamboo fiber (10TBF), 20 Vol% treated bamboo fiber (20TBF) and 10 Vol% plus corn starch treated bamboo fiber (STBF) was 0.058%, 0.050%, 0.18% and 0.19% respectively. Figure 5(a) shows the boundary conditions and applied load and Fig. 5(b) shows the mesh type.

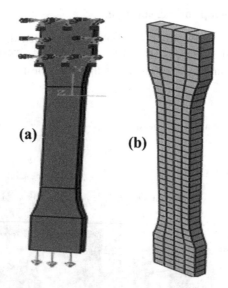

Fig. 5. The ABAQUS CAE tensile test FE analysis. (a) boundary conditions and (b) mesh type

2.4   Digital Image Correlation (DIC) Experiment

For the purpose of digital image correlation (DIC) analysis, a 120 mm × 15 mm × 5 mm tensile test specimens with 6 mm diameter center hole has been prepared from pure bamboo fiber, 10 Vol% TBF, 20 Vol% TBF and 10 Vol% TBF plus corn starch soaking for 30 min treated bamboo fiber/polyester resin composite materials. To capture the stress field distribution around the circular hole during the DIC tensile test, the surface of the specimen was cleaned and painted with black and white paints. In addition to that, the position of the camera has been adjusted at 90° to the surface of a specimen. Subsequently, a continuous video was recorded and saved during the tensile test process [21]. The recorded videos were analyzed in GOM correlate soft-ware strain analysis to calculate the strain fields present in the composite sample specimen materials. The DIC experimental test setup has been represented as shown in Fig. 6 below.

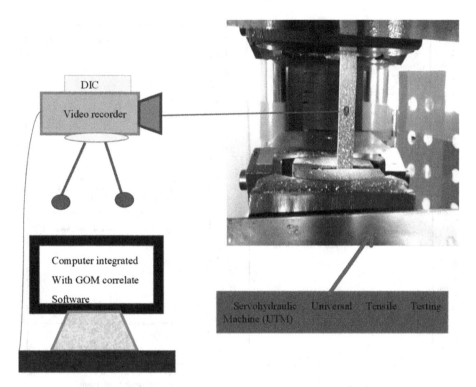

Fig. 6. Schematic representations of DIC experiment tensile test setup.

3 Results and Discussions

3.1 Tensile Test Experimental Measurements and Results

As illustrated in Fig. 7 and Table 1, the mechanical properties of pure bamboo fiber reinforced polyester composite have the maximum values. However, the flexibility and its industrial applications of the as-extracted pure bamboo fiber are very low compared to the processed (treated) bamboo fibers. To exploit the potential applications of bamboo, the bamboo fiber chemical solution treatment is cost-effective and an easy approach. In this study, NaOH solution treatment has been considered to remove the unwanted parts of the bamboo fiber to enhance the required properties. As shown in Table 1 below, the 10 Vol% NaOH plus corn starch soaking for 30 min treatment of bamboo fiber improves the yield strength and elongation properties compared to 10 Vol % NaOH, and 20 Vol% NaOH solution treated bamboo fiber polyester resin composite materials. As observed in Fig. 2, the 10 Vol% NaOH plus corn starch soaked for 30 min treated bamboo fiber surface roughness looks improved compared to the results obtained by 10 Vol% NaOH, and 20 Vol% NaOH solution treated bamboo fibers as shown in Fig. 3 which indicates the significant effect of corn starch to improve the bamboo fiber surface roughness.

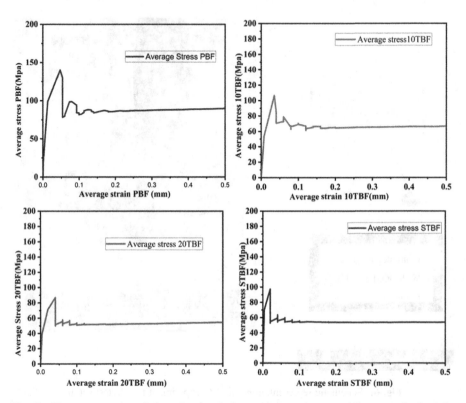

Fig. 7. The stress-strain relations bamboo/polyester composite materials were obtained by experimental tensile test.

The ultimate tensile strength (UTS) and young's modulus of a 10 Vol% NaOH treated bamboo fiber shows the maximum values compared to the 20 Vol% NaOH treated (20TBF) and the 10 Vol% NaOH plus corn starch soaked for 30 min treated bamboo fiber reinforced polyester resin composites. The results obtained from the experimental tensile test lead to the generalization that the use of a higher volume percentage of NaOH reduces the brittleness and rigidity of bamboo fiber. Furthermore, the use of corn starch integrated with NaOH can enhance the ductility and surface roughness of bamboo fiber.

Table 1. Mechanical properties of the average tensile strength of bamboo fiber/polyester resin composite materials

Treatment type	Mechanical properties of composite materials			
	Yield strength (MPa)	Ultimate strength (UTS) (MPa)	% Elongation @ break	Young's Modulus (GPa)
Pure bamboo (PBF)	98.93	139.98	5.56%	14.84
10TBF	54.05	106.43	3.86%	10.68
20TBF	39.81	86.86	3.189%	7.14
Corn starch TBF	70.21	97.5	5.245%	8.78

3.2 Finite Element (FE) Analysis Results Using ABAQUS CAE

The finite element analysis using ABAQUS Software gives similar trends of stress variations with the experimental tensile test results. As shown in Fig. 8 (a), the maximum stress was recorded in the untreated bamboo fiber. Next to the untreated bamboo fiber, the 10 Vol% NaOH solution treated bamboo fiber showed the maximum stress value as shown in Fig. 8 (b). Due to the loss of brittleness and rigidity of fiber, the 20 Vol% NaOH and 10 Vol% NaOH plus corn starch soaking treatment lead to lower stress values compared to the previously described treatment solutions.

3.3 Digital Image Correlation (DIC) Analysis Results

The DIC strain measurement was done by using the GOM correlate software integrated with tensile test experiments. The DIC analysis can give detailed information on the fiber-matrix interface bonding and the effects of surface/subsurface inclusion distributions on the stress-strain distribution patterns. As shown in Fig. 9, the stress field fluctuations are very high, even though the stress field values are maximum at the final recording time. The highest stress field fluctuation in the untreated bamboo fiber reinforced polyester composite indicates the highest mismatch of mechanical properties between the fiber and the matrix. Compared to all the four DIC specimens, the 20 Vol% NaOH treated bamboo fiber reinforced polyester composite shows the uniform stress field distributions as shown in Fig. 11, due to its enhanced surface roughness which can lead to strong bonding between the fiber and matrix interface. Similarly, the fiber surface roughness enhanced by corn starch soaking treatment leads to both stress field uniformity and stress carrying capacity of the composite as illustrated in Fig. 12 (Fig. 10).

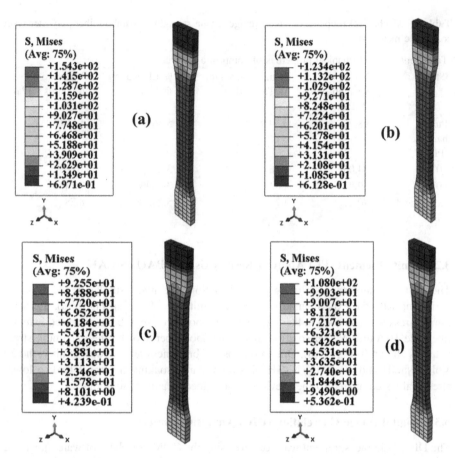

Fig. 8. ABAQUS finite element (FE) analysis results in the contour plot. (**a**) pure, (**b**) 10 Vol% NaOH treated, (**c**) 20 Vol% NaOH treated, and (**d**) 10 Vol% NaOH plus corn starch soak for 30 min treated bamboo fiber reinforced polyester composites

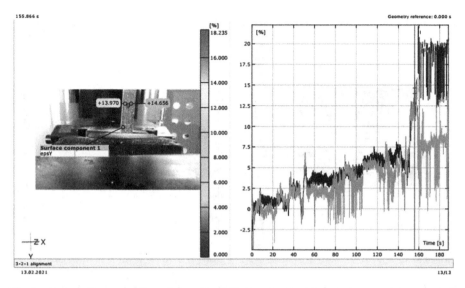

Fig. 9. DIC tensile test strain analysis using GOM correlate software for untreated bamboo fiber

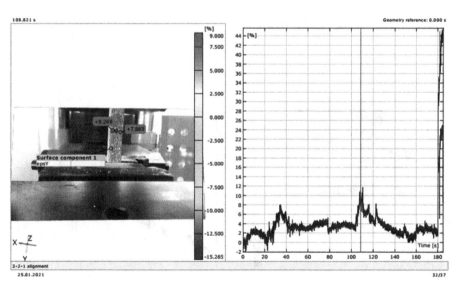

Fig. 10. DIC tensile test strain analysis using GOM correlate software for 10 Vol% NaOH treated bamboo fiber.

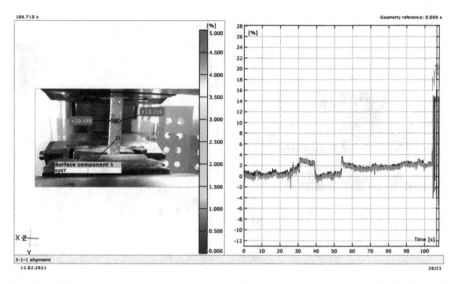

Fig. 11. DIC tensile test strain analysis using GOM correlate software for 20 Vol% NaOH treated bamboo fiber.

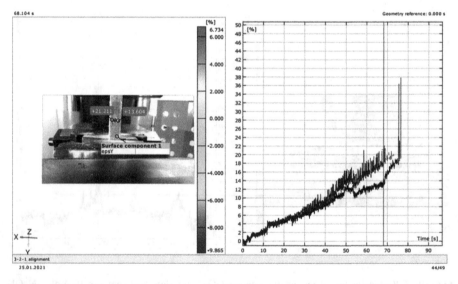

Fig. 12. DIC tensile test strain analysis using GOM correlate software for 10 Vol% NaOH plus corn starch treated bamboo fiber.

4   Conclusions

The results obtained from the experimental and finite element analysis lead to the following conclusions:

- The use of a higher volume percentage of NaOH treatment chemicals leads to improved uniform stress field distributions on the surface of bamboo fiber polyester resin composite materials specimens.
- The untreated bamboo fiber has higher strength, however; the DIC analysis indicated the non-uniformity of stress field distributions which indicates the presence of higher con-tents of inclusions.
- The 10 Vol% NaOH treated bamboo fiber has high strength next to untreated bamboo fiber.
- The 10 Vol% NaOH treated bamboo fiber plus corn starch soaking leads to good elastic and elongation properties compared to other treatment processes.
- In general, the NaOH chemical treatment of bamboo fiber reduces the brittleness of the fiber and improves the surface roughness and its ductile properties.

References

1. Elanchezhian, C., Ramnath, B.V., Ramakrishnan, G., Rajendrakumar, M., Naveenkumar, V., Saravanakumar, M.K.: Review on mechanical properties of natural fiber composites. Mater. Today Proc. 5(1), 1785–1790 (2018). https://doi.org/10.1016/j.matpr.2017.11.276
2. Redda, D., Alene, A.: Experimental analysis of bamboo and e-glass fiber reinforced epoxy hybrid composite. J. Mater. Sci. Eng. 6, 153–160 (2016). https://doi.org/10.17265/2161-6221/2016.5-6.005
3. Yvonne, K.S., Mahani, Y., Razak, W., Sofiyah, M.R., Razali, M.H.: Properties of epoxy-hybrid composite using bamboo fiber and Salacca Zalacca fruit skin powder. Mater. Today Proc. 5(10), 21759–21764 (2018). https://doi.org/10.1016/j.matpr.2018.07.029
4. Popat, T.V., Patil, A.Y.: A review on bamboo fiber composites. Iconic Res. Eng. J. 1(2), 54–72 (2017)
5. Shinde, A., Veer, S., Shinde, T., Sagale, P., Kamble, D.P.: A review on extraction methods of bamboo fibers and banana fibers. Int. J. Recent Trends Eng. Res. 4(5), 7–12 (2018). https://doi.org/10.23883/IJRTER.2018.4283.ITJSJ
6. Yikuno, K.E.: The indigenous bamboo forests of Ethiopia : an overview. AMBIO J. Human Environ. 29(8), 518–521 (2016). https://doi.org/10.1579/0044-7447-29.8.518
7. Senthilkumar, K., et al.: Mechanical properties evaluation of sisal fiber reinforced polymer composites: a review. Constr. Build. Mater. 174, 713–729 (2018). https://doi.org/10.1016/j.conbuildmat.2018.04.143
8. Zakikhani, P., Zahari, R., Sultan, M.T.H., Majid, D.L.: Bamboo fibre extraction and its reinforced polymer composite material. Int. J. Chem. Biomol. Metall. Mater. Sci. Eng. 8(4), 271–274 (2014)
9. Banga, H., Singh, V.K., Choudhary, S.K.: Fabrication and study of mechanical properties of bamboo fibre reinforced bio-composites. Innov. Syst. Des. Eng. 6(1), 84–99 (2015)
10. Singh, B., Gupta, G.: Physico-mechanical characterization of bamboo-glass fiber reinforced polyester composites filled with pine needle 7(5), 20–23 (2016)
11. Retnam, S.J., Edwin Raja Dhas, J.: A review on extraction of bamboo fibres and its properties, pp. 2347–7601 (2017)
12. Phong, N.T., Fujii, T., Chuong, B., Okubo, K.: Study on how to effectively extract bamboo fibers from raw bamboo and wastewater treatment. J. Mater. Sci. Res. 1(1), 144–155 (2011). https://doi.org/10.5539/jmsr.v1n1p144

13. Bongarde, U.S., Shinde, V.: Review on natural fiber reinforced polymer composites. Int. J. Eng. Sci. Innov. Technol. 3(2), 431–436 (2014)

14. Asim, M., Jawaid, M., Saba, N., Ramengmawii, Nasir, M., Sultan, M.T.H.: Processing of Hybrid Polymer Composites-A Review. Elsevier Ltd. (2017)

15. Hamidon, M.H., Sultan, M.T.H., Ariffin, A.H., Shah, A.U.M.: Effects of fiber treatment on mechanical properties of Kenaf fiber-reinforced composites : a review. J. Mater. Res. Technol. 8(3), 3327–3337 (2017)

16. Ezema Ike-Eze, I.C., Aigbodion, V.S., Ude, S.N., Omah, A.D., Offor, P.O.: Experimental study on the effects of surface treatment reagents on tensile properties of Banana fiber reinforced polyester composites. J. Mater. Environ. Sci. 10(5), 402–410 (2019). Available: http://www.jmaterenvironsci.com

17. Mehta, R.: Experimental Study on Application of Different Sizing Agents, December 2018 (2019)

18. Hamidon, M.H., Sultan, M.T.H., Ariffin, A.H., Shah, A.U.M.: Effects of fiber treatment on mechanical properties of kenaf fiber-reinforced composites: a review. J. Mater. Res. Technol. 8(3), 3327–3337 (2019). https://doi.org/10.1016/j.jmrt.2019.04.012

19. Ramachandran, M., Bansal, S., Fegade, V., Mpstme, R.: Analysis of bamboo fibre composite with polyester and epoxy resin. Int. J. Text. Eng. Process. 1(4), 2395–3578 (2015)

20. Manalo, A.C., Wani, E., Azwa, N., Karunasena, W.: Effects of alkali treatment and elevated temperature on the mechanical properties of bamboo fiber e polyester composites. Compos. Part B 80, 73–83 (2015). https://doi.org/10.1016/j.compositesb.2015.05.033

21. Shi, L., Zhang, X., Zhang, L., Wang, C., Wang, J.: Application of digital image correlation technique in stress and strain measurement. In: Asia Pacific Conference for Non-Destructive Testing (APCNDT 2017), Singapore, pp. 1–7 (2017)

Investigation of Halide Ion Release Tunnels of Haloalcohol Dehalogenase from Agrobacterium Radiobacter AD1; Computational Study

Aweke Mulu Belachew[1,3(✉)] and Tang Laxia[1,2]

[1] School of Life Science and Technology, University of Electronic Science and Technology of China, Chengdu 610054, China
aweke.mulu@aastu.edu.et
[2] Centers for Informational Biology, University of Electronic Science and Technology of China, Chengdu 610054, China
[3] College of Applied Science, Addis Ababa Science and Technology University, P.O.BOX 16417 Addis Ababa, Ethiopia

Abstract. The Halohydrine dehalogenase (HheC), active site is buried deep inside the structure of the enzyme and to enter the active site, the substrate must cross via the body of the enzyme called tunnels. In several studies revealed that they have been influenced substrate selectivity, stability and activity of enzymes. Know a day, identifying and understanding how tunnels exert selectivity, stability, and activity regulation of enzymes have been growing interest in the fields of computational approach and enzyme engineering. As far as, the HheC concerned studies suggest that the release of chloride ion determines the overall activity of the enzyme and thus tunnels are assumed to exist. Swiss-Modell, Auto dock 3.2, Gromacs 5.2.1, Caver 3.0, and RAMD computational techniques were applied to identify and analyze tunnels and how chloride ions migrate through these tunnels. The purpose of this study is to identify tunnels and analyzes how to influence Chloride ion-releasing activity in the HheC enzyme and provide prerequisite data for wet-lab experiment used to improve overall activity. In this study, we found the presence of Chloride ion narrowed tunnels compare to free HheC enzyme. Moreover, conformation difference, tunnel lining residues and bottle-neck residues were identified for next wet-lab experiment. Future wet-lab investigations to validate the role of residues that are found in tunnel lining could be needed to engineer the activity of HheC.

Keywords: Halide ion release tunnels · Halohydrine dehalogenase · Caver · Molecular dynamic simulation

1 Introduction

Recent experimental developments have revealed the biocatalytic properties of Halohydrine dehalogenase (HHDHs) toward both aromatic and aliphatic Halohydrine to yield Hydrogen, chloride and epichlorohydrine [1, 2]. The field has gradually broadened to computational study as the crystal structure of enzymes purified and determined. The

© ICST Institute for Computer Sciences, Social Informatics and Telecommunications Engineering 2022
Published by Springer Nature Switzerland AG 2022. All Rights Reserved
M. L. Berihun (Ed.): ICAST 2021, LNICST 412, pp. 365–376, 2022.
https://doi.org/10.1007/978-3-030-93712-6_25

Halohydrine dehalogenase (HheC) from the bacterial species Agrobacterium radiobacter strain AD1 has always been under constant investigation [1–3]. This enzyme has homo tetramer domain and each monomer with seven beta strand and extended C-terminus [3]. In the past two decades, the stretch of the C-terminal amino acids, halide binding site amino acids, and active site entrance amino acids have played a significant role in HheC engineering research [2, 4, 5]. This field closely follows the pattern of improving HheC enzyme activity, selectivity and stability by engineering aforementioned sites. However, the active site is buried inside the structure of the HheC, and substrates, as well as products, pass through the body of the enzyme through a tunnel [2]. Moreover, a study has shown that tunnels differentiation among substrates, synchronization of the order of catalytic steps, and reactions that require the number of substrates [14]. Chloride ion releasing tunnel has been shown significant impact on the activity, stability, and selectivity of the HheC tunnel [1, 2, 4, 5]. The available data is limited and no previous study has focused on number and chloride ion egress tunnels and egress kinetics study of HheC enzyme. An approach similar to ours has been presented before in [6] showed that a halide releasing tunnel conformational change preceding the release of halide ion from the active site structure of HheC. Despite the success of this work [6] in certain aspects, it still suffers from short simulation time to produce ensemble structures for tunnel computation. Some other prior work has examined this issue but, the focus was more on the conformational change that occurs in the loop region and lead solvation of the active site that facilitates halide ion escape from haloalkane dehalogenase [4, 5]. This method extends prior work by its unique consideration of the chloride ion release pathway, identification of tunnel lining residues for engineering the accessibility of tunnels and conformational change of HheC tunnels. In general work in this area is in its infancy and is somewhat limited to tunnel selectivity for entry/release of a specific substrates and products.

Until now, tunnels have been studied by using X-ray crystallography, steady-state kinetics, pre-steady-state kinetics, and molecular modeling approach [30, 31]. However, tunnels shape and physicochemical properties regularly change due to influence of thermal, ligand and substrates binding, solvent, and other changes in the surrounding environment [32]. A combination of wet-lab and dry studies is often required to examine the conformational change of enzymes tunnels [31]. Therefore, this extends a dynamic outlook for the enzyme engineers as frequently the dynamics of the enzyme active site are limited to optimize the reactive substrate binding. Recent theoretical developments have revealed that, there are a number of methods that can be used to investigate product releasing tunnel pathway. A number of works have been reported by using Random Acceleration Molecular Dynamics, Steered Molecular Dynamics, Metadynamics and Dynamic Map Ensemble Approaches [5–11]. In other word, dry experiments could form a close relation with wet experiment. In this work, we characterize different aspects of tunnels by using a CAVER 3.0, Gromacs and RAMD simulation in both free enzyme and chloride ion-enzyme complex. This strategy is common in proteins tunnel computation studies. For instance, it has computed tunnels in β2-adrenergic receptor, human cytochrome P450 enzymes, haloalkane dehalogenase and liver fatty acid binding protein [8–11]. As far as we know, no preceding study has investigated halide releasing tunnels. However, this issue has been considered by recent work [6] with a very short simulation time, which is unreasonable. Moreover, few studies have focused on indirect study on tunnel activity. To overcome the short-comings of previous studies outlined above, we propose molecular dynamic simulation for 100 ns. In this work we look to improve our earlier approach in two key areas, the RAMD simulation of novel chloride releasing tunnels and key structural changes that take place during chloride dissociation. In analogy with other procedures, this approach has the advantage of giving us an idea to render novel mechanistic insights into HheC tunnel wet-lab engineering. After rigorous examination, it was discovered that tunnels structure and flexibility difference between halide-enzyme complex and free enzyme based on root-mean-square fluctuation (RMSF), root mean-square deviation (RMSD) and evolution of secondary structures with time. Further investigation can be under-taken to explore tunnel lining residues and bottleneck residues. There are some major modifications planned in the future development of experimental study.

2 Results and Discussion

This study incorporates molecular dynamics (MD) simulation, Caver 3.0 and random accelerate molecular dynamics (RAMD) simulation techniques to investigate the chloride ion releasing tunnels in 100 ns simulated HheC chloride ion complex and free HheC enzymes. This technique utilizes a structures consist of free-HheC enzyme and HheC-chloride ion complex, which stabilized by isothermal-isobaric NPT and NVT ensembles based classical MD simulation for 1000 ps (Sup Fig. 1). Next, we evaluated the residue RMSD to analyze the residue behavior of both free-HheC enzyme and HheC-chloride ion complex during 100 ns simulations. In the literatures, RMSD has been extensively investigated to measures protein flexibility, effect of bound substrate and product to control active site accessibility as well as, the average distance between backbone atoms [22, 23].

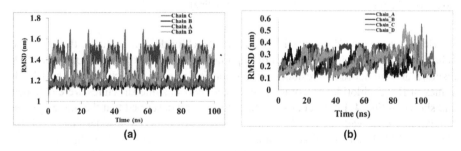

Fig. 1. The root-mean-square deviation (RMSD) value for A) Free HheC-enzyme, and B) HheC-Chloride ion complex analysis chain A (Blue), Chain B (black), Chain C (red) and Chain D (green) (Color figure online)

According to the result of the RMSD plot, all free HheC chains showed equili-bration throughout the simulation, and chain D revealed high flexibility between 10–20 ns, 20–30 ns, 40–50 ns, and 58–60 ns (Fig. 1). In HheC-Chloride ion complex types, conformational flexibility reduced and destabilized by the binding of chloride ion compare to free HheC enzyme, as revealed from the RMSD calculation (Fig. 2). Other groups confirmed that binding of ligand to HheC enzyme decreased and destabilized backbone flexibility, which is consistence with this study [2, 23, 24]. The RMSD presented here, used to test for conformations characteristics and confirm which of the regions of high mobility adequately illustrate the differences on the conformational sampling between free-HheC and HheC-Chloride Ion Complex over 100 ns. In the course of the last 100 ns simulations, the RMSD values for HheC-Chloride ion complex chains decrease with average values from 0.1 nm to 0.4 nm and remain unstable throughout simulation time. Here, free HheC enzyme back bone displayed mean RMSD estimations between 1.1 Å and 1.5 Å. In comprehensive, a higher backbone RMSD value indicated greater movement; conversely, lower residue RMSD value indicates lower movement. Evidence from several MD studies indicated that RMSD used to understand enzymatic mechanisms and to investigate selective unbinds [25, 30].

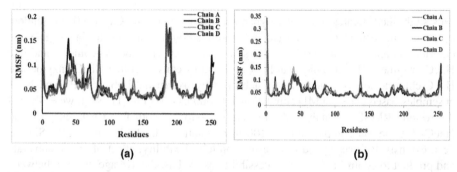

Fig. 2. RMSF results for backbone atoms of A) free-HheC enzyme and HheC-Chloride ion complex chain A (Blue), Chain B (black), Chain C (green) and Chain D (red), which are plotted along with the residues (gray bars). (Color figure online)

Here, we proposed to predict whether the chloride ion disturbs the dynamic behavior of HheC residues, which are important to investigate the role of bottle-neck residues and tunnel-lining residues in chloride ion releasing mechanism. The RMSF values of HheC-chloride ion complex and free-HheC enzyme structures were obtained and shown in Fig. 4. Interpretation of fluctuation score described that the higher degree of flexibility observed in free-HheC enzyme structures between residues 80–100, 150–189, and 200–248 than HheC-chloride ion complex structures (Fig. 2a). The root-mean-square-fluctuation (RMSF) of the backbone revealed comparable motion in the inside of free-HheC and HheC-chloride ion complex (Fig. 2b). As seen in the figure, aforementioned residues of HheC-chloride ion complex produced the clear changes, which mainly concentrate the region between 80–100, 150–189, C-terminus and 200–248 and a portion of 250 residues, surrounding the exit of the chloride ion tunnels (Fig. 4b). In this position the free HheC enzyme showed higher flexibility. Several landmark studies, observed the loop secondary structures tend to fluctuate more than others molecular moieties [25, 30].

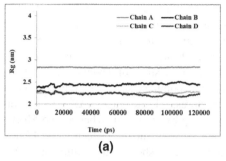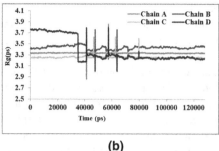

(a)   (b)

Fig. 3. Time evolution of the radius of gyration (Rg) values for A) HheC-Chloride ion complex B) free-enzyme analysis chain A (Blue), Chain B (black), Chain C (green) and Chain D (red), which are plotted along with the time (gray bars) (Color figure online)

The radius of gyration plot for the backbone of HheC enzyme models versus time at 300 K is shown in Fig. 3. To observe the outcome of the chloride ion on HheC enzyme packing, the radius of gyration (Rg) was calculated. The higher Rg values indicate loose packing of HheC structure, which means conformation that is more flexible. In this context, significant difference between free-HheC and HheC-chloride ion complex observed according to Rg analysis (Fig. 3). Rg value for free-HheC showed higher value between 3.1–3.5 nm and except, Chain D remain unstable until the end of 4 ns simulation (Fig. 2b). This implies that there is high probability to re-duce compactness of HheC Enzyme between during simulation. Studies have demonstrated the strong and consistent link between small molecule interactions, and their role in conformational rearrangement and dynamics in biocatalysts [30].

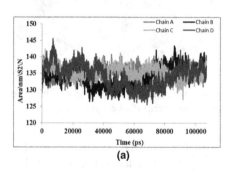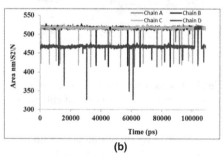

(a)   (b)

Fig. 4. Solvent accessibility surface area (SASA) analysis for A) the HheC-chloride ion complex and B) free-HheC enzyme structures chain A (Blue), Chain B (black), Chain C (green) and Chain D (red), which are plotted along with the time (gray bars). (Color figure online)

Similarly, solvent dynamics inside the biomolecule solvation layer play vital part in enzyme catalysis, but thoughtful of its role is delayed by its complexity [26, 28, 30]. Here, we studied Solvent accessibility surface area SASA analysis between the HheC-chloride ion complex and free-HheC enzyme structures. Increased value of SASA in the HheC-chloride ion complex indicates its comparatively not wrinkled nature as compared to the free-HheC enzyme. Change of SASA in HheC-chloride complex and free-HheC enzymes shown in Fig. 4. For all chains in free-HheC enzyme structures showed similar fashion of deviation until 100 ns from the initial structure (Fig. 4a). HheC-chloride ion complex structures showed similar fashion of deviation until 100 ns from the initial structure, but HheC-chloride ion complex structure showed greater value of SASA than free-HheC enzyme structures. The average SASA value was between 450–550 nm in HheC-chloride ion complex (Fig. 4b), whereas the HheC-chloride ion complex structures showed average SASA value of between 130–145 nm, respectively, as depicted in Fig. 4a. Literature review showed that different SASA structures have been seen for Apo-enzyme and Holo-enzyme experimental and computational studies [26, 28, 30]. Inconsistent with other studies the accessibility of active sites is being controlled by chloride ion binding and unbinding. From this stand-point, SASA could be considered tunnels as closed or open and shown the active site isolated from or connected to the bulk solvent.

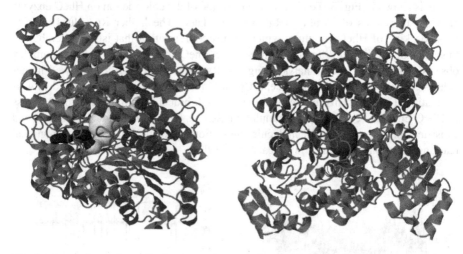

Fig. 5. Comparison of the HheC-chloride ion complex (left) and free HheC (right). The main tunnel is closed by the introduced chloride ion (in blue and green) (Color figure online)

For this investigation, we examined the tunnels assembled from each snapshot using CAVER 3.0.2 [29]. It has been experimentally demonstrated that Ser132, Tyr145 and Arg149 active site residues and we employed as starting point of tunnels computation. Our results demonstrated that there are three significant tunnels i.e. one tunnel from free HheC and two tunnels from HheC-Chloride ion complex, with clustering threshold of the pathway at 4.0 Å (Table 1). Chloride discharging tunnels revealed in Fig. 5. In this investigation, two tunnels identified in HheC chloride ion complex, while one tunnel found in free HheC, with clustering threshold of the pathway at 4.0 Å. In line with previous studies, tunnels width and length used to assess geometric based tunnel identification programs [2]. Therefore, we showed that top four tunnels with shorter length and wider structure were identified (Table 1). Here we compare the results of the HheC chloride ion complex tunnels with that of the free HheC tunnels. This showed that chloride ion narrowing tunnels. A similar pattern of results obtained in priorities. There aren't distinct tunnels with preferences higher than that shown in Table 1. In the meantime, amino acids lining up tunnels, as well as residues creating bottlenecks tunnels were recognized. Thoroughly, twenty-eight (28) essential residues were revealed in the bottleneck and tunnels by caver 3.0.2. From these results several new important residues such as, 84 P, 137 G, 186 F, 245 M and 248 R, 162 Q, 232 L, 233 T, 162 Q, 247 Q, 177 Y, 187 Y, 191 P, 192 W, 195 E, 197 Q, 198 H, 201 H, 204 K, 205 V, 236 V, 238 W, 243 F, 244 P, 86 F, 138 P, 139 W, 140 K, 141 Q, 142 L, 165 Q, and 160 S found in tunnel-2 and tunnel-3 (Table 1). Our results demonstrated that new important residues that we discovered are located in the bottlenecks and tunnels of both free HheC and HheC-chloride ion complex. These include 131 T, 132 S, 134 T, 130 I, and 133 A. Furthermore, sections close to the individual tunnels revealed the most vital conformational variation inside free HheC (Fig. 2). Conversely, thought of the chloride ion release occasion by classical MD simulation was not satisfactory owing to the very robust electrostatic interactions between chloride ion and tunnel site residues. Therefore, RAMD simulation was desirable. The majority of prior research has applied RAMD to a wide range of proteins tunnel engineering for modifying activity [6, 7, 9]. In the context of this study, after a series of MD simulation and CAVER analysis, RAMD simulation was executed on the fifty various data structures of HheC chloride ion complex, which were extracted from classical MD simulation. Recent theoretical developments have revealed that 0.85 kcal Å−1 mol−1 force applied on chloride ion. In this study, when the random 0.85 kcal Å−1 mol−1 force applied on chloride ion, it destabilized the interactions between the chloride ion and tunnel residues and finally explored a new direction to exit. In line with previous CAVER analysis chloride ion throwing out through two dissimilar tunnels: tunnels B and C (Table 1).

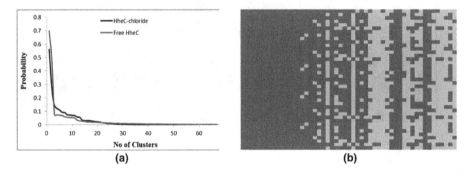

Fig. 6. A) Probabilities of the 67 largest clusters of free HheC-(red) and HheC-Chloride-(black) enzyme, B) Heat map reflecting the time progression of bottleneck radii of private tunnel clusters. Per row corresponds to one cluster of 10000 pictures. The gray color symbolizes that no tunnel from an assigned cluster was recognized in a given picture.(Color figure online)

During tunnel computation, the structure produces dozens of tunnels, which are difficult to determine the steadiness of distinct tunnels over time. Here, we focused on the tunnel that is persisted throughout the simulation and serves as the chloride ion release pathway and for further detailed exploration. For this study tunnels in one static image with a heat map exhibits every distinguished tunnel in the molecular dynamics in Fig. 6b. A rectangle in the heat map corresponds to the bottleneck of a tunnel at a distinct position in time and the intensity encodes the bottleneck size. The paint slider to the right outlines the plotting of bottleneck size to paint. A lower limit of the acceptable bottleneck extent can be interactively quantified on the paint slider. Bottlenecks under this boundary are shown in white. A vertical line in the all tunnel heat agrees to the time-based development of a specific tunnel over time. White rectangles on such a line specify time steps where the tunnel is either closed or it is too small for the examined ligand. A horizontal line corresponds to all the tunnels given at a specific point in time. In this study, tunnel is fixed according to their significance from left to right and at the left of the heat map the most encouraging tunnels are shown. The importance of a given tunnel is calculated by averaging the sum of tunnel throughputs over all pictures. If the tunnel is closed at given picture, zero value is used, which rejects further consideration. And also, transient tunnels are depicted in the right part of the heat map and showed the temporal location of the open part of the tunnel. Generally, this shows graphic variance if the tunnel is open for a continuous serving of time or if the time steps when the tunnel is open are dispersed discontinuously throughout the molecular dynamics and govern if the chloride ion could be followed the tunnel. This is a candidate for further exploration.

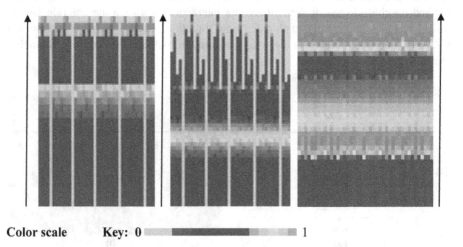

Color scale   Key: 0 ▬▬▬▬▬▬▬▬ 1

Fig. 7. Heat map visualizing the time evolution of the tunnel profile for 100 ns simulation. The first two columns depict the average profile for the HheC-Chloride complex and the third column outlines free HheC pictures. The color of an element with coordinates x and y signifies the radius of a presented tunnel in 10000 snapshots and 625 distance interval.

After the filtering stage, we explored the top three selected tunnels as shown in Fig. 7 by using bottle-neck. Here, we used different bottleneck sizes and compute with various frames of the bottleneck, which restricts the maximal size of relevant chloride ion outlet. As shown in Fig. 7 We address this problem by including an interactive Single Tunnel Heat Map. In this context, we performed the tunnel analysis several times, with a small bottleneck radius between 0.5–0.9 Å. The Single Tunnel Heat Map representation now displays only one tunnel from free-HheC and two from HheC-chloride ion complex at a time (Fig. 7). The upright axis again signifies the time domain. The horizontal axis now signifies the tunnel length and the color of separate rectangles encrypts the thickness of the tunnel at conforming positions along the tunnel centerline. The grey rectangles depict that the tunnel is closed or the bottle-neck size is below the user-defined threshold. We can use the pre-computed information about the tunnel thickness in the closed parts as well which is fixed as grey value. Darker grey values link to smaller bottle-neck widths of the closed tunnel. Mostly, we get an overview of the tunnel behavior of HheC when changing the minimum bottleneck size, which helps them to discovery an appropriate threshold value. This value then outlines the maximal size of a chloride ion which could be transported via this tunnel. An all Tunnels Heat Map is a much more collected image as compared to the Single Tunnel Heat map. In an All Tunnel Heat map a tunnel is reduced to its bottleneck, whereas in a Single Tunnel Heat map the complete tunnel at an exact idea in time is given. By studying the throughput of tunnels using the all Tunnel Heat map and Single Tunnel Heat map, selected candidate tunnels for the transport of a chloride ion of a specified size to the HheC active site.

Table 1. Features of tunnels in HheC-chloride complex and free-HheC enzymes. Tunnels B, C in HheC-chloride complex and tunnel B in free-HheC, respectively

Tunnels	Bottleneck Radius	Tunnel length	Priority	Tunnels residues	Bottleneck residues
Tunnel-A	1.046 ± 0.05	14.14 ± 0.007	0.60	12 F,83 A,84 P,86 F, 130 I, 131 T,132 S, 133 A, 134 T, 139 W, 142 L, 145 Y, 149 R, 175 P, 176 Q,177 Y, 178 L, 184 P, 185 Y, 186 F, 187 Y, 188 P, 192 W, 249 M, 80 N, 82 F, 85 Q, 174 G	P138, K161,P244, M245, I246, G137, G242, 249W, 186F, 84P, 187 Y,184 P,139 W,185 Y, 86 F, 145 Y
Tunnel-B	0.9 ± 0.003	15.9 ± 0.1	0.56	131 T,132 S,134 T, 135 P, 136 F, 145 Y, 149 R, 150 A, 152 A, 153 C, 154 T, 157 N, 161 K, 235 Q, 236 V, 238 W, 138 P, 130 I, 133 A, 146 T, 147 S, 148 A, 151 G, 174 G, 234 G, 237 F, 137 G and 151 G	132 S, 149 R, 131 T, 135 P,133 A, 153 C,134 T, 150 A,174 G, 146 T, 238 W, 145 Y, 152 A and 148 A
Tunnel-C	0.87 ± 0.001	12.3 ± 0.02	0.499	131 T,132 S, 134 T,135 P, 136 F,145 Y,149 R,150 A, 152 A,153 C,154 T,157 Q, 160 S, 161 K,165 E,235 Q, 236 V, 238 W, 86 F,135 P, 136 F, 138 P, 139 P, 140 K, 141 Q,142 L, 150 A,153 C, 154 T,157 E, 177 Y,187 Y, 191 P, 192 W, 195 E, 197 Q,198 H, 201 H, 204 K,205 V, 236 V, 238 W, 243 F, 244 P, 246 I, 247 Q, 130 I, 133 A, 146 T, 147 S,148 A,151 G, 162 Q, 174 G,232 L,233 T,234 G,237 F,84 P, 137 G, 186 F,245 M, and 248 R	132 S,149 R, 131 T,135 P, 133 A,153 C, 134 T,150 A, 174 G,146 T,238 W,145 Y, 152 A, and 148 A

The enzyme backbone conformation altered during chloride ion detachment, with spin of a few residue side chains further increasing the opening of tunnel A to let release of the chloride ion (Fig. 4a). Tunnel B lies between the 82–87 loop and 95–120 loop being on the reverse side from tunnel A. Certain parts of tunnel B were thought to be flexible, which specified that an open pathway could form at this region (Fig. 4b). Tunnel C is lined mostly by 82–87 loop. In this region, it is not a predominantly easy process to untie the side-chain packing of hydrophobic residues, so C was the tunnel least regularly used for ligand detachment (Fig. 4c). Meanwhile, we recognized key residues controlling the exit and entrance of HheC tunnels as showed in Table 1. Identification of the detachment ways will offer further mechanistic insights into HheC, which will benefit modification of HheC activity.

3 Conclusions

In this study, extensive MD simulations, CAVER 3.0 and RAMD were performed to examine the chloride ion releasing tunnel of HheC. Tunnels that facilitate the release of chloride ion in the free HheC and HheC-chloride complex enzymes were considered, and it was established that binding of chloride ion could meaningfully narrow the tunnels. Moreover, a conformational cluster analysis of the tunnel loop region specified its vital role in narrowing the chloride ion releasing tunnels. And also, amino acids making up tunnels and tunnel bottlenecks were identified. It was found that all three active site residues were located along the tunnel-site loop region, with the majority being situated along the main part of the enzyme. These findings provide a potential explanation for the conformational variation of the tunnel-site loop induced by the binding of chloride ions. Future research should consider the potential effects of engineering residues making up tunnels and tunnel bottlenecks more carefully, and their roles on activity of enzyme further inspect experimentally.

References

1 van Hylckama Vlieg, J., et al.: Halohydrin Dehalogenases are structurally and mechanistically related to Short-Chain Dehydrogenases/Reductases. J. Bacteriol. **183**(17), 5058–5066 (2001)

2 Tang, L., Torres Pazmiño, D., Fraaije, W.M., de Jong, M.R., Dijkstra, B.W., Janssen, D.B.: Improved catalytic properties of Halohydrin Dehalogenase by modification of the Halide-Binding Site. Biochemistry, **44**(17), 6609–6618 (2005)

3 Koopmeiners, J., et al.: HheG, a Halohydrin Dehalogenase with activity on cyclic epoxides. ACS Catal. **7**(10), 6877–6886 (2017)

4 Tang, X.L., Ye, G.Y., Wan, X.Y., Li, H.W., Zheng, R.C., Zheng, Y.G.: Rational design of halohydrin dehalogenase for efficient chiral epichlorohydrin production with high activity and enantioselectivity in aqueous-organic two-phase system. Biochem. Eng. J., **161**, 107708 (2020)

5 Estévez-Gay, M., Iglesias-Fernández, J., Osuna, S.: Conformational landscapes of Halohydrin Dehalogenases and their accessible active site tunnels. Catalysts **10**(12), 1403 (2020)

6 Tao, Y.: Theoretical and computational research on halide ion release channel of Haloalcohol Dehalogenase from Agrobacterium Radiobacter AD1. Unpublished Manuscript (2014)

7 Pan, Q.R., Li, M., Wang, B., Huang, H., Han, W.: Random acceleration and steered molecular dynamics simulations reveal the unbinding tunnels in adenosine deaminase and critical residues in tunnels. RSC Adv. **10**, 43994 (2019)

8 Potterton, A., et al.: Ensemble-based steered molecular dynamics predicts relative residence time of A2A receptor binders. J. Chem. Theory Comput., **15**, 3316–3330 (2019)

9 Vilar, S., Karpiak, J., Berk, B., Costanzi, S.: In silico analysis of the binding of agonists and blockers to the β2-adrenergic receptor. J. Mol. Graph. Model. **29**(6), 809–817 (2011)

10 Akram, M., Waratchareeyakul, W., Haupenthal, J., Hartmann, J.W., Schuster, D.: Pharmacophore modeling and in Silico/in Vitro screening for human cytochrome P450 11B1 and cytochrome P450 11B2 inhibitors. Front. Chem. https://doi.org/10.3389/fchem. 2017.00104

11 Daniel, L., Buryska, T., Prokop, Z., Damborsky, J., Brezovsky, J.: Mechanism-based discovery of novel substrates of Haloalkane Dehalogenases using in silico screening. J. Chem. Inf. Model **55**(1), 54–62 (2015)

12 Mujwar, S., Kumar, V.: Computational drug repurposing approach to identify potential fatty acid-binding Protein-4 inhibitors to develop novel antiobesity therapy. Assay Drug Dev. Technol. **18**(7), 1–20 (2020)

13 Gordon, J.C., Myers, J.B., Folta, T., Shoja, V., Heath, L.S., Onufriev, A.: H++: a server for estimating pKas and adding missing hydrogens to macromolecules, Nucleic Acids Res. **33**, W368–71 (2005)

14 Laskowski, R.A., MacArthur, M.W., Thornton, J.M.: PROCHECK: validation of protein structure coordinates, in International Tables of Crystallography, Volume F. In: Rossmann, M.G., Arnold, E. (eds.) Crystallography of Biological Macromolecules, pp. 722–725. Dordrecht, Kluwer Academic Publishers, Netherlands (2001)

15 Hess, B., Kutzner, C., van der Spoel, D., Lindahl, E.: GROMACS 4: algorithms for highly efficient, Load-Balanced, and scalable molecular simulation. J. Chem. Theory Comput. **4**(3), 435–447 (2008)

16 MacKerell, A.D., et al.: J. Phys. Chem. B. **102**, 3586–3616 (1998)

17 Wang, J., Wolf, R.M., Caldwell, J.W., Kollman, P.A., Case, D.A.: Development and testing of a General Amber Force Field. J. Comput. Chem. **25**(9), 1157–1174 (2004)

18 Jorgensen, W.L., Chandrasekhar, J., Madura, J.D., Impey, R.W., Klein, M.L.: Comparison of simple potential functions for simulating liquid water. J. Chem. Phys. **79**, 926 (1983)

19 Vardeman, F.C., Stocker, M.K., Gezelter, J.D.: The Langevin Hull: constant pressure and temperature dynamics for non-periodic systems. J. Chem. Theory Comput., **7**(4), 834–842 (2012)

20 Humphrey, W., Dalke, A., Schulten, K.: VMD: visual molecular dynamics. J. Mol. Graph. **14**(1), 33–38 (1996)

21 Schrodinger, L.L.C.: Book the PyMOL Molecular Graphics System, Version 1.3r1. The PyMOL Molecular Graphics System, Version 1.3r1 (2010)

22 Sargsyan, K., Grauffel, C., Lim, C.: How molecular size impacts RMSD applications in molecular dynamics simulations. J. Chem. Theory Comput. **13**(4), 1518–1524 (2017)

23 dos Santos, G.E., Fariab, X.R., Rodrigues, R.C., Bello, L.M.: Molecular dynamic simulations of full-length human purinergic receptor subtype P2X7 bonded to potent inhibitors. European J. Pharm. Sci. **152**, 105454 (2020)

24 Cui, Y.L., et al.: Structural and dynamic basis of human cytochrome P450 7B1: a survey of substrate selectivity and major active site access channels. Chem. European J. **19**(2), 549–557 (2013)

25 Mortier, J., Rakers, C., Bermudez, M., Murgueitio, M.S., Riniker, S., Wolber, G.: The impact of molecular dynamics on drug design applications for the characterization of ligand–macromolecule complexes. Drug Discovery, **20**(6), 1–17 (2015)

26 Verma, R., Mitchell-Koch, K.: In silico studies of small molecule interactions with enzymes reveal aspects of catalytic function. Catalysts **7**(7), 212 (2017)

27 Du, X., et al.: Insights into protein–ligand interactions: mechanisms, models, and methods. Int. J. Mol. Sci. **17**(2), 144 (2016)

28 Schwartz, S.D., Schramm, V.L.: Enzymatic transition states and dynamic motion in barrier crossing. Nat. Chem. Biol. **5**, 551–558 (2009)

29 Marques, S.M., Bednar, D., Damborsky, J.: Computational study of protein-ligand unbinding for enzyme engineering. Front. Chem. **6**(650), 1845–1852 (2018)

30 Prokop, Z., Gora, A., Brezovsky, J., Chaloupkova, R., Stepankova, V., Damborsky, J.: Engineering of protein tunnels: keyhole-lock-key model for catalysis by the enzymes with buried active sites. In: Protein Engineering Handbook, vol. 3, pp. 421–464. WileyVCH, Weinheim (2012)

31 Chovancova, E., et al.: CAVER 3.0: a tool for the analysis of transport pathways in dynamic protein structures. PLoS Comput. Biol., **8**(10), e1002708 (2012)

32 Pierce, L., Ferrer, R.S., McCammon, A., de Oliveira F.A., Walker, C.R.: Routine access to millisecond time scale events with accelerated molecular dynamics. J. Chem. Theory Comput., **8**(9), 2997-3002 (2012)

33 de Jong, R.M., et al.: Structure and mechanism of a bacterial haloalcohol dehalogenase: a new variation of the short-chain dehydrogenase/reductase fold without an NAD (P) H binding site. EMBO J. **22**, 4933-4944 (2003)

34 de Jong, R.M., Tiesinga, J.W.J., Villa, A., Tang, L., Janssen, B.D., Dijkstra, W.B.: Structural basis for the Enantioselectivity of an Epoxide Ring Opening Reaction Catalyzed by Halo Alcohol Dehalogenase HheC. J. Am. Chem. Soc., **127**(38), 13338–13343 (2005)

35 Cook, I., Wang, T., Almo, C.S., Kim, J., Falany, N.C., Leyh, S.T.: The gate that governs sulfotransferase selectivity. Am. Chem. Soc., **52**(2), 415–424 (2013)

36 Bottaro, S., Lindorff-Larsen, K.: Biophysical experiments and biomolecular simulations: a perfect match? Science **361**, 355–360 (2018)

Effect of Annealing on the Photoluminescence Intensity of Gehlenite:Eu Doped Phosphor Prepared in Different Gas Atmospheres

Fetene Fufa Bakare[1,2($\boxtimes$)], Abadi Hadush Tesfay[3],
and Shao-Ju Shih[4($\boxtimes$)]

[1] Department of Advanced Materials Science and Engineering Center
of Excellence, Adama Science and Technology University, Adama, Ethiopia
fetene.fufa@astu.edu.et

[2] Department of Materials Science and Engineering, Adama Science
and Technology University, Adama, Ethiopia

[3] Department of Chemistry, Axum University, Tigray, Ethiopia

[4] Department of Materials Science and Engineering, National Taiwan University
of Science and Technology, Taipei, Taiwan
shao-ju.shih@mail.ntust.edu.tw

Abstract. Europium doped gehlenite phosphor glassy powders were successfully prepared by spray pyrolysis followed by annealing under air, N_2 and N_2/H_2 treated gases. In this paper, it is of great attention and importance to find that the reductions of Eu^{3+} to Eu^{2+} ions can be realized. To identify the oxidations of europium ions, the X ray photo spectroscopy (XPS) was used. The photoluminescence (PL) properties intensively studied under different excitation in which the result shows that the europium doped phosphor gehlenite glassy powders emit a strong red light in air and N_2 treated gases; while under N_2/H_2 treated gas, blue light was observed.

Keywords: Gehlenite · Photoluminescence · Air · N_2 and N_2/H_2 · Eu^{2+}/Eu^{3+} · Spray pyrolysis

1 Introduction

It is known that aluminosilicates have excellent chemical and thermal stability, good corrosion resistance and low cost, which can be used in different fields of applications such as, in the areas of sensors, security labels, compact fluorescent lamps (CFLs), and field emission displays (EDs), white light emitting diodes (WLEDs) and excellent phosphor hosts [1–7]. Recently among, the aluminosilicate group amorphous gehlenite materials have superior photoluminescence properties when doped with rare earth metal ions [8].

Rare-earth ions doped gehlenite ($Ca_2Al_2SiO_7$) have been widely investigated for the last few decades [9]. For example, Er^{3+} and Nd^{3+} ions doped $Ca_2Al_2SiO_7$ have large absorption bands which enhance, for the fabrications of laser typed pumped materials. Zhang et al. have reported $Ca_2Al_2SiO_7$:Eu^{3+} as a potential red phosphor used in WLEDs [10]. Eu^{3+} is commonly, used in luminescence studies due to its intra

M. L. Berihun (Ed.): ICAST 2021, LNICST 412, pp. 377–387, 2022.
https://doi.org/10.1007/978-3-030-93712-6_26

transition electrons and the longlife times of the excited states. Most, red phosphors activated by Eu^{3+} ion were extensively reported, for example, $LiEu(PO_3)_4$ [11] and $Na_5Eu(WO_4)$ [12]. These phosphors can be effectively excited by the ultravio-let LED along with orange/red emission originating from the $^5D_0$ ^7F_J (J = 0, 1, 2, 3, 4) [13]. In addition, Eu^{2+} ions are more sensitive to the ligand field and luminescent color strongly depend on the host lattices in which the emission colors change, for example from blue to yellow (and even red). Its emission wavelength strongly depends on the nature of the host lattice due to the participations of d orbitals ($4f^65d^1 \rightarrow 4f^7$) [6]. In the previous report, Eu^{2+} ions are mainly obtained at eleveated temperature solid state reaction under specific atmospheres such as reducing atmosphere (N_2/H_2, H_2 and CO) [14, 15]. Haoyi et al. reported that Eu^{2+} ions doped $Ca_2Al_2SiO_7$ are prepared by solid state reaction method in which a blue-green emission were observed [16].

Several methods have been used for the synthesizes of phosphors materials. Among these methods: solid state reaction [17], sol-gel [1] and spray pyrolysis methods have been used. Solid- state reaction is a conventional method, but has some demerits such as, high heating temperature, low chemical uniformity, and large average particle size [18]. To improve these drawback, sol-gel methods were suggested, which resulted fine particle sizes and low preparation temperatures. However, they also have limitations such as, difficulties in powder morphology controlling and huge energy loss for the removal of residue during calcination process [19]. Thus, problems may reduce the enhancement of luminescent properties of phosphor particles. To overcome those limitation spray pyrolysis methods were used [20].

Particles prepared using spray pyrolysis method are chemical uniform in size and composition, spherical morphology and non-agglomeration, because of the microscale reactions that proceed inside a droplet [21, 22]. In additions, spray pyrolysis has many advantages such as its low annealing temperature, cost effective, high purity, fast process and continuous processes [23–25]. Shih et al. reported that, the gehlenite doped europium was prepared by spray pyrolysis methods were successfully prepared in which red emissions was obtained [8]. In this work we propose a single phosphor material to produce more than one color emissions in different atmospheric condition.

In this paper, a novel gehlenite: Eu glassy powders phosphors was systematically, studied under air, N_2 and N_2/H_2 treated gases. Additionally, for the determination of the atomic composition the oxidation state of europium ions was estimates, from peak area. We believe this work will greatly promote the development and application of the europium doped gehlenite phosphors.

2   Experimental Procedures

2.1   Preparation of Gehlenite: Eu Doped Glassy Powders

For the preparation of gehlenite: Eu doped glassy powder, aluminum nitrateenneahydrate (AlN), (AlN) (Al $(NO_3)_3.9H_2O$, 99%, Alfa Aesar), calcium nitrate tetrahydrate (CaN) (Ca $(NO_3)_2.4H_2O$, 99%, Alfa Aesar, Heysham, UK), tetraethylorthosilicate (TEOS) ($C_8H_{20}O_4Si$, 98%, Acros, Pittsburgh, PA) and europium oxide (Eu_2O_3, 99%, Alfa Aesar) were used. All chemicals were mixed and stirred at room temperature for

24 h with DI water. Then, the precursor, of the mixture was atomized by ultrasonic to form a droplet. The small droplets were supplied to the three different region temperatures, i.e., evaporation, calcination, and cooling at 250, 1000, and 350 °C, respectively. The phosphor particles produced were collected inside the metal cylinder wall. Finally, the collected powders prepared were treated at 800 °C for 1 h inside a tubular furnace under an air, N_2 and N_2/H_2 gases with the heating and cooling rate of 5 °C/min.

2.2   Characterization

The phase compositions of gehlenite: Eu phosphor particles prepared under air, N_2 and N_2/H_2 treated gases were examined, using XRD (D2 Phaser, Bruker, Karlsruhe, Germany), with Cu-Kα radiation, has used to obtain the XRD patterns with the range from 20° to 80° and with the scanning rate of 6°/ min. The surface morphology of gehlenite: Eu phosphors particles prepared under air, N_2 and N_2/H_2 treated gases were examined using scanning electron microscope (SEM, JSM-6500F, JEOL, Tokyo, Japan). Photo luminescent properties were determined using Xe-ramp as the excitation source. All the luminescence characterization of the phosphors was carried out at room temperature using a fluorescence spectrometer (FP-8500, JASCO, Tokyo, Japan). A Xenon lamp of 150 W was used as the excitation light source to record the spectra of gehlenite: Eu doped powders at a wavelength of 254 and 394 nm. The surface compositions of europium ions, oxidation state and the binding energies of the 3d core levels were determined by X-ray photoelectron spectroscopy (XPS, Perkin-Elmer PHI 5600, and Waltham, MA, USA). All measurements were carried out at the room temperature.

3   Results and Discussion

Figure 1 shows the phase composition of the gehlenite: Eu phosphor glassy powders treated in air, N_2 and N_2/H_2 gases. The XRD spectra showed that all powders have a broad band between 23° and 38°, indicating the absence of the crystalline phase for a glassy structure. In short, the gehlenite: Eu phosphor glassy powders treated in air, N_2 and N_2/H_2 gases treated exhibited the amorphous phase. Furthermore, the dopant didn't influence the structure of the prepared specimen.

The surface morphologies of the all powders were observed with FE-SEM, as shown in Fig. 2(a)–(c). As seen from Fig. 2, the image seems like similar, spherical and smooth shape in air, N_2 and N_2/H_2 treated gases, which was the morphology, does not influenced under thus gases treatment. Based on statistical measurement, the average particle sizes prepared phosphors are calculated from 300 particles were, 1.39 ± 0.52 μm, 1.32 ± 0.72 μm and 1.25 ± 0.5 μm in air, N_2 and N_2/H_2 treated gases respectively. In addition, the spherical and smooth, morphology which is considered to be of benefit in enhancing Photoluminescence properties [22].

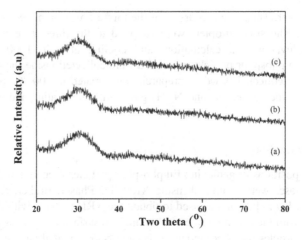

Fig. 1. XRD patterns of gehlenite: Eu phosphor glassy powders treated in (a) air, (b) N_2 and (c) N_2/H_2-gases treated.

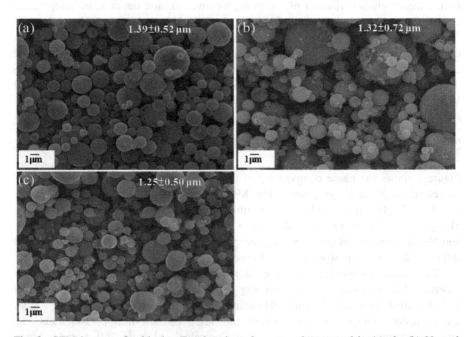

Fig. 2. SEM images of gehlenite: Eu phosphor glassy powders treated in (a) air, (b) N_2 and (c) N_2/H_2 gases treated.

To confirm the presence of Eu^{2+} and Eu^{3+} ions, all prepared powders were analysis by XPS techniques. X-ray photoelectron spectra (XPS), results were shown in Fig. 3 There were four photoelectron emission signals at the binding energy range between 1120 and 1180 eV in the XPS spectrum for gehlenite: Eu phosphor particles prepared under air, N_2 and N_2/H_2 treated gases in Fig. 3. From Fig. 3(a) two broad band peaking were observed at 1124.23 eV and 1133.79 eV, which is ascribed to Eu^{2+} $3d_{5/2}$ and Eu^{3+} $3d_{5/2}$, respectively. The other two band peaking were observed at 1153.94 eV and 1163.70 eV, which belongs to Eu^{2+} $3d_{3/2}$ and Eu^{3+} $3d_{3/2}$, respectively. In addition, in Fig. 3(b) there are four photoelectron emissions signals were observed at binding energy of 1124.44, 1133.82, 1154.09 and 1163.76 eV which attributed to Eu^{2+} $3d_{5/2}$, Eu^{3+} $3d_{5/2}$, Eu^{2+} $3d_{3/2}$ and Eu^{3+} $3d_{3/2}$ respectively. Lastly, in Fig. 3(c) four photo-electron emissions were observed at the binding energy of 1124.23, 1133.87, 1153.77 and 1163.55eV belongs to Eu^{2+} $3d_{5/2}$, Eu^{3+} $3d_{5/2}$, Eu^{2+} $3d_{3/2}$ and Eu^{3+} $3d_{3/2}$ respectively. The binding energy difference between the trivalent and divalent states is about $\sim 9.1eV$, in which similar discussions were given for the Eu ion in $KBaPO_4$: Eu phosphor as well [26].

The emission spectra of Eu ions doped gehlenite glassy powder treated are shown in Fig. 4(a) (λ_{ex} = 254 nm) and (b) (λ_{ex} = 394 nm) under air, N_2 and N_2/H_2 gases treated.

The emission spectrum of the gehlenite: Eu phosphor glassy powder from Fig. 4(a) were measured by adjusting the excitation at 254 nm, which exhibits a broadband at 400 nm and it attributed to $4f^65d \rightarrow 4f^7$ transitions of Eu^{2+}. Up on 254 nm UV excitation, the gehlenite: Eu^{2+} phosphor shows a strong blue emission band with a peak between 360–470 nm, which is attributed to the 5d-4f allowed transition of Eu^{2+} ions. Furthermore, for transitions of Eu^{3+} ions there is the existence of narrower peaks between 550 and 750 nm due to the $^5D_0 \rightarrow {}^7F_J$ (J = 1–4) transitions. From Fig. 4(b), there are two main emission peaks at 613 nm and 592 nm which is assigned to the induced electric dipole (ED) transition $^5D_0 \rightarrow {}^7F_2$ and magnetic dipole (MD) transition $^5D_0 \rightarrow {}^7F_1$ of Eu^{3+}. The magnetic dipole transition appears due to both centrosym-metric and non centrosymmetric lattice centres, whereas the induced electric dipole transition appears when Eu^{3+} ions occupy non-centrosymmetric lattice centres. The relative intensity ratio of the $^5D_0 \rightarrow {}^7F_1$ and $^5D_0 \rightarrow {}^7F_2$ transitions strongly depends on the local symmetry of the Eu^{3+} ions [27].

As mentioned in Table 1 the atomic composition of sample prepared under air, N_2 and N_2/H_2 treated gases were calculated from the XPS analysis for both Eu^{2+} and Eu^{3+} ions. Atomic composition of Eu^{2+} in percentage under air, N_2 and N_2/H_2 treated was 56.33%, 50.65% and 61.67% respectively. Comparatively, N_2/H_2 treated Eu-doped gehlenite glassy powders were 61.67% (Eu^{2+}) in which the highest intensity of blue emitted color was obtained at excitation of 254 nm compare to air and N_2 treated gases. However, in air and N_2 treated Eu-doped gehlenite glassy powders were 56.33% and 50.65% respectively. The photoluminescence intensity recorded for air and N_2 treated gases at the excitation of 254 nm was low which suppressed their emissions due to

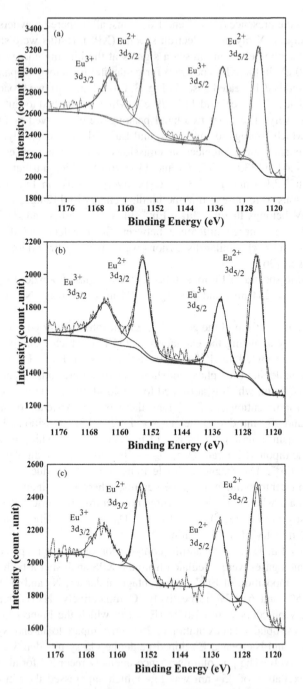

Fig. 3. XPS spectra of the Eu 3d peaks of gehlenite: Eu phosphor glassy powders treated in (a) air, (b) N_2 and (c) N_2/H_2-gases treated. Solid line represents the experimental spectrum (after background subtraction) and the dotted lines are the results with curve fitting.

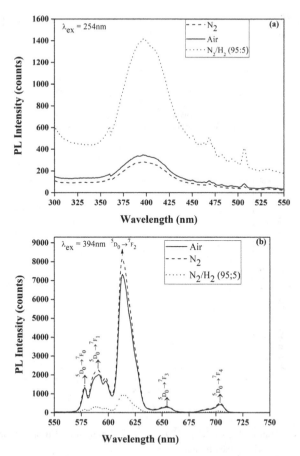

Fig. 4. PL spectra of gehlenite: Eu phosphor glassy powder (a) (λ_{ex} = 254 nm) and (b) (λ_{ex} = 394 nm) treated in air, N_2 and N_2/H_2 gases treated.

reduction of Eu^{3+} to Eu^{2+} ions, whereas at the excitations of 394 nm the highest intensity of red emission was obtained. From this analysis the N_2/H_2 treated were the appropriate for blue emissions in which it favored to Eu^{2+} ion but under air and N_2 treated shows better red emissions. Generally, two colors from a single phosphor material were successfully obtained under air, N_2 and N_2/H_2 treated gases.

Figure 5 shows the ratio of the integrated emission intensity caused by the ($^5D_0$ $^7F_2$) transition to the ($^5D_0 \rightarrow {}^7F_1$) transition of Eu^{3+} ions, i.e., ($^5D_0 \rightarrow {}^7F_2$) / ($^5D_0$ $^7F_1$). As we seen from Fig. 5 the intensity ratios of N_2 treated gases where higher than in air and N_2/H_2 treated gases. The values of intensity ratios are 3.64, 3.69 and 3.16 in air, N_2 and N_2/H_2 treated gases respectively.

Table 1. Compositions of Eu^{2+} and Eu^{3+} ions from XPS data of Eu-doped gehlenite glassy powders treated in air, N_2 and N_2/H_2 gases treated.

Atmospheric gases	Peak area						Atomic composition (%)	
	Eu^{3+} $3d_{5/2}$	Eu^{2+} $3d_{5/2}$	Eu^{3+} $3d_{3/2}$	Eu^{2+} $3d_{3/2}$	$\sum Eu^{3+} + Eu^{3+}$ $3d_{5/2}\ 3d_{3/2}$	$\sum Eu^{2+} + Eu^{2+}$ $3d_{5/2}\ 3d_{3/2}$	Eu^{2+}	Eu^{3+}
N_2	3944.4	4333.1	4263.9	4097.2	8208.3	8430.3	50.7	49.4
Air	2393.3	3256.9	2419.1	2952.4	4812.4	6209.3	56.3	47.6
N_2/H_2	1879.7	3097.9	1458.8	2271.4	3338.5	5369.3	61.6	38.3

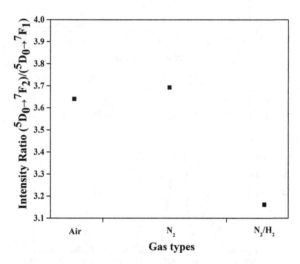

Fig. 5. PL Intensity Ratio $(^5D_0 \rightarrow {}^7F_2) / (^5D_0 \rightarrow {}^7F_1)$ of gehlenite: Eu phosphor glassy powder treated in air, N_2 and N_2/H_2 gases treated.

The significance of $(^5D_0 \rightarrow {}^7F_2) / (^5D_0 \rightarrow {}^7F_1)$ offers how far the Eu^{3+} ion deviates from the Centro symmetry, i.e., a measure of the site symmetry of Eu^{3+} ion. The intensity ratio of N_2 treated where greater, than air and N_2/H_2 treated. This larger in intensity ratio which results better color purity for red emissions [28]. The ratio was relatively the similar in air and N_2 treated, but at N_2/H_2 treated lower intensity ratio. Thus, the environment around the Eu^{3+} ions was changed under different atmospheric conditions. In other words, the asymmetric ratio increases with decreasing the degree of distortion from the inversion symmetry of the local environment of Eu^{3+} ions [27]. This effect can be explained by the preparation method in which the sample was conducted under air and N_2 treated less reduction takes place. However, sample conducted under the N_2/H_2 treated, europium is mainly in the form of divalent in which reduction were realized compare to the air and N_2 treated.

4   Conclusions

Photoluminescence properties of europium doped gehlenite have been measured at a different excitation wave length in which the prepared sample in air treated, N_2 treated and N_2/H_2 treated were successfully studied. The atomic composition of Eu^{3+} and Eu^{2+} ions were obtained from peak area with irrespective of binding energy. The photoluminescence properties of both Eu^{3+} and Eu^{2+} ions in phosphor glassy powder shows red and blue emission were obtained at different excitation wavelength respectively, which gives a crucial hint on developing new phosphors with different rational designs in the future. The XPS results revealed that the europium (Eu^{3+}) ion doped gehlenite phosphor with N_2 treated > air treated > N_2/H_2 treated shows better red emission intensity. Whereas, for blue emissions the effect of atmospheric gases i.e., N2 treated < air treated < N_2/H_2 treated was obtained for Eu^{2+} ion doped gehlenite phosphor. The intensity ratio (R) in N_2 treated was the highest values compare to air treated and N_2/H_2 treated.

Acknowledgments. This work was supported by Adama Science and Technology University and financial support from the National Science Council of Taiwan.

Conflicts of Interest: The authors declare no conflict of interest.

References

1. Tiwari, G., Brahme, N., Bisen, D.P., Sao, S.K., Sharma, R.: Thermoluminescence and Mechanoluminescence properties of UV-Irradiated $Ca_2Al_2SiO_7$:Ce^{3+}, Tb^{3+} Phosphor. Phys. Proc. **76**, 53–58 (2015). https://doi.org/10.1016/j.phpro.2015.10.010
2. Luo, Y., Xia, Z.: Effect of partial nitridation on the structure and luminescence properties of melilite-type $Ca_2Al_2SiO_7$:Eu^{2+} phosphor. Opt. Mater. **36**(11), 1874–1878 (2014). https://doi.org/10.1016/j.optmat.2014.03.032
3. Jiang, W., Fu, R., Gu, X., Zhang, P., Coşgun, A.: A red-emitting phosphor $LaSr_2AlO_5$: Eu^{3+}/ Eu^{2+} prepared under oxidative and reductive atmospheres. J. Lumin. **157**, 46–52 (2015). https://doi.org/10.1016/j.jlumin.2014.07.018
4. Bernardo, E., Fiocco, L., Prnová, A., Klement, R., Galusek, D.: Gehlenite:Eu^{3+} phosphors from a silicone resin and nano-sized fillers. Opt. Mater. **36**(7), 1243–1249 (2014). https://doi.org/10.1016/j.optmat.2014.03.007
5. Sahu, I.P., Bisen, D., Brahme, N., Tamrakar, R.K.: Enhanced luminescence performance of $Sr_2 MgSi_2 O_7$: Eu^{2+} blue long persistence phosphor by co-doping with Ce^{3+} ions. J. Mater. Sci. Mater. Electron. **27**(1), 554–569 (2016)
6. Peng, M., Hong, G.: Reduction from Eu^{3+} to Eu^{2+} in $BaAl_2O_4$: Eu phosphor prepared in an oxidizing atmosphere and luminescent properties of $BaAl_2O_4$: Eu. J. Lumin. **127**(2), 735–740 (2007)
7. Bouchouicha, H., et al.: Synthesis and luminescent properties of Eu^{3+}/Eu^{2+} co-doped calcium aluminosilicate glass–ceramics. J. Lumin. **169**, 528–533 (2016). https://doi.org/10.1016/j.jlumin.2014.11.054

8. Shao-Ju, S., Yu-Chien, L., Shih-Heng, L., Chin-Yang, Y.: Correlation of morphology and photoluminescence properties of gehlenite: Eu glassy phosphors. Int. J. Appl. Ceram. Technol. **14**(1), 56–62 (2017). https://doi.org/10.1111/ijac.12616

9. Lopez-Iscoa, P., et al.: Effect of partial crystallization on the structural and luminescence properties of Er^{3+}-doped phosphate glasses. Materials **10**(5), 473 (2017)

10. Penghui, Y., Xue, Y., Hongling, Y., Jiang, T., Dacheng, Z., Jianbei, Q.: Effects of crystal field on photoluminescence properties of $Ca_2Al_2SiO_7$: Eu^{2+} phosphors. J. Rare Earths **30** (12), 1208–1212 (2012)

11. Wiglusz, R., Pazik, R., Lukowiak, A., Strek, W.: Synthesis, structure, and optical properties of LiEu $(PO_3)_4$ nanoparticles. Inorg. Chem. **50**(4), 1321–1330 (2011)

12. Huang, J., Loriers, J., Porcher, P., Teste de Sagey, G., Caro, P., Levy-Clement, C.: Crystal field effect and paramagnetic susceptibility of $Na_5Eu(MoO_4)_4$ and $Na_5Eu(WO_4)_4$. J. Chem. Phys. **80**(12), 6204–6209 (1984)

13. Cai, J., Pan, H., Wang, Y.: Luminescence properties of red-emitting Ca_2 Al_2 SiO_7: Eu^{3+} nanoparticles prepared by sol-gel method. Rare Met. **30**(4), 374 (2011)

14. Grandhe, B.K., et al.: Reduction of Eu^{3+} to Eu^{2+} in $NaCaPO_4$: Eu phosphors prepared in a non-reducing atmosphere. J. Alloy. Compd. **509**(30), 7937–7942 (2011). https://doi.org/10.1016/j.jallcom.2011.05.044

15. Xie, H., Lu, J., Guan, Y., Huang, Y., Wei, D., Seo, H.J.: Abnormal reduction, $Eu^{3+} \rightarrow Eu^{2+}$, and defect centers in Eu^{3+}-doped pollucite, $CsAlSi_2O_6$, prepared in an oxidizing atmosphere. Inorg. Chem. **53**(2), 827–834 (2013)

16. Wu, H., Hu, Y., Ju, G., Chen, L., Wang, X., Yang, Z.: Photoluminescence and thermoluminescence of Ce^{3+} and Eu^{2+} in $Ca_2Al_2SiO_7$ matrix. J. Lumin. **131**(12), 2441–2445 (2011). https://doi.org/10.1016/j.jlumin.2011.06.024

17. Yang, P., Yu, X., Yu, H., Jiang, T., Zhou, D., Qiu, J.: Effects of crystal field on photoluminescence properties of $Ca_2Al_2SiO_7$:Eu^{2+} phosphors. J. Rare Earths **30**(12), 1208–1212 (2012). https://doi.org/10.1016/S1002-0721(12)60207-5

18. Teixeira, V.C., Montes, P.J.R., Valerio, M.E.G.: Structural and optical characterizations of $Ca_2Al_2SiO_7$:Ce^{3+}, Mn^{2+} nanoparticles produced via a hybrid route. Optical Mater. **36**(9), 1580–1590 (2014). https://doi.org/10.1016/j.optmat.2014.04.037

19. MG, L., Shi-Chang, Z., JG, V.: Ceramic powder synthesis by spray pyrolysis. J. Am. Ceram. Soc. **76** (11), 2707–2726 (1993). https://doi.org/10.1111/j.1151-2916.1993.tb04007.x

20. Kang, Y.C., Chung, Y.S., Park, S.B.: Preparation of YAG: Europium red phosphors by spray pyrolysis using a filter- expansion aerosol generator. J. Am. Ceram. Soc. **82**(8), 2056–2060 (1999)

21. Wang, W.-N., Widiyastuti, W., Ogi, T., Lenggoro, I.W., Okuyama, K.: Correlations between crystallite/particle size and photoluminescence properties of submicrometer phosphors. Chem. Mater. **19**(7), 1723–1730 (2007)

22. Kang, Y.C., Park, S.B.: Morphology of (YxGd1-x) BO_3: Eu phosphor particles prepared by spray pyrolysis from aqueous and colloidal solutions. Jpn. J. Appl. Phys. **38**(12B), L1541 (1999)

23. Park, Y.J., Kim, Y.J.: Blue emission properties of Eu-doped $CaAl_2O_4$ phosphors synthesized by a flux method. Mater. Sci. Eng., B **146**(1), 84–88 (2008). https://doi.org/10.1016/j.mseb.2007.07.048

24. Sohn, J.R., Kang, Y.C., Park, H.D.: Morphological control of Y_2O_3: Eu phosphor particles by adding polymeric precursors in spray pyrolysis. Jpn. J. Appl. Phys. **41**(5R), 3006 (2002)

25. Kang, Y.C., Park, H.D., Park, S.B.: The effect of metal chloride fluxes on the properties of phosphor particles in spray pyrolysis. Jpn. J. Appl. Phys. **39**(12B), L1305 (2000)

26. Wanjun, T., Donghua, C.: Photoluminescent Properties of ABaPO$_4$: Eu(A= Na,K) Phosphors Prepared by the Combustion-Assisted Synthesis Method. J. Am. Ceram. Soc. **92**(5), 1059–1061 (2009)
27. Koparkar, K., Bajaj, N., Omanwar, S.: Effect of calcination temperature on structural and optical properties of europium (III) doped SrO–Y$_2$O$_3$ phosphor. J. Mater. Sci. Mater. Electron. **26**(5), 2748–2753 (2015)
28. Park, K., Kim, H., Hakeem, D.A.: Effect of host composition and Eu^{3+} concentration on the photoluminescence of aluminosilicate (Ca,Sr)$_2$Al$_2$SiO$_7$:Eu^{3+} phosphors. Dyes Pigm. **136** (70), 77 (2017). https://doi.org/10.1016/j.dyepig.2016.08.022

Energy Science, Engineering and Policy

Investigation of Solar Chimney Power Plant and Experimental Analysis of Energy Yield from Small Size Draft Tube and Solar Collector

Ashenafi Tesfaye Bicks[1](✉), Solomon Tesfamariam Teferi[2], and Tewodros Walle Mekonnen[2]

[1] Departmnet of Mechanical Engineering, University of Gondar, Gondar, Ethiopia
[2] Addis Ababa Institute of Technology, Addis Ababa University, Addis Ababa, Ethiopia

Abstract. The Solar chimney power plant is a naturally driven power generating system. In this research, a solar chimney power plant is studied by developing an experimental model for a maximum power output of 32 W. The performance of large-scale electricity generation from the plant is predicted by analyzing different geometrical configurations. CFD model is used to study flow characteristics of air temperature inside the collector. Then, for 30 kW power output, the selected optimized dimensions are: chimney height, collector diameter, chimney diameter, and collector height are estimated to be 15 m, 15 m, 0.2 m, and 0.2 m respectively. For a fixed chimney diameter and collector height, an increase in height of the chimney raises the power output until it reaches the designed optimum height, an increase in chimney height beyond the optimum value will result in an energy loss due to lower total pressure difference caused by frictional pressure rise. The experimental model developed is scaled down to a chimney height of 3 m and collector diameter of 2 m with a maximum power output of 32 W. In the experiment, the characteristics of the temperature inside the collector are studied by varying the height of the collector above the ground. The temperature difference between collector exit and collector inlet from the comparison of experimental and simulated modeled are in good agreement. It was found that the implementation of a solar chimney power plant is technically feasible for the generation of electrical energy up to the desired potential by adjusting chimney height and collector diameter.

Keywords: Solar energy · Solar chimney power plant · Solar collector · Optimum chimney height · Collector height

1 Background

The cause for the serious environmental problem is primarily an increase in global fossil fuel consumption for electrical energy generation and other needs. According to the study by different experts, it was predicted that if we do not shift the source of energy generation to a cleaner source, climate change will cause a significant problem

M. L. Berihun (Ed.): ICAST 2021, LNICST 412, pp. 391–412, 2022.
https://doi.org/10.1007/978-3-030-93712-6_27

in our universe. Today, fossil fuels are the primary fuel source and are still widely used for major electricity generation around the world. According to the report of (Renewable and Agency 2017), the energy consumption for electricity production worldwide is projected to increase up to 2040 G.C.

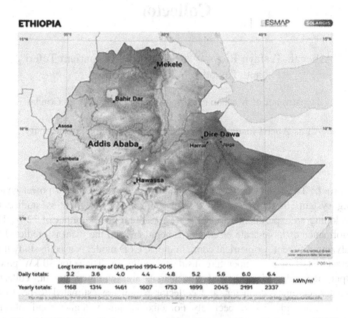

Fig. 1. Ethiopian Solar resource map (Renewable and Agency 2017)

Clean Electrical energy can be generated by a different mechanism using solar energy and other natural resources worldwide. For example, in developing countries like Ethiopia, it is estimated that a daily solar radiation potential varies between (3.2–6.4) kwh/m^2 as shown in Fig. 1. However, based on a report by (Renewable et al. 2012) electrical energy generation majority share (92.5%) comes from hydro-power, which only covers 38% of the total energy demand of the population. It can be concluded that the conversion of solar energy resources into useful energy is at its primary stage.

The solar chimney power plant is a form of solar energy conversion system, which is studied by several researchers in various countries but the first pilot plant of the solar chimney power plant was built in Spain in 1982. The project was functional for more than 8 years but it was considered inefficient as a result different researcher has conducted an experiment and made an improvement in its performance (Gannon and Backström 2003). The solar chimney power plant is a naturally driven power generating system. It converts solar energy first into thermal energy then into kinetic energy finally into electrical energy. It combines the concept of solar air collectors and a central updraft chimney to generate a solar-induced convective flow which drives turbines to generate electricity. Electricity generation from solar radiation by air convection works when the air beneath the collector gets heated, its density decreases. The buoyance force and the pressure difference between the top and base of the chimney push the air upward. Part of this heat is converted to mechanical energy by the axial flow turbine mounted at the base of the chimney.

In 2010, (Koonsrisuk et al. 2010), Studied the effect of tower area change in a solar chimney power plant. The study showed that the tower area change affects the efficiency and the mass flow rate through the plant. The velocity increases at the top of a convergent tower, the mass flow rate remains similar to that of a constant area tower. For a divergent tower design, velocity increases near the base of the chimney, and the maximum kinetic energy also occurs at the base of the chimney.

In 2010 (Hamdan 2010), studied an analytical model. In the analysis, it is considered that a simplified Bernoulli's equation combined with fluid dynamics and ideal gas equation using EES solver to predict the performance of the solar chimney power plant. The study showed that the height and diameter of the solar chimney are the most important design variables for solar chimney power plants. However, the collector area has a small effect on second-law efficiency but a strong effect on harvested energy. (Ming et al. 2016), established a simple analysis of the air flowing through the solar chimney power plant and also studied the thermodynamic cycle of the solar chimney power plant. They also developed a mathematical model of ideal and actual cycle efficiencies for medium-sized and large-sized solar chimney power plants. Brayton cycle corresponding to medium-scale solar chimney power generation system is 1.33% and 0.3% respectively, while the ideal efficiency of large scale SC system with chimney height 1000 m is 3.33%, while the maximum value of the actual efficiencies is 0.9%. The results from their work were used as a theoretical guideline for designing and building a commercial-size solar chimney power plant in China.

In 2019 (Fallah and Valipour 2019), investigated the performance of solar chimney power plants with and without artificial roughness using a three-dimensional simulation. In the analysis, without artificial roughness, the airflow in the collector accelerates gradually and runs centripetally to the base of the chimney with energy being absorbed from the ground surface of the collector, and average velocity at the base of the chimney reaches 9.25 m/s. Also, the power of the SCPP is equal to 46.1 kW. But with artificial roughness, the negative influences are evident, creating friction in the flow path, the airflow at the chimney bottom is deflected with an average velocity of less than 9.25 m/s and it reaches 8.88 m/s and the power is reduced by about 5%. It is found that the artificial roughness in SCPP improves heat transfer, but reduces velocity; therefore, there is an optimal dimension and location for it. Geometrically, the location of this roughness near the collector entrance has a better performance than other locations, but this change of locations has little impact on the performance of SCPP.

In a solar chimney power plant system turbine is the main component which will be used as the power-producing unit. The main purpose of the turbine is to convert the kinetic energy of heated air into mechanical energy using the turbine rotors. To have easier installation and maintenance turbines are usually placed at the base of the chimney. The turbine of SCPP is usually an axial flow type turbine. The operation and design of modern wind turbines could be applied to the solar chimney but in comparison, solar chimney turbines have a much higher energy extraction per unit flow and are more similar to gas turbines. Solar chimney turbines have a greater pressure drop than wind turbines and require more blades but not as many as gas turbines. It was found that wind turbine blades can be treated accurately as individual airfoils. This is not the case in the solar chimney turbine due to the higher blade solidity (blade chord to pitch ratio). The pitch angle of the blades can be adjusted like wind turbines but due to the flow being enclosed in an SCPP like a gas turbine, the turbine may have radial inflow guide vanes. The blades required for the solar chimney turbine are of low solidity when compared to gas-turbine turbo machinery but they cannot be treated accurately as single blades like those of wind turbines (von Backström and Gannon 2004).

Under this study, a small-scale solar chimney power plant is designed and experimentally investigated for the generation of 30 kW electrical energy. The optimum geometry for the desired output is analyzed by varying collector diameter, chimney height, and chimney diameter. The experimental model is designed to validate the simulation conducted using the CFD model. The developed model is scaled down to a chimney height of 3 m and collector diameter of 2 m for simplicity during an investigation. Using the CFD model the analyzed power output for a chimney height of 3 m, collector diameter of 2 m, 0.16 m chimney diameter, and 0.17 collector height from the ground provides 32 W power output which is 6% higher than the actual experiment of the same geometrical size. The measured data in the experimental result is 93.75% reliable with a deviation of 6.25% relative to the simulated result. The variation is mainly caused by the weather condition instability since the draught occurred in 2015 (USAID 2016). As a result recorded value between the CFD and experimental model is maximum since during the testing process the solar radiation intensity is not steady as anticipated in the historical data Moreover analysis is conducted for the prediction of maximum power output from this plant within the geometrical size of chimney height up to 60 m and collector diameter up to 25 m by fixed chimney diameter at 0.2 m and collector height at 0.2 m.

2   Material and Methods

a. Design of Solar Chimney Power Plant: A Case Study

The study of a solar chimney power plant is performed by combining, a theoretical design of technical parameters and simulation of the main component using CFD tools. To select a geometrical configuration for desired 30 kW power out, MATLAB software is used as an optimization tool. For the analysis of temperature and thermal characteristics inside the collector, ENERGY 2D is used as computational fluid dynamics (CFD) tool, it is also used to simulate the temperature variation in all dimensions of Collector sides. The actual prototype shown in Fig. 2 is designed to generate power out of 32 W maximum. The axial flow turbine is installed in between the collector exit and chimney inlet and the generator is placed at the ground beneath the turbine.

Fig. 2. Experimental Solar chimney power plant at the test site.

For the design of the solar chimney power plant, a mathematical equation is developed by considering the basic concept of conservation of energy, thermodynamic, momentum, and continuity equation. The collector material used in the experimental model is polyvinyl chloride (PVC) with optical property shown in Table 1.

Table 1. Optical property of polyvinyl chloride collector material

Material	Symbol	Value
Collector absorptivity (PVC)	αc	0.3
Collector transmissivity	T_c	0.7
Collector roughness length	e_{rc}	0.002 m
Emissivity of canopy	ε	0.85

i. Air standard cycle of SCPP cycle and the surrounding air expansion

In a solar chimney power plant (SCPP) cycle analysis compression takes place in the environment as shown in Fig. 3, this makes the cycle different from the gas turbine cycle where the compression takes place in the system. In an ideal gas turbine power, the expansion process entirely takes place inside the turbine. However, in solar chimney power plant expansion takes place first in the turbine in processes 2–3, and the remaining takes along the chimney system. Cooling process 4–5 is not inside the power plant. The exhaust air is mixed with the ambient air at state 5 and cooled back to state 1 as shown in Fig. 4.

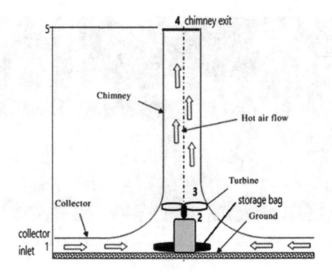

Fig. 3. Solar chimney power plant with generator and storage unit.

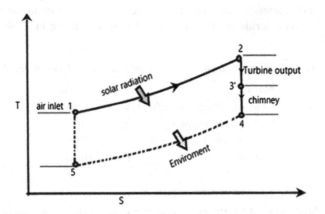

Fig. 4. T-S diagram of solar chimney power plant air standard cycle

The total heat input is;

$$Q_i = \dot{m} \times (h_2 - h_1) = \dot{m}C_P(T_2 - T_1) \tag{1}$$

The Expansion energy to lift the air to state 4:

$$P_{lift} = \dot{m} \times g \times H_{chim} \tag{2}$$

The energy exchange is isentropic since the friction and heat transfer are negligible. Then the value of enthalpy (Δh) can be equated to the amount of air that has descended in the atmosphere after having been cooled from chimney exit temperature. So, the enthalpy change in the chimney becomes;

$$\Delta h = g \times \Delta H_{chim} = Cp \times (T_1 - T_5) \tag{3}$$

Then the turbine shaft power becomes;

$$P_{shaft} = \dot{m} \times Cp \times (T2 - T3) - \dot{m} \times Cp \times (T_1 - T_5) \tag{4}$$

ii. Momentum equation

Figure 5 shows the instantaneous fluid flow through the area beneath the collector.

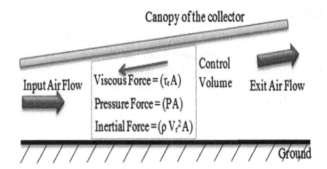

Fig. 5. The force that acts inside the bottom of the collector

Balance of forces of airflow inside the collector can be obtained by applying Newton's second law for partial control volume:

$$\frac{\partial(\rho V_r^2)}{\partial r} = -\frac{\partial P}{\partial r} + \frac{\partial \tau_r}{\partial r} + \rho g \tag{5}$$

iii. Continuity equation

The continuity equation of the collector for radial flow shown in Fig. 6 is written as;

$$(\rho_1 V_r A_{COLL})in = (\rho_2 V_r A_{COLL})out \tag{6}$$

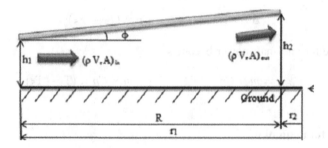

Fig. 6. Radial section of the collector

iv. Energy Conservation

The total energy per area of the collector shown in Fig. 7 is the sum of;
Heat gain into the glazing = heat lost from the glazing
Heat gain into the absorber = heat lost from the absorber
Heat gain into the fluid = heat lost from the fluid
Heat gain into the ground = heat lost from the ground

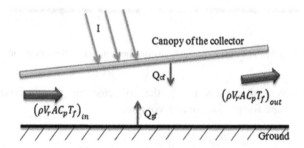

Fig. 7. Energy balance diagram for SCPP system.

In a solar chimney power plant, the flow of the fluid is due to natural convection. Natural convection is when the fluid is driven by local density difference while mixed convection flows occur when the convection of fluid is driven by both a pressure gradient and buoyancy forces. The resistance diagram for all heat transfer modes in the solar chimney power plant system is shown in Fig. 8.

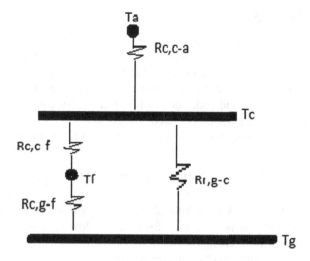

Fig. 8. Resistance diagram for all heat transfer modes in SCPP

In the CFD analysis, the model is investigated by the characteristics of the fluid flow inside the collector shown in Fig. 9. In the simulations, steady-state analysis is considered by creating an environment of updraft solar chimney power plant as per the design.

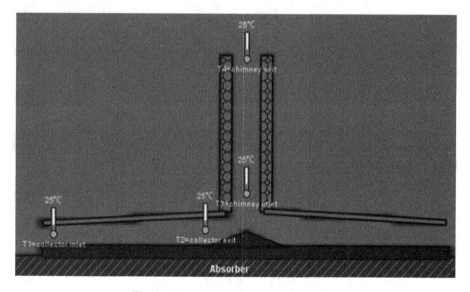

Fig. 9. Thermal boundary condition setting

b. **Design methodology**

To calculate the available power output from the plant an assumption for pressure ratio between chimney inlet, (P3) and collector exit (P2) will be made initially as, P_3/P_2. The collector inlet pressure P1 is assumed as Patm = 0.77 bar (atmospheric pressure at inlet @$T_1 = 25\,°C$). This power plant is open to the environment, pressure variation between the collector inlet and collector exit is neglected. By considering the number stationed in Fig. 3 all the parameters are equated as follows.

The collector exit temperature is found from the energy equation;

$$q''A_{gz} = \frac{1}{2}\dot{m} \times \left(v_2^2 - v_1^2\right) + \dot{m} \times Cp(T_2 - T_1) \tag{7}$$

According to (Koonsrisuk and Chitsomboon 2013) frictional effect is ignored since the velocity in this region is quite low. Because the flow is in the very low Mach number regime, the kinetic energy contribution can be neglected.

Then the above equation will be re-written as:

$$q''A_{gz} = \dot{m}Cp(T_2 - T_1) \tag{8}$$

This shows that the mass flow rate is inversely proportional to the collector temperature rise, Since the mass flow rate is assumed to be constant, then collector area can be found from (Koonsrisuk and Chitsomboon 2013) equation.

$$T_2 = T_1 + \frac{q''A_{gz}}{\dot{m}Cp} \tag{9}$$

Heat flux q'' incident on the surface of the glazing, with an overall heat loss coefficient value of: $U_t = 5\ W/m^2K$

$$q'' = (\alpha \times \tau) \times G_r - U_t \times \Delta T \tag{10}$$

The work extraction process at the turbine is assumed to be an isentropic process, Temperature of air at the entrance of chimney or turbine exit (T_3) can be calculated from the equation below;

$$T_3 = T_2\left(P_3/P_2\right)^{\frac{\gamma-1}{\gamma}} \tag{11}$$

Then the pressure P4 at the chimney exit can be found from the following equation;

$$P_4 = P_1\left(1 - \left(\frac{g*H_{chim}}{Cp*T_1}\right)^{Cp/R}\right) \tag{12}$$

From the ideal gas constant the density of each state can be written as;

$$\rho = \frac{P}{RT} \tag{13}$$

To determine the density at the chimney outlet the temperature at that state should be known; According to the (Backström et al. 2000) equation of temperature at chimney exit T_4 becomes;

$$T_4 = T_3 - g \times \frac{H_{chim}}{Cp} \tag{14}$$

Now recall that the above parameter is computed by the assumed value of pressure P_3, so this result has to be validated by equation developed by (Backström et al.2000) for actual P_3.

Pressure at the chimney inlet or turbine outlet;

$$P_{3actual} = P_4 + 0.5 \times (\rho_3 + \rho_4) \times g \times H_{chim} + \left(\frac{\dot{m}}{A_{gz}}\right)\left(\frac{1}{\rho_4} - \frac{1}{\rho_3}\right) \tag{15}$$

The tower (chimney) converts the heat flow produced by the collector into kinetic energy (convection current) and potential energy (pressure drop at the turbine). The density difference caused by the temperature rise in the collector works as a driving force.

The lighter column of air in the tower is connected with the surrounding atmosphere at the base (inside the collector) and the top of the tower, and thus acquires lift. The pressure difference Δp_{tot} is produced between tower base (collector outlet) and the ambient;

The pressure difference can be written as;

$$\Delta p_{tot} = g \times \int_0^{H_{chim}} (\rho_2 - \rho_4)dH \tag{16}$$

The pressure difference can be re-written as;

$$\Delta p_{tot} = g \times (\rho_2 - \rho_4) \times H_{chim} \tag{17}$$

The useful driving pressure is;

$$P_t = \Delta p_{tot} - P_f \tag{18}$$

Where P_f = frictional pressure drops.

Then the velocity at the chimney entrance V_2 can be found from (Zhou et al. 2010);

$$V_2 = \frac{G(\tau \times \alpha) \times A_{gz} - \beta(\Delta T_a \times A_{gz})}{\rho_{air} A_{chim} C_p (\Delta T)} \tag{19}$$

Then, $\Delta T_a = (T_{pm} - T_1)$.

i. Mean plate temperature (T_{pm})

$$T_{pm} = T_1 - \frac{Q_{useful}}{A_{gz} \times \beta \times F_R} \times (1 - F_R) \tag{20}$$

ii. Collector Heat removal factor (F_R)

$$F_R = \frac{\dot{m} \times C_P}{A_{gz} \times \beta} \left(1 - \exp \left(\frac{A_{gz} \times \beta \times F'}{\dot{m} \times C_P} \right) \right) \tag{21}$$

The theoretical **power extracted** by the turbine can be determined from the energy equation and Gibbs relation from classical thermodynamics;

$$P_{out} = \eta_{tur} \times P_t \times V_2 \times A_{gz} \tag{22}$$

So, to calculate the theoretical power output using Eq. (22), the solution procedure is shown in Fig. 10 has to be followed. The power output from this plant is mainly dependant on the area of the collector, chimney diameter, and chimney height so it can be seen that increasing the area of the collector will have a direct impact on power output, so the longer the collector diameter the higher the power output, the total pressure P_t is also the effect of chimney height and diameter so an increase in two parameters will result in increased power output. The atmospheric pressure is assumed to be below 1 bar at the collector exit or chimney inlet (P_2) due to the shape of a low-pressure trough (dome). The pressure is lower at this point due to warm air advection. At the collector exit and chimney inlet, the warm air is less dense than the air replacing it, as a result, surface pressure at P_2 will fall below 1 bar. The pressure at collector inlet pressure P_1 is assumed to be the same as the pressure in the collector exit for simplicity during analysis.

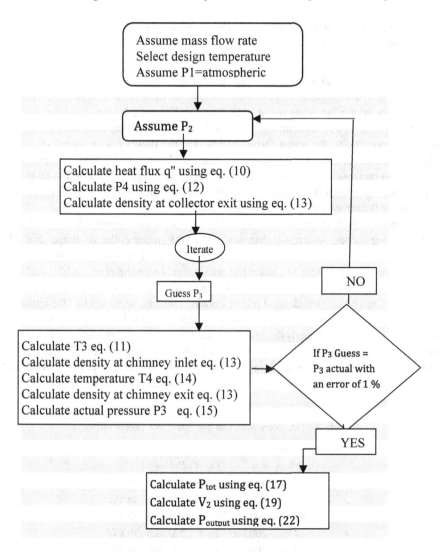

Fig. 10. Solar chimney power output solution procedure

3   Result and Discussion

In this study, the optimum geometrical size of the solar chimney power plant main component is selected at different collector diameter, chimney height that provides maximum power output. In the analysis, the influence of different parameters on the power output has been investigated as shown in the following sections.

3.1 Optimization of Solar Chimney Power Plant for Different Geometrical Size

I. Power Output vs Diameter of Glazing (Collector)

In the analysis, the variation of power output with an increase in a collector diameter is simulated by fixing the diameter of a chimney at 200 mm, the height of the collector from the ground at 200 mm, and varying the height of the chimney from 5 m–15 m as shown. According to the result shown in Fig. 11, the power output increases linearly with an increase in collector diameter and chimney height. In the investigation, it was seen that an increase in diameter of the collector creates a good condition to an inlet air to gain more heat until it reaches to chimney inlet since the longer air it takes the air to reach the collector exit the more it gets heated.

The analysis conducted was used to predict the optimum geometrical size for the 30 kW power output. As a result chimney height of 9 m and collector diameter of 22 m is optimum size as shown in Table 2. It should be noted that collector diameter should be as minimum as possible to reduce the area coverage by the plant. Additionally, the analysis showed that using the indicated fixed-parameter a chimney height must be more than 6 m to reach the desired power output. This can be varied by (Dehghani and Mohammadi 2014); they presented an optimal geometrical selection based on need and population size. In the analysis, the simulated Scatter distribution of the collector diameter with population, accordingly for a population size of the optimal range of collector diameter is between 200 and 1200 m while the allowable range is between 100 and 1500 m at an indicated other fixed geometrical area and total cost.

Table 2. Geometry selection for 30kW for power output

Options	Geometry				Power(kW)
	Hchim	hc1	Dcoll	Dchim	
1	3 m	200 mm	30 m	200 mm	15 kW
2	6 m	200 mm	28 m	200 mm	30 kW
3	9 m	200 mm	22 m	200 mm	30 kW
4	12 m	200 mm	16 m	200 mm	30 kW
5	15 m	200 mm	13 m	200 mm	30 kW

II. Height of Chimney Versus Power Output

The result shown in Fig. 12 was conducted by varying the height of the chimney and diameter of the collector while fixing the diameter of the chimney and collector height from the ground at 200 mm each. The result shown in Fig. 12 illustrates the optimum chimney height that gives the maximum power output for a certain collector diameter, chimney height, and collector height from the ground. For the case study under consideration, for simplicity and less collector area coverage, option three (3) is selected for the application of 30 kW power output, with a chimney height of 17 m and 17 m of collector diameter as shown in Table 4. Moreover, by keeping the fixed parameters and increasing the chimney height up to 45 m and the collector diameter of 25m more than 350 kW power output can be achieved as shown in Fig. 11. However, increasing the chimney height above 45 m will result in power loss caused by the total frictional pressure drop in the chimney (draft tube) system.

It can be verified based on the investigation carried out by (Asnaghi and Ladjevardi 2012); they conducted an investigation in energy generation from the solar chimney power plant at 4 selected regions in Iran. According to their analysis, the considered solar chimney power plant is predicted to produce electrical power from 175 MWh–265 MWh in different months of the year. In the analysis, it is assumed that the turbine can create a 120 Pa pressure difference with an overall conversion efficiency of 4%.

Table 3. Chimney height selection for 30 kW

Options	Geometry				Power (kW)
	Dchim	Dcoll	Hchim	hc1	
1	200 mm	5 m	60 m	200 mm	21 kW
2	200 mm	10 m	28 m	200 mm	30 kW
3	200 mm	17 m	17 m	200 mm	30 kW
4	200 mm	20 m	9 m	200 mm	30 kW
5	200 mm	25 m	7 m	200 mm	30 kW

3.2   CFD Analysis of Solar Chimney Power Plant with Same Geometrical Size to the Experiment

a) Height of Chimney vs Power Output

For specific geometrical setup listed in Table 3, an increase in the height of the chimney above 62 m at fixed collector height from the ground (hc1 = 170 mm), the diameter of the chimney (Dchim = 160 mm), the diameter of the collector (Dcoll = 2 m) will result in a decrease in power output generation, the decrease in the power is caused by the domination of a frictional pressure along with the chimney(draft tube). When a chimney height reaches 107 m the power output equal to zero means frictional pressure loss is equal to useful driving pressure. Therefore, for the indicated fixed parameters shown the optimum chimney height for useful energy production is 58 m as shown in Fig. 13.

Table 4: Geometry specification for a model developed

No.	Parameter	Value	Symbol
1	Chimney height	3 m	H_{chim}
2	Collector diameter	2 m	D_{coll}
3	Chimney diameter	0.16 m	D_{chim}
4	Collector height from the ground	0.170–0.4 m	h_{c1}

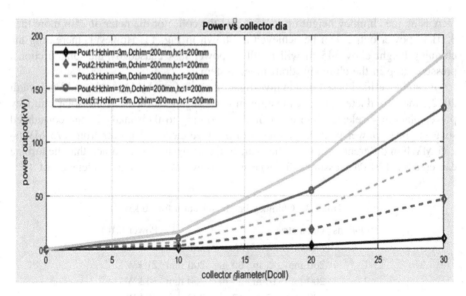

Fig. 11. collector diameter vs power output.

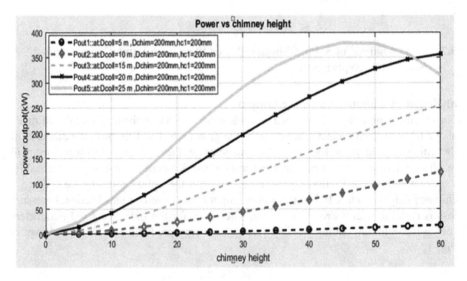

Fig. 12. Chimney height versus power output

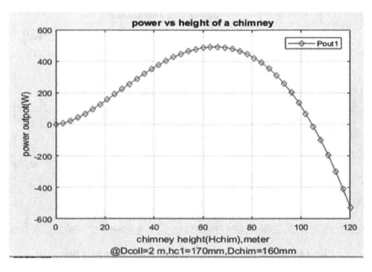

Fig. 13. Power versus chimney height for experiment

The experimental study under consideration, the developed model of the solar chimney power plant is constructed with 3-m chimney height and 2-m collector diameter (with an aperture area of 3.97 m^2) which provides a maximum power output of 32 W as shown in Fig. 13. Under a fixed chimney height from the ground (hc1 = 0.170 m), collector diameter (Dcoll = 2 m), and chimney diameter (Dchim = 0.16 m), the optimum chimney height is 52 m, an increase in chimney height beyond 52 m will result in power loss due to frictional pressure drop in a chimney.

b) Collector Diameter vs. Power Output

According to the analysis shown in Fig. 14, for a fixed chimney height from the ground (hc1 = 0.170 m,), collector diameter (Dcoll = 2 m) and chimney diameter (Dchim = 0.16 m, an increase in the diameter of the collector up to 3 m will increase the power output of the plant up to maximum power output of 9 kW. When the collector diameter exceeds more than 5 m, the rate of power production increases more than twice. As a result, it can be concluded that solar chimney power plant is more economical for larger-scale than small-scale electrical power generation.

c) Pressure (P$_t$) Versus Height of the Chimney

At a fixed parameter of chimney diameter, collector diameter, collector exit temperature, and height of the collector from the ground of 0.16 mm, 2 m, 315 K and 0.17 mm respectively. The useful pressure (Pt) increases until the chimney height reaches 58 m, beyond this height of the chimney the pressure tends to dramatically drop down due to

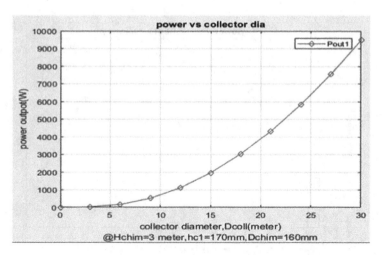

Fig. 14. Power output versus collector diameter idea that solar

the cumulative effect of frictional pressure loss. At a fixed parameter useful pressure is zero when the chimney height reaches 103 m this results in zero power output of the solar chimney power plant. So, the maximum allowable chimney height for this designed solar chimney power plant is 58-m unless if the is no change in the fixed-parameter as shown in Fig. 15.

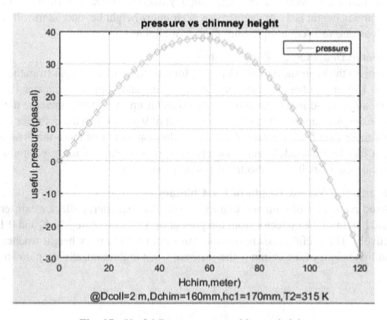

Fig. 15. Useful Pressure versus chimney height

3.3 Actual Prototype Experimental Result

In the experimental analysis the temperature is recorded for three consecutive days starting from May 21/18–May 23/18 for collector height of the 170 mm and 400 mm from the ground as shown in Fig. 16. An average was taken in every 5-min recording due to the instability of the weather condition. The maximum collector exit temperature reading of 41.7 °C was recorded at mid-day at 12 : 44 h. This can be validated by the experimental investigation conducted by (Lal et al. 2016), according to their study the maximum air temperature and velocity in the collector area are found to be 42.4 °C and 12.2 m/s respectively at 14:00 h of the typical day with approximately with the same geometrical size compared to prototype in this study. The maximum solar radiation is measured to be 820 W/m^2 at noon. The maximum ambient temperature is found to be 42 °C at 14:00 h of the typical day.

According to the measured data in this study, the collector exit temperature is relatively lower throughout the day for a collector height of 400 mm compared to a 170 mm collector height. So, it can be concluded that whenever the height of the collector from the ground is higher, the collector exit temperature will be lower at indicated fixed geometrical configurations, since the hotter air beneath the collector is taken away by local wind speed recorded during the experiment ranging above 6.8 m/s which is 22.2% above the yearly average wind speed of 5.3 m/s in Addis Ababa and the air with higher density flows over the collector instead of going beneath the collector.

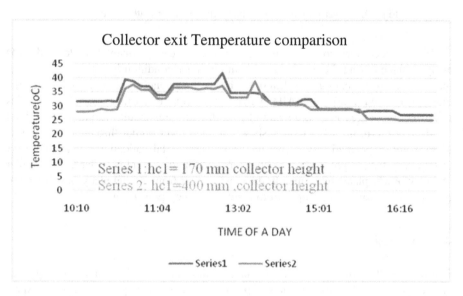

Fig. 16. Collector exit temperature comparison for different collector heights from the ground

I. Power Output vs Time of the Day

The validation for both simulated models and experimental result power output depends on the temperature difference throughout the day. So, the power output of the actual experiment varies from 8 W – 32 W, maximum power output was recorded during the mid-day at 12 : 44 PM and minimum at 15 : 19 PM. While, the simulated model power output varies from 20 W – 34 W, maximum at 13 : 20 PM and minimum at 10 : 10 AM as shown in Fig. 17.

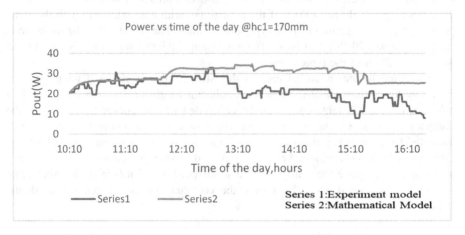

Fig. 17. Power output for an actual experiment vs mathematical model

The recorded variation is slightly different for the experimental model and CFD analysis since during the testing process the weather condition is not steady as anticipated in the historical data. In Ethiopia, the weather condition is not stable since the draught occurred in 2015 (USAID 2016). In the actual experiment, the characteristics of power output are rough as a result of collector exit temperature variation throughout the day. While in the CFD model, show that the power output throughout the day is uniform for a specified time of the day. So experimental validation is mandatory for this system before proceeding to the construction of medium to large scale solar chimney power plant, subsequently drawing a result from a CFD analysis will lead to over prediction of power output from a solar chimney power plant.

4 Conclusions

In this study, the experimental model and CFD model of the solar chimney power plant are developed for the investigation of power generation. Comparison between experimental result and CFD model shows a slight variation in maximum power output. In the CFD model total power output of 34 W is recorded for collector diameter (Dcoll = 2 m), chimney diameter (Dchim = 0.16 m), and collector height from 0.17 m up to 0.4 m above the ground, whereas in the experiment 32 W power output is recorded for same geometrical size. However in the daily power out the experimental model has an unsteady result relative to the CFD model. Additionally, optimization of the solar chimney power plant is investigated. Under a fixed chimney height from the ground (hc1 = 0.170 m,), collector diameter (Dcoll = 2 m), and chimney diameter (Dchim = 0.16 m), the optimum chimney height is 52 m, an increase in chimney height beyond 52 m will result in power loss due to frictional pressure drop in a chimney. Therefore, optimum chimney height for a desired potential has to be determined before the actual power plant's development. Moreover, the study investigates the power output for a larger size. For the design of 30 kW power output, the chimney height of 15 m and collector diameter of 15 m at a fixed chimney diameter of 0.2 m and 0.2m height of the collector from the ground is the optimum size. However, making any modification to the fixed parameters results in a new optimum chimney height and collector diameter. Increasing the collector diameter increases collector exit temperature resulting in an increased power output of the plant since the longer air takes to reach the collector exit the more it gains heat. So an increase in collector diameter will increase power output. The temperature measured from the experimental study and analytical model has similarities and variations throughout the day. It should be noted that the result from the analytical model may lead to over-prediction of power output from the plant, so it is important to test the potential of the system by developing an actual experimental model before developing a large-scale solar chimney power plant.

Nomenclature

Abbreviation and symbol	Abbreviation and symbol	Greek symbols
abs: absorber	Q : Heat gain $[W/m^2]$	α: absorption coefficient
E_{eff} : Effectiveness of coefficient	T_a : Temperature of the air inside the collector [K]	B: coefficient of volumetric thermal expansion,1/K
gz :glazing	T_{pm} : Mean plate temperature [K]	Δp :pressure drop, Pa
h_{c1} : Glazing height from ground at entrance[m]	Tp : Average temperature of a plate [K]	g : specific heat ratio
h_{c2} : Glazing height from ground at exit[m]	T_1 : Temperature at collector inlet	η: Efficiency
H : Chimney height[m]	T_2 : Temperature at collector exit	μ : dynamic coefficient
Δp_{tot} : Total pressure difference	T_3 : Temperature at chimney inlet	f:friction factor
P_1 : Pressure at collector inlet	T_4 : Temperature at chimney exit	v: viscosity
P_2 : pressure at collector exit	SCPP : solar chimney power plant	τ: transmittance
P_3 : pressure at chimney inlet	V : Flow velocity $[m/s]$	γ :isentropic constant
P_4 : pressure at chimney exit	Agz=area of the glazing	ρ = Air density, kg/m3
Rc,c-a: heat transfer from collector to ambient by convection	Vr:radial velocity of air(m/s)	
Rr,g-c: heat transfer from ground to collector by radiation	q'':Heat flux in W/m^2	
Rc,c-f: Heat transfer from collector to the fluid(air) by convection	Rc,g-f: heat transfer from ground to fluid by convention	

Acknowledgments. The authors of this manuscript are thankful to Addis Ababa institute of technology laboratory directorate for their cooperation in providing necessary tools during experiment development.

Author Contributions. Ashenafi Tesfaye is the main author of this manuscript under the guidance of Solomon T/Mariam and Tewodros walle. All authors read and approved the final manuscript.

Funding. It is to declare that no funding for research has been received during data collection, design, and experimentation from any funding agency.

Availability of Data and Material. The data sets supporting the conclusion of this article are included within the article.

Competing Interest. The authors declare that they have no competing interests.

References

Asnaghi, A., Ladjevardi, S.M.: Solar chimney power plant performance in Iran. Renew. Sustain. Energy Rev. **16**(5), 3383–3390 (2012). https://doi.org/10.1016/j.rser.2012.02.017

Backström, T.W.V., Gannon, A.J., Backstro, T.W.V.: Solar chimney cycle analysis with system loss and solar collector performance with system loss and solar (2000). https://doi.org/10.1115/1.1314379

Dehghani, S., Mohammadi, A.H.: Optimum dimension of geometric parameters of solar chimney power plants - A multi-objective optimization approach. Sol. Energy **105**, 603–612 (2014). https://doi.org/10.1016/j.solener.2014.04.006

Fallah, S.H., Valipour, M.S.: Evaluation of solar chimney power plant performance: the effect of artificial roughness of collector. Sol. Energy **188**(May), 175–184 (2019). https://doi.org/10.1016/j.solener.2019.05.065

Gannon, A.J., Backström, T.V.: Solar chimney turbine performance. J. Sol. Energy Eng.-Trans. Asme **125**, 101–106 (2003)

Hamdan, M.O.: Analysis of a solar chimney power plant in the Arabian Gulf region. Renew. Energy, 1–6 (2010). https://doi.org/10.1016/j.renene.2010.05.002

Koonsrisuk, A., Lorente, S., Bejan, A.: Constructal solar chimney configuration. Int. J. Heat Mass Transf. **53**(1–3), 327–333 (2010). https://doi.org/10.1016/j.ijheatmasstransfer.2009.09.026

Koonsrisuk, A., Chitsomboon, T.: Mathematical modeling of solar chimney power plants. Energy **51**, 314–322 (2013). https://doi.org/10.1016/j.energy.2012.10.038

Lal, S., Kaushik, S.C., Hans, R.: Experimental investigation and CFD simulation studies of a laboratory scale solar chimney for power generation. Sustain. Energy Technol. Assess. **13**, 13–22 (2016). https://doi.org/10.1016/j.seta.2015.11.005

Ming, T.Z., et al.: Simple analysis on thermal performance of solar chimney power generation systems. 9671(December) (2016) https://doi.org/10.1179/014426009X12519696923902

Renewable, I., Agency, E.: Renewable Energy Statistics 2017 Statistiques D ' Énergie Renouvelable 2017 Estadísticas De Energía (2017)

Renewable, U., Program, E., Final, D.: Federal Democratic Republic of Ethiopia Ministry of Water and Energy. January (2012)

USAID: El niño in ethiopia, a real-time review of impacts and responses 2015–2016, 28 March 2016. http://www.agri-learning-ethiopia.org/wp-content/uploads/2016/06/AKLDP-El-Nino-Review-March-2016.pdf

von Backström, T.W., Gannon, A.J.: Solar chimney turbine characteristics. Sol. Energy **76**(1–3), 235–241 (2004). https://doi.org/10.1016/j.solener.2003.08.009

Zhou, X., Xiao, B., Liu, W., Guo, X., Yang, J., Fan, J.: Comparison of classical solar chimney power system and combined solar chimney system for power generation and seaw (2010)

Design and Manufacturing of an Institutional Mirt Stove with Waste Heat Recovery System

Tesfaye Wondatir Mihretie[1]([⊠]) and Nigusse Mulugeta[2]

[1] School of Research and Post Graduate Studies Energy Center, Bahir Dar Institute of Technology, P.O.Box 26, Bahir Dar, Ethiopia
[2] Faculty of Mechanical and Industrial Engineering, Bahir Dar Institute of Technology, Bahir Dar University, P.O.Box 26, Bahir Dar, Ethiopia

Abstract. In the present study the performance of an institutional mirt stove with waste heat recovery system was designed and investigated. The waste heat recovery system is designed to utilize the heat of waste gases of institutional mirt stove as a source of energy for the purpose of injera baking on the secondary mitad. Beside to this main design improvement, adding fuel supporting structure like grates to allow ash falls through it and air to be entered under-neath the fuel and ash collection boxes and ash removal openings below each grate were provided. The performance of the improved stove was compared with that of the existing institutional mirt stove through controlled cooking test method. The result shows that the improved stove saved up to 16% fuel wood and 14% cooking time as compared to the existing institutional mirt stove. During the test a temperature of about 216.3 °C on the surface of a secondary mitad is achieved and injera is baked on this surface. Finally, the techno-economic analysis shows that the improved institutional mirt stove with waste heat recovery for injera baking system is economically feasible.

Keywords: Improved institutional mirt stove · Waste heat recovery system · Specific fuel consumption · Total cooking time

1 Introduction

Around 90% of the institutional kitchens in Ethiopia depend on biomass for cooking and baking, for which traditional stoves are often used [1]. The three-stone fireplace and many of institutions use pots or mitads which are inbuilt with cement, clay or bricks. However, both of these cooking or baking technologies are thermally as well as environmentally inefficient and hence create higher amount of waste heat and problems for users.

In the mid-1990s the World Bank assisted Cooking Efficiency Improvement and New Fuels Marketing Project implemented by the Ministry of Mines and Energy adopted the improved household "injera" (a traditional flat-bread) baking stove, also known as mirt stove [2]. In the mid-2010s, Energising Development (EnDev) implemented "Efficient stoves for bakeries in Ethiopia project" introduced a different version of modified mirt stoves. Small holding injera bakers use a single stove for their daily baking. Others, such as cooperative micro-enterprises use different versions of modified

M. L. Berihun (Ed.): ICAST 2021, LNICST 412, pp. 413–424, 2022.
https://doi.org/10.1007/978-3-030-93712-6_28

mirt stoves, which cluster two or more stoves so that they use a single chimney, with additional parts for collecting the smoke from the individual stoves, it is called Institutional mirt stove [3, 4].

Even if institutional mirt stove is among the improved designed stove, it has some drawbacks, like high amount of waste heat by the flue gas, difficulty of ash removing system and the radiative heat coming off the chimney cause the bakeries inconvenience, this is because, an experimental study [5] showed, the four-tipped star shape structure for chimney supporting is cracked in the areas where it received high temperature of exhaust flue gasses.

Baking is an essential way of preparing food from raw staple crops. Many different varieties of bread and pastry have emerged from regional traditions around the world. Baking involves very high temperatures (around 180–220 °C) and therefore requires a larger amount of thermal energy input than is required for cooking. The availability and price of fuel is therefore crucial for bakeries, as it constitutes their largest operating cost [6].

Effect of waste heat recovery on different types of biomass stoves was discussed and its impact on efficiency enhancement was determined [7].

Improving stoves is an effective way of improving the environment and serving communities.

Recent field tests have shown that improvements in air control and firebox design is currently the most effective and socially acceptable stove design modification. Waste heat utilization from flue gas is one option to increase the heat transfer efficiency of a stove [8].

Thus to reduce the problems associated with using institutional mirt stove, in this work institutional mirt stove with waste heat recovery system, which uses waste heat from the exhaust flue gases of institutional mirt stove as the source of energy for secondary injera baking oven is expected to include the following benefits: Saves money and time in acquiring fuel, reduced fuelwood consumption and total baking time.

This work focused on utilizing waste heat as a source of energy for injera baking oven (as recovery device). Because baking injera consumes the largest share of wood fuel and time for bakeries in the institution.

The main objective of this work is to design, manufacture an experimental prototype improved institutional mirt stove with waste heat recovery system that enhances heat transfer from exhaust flue gases to the secondary injera baking oven and to compare the performance of the improved institutional mirt stove with waste heat recovery system and the traditional stove are compared through test.

2 Materials and Methods

The commonly used traditional institutional mirt stove does not contain any features that will help in the effectively usage of energy and conversion process as efficient is shown in Fig. 1(a). The proposed model of improved institutional mirt stove with waste heat recovery system design is shown in Fig. 1(b).

(a). Model of stoves Existing institutional mirt stove

(b). Model of stoves Improved institutional
mirt with waste heat recovery system.

Fig. 1. (a). Model of stoves Existing institutional mirt stove (b). Model of stoves Improved institutional mirt with waste heat recovery system.

The main materials that are required for the work are clay plate (mitad), fired brick, cement, construction hollow block, iron rod, red ash and sheet metal. The materials selection is based on local availability and cost affordability.

The main components of the improved institutional mirt stove considered in this model are:-

Mirt Stoves. There are four independent mirt stoves. Each stove has four parts fit to make a cylindrically shaped enclosure (about 660 mm in diameter and 240 mm high). The cylindrical enclosure of each mirt stoves has two openings. The first opening, which has a semi-elliptic shape, is at the lower front of the enclosure and is about 240 mm wide and 110 mm high. It is used as fuel and air inlet. The second is at the rear up, where the enclosure is fitted with the inlet duct of exhaust flue gas to the flue chamber of the secondary injera baking mitad, as smoke outlet. This opening is of rectangular cross section and has a dimension of 190 mm width and 70 mm height.

Structure: The stoves supporting structure was designed to have 2290 mm × 2290 mm overall dimensions in ordered to support four independent mirt stoves and secondary injera baking assembly of 660 mm diameter which located at the center of the top platform. The height of the structure was designed to be 700 mm.

Mitad: It is a flat and circular pan commonly about 500 to 600 mm in diameter and traditionally used over large clay hearths to bake injera. The secondary baking mitad is considered to be 20 mm thick and 580 mm in diameter, which is equivalent to the size of primary baking mitads and also available in the local market.

Flue Chamber: The flue chamber is basically cylindrically shaped enclosure whose axis is vertically oriented. The cylindrical enclosure is made when four identical mating pieces of walls match together to form a cylindrically shaped enclosure. Its outer diameter was designed to be 660 mm and 60 mm wall thickness and 140 mm high.

The top part of the walls of the enclosure was provided 20 mm slotted rim for resting the secondary mitad.

Ducts: Four flue gases inlet ducts between each mirt stoves and flue chamber were constructed by maintaining constant cross sectional area of smoke outlets of each mirt stoves 190 mm by 70 mm and.one flue gases outlet duct opening was built with cross sectional area of 180 mm by 180 mm, that was considered to be equivalent to the chimney internal area, at the center of the housing of the flue chamber. The height of the outlet duct inside the flue chamber was considered to be 100 mm.

Grates: Four rectangular plates, made of 10 mm dia. MS iron rods were designed for holding fuel wood and allowing ash to be fall through to ash collector boxes. Each rod was welded 10 mm apart from others. The overall dimensions of each grate were considered to be 360 mm by 360 mm.

Ash Collector Boxes and Ash Outlets: Ash collector boxes and ash removal openings have been introduced below each grate. The size of each ash collector is 380 mm × 380 mm and 250 mm height. Each ash outlet ports of size 200 mm × 200 mm is used to dispose the ash from the ash collector box of each independent mirt stoves.

Chimney: The chimney, made of sheet metal of 1.5 mm thickness, has circular cross section about 200 mm in diameter and 2 m in height which is equivalent to the existing institutional mirt stove chimney size.

2.1   Model of Waste Heat Recovery System Components

The main components of the waste heat recovery system for injera baking considered in this model are as shown in the Fig. 2 below.

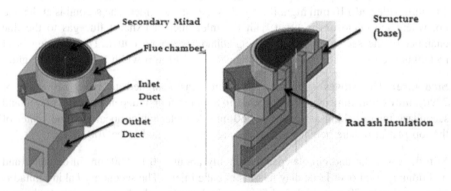

(a) 3D model of waste heat recovery System

(b) Cross sectional view of 3D model of waste heat recovery system

Fig. 2. (a) 3D model of waste heat recovery System (b) Cross sectional view of 3D model of waste heat recovery system

2.2   Working Principle of the Experimental Model

The working principle of the experimental model as can be observed from Fig. 3; Fuel wood was burnt in each independent mirt stove combustion chambers over their grates and baking on each primary mitads is done by direct flame produced from fuelwood, while baking on the secondary mitad is done by the heat of hot exhaust flue gases coming out from each independent mirt stoves.

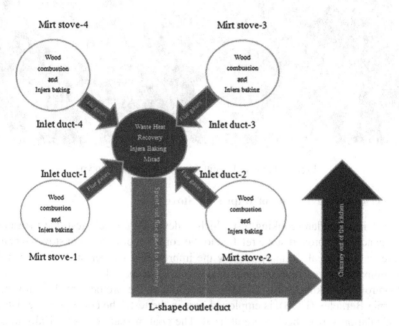

Fig. 3. Working principles and flue gases passage of the experimental model.

The bottom of the secondary baking pan was exposed to the hot flue gases. Thus heat was transferred from the hot flue gases to the baking pan by convection and conduction heat transfer mechanisms. After giving the energy to the baking mitad the spent flue gases are led out of the kitchen through the L- shape rectangular duct to chimney and finally to the environment through chimney stack.

2.3   Manufacturing of Stove Model

As per the design of improved Institutional mirt stove model shown in Fig. 4. for manufacturing the stove Bahir Dar University (BIT Campus) injera baking kitchen and the Research workshop is sufficient enough.

Fig. 4. Improved institutional mirt stove prototype

2.4   Performance Testing of Improved Stove

The CCT is a standard cooking test which is designed for field test that measures the performance of improved stove relative to the common or traditional stoves when cook prepares a local meal. It analyzes how the improved stove performs to save fuel and time compared to common or traditional cooking methods [9].

Controlled cooking test (CCT) [9], according to the protocol of the University of California-Berkeley (UCB), is employed here in the test. The corresponding data entry and calculation spreadsheets were utilized. The goal of such test is basically to get the value of specific fuel consumption of a stove, which is the amount of fuel used to produce a unit amount of food expressed in units of g/kg. This is the main parameter used for comparing the improved stove against the baseline stove. The total time of producing a certain amount of food is also a measure of stove performance. Therefore total time of production of injera was recorded for each of the baking sessions.

During the test, the amount of batter, the weight of the fuel used, the elapsed time, the weight of charcoal and container, the weight of a cooking pot, total weight of cooked food, the total number of injera baked, the equivalent dry wood consumed, moisture content of the wood, air temperature of the day and the surface temperature of the secondary mitad were recorded.

Instruments used for performing CCT are balance; stopwatch; thermometer; a handheld moisture tester.

2.5   Economic Analysis

The benefit-cost and payback period analyses were used to determine the economic acceptability of the improved stove.

Payback period is the number of years required to recover the initial investment in full with the help of the stream of annual cash flows generated by the project. The cash flow is assumed to be constant throughout their useful life time of the improved stove. Payback period can be calculated using Eq. 1 [10].

$$Payback = \frac{Annual\ Cash\ flow}{Initial\ Investment} \tag{1}$$

Benefit-cost Ratio: is the ratio of the net benefits to costs of the project. If the benefit-cost ratio is greater than or equal to one, accept the project as economically justified for the estimates and discount rate applied. The conventional benefit/cost ratio is calculated by Eq. 2 [10].

$$Benefit/cost = \frac{present\ Worth\ of\ Cost}{Present\ Worth\ of\ Benefit} \tag{2}$$

The cost of the project is in present worth. The benefits gain by the improved stove throughout their useful life time is future worth and should be converted into present worth by Eq. 3 [10].

$$P = F \times (1 + i)^{-n} \tag{3}$$

Where: p is the Present worth; F is the future worth; i-is interest rate in percent, and n is the number of useful life years of the stove.

3   Results and Discussion

3.1   Equivalent Dry Wood Consume

A comparison of institutional mirt stove and improved stove has been made with their respective average equivalent dry wood consumed during the test. The results obtained are presented in Fig. 5.

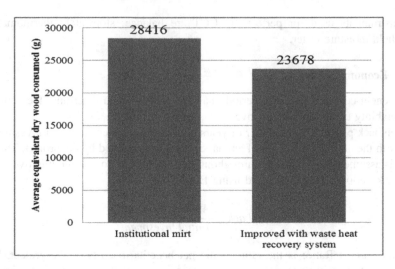

Fig. 5. Equivalent dry wood consumed by each stove.

As shown in Fig. 5, the amount of fuel wood to bake 117 injera was relatively low for improved stove as compared to institutional mirt stove. Institutional mirt stove registered a higher average fuel wood consumption, which is 28416 g and improved stove with 23678 g of fuel wood consumption. The equivalent dry fuel consumed per injera was 202 g with improved stove and 243 g with Institutional mirt stove. Fuel consumption is reduced by 41 g per injera as a result of using improved stove. This indicates that improved stove has fuel saving potential over institutional mirt stove by 16.9%.

3.2 Specific Fuel Consumption

As it can be seen in Fig. 6, Institutional mirt stove has the higher average specific fuel consumption of 625 g/kg. Improved stove was found 525 g/kg average specific fuel consumption. The direct output of CCT version 2.0 software results showed that there is a significant difference between the stoves at 95% confidence interval. Institutional mirt stove and improved stove was significant with percentage difference of 16%. This suggests that improved stove was 16% more efficient or saved up to 16% of the fuel wood per kg of Injera.

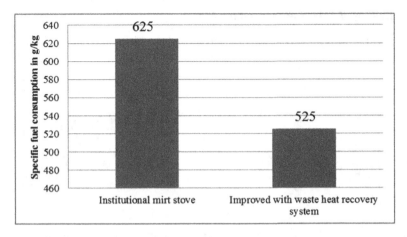

Fig. 6. Specific fuel consumption of the two stoves

3.3 Cooking Time

From the result shown in Fig. 7, it was observed that improved stove was found to have low mean cooking time. Institutional mirt stove had an average cooking time of 111 min as compared to 96 min of the improved stove. The difference in cooking time between stoves was statically significant at 95% confidence interval. This indicated that improved stove is saved up to 14% cooking time. Therefore, the improved stove gives lower cooking time than institutional mirt stove.

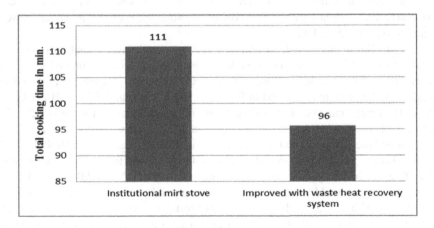

Fig. 7. Average cooking time of stoves

3.4   Baking of Injera on Secondary Mitad

The activities during injera baking on the secondary mitad were shown in the Fig. 8.

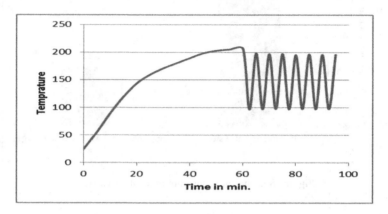

Fig. 8. Temperatures of secondary baking pan surface during baking cycles

3.5   Techno-Economic Evaluation of Improved Institutional Mirt Stove

The amount of fuel wood saved during baking process using the improved stove was the benefits gain from the project. The initial investment cost of the improved stove is taken as costs of the project. Considering the durability of materials used to manufacture the stove it was estimated to have a life span of 7 years.

The Initial investment of improved stove was the sum of raw material cost, machining cost and labor cost. The cost of manufacturing of the improved stove is found to be 10,496.63 ETB.

The amount of wood fuel consumption per injera with institutional mirt stove was obtained to be 0.243 kg per injera while it was 0.202 kg for an improved stove. The difference in the consumed fuel wood was about 0.041 kg per injera. From the survey conducted, the price of fuel wood at Bahir Dar town was found 3.21 ETB per kg and the daily average number of injera baked on one institutional mirt stove is 1200. The annual fuel wood saved per one stove is 17,958 kg. Hence the bakers save 57,645 birr per year and the cost saved through the useful life time (7 years) was ETB 403,515.26.

The benefit gain from improved stove was the cost saved from fuel wood purchase. Therefore, the benefit gain from improved stove was 403,515.26 ETB. This value was future worth and should be converted to present worth by the current saving interest of the country which is 5%. Thus, the present worth of benefit was ETB 316,165.55. Therefore, the benefit/cost ratio of improved stove was 30.12. This indicates that the project was economically feasible.

The annual cash flow for improved stove was the cost of fuel wood saved from purchase per year which is obtained ETB 57645.18 per year. Therefore, the payback period of improved stove was found 0.18 year or 2.2 months only.

4   Conclusions

A country's socio-economy cannot show progressive development unless energy is explored, developed, distributed and utilized in an efficient and appropriate way. Therefore, this work introduced the utilization of waste heat from exhaust flue gases of institutional mirt stove and recovered for the purpose of injera baking process in order to improve the performance of the stove. In this experimental study a more efficient and improved institutional mirt stove with waste heat recovery system was de-signed, manufactured and the performance of improved institutional mirt stove was compared with that of traditional institutional mirt stove through controlled cooking test method.

Based on the results obtained during the experimentation following conclusions could be drawn:

The surface temperature of the secondary baking mitad in the experiment was measured and about 216.3 °C was registered; so that it was possible to bake nice injera. The baking cycle took about five minutes. It could be inferred that it was possible to bake injera using the heat of exhaust flue gases from institutional mirt stove as energy source.

The controlled cooking test of the improved stove revealed that the time required for baking 117 injera was 15 min and 4.797 kg less fuel than traditional institutional mirt stove thus 14% time and 16% fuel saved in the improved stove.

The kitchen environment was free from radiative heat coming out of the chimney. The stove was easy to operate (bake) on it and also to remove ash.

The estimated cost of the system was ETB 10,496.63 with 0.18 year payback period and benefit cost ratio of 30.12. It could be inferred that the improved stove is technically as well as economically feasible in the present energy context.

Acknowledgment. The author would also like to thank the members of energy center in Bahir Dar Insti-tute of Technology, my co- advisor Mr. Getu Almaywu and Mr. Negese Yayu for their support, encouragement, and invaluable comments during the research work. I also appreciate the support of Temirenesh, Alem, and the entire members of the Injera bakeries at the Bahir Dar Institute of Technology.

Finally, author special thanks go to all my family: my lovely mother Shimbra Hailu, my father Wondatir Mihiretie and my sister Abay Wondatir, without whom this study could not have taken place.

References

1. Commercial production of energy efficient biomass stoves for the commercial/institutional sector, DFID KAR 6848, June 1999
2. Douglas, F., et al.: Comparative International Review of Stove Programs, s.l.: The World Bank Washington, D.C. (1994)
3. GIZ, Efficient Stoves for Bakeries Ethiopia, Eschborn (2013)
4. Energising Development (EnDev) Ethiopia Improved Cook Stoves (ICS), September 2014
5. Anteneh, G.: Stove Testing Results: a Report on Controlled Cooking Test Results Performed on Mirt with integrated chimney and Institutional Mirt Stoves (2011)

6. Abdulkadir, A.H., Demiss, A., Ole, J.N.: Performance Investigation of Solar Powered Injera Baking Oven for Indoor Cooking, pp. 186–196. ISES solar world congress proceedings, Kassel (2011)
7. Lokras, S.S.: Development and dissemination of fuel-efficient biomass burning devices. J. Indian Inst. Sci. **92**(1), 99–110 (2012)
8. Baldwin, S.F.: Biomass Stoves Engineering Design, Development and Dissemination, Arlington, Virginia: Volunteers in Technical Assisstance (with center for Energy and Environmental Studies, Princeton University) (1987)
9. Bailis, R.: Controlled Cooking Test, Version 2.0.University of California-Berkley, Pre-pared for Household Energy and Health Program of Shell Foundation (2004)
10. Newnan, D.G., Eschenbach, T.G., Lavelle, J.P.: Engineering Economic Analysis, 9th edn. Oxford University Press, New York (2004)

Experimental Investigation of Double Exposure Solar Cooker with an Asymmetric Compound Parabolic Concentrator

Lamesgin Addisu Getnet[✉] and Bimrew Tamrat Admassu

Bahir Dar Institute of Technology, Bahir Dar University, Bahir dar, Ethiopia

Abstract. This work provides the experimental test results and findings of solar cooker developed in Bahirdar. The cooker is double exposure type consisting of plane reflectors being fixed on top glazing and an asymmetric compound parabolic concentrator fixed on the side wall. It has a box casing with an aspect ratio of 2.66 and overall dimension of 920 mm × 343 mm × 400 mm. Stagnation tests were conducted on the double exposure and conventional solar box cooker. From the test maximum absorber plate temperature of 145 °C for the double exposure and 122 °C for the conventional cooker have been achieved at 12: 30 PM and 12:40 PM respectively. The respective first figure of merit values were found to be 0.123 and 0.088, the former satisfying minimum requirement as per BIS. Water or load test conducted indicates as it has taken 2 h and 30 min for 2 L of water to boil in the double exposure solar cooker while in conventional cooker water doesn't reach its boiling point, being heated to a maximum temperature of 88 °C. For the food cooking, 1 kg of rice distributed in two pots was cooked in 1 h and 35 min, starting from 10:00 AM. 1 kg of bean was cooked in 2 h and 45 min. The double exposure cooker is therefore able to cook hard meals like bean and soft meals like rice and spaghetti two and four times per day respectively. This food cooking result has good implication that if intensive work is done, solar cookers can be disseminated into and used by the society.

Keywords: Double exposure solar cooker · Conventional solar cooker · Vertical glass cover · Food cooking test

1 Introduction

One of the world's great concerns today is energy. Whatever its forms and its source, it is needed by every society and sector or organization in the world for different applications. Cooking is the prime activity made by every society, that needs a great percentage of energy needs of the world. In developing countries biomass, specifically firewood, is the major energy source for cooking. Even though it is considered as a renewable energy source, it has series draw backs. Deforestation leading to famine and draught, air pollution due to fire wood burning, health problems and risk of kitchen burning due to fire wood cooking are some of the problems facing this energy sector. This makes the research community to focus attention on the free, abundant and clean energy source: solar energy! This can be harnessed by devices for different energy

© ICST Institute for Computer Sciences, Social Informatics and Telecommunications Engineering 2022
Published by Springer Nature Switzerland AG 2022. All Rights Reserved
M. L. Berihun (Ed.): ICAST 2021, LNICST 412, pp. 425–442, 2022.
https://doi.org/10.1007/978-3-030-93712-6_29

needing applications. Solar cooking is the most viable, simplest and direct application of solar energy [1, 2].

Solar cooker is a device which utilizes solar energy to cook food, and enable processes like pasteurization and sterilization. The focus of this work is on solar box cookers due to its ease of manufacturing and lower attendance for manual tracking. Researches on solar cooking from the first solar box cooker till now played a vital role for solar cookers to be efficient, cost effective and socially viable. The developments include material type, size and orientation of the cooker as a whole or components: absorber plate, reflector, cooking vessel, glass cover and insulation [1, 3]. The literatures reviewed here after are to catch up the modifications in researches on size and orientation of components.

S. Mahavar et al. [4–6] have designed and tested a solar box cooker for a single family, by making the cooker very light weight, increasing the performance and to have a relatively low cost. They also determined the optimum load range for the solar cooker at which the total cooking time together with other cooker performance parameters would be better to be 1.2–1.6 kg. F. Yettou et al. [7] have compared the performances of two box type solar cookers having horizontal and inclined aperture apertures. The cooker with inclined aperture was observed to have better performance than horizontal one due to increase of absorption area. Sethi et al. [8] also have designed and developed an inclined solar box cooker with one reflector. Tests were conducted on this developed cooker and compared the results with the horizontal cooker having similar dimension and material, showing that the former has a better performance.

Reflectors in solar technologies are used to increase the amount of solar radiation intensity falling on the absorber surface. The increase in number of reflectors increases the performance. Zied Guidar et al. [9] have designed and constructed a box cooker with four outer reflectors. Test conducted and performance calculated reveals as the first figure of merit is 0.14, which is greater value compared to the cooker without reflector. Absorber plate temperature was 133 °C which is better than the later. Amanuel Weldu et al. [10] designed and experimentally investigated a box type solar cooker with single reflector that can be optimally tracked every hour. The test results show that, the performance is better than cooker with fixed reflectors, which in turn is better than solar cookers without reflectors. But the boiling time is not less than 3 h for the optimally tracked one, which should be enhanced.

The common problem for many box type cookers is their need for frequent tracking in order to capture sunlight effectively in sunshine hours. There are many scholars who did to improve the tracking and make it to be performed little times per day, per month or per week or make it non tracking. Mirdha et al. [11] have tried a variety of combination of reflectors to have high value of collection coefficient for reflectors and reduced adjustment periods. The final cooker developed has fixed vertical wall reflector facing to south along with another south facing reflector on its lid which is trackable. It had side mirrors to remove permanent movement of the cooker throughout the day in the direction of the sun, as it goes from east to west. Harmim et al. [12] have developed and tested a solar box cooker having ACPC fixed on vertical side wall of the cooker. The cooker itself is fixed on the wall of south facing building, so that indoor cooking is being made, which is socially viable.

Solar cookers were also designed to increase solar absorption by exposing the absorber plate for solar radiation from different directions, albeit it was receiving solar energy from above horizontal glazing in earlier times. Saravanan and Janarathanan [13] have developed a double exposure cooker and compared its performance with the conventional cooker exposed only from above. This cooker is so huge in size requiring wider location area more than a simple kitchen house. In addition, arranging the side reflectors to keep timely movement of sun is also a difficult task. Increasing the number of reflectors increases the performance of the cooker. In addition, tracking the reflectors based on movement of sun, also increases the performance [9]. Scholars also have noticed that outer reflectors fixed on the box cookers have a drawback, as tracking of reflectors needs continuous attending and also the reflector by itself increases size of the cooker. Mulu Bayray et al. [14] have designed a box cooker with internal reflectors, whose performance have been better than solar cookers without reflectors. But still such cookers have low performance, taking long cooking hours. Solar cookers were also developed with non-tracking concentrators aimed both at increasing performance and cooking to be made unattended [15].

In spite of such efforts being made on solar box cookers, they are not widely used. Specifically, in Ethiopia, the technology is unknown by the society. Great effort is expected from scholars to make it socially viable, efficient and disseminate towards the society. Most of highly populated countries including Ethiopia are blessed with high solar radiation in the range of 5–7 KWh/m^2 and have shiny days on average of 275 days per year. Therefore, it can easily be said that solar cookers in Ethiopia have higher potential on being a supplement for energy demand of cooking if efforts are made for cases mentioned before [16].

Even though efforts are made to reduce the cooking time, they are not compatible with the rural society. For instance, solar box cookers with tracking plane reflectors have been seen to be tracked every hour, day or in the interval of some specified time. Double exposure solar cookers discussed so far requires very wide space [13]. Some also have a series of flat plates, fixed on parabolic path from below of box cooker. These flat plates are tracked continuously throughout the day following solar path, and this is difficult to operate for the illiterate rural society (the case for Ethiopia). Even though it is possible to operate, standing outside for follow up at sunny day is the other side effect. It was seen in literatures, there have been works to develop solar cookers with non-tracking reflectors. But their performance is lower than other box cookers [17, 18].

In this work it is intended to develop double exposure solar cooker that does not require frequent tracking and perform as good as trackable plane reflectors. This is made by adding asymmetric compound parabolic concentrator to the vertical side of the box casing, on conventional solar box cookers which have plane reflectors.

Compound parabolic concentrator is a non-imaging concentrator that is used for concentrating all solar radiation falling on it to the receiver at a wider limit called acceptance angle. It has been used for high temperature application that does not require frequent tracking, once it is installed in appropriate direction. When the parabolic concentrators are asymmetric, it can be integrated with vertical walls of a box and buildings for facade integration. These have been normally used for indoor cooking and photovoltaic generation with building integration [12, 19–21].

2   Materials and Methods

2.1   Design and Description of the Developed Solar Cooker

The box casing dimensions was determined by considering the amount of energy it would intercept by absorber from the reflector. In doing so, the amount of energy required to cook a specified food is determined and then used to size box dimensions.

2.1.1   Cooking Load

Rice is to be cooked as a sample once for a family and the ratio of water needed for the specified amount of rice is taken from literature. For the 0.5 kg of rice, which is the average consumption for a family the amount of water needed is 1.25 L [22].

In cooking, there is a specific range of load that is optimum in terms of cooking time, and other performance parameters like thermal efficiency, figures of merit. For a family cooker the optimum amount of load to be cooked was determined to be 1.2–1.6 kg [11]. Hence, the water amount calculated for the family cooking is in the optimum load range.

The energy required at the cooking pot which is to be determined is equal to the sensible heat load of water and food ingredients in cooking, plus energy needed for maintaining boiling temperature due to loss of energy through evaporation of water during or before boiling temperature. The sensible heat load is calculated from the temperature increment of water from its initial value of ambient temperature to the cooking temperature which can be taken as boiling temperature of water.

To know the full load, the ingredients to be used in the cooking, should be specified. Ingredients used for cooking it are: onion and oil. Compared with the water and rice, the other ingredients are very small in proportion. So, cooking load can be determined from the two with a certain percentage increment.

$$E_s = m_w c_{pw} \Delta T + m_r c_{pr} \Delta T \qquad (2.1)$$

The given quantities and physical properties are $m_w = 1.25$ kg, $c_{pw} = 4.22$ kJ/kg.K, $m_r = 500$ g, $c_{pr} = 1.8$ kJ/kg.k and ΔT is temperature difference between the boiling and average ambient temperature of water, which are 94 °C and 21 °C respectively. Substituting these numerical values into the equation, the value of total energy required is 432.525 kJ. It is the total amount of sensible energy required at the cooking pot throughout the cooking period.

It is found from literatures that the amount of energy needed for maintaining cooking temperature can be approximated as one third of sensible heat energy required [23]. The total energy required for cooking is then,

$$E_t = E_s + \frac{1}{3} E_s = 576.7 \text{ KJ} \qquad (2.2)$$

This thermal energy is acquired from the incoming solar radiation. In the cooking period, there are many convections, radiation and conduction losses from the pot and other cooker components like glass cover and absorber plate. Hence the calculated energy value is the net energy at cooking pot irrespective of these losses.

2.1.2 Box Casing

This is the parallelepiped shape on which other components are attached and inside which the cooking pot is placed. The height and width of cooker are determined by considering: pot size, insulation, reflectors to be added (as the box should be structurally able to carry plane and parabolic reflectors) provided that absorber plate inside it is able to capture sufficient energy for cooking. Rectangular shaped solar box cookers perform better than square shaped once. The optimum length to width ratio for box type cookers was determined to be 2.66 [24]. Hence length can be calculated using this ratio, once the height and width are determined based on the above considerations.

The box casing can be made from locally available humanitarian waste materials like cardboards and stronger materials like wood, ply wood and steel. Each material has its own merits over the others. The box casing in this study should be structurally able to support the ACPC at its walls and from upper glazing. It would also be good if it has lower thermal conductivity so that it would have insulating property to retain heat. The box material is taken to be plywood due to its higher strength and availability, cheapness and lower thermal conductivity (serving as insulation also).

Since any design problem goes in either of the two methods (determining size and dimensions with given operating parameters and vice versa), in this study the sizes of different parts of the cooker would be determined from the heat load calculated before.

Determination of the size of box casing includes the design of basic components of the cooker like absorber tray, reflector and glazing. This is because the casing is used to hold up all these components together serving as a basic component for the cooker assemblage.

The width of box includes the diameter of cooking pot, sufficient gap for air circulation, insulation. It is possible to simply consider these factors and assign certain numerical value. But it is impossible to know whether this width of box with the length can intercept the desired solar insolation to get the total energy calculated before. Hence, width of box should be calculated based on the energy requirement.

The following assumptions are taken, which are mostly valid for many solar cookers developed so far, for calculation start up and sizing of components.

- The cooker would have an overall efficiency of 30%.
- Cooking would be achieved in 1.5 h (Many recent solar cookers can cook in 1.5–2 h period)

The efficiency and cooking time values are taken based on the following reasons. Many solar box cookers have thermal efficiency in the range of 25–35%. Solar box cookers which are smaller in size have thermal efficiencies around the upper limit of the above range [10, 25]. Solar box cookers having greater sizes have efficiencies around the lower limit of the range given [18]. The solar cooker developed in this work is aimed at achieving cooking without tracking of reflectors. To achieve this, there is a stepped absorber plate: Horizontal absorber plate at bottom of cooker and vertical absorber plate for absorbing solar radiation from ACPC. When doing this, the size of absorber plate and its area increases. Increased in absorber plate area also brings increased heat loss. Hence, the efficiency may not be improved. So, the author picks a numerical value for the cooker efficiency from this range.

The total energy required at the pot is related with solar insolation as

$$\eta = \frac{E_t}{IAt} \tag{2.3}$$

A, is intercept area of the solar cooker which includes effective area of glazing and reflectors, and the numerator is the total energy required which is calculated from the ratio of average solar daily radiation to sunshine hour for the experimental location: Bahir Dar.

$$I = \frac{Averagedailysolarisolation}{sunshinehours}$$
$$= 726 \, w/m^2$$

The calculated solar irradiance is the average global irradiance on horizontal surface. Substituting these values of variables gives an intercept area to be $A = 0.48 \, m^2$.

In solar collectors, the reflectors have significant effect on the solar energy collection. Researches conducted on the investigation of the effect of reflectors on solar radiation captured have showed as the addition of reflectors can increase radiation capture 1.5–2 times than cookers without reflectors [10, 26]. This increase in collection coefficient is due to the increased aperture area by addition of reflectors. There is no exact mathematical equation that relates the aperture and absorber areas. Hence, this collection coefficient is used for rough estimation of the absorber area from the aperture area calculated in Eq. (2.3).

$$A = 1.5 A_{ab} \tag{2.4}$$

Where A_{ab} is absorber area, which is calculated to be $0.32 \, m^2$. This absorber area is the product of its length and width. The optimum length to width ratio for rectangular box cookers is 2.66 [18].

$$A_{ab} = lw = (2.66w)w \tag{2.5}$$

From Eq. 2.5 the width of absorber plate and hence the width of the solar cooker is 0.343 m, and the length is also calculated to be 0.92 m.

The box height should be enough for what was mentioned in the case of width. In addition, the vertical absorber plate which absorbs the solar radiation from asymmetric compound parabolic reflectors should be larger in size, as the aperture should have sufficient gap. It is taken to be 40 cm. Therefore, overall dimension of the box casing is 920 mm × 343 mm × 400 mm. The cooker is made of plywood of 20 mm thickness, with openings from two sides for loading and unloading of cooking utensils (Fig. 1).

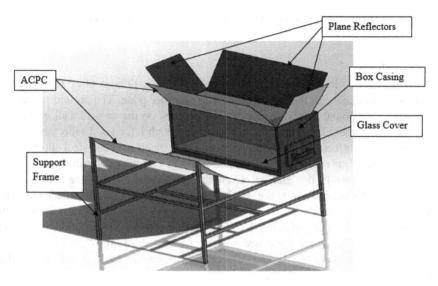

Fig. 1. Developed solar cooker

2.1.3   Glazing

Glazing in a solar technology indicates glasses or plastics used in collector and solar cooker coverings. In solar box cookers it covers the absorber plate allowing sunshine to reach it. It does so for preventing rain, wind, and cold from reaching the plate surface that will cause loss of heat. The transparent cover (glazing) is used to reduce convection losses from the absorber plate through the restraint of the stagnant air layer between the absorber plate and the glass. It also reduces radiation losses from the collector. The glass is transparent to the short-wave radiation received from the sun but it is nearly opaque to long-wave thermal radiation emitted by the absorber plate. Although glass is virtually opaque to the long wave radiation emitted by collector plates, absorption of that radiation causes an increase in the glass temperature and a loss of heat to the surrounding atmosphere. Water white (low iron) glass is better in transmittance than polyester and window glass and it is selected in this work for its good transmittivity [27]. The top and front sides of the box casing in this study are covered with 4 mm thick white glasses, which allows solar absorption from top and front sides that are reflected from the plane and compound parabolic reflectors respectively.

The solar radiation passing into the box casing through the glazing is then absorbed by the absorber plate. It is a metal sheet of high thermal conductivity painted black, for changing the absorbed solar energy into thermal energy.

To reduce the heat loss to the environment, an insulation material of low thermal conductivity is provided between plywood casing and absorber plate. Fiberglass of insulation 40 mm thickness is used [27]. The thickness of this insulation is made to be lower than the recommended value for solar box cookers, as the box casing made of plywood by itself is highly insulating material. The 4 cm fiber glass is to be used at the bottom and rear view of the box. The material of box casing is made with plywood of 2 cm thickness.

2.1.4   Reflector

The reflectors used in this study are of two types. The first one is plane reflectors that reflect solar radiation on the top to horizontal absorber plate. The second reflector is asymmetric compound parabolic reflector that is fixed on the vertical wall of the box. Aluminum foil is used for the reflective material which have good reflectance unless there are many surfaces wrinkling upon it, and it is glued over the steel sheet [27].

The size of plane reflector is determined in a way that the solar radiation striking it should reflect towards the glazing. Even though increasing the size increases the amount of reflected radiation, the shadow effect of higher width reflectors would decrease the performance. Also, solar radiation may reflect from one mirror to the opposite one and again reflected back to the atmosphere. The optimum size for reflectors is taken to be the same size as cooker box width [28].

The specifications of the developed solar cooker are summarized and presented as follows in Table 1.

Table 1. Specifications of the developed solar cooker

SN	Component name	Specification	Material used
1	Box casing	343 mm × 920 mm × 400 mm	Ply wood of thickness 2 cm
2	Absorber plate	343 mm × 920 mm; 400 mm × 920 mm (Stepped absorber plate)	Aluminum metal 0.4 mm thick
3	Glazing	343 mm × 920 mm; 400 mm × 920 mm (Horizontal and vertical	White glass
4	Reflector	Plane reflectors: 2 (343 mm × 920 mm); 2(343 mm × 400 mm) ACPC with concentration ratio of 2.92	Aluminum foil of 0.86 spectacular reflectance
5	Insulation	343 mm × 920 mm; 400 mm × 920 mm; 2(343 mm × 400 mm)	Fiber glass with 4 cm thickness

2.2   Experimental Setup

The experimental work is conducted in Bahr dar Institute of Technology, Ethiopia. The box cooker is fixed with south facing orientation, as asymmetric compound parabolic concentrators on northern hemisphere should face to south [28]. The tests were conducted as per the international standards of solar cooker test procedures [29–31].

Absorber temperature, ambient temperature, temperature of water being heated and solar radiation are recorded every 10 min, so that these properties are used to evaluate performance measuring parameters like first and second figure of merit, cooking power. All experiments were started at 10:00 a.m. and continued until 4:00 p.m.

The performance of the developed DESC was compared with other cookers performances reviewed from literatures. In addition, a test was conducted on the same developed cooker by covering the vertical glazing by insulation material, plywood. This is used as a controlled set up to see the effect of addition of ACPC on the conventional box cooker with plane reflectors.

K type thermocouples were used to measure various component temperatures of the developed cooker (Accuracy of 0.1% reading + 0.7 °C). Simultaneously, solar intensity was measured by TM-207 Solar meter (3 ½ digits display with maximum reading of 2000 W/m^2) (Fig. 2).

Fig. 2. The manufactured solar cooker on test

Fig. 3. Experimental setup of the box cooker

3 Thermal Performance Parameters

The performance of solar cookers depends on the climatic conditions and design parameters. The climatic conditions which affect the performance of solar cookers are solar insolation, ambient temperature and wind speed. Solar cookers of any type should be tested and their performance should be expressed in terms of some parameters for comparison with cookers designed and tested at different time and places. These parameters of performance evaluation include: first and second figure of merit, standardized cooking power.

3.1 First Figure of Merit

First figure of merit is defined as the ratio of optical efficiency to overall heat loss coefficient. It is the measure of differential temperature gained by plate absorber at a particular level of solar radiation. Stagnation test is conducted to evaluate this parameter in which the solar box cooker is exposed to solar radiation without any load. The mathematical expression is as follows [5–7].

$$F_1 = \frac{\eta_o}{U_L} \tag{3.1}$$

First figure of merit value ensures that the glass covers have good optical transmission and the cooker have lower heat loss coefficient. According to bureau of Indian Standards solar box cookers are grouped into grades A and B. A box cooker with first figure of merit value greater than 0.12 is graded A, whereas cookers having first figure of merit less than 0.12 are graded B [30].

It is determined experimentally as

$$F_1 = \frac{T_{ps} - T_{amb,s}}{I} \tag{3.2}$$

3.2 Second Figure of Merit

Second figure of merit indicates the effectiveness of the heat transfer from the absorber plate and the inside air to contents of the cooking pots. For a box cooker to be said good in heat transfer from vessel to the food contents, the second figure of merit should be greater than 0.4 [30]. It is evaluated under full load conditions and expressed mathematically as Eq. (3.3)

$$F_2 = \frac{F_1(m_w C_w)}{At} \ln \left[\frac{\left\{1 - \frac{1}{F_1}\left(\frac{T_{w1}-T_{amb}}{I}\right)\right\}}{\left\{1 - \frac{1}{F_1}\left(\frac{T_{w2}-T_{amb}}{I}\right)\right\}} \right] \tag{3.3}$$

Where, I and T_{amb} is average solar insolation and ambient temperature recorded during the test period, for increasing water temperature from a certain initial temperature, T_{w1} to T_{w2} in the time interval, t [31]. The upper limit of the water temperature, Tw2 is taken us the boiling or saturation temperature at atmospheric pressure of the environment. However, this has a drawback. Since the rate of variation of water temperature approaches zero as the water temperature approaches saturation temperature, there is a great uncertainty in deciding the termination point of time interval t. Therefore, the upper limit of sensible heating (T_{w2}) should be fixed in the temperature range lower than this temperature by 5 °C–10 °C. Initial temperature, Tw1 could be taken at some value (say, midway) between the ambient and the boiling point [32].

3.3   Cooking Power

Cooking power is the time rate of useful energy gain by the cooker in the cooking or heating period. It is obtained by multiplying the heat capacity of water being heated with the temperature change in the given time interval and dividing the result to the time interval [29].

$$P = \frac{m_w C_w (T_{w2} - T_{w1})}{t} \qquad (3.4)$$

This cooking power cannot be directly used for comparing solar cookers at different locations. Hence, it is standardized to the form in Eq. 3.5. The standard cooking power is calculated by correcting cooking power calculated before in to a standard solar radiation of 700 W/m². It is calculated by multiplying the interval cooking power by 700 W/m² and dividing the result by the average insolation recorded in the interval [29].

$$Ps = \frac{m_w C_w (T_{w2} - T_{w1}) \times 700}{It} \qquad (3.5)$$

3.4   Thermal Efficiency

The thermal efficiency of the solar cooker is calculated to know how much is this cooker converting the available solar radiation into useful heat energy that is manifested in the temperature increment of cooking pot contents. Mathematically it is expressed as the ratio of desired output to input energy [10].

$$\eta = \frac{m_w c_{pw} \Delta T}{\alpha \tau I A t} \qquad (3.6)$$

Where α is the absorbance property of the aluminium absorber plate and τ is transmittance of the glass cover whose values are 0.84 and 0.89 respectively [12].

4   Results and Discussion

4.1   Stagnation Test

Stagnation test is experiment conducted when the solar cooker is exposed to solar radiation without any load. This test was made for 4 days (24/12/2018–27/12/2018), 2 for each of the solar cooker types: modified and conventional cooker. The absorber plate temperature and solar intensity variation through out the day is shown graphically in Fig. 3. As seen on the graph the maximum absorber temperature of 145 °C and 122 °C were recorded respectively at 12:30 PM and 12:40 PM respective times, with the stagnation solar intensity of 920 W/m² and 917 W/m² respectively. Saravanan et al. [13] have designed a double exposure solar cooker and conducted experiment, the test results showing as the stagnation temperature of 102 °C reached after 3 h. Stagnation test results for solar box cookers developed by different scholars reached stagnation

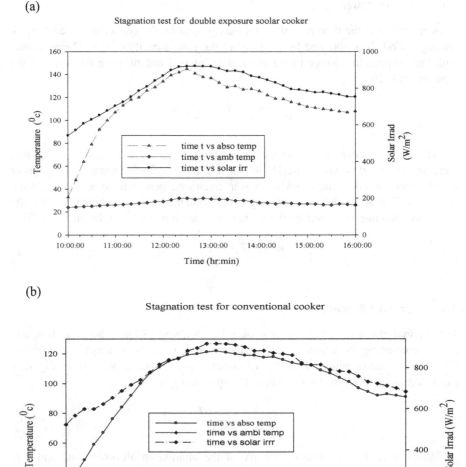

Fig. 4. Thermal performance curve for (a) double exposure cooker and (b) conventional cooker

temperatures of 118 °C, 119 °C, 161 °C [15, 25, 32]. Hence the developed cooker can be categorized as high performing cooker, as absorber plate temperature is one of parameters indicating solar cookers performance [32]. The plot of absorber plate and solar intensity throught the day is shown in Figs. 4 and 5.

Variations of absorber plate temperatures for the two cookers

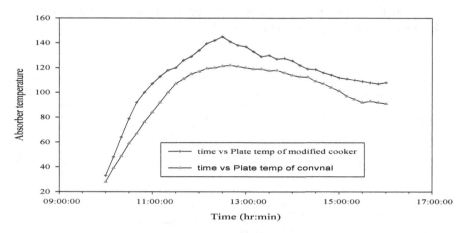

Fig. 5. Variation of absorber plate temperatures for the two cookers

The absorber plate temperature curves in Fig. 4 indicate that, addition of the ACPC on the conventional cooker would increase absorber plate temperature at all times of the test period.

The first figure of merit calculated based on Eq. (3.1) gives, 0.123 for the double exposure cooker and 0.097 for conventional cooker.

The bureau of Indian standards for solar cookers classifies cookers in to major categories by the first figure of merit. Grade A cookers are required to have a minimum value of 0.12 first figure of merit and those cookers having lower figure of merit than 0.12 are classified as Grade B. Therefore, stagnation test results in this work indicate that the modified cooker is Grade A [30].

4.2 Load Test (Water Heating Test)

This test was made with a 2 kg of water load on 2 pots evenly distributed in the cooker (28/12/2018 – 30/12/2018). It is conducted for 3 days, 2 for the modified (graph is done only for one day, as the two days data have almost similar pattern) and one for conventional one.

In this work T_{w2} is taken to be 90 °C as boiling temperature of water in Bahir dar is 94 °C. With these temperature ranges and other parameters known, and the result gives F2 to be 0.41. According to bureau of Indian Standards solar cookers with F2 value greater than 0.4 are taken as good, which this cooker also satisfies [30].

The maximum cooking power calculated based on Eq. (3.6) is 125.1 W and 111.2 W for the modified and conventional cooker respectively, while the minimum value is 16.7 W and 13.9 W respectively. This large value of cooking power indicates greater solar intercept area (and the cooker of coarse is as such), and minimum value indicate poor insulation [29]. The indication of poor insulation is due to increased heat loss through two glass covers, not double glazing, but the vertical and horizontal covers on top and front face.

The variations of temperature values for different components and solar insolation with time are shown graphically in Fig. 6 and 7.

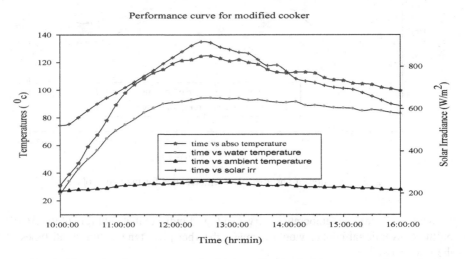

Fig. 6. Thermal performance curve for load test for the double exposure solar cooker.

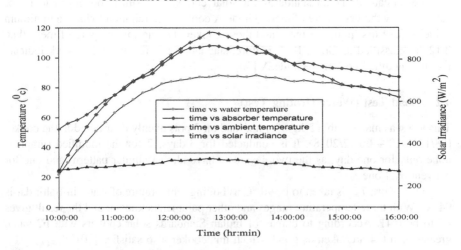

Fig. 7. Thermal performance curve for load test for the conventional cooker.

4.3   Food Cooking Test

In addition to the international test standards and parameters, actual cooking of different food types have also been made. This is why the solar cooker was also developed. Figure 8 shows foods cooked in these cooking days.

Fig. 8. Foods *Cooked by the developed DESC*.

The test conducted on December 31/2018 and January 1/2019 shows that one kg of rice was cooked in 1 h and 35 min, the cooking starting at 10:00 h. It seems to be contradictory that, water boils after 2 h and 30 min but the rice is cooked in smaller time duration than this boiling time of water. This is because, the cooking was made by adding proportional amount of water and rice together, so that cooking is achieved below boiling temperature of water. It is known that food can be cooked in temperature range of 60–90 °C [18]. 1 kg of bean was cooked in 2 h and 45 min, so that for hard foods it is possible to cook two meals per day.

This is best cooker performance when compared with many of solar box cookers developed till now. The nontracking reflector solar cooker developed by Nahar was able to cook soft and hard foods in 2 and 3 h respectively [15]. Rice cooking also conducted on box cooker with wiper mechanism was cooked in 91 min [25]. Different types of food in double exposure cooker, developed by Amer, were cooked in the ranges of 1 h and 30 min up to 2 h and 45 min [33].

4.4 Thermal Efficiency

Substituting the following numerical values, which was given in test period or calculated before, in to Eq. (3.6).

$m_w = 2\,kg$, $C_w = 4180\,\frac{J}{kgk}$, $t = 9000\,s$, Aperture area $A = 0.47$ m2, Iavg = 738 W/m2, $\Delta T = 94{-}25 = 69\ °C$.

gives, thermal efficiency of the cooker is 27%. This relatively low efficiency is due to increased heat losses from the glass covers. It is known that increase in glass cover and absorber area also leads to increased loss, even though the net value of energy capture is positive. Although this number is comparatively lower than recent solar box cookers being developed, the actual performance on cooking is so good. Satisfactory cooking ability is due to higher amount of solar energy aperture area, the summation of plane reflector and ACPC apertures.

5 Cost and Affordability

The cost of the developed solar box cooker is shown in Table 2.

Table 2. Cost of the developed cooker

Component/material	Measurement unit	Total size	Total cost (Birr)
Aluminum sheet metal	Area (m²)	0.743 × 0.92	800
Steel sheet	Area (m²)	2.5 × 0.92	1200
Aluminium foil	Small Roll	1	100
Plywood	Area (m²)	2 (0.743 × 0.92)	150
Glass cover	Area (m²), thickness	0.743 × 0.92	320
Insulation	Area (m²), thickness (cm)	0.743 × 0.92 × 4	300
Angle iron for support	Length (m)	12 m	800
Glue	Number	1	90
Paint ink	Litre	1	90
Labour cost (one person)	Number of days	2	800
Total cost			4650

This total cost of 4650 Birr, is affordable by most of the rural society. The addition of asymmetric compound concentrator, does not have significant effect on the cost. The cost of the cooker is not comparable with the advantages it would bring in terms of decreasing deforestation and decreasing labor work in searching for wood from abroad.

6 Conclusion and Recommendation

Conclusion

The stagnation and water load tests conducted on the developed solar cooker, indicate that the addition of asymmetric compound solar collector would have significant increment to the performance than the conventional solar box cooker. The food cooking also indicates as it is possible to use this cooker for cooking applications especially those which does not require frequent stirring. The cost of the developed cooker is also affordable.

Recommendation

✓ Research works have to be done on increasing performance of solar cookers with out or with minimum tracking requirement, but with increased collection coefficient for reflectors, that can be easily used by the rural society.

✓ Increase in absorber area, also leads to increased heat loss. Researches in these areas should focus on optimizing geometry of the cooker for decreasing heat loss.

References

1. Cuce, E., Cuce, P.M.: A comprehensive review on solar cookers. Appl. Energy **102**, 1399–1421 (2013)
2. Muthusivagami, R.M., Velraj, R., Sethumadhavan, R.: Solar cookers with and without thermal storage—a review. Renew. Sustain. Energy Rev. **14**, 691–701 (2010)
3. Panwara, N.L., Kaushika, S.C., Kothari, S.: State of the art of solar cooking: an overview. Renew. Sustain. Energy Rev. **16**, 3776–3785 (2012)
4. Mahavar, S., Sengar, N., Rajawata, P., Verma, M., Dashora, P.: Design development and performance studies of a novel Single Family Solar Cooker. Renew. Energy **47**, 67–76 (2012)
5. Mahavar, S., Rajawat, P., Punia, R.C., Sengar, N., Dashora, P.: Evaluating the optimum load range for box-type solar cookers. Renew. Energy **74**, 187–194 (2015)
6. Mahavar, S., Rajawat, P., Marwal, V.K., Punia, R.C., Dashora, P.: Modeling and on-field testing of a Solar Rice Cooker. Energy **49**, 404–412 (2013)
7. Yettou, F., Azoui, B., Malek, A., Panwar, N.L.: Comparative assessment of two different designs of box solar cookers under Algerian sahara conditions. Revue des Energies
8. Sethi, V.P., Pal, D.S., Sumathy, K.: Performance evaluation and solar radiation capture of optimally inclined box type solar cooker with parallelepiped cooking vessel design. Energy Convers. Manage. **81**, 231–241 (2014)
9. Guidara, Z., Souissi, M., Morgenstern, A., Maalej, A.: Thermal performance of a solar box cooker with outer reflectors: numerical study and experimental investigation. Solar Energy **158**, 347–359 (2017)
10. Weldu, A., et al.: Performance evaluation on solar box cooker with reflector tracking at optimal angle under Bahir Dar climate. Sol. Energy **180**, 664–677 (2019)
11. Mirdha, U.S., Dhariwal, S.R.: Design optimization of solar cooker. Renew. Energy **33**, 530–544 (2008)
12. Harmim, A., Merzouk, M., Boukar, M., Amar, M.: Design and experimental testing of an innovative building-integrated box type solar cooker. Sol. Energy **98**, 422–433 (2013)

13. Saravanan, K., Janarathanan, B.: Comparative study of single and double exposure Box-type solar cooker. International Journal of Scientific & Engineering Research, vol. 5, no. 5, May-2014 620 ISSN 2229–5518

14. Kahsay, M.B., Paintin, J., Mustefa, A., Haileselassiea, A., Tesfay, M., Gebray, B.: Theoretical and experimental comparison of box solar cookers with and without internal reflector. Energy Procedia **57**, 1613–1622 (2014)

15. Nahar, N.M.: Design and development of a large size non-tracking solar cooker. J. Eng. Sci. Technol. **4**(3), 264–271 (2009)

16. Asfafaw, H.T., Mulu, B.K., Ole, J.N.: Design and development of solar thermal Injera baking: steam based direct baking. Energy Procedia **57**, 2946–2955 (2014)

17. Negi, B.S., Purohit, I.: Experimental investigation of a box type solar cooker employing a non-tracking concentrator. Energy Convers. Manage. **46**, 577–604 (2005)

18. Folaranmi, J.: Performance evaluation of a double-glazed box-type solar oven with reflector. Journal of Renewable Energy, pp. 1–8 (2013)

19. Harmim, A., Merzouk, M., Boukar, M., Amar, M.: Solar cooking development in Algerian Sahara: towards a socially suitable solar cooker. Renew. Sustain. Energy Rev. **37**, 207–214 (2014)

20. Harmim, A., Merzouk, M., Boukar, M., Amar, M.: Mathematical modeling of a box-type solar cooker employing an asymmetric compound parabolic concentrator. Sol. Energy **86**, 1673–1682 (2012)

21. Harmim, A., Belhamel, M., Boukar, M., Amar, M.: Experimental investigation of a box-type solar cooker with finned absorber plate. Energy **35**, 3799–3802 (2010)

22. Harmim, A., et al.: Design and experimental testing of an innovative building-integrated box type solar cooker. Sol. Energy **98**, 422–433 (2013)

23. Sonesson, U., Janestad, H., Raaholt, B.: Energy for Preparation and Storing of Food - Models for calculation of energy use for cooking and cold storage in households. SR 709 ISBN 91-7290-224-8

24. Farooqui, S.Z.: Angular optimization of dual booster mirror solar cookers – Tracking free experiments with three different aspect ratios. Sol. Energy **114**, 337–348 (2015)

25. Ademe, Z., Hameer, S.: Design, construction and performance evaluation of a Box type solar cooker with a glazing wiper mechanism. AIMS Energy **6**(1), 146–169 (2018)

26. Pejack, E.: Technology of solar cooking. Self-published on Internet. Prof. at University of the Pacific (2003)

27. Duffie, J.A., Beckman, W.A.: Solar Engineering of Thermal Processes. 2013 by John Wiley & Sons, 5th Edition (2013)

28. Funk, P.A.: Evaluating the international standard procedure for testing solar cookers and reporting performance. Sol. Energy **68**(1), 1–7 (2000)

29. Bureau of Indian Standards (BIS) IS 13429, Indian Standard (IS 13429) (2000)

30. Mullick, S.C., et al.: Thermal test procedures for box type solar cookers. Sol. Energy **39**(4), 353–360 (1987)

31. Varshney, G.S.: Testing of Solar Box Cookers: A Review. JETIR (ISSN-2349-5162), vol. 4, no. 12, December 2017

32. Saxena1, A., Karakilcik, M.: Performance evaluation of a solar cooker with low-cost heat storage material. Int. J. Sustain. Green Energy **6**(4), 57–63 (2017)

33. Amer, E.H.: Theoretical and experimental assessment of a double exposure solar cooker. Energy Convers. Manage. **44**, 2651–2663 (2003)

Exergy and Economic Analysis of Modified Mixed Mode Solar *Injera* Dryer

Senay Teshome Sileshi[1]([⊠]) [iD], Abdulkadir Aman Hassen[2],
and Kamil Dino Adem[2]

[1] School of Mechanical and Industrial Engineering, Dire Dawa Institute
of Technology, Dire Dawa University, Dire Dawa, Ethiopia
senay.teshome@ddu.edu.et
[2] School of Mechanical and Industrial Engineering, Addis Ababa Institute
of Technology, Addis Ababa University, Addis Ababa, Ethiopia

Abstract. In Ethiopia *injera* is consumed by most of the population. However, the application of solar dryers in drying *injera* is not a common practice. The aim of this study is to evaluate the performance of a modified mixed mode solar *injera* dryer which integrates a vertical air distribution channel using energy and exergy analysis and to determine the economic significance. The overall drying efficiency of the modified dryer in drying *injera* was found to be 10% and it takes around 4 h to reduce the moisture content to 0.14 g water/g solids. In drying *injera*, an even temperature distribution of drying air was observed over the drying trays with 2 °C temperature difference. The embodied energy of the modified dryer was obtained to be 765.46 kWh. The overall exergy efficiency of the modified dryer was found to be 13.2% and the result indicated that the exergy efficiency has an inverse relation with exergy loss. The exergy losses of the bottom and top trays were found to have very similar values and the exergy losses were observed to have monotonic relation with exergy inflow and an inverse relation with moisture content. From the economic analysis the saving per day of the modified dryer turns out to be 111.48 ETB/day and the cumulative present worth of the annual savings by using the modified dryer was found as 154,459 ETB with payback period of 104 drying days. This solar *injera* dryer will be a cost-effective choice for mass producers of dried *injera*.

Keywords: Mixed mode dryer · *Injera* drying · Exergy analysis · Economic analysis · Embodied energy

1 Introduction

The most important food in Ethiopian is *injera*. *Injera* is a fermented bread which is prepared from teff (*Eragrostistef*) [1]. *Injera* is rich in fiber and it is free from gluten [2]. Traditionally, *injera* is stored and preserved most of the time using open sun drying. Open sun drying is a traditional method and it suffers from may drawbacks like, prolonged drying, susceptibility to infestation and uncontrolled drying. This results deterioration in the quality of drying food [3]. Food preservation is possible by

© ICST Institute for Computer Sciences, Social Informatics and Telecommunications Engineering 2022
Published by Springer Nature Switzerland AG 2022. All Rights Reserved
M. L. Berihun (Ed.): ICAST 2021, LNICST 412, pp. 443–463, 2022.
https://doi.org/10.1007/978-3-030-93712-6_30

implementing appropriate drying technology. Conventional dryers uses substantial amount of energy that leads to an adverse environment impact due to greenhouse gas emission and increases the cost of dried product [4]. To overcame this problem, application of solar energy is an alternative approach for drying food, as it is abundant, renewable, inexpensive and environmentally friendly [5]. Solar food dryer helps to prevent the microbial growth and by lowering the moisture content it improvs shelf-life of food [6, 7].

For low temperature drying, mixed mode solar dryers were very efficient and found to retain the quality of dried food products [6, 8]. Mixed mode solar drying system comprises a flat plate solar collector and drying chamber. In this system, the transmitted solar radiation from a transparent cover is converted into heat through both components and utilized in the drying chamber to extract the moisture contained in the food [4].

Ethiopia is one of the countries with diverse climate condition and it is favorable for solar drying application due to availability of sufficient sunshine [9]. Solar dryers could be an effective solution to improve the economic benefit of the society by improving value-added food products locally. Since, solar dried food product are considered as branded product, the profit is certainly higher than traditionally dried food products [10–12]. Also, applying this technology will present good employment opportunity, create income generating system and helps in enhancing the nutritional standards and foreign exchange opportunity of the country [9].

The aim of design and optimization of drying system is to maximize the moisture loss of the dried product with minimum energy consumption. Consequently, quality and quantity of energy consumed during food drying process have to be evaluated to measure overall thermal performance of drying system [13]. Energy analysis of solar dryer using first law of thermodynamics helps to identify the type and amount of energy which flows through the drying system, but not the quality and losses due to irreversibility of energy [7]. Exergy analysis of solar dryer based on second law of thermodynamics will overcome the constraints of energy analysis [14]. Using energy and exergy analysis will give a clear idea about the performance of a dryer and helps to optimize the drying process [15].

Prakash et al. [16] conducted environomical analysis with energy and exergy analysis to evaluate modified greenhouse dryer operating in active and passive modes. The payback period was found to be 1.89 and 1.11 years and the embodied energy was found to be 628.73 kWh and 480.277 kWh. The exergy efficiency was in the range 30% to 78% and 29% to 86% for active and passive modes, respectively. Fudholi et al. [17] performed energy and exergy analyses on an indirect solar dryer operating in a forced mode and the experimental result showed a drying and exergy efficiency of 13% and 57%, respectively. Also, the specific energy consumption (SEC) was observed to be 5.26 kWh/kg with maximum exergy loss of 238.4 W.

Celma and Cuadros [18] applied energy and exergy to evaluate a passive natural convection solar dryer. It was observed that the exergetic efficiency decreases as drying chamber inlet temperature increases. Fudholi et al. [19] tested indirect type active solar seaweed dryer and the result indicated a drying efficiency of 27% and exergy efficiency of 30%.The improvement potential and SEC of the solar drying were found to be 247 W and 2.62 kWh/kg, respectively. Akpinar et al. [20] performed energy and exergy analyses using a cyclone dryer and the result showed exergy loss in a range from 0 to 1796 J/s. Also, it was observed that the exergy loss took place mainly in the first tray.

Even though, there are several studies on solar dryers for drying different food products [5, 21–28]. Also, few studies have been reported in improving the uneven distribution of drying air through drying chamber of mixed mode dryers [24, 29–31]. None of the published papers addressed *injera* drying using a modified mixed mode solar dryer with a comprehensive long term economic and exergy analysis. Therefore, the purpose of this study was to design and perform energy and exergy analysis with economic analysis of a modified mixed mode solar *injera* dryer with a vertical air distribution channel integrated into a drying chamber.

2 Material and Methods

2.1 Experimental Setup

The modified dryer contains, flat plate collector and drying chamber and it is constructed using locally accessible material (Fig. 1). The flat plate solar collector (1 m 2 m) with air depth of 0.1 m and tilted at an angle of 13° from horizontal was constructed. The slop of the flat plate collector was taken as the latitude of the site for optimum year-round incident solar radiation collection [32]. But to prevent accumulation of rain water during rainy season, the collector tilt was modified. The collector top was covered with 5 mm transparent window glass. The absorber was black painted galvanized sheet metal and between the absorber and plywood bottom cover there is heat insulation with 10 mm air gap and 50 mm sawdust. The drying chamber with 2.2 m height and 1.5 m depth holds three parts, a plenum chamber, vertical air distribution channel and four drying trays. The vertical air distribution channel was constructed from black painted galvanized sheet metal and it is a unique feature integrated into the drying chamber to facilitate uniform air distribution throughout the drying chamber trays. The roof of the drying chamber was covered using corrugated polycarbonate sheet which helps to transmit solar radiation to the drying chamber.

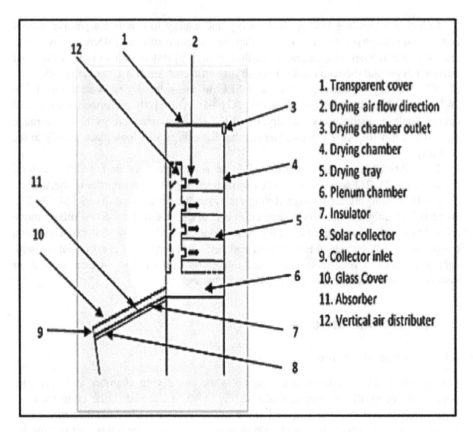

1. Transparent cover
2. Drying air flow direction
3. Drying chamber outlet
4. Drying chamber
5. Drying tray
6. Plenum chamber
7. Insulator
8. Solar collector
9. Collector inlet
10. Glass Cover
11. Absorber
12. Vertical air distributer

Fig. 1. Schematic view of modified mixed mode natural convection solar *injera* dryer

2.2 Experimental Procedure

To perform the experiment a month of August was chosen to represent an environment with low solar radiation. This condition will help to evaluate the performance of the dryer in a worst-case scenario and ensures the ability of the dryer to operate all year round. The experiment was conducted from 09:30 am till 14:30 pm. Before starting the experiment, the dryer was run for an hour to attain steady state condition through the modified dryer (Fig. 2 (a) and (b)).

To measure the temperature distribution at different locations K-type thermocouples were installed with an accuracy of ±0.2 °C at six locations and readings were taken every 5 min [33] using LabVIEW 2017 Data Acquisition system (DAQ) which is connected to a PC and the data was interpreted using Excel 2017. To measure the air velocity an anemometer integrated in (Extech's Model 45170) was used with ±0.03 m/s accuracy.

Injera with an approximate weight of 1.13 kg was purchased from local *injera* providers and used the same day for the experiment after sliced manually in rectangular shape (50 × 40 mm) [34]. The moisture content of *injera* before drying was determined following the recommendation by ASTM 2014 [35] and it was found to be 1.9 g water/g solids after drying *injera* in an oven for 24 h at 105 °C. To determine the weight change of *injera* through the experiment samples with approximate weight of 128 g were collected in 30 min interval from the drying trays and weight measurement was performed by using an electric balance (Ohaus Explorer) with ±0.001 g accuracy until desired final moisture content was achieved [33].

Fig. 2. Photographic view of the experimental setup

2.3 Energy Analysis of Modified Solar Dryer

Energy analysis of the designed solar *injera* dryer is evaluated using different methods implemented by different authors [23, 36–39] and these parameters were evaluated using the equations below.

$$SEC = \frac{E_t}{M_w} \tag{1}$$

$$SMER = \frac{1}{SEC} \tag{2}$$

$$\eta_d = \frac{M_w L_v}{E_t} \tag{3}$$

Where, M_w is the amount of moisture removed from *injera* and can be calculated from Eq. 4 [40].

$$m_w = \frac{M_w(M_i - M_f)}{100 - M_f} \qquad (4)$$

Daily thermal output (E_d) of the modified *injera* dryer is calculated using Eq. 5 and to account for the energy required to increase the sensible heat of *injera* by 15% and by 10% for heat loses from different parts of the dryer. The annual thermal output of the dryer per batch of dried *injera* (E_{an}) is calculated using the daily thermal output and the total sunshine days per year of the specific location and it is given by Eq. 6 [41].

$$E_d = \frac{M_w \times L_v}{3.6 \times 10^6} \qquad (5)$$

$$E_{an} = E_d \times N_d \qquad (6)$$

The sunshine days (N_d) in a year and the drying days (N_b) per batch were taken as 212 days [42] and 2 days/batch, respectively. The energy payback time of the dryer is estimated using Eq. 7 [43].

$$\text{EPBT} = \frac{EE}{E_{an}} \qquad (7)$$

Finally, the embodied energy of various materials used in fabrication of the dryer were calculated and presented in Table 1.

Table 1. The embodied energy of dryer

S. no.	Material	Embodied energy coefficient (kWh/kg)	Quantity (kg)	Total embodied energy (kWh)	Ref
1	GI sheet	9.67	17.75	171.59	[44]
2	Paint (solvent based)	27.25	5.00	136.25	
3	Plywood	2.88	80.95	233.86	
4	Timber	0.55	31.80	17.67	
5	Polycarbonate	10.19	3.69	37.66	
6	Glass sheet	4.41	25.00	110.42	
7	Steel wire mesh tray	9.66	1.50	14.50	
8	Fittings				
	Hinges	55.28	0.20	11.06	
	Handle	55.28	0.10	5.52	
	Steel common nails	9.67	1.50	14.51	
	Door lock	55.28	0.02	1.38	
9	Sawdust	0.55	19.90	11.06	[45]
	Total			**765.46 kWh**	

2.4   Exergy Analysis

The exergy equation for steady state system based on second law of thermodynamics is shown in Eq. 8 [46].

$$E_x = \dot{m}_{da} \times C_{pda} \left[(T - T_{amb}) - T_{amb} \times \left(\ln \frac{T}{T_{amb}} \right) \right] \tag{8}$$

The exergy inflow to the drying chamber of the modified dryer comprises the drying air flowing from the collector and the incident radiation passing through the top transparent cover of the drying chamber and it is calculated using Eq. 9 and 10 [39, 47, 48].

$$E_{x,dc_{in}} = E_{x,T1_{in}} = \dot{m}_{da} \times C_{pda} \left[(T_{dc,in} - T_{amb}) - T_{amb} \times \left(\ln \frac{T_{dc,in}}{T_{amb}} \right) \right] \tag{9}$$

$$E_{x,dc,rad_{in}} = I \times \tau \times \alpha \times A_d \left(1 - \frac{T_{amb}}{T_{sky}} \right) \tag{10}$$

Where, T_{sky} is taken as $\frac{3}{4} T_s$, which results T_{sky} to be 4,077 °C and T_s is the black body temperature of the sun [39, 48].

The exergy outflow and losses from drying tray one and drying chamber is calculated using Eq. 11–14, respectively [49].

$$E_{x,T1_{out}} = \dot{m}_{da} \times C_{pda} \left[(T_{T1,out} - T_{amb}) - T_{amb} \times \left(\ln \frac{T_{T1,out}}{T_{amb}} \right) \right] \tag{11}$$

$$E_{x,dc_{out}} = \dot{m}_{da} \times C_{pda} \left[(T_{dc,out} - T_{amb}) - T_{amb} \times \left(\ln \frac{T_{dc,out}}{T_{amb}} \right) \right] \tag{12}$$

$$E_{x,T1_{loss}} = E_{x,T1_{in}} - E_{x,T1_{out}} \tag{13}$$

$$E_{x,dc_{loss}} = E_{x,dc_{in}} - E_{x,dc_{out}} \tag{14}$$

Exergy efficiency for drying tray one and drying chamber is calculated using Eq. 15 [20].

$$\eta_{E_x} = 1 - \frac{E_{x,loss}}{E_{x,dc_{in}}} \tag{15}$$

The optimum improvement of exergy efficiency is achieved when the exergy loss from the modified mixed mode solar *injera* dryer is reduced. This improvement potential (*IP*) of the *injera* dryer is given by Eq. 16 [37].

$$IP = (1 - \eta_{E_x}) E_{x,loss} \tag{16}$$

2.5   Economic Analysis

Economic analysis of the modified dryer is evaluated using, the annualized cost analysis, life cycle analysis and payback period [50]. The annualized cost of *injera* drying is evaluated by Eq. 17 [51].

$$C_a = C_{ac} + C_m - V_a + C_{rf} + C_{re} \tag{17}$$

The annualized capital cost (C_{ac}) and salvage value (V_a) of the *injera* dryer are calculated using Eq. 18 and 19, respectively [52].

$$C_{ac} = C_{cc} \times F_c \tag{18}$$

$$V_a = V \times F_s \tag{19}$$

where, F_c and F_s are defined by Eq. 20 and 21, respectively [52].

$$F_c = \frac{d \times (1+d)^n}{(1+d)^n - 1} \tag{20}$$

$$F_s = \frac{d}{(1+d)^n - 1} \tag{21}$$

The cost of *injera* drying (C_s) per kilogram of dried *injera* and amount of *injera* dried (M_y) per year using the modified dryer are evaluated by Eq. 22 and 23, respectively [50].

$$C_s = \frac{C_a}{M_y} \tag{22}$$

$$M_y = \frac{M_d * N_d}{N_b} \tag{23}$$

For an electric *injera* dryer, which can dry the same amount of *injera* by substituting the modified dryer, the annual running fuel cost (C_{rf}) can be evaluated by using the equation below [50].

$$C_{rf} = \frac{M_y\left[\left(\frac{M_c}{100}\right) \times L_v \times C_e\right]}{\eta_e \times 3600} \tag{24}$$

Where, M_c is the moisture content of *injera* in dry basis and evaluated using Eq. 25 [5].

$$M_c = \left(\frac{M_f - M_d}{M_d}\right) \times 100 \tag{25}$$

In the life cycle savings method, the savings per *injera* drying days in the base year and the present worth of the annual savings over the life time of the modified dryer will be evaluated.

The cost of fresh *injera* per kilogram of dried *injera* is evaluated by Eq. 26 [50].

$$C_{dp} = C_{fp} \times \left(\frac{M_f}{M_d}\right) \tag{26}$$

The expense required in drying 1 kg of *injera* (C_{ds}) is evaluated for the solar *injera* dryer and electric *injera* dryer by adding the fresh *injera* cost (C_{dp}) with the cost of *injera* drying (C_s) [50].

$$C_{ds} = C_{dp} + C_s \tag{27}$$

By drying *injera* using modified dryer, the saving per kilogram (S_{kg}) in the base year can be evaluated by Eq. 28 [50].

$$S_{kg} = C_b - C_{ds} \tag{28}$$

The savings due to *injera* drying using the modified dryer per batch (S_b) and also per day (S_d) in the base year can be calculated using Eq. 29 and 30, respectively [50].

$$S_b = S_{kg} \times M_d \tag{29}$$

$$S_d = \frac{S_b}{N_b} \tag{30}$$

The annual savings (S_j) and the present worth (P_j) of *injera* drying using the modified mixed mode solar dryer in the jth year can be found by using Eq. 31 and 32 [50].

$$S_j = S_d \times N_d \times (1+i)^{j-1} \tag{31}$$

$$P_j = F_{pj} \times S_j \tag{32}$$

$$F_{pj} = \frac{1}{(1+d)^j} \tag{33}$$

Finally, the payback period (N) is evaluated by the equation below [53].

$$N = \frac{\ln\left(1 - \left(\frac{C_{cc}}{S_1}\right) \times (d-i)\right)}{\ln\left(\frac{1+i}{1+d}\right)} \tag{34}$$

3 Result and Discussion

3.1 Performance of Modified Dryer

The drying air temperature distribution through the dryer is shown in Fig. 3. During the experiment the average ambient temperature was recorded as 21 °C with solar radiation of 402 W/m². From the result it can be observed that the drying air temperature from the collector outlet was more than the ambient throughout the experimental period. This indicates that the dryer can provide sufficient amount of temperature for drying *injera* over the entire drying hour [33].

The extent of temperature variation between drying trays were found to be insignificant and it was within a narrow range of about 2 °C (Fig. 3). This uniform temperature distribution over the modified dryer could be the result of the air distribution channel and this indicates the use of this configuration will increase the efficiency of solar dryers.

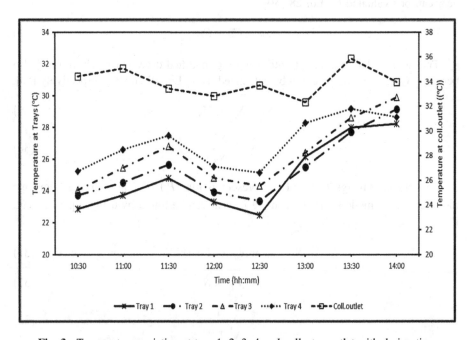

Fig. 3. Temperature variation at tray 1, 2, 3, 4 and collector outlet with drying time

The change in moisture content of injera over the experiment is shown in Fig. 4. The result indicates that to dry injera to a moisture content of 0.14 g water/g solids using the modified dryer, it takes around 4 h and the moisture content of injera was observed to decrease as drying time advances.

It was noted that the drying chamber temperature was affected as the moisture content of *injera* decreases since at the final stages of the experiment it starts to increase.

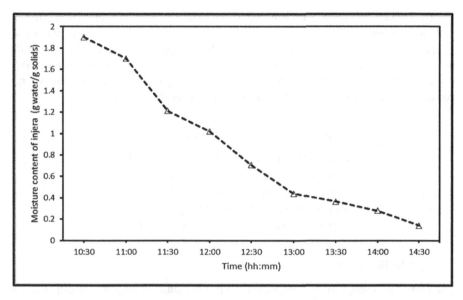

Fig. 4. The change in moisture content of *injera* with respect to drying time

3.2 Energy Performance of the Solar Dryer

The change in useful energy gain from the solar collector and the solar radiation on the collector is shown in Fig. 5. It can be seen from this result that the energy gain of the drying air from the collector increases as solar radiation decreases. The average value of energy gain from the collector was 2.1 kJ/s at corresponding solar radiation of 402 W/m^2.

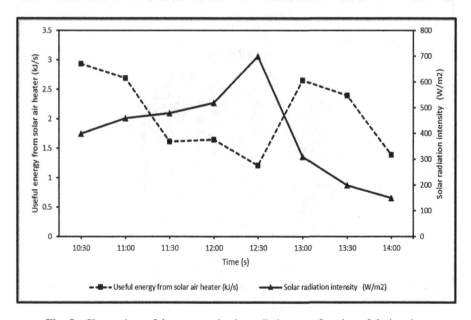

Fig. 5. Change in useful energy and solar radiation as a function of drying time

To evaluate the overall performance of the modified dryer the selected parameters with their computed results are presented in Table 2. Madhlopa and Ngwalo [54] specified a drying efficiency between 10 to 15% for natural convection dryers and the result from our study lies in this range. However, if the dryer was loaded to the design capacity, the results of this parameters could change particularly the specific energy consumption would decrease, while the drying efficiency increases.

Table 2. Performance parameters of the dryer

Parameters and performance	Unit	Value
Daily thermal output	kWh	4.01
Specific energy consumption	kWh/kg	6.9
Specific moisture extraction rate	kg/kWh	0.14
Drying efficiency	%	10%

3.3 Embodied Energy

The embodied energy of the materials used in the manufacturing the modified mixed mode solar dryer is shown in Table 1 and the percentage share is shown in Fig. 6. The percentage share of plywood was found to be the highest compared to the other materials used. The total embodied energy in the modified dryer was computed to be 766 kWh (Table 1) and the energy payback time (*EPBT*) was found to be 1.8 years. The result of the energy payback time could be considered as very low, when compared to [36, 55] reported values of 4.36 and 3.53 years.

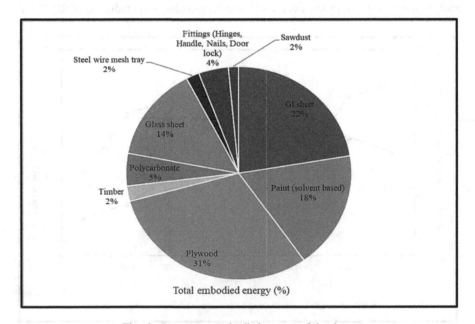

Fig. 6. Percentage embodied energy of the dryer

3.4 Exergy Analysis Result of the Modified Dryer

Figure 7 shows the exergy band diagram of the dryer which is obtained from the exergy analysis.

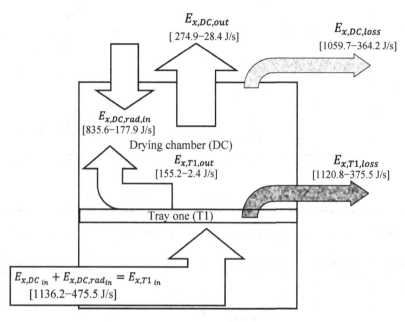

$E_{x,DC,out}$
[274.9–28.4 J/s]

$E_{x,DC,loss}$
[1059.7–364.2 J/s]

$E_{x,DC,rad,in}$
[835.6–177.9 J/s]

Drying chamber (DC)

$E_{x,T1,out}$
[155.2–2.4 J/s]

$E_{x,T1,loss}$
[1120.8–375.5 J/s]

Tray one (T1)

$E_{x,DC\ in} + E_{x,DC,rad_{in}} = E_{x,T1\ in}$
[1136.2–475.5 J/s]

Fig. 7. Exergy band diagram of the modified dryer

The exergy in, out and loss during the drying experiment are shown in Fig. 8 and Fig. 9 for drying chamber and drying tray one, respectively. The exergy in and out from drying chamber and drying tray one varies between 1136.2 to 475.5 J/s and 274.9 to 28.4 J/s and 1136.2 to 475.5 J/s and 155.2 to 2.4 J/s, respectively. The change in exergy flowing in and out over the experimental period can be explained by the variation in solar radiation [46]. Similarly, exergy loss from drying chamber and drying tray one varies between 1059.7 to 364.2 J/s and 1120.8 to 375.5 J/s, respectively. Also, the change in exergy loss can further be related to the change in moisture content of injera over the drying experiment [20]. The exergy loss from drying chamber and drying tray one was observed to be almost identical. This can indicate that the energy utilized by the dried *injera* located at different trays was equivalent. Since the exergy losses of the drying chamber were equal to exergy losses from drying tray four.

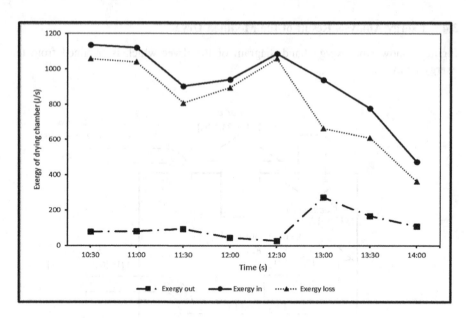

Fig. 8. Exergy in, exergy out and exergy loss with drying time for drying chamber

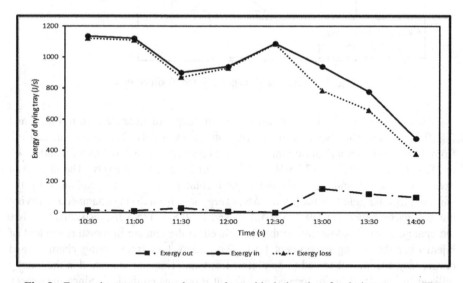

Fig. 9. Exergy in, exergy out and exergy loss with drying time for drying tray one (T1)

The change in exergy efficiency with respect to exergy loss for drying tray one is shown in Fig. 10. The exergy efficiency for drying tray one ranges from 0.22% to 21.1%. The exergy efficiency was found to be lower and steady for about the first two hours of the drying process and then it starts to increase when the exergy loss starts to decrease. The higher exergy loss and lower exergy efficiency indicates that the energy contained in the drying air was utilized effectively in drying *injera*. The exergy loss was observed to decline when the moisture content of *injera* decrease as the drying process advances (Fig. 11) and similar pattern was observed in Akpinar et al. [20].

Similar pattern was also observed with the drying chamber exergy efficiency and loss. The exergy efficiency of the drying chamber was obtained to vary from 2.6% to 29.3%. The value of improvement potential was calculated to be in the range from 278.8 J/s to 1032 J/s. It was noted that as drying time progresses the exergy efficiency rises and improvement potential declines. Similar pattern was reported by Lakshmi et al. [39] between the exergy efficiency and improvement potential.

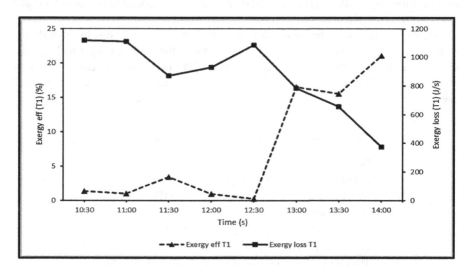

Fig. 10. Exergy loss and exergy efficiency for drying tray one (T1)

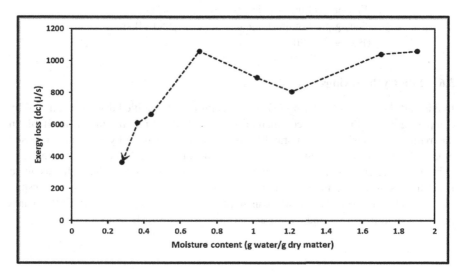

Fig. 11. Variation in exergy loss with moisture content for injera drying

3.5 Annualized Cost

To perfume the economic analysis different assumptions were implemented. The values of C_m and V were considered to be 10% of the C_{ac} and the interest rate was considered as the sum of the inflation rate and real interest rate [12, 50]. Also, additional parameters which were used in the analysis are presented in Table 3 and this parameter values are considered based on the economic condition in Ethiopia.

The annual drying capacity of a single modified solar *injera* dryer was evaluated and found to be 509 kg of *injera*. The annualized cost was evaluated for drying *injera* using the modified solar dryer and electric dryer and it was found to be 2,466 ETB and 3,403 ETB, respectively.

Similarity the cost of drying one kilogram of *injera* was evaluated for both drying methods and the result shows that drying *injera* using the modified dryer will cost 4.8 ETB while using electric dryers will cost 6.7 ETB. The result indicates that using modified solar dryer will reduce the cost of *injera* drying by 2 ETB per kilogram of dried *injera*.

Table 3. Parameters used in the economic analysis of the modified dryer

Parameters	Values
Capital cost for single modified dryer	10,000 ETB
Inflation rate	11%
Real interest rate	7%
Interest rate	18%
Life span of the modified dryer	10 years
The average domestic cost of electricity	0.77 ETB/kWh
Cost of fresh *injera* (for one kilogram)	21 ETB/kg
Capital cost for single electric dryer	12,500 ETB
Efficiency of the electric dryer	0.75%
Selling price of dried *injera*	95 ETB/kg

US$1 = ETB 40

3.6 Life Cycle Savings

In this part the savings by drying *injera* in this proposed modified dryer is evaluated by comparing it with the cost of commercially available dried *injera* which is available in the market and considered as a branded dried *injera*. The saving by using the proposed modified dryer for drying *injera* was found to be 111.48 ETB in a single drying day. Other results related to life cycle savings analysis are presented in Table 4. It was noted from this result that an annual saving present worth of 154,459 ETB over the lifespan of the modified dryer. This result can imply that by investing 10,000 ETB on this proposed modified dryer today, a user can save 154,459 ETB today.

3.7 Payback Period

The payback period was evaluated and the time needed to cover the initial investment by the savings from using the modified dryer was determined to be 0.49 years or 104 drying days. This result can indicate that the dryer will operate without any cost for around 9.5 years. This can be explained by the materials used in the fabrication of the dryer which were locally accessible and inexpensive. In addition, the dryer was construct by locally available skilled workers with minimum cost.

Table 4. Results of the life cycle saving analysis for the modified dryer over the lifespan of ten years

Year	Annualized cost (ETB)	Annual savings (ETB)	Present worth of annual saving (ETB)	Present worth of cumulative saving (ETB)
1	2,466.00	23,633.76	20,028.61	20,028.61
2	2,466.00	26,233.47	18,840.47	38,869.08
3	2,466.00	29,119.16	17,722.82	56,591.90
4	2,466.00	32,322.26	16,671.46	73,263.36
5	2,466.00	35,877.71	15,682.48	88,945.84
6	2,466.00	39,824.26	14,752.16	103,698.00
7	2,466.00	44,204.93	13,877.03	117,575.04
8	2,466.00	49,067.47	13,053.82	130,628.86
9	2,466.00	54,464.89	12,279.44	142,908.30
10	2,466.00	60,456.03	11,551.00	154,459.30

4 Conclusion

The performance of the modified dryer was evaluated based on the energy and exergy analysis and finally the economic analysis of the proposed dryer was performed. The temperature over *injera* drying trays was observed to have an even distribution. To dry *injera* to the final moisture content of 0.14 g water/g solid it took around 4 h. The SEC and drying efficiency of the modified dryer were 6.9 kWh/kg and 10%. The total embodied energy and the energy payback time of the modified dryer was computed to be 766 kWh and 1.8 years, respectively.

From the exergy analysis it was observed that the exergy losses of the modified dryer decrease as the drying process progress and as the moisture content of *injera* reduces. Also, the exergy losses of the bottom and top *injera* drying trays were found to be very similar and this indicated that *injera* dried at different levels of drying trays were exposed to uniform drying energy. The value of exergy efficiency was observed to ranges from 2.6% to 29.3% and it increase as the value of exergy loss decreases.

The economic analysis of the modified dryer indicated that the cost of drying *injera* using electric dryer will cost 40% more when compared with the proposed modified dryer. The cumulative present worth of the modified dryer was evaluated to be 154,459 ETB with a very low payback time of 104 drying days.

Finally, the result indicates that *injera* drying using the modified dryer will benefit users by reducing the drying time because of the higher temperature in the drying chamber and will improve the quality of dried *injera*. Evaluating a dryer using energy, exergy and economic analysis will give significant insight about the system.

Acknowledgment. Authors of this paper would like to thank the School of Mechanical & Industrial Engineering, Institute of Technology of Dire Dawa University and Addis Ababa University for funded the study, and the technical staff who constructed the modified dryer.

References

1. Baye, K.: Nutrient composition and health benefits, pp. 371–396 (2005)
2. Ashagrie, Z., Abate, D.: Improvement of Injera shelf life through the use of chemical preservatives. Afr. J. Fodd Agric. Nutr. Dev. **12**, 6409–6423 (2012)
3. Pardhi, C.B., Bhagoria, J.L.: Development and performance evaluation of mixed-mode solar dryer with forced convection. Int. J. Energy Environ. Eng. **4**, 23 (2013). https://doi.org/10.1186/2251-6832-4-23
4. Chauhan, P.S., Kumar, A., Nuntadusit, C.: Thermo-environomical and drying kinetics of bitter gourd flakes drying under north wall insulated greenhouse dryer. Sol. Energy **162**, 205–216 (2018). https://doi.org/10.1016/j.solener.2018.01.023
5. Lingayat, A., Chandramohan, V.P., Raju, V.R.K.: Design, development and performance of indirect type solar dryer for banana drying. Energy Procedia **109**, 409–416 (2017). https://doi.org/10.1016/j.egypro.2017.03.041
6. Dhalsamant, K., Tripathy, P.P., Shrivastava, S.L.: Effect of pretreatment on rehydration, colour and nanoindentation properties of potato cylinders dried using a mixed-mode solar dryer. J. Sci. Food Agric. **97**, 3312–3322 (2017). https://doi.org/10.1002/jsfa.8181
7. Mugi, V.R., Chandramohan, V.P.: Energy and exergy analysis of forced and natural convection indirect solar dryers: estimation of exergy inflow, outflow, losses, exergy efficiencies and sustainability indicators from drying experiments. J. Clean. Prod. **282**, 124421 (2021). https://doi.org/10.1016/j.jclepro.2020.124421
8. Zaman, M.A., Bala, B.K.: Thin layer solar drying of rough rice. Sol. Energy **42**, 167–171 (1989). https://doi.org/10.1016/0038-092X(89)90143-6
9. Wakjira, M.: Solar drying of fruits and windows of opportunities in Ethiopia. African J. Food Sci. **4**, 790–802 (2010)
10. Anum, R., Ghafoor, A., Munir, A.: Study of the drying behavior and performance evaluation of gas fired hybrid solar dryer. J. Food Process Eng. **40**, e12351 (2017). https://doi.org/10.1111/jfpe.12351
11. Singh, S., Singh, P.P., Dhaliwal, S.: Multi-shelf portable solar dryer. Renew. Energy **29**, 753–765 (2004). https://doi.org/10.1016/j.renene.2003.09.010
12. Sreekumar, A.: Techno-economic analysis of a roof-integrated solar air heating system for drying fruit and vegetables. Energy Convers. Manag. **51**, 2230–2238 (2010). https://doi.org/10.1016/j.enconman.2010.03.017
13. Rani, P., Tripathy, P.P.: Drying characteristics, energetic and exergetic investigation during mixed-mode solar drying of pineapple slices at varied air mass flow rates. Renew. Energy **167**, 508–519 (2021). https://doi.org/10.1016/j.renene.2020.11.107
14. Tiwari, G.N., Sahota, L.: Exergy and Technoeconomic Analysis of Solar Thermal Desalination. Elsevier Inc. (2018)

15. Dincer, I.: Exergy as a potential tool for sustainable drying systems. Sustain. Cities Soc. **1**, 91–96 (2011). https://doi.org/10.1016/j.scs.2011.04.001

16. Prakash, O., Kumar, A., Laguri, V.: Performance of modified greenhouse dryer with thermal energy storage. Energy Rep. **2**, 155–162 (2016). https://doi.org/10.1016/j.egyr.2016.06.003

17. Fudholi, A., Sopian, K., Yazdi, M.H., et al.: Performance analysis of solar drying system for red chili. Sol. Energy **99**, 47–54 (2014). https://doi.org/10.1016/j.solener.2013.10.019

18. Celma, A.R., Cuadros, F.: Energy and exergy analyses of OMW solar drying process. Renew. Energy **34**, 660–666 (2009). https://doi.org/10.1016/j.renene.2008.05.019

19. Fudholi, A., Sopian, K., Othman, M.Y., Ruslan, M.H.: Energy and exergy analyses of solar drying system of red seaweed. Energy Build. **68**, 121–129 (2013). https://doi.org/10.1016/j.enbuild.2013.07.072

20. Akpinar, E.K., Midilli, A., Bicer, Y.: Energy and exergy of potato drying process via cyclone type dryer. Energy Convers. Manag. **46**, 2530–2552 (2005). https://doi.org/10.1016/j.enconman.2004.12.008

21. Mahapatra, A., Tripathy, P.P.: Thermal performance analysis of natural convection solar dryers under no load condition: experimental investigation and numerical simulation. Int. J. Green Energy **16**, 1448–1464 (2019). https://doi.org/10.1080/15435075.2019.1671417

22. Erick César, L.V., Ana Lilia, C.M., Octavio, G.V., et al.: Thermal performance of a passive, mixed-type solar dryer for tomato slices (Solanum lycopersicum). Renew. Energy **147**, 845–855 (2020). https://doi.org/10.1016/j.renene.2019.09.018

23. Dejchanchaiwong, R., Arkasuwan, A., Kumar, A., Tekasakul, P.: Mathematical modeling and performance investigation of mixed-mode and indirect solar dryers for natural rubber sheet drying. Energy Sustain. Dev. **34**, 44–53 (2016). https://doi.org/10.1016/j.esd.2016.07.003

24. Abubakar, S., Umaru, S., Kaisan, M., et al.: Development and performance comparison of mixed-mode solar crop dryers with and without thermal storage. Renew. Energy **128**, 285–298 (2018). https://doi.org/10.1016/j.renene.2018.05.049

25. Wang, W., Li, M., Hassanien, R.H.E., et al.: Thermal performance of indirect forced convection solar dryer and kinetics analysis of mango. Appl. Therm. Eng. **134**, 310–321 (2018). https://doi.org/10.1016/j.applthermaleng.2018.01.115

26. Madhlopa, A., Jones, S., Kalenga, S.J.: A solar air heater with composite–absorber systems for food dehydration. Renew. Energy **27**, 27–37 (2002). https://doi.org/10.1016/S0960-1481(01)00174-4

27. Musembi, M.N., Kiptoo, K.S., Yuichi, N.: Design and analysis of solar dryer for mid-latitude region. Energy Procedia **100**, 98–110 (2016). https://doi.org/10.1016/j.egypro.2016.10.145

28. Hajar, E., Rachid, T., Najib, B.M.: Conception of a solar air collector for an indirect solar dryer. Pear drying test. Energy Procedia **141**, 29–33 (2017). https://doi.org/10.1016/j.egypro.2017.11.114

29. Misha, S., Mat, S., Ruslan, M.H., et al.: Review on the application of a tray dryer system for agricultural products. World Appl. Sci. J. **22**, 424–433 (2013). https://doi.org/10.5829/idosi.wasj.2013.22.03.343

30. Margaris, D.P., Ghiaus, A.: Dried product quality improvement by air flow manipulation in tray dryers. J. Food Eng. **75**, 542–550 (2006). https://doi.org/10.1016/j.jfoodeng.2005.04.037

31. Mathioulakis, E., Karathanos, V.T., Belessiotis, V.G.: Simulation of air movement in a dryer by computational fluid dynamics: application for the drying of fruits. J. Food Eng. **36**, 183–200 (1998). https://doi.org/10.1016/S0260-8774(98)00026-0

32. Duffie, J.A., Beckman, W.A.: Solar Engineering of Thermal Processes, 4th edn. Wiley, Hoboken (2013)

33. Leon, M.A., Kumar, S., Bhattacharya, S.C.: A comprehensive procedure for performance evaluation of solar food dryers. Renew. Sustain. Energy Rev. **6**, 367–393 (2002)
34. Sileshi, S.T., Hassen, A.A., Adem, K.D.: Drying kinetics of dried injera (dirkosh) using a mixed-mode solar dryer. Cogent Eng. **8**, 1–19 (2021). https://doi.org/10.1080/23311916.2021.1956870
35. ASTM: ASTM D2974-14: Standard test methods for moisture, ash, and organic matter of peat and other organic soils. ASTM International, West Conshohocken (2014)
36. Shrivastava, V., Kumar, A.: Embodied energy analysis of the indirect solar drying unit. Int. J. Ambient Energy **38**, 280–285 (2017). https://doi.org/10.1080/01430750.2015.1092471
37. Fudholi, A., Sopian, K., Alghoul, M.A., et al.: Performances and improvement potential of solar drying system for palm oil fronds. Renew. Energy **78**, 561–565 (2015). https://doi.org/10.1016/j.renene.2015.01.050
38. Rabha, D.K., Muthukumar, P., Somayaji, C.: Energy and exergy analyses of the solar drying processes of ghost chilli pepper and ginger. Renew. Energy **105**, 764–773 (2017). https://doi.org/10.1016/j.renene.2017.01.007
39. Lakshmi, D.V.N., Muthukumar, P., Layek, A., Nayak, P.K.: Performance analyses of mixed mode forced convection solar dryer for drying of stevia leaves. Sol. Energy **188**, 507–518 (2019). https://doi.org/10.1016/j.solener.2019.06.009
40. Ayensu, A.: Dehydration of food crops using a solar dryer with convective heat flow. Sol. Energy **59**(4–6), 121–126 (1997). https://doi.org/10.1016/S0038-092X(96)00130-2
41. Prakash, O., Kumar, A.: Environomical analysis and mathematical modelling for tomato flakes drying in a modified greenhouse dryer under active mode. Int. J. Food Eng. **10**, 669–681 (2014). https://doi.org/10.1515/ijfe-2013-0063
42. Shahin, M.: Chapter 3 Climate of the Nile Basin. Dev. Water Sci. **21**, 59–111 (1985). https://doi.org/10.1016/S0167-5648(08)70762-7
43. Eltawil, M.A., Azam, M.M., Alghannam, A.O.: Energy analysis of hybrid solar tunnel dryer with PV system and solar collector for drying mint (MenthaViridis). J. Clean. Prod. **181**, 352–364 (2018). https://doi.org/10.1016/j.jclepro.2018.01.229
44. Baird, G., Alcorn, A., Haslam, P.: The energy embodied in building materials - updated New Zealand coefficients and their significance. IPENZ Trans. **24**, 46–54 (1997)
45. Pullen, S.: Embodied energy of building materials in houses (1995)
46. Akbulut, A., Durmuş, A.: Energy and exergy analyses of thin layer drying of mulberry in a forced solar dryer. Energy **35**, 1754–1763 (2010). https://doi.org/10.1016/j.energy.2009.12.028
47. Akpinar, E.K., Midilli, A., Bicer, Y.: The first and second law analyses of thermodynamic of pumpkin drying process. J. Food Eng. **72**, 320–331 (2006). https://doi.org/10.1016/j.jfoodeng.2004.12.011
48. Ndukwu, M.C., Simo-Tagne, M., Abam, F.I., et al.: Exergetic sustainability and economic analysis of hybrid solar-biomass dryer integrated with copper tubing as heat exchanger. Heliyon **6**, e03401 (2020). https://doi.org/10.1016/j.heliyon.2020.e03401
49. Midilli, A., Kucuk, H.: Energy and exergy analyses of solar drying process of pistachio. Energy **28**, 539–556 (2003). https://doi.org/10.1016/S0360-5442(02)00158-5
50. Singh, P.P., Singh, S., Dhaliwal, S.S.: Multi-shelf domestic solar dryer. Energy Convers. Manag. **47**, 1799–1815 (2006). https://doi.org/10.1016/j.enconman.2005.10.002
51. Sodha, M.S., Chandra, R., Pathak, K., et al.: Techno-economic analysis of typical dryers. Energy Convers. Manag. **31**, 509–513 (1991). https://doi.org/10.1016/0196-8904(91)90085-W
52. Kumar, A., Kandpal, T.C.: Solar drying and CO2 emissions mitigation: potential for selected cash crops in India. Sol. Energy **78**, 321–329 (2005). https://doi.org/10.1016/j.solener.2004.10.001

53. Desa, W.N.Y.M., Fudholi, A., Yaakob, Z.: Energy-economic-environmental analysis of solar drying system: a review. Int. J. Power Electron. Drive Syst. **11**, 1011–1018 (2020). https://doi.org/10.11591/ijpeds.v11.i2.pp1011-1018
54. Madhlopa, A., Ngwalo, G.: Solar dryer with thermal storage and biomass-backup heater. Sol. Energy **81**, 449–462 (2007). https://doi.org/10.1016/j.solener.2006.08.008
55. Barnwal, P., Tiwari, G.N.: Life cycle energy metrics and CO2 credit analysis of a hybrid photovoltaic/thermal greenhouse dryer. Int. J. Low Carbon Technol. **3**, 203–220 (2008). https://doi.org/10.1093/ijlct/3.3.203

Energy Management Control System for Hybrid Renewable Energy Power Sources

Sintayehu Alemnew Hailu[1]([✉]) [ID], Getachew Biru Worku[2] [ID], and Minyamer Gelawe Wase[3] [ID]

[1] Kotebe Metropolitan University, Addis Ababa, Ethiopia
[2] Addis Ababa University, Institute of Technology, Addis Ababa, Ethiopia
[3] Adama Science and Technology University, Adama, Ethiopia

Abstract. Ethiopia is a developing country, where population living in the country side still does not have access to electricity – for the most part. The majority of the population in the rural areas uses fossil fuels for house hold use. Fossil fuels are friendly to the environment. Renewable energy sources are alternative solutions to mitigate these problems. Ethiopia is endowed with numerous renewable energy resources naturally. The major ones are small-scale hydropower, biomass, and solar power. This paper deals with the design and implementation of a hybrid power generation energy management system to be used in the Benti rural village of Fogera Wereda. Managing the different energy sources is discussed in detail. The Fogera site consists of 426 households with a total electric power demand of 120 kW. To satisfy this demand, 50%, 30%, and 20% are to be contributed from hydro, solar, and Biomass power system generations respectively. A fuzzy logic controller is used as the main component of the power management system. The controller monitors the demand coming from the loads and which sources are available to switch to the appropriate power supply regularly.

Keywords: Hybrid · Solar · Biomass · Hydropower · Fuzzy logic controller

1 Introduction

Ethiopia is naturally gifted with several renewable energy sources which can be used as a source of electrical energy. A few of the major ones are hydropower, biomass, wind, and solar energy which can be utilized separately or in combination. Be that as it may, conventional biomass energy is the overwhelming source of energy within the country range for about 83% of the full population of Ethiopia [1]. Village electrification may be a pivotal step for moving forward the socio-economic conditions of provincial zones and by and large advancement of the nation [2]. The nation includes a gigantic renewable vitality potential that has not yet been evaluated for rural charge. In case country communities are provided with cutting edge power from renewable vitality assets, the vitality utilization of the nation increments and after that the business of its populace will be moved forward. Nonetheless, there are many adverse effects of continual use of traditional biomass energy, such as the continuous deforestation, the scarcity of natural resources and the rising cost of household fuels. In particular, the

M. L. Berihun (Ed.): ICAST 2021, LNICST 412, pp. 464–479, 2022.
https://doi.org/10.1007/978-3-030-93712-6_31

gathering of firewood has increased the physical strain on the women and children usually entrusted with this task; and rising oil import costs have hurt Ethiopia's trade balance and caused a shortage of foreign exchange (Fig. 1).

Fig. 1. Lack of electricity accesses and its consequences in rural village (Source: Fogera woreda city administration)

In order to mitigate those problems, the worldwide attentions are given to renewable energy technologies. Connecting the majority of rural areas to the main electrical grid requires a huge investment and effort. The micro-grids can be a cost-effective solution for such rural areas. Through previous work, researchers have attempted to combine and hybridize different energy sources. Siddhartha Gobina [3] proposed an optimal sizing based on a genetic algorithm of an autonomous hybrid solar battery/biomass power supply system to meet the energy demand of a typical village on Sagar Island. Melakou. M [4] developed a hybrid renewable energy generation based on a fuzzy logic controller for the village of Barsoma. rural districts in Ethiopia. J. P. Sharma [6] proposed an autonomous hybrid energy system model for universities. Martin Galad et al. [7, 10, 11] discussed a module design of photovoltaic solar cells for an autonomous renewable system. However, their work was only based on the design and modeling of the hybrid power systems. Hybrid power systems need to be controlled depending on the power demand and energy resource availability of the village. This paper introduces the hybrid power system management based on the fuzzy logic controller. The fuzzy logic is responsible to switch the available power system sources depending on the power demand. In this work, storage systems (Batteries) are not considered, due to cost factor. This research focuses on AC power systems, which is generated from hybrid energy sources and how it is controlled to meet the power demand.

2 The Proposed Hybrid System

The proposed hybrid system combines solar, micro-hydro and biomass renewable energy sources as shown in Fig. 2. Its ability to meet energy demand depends on climate data, area location and household size. These conditions will determine the different operating modes of the system. The controller is responsible for meeting customer energy demands and improving system efficiency. The controller detects the demand on the load side and switches the source accordingly to meet the demand on the customer side based on the availability of energy resource.

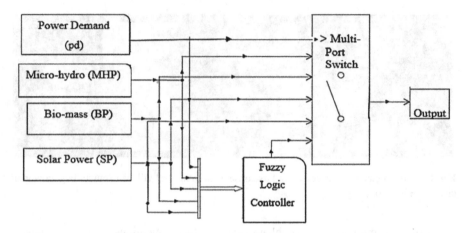

Fig. 2. Block diagram of proposed hybrid system

In principle, these techniques are evaluated by the energy balance between total production and total demand. A full-fledged controller is essential to efficiently manage the operation of production subsystems. It depends on the amount of load; the controller makes the appropriate decision to switch the multiport switch to the desired load demand output.

3 Energy Demand

Evaluation of the total energy consumption of the study area is the first step taken to design an electric power system [4]. The size and cost of implementing hybrid system components is strongly influenced by the size of the electrical load. Determination of village load was carried out for 426 families with an average of four members per family unit; representing a population of 1704 (source: the city administration). Load estimation is carried out by identifying the type, daily operating hours, number of equipment and their evaluation. As a result, the total energy consumption is estimated using the general formula;

Energy consumption(kWh) = number of appliances used ∗ power rating of each appliance (W) ∗ hours of operation/1000.

Energy demands in the village is estimated by assuming the following uses for the average household: lighting (100% of population), 4 water pumping motors for irrigation, Radio (70% of population), TV (70% of population), household refrigerator (25% of population), cooking stove (10% of population), and Injera Mitad (7% of population). Due to the high energy demand of Injera Mitad and cooking stoves, the number of users is small. The elementary school (10 lighting each consuming 130w, 8-fluorescent lamps each consuming 52 W, one copy machine consuming 900 W, and one computer consuming 300 W,) and clinic (8 lighting each consuming 104 W, 4 fluorescent lamps each consuming 26 W, one vaccine refrigerator consuming 100 W, microscope consuming 15 W, water heater consuming 1000 W, and one computer consuming 30 W) are considered as loads as shown in Table 1. Load profiles for each village were available due to the courtesy of the administrative officers of Fogera Wereda and Benti Kebele combined with the observed previous trends from similar villages that had recently been electrified.

Table 1. Total energy consumption of Benti village.

Time	Total Load (kWh)					
	Energy Household	Public loads	Energy In church	Energy in clinic	Energy in school	Total load Energy
0:0-1:0	10.65	-	0.026	0.126	-	10.802
1:0-2:0	10.65	-	-	0.1	-	10.75
2:0-3:0	10.65	-	-	0.1	-	10.75
3:0-4:0	10.65	-	-	0.1	-	10.75
4:0-5:0	16.188	-	-	0.1	-	16.288
5:0-6:0	105.222	-	0.134	0.1	-	106.122
6:0-7:0	108.63	-	0.134	0.1	-	108.864
7:0-8:0	44.73	-	-	0.1	-	44.83
8:0-9:0	44.73	9.5	-	1.115	-	55.345
9:0-10:0	44.73	9.5	-	1.415	-	55.645
10:0-11:0	44.73	-	-	0.4	1.2	46.33
11:0-12:0	44.73	-	-	0.1	0.300	45.13
12:0-13:0	108.63	-	-	0.1	-	108.73
13:0-14:0	44.73	-	-	0.1	-	44.83
14:0-15:0	44.73	9.5	-	1.115	0.3	55.645
15:0-16:0	44.73	9.5	-	1.415	0.3	55.945
16:0-17:0	44.73	-	-	0.4	0.9	46.03
17:0-18:0	44.73	-	0.080	0.1	-	44.91
18:0-19:0	136.32	-	0.184	0.204	0.182	136.89
19:0-20:0	72.42	-	0.160	0.204	0.234	73.018
20:0-21:0	72.42	-	0.026	0.152	0.104	72.702
21:0-22:0	57.51	-	-	0.152	0.052	57.714
22:0-23:0	21.726	-	-	0.126	0.052	21.904
23:0-24:0	10.65	-	-	0.126	-	10.776
Total load Energy	1199.616	38	0.744	8.085	3.624	1250.069

(Source: Fogera woreda city administration)

The total daily electricity consumption by households, commercial expenses (health centers, churches, schools) and general expenses are 1199,616 kWh, 12,453 kWh, 38 kWh, respectively. The total daily electricity consumption of Benti village is around 12050.069 kWh. Figure 3 shows the total load profile of the village. Peak loads are at

7 pm, 8 pm, 9 pm as most households use lamps. The minimum load is around 22:00 to 06:00 because the energy consumption late at night is minimal. Figure 3 shows the daily load profile of Benti village.

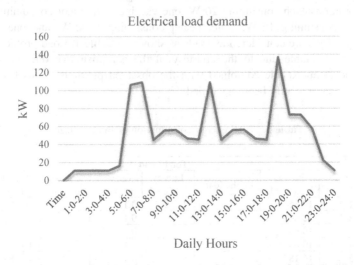

Fig. 3. Load profile of Benti village (Source: Fogera woreda city administration)

The total daily energy consumption of the selected village location is around 12050.069 KWh, and from here, the annual energy consumption is 12050.1 kWh 365 i.e., 4398275.185 kWh (4398,275 MWh). The average load demand (LD) per hour is 52.1 kW and the peak load (PL) is calculated by dividing the average load demand by the load factor (LF) and taking a load factor of 0.6.

$$PL = \frac{LD}{LF} = \frac{52.1\ kW}{0.6} = 86.8$$

Installed capacity = peak load + loss, and assuming a loss of 7% of peak load (PL) which gives 6.076 kW, the installed capacity is 86.6 kW + 6.076 kW = 92. 876 kW. Accordingly, the total electrical energy demand of the village becomes 92.876 kW.

a. **Forecasting load demand after 10 years**

The current total daily household electricity consumption is 11999.6 kWh. Consumption per household (U) = annual energy consumption (A) number of households (N).

$$U_{230} = 437.85\ MWh \div 426 = 1027.84\ kWh$$

$$\log G = 1.28 + C_1 + \ldots\ldots - K_1 \times K_2 \ldots K_N 0.155\log u \tag{1}$$

where, G = annual percentage growth in per household consumption, U is annual kWh usage per household, C_1.... etc. are constants for household's growth (2.3%) and others. $K_1, K_2....K_N$ are constant assumed to be one.

$$\log G = 1.28 + C_1 - 0.15 \log u, C_1 = 0.05 \times PR, C_1 = 0.115$$
$$\log G = 1.28 + C_1 - 0.15 \log 1027.84,$$
$$\log G = 1.28 + 0.115 - 0.45178$$
$$\log G = 0.9432, G = 10^{0.9432} = 8.77$$

By 2030 the annual KWh usage per household is estimated via:

$$U_{230} = U_{230} \times (1 + \frac{G}{100})^{10} \div (1 + \frac{PR}{100})^{10} \quad (2)$$

$$U_{230} = 1027.84 \times (1 + \frac{8.77}{100})^{10} \div (1 + \frac{2.3}{100})^{10} = 1897.8\,\text{kWh}.$$

Number of house hold (HS) for 2030

$$HS_{230} \times (1 + \frac{PR}{100})^{10} = 426 \times (1 + \frac{2.3}{100})^{10} = 535\,\text{Households}$$

Energy consumption per household for 2030 = 1897.8 kWh × 535 = 1015.3 MWh

$$\text{Peak load demand} = \frac{\text{Annual energy consumption}}{\text{total time of the year}} = \frac{1015.3}{365} = 115.9\,\text{kW}$$

Table 2. Public and commercial loads forecast

Load type	Commercial loads			Public loads	
	Health centers	Schools	Churches	Mills	Pumps
Present condition	1	1	1	1	1
kW	0.336	0.15	0.031	1.25	0.333
Total kW	2.1				
10 years plan	1	1	1	1	2
kW	0.66	0.65	0.25	2	0.666
Total kW	4.1				

The commercial and general load needs of Benti village for the next 10 years are shown in Table 1. According to the 2020–2030 plan for the Benti village GC, the total commercial electricity demand and public load is assumed to be 4.1 kW working 10 h a day. Therefore, the total energy consumption is 4 kWh. This shows that commercial and industrial expenses will grow very rapidly due to the growth of schools, health centers, irrigation, rice production and others. Thus, the total electricity demand of Benti Village for the year 2030 is 120 kW (Table 2).

4 Fuzzy Logic Controller (FLC) for the Hybrid System

In this paper, FLC is used to monitor and regulate the power supplied by the hybrid system to electrify the village. Fuzzy logic is one type of artificial intelligence-based technique [8]. It consists of three main steps: fuzzification, fuzzy inference with knowledge base, and defuzzification which is shown in Fig. 4.

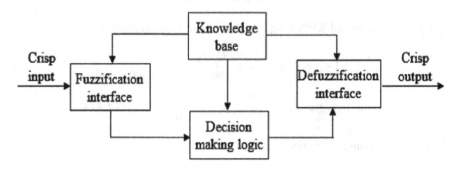

Fig. 4. The general architecture of the fuzzy logic controller [8]

Fuzzification is the process of converting crisp sets into fuzzy sets. This process is known as fuzzy inference [9]. Fuzzy inference systems come in two types: Mamdani-type and Sugeno-type which differ in the way outputs are resolved. In order for the actual system to use the output, the fuzzy logic must convert the internal fuzzy output variable to a sharp value. This conversion process is called defuzzification. Fuzzy logic design provides an effective way of controlling power systems. It first watches the load and switches the appropriate power sources to meet the demand from the costumers.

a. Fuzzy Interface Model

The main steps taken when designing the FLC are specifying the constraints, setting the linguistic variables, and setting rules for controllers. The fuzzy logic controller in this work has four inputs and one output. The linguistic input variables of the FLC are Solar power (Sp), Microhydro-power (Mhp), Biomass power (Bp) and Power demand (PD), and the single linguistic output variable is out power (Po). Each input linguistic variable is specified by three linguistic values namely Low, Medium and Large. The output linguistic variable has Mhp only, Mhp + Sp, Mhp + Bp, Mhp + Sp + Bp linguistic values. The fuzzy interface model in the fuzzy toolbox is developed as shown Fig. 5.

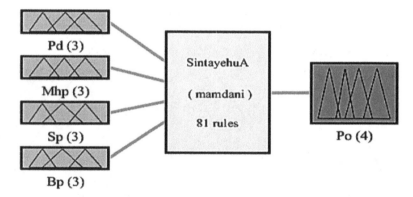

Fig. 5. Fuzzy interface model

Hence there are 4-inputs each has 3-membership functions and one output which has 4-membership functions. As a result, there are 81 fuzzy if then rules. From the total of 81-rules, 10-if then rules are shown below.

1. If (Pd is Low) or (Mhp is L) or (Sp is L) or (Bp is L) then (Po is Mhp+Sp) (1)
2. If (Pd is Low) or (Mhp is L) or (Sp is L) or (Bp is M) then (Po is Mhp+Bp) (1)
3. If (Pd is Low) or (Mhp is L) or (Sp is L) or (Bp is H) then (Po is Mhp+Bp) (1)
4. If (Pd is Low) or (Mhp is L) or (Sp is M) or (Bp is L) then (Po is Mhp+Sp) (1)
5. If (Pd is Low) or (Mhp is L) or (Sp is M) or (Bp is M) then (Po is Mhp+Sp) (1)
6. If (Pd is Low) or (Mhp is L) or (Sp is M) or (Bp is H) then (Po is Mhp+Bp) (1)
7. If (Pd is Low) or (Mhp is L) or (Sp is H) or (Bp is L) then (Po is Mhp+Sp) (1)
8. If (Pd is Low) or (Mhp is L) or (Sp is H) or (Bp is M) then (Po is Mhp+Sp) (1)
9. If (Pd is Low) or (Mhp is L) or (Sp is H) or (Bp is H) then (Po is Mhp+Sp) (1)
10. If (Pd is Low) or (Mhp is M) or (Sp is L) or (Bp is L) then (Po is Mhp+Sp) (1)

For the FLC design the triangular membership function justified the inputs; Mamdani inference system was tasked with rule processing, and center of gravity analyzed and processed defuzzification [9]. Membership function for each input-output linguistic values was assigned and the possible operational rules were generated. Next, the rules of the controller for the input values if the output were evaluated for suitability. To see the overall performance of the hybrid system, components are assumed to produce a random signal.

A) Membership Function of Power Demand (PD)

Membership function has three linguistic values which are Low (0 22.5 45), Medium (30 60 90), and Large (60 90 120) as shown in Fig. 6.

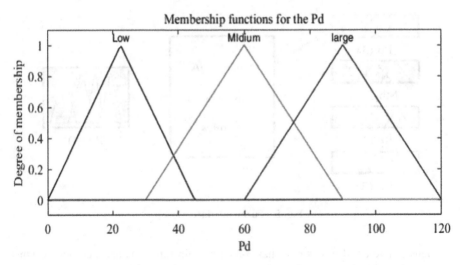

Fig. 6. Membership function of power demand

B) Membership Function of Micro-Hydropower (Mhp)

Mhp is the second input linguistic variable having three linguistic values: Low (0 13.5 27.5), Medium (18.3 32.08 45.83), Large (36.6 51.3 66) as shown in Fig. 7.

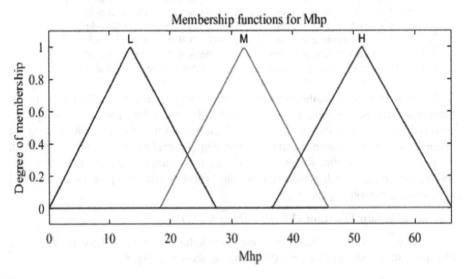

Fig. 7. Membership function of micro-hydro power

C) Membership Function of Solar Power (Sp)

The third input to the linguistic variable is the Solar Power which has three linguistic values, Low (0 6.66 13.33), Medium (6.66 16.67 26.67), Large (20 28 40) as shown in Fig. 8.

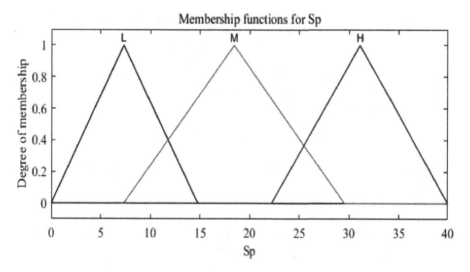

Fig. 8. Membership function of solar power

D) Membership Function of Biomass Power (BP)

Biomass power is the fourth input also having three linguistic values, Low (0 5 9.99), Medium (5 12.5 20), Large (15 21 27) as shown in Fig. 9.

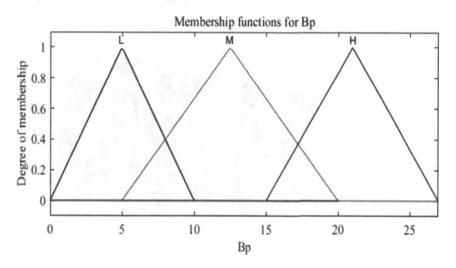

Fig. 9. Membership function of Biomass power (BP)

E) Membership Function of Output Power (Po)

Amongst output linguistic variables output power is the sole variable which has three linguistic values: Mhp-only (0 18.75 37.5), Mhp + Sp (30 45 60), Mhp + Bp (45 67.5 90), Mhp + Sp + Bp (75 97.5 120) as shown in Fig. 10.

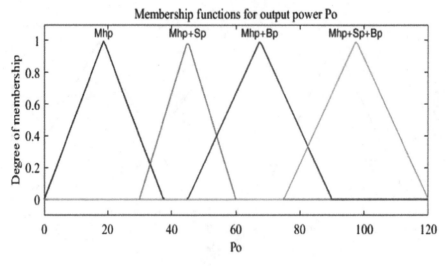

Fig. 10. Membership function of output power (Po)

The designed fuzzy logic model for the hybrid system can be seen in the 3D surface view of the model as shown in Fig. 11.

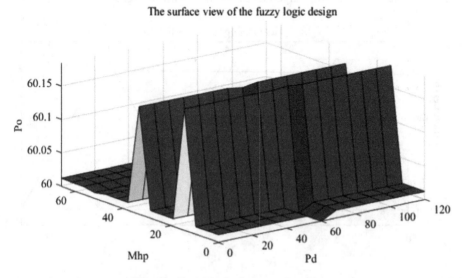

Fig. 11. Fuzzy logic design surface view

F) Integration of the fuzzy logic controller with the forecasted model in Simulink model

Here is a fuzzy logic controller model with four inputs and one output. The rule corpus has been written in the checkbox. The system is managed according to the established rules. Solar power (Sp), micro hydro power (Mhp), biomass power (Bp) and power demand (Pd) are the controller input parameters as shown in Fig. 12 Simulink Models. The Gaussian random signal generator is assumed to be in the form of power coming from each component of the power source. The multiport conditional switch will perform actions based on the rules coded in the fuzzy logic controller.

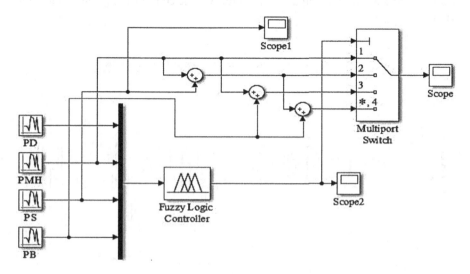

Fig. 12. The block diagram representation of the hybrid system

Since these renewable sources are discontinuous in nature, the values of all of these input sources will vary over time. To check if the controller can accommodate this variation and make the correct final decision on the multiport switch, a Gaussian random number generator is used. The generator is selected as input for these five variables (power required, micro hydroelectric power generation, solar energy and biomass energy). A couple of scenarios were hypothesized to verify the functionality of this smart controller, which are given below.

5 Simulation Result and Analysis

The designed fuzzy logic controller, is evaluated under different operating conditions, such as: whether the solar radiation is low or not, the range is high and the rice husk is medium and other conditions. However, a random number is assigned to the controller to determine the proper functionality of the controller. The scope shows the power output. This means that the output power that will provide the required power ranging from 0–120 kW,

Case Study One: If the demand power PD is 100 kW, Mhp is 60 kW, Sp is 20 kW, and Bp is 20 kW then the output power of fuzzy logic controller is given on the figure below.

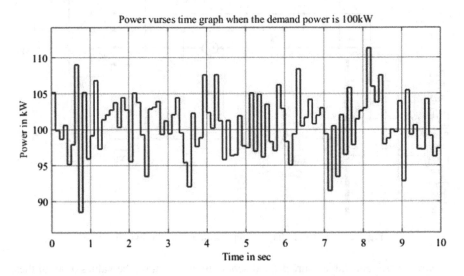

Fig. 13. Simulation result of fuzzy logic controller case one

The controller selects the power source appropriately to serve the power demand of customer. In this particular case, the power demand is about 100 kW. The available power resources will be from the respective energy sources: Mhp = 60 kW, Sp = 20 kW, and Bp = 20 kW and as illustrated in Fig. 13.

Case Study Two: If for example the power demand PD is 40 kW, Mhp = 25 kW, Sp = 15 kW, and Bp = 0 kW, then the output power is indicated as shown in the Fig. 14.

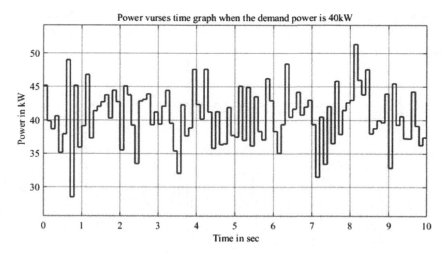

Fig. 14. Simulation result of fuzzy logic controller case two

Case Study Three: Assuming the power demand PD is 80 kW, Mhp = 55 kW, Sp = 10 kW and Bp = 15kW, then the output power of Fuzzy Logic Controller will be indicated as in the Fig. 15.

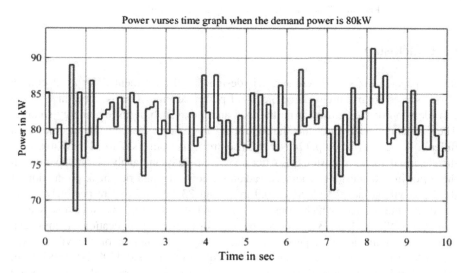

Fig. 15. Simulation result of fuzzy logic controller case three

Case Study Four: If for example the power demand PD is 60 kW, Mhp = 25 kW, Sp = 30 kW and Bp = 5kW, then the output power of fuzzy logic controller will be indicated as in the Fig. 16.

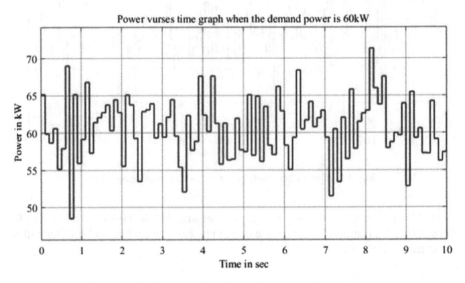

Fig. 16. Simulation result of fuzzy logic controller case three

6   Conclusion

In this paper a fuzzy logic controller is designed and implemented for a selecting a power source from a multisource electrical power scheme. This is done through the consideration of the demand from the load and the availability of the energy sources. The simulation results show that the controller can properly serve the intended power in different scenarios (the output power from controller is from 5 kW to 120 kW to satisfy the electric demand of customer). After a detailed study and analysis, we have drawn the following conclusions. The solar radiation, flow rate, and rice husk production of the Benti village are 5.4 kWh/m^2, 0.9 m^3/s, and 33.246 MT/day respectively. Load profile of the village, which consisted of about 426 households, was assessed as 1199.616 kWh, 12.453 kWh, 38 kWh per day for household applications, commercial loads, and public loads respectively. The energy consumption of the village was forecasted for 10 years using a suitable technique to be around 4398.275 MWh from 1015.3 MWh of the base year. From the load assessment survey, the total electric demand of Benti village was 120 kW. To meet this demand, the PV, Micro-hydro and Bio-mass, supply account 30%, 50% and 30% of the total 120 kW power demand, respectively. The intelligent controller makes intelligent decisions by sensing the type and amount of resource available, and then selecting—the appropriate alternative source based on the power demand.

References

1. Federal Democratic Republic of Ethiopia Ministry of Water and Energy: Scaling - Up Renewable Energy Program Ethiopia Investment Plan (2012)
2. Kumaravel, S., Ashok, S.: An Optimal Stand-Alone Biomass/Solar-PV/PicoHydel Hybrid Energy System for Remote Rural Area Electrification of Isolated Village in Western-Ghats Region of India. Department of Electrical Engineering, National Institute of Technology Calicut, Calicut, Kerala, India (2012)
3. Siddhartha Gobina Deb: Optimal Sizing of a Stand-alone Solar-Wind-Battery DG/Biomass Hybrid Power System to Meet the Load Demand of a Typical Village at Sagar Island Using Genetic Algorithm. Master thesis, Jadavpur University (2012)
4. Melaku, M.: Fuzzy logic controller-based hybrid renewable power generation for Barsoma village (2014)
5. Girma, Z., Braun, M.: Techno economic assessment and optimization study of hybrid power system using homer software for electrification of rural district in Ethiopia. Int. J. Renew. Energy Res. Inst. Wind Energy Technol. 3(3), 627–639 (2013)
6. Sharma, J.P.: A Standalone Hybrid Energy system modelling for Academic institution, October 2015
7. Galadm, M., Spanik, P.: Design of Photovoltaic Solar Cell Module for Stand-alone Renewable System (2014)
8. Espitia, H., Soriano, J., Machón, I., López, H.: Design methodology for the implementation of fuzzy inference systems based on boolean relations. MDPI: Electronics **8**, 1–28 (2019)
9. Shezan, S., et al.: Fuzzy logic implementation with MATLAB for solar-wind battery-diesel hybrid energy system. Department of Electrical and Electronic Engineering, Faculty of Engineering, Uttara University, Dhaka, Bangladesh, vol. 2 (2016)
10. Lau, K.Y., Yousof, M.F.M., Arshad, S.N.M., Anwari, M., Yatim, A.H.M.: Performance analysis of hybrid photovoltaic/diesel energy system under Malaysian conditions. Energy **35** (8), 3245–3255 (2010)
11. of Rural District in Ethiopia. Int. J. Renew. Energy Res. Inst. Wind Energy Technol. 3(3)

Comparison of Thermal and Emissions Performance on Three Stoves for Distilling Areke, A Traditional Ethiopian Beverage

Temesgen Assefa Minale[1(✉)] and Kamil Dino Adem[2]

[1] Bahir Dar Institute of Technology, Bahir Dar University, Bahir Dar, Ethiopia
[2] Addis Ababa Institute of Technology, Addis Ababa University, Addis Ababa, Ethiopia

Abstract. *Areke* is a traditionally fermented and distilled beverage. And it is one of the frequently consumed drinks in semi-urban and rural areas of Ethiopia. Also, it is a drink for most people in the country. Regarding its preparation, it is brewed using a three-stone fire which consumes a large amount of firewood and generates significant indoor air pollution. The evaluation and comparison of thermal and emissions performance of existing cook stoves employed for *Areke* distillation may help the rural poor and semi-urban population to reduce the economic and health costs associated with its preparation. In doing so, Control Cooking Test (CCT) protocol was employed for all the three types of stoves: a three-stone fire, traditional *Areke* stove, and *Mirt Areke* stove. The test results showed that *Mirt Areke* stove reduced fuel use by 51% compared to the three-stone fire while the improvement made by the traditional *Areke* stove is 36%. Indoor air pollution indicators of CO, $PM_{2.5}$ and PM_{10} also showed a reduction by 29%, 53%, and 52%, respectively, while comparing *Mirt Areke* stove with three-stone fire. In the case of a traditional *Areke* stove, the percentage increase in CO is 14.3% while percentage reduction in $PM_{2.5}$, and PM_{10}, is 17.9% and 18.3%, respectively. These results indicate that the improved *Mirt Areke* stove has a better performance than the traditional *Areke* stove.

Keywords: *Areke* · Improved cook stove · Distillation · Indoor air pollution

1 Introduction

Ethiopia is one of the countries where a wide variety of traditionally fermented beverages are produced on a fairly small scale, usually for local consumptions. The various traditional fermented beverages are produced on a fairly small scale and usually used for local consumption. To mention just a few of varieties of *Tella, Tej, Borde, Areke, Karibo,* and *Korefe* are consumed in Ethiopia (Tafere 2015). The preparation of many indigenous or traditionally fermented beverages is still a household art (Tafere 2015). *Areke* is usually brewed in rural and semi-urban areas and is used more commonly by farmers and semi-urban dwellers than by people who live in the cities (WHO 2004).

In order to prepare *Areke*, spherical round ceramic pot is filled with *difdif* (a mixture of malt, hops and water left to ferment for 5 days in warm zone and for twelve days in cold zone). *Difdif* is the main mash to *tinsis* (which is usually a mixture of malt, *gesho*

M. L. Berihun (Ed.): ICAST 2021, LNICST 412, pp. 480–491, 2022.
https://doi.org/10.1007/978-3-030-93712-6_32

(hops), and water kept for 4–5 days in a closed container). In the start, firewood is ignited to begin the combustion until the *difdif* becomes warmer. At a later stage, the quantity of firewood is slowly reduced until it reaches one piece. In the meantime, the vapour from the boiled difdif flows through the *Mekane* (condenser tube) and is collected in the canteen which then is immersed into water at ambient temperature. Due to the transfer of heat, the water gets warmer and warmer. Then, the distillation of the *Areke* continues until it becomes complete. There are signs which show that the completion of the activities, i.e., excessive alcoholic odor and knocking sound.

In most of the rural areas of Ethiopia, *Areke* is still distilled using the three-stone fire. A study conducted in one of the regional towns of Ethiopia, *Arisi Negle*, showed that the indoor air pollution of *Areke* distillation is higher than the WHO standard. The CO and PM concentrations were 68.81 ppm and 3.11 mg/m^3, respectivley during distillation (Mohammed 2008). The Controlled Cooking Test (CCT), where seven pots with separate fuel supply were placed in a single room, resulting in reductions of specific fuel consumption by 4.4% and the time required for brewing the beverage by 22% upon using the improved stove made out of bricks. The improved *Areke* stove has showed a reduction by 52% and 57% in CO and PM, respectively during the whole distillation process (Woldeselassie 2008). *Areke* distillation using biogas stove was also studied in the same location and between 0.6 m^3 to 1 m^3 of biogas is consumed to distill a liter of *Areke*. The finding also suggested that a significant amount of fire wood consumption could be replaced with biogas for distilling *Areke* in the town (Mengiste 2010).

Similar with other biomass cooking technologies in the country which are used for cooking, baking and brewing, *Areke* distillation using three stone fire causes two of the top leading deaths, which are neonatal disorders and lower respiratory infections, i.e., responsible for the majority of deaths relating to indoor air pollution (GBD 2018).

A number of initiatives were taken to improve the three-stone fire cook stoves for cooking (GIZ-ECO 2011b) and baking (Adem et al. 2019; GIZ-ECO 2011a). However, the *Areke* distillation stove has been a neglected area of research. The indoor air problem associated with distilling Areke using a three-stone fire poses a serious health problem. Little effort has been made to evaluate the indoor air quality impacts arising from biomass combustion on *Areke* processing stoves. As a launching pad for research and development on improvement of *Areke* stoves, a standard performance evaluation is crucial. The number of spherical round ceramic pots and stoves varies from household to household ranging from 1 up to 10. So, using a single spherical round ceramic pot and stove as a baseline will help researchers and developers to base their improved design and make comparison.

So, the aim of this research is to experimentally evaluate the *Areke* stoves both the three-stone fire and the improved stoves using the CCT protocol. The result will help developers to disseminate a better performing *Areke* stove throughout the country for reducing firewood consumption, indoor air pollution and health impacts. The dissemination of improved *Areke* stove does not necessarily imply increasing intake of *Areke* rather any gain from the reduction of fuel consumption and indoor air pollution will benefit the household. The major beneficiaries are women and children (ERG 2014).

2   Materials and Methods

2.1   Description of the *Areke* Stove

Areke distillation process is a time consuming activity compared to other household cooking practices. On average, it takes from 2 to 2.5 h per batch excluding the time required to prepare the *difdif* (the processed grains). In the case of a single *Areke* processing unit, a single spherical round ceramic pot with single bamboo pipe and metal canteen is used for distilling *Areke*. As shown in Fig. 1((a) & (b)) the *difdif* is added into a *Ensera* (ceramic pot) where it is supported by three stones called three-stone fire stove. The ceramic pot has the same chemical composition and treatment as a ceramic pan for baking *injera* – Ethiopian flat bread. This stove is used for processing in a single pot where a number of pots could be arranged to produce *Areke* in a single room as shown in Fig. 1(c).

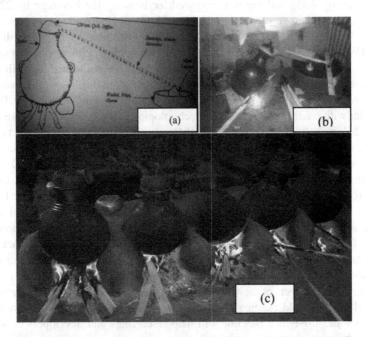

Fig. 1. *Areke* stoves: (a) Schematic representation of single pot, (b) Single pot *Areke* processing and (c) Multiple of number of pot for *Areke* processing

2.2   Mold Developed for *Mirt Areke* Stove

Since *Mirt injera* stoves *(injera is* Ethiopian flat bread*)* have been under dissemination for quite a number of years, producers have become comfortable to make *Mirt Areke* stove using similar approach. Due to its weight, performance and other conveniences, making the stove into two parts became mandatory. Thus, the final mold was taken to stove producers for a test and feedback was collected and further improvement made. Figure 2 shows the final modified mold was used for producing *Mirt Areke* stove. The CATIA software was also used to draw the detail workshop drawing of the stove.

Fig. 2. Final mold for *Mirt Areke* Stove

Three types of biomass cook stoves (three-stone fire, traditional, and *Mirt Areke* stove) were used to conduct the test. As the name is self-explanatory, the three-stone fire uses three-stones to support the spherical round ceramic pot where fuel is combusted to boil the content of the pot (Fig. 3a). This stove is used for various cooking applications. The second is the traditional *Areke* stove. It is locally made out of mud and finally painted with *wet dung* (Fig. 3b). The third type of stove is constructed with mortar and cement using mold of two halves to make the handling better for women as they are the major users of the stove (Fig. 3c).

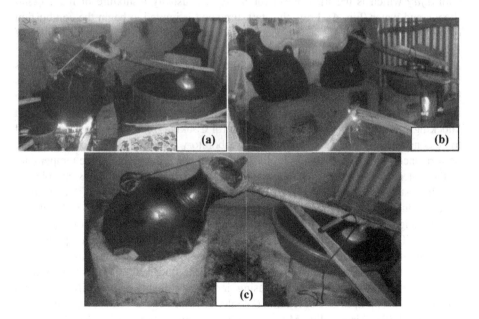

Fig. 3. *Areke* stoves: (a) three-stone fire, (b) traditional and (c) *Mirt Areke*

2.3   Firewood Characterization

The firewood which is eucalyptus tree cut into pieces and sun dried for at least three to four weeks, was used for conducting the *Areke* stoves tests. Representative samples were collected and prepared for the characterization of the wood. Table 1 indicates the characterization of the wood determined at the Geological Survey of Ethiopia according to ASTM standard (ASTM 1983).

Table 1. Basic characteristics of wood (Eucalyptus)

General characteristics	
Size (mm × mm × mm)	20 × 20 × 1000
Bulk density (kg m^{-3})	480
Moisture content (%)	5.64
Higher heating value (HHV) (MJ kg^{-1})	18.64
Proximate analysis	
Volatile matter (% db)	80.81
Fixed carbon (% db)	13.02
Ash content (% db)	0.54

2.4   Experimental Setup for *Areke* Stove

The experiment was conducted using three biomass stoves: three-stone fire, traditional stove and *Mirt Areke* stove. In order to make the presentation concise, a general experimental set-up is presented in Fig. 3. The spherical round ceramic pot is filled with *difdif* which is the main mash for *tinsis*, i.e., usually a mixture of malt, *gesho* (hops), and water (Fig. 4). From the start, firewood is ignited to begin the combustion of the fuel wood until the *difdif* becomes warmer. At a later stage, the quantity of firewood is slowly reduced until it reaches one piece. In the meantime, the evaporated *Areke* through *Mekane* (condenser tube) and is collected in the *canteen*. The *canteen* is immersed into water at ambient temperature. Due to the transfer of heat, the water gets warm. Then, the distillation of the *Areke* continues until it becomes complete. There are signs which show the completion of the activities, excessive alcoholic odor and knocking sound. In this experiment, the Control Cooking Test (CCT) protocol is used to be conducted by a professional cook at a laboratory setting was used to evaluate the performance of the *Areke* stoves (Bailis 2004). Following the protocol, the temperature of the water was recorded in 1 min interval until the distillation becomes complete.

The test for each type of stove (three-stone fire, tradtional, and *Mirt Areke* stove) were conducted in a typical Ethiopian kitchen, i.e., 2.5 m (length) × 3.5 m (width) × 2.5 m (height). According to the recommendation of the University of California (CEIHD 2005), the instruments used for measuring carbon monoxide, particulate matter, room tempeature, and relative humidity were placed at 100 cm from the edge of the combustion zone, at a height of 145 cm from the floor and at 150 cm away from openable doors. CO was measured using indoor air quality meter, KM 410 with accuarcy $\pm$ 30 ppm, $\pm$ 5% of reading (Wohler 2019). $PM_{2.5}$ and PM_{10} were measured using WP 6301 Air Quality Monitor with a detection range of 0 to 500 mg/m^3

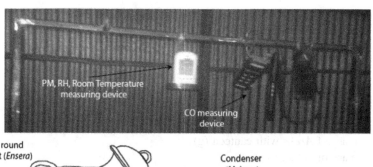

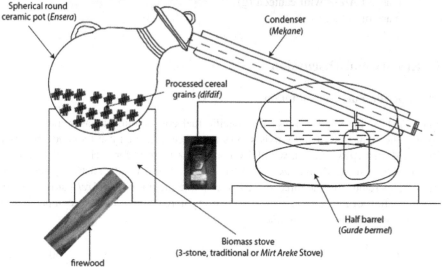

Fig. 4. Experimental Setup for *Areke* distillation stoves

(Vson 2019). For the conversion of CO unit from ppm to mg/min, we have taken into consideration the volume of the kitchen and time taken to brew *Areke* (CHSR 2019).

2.5   Performance Cacluations

The amount of fuel used to brew a gram of *Areke* was calculated for all the three stoves. A total of 9 tests were conducted for evaluating the performance of the three types of stoves under considerations where fuel use was used as one of the performance indicators. Equation (1), (2) and (3) were used in order to evaluate the equivalent firewood (f_d), net weight of food (W_f) and *SFC*.

$$f_d = (f_i - f_f) * [1 - (1.12 * m)] - 1.5 * m_{char} \qquad (1)$$

$$W_f = p_f - p \qquad (2)$$

$$SFC = \frac{f_d}{W_f} * 1000 \qquad (3)$$

Where,

SFC	Specific Fuel Consumption (g/g)
f_d	equivalent firewood (g)
f_i	initial weight of firewood (g)
f_f	final weight of firewood (g)
m	moisture content of firewood (%)
m_{char}	amount of char produced (kg)
W_f	net weight of *Areke* (g)
p_f	mass of *Areke* with canteen (g)
p	mass of canteen (g)

3   Results and Discussion

3.1   Specific Fuel Consumption

Figure 5 (left side y-axis) shows the specific fuel consumption measurements for all stoves. The right side of the y-axis shows the percentage fuel use reduction by traditional and *Mirt Areke* stoves, with 95% confidence interval for each stove, relative to the three-stone stove. Both *Areke* stoves showed substantial and statistically significant fuel savings relative to the three-stone stove. While the traditional *Areke* stove showed 36% reduction of fuel use. *Mirt Areke* stove registered 51% reduction compared with the three-stone stove as a baseline.

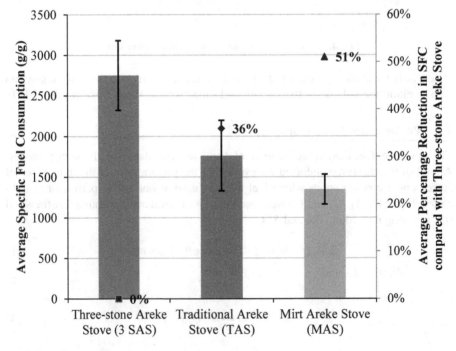

Fig. 5. Average specific fuel consumption (three-stone, traditional and *Mirt Areke* stoves)

In a similar study, a 4.4% reduction in specific fuel consumption was recorded in using a rectangular block stove which holds seven spherical round ceramic pots (Woldeselassie 2008). However, according to the experiment made on a single stove by this author, both the traditional and *Mirt Areke* stove exhibited a better performance in terms of specific fuel consumption. Since *Areke* distillery ceramic pot stove and *injera* baking pan stove have similar materials of construction, they can be compared in terms of their performance. In this regard, *Mirt and Gonzie*, improved enclosed *injera* baking stoves, showed a reduction in specific fuel consumption ranging between 24%–49% (Dresen et al. 2014; Feleke 2007; Gulilat 2011, Gulilat 2014; Jeldeti 2005; Teka 2013; Tufa 2012). Similarly, our performance test which was carried out on a single stove has showed reduction in specific fuel consumption of the same range.

3.2   Average Brewing/Cooking Time

The time to brew *Areke* is also an important indicator of stove performance. Depending on local conditions and individual preferences, stove users may value this indicator equivalent to fuel consumption. Time to brew is calculated from the difference between starting and finishing time of *Areke* processing activity. Figure 6 (left y-axis) shows the average brewing time for traditional and *Mirt Areke* stoves. Figure 5 (right – y-axis) on the other hand, indicates the percentage reduction of traditional and *Mirt Areke* stoves as compared to the three-stone fire stove with 95% confidence intervals.

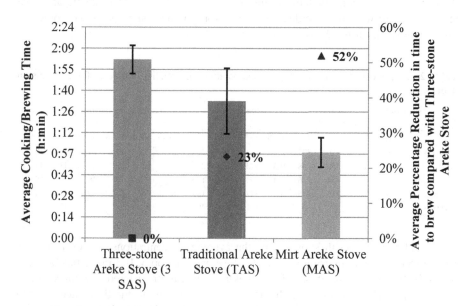

Fig. 6. Average brewing time (three-stone, traditional and *Mirt Areke* stoves)

Traditional *Areke* stove showed a reduction of 23% (29 min) brewing time as compared to the three-stone stove. However, *Mirt Areke* stove reduced the time by more than half of the time taken by three stone (52%; 1:04 h:min). Our finding shows a better reduction in time to brew using *Mirt Areke* stove which may show a good improvement for *Areke* brewing stoves. Woldeselassie (2008) achieved a 22% reduction in time to brew by using improved *Areke* stove where the computation was based on seven stoves or through spherical round ceramic pots which were used during the testing. However, in our test, a single stove was used during the whole period. One of the performance indicators, i.e., the time for brewing/cooking shows reduction on ceramic *injera* baking stove ranging between 5% to 17% (Feleke 2007; Gulilat 2011; Teka 2013; Tufa 2012). The cause for this variation of *injera* baking time could be further verified by other researchers in the area.

3.3   Indoor Air Pollution

The test result indicated that the average CO generated while the three-stone *Areke* stove is in use is around 14 ppm. Similarly, the average $PM_{2.5}$, and PM_{10} were 347 ppm and 387 ppm, respectively. In the case of *injera* baking on the three-stone fire, the recorded CO was 80 ppm which is higher than that of the *Areke* stove. This could be due to the less amount of firewood consumed (Yosef 2007). Table 2 indicates the average CO, $PM_{2.5}$, and PM_{10} room air temperature and relative humidity observed during the distillation of *Areke*.

The average concentration of CO, $PM_{2.5}$ and PM_{10} observed in the test room while using the traditional *Areke* stove were 16 ppm, 285 ppm, and 316 ppm, respectively. And, the average room air temperature and relative humidity were 25 °C and 43%. However, there were no recorded test results for making comparisons with other traditional stoves used for *Areke* brewing.

Table 2. Average CO, $PM_{2.5}$, PM_{10}, air temperature and relative humidity for a three-stone *Areke* stove

	CO (ppm)			$PM_{2.5}$			PM_{10}			Air Temperature (°C)			Relative Humidity (%)		
	3SAS	TAS	MAS	3SAS	TAS	MAS	3SAS	TAS	MAS	3SAS	TAS	MAS	3SAS	TAS	MAS
Test 1	14	20	15	256	332	182	283	369	215	26	25	27	34	40	35
Test 2	11	13	10	350	248	183	373	272	200	27	25	22	29	43	49
Test 3	16	14	4	434	276	124	504	308	140	27	24	23	28	46	48
Mean	14	16	10	347	285	163	387	316	185	27	25	24	30	43	44
STDev	3	4	6	89	43	34	111	49	40	1	1	3	3	3	8

In addition, the result showed that the average concentrations of CO, $PM_{2.5}$ and PM_{10} in the test room in using *Mirt Areke* stove, were 10 ppm, 163 ppm, and 185 ppm, respectively. In the case of *Mirt injera* baking stove, the registered CO concentration was 7.2 ppm which is less than the *Mirt Areke* stove, due to the difference in application of the stoves for baking rather than brewing (Yosef 2007). In the test room, the average temperature and relative humidity were 24 °C and 44%, respectively. And, the average amount of CO was 10 ppm whereas the average time taken to brew on *Mirt Areke* stove was 57 min. This observed CO value was lower than the WHO recommendation which is less than 30 ppm during one hour exposure (WHO 2010).

Similarly, this is less than the strong recommendation of WHO (2014) which is 0.59 g/min while taking into account the volume of the kitchen and time to brew stands at 0.0044 g/min.

Considering the three-stone *Areke* stove as a reference, the percentage reductions in CO and $PM_{2.5}$ in using *Mirt Areke* stove was better. If the whole tests were conducted under the hood, the results could have a different figure with better accuracy suggested for similar studies in the future. Now, there is a baseline data available for *Areke* stove which will help other researchers and developers to improve the existing *Areke* stove.

In addition to the improvement in the performance of *Mirt Areke* stove, the use of mold to produce the stove in a uniform structure will help users to attain similar results in using the stoves. A stove with a uniform structure was not possible in the case of traditional *Areke* stoves. But, this could be even made better if *Mirt Areke* stove is to be manufactured at industrial scale.

4 Conclusion

The three types of *Areke* distillation biomass cookstoves, a three-stone fire, tradtiional stove, and *Mirt Areke* stove, were tested for their performance in terms of fuel use and indoor air pollution. The test results showed that *Mirt Areke* stove reduces fuel use by 51 percent compared with the three-stone fire *Areke* stove. CO, $PM_{2.5}$, and PM_{10} were reduced by 29%, 53%, and 52%, respectivley.Similarly, the traditional *Areke* stove reduce fuel use by 36 percent compared with the three-stone fire *Areke* stove. CO increased by 14% while $PM_{2.5}$, and PM_{10} were reduced by 18% for both $PM_{2.5}$, and PM_{10} in the case of traditonal *Areke* stove.

Following the test results, the mold for *Mirt Areke* stove was prepared and tested for practical application. In order to replicate the *Mirt Areke* stove production, a detailed manufacturing drawing should be prepared and made ready for dissiminaton.

The tests conducted on biomass *Areke* stoves could be used as a baseline performance data for future improvements. Currently, dissiminating the *Mirt Areke* stove with its mold for producers in the country will save a large amount of fuel and decreases indoor air pollution for those who are currently engaged in the distillation of *Areke* around the country.

References

Adem, K.D., Ambie, D.A., Arnavat, M.P., Henriksen, U.B., Ahrenfeldt, J., Thomsen, T.P.: First njera baking biomass gasifier stove to reduce indoor air pollution, and fuel use. AIMS Energy 7(2), 19 (2019)

ASTM, American Society of Testing Materials: Annual book of ASTM standard, 19013 (1983)

Bailis, R.: Control Cooking Test (CCT) Version 2.0 (Household Energy and Health Programme, Shell Foundaition) (2004)

CEIHD, Center for Entrepreneurship in International Health and Development, School of Public Health University of California - Berkeley. Installing Indoor Air Pollution Instruments in a Home, Version 5.1 (2005). http://berkeleyair.com/wp-content/publications/guidelines-for-instrument-placement.pdf. Accessed 10 Aug 2016

CHSR, Center for Hazardous Substitute Research. Environmental Science and Technology Briefs for Citizens: Understanding Units of Measurement (2019). https://cfpub.epa.gov/ncer_abstracts/index.cfm/fuseaction/display.files/fileID/14285. Accessed 30 Sept 2019

Dresen, E., DeVries, B., Herold, M., Verchot, L., Müller, R.: Fuelwood savings and carbon emission reductions by the use of improved cooking stoves in an afromontane forest, Ethiopia. Land **3**(3), 1137 (2014)

ERG, Ethio Resource Group. Energy Efficiency Improvement in Areke Distillation System, Basona Werena Woreda, Amhara Regional State (2014)

Feleke, Y.A.: Assessing Environmental Benefits of Mirt Stove with Particular Reference to Indoor Air Pollution (Carbon Monoxide & Suspended Particulate Matter) and Energy Conservation. (Msc Thesis), Addis Ababa University, Addis Ababa, Ethiopia (2007)

GBD, Global Burden of Disease. Global, regional, and national age-sex-specific mortality for 282 causes of death in 195 countries and territories, 1980–2017: a systematic analysis for the Global Burden of Disease Study 2017. The Lancet **392**(10159), 1736–1788 (2018)

GIZ-ECO, Deutsche Gesellschaft fur Internationale Zusammenarbeit-Energy Coordination Office. Mirt Stove Ethiopia (2011a). https://energypedia.info/images/a/a0/GIZ_HERA_2012_Mirt_stove.pdf. Accessed 16 Sept 2019

GIZ-ECO, Deutsche Gesellschaft fur Internationale Zusammenarbeit-Energy Coordination Office. Tikikil Stove (2011b). Accessed 16 Sept 2019

Gulilat, A.: A Report on Controlled Cooking Test Results Perfomed on Mirt with integrated Chimeny and Institutional Mirt Stoves GIZ Energy Coordination Office (GIZ ECO-Ethiopia) report (2011)

Gulilat, A.: A Report on Controlled Cooking Test of Gonzie Stove GIZ Energy Coordination Office (GIZ ECO-Ethiopia) report (2014)

Jeldeti, G.W.: Factors Controlling Households Energy Use: Implication for the Conservation of the Environment. (Msc thesis), Addis Ababa University, Addis Ababa, Ethiopia (2005)

Mengiste, A.A.: The Potential of Biogas Energy in Supplementing the Household Energy needs for Areke Production: The Case of Arsi-Negele District, Oromia Regional State. (Msc thesis), Addis Ababa University, Addis Ababa (2010)

Mohammed, N.: Impact of 'Katikala' Production on the Degradation of Woodland and Vegetation and Emission of CO and PM during Distillation in Arsi-Negele Woreda, Central Rift Valley of Ethiopia. (Msc thesis), Addis Ababa University, Addis Ababa (2008)

Tafere, G.: A review on Tradtional Fermented Beverages of Etthipian. J. Nat. Sci. Res. **5**(15), 9 (2015)

Teka, W.G.: A Report on Controlled Cooking Test (CCT) Results on Awramba Stove (2013)

Tufa, A.Z.: A Report on Controlled Cooking Test Results Made on Multi-fuel and Chimney integrated Injear Baking Stoves GIZ Energy Coordination Office (GIZ ECO - Ethiopia) report (2012)

Vson, Vson Technology Co., Ltd. WP 6301 Air Quality Monitor (2019). http://www.vson.com.cn/English/contact/. Accessed 18 Aug 2019

WHO, World Health Organization. Global Status Report on Alcohol (2004)

WHO, World Health Organization. WHO guidelines for indoor air quality: selected pollutants (2010). http://www.euro.who.int/_data/assets/pdf_file/0009/128169/e94535.pdf. Accessed 03 Sept 2016

WHO, World Health Organization. WHO Guidelines for Indoor Air Quality: Household Fuel Combustion (2014)

Wohler, USA Inc. Indoor Air Quality Meter (2019). https://www.woehler-international.com/fileadmin/user_upload/woehler/resources/downloads/products/km410/manual/22718_BDA-KM410_de-en-nl.pdf. Accessed 18 Aug 2019

Woldeselassie, G.G.: Evaluating the Efficiency of Improved Local Liquor (Areke) Distilling Stove by Measuring the Indoor Air Emission. (Msc thesis), Addis Ababa University, Addis Ababa (2008)

Yosef, A.F.: Assessing Environmental Benefits of Mirt Stove with Particular Reference to Indoor Air Pollution (Carbon Monoxide & Suspended Particulate Matter) and Energy Conservation. (Msc), Addis Ababa University, Addis Ababa, Ethiopia (2007)

Challenges and Prospects of Hydro-Pumps for Small Scale Irrigation

Dessie Tarekegn Bantelay[1]([⊠]) [iD], Girma Gebresenbet[2],
and Bimrew Tamerat Admassu[1] [iD]

[1] Faculty of Mechanical and Industrial Engineering, Bahir Dar Institute
of Technology, Bahir Dar University, 26, Bahir Dar, Ethiopia
[2] Department of Energy and Technology, Swedish University of Agricultural
Sciences, SLU, Box 7032, 750 07 Uppsala, Sweden
girma.gebresenbet@slu.se

Abstract. Escalation of small-scale irrigation is supposed to be an essential requirement for the growth of the agricultural sector in developing countries. In Ethiopia intensification of small-scale irrigation has got a policy priority for rural poverty mitigation, growth, and building climate adaptation economy. The irrigated land in Ethiopia is not far from 5% of irrigable land, and only around 5% of available water resources are utilized annually. To maximize the effort deploying an environmentally friendly and less expensive technological alternative needs attention. In this regard, pressurized irrigation schemes that operate on renewable energies such as hydro-powered pumping contribute more. Even though the technology has an obvious advantage over the other pumping technologies, they are not been used gradually through time and are mostly ignored. The objective of this study was to conduct strengths, weaknesses, opportunities, and threats analysis on prospects of a hydro-powered pumping system for small-scale irrigation in Ethiopia. In this regard, important small-scale irrigation pump problems were examined and prospects and barriers of hydro-powered small-scale irrigation pumping systems were identified. A comparative study was conducted for comparative between existing pump types (Engine powered, Motor powered, and Manual) deployed in the community for small-scale irrigation. According to the study result, the hydro-powered pumps have better prospects for small-scale irrigation.

Keywords: Irrigation pump · Hydro-pump · Pump as turbine · Pump power · Renewable energy

1 Introduction

Escalation of small-scale irrigation schemes is supposed to be an essential precondition for the growth of the agricultural sector in Ethiopia. In Ethiopia intensification of small-scale irrigation has got a policy priority for rural poverty alleviation, growth, and building climate adaptation economy [1, 2]. The irrigated land in Ethiopia is not far from 5% of irrigable land [3], and only around 5% of available water resources are utilized annually [4]. A study revealed small-scale irrigation scheme operated and managed by a farmer is quite impressive and popular in recent years due to the rapid return and poverty alleviation. Therefore, the numbers of small irrigation schemes are increasing rapidly in

© ICST Institute for Computer Sciences, Social Informatics and Telecommunications Engineering 2022
Published by Springer Nature Switzerland AG 2022. All Rights Reserved
M. L. Berihun (Ed.): ICAST 2021, LNICST 412, pp. 492–505, 2022.
https://doi.org/10.1007/978-3-030-93712-6_33

sub-Saharan Africa and South Asia [5]. Even though there are a lot of influencing factors in agriculture, improving irrigation water access and control is a principal factor to improve smallholder farm production and consequently improving their livelihoods [6]. A way to achieve this goal is to intensify irrigation base farming using pumping facilities and increase production and productivity in the sector. However, many current irrigation systems operate on diesel-based pumping technologies. As a result, it is suffering from high operation and maintenance costs and it is strongly linked to air pollution due to the continuous use of expensive fossil fuel [7], thereby becoming cost-intensive for smallholder farming. Renewable energies, solar, wind, and hydropower, or a combination of them are an environmentally sound and less expensive substitute for small-scale irrigation [8]. From renewable energy-based pumping systems, hydro-powered pumping (HPP) systems have further advantages over other renewable energy (RE) based counterparts. These benefits include: I their energy source is typically more localized, concentrated, and predictable; (ii) they have a higher power-to-size ratio, making them more cost-effective; (iii) they are mechanically less complex and robust, requiring less maintenance and lasting longer; and (iv) they are typically more efficient (up to 85%) [9]. Despite these obvious advantages, most hydro-powered pump (HPP) technologies have not been used steadily over time, and are largely ignored [10]. There have been few studies on water turbine pump (WTP) design since the beginning of the twenty-first century, and the literature prior to 2000 is mostly theoretical study and design selection [11]. The objective of this study was to conduct a strength, weaknesses, opportunities, and threats (SWOT) analysis on the prospects of a hydro-powered pumping system for small-scale irrigation in Ethiopia.

2 Literature Review

Ethiopia is a country located in the East of Africa lies between 3° to 15°N latitude and 33° to 48°E longitudes, with a land area of about 1.097 million km^2. According to the World population review report, currently, Ethiopia has a population of about 105 million of which 83% live in rural areas [12]. Ethiopia has a diverse range of renewable energy resources that can be used to satisfy the country's electrification goals. Hydropower has a 45GW potential, the wind has a 10GW potential, geothermal has a 5GW potential, and sun irradiation ranges from 4.5 kWh/m^2/day to 7.5 kWh/m^2/day. [13]. Currently, Ethiopia has one of the lowest electricity consumption per capita in Africa. Distinguishing energy access and security is a critical factor for development; Ethiopia needs to handle key challenges associated with energy security and diversification of energy supply. Nowadays Ethiopia's total installed capacity of electric generation is about 4.5 GW (2019) mainly generated by hydro (90%) and followed by wind energy (7.6%) [14]. According to Ethiopia's country report in 2019, only about 45% of the country's population has access to electricity. The urban population has 97% access to electricity, while in rural areas electricity access remains extremely low at about 31% [15]. Nowadays, there is a severe deficiency of public finance for power expansion of African Governments from the World Bank and other multilateral and bilateral aid agencies, which had financed mega hydropower project development in the past [16]. So the countries have to focus on small and micro-hydropower development and direct applications, such as hydro-pumping.

2.1   Small Scale Irrigation

To persist with the rapid population growth and the corresponding need for food production, developing countries give great attention to affordable irrigation development. Since large-scale irrigation development needs huge finance, small-scale and on-farm water development and efficient use of water are receiving special attention. Many such small-scale farm water development projects depend on groundwater and low-level surface water for their water resources, and water lifting is a vital part of their use. Inexpensive small-scale irrigation can successfully build the flexibility of vulnerable farming households by reducing their dependency on erratic and unpredictable rainfall. While there is a tendency to replace some of the traditional devices with modern pump equipment, the majority of developing countries feel that the improvement of traditional facilities, which are locally produced, repaired, and used by farmers, must receive due attention. Furthermore, because of food shortage and the rising cost of energy, a modern means of lifting water with renewable energy is becoming increasingly important. One of these alternatives is a hydro-power pumping system.

One of the key causes for Ethiopia's sluggish agricultural growth is the sector's low percentage of total investment capital, which represents only 4.2% of the country's total investment capital [17]. As a result, land and labor productivity, as well as farm household income, are all at historically low levels. Furthermore, agriculture is reliant on natural rainfall and is susceptible to drought, which has a detrimental impact on farmer productivity and production. As a result, rural areas have a comparatively high poverty rate, with an average of 25.6%, compared to 14.8% in urban areas [17]. Additionally, World Bank data show that Ethiopian farmers have the lowest gross per capita farm income of 721.28 (USD) as compared to 4137.98 (USD) in china and 82,283.64 (USD) of Canada [18]. Therefore, Ethiopian farmers must make more efforts to transform the agriculture sector so that it reaches the level of modern agriculture and set long-term targets to achieve higher incomes.

2.2   Pump Power for Irrigation

The introduction of appropriate, sustainable, and successful small-scale irrigation [17] schemes requires attention to improving water management. A pump is the heart of most irrigation systems and if not properly selected leads to excessive pumping costs. In small-scale irrigation pumps are used to raise water from a lower to a higher elevation from which the water then flows through canals to the field requiring irrigation or to raise the water pressure head so that it can b transmission line e sprayed on the field using a sprayer. There are numerous types of pumps designed for various purposes. Surface centrifugal pumps installed above the water level are the most commonly used pumps. It is a mature technology. The basic difference that brings economical significance is the power drive. The most commonly used drive options are engine, motor, and manual.

Engine-driven (petrol and diesel) water pumps are still popular because they appear to be the most cost-effective alternative to solar pumping. However, there are other recurring costs associated with these pumps that drive up their price over time. They have short lifespans, require constant maintenance, and consume a lot of fuel.

Furthermore, they are extremely polluting, degrading air quality and emitting carbon dioxide, both of which contribute to climate change. Manual water pumps, such as Afridev, Pedal, Rope and Washer, and treadle pumps, are another option in addition to engine drive. A manual drive is required for these. These sorts of water pumps, while inexpensive, require a lot of time and labor to install and have a limited capacity. In addition, motor-driven (electric and solar) pumps are used as a small-scale irrigation pumping alternative. Even though electric-driven pumps are the most cost-effective choice, their use is limited due to the lack of power infrastructure. According to the international energy agency 2019 report, in Ethiopia, only 47% of the population has access to electricity as shown in Fig. 1. In contrast, with a solar water pump, the solar panels will keep providing free and clean energy. It doesn't need electricity or fuel and has a low maintenance requirement. Contrary to this the upfront cost of the solar water pumps barrier restricts its applicability.

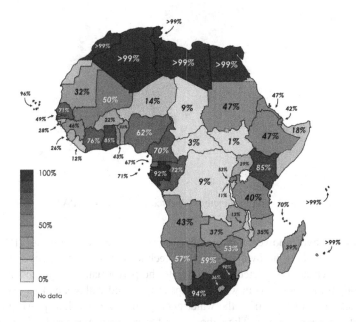

Fig. 1. Access to electricity in Africa by the proportion of the population, 2019 data (Source: the international energy agency)

In today's pump power research work hydro-power pump gets great attention. It is a water-lifting device in which the turbine and pump are coaxial or conjugating as a whole through gear transmission or designed as single equipment. The whole or part of the unit is submerged in water during operation. The turbine is the prime mover; the pump follows the turbine rotation under the action of definite water flow and head. Water is thus pumped to the upland areas where irrigation is needed. Simply considering the utilization of hydraulic energy, the water-turbine pump is a device of the highest hydraulic efficiency [19]. Water energy is applied directly to do work for lifting water, and no intermediate energy is lost through turbine transmission. Obviously,

under the same condition of hydraulic energy, lifting water by electrical power generated will inevitably cause a series of energy losses within the generator, transformer,
power transmission line, and electrical motor. So, the efficiency is much lower than that
of the water-turbine pump using the same hydraulic energy (Fig. 2).

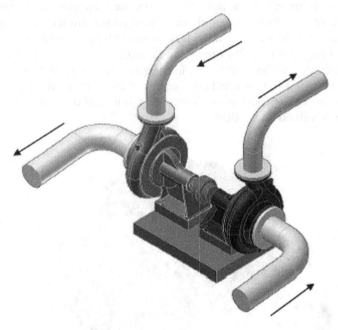

Fig. 2. Pump directly connected to the turbine (PAT)

One of the hydro-powered pumping systems is a pump as turbine (PAT) based
pumping system. It is innovative pumping technology. Currently, several emerging
types of research are conducted to investigate the performance of pumps as a turbine
for micro-hydropower plants in which pumps are coupled with generators externally. In
this indirect mode of operation, the water energy converted to shaft power using PAT
and transfer to a generator. Then the generator converts the mechanical energy to
electrical energy and transmits it to the pump motor. Finally, the electrical motor
coupled to the pump converts the electrical energy and transfer to pump shaft. On the
other hand, the direct method of connecting two pumps one as a turbine and the other
as a lifting device eliminates the need for hydroelectric power generation and the loss
of electric energy during intermediate energy conversion and transmission processes.
Furthermore, with a reasonable water turbine pump integration (WTP) design, the
energy utilization can be even higher than with other forms of water-lifting machinery
[20]. At the same time, it also saves a considerable amount of mechanical and electrical
equipment installation, and the corresponding infrastructure cost [21]. Figure 3 represents types of hydro-powered pumping (HPP) technologies.

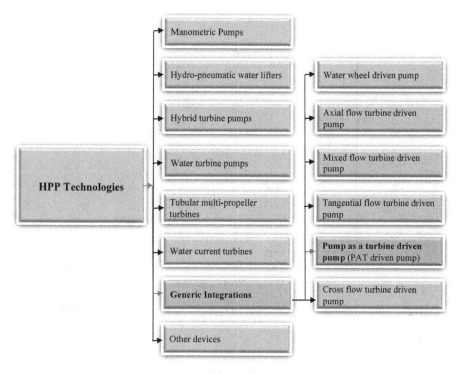

Fig. 3. Classification of hydro-powered pumping (HPP) technologies [10]

2.3 Pumps Suitable for PaT Application

The selection of the correct type and size of pump to use as a turbine is based on technical (head and flow rate available at the site) and economic issues (initial and operating cost). There are research results that testified that major types of centrifugal pumps can be used for reverse mode application [22]. The appropriate type and size of pump to be used for reverse mode application selected based on head and discharge required, as shown in Fig. 4 [23]. It is visible that axial pumps are suitable for low head and high flow rates; whereas, multistage radial pumps are appropriate for high head and low discharge sites. Recent evidence suggests that single-stage centrifugal and axial flow pumps are suitable for PAT application as compared with Francis, Pelton, and Kaplan turbines respectively [24, 25]. Even though it is possible to use double suction and in-line pumps for turbine mode application, they are less efficient than other pump types. But self-priming and Wet-motor submersible borehole pumps are not appropriate for turbine mode application due to the existence of a non-return valve. Likewise, dry-motor submersible pumps with fin cooling arrangements, are not suitable for turbine mode application due to overheating issues [26]. Despite the fact that the pump performs best when the head is between 13 and 75 m, the pump's lifetime cost lowers as the head increases [27].

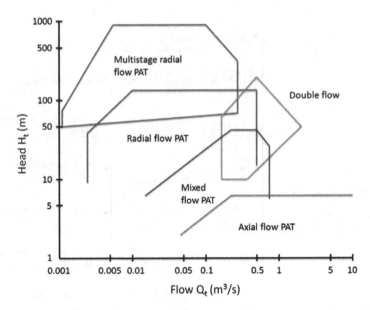

Fig. 4. Recommended range of different types of pumps to work as turbines [23].

3 Methods

To understand the scenario, along with the literature review, other documents of the case had been reviewed. In this study considering various reasons, the survey was conducted previously on different organizations, professionals, and small farm holders.

3.1 Assessment Areas

The purpose of this survey is to identify the gap in intensifying pump-based small-scale irrigation in selected woredas. The assessment area comprised Estie, Fogera, and Fareta woredas in the south Gondar zone and Bahir Dar Zuria, Semien Achefer, and Sekela woredas in the west Gojjam zone, Amhara Regional State of Ethiopia.

3.2 Sampling Method and Sample Sizes

The purpose of this survey was to measure customer satisfaction on existing pumping technology and the need for a new product, it didn't necessarily rely on having a statistically significant sample size. While it's important that the responses were accurate and represent how customers feel, taking a closer look at each answer in a customer satisfaction survey was taken. Table 1 presented the distribution of the sample. Quantitative and qualitative information was gathered from 322 small-scale farm holders who are using pump-based irrigation, 92 maintenance service providers, and 47 pump manufacturers and retailers. Individual household interviews were held with a total of 89 households. Focus group discussions (FGDs) were held with 5 groups having 8,12,8,11 and 10 members respectively. Both the household interviews and the FGDs were rearranged and held on sites.

Table 1. Distribution of sample

Woreda	Questioner		Interview	
	Male	Female	Male	Female
Estie	61	26	12	1
Fogera	67	29	16	0
Fareta	39	17	8	0
Bahir Dar Zuria	74	32	23	2
Semien Achefer	39	17	13	1
Sekela	42	18	13	0

The survey sample size determined as;

$$\text{Sample size} = \frac{\frac{z^2 \times p(1-p)}{e^2}}{1 + \left(\frac{z^2 \times p(1-p)}{e^2 N}\right)}$$

Where;

N = Population size, the number of farmers who are using a pump for small-scale irrigation.

e = Margin of error (percentage in decimal form),

z = z-score, it is the number of standard deviations a given proportion is away from the mean. for a confidence level of 99%, a z-score was taken at a value of 2.58.

Table 2 presented the Percentage share of pump types used by small farm holders for small-scale irrigation. Based on the survey result petrol engine pumps, rope and washer pumps and diesel engine pumps have 65%, 16%, and 12% share respectively.

Table 2. Percentage share of pump types used by small farm holders for small scale irrigation

S.N	Pump type	Share %
1	Electric motor pump	1.5%
2	Diesel engine pump	12%
3	Petrol engine pump	65%
4	Pedal pump	3%
5	Treadle pump	2%
6	Rope and washer pump	16%
7	Others	0.50%

3.3   Data Collection Methods

The assessment was conducted both in Amharic and English languages and data was gathered through Interviews, Focus group discussions, and structured questionnaires. The data focused on factors restricting farmers from using a water pump for small-scale irrigation, small-scale irrigation pump problems, factors which attribute more for poor performance and reliability of radial centrifugal pumps in small-scale irrigation, more vulnerable parts of pumps, and perception of the community on different types of pumps. Secondary data were gathered from current records of enterprises, government technology transfer offices, agriculture extension workers, farmer cooperatives and unions, NGOs & financial institutes.

3.4 Data Analysis

The data generated through the questionnaire was analyzed by employing the Statistical Package for Social Science (SPSS version 20) and MINITAB version 14. To analyze the data collected, descriptive methods such as frequency, percentage, average, and standard deviation were used. The Pearson correlation (r) was used to measure the linear association between the dependent and independent variables. It describes the strength of the relationship between the two variables. Multiple regressions were also used to allow additional factors to enter the analysis separately so that the effect of each independent variable can be estimated. quality function deployment (QFD) was used to define customer requirements and convert them into detailed engineering specifications and plans to produce the products that fulfill those requirements.

4 Results and Discussions

4.1 Assessment Findings

The client will usually specify the desired pump head and flow rate. The type and speed of the driver may also be specified. Speed is governed by considerations of cost and efficiency as well as drivers available to the client. Given these parameters, the task of the engineer is to minimize cost. Which cost to minimize, first cost or life-cycle cost, however, is an important consideration too. These considerations call for optimizing efficiency, reliability, and maintainability. For this reason, a survey was conducted to identify the customer's requirements in small-scale irrigation pumps. In the communities studied, most of the small farm holders as presented in Table 3 agreed on the pump based small-scale irrigation restricted by the serious quality problem in the sector (93.34%); high maintenance cost (96.81%); high Initial cost (82.61%); the energy source is not readily available and the cost is high (91.30%); awareness gap, there is a problem to select and use the right technology (74.47%); limited experience sharing culture with successful farmers (61.11%); important farm machinery is not properly introduced by the relevant body (71.74%); lack of quality water pump supplier (79.12%) and shortage of qualified maintenance experts (65.17%). However, significantly disagreed on government laws, policies and regulations are not conducive (81.52%); inadequacy of infrastructure such as power, water, road, etc. (86.18%) has influence; Lack of access to finance and loans and banks and credit institutions overstated requirement to finance on the sector (70.33%); the agriculture practice doesn't require it (95.50%); farmers who have already started using it in our area are not as effective as expected (98.86%) (Fig. 5).

Fig. 5. Small farm holders waiting for fuel (Left) and Treadle pumps disposed of due to quality defect in Ethiopia (Right) (Source: a survey on February 2021)

During the physical survey, the small-scale farmers have been hit by a severe fuel shortage in Ethiopia. long queues have been formed outside fuel stations waiting for hours and days to buy fuel for their pumps. Similarly, a huge number of Treadle pumps disposed of due to quality defects have been observed in manufacturing shops.

Table 3. Analysis of factors restricting small farm holders from deploying pump-based small-scale irrigation and users. (Source: a survey on February 2021)

S.N	Questionnaire	Strongly disagree	Disagree	Neutral	Agree	Strongly agree
1	This is because government laws, policies, and regulations are not conducive	59.78%	21.74%	7.61%	8.70%	2.17%
2	Inadequacy of infrastructure such as power, water, road etc.	64.89%	21.28%	7.45%	6.38%	0.00%
3	Because the pumps on the market have a high maintenance cost	1.06%	2.13%	0.00%	68.09%	28.72%
4	Lack of access to finance and loans; Banks and credit institutions overstated requirement to finance in the sector	21.98%	48.35%	25.27%	3.30%	1.10%
5	Due to the awareness gap, there is a problem with choosing and use the right technology	5.32%	19.15%	1.06%	46.81%	27.66%
6	Limited experience sharing culture with successful farmers	7.78%	18.89%	12.22%	36.67%	24.44%
7	It is because our agriculture practice doesn't require it	62.92%	32.58%	1.12%	1.12%	2.25%
8	This is because farmers who have already started using it in our area are not as effective as expected	78.41%	20.45%	0.00%	1.14%	0.00%
9	This is because the technologies we need have not been properly introduced by the relevant body	18.48%	7.61%	2.17%	42.39%	29.35%
10	Neither the pumps nor their accessories aren't widely available in the area	3.30%	7.69%	9.89%	51.65%	27.47%
11	The quality problem in the sector is so serious that we are afraid to buy and use it (They are not long-lasting)	3.33%	2.22%	1.11%	55.56%	37.78%
12	This is because it is not easy to find a professional who can provide qualified maintenance and professional support	26.97%	4.49%	3.37%	2.25%	62.92%
13	It's because of the high initial cost of the pumps we can't afford it	2.17%	11.96%	3.26%	51.09%	31.52%
14	The energy source is not readily available and the cost is high (They work with fossil fuel)	1.09%	2.17%	5.43%	63.04%	28.26%

Similarly, the failure rate of pump components is assessed and presented in Table 4 based on the secondary data obtained from the maintenance service provider. Accordingly, the majority of the pump failure is associated with a prime mover, fitting and fixtures, and impeller which accounts for a failure rate of 30.11%, 29.57%, and 14.52% respectively. Other mechanical failures associated with bearing, casing, diffuser, mechanical seal, and O-ring accounts for a failure rate of 25.80% only. So, an initial focus should be given to improve prime mover than to fitting and fixtures and impeller.

Table 4. Component's failure rate analysis for pumps used for small scale irrigation (Source: a survey on February 2021)

S.N	Problem source	Percentage share
1	Prime mover	30.11%
2	Fitting and fixtures	29.57%
3	Impeller	14.52%
4	Bearing	9.68%
5	Casing	5.91%
6	Diffuser	3.76%
7	Mechanical seal	3.76%
8	O-ring	2.69%

Considerably technical experts agreed that most of the pumps deployed in the community for small-scale irrigation have poor performance and untrustworthiness. Assessment made to point out the root causes of technical complications that affecting the intensification of pump-based small-scale irrigation. According to the assessment result, 75.63% of the technical expert agreed that the problem arises from the type and quality of the material from which they made and 67.79% of them agreed that It arises from inappropriate use. Other factors such as Manufacturing process limitations (35.03%), power source it uses (32.25%), design limitations (27.65%), and assembly limitations (1.88%) have a considerable effect (Table 5).

Table 5. Analysis of small-scale irrigation pumps limitation affecting intensification in the community (Source: a survey on February 2021)

S.N	Questionnaire	Strongly disagree	Disagree	Neutral	Agree	Strongly agree
1	Arise from on the type and quality of the material from which they made (75.63%)	4.73%	13.40%	6.24%	48.84%	26.79%
2	It is caused by inappropriate use (67.79%)	6.55%	19.02%	6.64%	41.74%	26.05%
3	Arise from Manufacturing process limitations (35.03%)	38.61%	22.77%	3.60%	21.44%	13.59%
4	Arise from the power source it uses (32.25%)	35.35%	25.74%	6.67%	18.90%	13.35%
5	Arise from design limitations (27.65%)	1.13%	0.56%	70.67%	26.52%	1.13%
6	Arise from assembly limitations (1.88%)	73.25%	24.49%	0.37%	1.13%	0.75%

4.2 Comparative Study

A survey was conducted for a comparative study of existing pump types deployed in the community for small-scale irrigation. These include engine-powered (diesel and petrol), motor-powered (electric and solar), and manual (Afridev, pedal, rope, and washer and treadle). Small farm holders pump requirements/constraints data collected using **a** market survey from farmers who came to purchase pumps for small scale irrigation, Information from the pump and spare suppliers, Information from maintenance service providers, and farmers complaints organized by agricultural extension workers.

The quality function deployment (QFD) study as presented in Fig. 6 at the initial stages were concerned with finding out what the small farm holders need actually in the pump. More than 22 requirements were identified through telephone interviews, face-to-face interviews, and customer complaint history. Then the customer's important requirements rating identified through questionnaires from farm holders, retailers, and maintenance service providers. According to the finding, the small farm holders rated long lasting 15.42%, low initial cost 15.17%, low operating cost 14.48%, low maintenance demand 13.53%, efficient 11.02%, safety 10.39%, low operation & maintenance skill requirement 10.07%, and better capacity (head) 9.92%. Then important engineering characteristics type of prime mover, cost of production, design life, use of standard parts, and several components identified to ensure customer satisfaction. Then the two highlighting conflicting characteristics correlated and target values stetted. According to calculated priority rank cost of production, type of prime mover, several components, use of standard parts, and design life have a high priority rank sequentially.

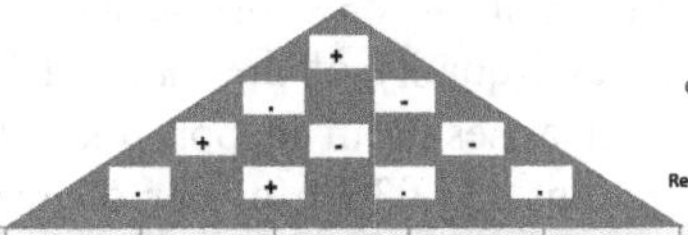

Correlation:	+	.	-
	Positive	No correlatio	Negative

Relationships:	9	6	3	0
	Strong	Moderate	Weak	None

1: low, 5: high Customer importance rating	Desired direction of improvement (↑,0,↓) Functional Requirements (How) → Customer Requirements - (What) ↓	Type of prime mover	Cost of production	Design life	Use of Standard Parts	Number of components	Weighted Score	Competitive evaluation (1: low, 5: high) Satisfaction rating	Solar Pump	Engine Pump	Manual Pump
4.60	Low operating cost	8	7	7	5	0	14.48%	4.5	4.5	1	2.5
4.30	Low maintenance demand	7	7	0	9	3	13.53%	4	4	1	2
3.20	Low operation & maintenance skill	8	0	1	6	9	10.07%	3	2	1	3
4.90	Long lasting	4	5	9	3	6	15.42%	4	3.5	3	4
3.30	Safety	3	3	0	0	6	10.39%	5	5	3.5	4.5
3.50	Efficient	3	6	1	0	9	11.02%	4.5	4	3	4.5
3.15	Better capacity (head)	1	3	1	0	0	9.92%	5	4	5	2
4.82	Low initial cost	7	9	6	9	7	15.17%	4	2	3	4
31.77											
	Technical importance score	169.39	170.53	115.07	138.98	156.14	1				
	Importance %	16939%	17053%	11507%	13898%	15614%	75011%				
	Priorities rank	2	1	5	4	3					

Fig. 6. Quality function deployment (QFD) to assess farmers pump requirement

The customer importance ratings and competitive comparison data were gathered during the customer requirement survey. Then based on the competitive evaluation result, a pump having a satisfactory rating of 4.5, 4, 3, 4, 5, 4.5, 5, and 4 for long-lasting, low initial cost, low operating cost, low maintenance demand, efficient, safe, low operation & maintenance skill and better capacity (head) respectively needed. When we review different possibilities hydro-powered pumps are the best alternative. Hydro-powered pumps use the energy of water. It does not require any other external sources of energy such as fossil fuel or electricity. As a result, it has zero operating costs and doesn't emit any greenhouse gas. The technology has a great contribution to the health and finances of the farmers and also supports the efforts in preventing environmental degradation.

5 Conclusion

In conclusion, this study shows that small-scale irrigation is restricted by the serious quality problem, high maintenance and initial cost, energy source and cost, awareness gap, limited experience sharing culture, lack of supplier, and shortage of qualified maintenance experts. Besides, the majority of the pump failure is associated with a prime mover, fitting and fixtures, and impeller which accounts for a failure rate of 30.11%, 29.57%, and 14.52% respectively. Other mechanical failures associated with bearing, casing, diffuser, mechanical seal, and O-ring accounts for a failure rate of 25.80% only. Moreover, considerable technical experts agreed that most of the pumps deployed in the community for small-scale irrigation have poor performance and untrustworthiness. The assessment made to point out the root causes of technical complications that affecting the intensification of pump-based small-scale irrigation. According to the assessment result, 75.63% of the technical expert agreed that the problem arises from the type and quality of the material from which they made and 67.79% of them agreed that it arises from inappropriate use. Other factors such as manufacturing process limitations (35.03%), power source it uses (32.25%), design limitations (27.65%), and assembly limitations (1.88%) have a considerable effect.

References

1. Ababa, A.: Ethiopia: Building on Progress A Plan for Accelerated and Sustained Development to End Poverty (PASDEP) (2006)
2. Zegeye, H.: Climate change in Ethiopia: impacts, mitigation and adaptation. Int. J. Res. Environ. Stud. 5(1), 18–35 (2018)
3. Sadoff, C.: Managing water resources to maximize sustainable growth: a World Bank water resources assistance strategy for Ethiopia (2008)
4. Aquastat, F.: Irrigation in Africa in figures: AQUASTAT Survey. FAO Water Report (2005)
5. Shah, T., Namara, R., Rajan, A.: Accelerating irrigation expansion in Sub-Saharan Africa: policy lessons from the global revolution in farmer-led smallholder irrigation. IWMI (2018)
6. Burney, J.A., Naylor, R.L.: Smallholder irrigation as a poverty alleviation tool in sub-Saharan Africa. World Dev. 40(1), 110–123 (2012)

7. Aliyu, M., et al.: A review of solar-powered water pumping systems. Renew. Sustain. Energy Rev. **87**, 61–76 (2018)
8. Gopal, C., Mohanraj, M., Chandramohan, P., Chandrasekar, P.: Renewable energy source water pumping systems—a literature review. Renew. Sustain. Energy Rev. **25**, 351–370 (2013)
9. Fraenkel, P.: Water-pumping devices: a handbook for users and choosers. Intermediate Technology London (1997)
10. Intriago Zambrano, J.C., Michavila, J., Arenas Pinilla, E., Diehl, J.C., Ertsen, M.W.: Water lifting water: a comprehensive spatiotemporal review on the hydro-powered water pumping technologies. Water **11**(8), 1677 (2019)
11. Zhou, D., et al.: Development and numerical performance analysis of a pump directly driven by a hydrokinetic turbine. Energies **12**(22), 4264 (2019)
12. Hailu, A.D., Kumsa, D.K.: Ethiopia renewable energy potentials and current state. AIMS Energy **9**(1), 1–14 (2021)
13. Mengistu, M., et al.: A review on biogas technology and its contributions to sustainable rural livelihood in Ethiopia. Renew. Sustain. Energy Rev. **48**, 306–316 (2015)
14. Van de Graaf, T.: International energy agency. In: Handbook of Governance and Security. Edward Elgar Publishing (2014)
15. Roszko-Wójtowicz, E., Grzelak, M.M.: Macroeconomic stability and the level of competitiveness in EU member states: a comparative dynamic approach. Oeconomia Copernicana **11**(4), 657–688 (2020)
16. Kalitsi, E.: Problems and prospects for hydropower development in Africa. In: The Workshop for African Energy Experts on Operationalizing the NGPAD Energy Initiative (2003)
17. (PDC), P.a.D.C., Poverty and economic growth in Ethiopia (1995/96–2015/16). Planning and Development Commission (PDC): Addis Ababa, Ethiopia (2018)
18. World Bank: World Development Indicators. World Bank, Washington, DC (2016)
19. Tsutsui, H.: Water lifting devices with renewable energy for agriculture in asian developing countries with emphasis on the Chinese experience. J. Irrig. Eng. Rural Plan. **1989**(17), 31–47 (1989)
20. Li, J., Gao, H., Hu, X.: An economic analysis of a turbine-driven feed water pump. Int. J. Simul. Syst. Sci. Technol. **17**, 3.1 (2016)
21. Sant, T., Buhagiar, D., Farrugia, R.N.: Offshore floating wind turbine-driven deep sea water pumping for combined electrical power and district cooling. In: Journal of Physics: Conference Series. IOP Publishing (2014)
22. Lueneburg, R., Nelson, R.: Hydraulic power recovery turbines, pp. 246–282 (1992)
23. Chapallaz, J.-M., Eichenberger, P., Fischer, G.: Manual on pumps used as turbines. Vieweg Braunschweig, Germany (1992)
24. Orchard, B., Klos, S.: Pumps as turbines for water industry. World Pumps **2009**(8), 22–23 (2009)
25. Derakhshan, S., Nourbakhsh, A.: Experimental study of characteristic curves of centrifugal pumps working as turbines in different specific speeds. Exp. Therm. Fluid Sci. **32**(3), 800–807 (2008)
26. Sharma, R.: Pumps as turbines (PAT) for small hydro. Indian J. Power River Valley Dev. **49**, 44–48 (1999)
27. Buse, F.: Using centrifugal pumps as hydraulic turbines (1981)

Numerical and Experimental Performance Investigation of Vertical-Axis Hydrokinetic Turbine

Muluken Temesgen Tigabu[1,3(✉)], D. H. Wood[2], and Bimrew Tamrat Admasu[3]

[1] BahirDar Energy Center, BahirDar Institute of Technology,
BahirDar University, P.O.BOX 26, Bahir Dar, Ethiopia
[2] Department of Mechanical and Manufacturing Engineering,
University of Calgary, Calgary, AB T2N 1N4, Canada
[3] Faculty of Mechanical and Industrial Engineering, BahirDar Institute
of Technology, BahirDar University, Bahir Dar, Ethiopia

Abstract. We presented the performance of H-type vertical axis hydrokinetic turbine (VAHKTs). To study the hydrodynamics of VAHKTs an analytical method using a double multi-stream tube (DMST) model was used and an experimental study was employed to validate the DMST results. The key difficulty in the development of VAHKTs technologies is the limited number of researches that show the actual performance under different water velocities. We developed a Matlab code to predict the performance and for validation experimental investigations were performed. The performance operational parameters of power coefficient (C_P) and torque coefficient (C_Q) were used with tips speed ratio (TSR). To validate the DMST and experimental results we used a reference turbine (RM2) developed by the USA Department of Energy's (DOE). A good agreement was found between the analytical and experimental results with the reference turbine. From the study, it is found that the C_P of VAHKTs show an increment and then decrease as the TSR increased. The operating region for VAHKTs is between $1.2 \leq TSR \leq 3.8$. The study illustrated that at $TSR \geq 4$ it is found that there is no power generation from VAHKTs. As s result, the Matlab code we developed based on DMST can be used as a cost effect and robust tool to design and predict the performance of VAHKTs.

Keywords: DMST model · RM2 reference turbine · Hydrodynamics performance · Power coefficient · VAHKTs

1 Introduction

Hydropower conversion is the use of energy contained in the flowing water into the mechanical rotation. It has been used to run wheels for grinding grain in ancient times and to generate electricity in modern times.

© ICST Institute for Computer Sciences, Social Informatics and Telecommunications Engineering 2022
Published by Springer Nature Switzerland AG 2022. All Rights Reserved
M. L. Berihun (Ed.): ICAST 2021, LNICST 412, pp. 506–521, 2022.
https://doi.org/10.1007/978-3-030-93712-6_34

A	Swept area m^2	N	Number of blades (-)
a_{up}	Upwind induction factor (-)	N_h	Number of stream tubes (-)
a_{dn}	Downwind induction factor (-)	Q	Torque (N.m)
c	Blade chord (m)	R	Rotor radius (m)
C_D	Drag coefficient (-)	Re	Reynolds number (-)
C_L	Lift coefficient (-)	V_{up}	Upstream velocity (m/s)
C_N	Normal force coefficients (-)	V_{dn}	Downstream velocity (m/s)
C_T	Tangential force coefficient (-)	V_e	Equilibrium velocity (m/s)
C_q	Torque coefficient (-)	V_∞	Free wind velocity (m/s)
C_P	Power coefficient (-)	W	Relative velocity (m/s)
F_N	Normal force component (N)	α	angle of attack
F_T	Tangential force component (N)	θ	azimuth angle

According to the International Renewable Energy Agency (IRENA) today, hydropower is among the most cost-effective means of generating electricity with a total installed capacity of 1308 GW worldwide and 3817 MW for Ethiopia in 2019. The basic principle of hydropower energy conversion is the use of water to drive the turbines. The energy contained in the water can be used to drive the turbine in two different ways, (1) by use of large reservoirs such as dams to store water and the stored water potential energy used to drive the turbine and (2) without dams and reservoirs, only the kinetic energy of the water is used to drive the turbine. However, recent criticisms have been raised against dam-based hydropower plants (for example, [19,20,25]) due to their versatile effect on the ecosystem, land use, and aquatic life. According to the status report of International Hydropower Association [2] the five years between 2015–2019, the growth in installed capacity was limited 2.1% and 1.2% in 2019.

On the other hand without dam hydropower plant has got considerable attention as an environmentally-friendly option due to smaller effect on the ecosystem. A key aspect of without dam hydropower is producing power at a smaller scale, the frequent term to describe such technologies is hydrokinetic turbines (HKTs). HKTs is a collective term used to refer to the energy generated from the moving water of the currents in oceans, tidal, rivers, and human-made water structures. HKT technologies can be categorized into two main groups by M. Anyi and B. Kirke [1], (1) the axial flow turbine and (2) the cross-flow turbine (other kinds of literature also used vertical axis). There are two types of cross-flow turbine – also called vertical axis turbines: The Savonius type (based on the drag force) and the Darrieus type turbines (based on the lift force). Furthermore, the Darrieus type can also be classified based on the type of rotor as helical or straight (H-type). A detailed review on the classification of HKTs is provided by [13], this paper will focus on H-type Darrieus Vertical axis hydrokinetic turbine (VAHKTs).

The merits of generating electricity using VAHKTs include simple structural components, independence to water current direction, generating power from any direction of the current, no need for a yaw mechanism, and easier maintenance. The working principle and design Methodology of HKTs are similar to the wind energy conversion system. For an equal cross-sectional area, a wind speed of 10 m/s has the same incoming kinetic power as a water flow speed of 1.1 m/s and in general, VAHKTs can be installed in a flow of water velocity starting from 0.5 m/s and above [8]. However, the wind energy sector is matured and at a fully commercialized stage while HKTs still in a developmental phase and have not been fully commercialized yet, due to their reliability and low power density [6]. The study of HKTs is a growing field of renewable energy research, and it can make a big difference to power communities in remote locations [23].

Due to poor conversion efficiency, the performance investigation of VAHKTs has received considerable critical attention such as [9,22,23]. However, most of the studies have been carried out and available in the open literature on the performance investigation of vertical axis wind turbines, experimental by [24, 26] Analytical parametric performance investigation by [4,14,17]. For VAHKTs limited studies are available on the actual performance of VAHKTs (for example, [12] presented the design consideration and performance of VAHKTs for river applications). However, the research efforts in HKTs technology are rather scarce and the knowledge base is quite deficient. Therefore, this study makes a major contribution to research on VAHKTs by investigating the actual performance.

The hydrodynamics of VAHKTs is quite complex due to variation in the local angle of attack, local relative flow velocity, tangential, and normal forces [8]. Several mathematical models have been developed to investigate the performance of VAHKTs, a detailed compressive review of these models is given by [7,11]. Under the current investigation, this paper used the double multi-stream tube model (DMST) which was first introduced by Paraschivoiu [16].

This paper aims to investigate the performance of VAHKTs using Analytical and experimental methodologies. A Matlab code based on DMST is used to predict the performance and further experimental results were used to validate the analytical method. The importance and originality of this study are that it explores the actual performance of VAHKTs and develops a cost effect prediction model for fast implementation and design. The findings should make an important contribution to the applicability of VAHKTs for remote regions in off-grid areas where the operating cost of fuel-based power generation is high.

2   Materials and Methods

2.1   Mathematical Formulation of the Hydrodynamics Model

The design methodology for VAHKTs shares similar principles with the vertical axis wind turbine. The philosophy applied to the study of vertical axis wind turbines is aerodynamics whereas for VAHKTs similar hydrodynamic models can be used. The total power generated from HKTs is determined in a similar fashion with that of wind energy converters as shown in Eq. (1);

$$P = \frac{1}{2}C_P \rho A V^3 \tag{1}$$

where C_P is the turbine power coefficient which typically lies between 0.2 and 0.4. V is the velocity, ρ is the water density, and A is the swept area of the rotor.

Double-multiple Stream Tube Model (DMST). is based on the calculation of flow velocity through the turbine by equating the stream-wise hydrodynamics force imparted on the blades with the rate of change of momentum. The key future of DMST is dividing the turbine swept area into two parts as upstream half-cycle of the rotor and downstream half-cycle of the rotor. Throughout this paper, the term 'up' will refer to the upwind half cycle and 'dn' for the downwind half cycle. DMST model is capable of calculating the difference in the induced velocities at the upstream (V_{up}) and downstream (V_{dn}). V_{up} and V_{dn} at each level of the rotor were obtained using the principle of two actuator disks (an ideal model used to represent the rotor as an infinitely thin disk) in tandem as illustrated in Fig. 1. Then by averaging the contribution of each stream- tubes the torque, power, lift, and drag can be calculated. In the DMST model the upcoming free stream velocity, V_∞, is reduced by interference factors of a_{up} in the upstream and a_{dn} in the downstream. The axial induction factors proceed by discretization of each disk into multiple stream tube models. Azimuthal discretization of stream tubes is the first step in DMST, each stream-tubes located by the Azimuthal angle as shown in Fig. 2. For simplicity, it can be considered that each stream tubes are parallel to each other and each stream tube can be assumed as independent of each other. The area occupied by each stream-tube A_i can be calculated by discretization the azimuthal angle to infinitesimal $\delta\theta$ as shown in Fig. 2.

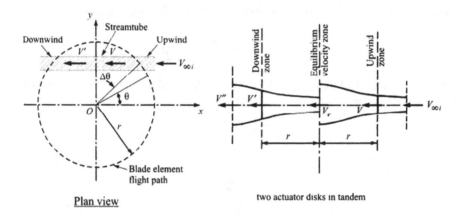

Fig. 1. Double multi stream-tube model diagram [15]

$$A_i = (R\delta\theta)(\delta h sin\theta_i) \qquad (2)$$

Hence, the induced V_{up}, at equilibrium, V_e, and V_{dn} is calculated using;

$$V_{up} = a_{up}V_\infty \qquad (3)$$
$$V_e = (2a_{up} - 1)V_\infty \qquad (4)$$
$$V_{dn} = a_{dn}(2a_{up} - 1)V_\infty \qquad (5)$$

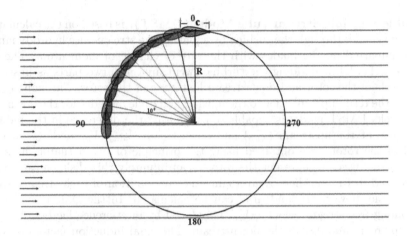

Fig. 2. Azimuthal discretization of stream tubes (shown in the straight lines), the azimuthal location of the blade is shown in the figure at every 10^0 for $0 \leq \theta \leq 90$

The remaining part of this section will present the DMST mathematical formulation for the upwind half cycle, the same procedure can be performed for the downstream half cycle only by replacing V_{up} by V_{dn}. The velocity diagram for DMST is expressed in Fig. 3 considering the pitch angle as zero. Then the local angle of attack can be calculated using the following equation,

$$\alpha = tan^{-1}\left(\frac{V_{up}sin\theta_i}{V_{up}cos\theta_i + \omega R}\right) \tag{6}$$

where TSR is calculated as $TSR = (\omega R)/V_\infty$, similar the relative velocity is expressed as follows;

$$w = \sqrt{(V_{up}cos\theta_i + \omega R)^2 + (V_{up}sin\theta_i)^2} \tag{7}$$

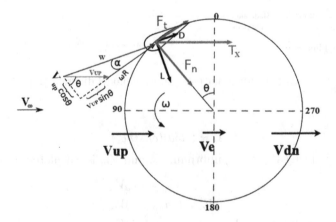

Fig. 3. Velocity triangle diagram and Force components [3]

The Reynolds number then can be computed as

$$Re = \frac{cw}{\nu} \tag{8}$$

After the velocity diagram is resolved the next step is to calculate the force components which are shown in Fig. 3. The normal force F_n and tangential force F_t can be expressed by the force coefficients for each as;

$$C_N = C_L \cos\alpha + C_D \sin\alpha \tag{9}$$
$$C_T = C_L \sin\alpha - C_D \cos\alpha \tag{10}$$

Then

$$F_n = \frac{1}{2} w^2 c \delta h C_N \tag{11}$$

$$F_t = \frac{1}{2} w^2 c \delta h C_T \tag{12}$$

The total effect of F_t and F_n on hydrofoil will create an axial force F_X, for one turbine blade it can be found by decomposing in the axial direction as

$$F_X = F_N \sin\theta_i - F_T \cos\theta_i \tag{13}$$

for N number of blades the total axial force will be

$$\overline{F_X} = N \frac{\delta\theta}{2\pi} F_X \tag{14}$$

Then the axial thrust coefficient computed as;

$$C_X = \frac{\overline{F_X}}{\frac{1}{2}\rho V_\infty^2 A} = \frac{Nc}{2\pi R} \frac{w^2}{V_\infty^2} \frac{1}{|\sin\theta_i|} (C_N \sin\theta_i - C_T \cos\theta_i) \tag{15}$$

The axial trust coefficient then computed with the momentum theory to solve the iteration scheme of DMST to find a_{up}

$$4a_{up}(1 - a_{up}) = C_X = \frac{\overline{F_X}}{\frac{1}{2}\rho V_\infty^2 A} = \frac{Nc}{2\pi R} \frac{w^2}{V_\infty^2} \frac{1}{|\sin\theta_i|} (C_N \sin\theta_i - C_T \cos\theta_i) \tag{16}$$

The calculations at downstream, as repeated previously, can be performed in a identical manner to those of the upstream by considering the following modification of the stream velocity as

$$V_{dn} = (1 - a_{up}) V_e = (1 - a_{dn})(1 - 2a_{up}) V_\infty \tag{17}$$
$$C_X^{dn} = 4a_{dn}(1 - a_{dn})(1 - 2a_{up})^2 \tag{18}$$

The torque, power, and power coefficient then can be determined as

$$T_i = \frac{1}{2}\rho W_{\infty,i}^2 c \Delta h C_{T,i} * R \tag{19}$$

$$T_{tot} = N_P \left[\frac{1}{2N_\theta} \left(\sum_{k=1}^{N_\theta} T_i^{up} + \sum_{k=1}^{N_\theta} T_i^{dn} \right) \right] \tag{20}$$

$$P = \Omega T_{tot} \tag{21}$$

$$C_P = \frac{P}{\frac{1}{2}\rho V_0^3 A} \tag{22}$$

2.2 Analytical Performance Predication of Vertical-Axis Hydrokinetic Turbines

To predict the performance of VAHKTs the process started by specifying the turbine geometric and working condition parameters. The design flow is shown in Fig. 4, to implement the design procedure a NACA 0021 hydrofoil was used. We refer to the design guideline proposed by [5] for optimizing the annual energy yield.

Using the flow chart shown in Fig. 4 a design specification parameter were developed for the performance prediction as shown in Table 1. The required water velocity data was referred from the work of [21], and the experimental result of the hydrofoil data for NACA 0021 was taken from the [18]. However, the data provided by the [18] only contain the range of $0 < \alpha < 180$ and limited Re. Hence, a panel method using an XFoil is available at https://web.mit.edu/drela/Public/web/xfoil/ to generate the hydrofoil data of the rang of $-20 \leq \alpha \leq 20$ for different Re of 50,000, 100,000, 200,000, 500,000, and 1,000,000 was used. For the other range of α the influence of Re is limited to the region of low α, Hence experimental data of [18] were used. Using the experimental result of [18] the relation for C_l and C_D above $\alpha > 20$ && $\alpha < -20$ a polynomial fit

Table 1. Geometric and working condition specification of VAHKTs

Parameters	Value
Radius of the rotor (m)	0.125
Diameter of the rotor (m)	0.25
Height of the blade (m)	0.4
Number of blades	3
Chord length (m) of the hydrofoil	0.03
Type of hydrofoil	NACA0021
Operating Reynolds number	50,000, 100,000, 200,000, 500,000, and 1,000,000
Kinematic viscosity of water at 20 °C (m^2/s)	1.004e − 6
Incoming velocity range (m/s)	0.75, 1.5, 2, 2.5, and 3

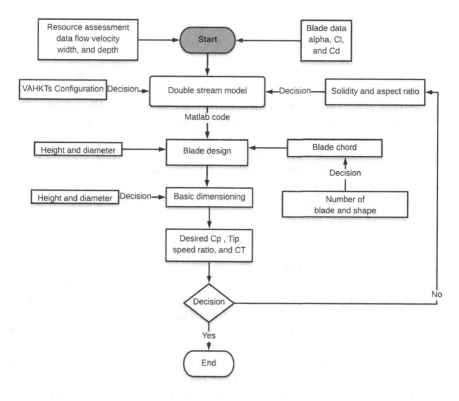

Fig. 4. Design flow chart for H-VAHKTs

were generated using a MATLAB cure fitting tool with the 4th order with the $R^2 = 0.9817$ at Coefficients with 95% confidence bounds and express as follows.

$$C_l = -1.232 \times 10^{-8}\alpha^4 + 8.605 \times 10^{-6}\alpha^3 - 0.0017\alpha^2 + 0.1047\alpha - 0.9 \quad (23)$$
$$C_D = 2.178 \times 10^{-8}\alpha^4 - 7.569 \times 10^{-6}\alpha^3 + 0.00056\alpha^2 + 0.01912\alpha - 0.3 \quad (24)$$

To predict the performance, equations presented in Sect. 2.1 were used to develop a Matlab code. The general Proceeder used to solve the DMST using a Matlab code is given as;

1. The analytical simulation using the DMST model begins by specifying the geometries and working conditions of VAHKTs a seen from Table 1.
2. Then the discretization of the rotor into 36 stream tubes was followed i.e. 18 stream tubes for each up and downstream of the rotor and the azimuthal discretization is performed for every 10^0.
3. The iterations initiated for the upstream section by a wild guess of $a_{up} = 1$.
4. Then the angle of attack, relative velocity, and Reynolds number calculated using Eq. (6), (7), and (8) respectively.

5. Using the Panel data of Xfoil and experimental data of [18] the C_l and C_D at different α were used to estimate the required C_D and C_N, Eq. (9) and (10) used.
6. The required hydrodynamics forces then calculated using Eqs. (11), (12), and (13).
7. Then the first induction factor is estimated using Eq. (16), then the iteration continues until the difference between the induction factors is $< 10^{-6}$.
8. Once the value of induction factor in desired range C_P is calculated for the up-stream of half the rotor using Eq. (22).
9. Then the same procedure is repeated for the other half of the downstream rotor by replacing the velocity relation given in Eq. (3), (4), and (5).
10. Finally the C_P for both half of the rotor will be added to get the total C_P.

2.3   Experimental Setup and Validation

The primary objective of the experimental work is to validate the results of DMST model performance prediction. The experiment was conducted based on a water loop flume of S6-MKII. S6-MKII flume is assembled from a modular section of 2 m length and 300 mm wide by 450 mm deep cross-section as shown in the schematic of Fig. 5. The experimental work is carried for a velocity of 1.2 m/s.

We developed the prototype of the VAHKT based on the specifications provided in Table 1, it is made with a thermoplastic polymer Polylactic Acid (PLA) material using a 3D printer. The 3D model and the developed prototype is as shown in Fig. 6.

The instruments used for measurements were a Valeport BFM002 S-N 2065 current meter to measure the velocity, a tachometer, to measure the angular velocity ω, and a load cell-based torque measurement, to measure T, as shown in Fig. 7.

The procedure we followed to conduct the experiment started by first placing the turbine's unit assembly in the test rig of the S6-MKII flume, then the experiment was started by measuring the upstream velocity using the current meter and then a 5 min. time has given the turbine to be in the fully developed rotation and ω was measured then we the torque measurements were carried out. The available C_P was calculated using the fowling equation;

$$C_P = \frac{T\omega}{1/2\rho A V^3} \tag{25}$$

To further validate both the experimental and DMST results we used also the experimental result of a reference model (RM2) developed by U.S. Department of Energy's (DOE) [10] the for validation, the specification of RM2 is given in Table 2.

Fig. 5. S6-MKII Test rig flume, the section shown in red is the location of the test. (Color figure online)

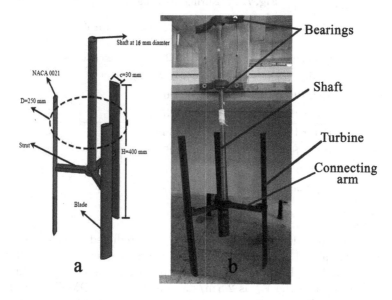

Fig. 6. (a) 3D model of the VAHKTS and (b) prototype used for the test

3   Results and Discussion

3.1   DMST Performance Evaluation

We developed a Matlab code to predict the performance of VAHKTs under different water velocities of 0.75, 1.5, 2, 2.5, and 3 m/s for each V_∞ we solve for

Fig. 7. Measuring instruments

Table 2. Specification of RM2 reference turbine

Parameter	RM2 turbine geometries
Blade Profile	NACA 0021
Max Blade Chord Length	0.0267 m
Rotor Height	0.323 m
Rotor Diameter	0.43 m
Rotor Shaft Diameter	0.0254 m
Solidity	0.047
Tip-Speed Ratios	1 to 4

different tip speed ratio of 1, 2, 3, 4) and C_P is predicted. For each case 1000 iterations were carried out, the convergence criteria are set to bellow 10^{-6}.

It is evident from Fig. 8 the maximum operating condition with high performance C_P is when the V_∞ is 2.5 m/s and at 2.5 TSR. DMST also provides insightful velocity distributions across the azimuthal location of the turbine. For example, referring to Fig. 9 the reduction of V_∞ by the turbine in the upwind and downwind of the rotor can be demonstrated when V_∞ of 1.5 m/s and 2.5 m/s and at 3 TSR. Figure 10 showed the contribution of each blade to the generation of torque, it can be shown that the first power starts produced by the first blade and then the second blade while blade three produces net zero positive torque.

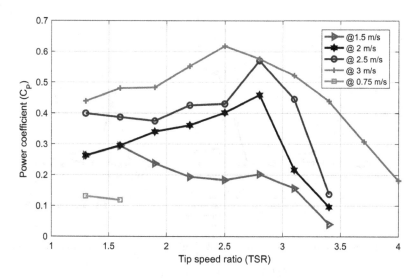

Fig. 8. DMST performance prediction of VAHKTS under different v_∞

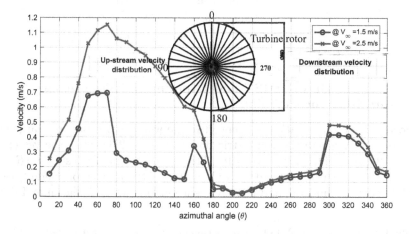

Fig. 9. Velocity distribution in the half up and down stream of the rotor.

3.2   Experimental Performance Evaluation

The experimental investigation were carried out to validate the DMST results at the V_∞ of 1.2 m/s, the TSR is calculated as $TSR = (\omega R)/V_\infty$. The result from measurement is summarized in the following Table 3.

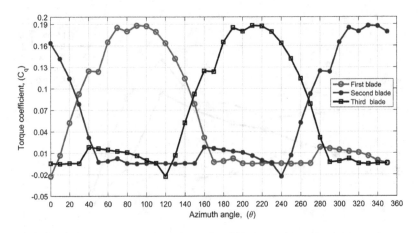

Fig. 10. Torque coefficient performance of single blade at different azimuthal angle

Table 3. Experimental results

	Measurements		TSR	C_P
	Torque (Nm)	ω (RPM)		
$V_\infty = 1.2\,\text{m/s}$	0.051	95	1.03	0.0115

3.3   Compression of DMST and Experimental Performance with Reference Turbine

Performance studies of RM2 reference turbine were carried out in a large open channel facility where the volumetric flow rate, $Q = 2.35\,\text{m}^3/s$, the velocity of $V_\infty = 1.2\,\text{m/s}$, and with $Re = 6.1 \times 10^4$. From the performance test at $TSR = 2.2$ Optimal performance occurred with $C_P = 0.07$. The comparison made between the DMST, experimental, and RM2 reference model, which is shown in Table 4;

Table 4. Compression of DMST and experimental performance with reference turbine, at $V_\infty = 1.2\,\text{m/s}$

TSR	DMST	Experiment	RM2
1.10	0.098	0.0115	0.007
1.33	0.165	–	0.017
1.55	0.2449	–	0.029
2.20	0.18	–	0.070
2.90	−0.0636	–	−0.05

From Table 4 C_P were over predicted by DMST, while the experimental and RM2 result showed a good agreement.

4   Conclusions

The purpose of the current study was to predict the performance of VAHKTs through DMST and experimental study. The Performance investigation using DMST was carried out for different water velocities. The DMST model showed that higher C_P is observed when TSR is 2.5 and the upcoming upstream velocity is 3 m/s. To validate the DMST model experimental studies were carried out, the experiments confirmed the Result obtained from DMST. Further compression is made by RM2 with the DMST and experimental which showed good consistency. The simulation tools are therefore useful for designing vertical axis turbines.

References

1. Anyi, M., Kirke, B.: Evaluation of small axial flow hydrokinetic turbines for remote communities. Energy Sustain. Dev. **14**(2), 110–116 (2010). https://doi.org/10.1016/j.esd.2010.02.003. https://www.sciencedirect.com/science/article/pii/S0973082610000128
2. International Hydropower Association: 2020 Hydropower Status Report — International Hydropower Association (2020). https://archive.hydropower.org/publications/2020-hydropower-status-report
3. Ayati, A.A., Steiros, K., Miller, M.A., Duvvuri, S., Hultmark, M.: A double-multiple streamtube model for vertical axis wind turbines of arbitrary rotor loading. Wind Energy Sci. **4**(4), 653–662 (2019). https://doi.org/10.5194/wes-4-653-2019. https://wes.copernicus.org/articles/4/653/2019/
4. Bangga, G., Dessoky, A., Lutz, T., Krämer, E.: Improved double-multiple-streamtube approach for H-Darrieus vertical axis wind turbine computations. Energy **182**, 673–688 (2019). https://doi.org/10.1016/j.energy.2019.06.083. https://www.sciencedirect.com/science/article/pii/S0360544219312149
5. Bianchini, A., Ferrara, G., Ferrari, L.: Design guidelines for H-Darrieus wind turbines: optimization of the annual energy yield. Energy Convers. Manag. **89**, 690–707 (2015). https://doi.org/10.1016/j.enconman.2014.10.038. https://www.sciencedirect.com/science/article/pii/S0196890414009194
6. Chica, E., Pérez, F., Rubio-Clemente, A., Agudelo, S.: Design of a hydrokinetic turbine, Medellin, Colombia, pp. 137–148, September 2015. https://doi.org/10.2495/ESUS150121. http://library.witpress.com/viewpaper.asp?pcode=ESUS15-012-1
7. Dai, Y.M., Gardiner, N., Sutton, R., Dyson, P.K.: Hydrodynamic analysis models for the design of Darrieus-type vertical-axis marine current turbines. Proc. Inst. Mech. Eng. Part M J. Eng. Marit. Environ. **225**(3), 295–307 (2011). https://doi.org/10.1177/1475090211400684. https://doi.org/10.1177/1475090211400684
8. Goude, A.: Fluid Mechanics of Vertical Axis Turbines: Simulations and Model Development. Ph.D. thesis, Uppsala University, Electricity (2012)
9. Güney, M., Kaygusuz, K.: Hydrokinetic energy conversion systems: a technology status review. Renew. Sustain. Energy Rev. **14**(9), 2996–3004 (2010). https://doi.org/10.1016/j.rser.2010.06.016. https://www.sciencedirect.com/science/article/pii/S1364032110001632

10. Hill, C., Neary, V.S., Gunawan, B., Guala, M., Sotiropoulos, F.: U.S. department of energy reference model program RM2: experimental results. https://doi.org/10.2172/1171458. https://www.osti.gov/biblio/1171458

11. Islam, M., Ting, D.S.K., Fartaj, A.: Aerodynamic models for Darrieus-type straight-bladed vertical axis wind turbines. Renew. Sustain. Energy Rev. **12**(4), 1087–1109 (2008). https://doi.org/10.1016/j.rser.2006.10.023. https://www.sciencedirect.com/science/article/pii/S136403210600164X

12. Khan, M., Iqbal, M., Quaicoe, J.: Design considerations of a straight bladed Darrieus rotor for river current turbines. https://doi.org/10.1109/ISIE.2006.295835

13. Khan, M., Iqbal, M., Quaicoe, J.: River current energy conversion systems: progress, prospects and challenges. Renew. Sustain. Energy Rev. **12**(8), 2177–2193 (2008). https://doi.org/10.1016/j.rser.2007.04.016. https://www.sciencedirect.com/science/article/pii/S136403210700069X

14. Moghimi, M., Motawej, H.: Developed DMST model for performance analysis and parametric evaluation of Gorlov vertical axis wind turbines. Sustain. Energy Technol. Assess. **37**, 100616 (2020). https://doi.org/10.1016/j.seta.2019.100616. https://www.sciencedirect.com/science/article/pii/S2213138819306691

15. Paraschivoiu, I.: Wind Turbine Design: with Emphasis on Darrieus Concept. Polytechnic International Press (2002). https://books.google.com.et/books?id=sefVtnVgso0C

16. Paraschivoiu, I.: Double-multiple streamtube model for studying vertical-axis wind turbines. J. Propul. Power **4**(4), 370–377 (1988). https://doi.org/10.2514/3.23076

17. Roh, S.C., Kang, S.H.: Effects of a blade profile, the Reynolds number, and the solidity on the performance of a straight bladed vertical axis wind turbine. J. Mech. Sci. Technol. **27**(11), 3299–3307 (2013)

18. Sheldahl, R.E., Klimas, P.C.: Aerodynamic characteristics of seven symmetrical airfoil sections through 180-degree angle of attack for use in aerodynamic analysis of vertical axis wind turbines. https://doi.org/10.2172/6548367. https://www.osti.gov/biblio/6548367

19. Soukhaphon, A., Baird, I.G., Hogan, Z.S.: The impacts of hydropower dams in the Mekong river basin: a review. Water **13**(3), 265 (2021). https://www.mdpi.com/2073-4441/13/3/265

20. Sovacool, B.K., Walter, G.: Internationalizing the political economy of hydroelectricity: security, development and sustainability in hydropower states. Rev. Int. Polit. Econ. **26**(1), 49–79 (2019). https://doi.org/10.1080/09692290.2018.1511449

21. Tigabu, M.T., Wood, D., Admasu, B.T.: Resource assessment for hydro-kinetic turbines in Ethiopian rivers and irrigation canals. Energy Sustain. Dev. **58**, 209–224 (2020). https://doi.org/10.1016/j.esd.2020.08.005. https://www.sciencedirect.com/science/article/pii/S0973082620302866

22. VanZwieten, J., et al.: In-stream hydrokinetic power: review and appraisal. J. Energy Eng. **141**(3), 04014024 (2015). https://doi.org/10.1061/(ASCE)EY.1943-7897.0000197

23. Vermaak, H.J., Kusakana, K., Koko, S.P.: Status of micro-hydrokinetic river technology in rural applications: a review of literature. Renew. Sustain. Energy Rev. **29**, 625–633 (2014). https://doi.org/10.1016/j.rser.2013.08.066. https://www.sciencedirect.com/science/article/pii/S1364032113006060

24. Wu, Y.K., Lin, H.J., Lin, J.H.: Certification and testing technology for small vertical axis wind turbine in Taiwan. Sustain. Energy Technol. Assess. **31**, 34–42 (2019). https://doi.org/10.1016/j.seta.2018.11.005. https://www.sciencedirect.com/science/article/pii/S2213138817300279

25. Zarfl, C., Lumsdon, A.E., Berlekamp, J., Tydecks, L., Tockner, K.: A global boom in hydropower dam construction. Aquat. Sci. **77**(1), 161–170 (2015). https://doi.org/10.1007/s00027-014-0377-0

26. Zeiner-Gundersen, D.H.: A vertical axis hydrodynamic turbine with flexible foils, passive pitching, and low tip speed ratio achieves near constant RPM. Energy **77**, 297–304 (2014). https://doi.org/10.1016/j.energy.2014.08.008. https://www.sciencedirect.com/science/article/pii/S036054421400944X

Artificial Intelligence Based Security Constrained Economic Dispatch of Ethiopian Renewable Energy Systems: A Comparative Study

Shewit Tsegaye[1(✉)], Fekadu Shewarega[2], and Getachew Bekele[3]

[1] Jimma University, 378 Jimma, Ethiopia
[2] University of Duisburg-Essen, 47057 Duisburg, Germany
fekadu.shewarega@uni-due.de
[3] Addis Ababa University, 385 Addis Ababa, Ethiopia
getachew.bekele@aait.edu.et

Abstract. In this study, a comparison of two artificial intelligence inspired solution methods employed to solve Security Constrained Economic Dispatch (SCED) of Ethiopian Renewable Energy Systems (ERES) is presented. The solution methods are Efficient & Parallel Genetic Algorithm (EPGA) and Hopfield Neural Network (HNN). This paper argues that employing intelligent SCED that considers power mismatch and intermittency of renewables can solve ERES's recursive blackouts. A simulation was conducted on MATLAB. According to the results, both solution methods provide the best solutions for their respective purposes. For providing accurate forecast & predictive control of intermittent generation, it is imperative to employ HNN. When obtaining global maxima of multi-objective function is required, it is recommended to employ EPGA. Generally, employing intelligent SCED is a key planning step in adopting smarter grids as it reduces the production cost and the number of blackouts while increasing the security level of ERES.

Keywords: Hopfield neural networks · Genetic algorithms · Security constraints · Economic dispatch · Renewable energy systems · Ethiopian power grid

1 Introduction

Access to a secure and affordable energy supply is a prominent prerequisite for economic growth of a developing country like Ethiopia. With a formidable dependency on hydropower, renewable generation is increasing from the current 0.3 GW of wind capacity to 2.4 GW by 2025, before reaching 3.6 GW by 2030. Concurrently, emerging grid-connected solar PV capacity extends to an impressive 3.3 GW by 2025 ahead of the 5.3 GW projected installed capacity [1]. The Ethiopian grid is now entirely prime-moved by renewable energy sources and the Ethiopian Growth and Transformation Plan (GTP) imply that this trend will continue [2, 3] in compliance with the country's Climate Resilient Green Economy (CRGE) strategy [1, 4, 5]. Even though the

© ICST Institute for Computer Sciences, Social Informatics and Telecommunications Engineering 2022
Published by Springer Nature Switzerland AG 2022. All Rights Reserved
M. L. Berihun (Ed.): ICAST 2021, LNICST 412, pp. 522–542, 2022.
https://doi.org/10.1007/978-3-030-93712-6_35

country's plans are promising, there are still challenges regarding demand-supply balance that lead to recursive electricity blackouts [4].

One of the main challenges of power system operation is that electrical energy is cumbersome to store in significant amounts. This aspect requires a continuous balance between generation and demand subject to operational constraints. The second challenge is related to the integration of intermittent renewable energy sources. Variability and intermittency of wind and solar are challenges that cannot be ignored. Integrating them with other sources, providing storage and probabilistic forecast are their corresponding possible solutions [6]. For example, integrating solar and wind with geothermal & hydro stabilizes a given electrical system by providing flexibility and reserve services [7].

Table 1. Unit-based partial outages and their reasons for outage (2015–2016)

Power plant	Unit	Outage (MW)	Reason
	UNIT I	29	Under frequency
	UNIT II	29	Under frequency
FINCHA	UNIT III	29	Under frequency
	UNIT IV	16	Under frequency
AMERTI	UNIT I	15	Under frequency
	UNIT II	15	Under frequency
GIBE I	UNIT I	10	Under frequency
	UNIT II	10	Under frequency
	UNIT I	102	Over-voltage
	UNIT II	99.2	Over-voltage
	UNIT II	12	Under frequency
AWASH II	UNIT II	10	Under voltage
	UNIT I	35	Under frequency
	UNIT II	35	Under frequency
MELKA	UNIT I	2.5	Over-current
	UNIT II	2.5	Over-current
	UNIT I	20	Under frequency
	UNIT I	10	Phase unbalance
ADAMA	ALL	16.4	Lost voltage
ASHEGODA	ALL	0.64	Lost voltage
ADAMA	ALL	14.64	Lost voltage
Total outage		704.38	

A daily power operation task which coins these two challenges is Security constrained Economic Dispatch (SCED). SCED is a process of planning generation schedules for generating units to completely and economically supply the demand while satisfying security constraints [8]. Here the argument for the importance of SCED hinges on the link among demand-supply imbalance, intermittency of renewables, and operational security needs [9]. There is growing evidence that most blackouts and outages of the Ethiopian power system are caused by poorly dispatched generating units [9, 10]. For one, under frequency and over frequency occur due to the imbalance between generation and load as presented in Table 1.

Official blackout report of the Ethiopian electric power from 2013 to 2016, reported 15 unit and plant blackouts. Contingencies such as natural incidents, equipment failures, and power mismatch caused these blackouts. Industries and commercial centers were not functional for an average of four months a year [5].

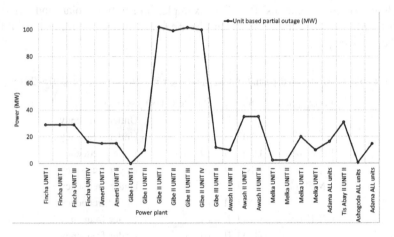

Fig. 1. Unit-based partial outages (2013–2016)

As determining an optimal solution of different functions with conflicting objectives is a moving target, a view of power system operation that ignores SCED is shortsighted [11, 12]. The recursive blackouts presented in Figs. 1 and 2 imply that the existing Ethiopian load dispatch center cannot address the challenges that the sector is facing in connection with intermittent renewables, power imbalance, and fluctuating demand.

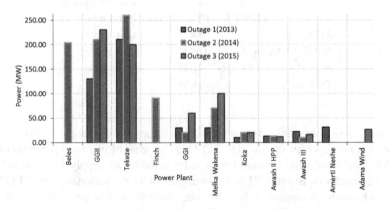

Fig. 2. Plant-based full outage samples (2013–2016)

This study utilized primary data such as forecasted load, interchange schedule, reserve requirements, transmission limits, generation cost offering, reserve limits, ramp rates and pre-scheduled generation level collected from generation-station control rooms and Ethiopian electric utility. This paper thus firmly chose to:

- Study and analyze ERES's potential, generation plan and capacity as supply side, demand profiles as demand side, of the supply-demand balance.
- Show the connection among recursive blackouts, reasons for an outage, intermittent renewables, power mismatch and SCED.
- Solve SCED of ERES using EPGA and HNN, and compare results.

2   Ethiopian Renewable Energy Systems

Integrating renewables without considering their economic and technical challenges leads to recursive blackouts and power service interruptions that subsequently affect the economic growth of the country [4]. For instance, in the Ethiopian power system, operation and planning decisions are carried out without the employment of economic dispatch. Ethiopia is gifted with various renewable energy resources. The estimated potential for hydropower is 45 GW, geothermal is 5 GW, and solar irradiation ranges from 4.5 kWh/m^2/day to 7.5 kWh/m^2/day [13, 14].

As of hydropower generation, large and small hydro potential estimates to 45 GW, of which 5% is only exploited. Wind potential is close to 1,350 GW but less than 1% of this potential is exploited [15]. The entire generation plan of ERES is depicted in Fig. 3. In a comprehensive construct, several papers presented renewable energy resource potential assessments and prospects of integrating renewable generation [15]. Hossain Mondal et al. [15] clearly articulated the prospects of improving energy efficiencies and mitigating greenhouse gasses emission of Ethiopian energy generation.

2.1   Generation Capacity

Electric power generation in Ethiopia currently depends on hydropower. At the same time, in 2012, only about 23% of the total population was connected to the national grid. The Ethiopian electricity grid is dominated by renewables, and the priority projects imply that this trend will continue. Geographic access to electricity is 56% with household connectivity of 25% and per capita electricity consumptions of 100 kwh/day [16, 17].

From a comprehensive understanding of the Ethiopian power grid, 99 power plants as renewable energy systems are identified. These include 48 operational power, 16 plants under construction, and 35 planned. Technology-wise, the planned power grid constitutes 35 hydropower plants, 18 geothermal power plants, 11 wind power plants, 9 solar power plants, and 21 renewable thermal power plants. In this study, the operational plants and plants that are under construction were used. Hence, the considered

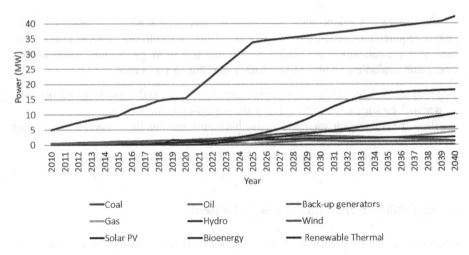

Fig. 3. Renewable generation capacity

renewable energy system constitutes 85 generating units and is dispatched for the projected year of 2025 according to the forecasted generation presented in Fig. 4.

2.2 Demand Forecast

The average annual growth in electricity demand from 2012 to 2013 was approximately 14% while electricity consumption per capita 60 Kw in the year 2012. According to [18], an estimated 23% population had access to electricity in 2012. Ethiopia faces a significant challenge while working to achieve sustainable development. Economic growth, population growth and industrialization greatly increase electricity demand [19]. To dress these challenges, the Ethiopian Electric power (EEP) is launching several projects considering demand for electricity to enhance its capacity in line with the growth of the country.

The electricity demand has doubled for the past 10 years and is expected to increase by 28%–32% per year in the next five years. GTP II aims to reach the power generation capacity of 17.3 GW and 21,728 km of transmission lines by 2020 [20]. These figures do not signify the effect of variable demand, recursive blackouts and intermittent generation. Most electric grids and utilities serve different customers of different sectors such as residential, commercial, and industrial as shown in Fig. 5. The electric usage is not the same for customers that belong to different sectors but somewhat similar for customers within the same sector [19].

To cope up with the growing demand's pace, intensive study on the demand profiles, accurate short-term planning, load forecast, and demand-supply balance should be provided. Apart from the prospects of empowering skilled workforce and advancing weak institutional capacity, providing economic and regulatory framework is a crucial power planning decision.

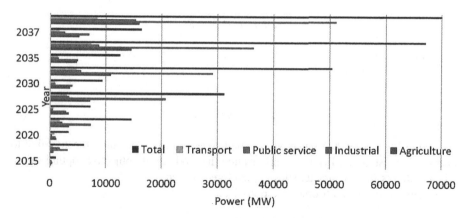

Fig. 4. Sector-wise demand forecast

2.3 Power Mismatch

To dispatch a power system, it is imperative to study supply and demand profiles. Supply refers to the existing generation capacity of the power system, while demand refers to the load of the grid. Ethiopia has a final energy consumption of around 40,000 GWh, whereof domestic appliances consume 4%, the transport sector consumes 3% and the industrial sector consumes 92%. Integrating renewables without considering their economic and technical challenges leads to recursive blackouts and power service interruptions that subsequently affect the economic growth of the country [21]. Ethiopia's current grid is inadequately maintained, and grid stability are already matters of concern, making the integration of renewables a heightened challenge.

Employing computationally efficient SCED can overcome these challenges. For example, with large reservoirs, hydropower can store energy over weeks, months, seasons or even years. Hydropower can therefore provide a full range of ancillary services such as spinning reserve, non-spinning reserve, operating reserves, responsive reserve, and contingency reserves that are required for high penetration of wind and solar [22]. To do this accurate dispatch interval, dispatch level and reserve allocation are needed. This way, the so-called 'duck curve' challenge of solar PV generation can be solved.

3   SCED Mathematical Formulation

3.1   Objective Functions

Power generating and operating cost functions, also known as objective functions rely on power flow output and forecasted values of demand determined for each dispatch interval [6, 23, 24]. The general form of SCED objective function is:

$$optimize f(x), x \in R^n \tag{1}$$

Subject to

$$h_k(x) = 0 \forall 1, 2...m \tag{2}$$

$$g_l(x) \leq 0 \forall 1, 2...L \tag{3}$$

Practically, the SCED objective function is non-linear and multi-objective due to operation constraints. Type of optimization method, multi objective optimization, which exhibits these characteristics is therefore selected.

General form of multi objective optimization is [6]:

$$Optimize f(x) = (f_1(x), f_2(x), f_{Nobj}(x)) \tag{4}$$

Subject to

$$g_l(x) = 0 \forall i = 1, 2...m$$

$$h_k(x) \leq 0 \forall k = 1, 2, ...K$$

$$x_i(1) \leq x_i \leq x_i(0) \tag{5}$$

This study uses the objective functions of the following renewable resources.

SCED for Hydro: $f_1(x)$ in the multi objective formulation represents objective function of hydro power generation [6, 8].

$$\min f_1(x) = C_h \sum_{i=1}^{N_{hg}} P_{hgj}(t) \tag{6}$$

Where

$$P_{hgj}(t) = \sum_{t=1}^{24} \sum_{i=1}^{N_G} 0.00981 \eta_i H_{ij} Q_{ij} \tag{7}$$

SCED for Wind: The power for assumed wind speed is given by [6, 12, 25]:

$$P_{wr} = \begin{cases} 0, for\ v_{wt} \leq v_i and\ v_{out} \geq 0 \\ P_{wr}(\dfrac{v_{wt} - v_i}{v_r - v_i}), for\ v_i \leq v_{wr} \leq v_{out} \\ P_{wr}, for\ v_r \leq v_{wt} \leq v_{out} \end{cases} \tag{8}$$

SCED objective function of wind generation is $f_2(x)$

$$f_2(x) = C_w \sum_{i=1}^{N_{WG}} P_{wgj}(t) + \sum_{t=1}^{24} \sum_{i=1}^{N_{WG}} C_R + C_P \tag{9}$$

C_R and C_P defined by $C_{Rw} + P_w j(t) - (P_{wr} j(t) - \alpha V)$, $C_{Pw} + ((P_w j(t) - \alpha V) - P_{wr} j(t))$ represent the reserve cost function and penalty cost function of wind power generation respectively. Reserve cost function helps to calculate the debit generated from the probability distribution function of variable wind speed [25]. The probability distribution function for the wind power output in the range of $(v_i \leq v \leq v_r)$ can be obtained using:

$$f_{pw} = \frac{K_{rvi}}{P_{wc}} \left[\frac{1 + \frac{h_{pw}(v_t)}{P_{wr}}}{C} \right]^{K-1} x e^{\left[\frac{h_{pw}(v_t)}{P_{wr}} \right]} K \tag{10}$$

Where K and C are Weibull probability distribution function factors.

$$K = (\frac{\sigma}{v_m})^{-1.086} \tag{11}$$

$$C = \frac{V_m}{T(1 + \frac{1}{K})} \tag{12}$$

SCED for Solar PV: The solar power output that can be extracted from a given solar irradiance G is [6, 10, 13]:

$$P_{sg}j(t) = P_{sg}(G) = P_{sr}j(\frac{G^2}{G_{std} + R_{ca}}) \tag{13}$$

And its corresponding objective function is represented by $f_3(x)$

$$f_3(x) = C_s \sum_{i=1}^{N_{sg}} P_{sg}j(t) + \sum_{t=1}^{24} \sum_{i=1}^{N_{sg}} C_R + C_P \tag{14}$$

Where for $0 < G < R$ ca:

$$P_{sg}j(t) = \sum_{t=1}^{24} \sum_{i=1}^{N_{sg}} (C_R + C_P) \tag{15}$$

C_R and C_P defined by $C_{RS} + P_s j(t) - (P_{sr} j(t) - \alpha V)$, $C_{PS} + ((P_s j(t) - \alpha V) - P_{Sr} j(t))$ represent the reserve cost function and penalty cost function of solar PV generation respectively. Reserve cost function helps to determine the debit produced from the probability distribution function of variable solar radiation. The probability distribution function for the power output of variable solar irradiance can also be determined using Weibull probability distribution function [6, 13, 21].

SCED of Renewable Thermal: Despite the difference in their constraints, renewable energy sources adapted from thermal power plants have similar objective function [21, 22]. Renewable thermal plants considered in this study include geothermal power plants, solar thermal power plants, biomass and waste to energy plants.

$$f_4(x) = C_{th} \sum_{i=1}^{N_{th}} P_{th}j(t) \left[\alpha_1 \sum_{i=1}^{N_{Gth}} F_{Gth}P_{Gth} + \alpha_2 \sum_{i=1}^{N_{Sth}} F_{Sth}P_{Sth} + \alpha_3 \sum_{i=1}^{N_{Bth}} F_{Bth}P_{Bth} \right] \quad (16)$$

Where

$$F_{th} = a_i P_{th}^2 + b_i P_{th} + c_i \quad (17)$$

$$F_{Gth} = a_i P_{Gth}^2 + b_i P_{Gth} + c_i \quad (18)$$

$$F_{Sth} = a_i P_{Sth}^2 + b_i P_{Sth} + c_i \quad (19)$$

$$F_{Bth} = a_i P_{Bth}^2 + b_i P_{Bth} + c_i \quad (20)$$

Security Index: Security index as an objective function that shows the severity of contingency during outages is considered and is introduced as an extension of SCED problem formulations in [6, 23, 26].

$$f_5(x) = f_{SL} = \sum_{i=1}^{NL} \left(\frac{P_{Gactive}}{P_{Gactive}^{max}} \right)^{2m} \quad (21)$$

Where N_L denotes the total number of transmission lines $P_{Gactive}$ and $P_{Gactive}^{max}$ represent active power flow and maximum active power flow at the kth line respectively.

3.2   Constraint Functions

In power systems, continuously respected operation constraints and limits ensure a reliable and secure operation of the system [6].

1. Demand and generation balance

$$P_D + P_L = \sum_{i=1}^{N_{hgg}} P_{hg} + \sum_{i=1}^{N_{wg}} P_{wg} + \sum_{i=1}^{N_{sg}} P_{sg} + \sum_{i=1}^{N_{th}} P_{th} \quad (22)$$

2. Generation limits

$$P_i^{min} \le P_i \le P_i^{max} \quad (23)$$

$$P_{min} \le 0.00981 \eta_i H_{ij} Q_{ij} \le P_{max} \quad (24)$$

$$0 \leq P_{w}j(t) \leq P_{wr} \tag{25}$$

$$0 \leq P_{s}j(t) \leq P_{sr} \tag{26}$$

$$0 \leq P_{h}j(t) \leq P_{hr} \tag{27}$$

3. Prohibited operating zones

$$P_i^{\min} \leq P_i \leq P_i^{Lj} \forall j = 1, 2...N_{Poz} \tag{28}$$

$$P_i^{V_j-1} \leq P_i \leq P_i^{lj} \tag{29}$$

$$P_i^{V_J-1} \leq P_i \leq P_i^{\max} \tag{30}$$

4. Transmission constraints: For transmission constraints Kron's loss equation is considered [23].

$$P_L = \sum_{i=1}^{n}\sum_{j=1}^{m} P_{gi}B_{ij}P_{gj} = B_{oo} + \sum_{i=1}^{n} B_{io}P_{gi} + \sum_{i=1}^{n}\sum_{j=1}^{m} P_{gi}B_{ij}P_{gj} \tag{31}$$

Where

$$B_{ij} = \frac{\cos(\theta_i - \theta_j)R_{ij}}{\cos\phi_i \cos\phi_j V_i V_J} \tag{32}$$

$$B_{oo} = \sum_{i=1}^{n}\sum_{j=1}^{m} P_{Di}B_{ij}P_{Dj} \tag{33}$$

$$B_{ij} = -\sum_{j=1}^{m}\left(B_{ij} + B_{ji}\right) \tag{34}$$

5. Security limits

$$S_1 \leq S_1^{\max} \forall l = 1, 2...N_L \tag{35}$$

$$\phi_j P(t) > o \forall j = 1, 2...N_C \tag{36}$$

6. Generator ramp rate limits

$$\max(P_i^{\min}, P_i^{t-1} - DR_i) \leq P_i(t) \leq \min(P_i^{\max}, P_i^{t-1} + DR_i) \tag{37}$$

7. Spinning reserve limits

$$\sum_{i=1}^{N_G} S_{Ri} \geq S_{Sr} \tag{38}$$

8. Water discharge and reservoir limits:

$$X_i^{\min} \leq X_i \leq X_i^{\max} \tag{39}$$

$$V_i^{\min} \leq V_i \leq V_i^{\max} \tag{40}$$

$$Q_i^{\min} \leq Q_{ij} \leq Q_j^{\max} \tag{41}$$

$$V_i^{\min} \leq V_{ij} \leq V_j^{\max} \tag{42}$$

$$V_{i,j+1} = V_{ij} - (Q_{ij} - q_i + S_{ij})\Delta t + \sum_{K \in K_j} (Q_{ij} + S_{kij} + I_j)\Delta t \tag{43}$$

9. Renewable generation penetration rate

$$P_w j(t) + P_s j(t) + P_h j(t) + P_{th} j(t) \leq \Psi P_D \tag{44}$$

Constraint (9) considers thermal (biomass, solar-thermal, geothermal), hydro, wind, and solar PV penetration ratios, ψ and ERES's penetration ratio is 97%.

4 Artificial Intelligence Methods

4.1 Hopfield Neural Networks (HNN)

1. *General Hopfield neural networks search mechanism formulation*
Setting values of the units to the specific start pattern initializes the Hopfield neural networks. The attractor pattern in Eq. (45) updates iteratively until the network converges. Hopfield networks proved that the attractors of the nonlinear phase spaces are stable, not periodic, or chaotic as in another systems. Convergence is therefore guaranteed, [24, 26, 27].

Hopfield neural networks learn by lowering the tolerance (ΔE) of states that the network must remember. This enables the network to function as an associative memory. This implies convergence to a remembered state if it is only a part of the state. The network recovers from a distorted input to a trained state that is most similar to the input. These properties are crucial, since a learning rule, satisfying them, is more biologically acceptable [28].

2. Hopfield neural networks flowchart

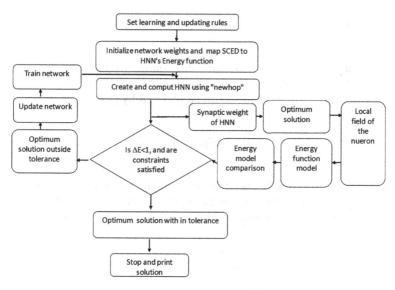

Fig. 5. Flow chart for HNN

3. Parameter Set-Up and Initialization

The attractor pattern in Hopfield Networks is a final stable state which should not change any value within its updating limit.

$$V_i^0 = P_{Gi}^{min} + rand(P_{Gi}^{max} - P_{Gi}^{min})$$

The initial values of inputs for these neurons are determined by the inverse sigmoid functions respective to the initial outputs of the continuous neurons representing power outputs of generating units [24, 28].

$$u_i^0 = \frac{1}{2\sigma} \ln \left(\frac{V_i^0 - P_{Gi}^{min}}{P_{Gi}^{max} - V_i^0} \right) \tag{45}$$

Neuron inputs come from two sources, one from the external inputs Ii and the other from the other neurons V_j. Where: U_i is the total neuron input to i, T_{ij} is the interconnection conductance from the neuron output of j to the input of neuron i, Ii denotes external input to neuron i, and V_j stands for the output of neuron j. The continuous variables of SCED are foundations for the continuous model of HNN [26, 28].

4. Mapping Economic Dispatch to Hopfield Neural Network

The objective function of an economic dispatch problem has two parts i) the operation & generation cost minimization part ii) the generation and computation error minimization part. To solve the economic dispatch problem the energy function is defined by combining the target functions with their constraints as [24, 28]:

$$E = A(P_D + P_L - \sum_{i=1}^{N} P_G)^2 + B \sum (a_i + b_i P_{Gthi} + c_i P_{Gthi}^2) + \left(\frac{C}{2}\right) P_L^2 \qquad (46)$$

Mapping the energy function to SCED determines synaptic strengths and external inputs of HNN. After replacing the output of unit i from P_{Gio} to P_{Gi}, and the transmission loss from P_{Lo} to P_L the loss can be obtained by [27]:

$$P_L = P_{Lo} + dP_L \cong P_{Lo} + \sum_{i=1}^{N} I_{Lio}(P_{Gi} - P_{Gio}) \qquad (47)$$

The energy function of HNN is formed by merging the objective functions and their corresponding constraint functions, using weight coefficients, which determine the weightage of each factor. This starts with the energy function of HNN given by [28]:

$$E = -\frac{1}{2} \sum_{i=1}^{N} \sum_{j=1}^{N} T_{Ij} V_i V_j - \sum_{i=1}^{N} I_i V_i \qquad (48)$$

The time derivative of this energy function should be negative in order to ensure convergence. HNN based SCED can be solved by the employment of the penalty function.

$$E = \frac{A}{2} \left(\sum_{i=1}^{N} (a_i P_{Gthi}^2 + b_i P_{Gthi} + c) \right) + \frac{B}{2} \left(P_L + P_D - \sum_{i=1}^{N} P_{Gthi} \right)^2 \qquad (49)$$

This energy function consists of an objective function also known as a cost function and design constraints function.

$$P_L = P_{Lo} + dP_L \cong P_{Lo} + \sum_{i=1}^{N} I_{Lio}(P_{Gi} - P_{Gio}) \qquad (50)$$

$$\frac{\partial P_L}{\partial P_{Gi} P_{Gio}} = 2 \sum_{i=1}^{N} B_{ij} P_{Gjo}(P_{Gi} - P_{Gio}) \qquad (51)$$

$$P_L = \sum_{i=1}^{N} \sum_{j=1}^{N} P_{Gio} B_{ij} P_{Gjo} + 2 \sum_{i=1}^{N} \sum_{j=1}^{N} B_{ij} P_{Gjo}(P_{Gi} - P_{Gio}) \qquad (52)$$

Mapping this equation into HNN, the computation should start by equating (54) and (55) to obtain the following set of equations.

$$T_{ii} = -Aa_i - B, T_{ij} = -B \tag{53}$$

$$I_i = B(P_D - P_L) - \frac{\lambda}{2}b_i \tag{54}$$

$$I_i = A(P_D + P_L) - \frac{Bb_i}{2} \tag{55}$$

A and B represent weighting factors where, A varies from 0.1 to 3, B is set to 1 and to 0.000055. A&B should be greater than or equal to zero. The relation that updates these values is called an adaptive calculation of weighting factors.

$$A = \frac{I_M + 0.5Bb_m}{P_G} \tag{56}$$

$$B = \frac{I_m - AP_D}{0.5b_m} \tag{57}$$

Where, $I_M = \left(\frac{1}{N_G}\right)\sum I_{ED_i}$, $b_m = \left(\frac{1}{N_G}\right)\sum b_i$ and $P_G = \sum P_{Gi}$, N_G is the number of committed generating units. In the selection procedure of weighting factors, A is associated with power mismatch (P_m), as it is assigned the highest priority over the other terms [9].

$$A(P_m)^2 \geq B(\Delta f_T) \tag{58}$$

$$A \geq B(\Delta f_T)/(P_m)^2 \tag{59}$$

The value of A is determined from any value of B and the value of weighting factor C is calculated by.

$$C = 2AP_m \tag{60}$$

4.2   Efficient Parallel Genetic Algorithm(EPGA)

1. *Parameter Set-Up and Initialization of the population*
Initialize the amount of generating units N and population size, NP and specify credible contingencies and. Population size and dimension randomly generate an initial vector Ptij. Ptij is the real power value of jth unit of the ith population randomly generated within the operating limits using [26, 29, 30];

$$P_{ij}^t = P_i^{\min} + rand(0, 1)(P_i^{\max} - P_i^{\min}) \tag{61}$$

Evaluate the fitness value of every vector Ptij according to the fitness function given below:

$$F_A = -(f_1(x) + f_2(x) + f_3(x) + f_4(x) + f_{Penality} + f_{Reserve} + f_{loss}) \tag{62}$$

Perform mutation operation on the target vectors to obtain new parameter vectors called mutant vectors using:

$$Z_{ij} = P^t_{ij} + F(P^t_{Rij} - P^t_{Rji}) \tag{63}$$

Perform crossover operation to create trial vectors from mutant and target vectors. If the generated random number value is less than or equal to the assumed value of the crossover constant, then the mutant vector is chosen, else the parent vector is chosen as given below. The considered crossover constant (C_R) must be within the domain of (0,1).

$$U^{t+1}_{ij} = \left\{ \begin{array}{l} Z_{ij}, if(R_{ij}) \leq C_R \\ P_{ij}, if(R_{ij}) \geq C_R \end{array} \right\} \tag{64}$$

Decide members to constitute the population of subsequent generation (t + 1). The new vector $U_{ij}^{(t+1)}$ is selected based on the comparison of fitness of both target vector, P_i and trial vector, U_i. Compute generation after generation to meet the stopping criteria t_{max} [26, 31] (Fig. 6).

2. *Genetic algorithm flowchart*

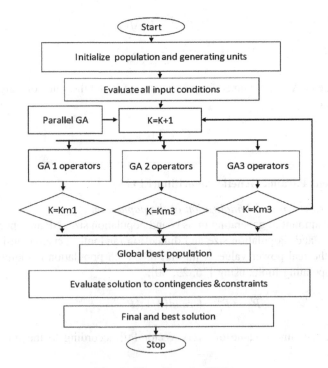

Fig. 6. Flow chart for EPGA

5 Results and Discussions

Figures 7 and 8 depict the simulation results including the behaviors of a particular Hopfield Neural Network. A dispatch comparison between different solution methods of a 3 unit fixed generation supplying a fixed demand is presented in Table 2. This comparison was done to indicate the robustness of HNN and EPGA.

Table 2. Comparison table between solution methods

Unit generation (MW)	MVMO solution	HNN solution	EPGA solution
P1	450	450	450
P2	324.66	322.85	321.91
P3	200.38	201.98	200.72
Pm (Mw)	-4.6×10^{-5}	-4.6×10^{-5}	-4.86×10^{-5}
Cost($/hr)	8236.20	8236.18	8206.18
Run time (sec)	0.125	0.105	0.115

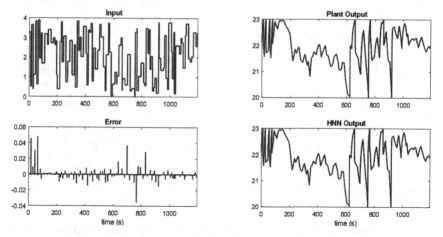

Fig. 7. Predictive control of variable renewable energy resources using neural networks for Ethiopian renewable energy systems

Predictive control enables the Hopfield net to lower the energy state that the net should remember as shown in Fig. 7. From weight positions plotted in Fig. 8, the attractor pattern on the final state, penalty function weights, and adaptive calculation of weighting factors can be obtained. HNN trains, learns and updates itself from feedback through weighting factors. In this study, errors and result fluctuations are considered as dispatch losses due to contingencies. This consideration helps in allocating contingency reserves.

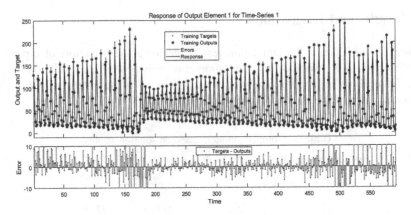

Fig. 8. Time series response of training the created GA-HNN

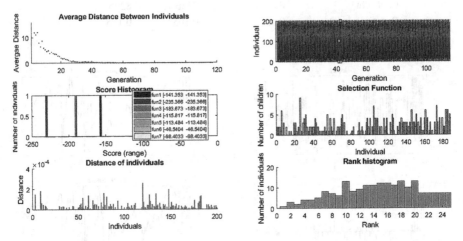

Fig. 9. Daily dispatch of Ethiopian renewable energy system using HNN enhanced EPGA

Figure 9 depicts daily dispatch of Ethiopian renewable energy systems altogether with the computational behaviors of EPGA. Unlike HNN, EPGA learns and updates itself from experiences through genealogy, natural selection and adaptation SCED is important for scheduling when/which generator to dispatch, determining how much reserve is need for spinning, standby, ramping, and contingency. As it is indicated in Table 3, the comparison of daily dispatches using both solution methods i.e. HNN and EPGA helps ERES concurrently increase its security level and reduce its generation cost.

Table 3. Comparison of HNN and EPGA.

Time	HNN Solution	EPGA Solution
1	⬇ 11847.04	⬇ 11847.04155
2	⬇ 11547.13	⬇ 11547.12606
3	⬆ 23394.17	⬆ 23394.16761
4	⬇ 11662.13	⬇ 11662.1314
5	⬇ 11768.15	⬇ 11768.15114
8	⬇ 11866.71	⬇ 11866.71086
7	⬇ 12034.89	⬇ 12034.88594
8	⬇ 12219.79	⬇ 12219.79114
9	⬇ 12543.93	⬇ 12543.93396
10	⬇ 13130.48	⬇ 13130.47914
11	⬇ 13397.93	⬇ 13397.92534
12	⬇ 13540.31	⬇ 13540.30971
13	⬇ 13260.92	⬇ 13260.92285
14	⬇ 12859.55	⬇ 12859.55294
15	⬇ 12431.65	⬇ 12431.65383
16	⬇ 12312.82	⬇ 12312.81593
17	⬇ 12017.45	⬇ 12017.45115
18	⬇ 12041.08	⬇ 12041.07891
19	⬇ 11757.06	⬇ 11757.05716
20	⬇ 11453.42	⬇ 11453.41733
21	⬇ 11424.6	⬇ 11424.6024
22	⬇ 11654.52	⬇ 11654.52416
23	⬇ 12368.03	⬇ 12368.02728
24	⬇ 12642.14	⬇ 12642.14203
Pm(MW)	3.22315E-05	3.16214E-05
P loss (MW)	36.78	36.23
Cost($/MW)	520,614.85	520,001.24
Run time (sec)	0.6875	0.2692

There is an important difference in the demand between weekdays and weekends. Furthermore, Mondays and Fridays being adjacent to weekends exhibit structurally different loads than Tuesday through Thursday. Day and night also, have a different share of load and generation effects Fig. 10. Thus helps to grasp the effect of weekend demand profiles on SCED of ERES.

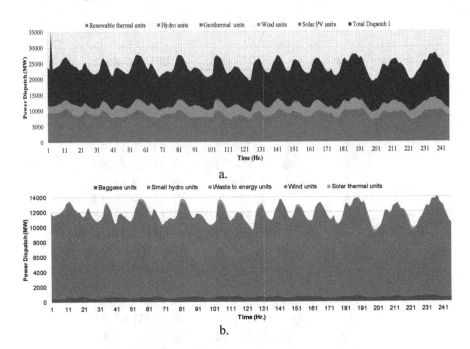

Fig. 10. Weekly dispatch Ethiopian renewable energy systems (a). Using HNN (b). Using EPGA

6 Conclusions

Recursive blackouts, frequent outages and power surges caused by intermittent renewables related contingencies, are the major obstacles of socio-economic advancement of the Ethiopian community. After the connections among these outages, reason of outages, and demand-supply imbalance are made, it is imperative to solve the challenges in connection with SCED. This paper thus argues that recursive blackouts can be reduced by employing computationally intelligent SCED of renewables that considers demand-supply imbalance, intermittency of renewables, variable demand and contingencies.

In the existing Ethiopian power grid, generation plan, load forecast, intermittency of renewable generation, storage constraints, contingencies, and ramping requirements are not considered. To date, there is no such practice in the Ethiopian power grid. For this reason, it is imperative to use AI based SCED of ERES. Renewable energy potential, generation capacity, and generation plan are analyzed for the supply side, whereas demand profiles are analyzed for the demand side of SCED of the Ethiopian power grid. Solving SCED of ERES using EPGA and HNN was carried out on MATLAB.

According to the results obtained, both solution methods provide the best solutions for their respective purposes. For providing accurate forecast and predictive control of intermittent generation, it is imperative to employ HNN. When obtaining global maxima of multi-objective function is required, it is recommended to employ EPGA.

References

1. Sarfi, V., Livani, H.: An economic-reliability security-constrained optimal dispatch for microgrids. IEEE Trans. Power Syst. **33**(6), 6777–6786 (2018)
2. Teeparthi, K., Vinod Kumar, D.M.: Multi-objective hybrid PSO-APO algorithm based security constrained optimal power flow with wind and thermal generators. Eng. Sci. Technol. Int. J. **20**(2), 411–426 (2017)
3. Zhu, D., Hug-Glanzmann, G.: Decomposition methods for stochastic optimal coordination of energy storage and generation. IEEE Power Energy Soc. Gen. Meet. **2014**, 1–5 (2014)
4. Jin, X., et al.: Security-constrained economic dispatch for integrated natural gas and electricity systems. Energy Procedia **88**, 330–335 (2016)
5. Zadeh, A.K., Zeynal, H., Nor, K.M.: Security constrained economic dispatch using multi-thread parallel computing. Int. J. Phys. Sci. **6**(17), 4273–4281 (2011)
6. Tsegaye, S., Shewarega, F., Bekele, G.: Security constrained economic dispatch of renewable energy systems. In: Delele, M.A., Bitew, M.A., Beyene, A.A., Fanta, S.W., Ali, A.N. (eds.) ICAST 2020. LNICSSITE, vol. 384, pp. 361–375. Springer, Cham (2021). https://doi.org/10.1007/978-3-030-80621-7_26
7. Hlalele, T.G., Naidoo, R.M., Bansal, R.C., Zhang, J.: Multi-objective stochastic economic dispatch with maximal renewable penetration under renewable obligation. Appl. Energy **270**, 115120 (2020)
8. Moreno, S.R., Kaviski, E.: Daily scheduling of small hydro power plants dispatch with modified particles swarm optimization. Pesqui. Operacional **35**(1), 25–37 (2015)
9. Damodaran, S.K., Kumar, T.K.S.: Hydro-thermal-wind generation scheduling considering economic and environmental factors using heuristic algorithms. Energies **11**(2), 353 (2018)
10. ElDesouky, A.A.: Security and stochastic economic dispatch of power system including wind and solar resources with environmental consideration. Int. J. Renew. Energy Res. **3**(4), 951–958 (2013)
11. Biswas, P.P., Suganthan, P.N., Qu, B.Y., Amaratunga, G.A.J.: Multiobjective economic-environmental power dispatch with stochastic wind-solar-small hydro power. Energy **150**, 1039–1057 (2018)
12. Jihane, K., Cherkaoui, M.: Economic dispatch optimization for system integrating renewable energy sources. AIP Conf. Proc. **1968**, 020023 (2018)
13. Bilil, H., Aniba, G., Maaroufi, M.: Multiobjective optimization of renewable energy penetration rate in power systems. Energy Procedia **50**, 368–375 (2014)
14. Suresh, V., Sreejith, S.: Economic dispatch and cost analysis on a power system network interconnected with solar farm. Int. J. Renew. Energy Res. **5**(4), 1098–1105 (2015)
15. Mondal, M.A.H., Bryan, E., Ringler, C., Mekonnen, D., Rosegrant, M.: Ethiopian energy status and demand scenarios: prospects to improve energy efficiency and mitigate GHG emissions. Energy **149**, 161–172 (2018)
16. Demissie, A.A., Solomon, A.A.: Power system sensitivity to extreme hydrological conditions as studied using an integrated reservoir and power system dispatch model, the case of Ethiopia. Appl. Energy **182**, 442–463 (2016)
17. Tucho, G.T., Weesie, P.D.M., Nonhebel, S.: Assessment of renewable energy resources potential for large scale and standalone applications in Ethiopia. Renew. Sustain. Energy Rev. **40**, 422–431 (2014)

18. Tenenbaum, B., Greacen, C., Siyambalapitiya, T., Knuckles, J.: From the Bottom Up: How Small Power Producers and Mini-Grids Can Deliver Electrification and Renewable Energy in Africa. The World Bank, Washington, D.C. (2014)
19. Guta, D., Börner, J.: Energy security, uncertainty and energy resource use options in Ethiopia: A sector modelling approach. Int. J. Energy Sect. Manag. 11(1), 91–117 (2017)
20. Master, D.M., Management, P.: The Challenges and Prospects of Electricity Access in Ethiopia (2018)
21. Brini, S., Abdallah, H.H., Ouali, A.: Economic dispatch for power system included wind and solar thermal energy. Leonardo J. Sci. 8(14), 204–220 (2009)
22. E. T. H. No, D. O. F. Sciences, E. T. H. Zurich, and E. T. H. Zurich, "ii c 2013 Maria Vrakopoulou All Rights Reserved 6(237)
23. Tsegaye, S., Shewarega, F., Bekele, G.: A review on security constrained economic dispatch of integrated renewable energy systems. EAI Endorsed Trans. Energy Web 21, e13 (2020)
24. Tsegaye, S., Shewarega, F., Bekele, G.: Hopfield neural network-based security constrained economic dispatch of renewable energy systems. EAI Endorsed Trans. Energy Web Online First 35, 1–14 (2021)
25. Cheng, W., Zhang, H.: A dynamic economic dispatch model incorporating wind power based on chance constrained programming. Energies 8(1), 233–256 (2015)
26. Tsegaye, S., Bekele, G.: Optimal generation dispatch of Ethiopian power system using hybrid genetic Algorithm-Hopfield neural network. EAI Endorsed Trans. Energy Web 18 (37), 1–15 (2021)
27. Yalcinoz, T., Cory, B.J., Short, M.J.: Hopfield neural network approaches to economic dispatch problems. Int. J. Electr. Power Energy Syst. 23(6), 435–442 (2001)
28. Salcedo-Sanz, S., Yao, X.: A hybrid Hopfield network-genetic algorithm approach for the terminal assignment problem. IEEE Trans. Syst. Man Cybern. Part B Cybern. 34(6), 2343–2353 (2004)
29. Gupta, N., Gaba, G.S., Singh, H., Gill, H.S.: A new approach for function optimization using hybrid GA-ANN algorithm. Int. J. Eng. Res. Appl. 2(2), 386–389 (2012)
30. Yeh, W.C., et al.: New genetic algorithm for economic dispatch of stand-alone three-modular microgrid in DongAo Island. Appl. Energy 263, 114508 (2020)
31. Ciornei, I.: Novel hybrid optimization methods for the solution of the economic dispatch of generation in power systems (2011)

Facile Preparation and Electrochemical Investigations of Copper-Ion Doped α-MnO₂ Nanoparticles

Nigus Gabbiye Habtu[1,3(✉)], Ababay Ketema Worku[1],
Delele Worku Ayele[1,2(✉)], Minbale Admas Teshager[4],
and Zerihun Getahun Workineh[5]

[1] Bahir Dar Energy Center, Bahir Dar Institute of Technology,
Bahir Dar University, P.O. BOX 26, Bahir Dar, Ethiopia
{nigus.gabiye,Delele.worku}@bdu.edu.et
[2] Department of Chemistry, Bahir Dar University,
P.O. Box 79, Bahir Dar, Ethiopia
[3] Department of Chemical Engineering, Bahir Dar Institute of Technology,
Bahir Dar University, P.O. Box 26, Bahir Dar, Ethiopia
[4] Department of Chemistry, Debre Markos University,
P.O. Box 269, Debre Markos, Ethiopia
[5] Department of Materials Science and Engineering, Bahir Dar University,
P.O. BOX 79, Bahir Dar, Ethiopia

Abstract. Copper doped MnO₂ nanoparticles have been developed by co-perception technique without using any surfactants and templates. The physiochemical and thermal properties of the as-prepared nanoparticles have been analysed by X-ray diffraction (XRD), Fourier transform infrared (FTIR) spectroscopy, and Thermogravimetric analysis (TGA) and/or Differential thermal analysis (DTA). The catalytic performance of MnO₂ and Cu doped MnO₂ nanoparticles have been assessed via cyclic voltammetry (CV). The crystal structure of MnO₂ and Cu doped MnO₂ nanoparticles was the sharply crystallized α-MnO₂. However, the Copper dopant has no noticeable influence on the crystallization of MnO₂ as determined by the results of XRD analysis. The formation of M-O (M = Mn, Cu) was confirmed from FTIR study. Cu-doped MnO₂ nanoparticles showed improved thermal stability as confirmed by TGA/DTA analysis. The doping amount had a high impact on the catalytic performance of the Cu-MnO₂ nanoparticles. The Cu-MnO₂ nanoparticles showed better catalytic performance as compared to pure MnO₂. Hence, Cu-doped MnO₂ nanoparticles showed improved catalytic activity and thermal stability.

Keywords: Copper-ion · α-MnO₂ nanoparticles · Co-perception technique · Oxygen reduction reaction

M. L. Berihun (Ed.): ICAST 2021, LNICST 412, pp. 543–553, 2022.
https://doi.org/10.1007/978-3-030-93712-6_36

1 Introduction

Oxygen reduction reaction (ORR) is the principal kinetically restricting the air electrode reaction in energy conversion and storage technologies such as rechargeable metal-air batteries (MABs) and supercapacitors [1, 2]. Preparing electrocatalysts for ORR is a critical issue. Thus, the most extensively used ORR catalysts are yet platinum (Pt) based nanoparticles due to their best performance [3, 4]. However, the practical utilization of Pt for ORR is limited because of its low abundance and high cost [5, 6]. Hence, different kinds of materials such as metal alloys, transition metal oxides, metal oxide, and hybrid materials were mostly used electrocatalysts for ORR [7]. However, utilizing cheap and active oxygen electrocatalysts for ORR remains a big problem [8]. Among these MnO_2 has been used as an electrocatalyst for ORR due to its abundance, novel electrocatalytic performance, low price, and environmentally friendly characteristics. MnO_2 can exist with five types of crystal phases (α-, β-, γ-, δ-, and λ-MnO_2) [9, 10]. The catalytic activity of MnO_2 depends greatly on the crystallographic arrangement, following the order of $\alpha \approx \delta > \gamma > \lambda > \beta$ as stated in the literatures [11, 12]. Investigation on MnO_2 as oxygen electrocatalysts for the ORR associated with the influence of the structure, composition, and morphology, on the catalytic activity [13]. Hence, the most studies have been focused in enhancing the ORR activity via compositing or doping MnO_2 with different transition metals, such as copper (Cu), silver (Ag), iron (Fe), nickel (Ni), and cobalt (Co) doped MnO_2 electrode for ORR application, which change electronic structure and electrochemical performance [14]. To improve these challenges, MnO_2 has been combined with other materials to obtain good electrochemical performance, such as nanocomposites, nanotube @MnO_2, graphene@MnO_2, carbon Co_3O_4@MnO_2, and CuO@MnO_2 [15]. In addition, cation doping has been proven to be an effective method to improve the conductivity of materials. Copper cation is considered to be one of the most suitable candidates for cation doping, as an effective doping cation to enhance the electrochemical performance. However, it is still a challenge to gain high-performance MnO_2 nanomaterials via a low-cost and simple preparation method [16]. Until, similar studies on Cu^{2+} doped MnO_2 nanoparticles for ORR utilization have not been reported very well [17, 18]. Hence, various techniques were applied for the development of doped MnO_2 which includes thermal decomposition, simple reduction [19], solid-phase process, hydrothermal [20], microwave, physical vapour deposition [21], chemical vapour deposition, electro deposition, sol-gel process, aerosol processing, and co-precipitation [22, 23]. Here we have reported the simple co-precipitation technique for the development of different levels of (0.025–0.1M) Cu-ion doped in MnO_2 nanoparticles for ORR application. This study investigates the synthesis of high-performance Cu-ion doped MnO_2 nanoparticles via a low-cost and simple preparation method in an alkaline medium.

2 Materials and Methods

2.1 Chemicals

All chemical were purchased in alpha chemika (India) and utilized without any purifying. Distilled water (DW) was utilized to prepare all solutions. Manganese sulfate monohydrate (99%, $MnSO_4.H_2O$), NaOH solution, potassium permanganate (99.5%, $KMnO_4$), ethanol, and Copper sulfate pentahydrate ($CuSO_4.5H_2O$) were used as precursors.

2.2 Preparation of α-MnO₂ Electrocatalysts

Cu-doped α-MnO₂ and α-MnO₂ nanoparticles were synthesized via co-perception technique. Firstly, 0.3M of $MnSO_4.H_2O$ was dissolved in 40 mL of DW and stirred. Then, $CuSO_4.5H_2O$ desired mole of (0.025, 0.05, 0.075, and 0.1 M) prepared in 40 mL of DW was added dropwise. Additional, 0.2M of potassium permanganate dissolved in 60 mL of DW was added dropwise to the mixture of $MnSO_4.H_2O$ and $CuSO_4.5H_2O$. Adjust the pH of the solution to12 by adding 0.2 M NaOH. After 5 h of stirring at 80 °C the precipitate of Cu doped MnO₂ nanoparticles were obtained. The product was filtered and cleaned with DW. The as-prepared nanoparticles have been dried at 100 °C for 12 h to evaporate water and volatile components. Finally, the as-prepared products were annealed at 500 °C for 3 h. Figure 1 shows schematic illustration of Cu-MnO₂ electrocatalysts preparation via co-precipitation approach.

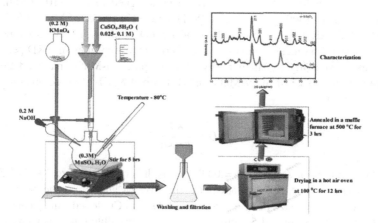

Fig. 1. Schematic illustration of Cu-MnO₂ electrocatalysts preparation by co-precipitation technique.

2.3 Characterization Techniques

The functional groups and other impurities exist in as-prepared samples have been determined via Fourier Transform Infrared spectroscopy (FTIR) (JASCO MODEL FT-IR 6660) in the wavelength range of 400–4000 cm^{-1}. The thermal property was studied by using TGA/DTA analysis. The XRD patterns of the synthesized nanoparticles were investigated by XRD (SHIMADZU, MAXima_X XRD-7000) with Cu-K$_\alpha$ radiation. Electrochemical analyses were conducted by three electrode CHI760E electrochemical workstation.

2.4   Electrochemical Measurements

A Glassy Carbon Electrode (GCE) of 3 mm has been used as a working electrode. Moreover, the electrode was sonicated with DW and ethanol for 10 min. Ag/AgCl (with an electrolyte of 0.1 M KOH) and Pt coil were utilized as a reference and counter electrodes, respectively. Then, 5 mg of MnO$_2$ and Cu-doped α-MnO$_2$ nanoparticles dispersed in a solution of 1 mL (2:1 v/v water/isopropanol mixed) was drop cast (15 mL) constantly on to the GCE electrode surface and dried. Cyclic voltammetry (CV) was conducted at a sweep rate of 50 mV s^{-1} in the range of +0.1 and −0.7 V.

3   Results and Discussion

3.1   Structural Analysis

The structure and phase purity of MnO$_2$ and Cu-doped MnO$_2$ nanoparticles were analysed by XRD in a 2θ range of 10–80°. Figure 2 illustrates the XRD pattern of MnO$_2$ and Cu-doped MnO$_2$ nanoparticles. As provided in Fig. 2, sharp diffraction peaks had been located at 2θ of 12.67°, 17.99 °, 28.67°, 37.49°, 41.89°, 49.77°, 56.15°, 60.11°, 65.34°, 69.39°, 72.88°, which could be assigned to the (110), (200), (310), (211), (301), (411), (600), (521), (002), (541), and (312) planes of MnO$_2$ (*JCPDS 00-44-0141*). Both XRD peaks shows phase of α-MnO$_2$ with tetragonal structure. However, with Cu dopant increasing copper oxides or other impurities of XRD peaks were not remarked, showing the high purity of as-prepared α-MnO$_2$ nanoparticles. The Average crystallite size of the α-MnO$_2$ and Cu doped MnO$_2$ were computed through Scherer equation.

$$D = \frac{K\lambda}{\beta\cos\theta} \tag{1}$$

where "K" is the Scherer constant = 0.89, "D" is the crystallites size, "λ" = 1.5406 Å (wavelength of X-rays), "β" (in radians) is the FWHM and "θ" is the peak position. The average crystallite size determined for α-MnO$_2$ and Cu doped MnO$_2$ nanoparticles were found to be 4.1 nm and 5.3 nm, respectively. Crystallite size was increased after the doping of copper due to Cu addition into the tunnels.

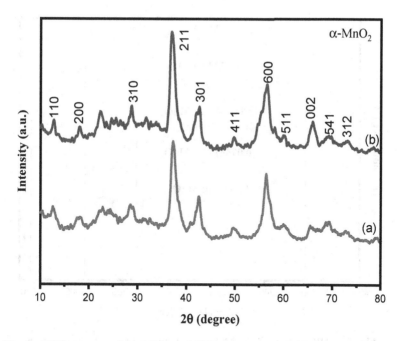

Fig. 2. XRD patterns of (a) MnO_2 and (b) 0.01 M Cu-doped MnO_2 nanoparticles.

3.2 Functional Group Study

FTIR spectra of un-doped MnO_2 and Cu-doped MnO_2 nanoparticles were analysed in the range of 4000–400 cm^{-1}, to investigate the functional groups on the surface of as-prepared materials, and displayed in Fig. 3. The bands located at 3425 cm^{-1} may be because of the stretching vibrations of hydroxyl groups. The peaks at 1647 and 1097 cm^{-1} are corresponding to the bending vibration of structural OH^- and H_2O. The peaks observed at around 521 cm^{-1} are ascribed to the metal-oxygen (M–O) bending vibrations of MnO_2 and Cu doped in MnO_2. The results obtained via the FTIR analysis confirm that Cu doped in MnO_2 nanoparticles was successfully developed. Thus, after doping with cu-ion the peaks at 3425 and 1647 cm^{-1} are stronger than those of the pure MnO_2, which indicates that cations dopant could facilitate the formation of hydroxyl OH^- or H_2O molecules.

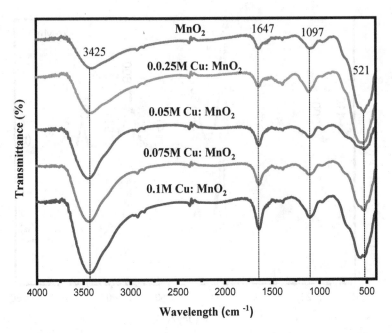

Fig. 3. FTIR spectra of pure MnO_2, and Cu doped α-MnO_2 nanoparticles.

3.3 Thermal Properties

To examine the thermal characteristics of MnO_2 and Cu doped MnO_2, TGA/DTA investigation have been examined in the temperature range of 30 °C–900 °C. The analysis was conducted with an increment of 10 °C per min in air atmosphere (Fig. 4). The TGA curve of MnO_2 displays three main weight losses in the temperature range of 30–129 °C, 130–534 °C, and 535–596 °C as shown in Fig. 4(a). The primary weight loss (0.38 mg) is associated with physically adsorbed water molecules, and the next (0.58 mg) corresponds with the phase change of MnO_2 to Mn_2O_3. Finally, the third phase of weight loss is associated with the phase change of Mn_2O_3 to Mn_3O_4. Hence, the analysis was started with 8 mg of MnO_2 and after exposed to 900 °C temperature, the remaining mass of MnO_2 was 6.85 mg with 14.38% weight loss. In the DTA analysis, the two endothermic and the exothermic peaks observed at 122 °C, 603 °C, and 807 °C indicates the elimination of physisorbed species, and the phase change from MnO_2 to Mn_2O_3 and Mn_3O_4, respectively. Similarly, The TGA curve of Cu doped MnO_2 exhibits three main weight losses in the temperature range of 30–315 °C, 316–534 °C, and 535–868 °C as shown in Fig. 4(b). The first weight loss (0.6 mg) ascribed to physisorbed species and the next (0.19 mg) is associated with the phase change of MnO_2 to Mn_2O_3. Finally, the third stage of weight loss (0.2 mg) is associated with the phase change of Mn_2O_3 to Mn_3O_4. Thus, the analysis was started with 8 mg of MnO_2 and after exposed to 900 °C temperature, the remaining mass of Cu doped MnO_2 was

7.01 mg with 12.34% weight loss. In the DTA analysis, the endothermic and the two exothermic peaks observed at 122 °C, 603 °C, and 807 °C indicates the elimination of physisorbed species, and the phase change from MnO_2 to Mn_2O_3 and Mn_3O_4, respectively. From the analysis Cu-doped MnO_2 nanoparticles showed good thermal stability with 12.34% weight loss.

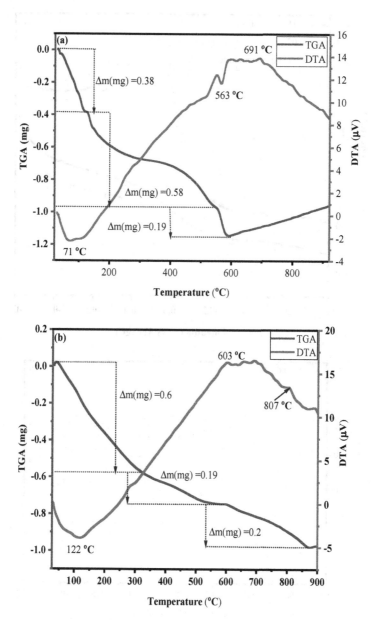

Fig. 4. TGA and DTA curve of (a) MnO_2 and (b) 0.1 M Cu doped α-MnO_2 nanoparticles.

3.4   Electrochemical Property Analysis

The ORR catalytic activity of the modified electrodes was investigated by CV in O_2 saturated in 0.1 M KOH aqueous solution at the scan rates of 50 mV s^{-1}, as shown in Fig. 5. The reduction peak was measured at -0.462V (vs. Ag/AgCl) for pure α-MnO$_2$.

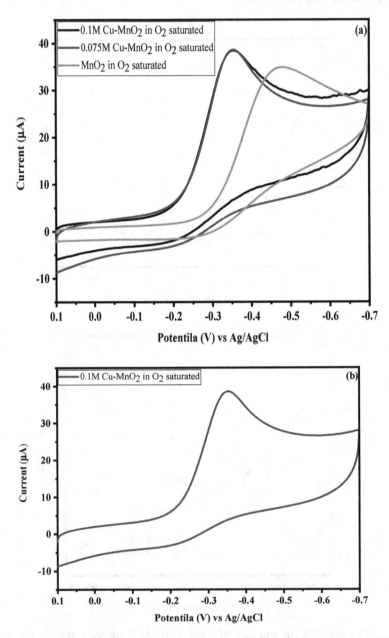

Fig. 5. CV curve of: (a) MnO$_2$ and Cu doped α-MnO$_2$ nanoparticles, (b) 0.1Cu doped MnO$_2$ of 20 cycles, at a scanning rate of 50 mVs^{-1}.

However, 0.075 and 0.1Cu doped MnO_2 showed enhanced reduction peak at -0.349 V (vs. Ag/AgCl) as shown in Fig. 5 (a). Hence, to determine the electrode stability of the Cu doped MnO_2 catalyst, a series of CV scans (of 20 cycles), at a scanning rate of $50 \, mVs^{-1}$, for 0.1Cu doped MnO_2 nanoparticles was taken out as displayed in Fig. 5 (b). The result reveals that the positions of reduction peak of electrode did not exhibit any notable variation with the increasing cycles, showing excellent electrode stability [24]. Overall, the CV analysis confirmed that Cu doped α-MnO_2 is a promising ORR oxygen electrocatalyst.

4   Conclusions

In this paper, the structural, thermal and, electrochemical characteristics of MnO_2 and Cu-doped MnO_2 nanoparticles with different Cu concentrations synthesized by co-prescription technique have been studied. The XRD patterns showed that Cu ions substituted Mn ions without altering the tetragonal structure up to 0.1 M Cu-doping. However, the Crystallite size increases from 4.1 nm to 5.3 nm with an increment of dopant concentration to 0.1 M. TGA/DTA analysis confirmed that Cu doped MnO_2 nanoparticles show an improved thermal property. The catalytic characteristics of MnO_2 and Cu doped MnO_2 nanoparticles as an effective electrocatalyst for ORR in alkaline media were studied via CV. The catalytic activity of as-prepared catalysts was exactly connected with its crystal structure. The results gained in this study show that, the Cu doped MnO_2 nanoparticles possess higher catalytic activity than MnO_2 for ORR. Additionally, the CV measurements confirm that the dual impact within Cu and Mn improves the performance by breaking of O-O bond in oxygen. Hence, the excellent electrochemical properties of Cu doped MnO_2 nanoparticles for ORR addresses it as a promising candidate in different oxygen electrocatalytic utilization such as fuel cells and MABs.

Acknowledgements. This work was supported by Bahir Dar University, Bahir Technology of Institute, Bahir Dar Energy Center.

Conflicts of Interest. There is no conflict of interest concerning this article.

References

1. Poonguzhali, R., Shanmugam, N., Gobi, R., et al.: Effect of thermal annealing on the structural, morphological and super capacitor behavior of MnO2 nanocrystals. Mater. Sci. Semicond. Process. **27**, 553–561 (2014). https://doi.org/10.1016/j.mssp.2014.07.044
2. Zhu, J., Baig, S.A., Sheng, T., et al.: Fe3O4 and MnO2 assembled on honeycomb briquette cinders (HBC) for arsenic removal from aqueous solutions. J. Hazard. Mater. **286**, 220–228 (2015). https://doi.org/10.1016/j.jhazmat.2015.01.004
3. Lim, Y.G., Kim, H.J., Park, K.: A novel method for synthesizing manganese dioxide nanoparticles using diethylenetriamine pentaacetic acid as a metal ion chelator. J. Ind. Eng. Chem. **93** (2021). https://doi.org/10.1016/j.jiec.2020.10.019

4. Worku, A.K., Ayele, D.W., Habtu, N.G.: Recent advances and future perspectives in engineering of bifunctional electrocatalysts for rechargeable zinc–air batteries. Mater. Today Adv. **9**, 100116 (2021). https://doi.org/10.1016/j.mtadv.2020.100116

5. Baral, A., Satish, L., Padhy, S.K., et al.: Structure and activity of lysozyme on binding to lithium-manganese oxide nanocomposites prepared from seabed nodule. J. Phys. Chem. Solids **151** (2021).https://doi.org/10.1016/j.jpcs.2020.109794

6. Jõgi, I., Levoll, E., Raud, J.: Plasma oxidation of NO in O2:N2 mixtures: the importance of back-reaction. Chem. Eng. J. **301**, 149–157 (2016). https://doi.org/10.1016/j.cej.2016.04.057

7. Zhang, Y., Yue, D., Fang, D., et al.: Enhanced darkening effect from the interaction of MnO2 and oxygen on the component evolution of amino-phenolic humic-like substances. Chemosphere **263** (2021). https://doi.org/10.1016/j.chemosphere.2020.127956

8. Asiri, S.M.M., Cevik, E., Sabit, H., Bozkurt, A.: Alginate-guided size and morphology-controlled synthesis of MnO2 nanoflakes. Soft. Mater. **18** (2020). https://doi.org/10.1080/1539445X.2019.1672192

9. Cruz-Díaz, M.R., Arauz-Torres, Y., Caballero, F., et al.: Recovery of MnO2 from a spent alkaline battery leach solution via ozone treatment. J. Power Sources **274** (2015). https://doi.org/10.1016/j.jpowsour.2014.10.121

10. Ge, X., Liu, J., Song, X., et al.: Hierarchical iron containing γ-MnO2 hollow microspheres: a facile one-step synthesis and effective removal of As(III) via oxidation and adsorption. Chem. Eng. J. **301**, pp. 139–148 (2016). https://doi.org/10.1016/j.cej.2016.05.005

11. Wang, J., Tao, H., Lu, T., Wu, Y.: Adsorption enhanced the oxidase-mimicking catalytic activity of octahedral-shape Mn3O4 nanoparticles as a novel colorimetric chemosensor for ultrasensitive and selective detection of arsenic. J. Colloid Interface Sci. **584**, 114–124 (2021). https://doi.org/10.1016/j.jcis.2020.09.107

12. Ning, P., Lin, X., Wang, X., Cao, H.: High-efficient extraction of vanadium and its application in the utilization of the chromium-bearing vanadium slag. Chem. Eng. J. **301**, 132–138 (2016). https://doi.org/10.1016/j.cej.2016.03.066

13. Zhou, S., Shang, H., Luo, J., et al.: Organoarsenic conversion to As(III) in subcritical hydrothermal reaction of livestock manure. J. Hazard. Mater. **402** (2021). https://doi.org/10.1016/j.jhazmat.2020.123571

14. Maity, J.P., Chen, C.Y., Bhattacharya, P., et al.: Advanced application of nano-technological and biological processes as well as mitigation options for arsenic removal. J. Hazard. Mater. **405** (2021). https://doi.org/10.1016/j.jhazmat.2020.123885

15. Worku, A.K., Ayele, D.W., Habtu, N.G., et al.: Enhancing oxygen reduction reaction activity of ε-MnO2 nanoparticles via iron doping. J. Phys. Chem. Solids **157**, 110207 (2021). https://doi.org/10.1016/j.jpcs.2021.110207

16. Worku, A.K., Ayele, D.W., Habtu, N.G., et al.: Recent progress in MnO2-based oxygen electrocatalysts for rechargeable zinc-air batteries. Mater. Today Sustain. 100072 (2021). https://doi.org/10.1016/j.mtsust.2021.100072

17. Wu, K., Liu, T., Xue, W., Wang, X.: Arsenic(III) oxidation/adsorption behaviors on a new bimetal adsorbent of Mn-oxide-doped Al oxide. Chem. Eng. J. **192**, 343–349 (2012). https://doi.org/10.1016/j.cej.2012.03.058

18. Ding, B., Zheng, P., Ma, P., Lin, J.: Manganese oxide nanomaterials: synthesis, properties, and theranostic applications. Adv. Mater. **32**, 1905823 (2020). https://doi.org/10.1002/adma.201905823

19. Sun, H., Xu, K., Huang, M., et al.: One-pot synthesis of ultrathin manganese dioxide nanosheets and their efficient oxidative degradation of Rhodamine B. Appl. Surf. Sci. **357**, 69–73 (2015). https://doi.org/10.1016/j.apsusc.2015.08.258

20. Feng, L., Xuan, Z., Zhao, H., et al.: MnO2 prepared by hydrothermal method and electrochemical performance as anode for lithium-ion battery. Nanoscale Res. Lett. **9**, 290 (2014). https://doi.org/10.1186/1556-276X-9-290

21. Soejima, T., Nishizawa, K., Isoda, R.: Monodisperse manganese oxide nanoparticles: synthesis, characterization, and chemical reactivity. J. Colloid Interface Sci. **510**, 272–279 (2018). https://doi.org/10.1016/j.jcis.2017.09.082

22. Qin, M., Zhao, H., Yang, W., et al.: A facile one-pot synthesis of three-dimensional microflower birnessite (δ-MnO2) and its efficient oxidative degradation of rhodamine B. RSC Adv. **6**, 23905–23912 (2016). https://doi.org/10.1039/C5RA24848E

23. Chen, Y., Tian, Y., Qiu, Y., et al.: Synthesis and superior cathode performance of sandwiched LiMn2O4@rGO nanocomposites for lithium-ion batteries. Mater. Today Adv. **1**, 100001 (2019). https://doi.org/10.1016/j.mtadv.2018.12.001

24. Zhang, X., Yu, P., Zhang, D., et al.: Room temperature synthesis of Mn3O4 nanoparticles: characterization, electrochemical properties and hydrothermal transformation to γ-MnO2 nanorods. Mater. Lett. **92**, 401–404 (2013). https://doi.org/10.1016/j.matlet.2012.11.022

Performance and Stability of Halide Perovskite Solar Cells in Bahir Dar Climatic Conditions

Getnet M. Meheretu[1,2,6,7(✉)], Getasew A. Wubetu[1], Bart Roose[6],
Amare Kassew[4], Hailu Shimels[5], Seifu A. Tilahun[3],
Elizabeth M. Tennyson[6], and Samuel D. Stranks[6,7]

[1] Energy Center, Bahir Dar Institute of Technology, Bahir Dar University,
Bahir Dar, Ethiopia
[2] Department of Physics, College of Science, Bahir Dar University,
Bahir Dar, Ethiopia
[3] Faculty of Civil and Water Resources Engineering, Bahir Dar Institute
of Technology, Bahir Dar University, Bahir Dar, Ethiopia
[4] Faculty of Electrical and Computer Engineering, Bahir Dar Institute
of Technology, Bahir Dar University, Bahir Dar, Ethiopia
[5] Faculty of Mechanical and Industrial Engineering, Bahir Dar Institute
of Technology, Bahir Dar University, Bahir Dar, Ethiopia
[6] Department of Physics, Cavendish Laboratory,
University of Cambridge, Cambridge, UK
[7] Department of Chemical Engineering and Biotechnology,
University of Cambridge, Cambridge, UK

Abstract. Perovskite solar cells are one of the most promising solar cell technologies, showing rapid development in power conversion efficiency (PCE). In this work, the performance and stability of triple-cation perovskite solar cells under continuous outdoor illumination in Bahir Dar climatic conditions and also the luminescence properties using steady-state photoluminescence (PL) spectroscopy has been studied. The work is conducted to study the electrical characterisation of the device under investigation in outdoor testing under ambient conditions to study the open-circuit voltage, short-circuit current density, fill factor, and efficiency of the device and obtained a PCE of above 16%, and a fill factor of above 60% with strong PL peak emission at 757 nm.

Keywords: Perovskite solar cells · Stability · Performance · Optoelectronic properties · Band gap tenability · PL spectroscopy

1 Introduction

Perovskite solar cells are one of the promising solar cells that attracted great attention for many researchers in the last few years. Recent studies show that single junction perovskite photovoltaic (PV) cells achieved power-conversion efficiency (PCE) of 25.5% and planar silicon/perovskite tandem cells achieved a PCE of 29% [1–4].

The performance and stability of the perovskite solar cells depend on the charge carrier recombination, band structure, compositional engineering, and external environmental exposures [5, 6]. The operation of a solar cell is governed by semiconductor

© ICST Institute for Computer Sciences, Social Informatics and Telecommunications Engineering 2022
Published by Springer Nature Switzerland AG 2022. All Rights Reserved
M. L. Berihun (Ed.): ICAST 2021, LNICST 412, pp. 554–564, 2022.
https://doi.org/10.1007/978-3-030-93712-6_37

physics; under illumination electrons and holes are generated and subsequently extracted and transported through the external circuit. The band gap ultimately governs the achievable PCE through the Shockley-Queisser (SQ) limit [1, 5]. The main electrical parameters that are used to characterise the performance of perovskite solar cells are: the power-conversion efficiency (PCE), short-circuit current density (J_{sc}), fill factor (FF), and open-circuit voltage (V_{oc}) [5]. The current density when there is no bias voltage is referred to as the short-circuit current density, while the voltage for which no current is extracted is termed as the open circuit voltage, i.e. J $(V = 0) = J_{sc}$, V $(J = 0) = V_{oc}$. The PCE of a solar cell can be expressed as [7]

$$P_{CE} = \frac{I_{out}}{I_{in}} = \frac{V_m J_m}{I_{in}} \tag{1}$$

where V_m and J_m are the voltage and current density respectively at the maximum power point density, I_{in} the power in the incident light and I_{out} the generated electrical power.

The FF of a solar cell describes the squareness of the J-V curve, which is determined by series and shunting resistance and is expressed as [8]

$$FF = \frac{V_m J_m}{V_{oc} J_{sc}} \tag{2}$$

Therefore, the PCE is can be expressed in the form [9]:

$$P_{CE} = \frac{V_m J_m}{I_{in}} = \frac{FF \times V_{oc} \times J_{sc}}{I_{in}} \tag{3}$$

Perovskite solar cells use hybrid organic-inorganic lead (Pb) halide perovskite as the light absorbing material. Perovskites have an ABX_3 crystal structure (Fig. 1), where A is a large cation (typically methylammonium (CH_3NH_3), formamidinium (CH $(NH_2)_2$) or cesium), B a divalent metal cation (Pb) and X is a halide anion (usually I or Br). The crystal structure and stability of perovskites can be determined by the Goldschmidt tolerance factor (t) and expressed as [10–14].

$$t = \frac{1}{\sqrt{2}} \frac{(R_A + R_X)}{(R_B + R_X)} \tag{4}$$

where R_A, R_B, R_X are radii of the ions A, B, and X respectively.

The most reproducible and highest performing cells employ mixed cation, mixed anion configurations which use a mixture of formamidinium and methylammonium as the monovalent cations as well as inorganic cesium. The triple cation perovskite configuration resulting from this composition posseses high thermal stability, contain less phase impurities and are less sensitive to processing conditions.

Halide perovskites have excellent optoelectronic properties, which makes them ideal for solar cell applications. The weak exciton binding energy and a high dielectric constant enable the dissociation of excitons to free electrons and holes. Furthermore,

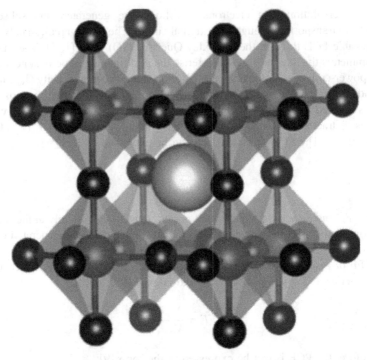

Cation Metal Halide

Fig. 1. Crystal structure of perovskites [adapted from reference [15, 16].

halide perovskites possess a tuneable direct bandgap, have a large absorption coefficient, low defect density, small Urbach energy, and long diffusion length [17–19].

Perovskites have excellent optoelectronic properties; however, it has intrinsic chemical instability of the absorber layer leading to degradation of the electronic properties [20]. There are also extrinsic instabilities that are usually caused by ions migration, exposure to visible and UV light, heat [21, 22], humidity and oxygen. Studies show that compositional engineering of the aforementioned mixed cation, mixed anion configurations perovskite can drastically increase stability. In addition, the electron transport layer (ETL), and hole transport layer (HTL) can promote instabilities stabilities as well [23, 24]. The stability of the perovskite solar cell can be improved using hybrid organic-inorganic cations of mixed halide with appropriate encapsulation. Passivation treatment with organic materials can reduce the defects in the perovskite surface and inhibits moisture entry into the device that can enable the device to better withstand degradation [15, 25–30].

Cesium based triple cations have high PCE and higher bandwidth than their corresponding non-cesium containing perovskites, and have attracted great attention for perovskite-based tandem cells for strong absorption of light in the whole solar spectrum. These cations essentially contains (CH_3NH_3), $(CH(NH_2)_2$ as monovalent organic cations, and cesium as inorganic cation to form triple cation [31, 32].

Since its emergence, perovskite solar cells show a rapid development that can surpass the solar technology performance within ten years and has achieved a PCE of 25.2%. In addition to its rapid enhancement in performance, its intrinsic optoelectronic properties, low-cost and ease of production have attracted great attention [33, 34]. Nevertheless stability is still the main challenge that hinders the commercialization of perovskite solar cell technology.

There is a possibility to improve the performance by changing the composition, and the device architecture [10, 12, 34, 35]. Researchers conducted on the degradation of PSCs shows that cells stored in the dark exhibited optimum stability, while cells stored in outdoor conditions degrades faster, and encapsulated solar cells stored outdoor condition could be completely dead within a month due to external environmental effects light sunlight exposure. Besides, some electrodes like silver undergo accelerated decomposition reactions in the outdoor conditions [6]. Different researches have been conducted using different metal oxide transport layers to promote the performance and stability of perovskite solar cells by changing the thickness of the absorber layer [33–35]. Many researchers used different mechanisms to increase the stability PSCs, and achieved some promising results [35, 36]. However, some of the researches are carried out under indoor controlled conditions, which cannot be viable for commercial applications; the performance, and stability achieved in outdoor conditions can still be improved by changing the device architecture, and passivation defects.

In this work, outdoor performance and stability of cesium containing triple-cation perovskite solar cells in Bahir Dar climatic conditions have been studied. The work encompasses the J-V sweep of the device under dark conditions, forward scan, reverse scan, and cyclic scan under outdoor solar radiation illumination of encapsulated devices and steady-state PL measurements. As an extension, the proposed and ongoing work aims to improve the performance and stability of perovskite solar cells by changing the device architecture.

2 Materials and Methods

2.1 Device Preparation

All chemicals were purchased from Sigma-Aldrich, unless stated otherwise. Fluorine doped tin oxide coated glass slides were cleaned by sonication in 2% Hellmanex solution for 15 min. The substrate was cleaned with deionized water and ethanol followed by sonication with acetone and isopropanol for 15 min each. It was then further treated with UV ozone for 15 min directly before compact layer deposition.

TiO_2 compact layer was deposited by spray pyrolysis from a precursor solution consisting of 0.4 ml acetylacetonate, 0.6 ml titanium diisopropoxide bis (acetylacetonate) and 9ml ethanol at 450 °C. After cooling down to room temperature, mesoporous TiO_2 was deposited by spincoating TiO_2 paste (150 mg/ml in ethanol, Greatcell Solar) at 4000 rpm for 20 s, followed by annealing at 450 °C for 30 min. Substrates were cooled down to 150 °C and immediately transferred to a nitrogen filled glovebox for perovskite deposition. Mixed halide cation perovskite films were deposited from a precursor solution containing FAI (1 M, Greatcell Solar), PbI_2 (1.1 M, TCI), MABr (0.2 M, Greatcell

Solar), $PbBr_2$ (0.2 M, TCI) and CsI (0.075 M) in anhydrous DMF:DMSO 4:1 (v:v). The perovskite solution was spin-coated using a two-step program, 1000 and 6000 rpm for 10 and 20 s respectively. While carrying out the second spin coating step 200 µl of chlorobenzene was dripped on the spinning substrate 5 s before the end of the program. The substrates were then treated with heat by annealing at 100 °C for 1 h in a nitrogen glove box. Subsequently, the substrates were cooled down for a few minutes and a Spiro-OMeTAD (Merck) solution (70 mM in chlorobenzene) doped with bis (trifluoromethylsulfonyl)imide lithium salt (Li-TFSI), tris(2-(1H-pyrazol-1-yl)-4-tert-butylpyridine)-cobalt(III)tris(bis(trifluoromethylsulfonyl)imide) (FK209, Dyenamo) and 4-tert-butylpyridine (TBP) was spincoated at 4000 rpm for 20 s. The compositional molar ratio of additives to spiro-OMeTAD were: 0.5, 0.03 and 3.3 for Li-TFSI, FK209 and TBP, respectively. Finally, 70 nm of gold was thermally evaporated under high vacuum on top of the HTM [11, 12, 15, 27, 29, 37]. Ten identical encapsulated devices/samples were prepared from the same composition. The basis for selecting these compositions is to promote stability without significantly affecting the performance. If the concentration of inorganic components high, it will significantly affect the performance.

2.2   Device Characterisation

The J-V characteristics of the devices were performed using Keithley 2400 source meter with I-V tracer software under dark conditions, and the outdoor environment under ambient Bahir Dar climatic conditions. The samples were nominally identical replicates labeled as 1 to 7. The devices numbers 1, 2 & 4 are not included in the illumination result. The first sample was used for dark current measurement and familiarisations for indoor measurements using mercury lamps; the second sample was damaged during the measurement, fourth sample electrode was difficult to locate its detection because of its encapsulation.

The incident power illuminated on the device is regularly measured with a lux meter which detects light in the visible spectral range. Its measurements are converted into mW/cm^2 using the 1-sun (100 mW/cm^2) radiation as a standard factor to include the UV-spectrum of the solar radiation. There is no readily available standard conversion between solar irradiance and Lux. In this report, solar Irradiance of 1 Sun (1,000 W/m^2) equals approximately 120,000 lx which was developed based on measurement uncertainties, equipment calibration accuracy, and standards' data conversion factor has been used [38]. Moreover, it was difficult to know when the AM 1.5 equivalent is shining on the solar cell as the measurements in outdoor conditions. This causes some errors on the reported input power radiation and then on the efficiency. The J-V scanning was carried out in the forward scan (from V_{sc} to V_{oc}) and backward scan (from V_{oc} to V_{sc} is) directions as well as single cycle scan (from V_{sc} to V_{oc} and then back to V_{sc}) patterns for the first seven devices. The remaining three Devices were reserved for spectroscopy measurements. Figure 2 depicts the schematic diagram of the J-V characterization of the setup.

Steady-state photoluminescence (PL) spectroscopy emission measurements were performed with an excitation wavelength of 500 nm at a scan rate of 600 nm/min. The peak obtained gives information about the charge carrier recombination rates. Based on

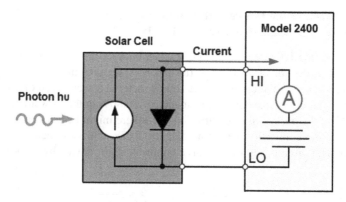

Fig. 2. Schematic diagram of the J-V measurement using Keithely 2400.

the measured values of PL, the performance and stability tests of the encapsulated devices, the following results are obtained.

3 Results and Discussions

3.1 J-V Characteristics of the Device Under Dark Current Measurement

Figure 3 illustrates a representative current-voltage characteristic of the perovskite solar cells. The curve shows that series resistance is low and shunting resistance high, as required for efficient solar cells.

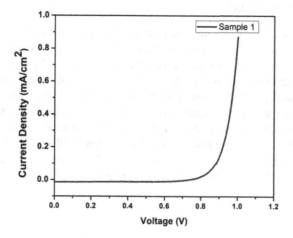

Fig. 3. I-V curve of perovskite device in the dark.

3.2   J-V Sweep of the Device with Outdoor Illuminations, Forward and Reverse Scans (from 12 PM–1 PM)

Figure 4 shows the J-V sweep of Sample 7 under outdoor illumination. The sweep scan is performed in the forward direction (a) and reverses direction (b) by scanning the voltage and measuring the current of the source meter at a scan speed of 40 mV/s. The results show that the device has a performance of 16.80% in the forward scan direction and 14.32% in the backward scan direction. Still there might be errors arising from the estimation of the conversion between solar irradiance and Lux meter as well as the active area. The discrepancy of the curve confirms slight device hysteresis.

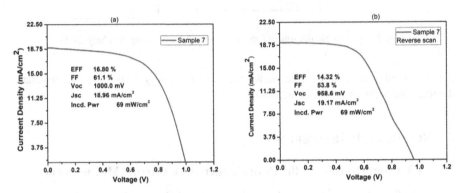

Fig. 4. (a) Forward and (b) reverse J-V scans under outdoor illumination

3.3   J-V Sweep of the Device with Outdoor Illuminations, Cycle Scan (from 12 PM–1 PM)

The curves in Fig. 5 show the one-cycle scan of Sample 3 (a) and 7 (b) under outdoor testing conditions. It was observed that after a careful scan, the source meter is in the off state with output in an open circuit scheme measurements. The performance of the J-V sweep of the device shows that the device demonstrates hysteresis manifested by lack of curve overlap and variation of solar cell parameters. The differences observed in the two curves are due to the presence of mobile ions and trap states. Mobile ions can cause change in the crystal structure and hence the difference of the observation of defects tolerance of the halide perovskites. The trap states affect the diffusion of charge carriers by restricting the mobility of these carriers. The effect and categorisation of the devices were based on the measured values performed repeatedly in the indoor controlled environment.

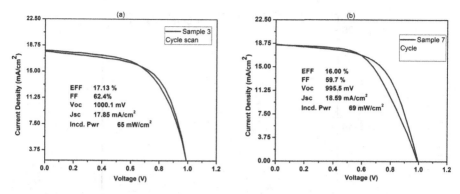

Fig. 5. Cyclic scan (a) sample-3 and (b) sample-7 of the same devices under outdoor illumination.

3.4   Device Performance and Stability Test Summary

Table 1 shows the performance and reproducibility test of 4 identical devices. The measurements were conducted from 28th January to 2nd February 2021 from 11 AM-3 PM. The results obtained a large variability in solar cell parameters, except for V_{oc}. The variability in J_{sc} may be explained by varying climatic conditions and slight variations in the active area size.

Table 1. Performance and reproducibility test (averages)

Sample	Scan Direction	Eff. (%)	FF (%)	Voc (V)	Jsc (mA/cm²)	I_{in} (mW/cm²)
Sample 3	Forward	16.3	61.3	1.00	17.3	65
Sample 3	Backward	15.1	55.4	0.98	18.0	65
Sample 5	Forward	13.4	47.1	0.97	19.1	65.14
Sample 5	Backward	10.5	56.4	1.00	18.6	100
Sample 6	Forward	17.2	61.9	1.00	17.0	100
Sample 6	Backward	13.7	57.2	0.97	17.1	100
Sample 7	Forward	14.2	52.7	1.00	16.7	62
Sample 7	Backward	13.6	51.8	0.99	16.5	62

3.5   Steady State Photoluminescence Spectroscopy

Figure 6 displays the steady-state PL emission spectra of the perovskite device as a function of wavelength using a deuterium lamp at an excitation wavelength of 500 nm. The result indicates the existence of strong emission at 757 nm (1.64eV). The emissions peak has been a Gaussian line shape with full width at half maximum (FWHM) of 45 nm resolution.

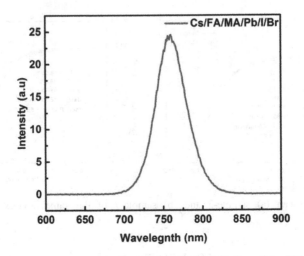

Fig. 6. Steady state PL measurement of encapsulated devices using deuterium lamp.

4   Conclusions and Future Work

In this study, a PCE of more than 16% is obtained, while researches used a baseline PCE of less than 17% with similar composition, but different concentration under indoor illumination [27]. It has been observed that the photovoltaic important solar cell parameters change with aging time. The PCE of the device under investigation changes under continuous illumination of the solar radiation. Sudden changes of the incident solar radiation due to cloud become a bottleneck to clearly articulate the degree of stability. While changing the scan directions, during the J–V measurements, the solar cell parameters changes, and the sweep shows a discrepancy between the forward and reverse scans, and hysteresis is observed in the cyclic scan which indicates that trap states and mobile ions are present in the device. The emission peak of the device has been studied using steady-state PL measurements and observed at that 758 nm. The results of our study are in agreement with other works performed [15, 29]. The triple cation concentration used in the preparation of the device, and its J–V characterization in the uncontrolled real outdoor environment in Bahir Dar climatic condition has not been done so far is the novelty of the work. Our future work will be monitoring the light intensity by continuously measuring the incident radiations using a lux meter/pyranometer to address variable outdoor conditions. By measuring operation continuously including in cloud events, working on extracting important information about how the cells respond **to shading** and then bounce back again will be the tasks to be carried out. Ideally, the device shall be left running for periods of weeks and track data the whole time to study the interrelationship between temperature and band-gap energies on the outdoor performance of device.

Testing the performance using a solar simulator to see its reproducibility with the outdoor measurements will be part of the work included in the package. The work will include treatments with additives to see their impact on the devices hysteresis and longer-term stability and explain the materials change after the operation. The work will be extended to synthesis/fabrication of the devices using optimum characterisation conditions and appropriate additives as well as assessing the potential of the techno-economic analysis of manufacturing the device locally.

Acknowledgements. The work is supported by **Engineering and Physical Sciences Research Council for (EPSRC), UK for Affordable Perovskite Solar Irrigation Systems for Small-holder Farmers in Ethiopia (APSISSFE), EPSRC Reference no EP/T02030X/1. Thus, the authors are** grateful the EPSRC for their financial support.

References

1. Yurui, M.Z., Ke, X., Lin, R., Luo, X., Han, Q., Tan, H.: Recent progress in the developing efficient monolithic all-perovskite tandem solar cells. J. Semicod. **41** 051201 (2020)
2. Zhao, Y., Ma, F., Gao, F., Yin, Z., Zhang, X., You, J.: Research progress in large-area Perovskite solar cells. Photonics Res. **8**, A1–A15 (2020)
3. Park, N.-G., Zhu, K.: Scalable fabrication and coating methods for perovskite solar cells and solar modules. Nat. Mate. **5**, 333–350 (2020)
4. Zhao, B.: Efficient light-emitting diodes from mixed-dimensional perovskites on a fluoride interface. Nat. Electron. **3**, 704–710 (2020)
5. Chen, J., Park, N.-G.: Causes and solutions of recombination in perovskite solar cells (2018)
6. Chauhan, A.K., Kumar, P.: Degradation in perovskite solar cells stored under different environmental conditions. Phys. D Appl. Phys. **50** 325105 (2017)
7. Idoko, L., Anaya-Lara, O., McDonald, A.: Enhancing PV modules efficiency and power output using multi-concept cooling technique. Energy Rep. **4**, 357–369 (2018)
8. Qiab, B., Wang, J.: Fill factor in organic solar cells. Phys. Chem. Chem. Phys. **15**, 8972 (2013)
9. Hossain, M.I., Qarony, W., Ma, S., Zeng, L.: Perovskite/Silicon tandem solar cells: from detailed balance limit calculations to photon management. Nano-Micro Lett. **11**, 58 (2019)
10. Green, M.A., Ho-Baillie, A., Snaith, H.J.: The emergence of perovskite solar cells. Nat. Phtonics **8**, 506–514 (2014)
11. Stranks, S.D., Snaith, H.J.: Perovskite Solar Cells (2016)
12. Olaleru, S.A., Kirui, J.K., Wamwangi, D., Roro, K.T., Mwakikunga, B.: Perovskite solar cells: the new epoch in photovoltaics. Solar Energy **196**, 295–309 (2020)
13. Ahmed, M.I., Habib, A., Javaid, S.S.: Perovskite solar cells: potentials, challenges, and opportunities (2015)
14. Chen, Y., Zhang, L., Zhang, Y., Gaoa, H., Yan, H.: Large-area perovskite solar cells – a review of recent progress and issues. Royal Soc. Chem. **8**, 10489–10508 (2018)
15. Tang, H., He, S., Peng, C.: A short progress report on high-efficiency perovskite solar cells. Nanoscale Res. Lett. **12**, 410 (2017)
16. Tennyson, E.M., Doherty, T.A..S., Stranks, S.D.: Heterogeneity at multiple length scales in halide perovskite semiconductors. Nat. Revi. Mater. **4**, 573–587(2019)
17. De Wolf, S., et al.: Organometallic halide perovskites: sharp optical absorption edge and its relation to photovoltaic performance. J. Phys. Chem. Lett. **5**(6), 1035–1039 (2014)

18. Lozano, G.: The role of metal halide perovskites in next-generation lighting devices. J. Phys. Chem. Lett. **2014**8(9), 3987–3997 (2014)
19. Stranks, S.D.: Electron-hole diffusion lengths exceeding 1 Micrometer in an Organometal Trihalide Perovskite Absorber. Science **342**(6156), 341–344 (2013)
20. Sivula, K.: Are organic semiconductors viable for robust, high-efficiency artificial photosynthesis? ACS Energy Lett. **5**(6), 1970–1973 (2020)
21. Juarez-Perez, E.J., Ono, L.K., Maeda, M., Jiang, Y., Hawash, Z., Yabing, Q.: Photode-composition and thermal decomposition in methylammonium halide lead perovskites and inferred design principles to increase photovoltaic device stability, J. Mater. Chem. A **6**, 9604 (2018)
22. Barker, F.A.J., et al.: Defect-assisted photoinduced halide segregation in mixed-halide perovskite thin. ACS Energy Lett. **2**(6), 1416–1424 (2017)
23. Stranks, S.D., Nayak, P.K., Zhang, W., Stergiopoulos, T., Snaith, H.J.: Formation of thin films of organic-inorganic perovskites for high-efficiency solar cells. Angew. Chem. Int. Ed. **54**(11), 3240–3248 (2015)
24. Howard, J.M., Tennyson, E.M. Neves, B.R.A., Leite, M.S.: Machine learning for perovskites' reap-rest-recovery cycle. Joule **3**, 325–337 (2019)
25. Chen, B., Rudd, P.N., Yang, S., Yuan, Y., Huang, J.: Imperfections and their passivation in halide perovskite solar cells. Chem. Soc. Rev. **48**, 3842 (2019)
26. Mahapatra, A., Parikh, N., Kumar, P., Kuma, M.: Changes in the electrical characteristics of perovskite solar cells with aging time. Molecules **25**, 2299 (2020)
27. Saliba, M.: Cesium-containing triple cation perovskite solar cells: improved stability, reproducibility and high efficiency (2016)
28. Abdi-Jalebi1, M., et al.: Charge extraction via graded doping of hole transport layers gives highly luminescent and stable metal halide perovskite devices. Friend Sci. Adv. **5**, eaav2012 (2019)
29. Jain, S.M., et al.: Vapor phase conversion of PbI2 to CH3NH3PbI3: spectroscopic evidence for formation of an intermediate phase. J. Mater. Chem. A **4**, 2630–2642 (2013)
30. Liu, Z., et al.: A holistic approach to interface stabilization for efficient perovskite solar modules with over 2,000-hour operational stability, Nat. Energy **5**, 596–604 (2020)
31. Mica, N.A.: Triple-cation perovskite solar cells for visible light communications. Photonics Res. **8**, A16–A24 (2020)
32. Ašmontas, S., et al.: Cesium-containing triple cation perovskite solar cells, coatings (2021)
33. Ghosh, A., Dipta, S.S., Shafaat Saud Nikor, S.K., Saqib, N., Saha, A.: Performance analysis of an efficient and stable perovskite solar cell and a comparative study of incorporating metal oxide transport layers. J. Opt. Soc. Am. B 37, 1966–1973 (2020)
34. PriyankaRoy, A.: Analysis of an efficient and eco-friendly CsGeSnI3 based perovskite solar cell: a theoretical study. Materials Today **44**, 2997–3000 (2021)
35. Kheralla, A., Chetty, N.: A review of experimental and computational attempts to remedy stability issues of perovskite solar cells. Heliyon **7**, e06211 (2021)
36. Aydin, E., et al.: Interplay between temperature and bandgapenergies on the outdoor performance of perovskite/silicon tandem solar cells. Nat. Energy **5**, 851–859 (2020)
37. Baena, J.P.C., et al.: Highly efficient planar perovskite solar cells through band alignment engineering. Energy Environ. Sci. **8**, 2928–2934 (2015)
38. Micheal, P.: A conversion guide: solar irradiance and lux illuminance (2020)

Numerical Investigations of Variable Pitch Straight-Bladed H-Darrieus VAWT

Temesgen Abriham Miliket[1]([✉]), Mesfin Belayneh Ageze[2],
and Muluken Temesgen Tigabu[1]

[1] Faculty of Mechanical and Industrial Engineering, Bahir Dar Energy Centre,
Bahir Dar Institute of Technology, Bahir Dar University, Bahir Dar, Ethiopia
[2] Addis Ababa Energy Center, Addis Ababa University, Addis Ababa, Ethiopia

Abstract. In this paper, we aim to develop low cost effective model for evaluating the aerodynamic design and performance of small scale straight blade H-Darrieus vertical axis wind turbine (VAWT). To optimize the rotor design the blades are modeled with variable pitch angle (β) configurations. To this end, DMST model was used to determine optimum pitch configuration at the minimum possible tip speed ratio (λ). Once the optimal design point was obtained, 2D unsteady computational fluid dynamics (CFD) simulation was carried out in order to describe the flow physics of the rotor. The power coefficient (Cp) obtained in DMST model was 0.464 which is in agreement with the present CFD simulation result computed by SST k-ω model (i.e. Cp = 0.4537) and wind tunnel experimental findings from literatures. This implies the performance of straight blade H-Darrieus VAWT with VP design is 37.2% better than one with the fixed pitch ($\beta = 0°$) blades. Hence, the present study delineates the performance of H-Darrieus wind turbine is dependent upon the turbine parameters, airfoil profile and desired blade pitch angle for sustainable power generation.

Keywords: Vertical axis wind turbine · Variable pitch blade · Double-multiple stream tube model · Computational fluid dynamics · Self starting · Power coefficient

1 Introduction

The wind is one of the most potential renewable energy resources in the world which utilizes wind turbines as a conversion machine. Among the types of wind turbines, H-Darrieus VAWT is the most popular one which yields higher power output at high wind speed. Despite this, the performance of the H-Darrieus wind turbine is relatively very low at low wind speed [1, 2]. Hence, attempts are devoted to exploring to enhance the aerodynamic performance of the rotor [3]. Associated with the rotor blade design, airfoil selection is the primary considerations. Symmetrical NACA-series are frequently used

© ICST Institute for Computer Sciences, Social Informatics and Telecommunications Engineering 2022
Published by Springer Nature Switzerland AG 2022. All Rights Reserved
M. L. Berihun (Ed.): ICAST 2021, LNICST 412, pp. 565–583, 2022.
https://doi.org/10.1007/978-3-030-93712-6_38

for straight blade H-Darrieus VAWT design [3]. However, these airfoil blades generate negative Cp at a low Reynolds number [4]. Contrarily, the power production of high solidity turbines became independent at high arbitrary Reynolds numbers [5]. To improve VAWT performance-enhanced shape airfoils such as S1046 airfoil become more effective for blade designs [6]. Hence, to afford enhanced wind turbine at low Reynolds number, blades to arm configuration also a crucial consideration. Based on the movement of the blade concerning the supporting strut, the blade of a wind turbine can be classified as either fixed or variable pitch. In a fixed pitch (FP) H-Darrieus wind turbine; airfoil blades, supporting struts, and tower are the main components [7]. The system doesn't need any blade pitch control mechanism rather it helps to minimize investment costs. However, it experienced much stalled time at a low tip speed ratio (TSR) [8], which may lead to catastrophic failure. Hence, researchers are coming with a variable pitch (VP) blade design that maintains the blade's angle of attacks (AoA) at required positions and reducing stalls. These designs are superior to overcome the self-starting problems and provide higher torque coefficients by allowing the blades to pitch cyclically [9, 10]. To allow the blade at optimum AoA through the rotor azimuth angle, the system can be managed by using either passive or active control systems [11, 12]. However small-scale VAWT are more fundamental with active pitch controls.

A wide range of analytical and computational studies has been carried out about the performance predictions of VAWT. However, due to the aerodynamic complexity of the H-Darrieus rotor research efforts are perusing enhanced modeling methods up-to-date. To acquire such analysis superimposing various model become a typical choice for robust performance investigations. DMST model developed by I.Paraschivoiu [13], is the combination of multiple stream tube (MST) model and double actuator disk (AD) theory [14, 15]. These models divide the rotor into upwind and downwind halves and account for any induction factor when VAWT is subjected to aerodynamic loadings [14]. DMST model used in [16], VP-VAWT with smaller AoA widen the rotor performance azimuth zone. DMST model and Prandtl's mathematics were used to evaluate the blade tip loss of FP and VP VAWT at rated TSR [17]. The result shows VP-approach achieves 18.9% performance growth. Also, detailed understandings of CFD helps to predict an accurate flow physics of VAWT. However, the selection of the physical model and turbulence affect the accuracy of the results [18]. Except for eddy simulations, all turbulence models in CFD have similar transport equations for turbulent kinetic energy (k) and turbulent dissipation rate(ε) [19]. But in the eddy simulation, the Prandtl numbers govern the turbulent diffusion and dispassion rate. The k-ε turbulence model is the most common turbulence model used in industrial applications. The main problems observed in k-ε turbulence models are not efficient to compute near-wall boundary flow with adverse pressure gradients [18]. However, the k-ω model has a low computational cost and better computational accuracy than the k-ε model. Besides that, the main drawback of the k-ω turbulence model is hard to converge and sensitive to initial conditions.

Hence, a robust turbulence model is required to capture near-wall and far-wall flow conditions for the accurate performance predictions of the turbine. The freestream inflow which is far away from the wall boundary is used the formulated SST k-ω turbulence model which can accurately be calculated for the separation [20]. Hence, SST k-ω turbulence model can achieve good results because of its capability of capturing proper behaviour in the near-wall layers or shear stress transports of the fluid and separated flow regions [21]. In the present study, the performances enhancement of straight-bladed H-Darrieus VAWT is carried out through DMST and CFD models.

2 Aerodynamic Analysis of H-Darrieus Rotor

The wind velocity at the rotor plane of each tandem disk can be defined by the induction factor [22, 23]. And also the wake velocity of upwind, equilibrium, and downwind half of the rotor can be determined reduced by induction factors [24, 25]. Hence the axial velocity through the upwind and downwind sides of the disks can be written as $V_e < V_i < V_\infty$ and $V_w < V_i' < V_e$ respectively. The main mathematical models which need for the DMST analysis are presented in this section, the details are available in [26] (Fig. 1).

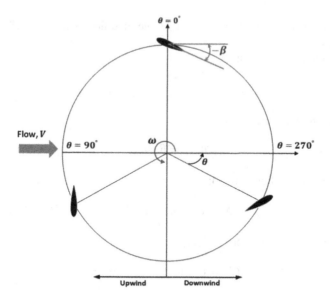

Fig. 1. Schematic of variable pitch VAWT [27].

Upwind induced velocity:

$$V = aV_\infty \tag{1}$$

Equilibrium induced velocity;

$$V_e = (2a - 1)V_\infty \tag{2}$$

Downwind induced velocity;

$$W_w = a'(2a - 1)V_\infty \tag{3}$$

Tip Speed Ratio (λ);

$$\lambda = \frac{\omega_r R}{V_\infty} \tag{4}$$

The angle of attack (α);

$$\alpha = \tan^{-1}\left(\frac{(1-a)\sin(\theta)}{\lambda + (1-a)\cos(\theta)}\right) \tag{6}$$

When we consider the blade pitch angle, the modified angle of attack [16, 17] can be written as:
The modified angle of attack (α_{mdf});

$$\alpha_{mdf} = \alpha - \beta(\theta) \tag{7}$$

Blade pitch angle (β);

$$\beta(\theta) = \beta_o \sin(\theta) \tag{8}$$

Normal force coefficient (CN);

$$CN = CL\cos(\alpha) + CD\sin(\alpha) \tag{9}$$

Tangential force coefficient (CT);

$$CT = CL\sin(\alpha) - CD\cos(\alpha) \tag{10}$$

Average thrust coefficient (C_T);

$$C_T = \left(\frac{Nc}{R}\right)\left(\frac{1}{2\pi}\right)\left(\frac{W}{V_\infty}\right)^2\left[CN - CT\left(\frac{\cos(\theta)}{\sin(\theta)}\right)\right] \tag{11}$$

Interference factor (f);

$$f = \frac{Nc}{8\pi R} \int\limits_{-\pi/2}^{\pi/2} \left(\frac{W}{V_\infty}\right)^2 (CN\sin(\theta) - CT\cos(\theta))d\theta \qquad (12)$$

Axial induction factor (a);

$$a = \frac{\pi}{\pi + f} \qquad (13)$$

Instantaneous torque (Qinst);

$$Q_{inst} = \frac{1}{2} C_T \rho c R W^2 h \qquad (14)$$

Average instantaneous torque (Qavg);

$$Q_{avg} = \frac{N}{2\pi} \int\limits_{-\pi/2}^{\pi/2} Q_{inst}d\theta \qquad (15)$$

Power coefficient (CP);

$$C_P = \lambda C_m \qquad (16)$$

Where Cm is the turbine moment coefficients (Fig. 2).

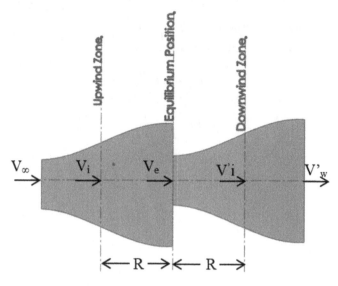

Fig. 2. Illustration of DMST model.

2.1   Double Multiple Stream Tube (DMST) Analysis

2.2   Computational Analysis

Governing Equations. A 2D pressure-based U-RANS formulation is used for numerical simulation and is a suitable solver for time-dependent analysis [28]. Semi-Implicit Method for Pressure Linked Equations (SIMPLE) algorithms with Second-order upwind scheme is selected for the spatial discretization method using finite volume analysis [29], for momentum, energy, and turbulence, as well as the bounded second-order implicit, are executed for the transient formulation [30]. Assuming the flow in the wind turbine is incompressible, continuity and momentum equation [31, 32] of unsteady flow can be written in the formula as in equations (16) and (17):

$$\nabla \cdot \left(\rho \vec{V} \right) = 0 \tag{17}$$

$$\frac{\partial (\rho u)}{\partial t} + \nabla \cdot \left(\rho u \vec{V} \right) = \frac{\partial p}{\partial x} + \frac{\partial \tau_{xx}}{\partial x} + \frac{\partial \tau_{yx}}{\partial y} \tag{18}$$

$$\frac{\partial (\rho v)}{\partial t} + \nabla \cdot \left(\rho v \vec{V} \right) = -\frac{\partial p}{\partial y} + \frac{\partial \tau_{yy}}{\partial y} + \frac{\partial \tau_{xy}}{\partial x} \tag{19}$$

Turbulence Modeling. In the present work SST-kω model introduced by [33] was used due to its better accuracy [34]. The general mathematical formulations of the SST-kω model [31], can be written as Eq. (20)

$$\frac{\partial (\rho k)}{\partial t} + \frac{\partial (\rho k u_i)}{\partial x_i} = \frac{\partial}{\partial x_j} \left(\Gamma_k \frac{\partial k}{\partial x_j} \right) + G_k - Y_k + S_K \tag{20}$$

$$\frac{\partial (\rho \omega)}{\partial t} + \frac{\partial (\rho \omega u_j)}{\partial x_i} = \frac{\partial}{\partial x_j} \left(\Gamma_\omega \frac{\partial \omega}{\partial x_j} \right) + G_\omega - Y_\omega + S_\omega \tag{21}$$

$$\Gamma_\omega = \mu + \frac{\mu_t}{\sigma_\omega} \tag{22}$$

$$\Gamma_k = \mu + \frac{\mu_t}{\sigma_k} \tag{23}$$

Where μ_t is the turbulent viscosity, σ_k and σ_ω are the turbulent Prandtl numbers for k and ω respectively.

$$\mu_t = \frac{\rho k}{\omega} \frac{1}{\max\left[\frac{1}{a^*}, \frac{SF_2}{a_1\omega}\right]} \qquad (24)$$

Where S (k,ω) is the strain rate magnitudes.

3 Methodology

3.1 DMST Model Solver Procedure

To calculate various parameters of the turbine the above simplified referred Eqs. (1) up to (16) are formulated with computer code developed in MATLAB R2019a software. Figure 3 illustrates the working loops of DMST algorisms; each half of the stream tube which classify into three main consecutive parameters i.e. impute parameters, calculated parameters, and output parameters. To begin the calculation process, first importing S1046 airfoil coordinate taken from University of Illinois at Urbana-champaign (UIUC) airfoil database to the foil tool and then the airfoils are imported to Q-blade to export the lifts (CL) and drag (CD) coefficients at different local Reynolds number with a corresponding angle of attack. To find intermediate working values, a linear interpolation method was used [35]. Following the input parameters, the calculations are initialized and an iterative process was used in the range $-\frac{\pi}{2} \le \theta_{up} \le \frac{\pi}{2}$ the upstream and downstream $\frac{\pi}{2} \le \theta_{dw} \le \frac{3\pi}{2}$ half interference factors of the turbine are computed until convergence is reached. Finally, optimum turbine performances are obtained based on the output parameters followed by the whole process.

3.2 Computational Fluid Dynamics (CFD) Method

ANSYS 19.2® fluent® commercial solver was used to understand the level of accuracy of the RANS equations using the SST-k-ω model in predicting the aerodynamic performance of the present model. To achieve computational accuracy 2D unsteady simulation was used for relevant H-Darrieus rotors computation [25]. Figure 4 demonstrates the geometry layout for the present simulation based on the information in Table 1.

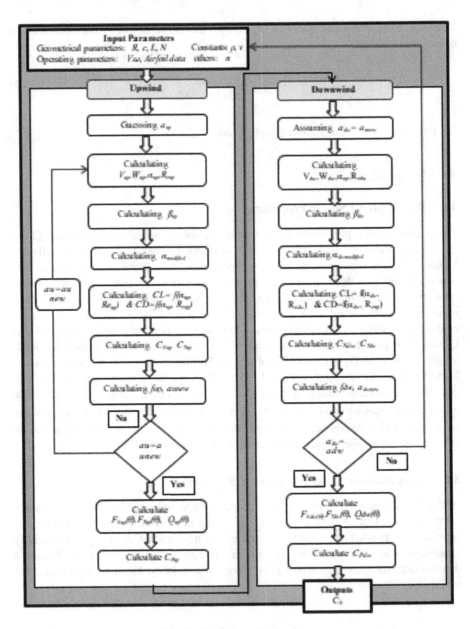

Fig. 3. DMST model algorism.

Table 1. Simulation parameters.

Parameters	Dimensions
Airfoil	S1046
c	0.09
R	1
N	3
Inlet velocity	9
Simulation type	2D unsteady
Model	SST-$k\omega$
Pitching mechanism	Fixed and variable

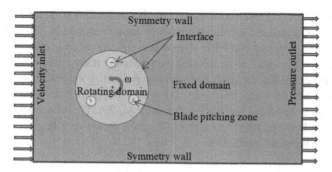

Fig. 4. Model geometry

Mesh Independence Study. To get improved quality of mesh spatial discretization, the triangular mesh has been taken place in the three sub-domains i.e fixed domain, rotating domain, and blades edge seen in Fig. 5. To obtain the grid-independent result, positioning the shape of surface mesh refinement on the computational sub-domain was done [30]. This can be achieved the relative velocity of the blade reaches a maximum value when the first mesh cell distance becomes at the nearest position. Hence the meshes are metric by the maximum Skewness value was 0.56488 at 0.043112 standard deviations. The mesh growth rate i.e element size of the blade subdomain to the blade edge was increased by 1.2 and its geometry consists of 401,877 nodes and 796,507 elements when the blade edges element sizes were 0.001 as several divisions.

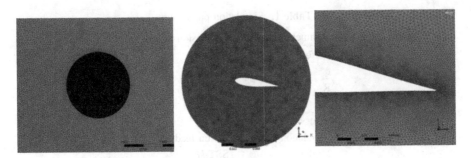

Fig. 5. Mesh generations; full domain, zoomed blade sub-domain, and around blade edges (left to right).

Solution Setup. A 2D pressure-based U-RANS formulation is used for numerical simulation and is a suitable solver for time-dependent analysis [28]. To capture implicit velocity-pressure coupling SIMPLE algorithms with the second-order upwind scheme were selected for the spatial discretization method using finite volume analysis [29, 30], which was executed for the unsteady simulations with good resolution. To compute dynamic force and unsteady flow field sliding mesh approach was used to behold the flow physics of the rotating and blade subdomain [6, 29]. This effectively computes the relative motion between fixed and rotating domains by interpolating the domain's flow quantity under transient conditions.

3.3   Models Validation

Once an optimized simulation is done, immediate comparisons were performed with experimental scientific pieces of literature which were conducted on small scale VAWT. The turbine design specifications are presented in Table 3 the torque calculated by CFD simulations well agreed with Yang et al. [36] presented in Fig. 6. Except for a little overestimation of the current investigations the results are well agreed with the previous work. This delay was due to the 3D simulation effect at low TSR rather than the airfoil type used (Table 2).

Table 2. Comparison literatures.

Dimensions	N	c (m)	l(m)	S(m^2)	V (m/s)	Airfoil type
I. Paraschivoiu; 2002 [25] (Sandia 2m)	3	2	5.877	2.5944	variable	NACA0012
Yang et al.; 2018 [36]	2	2	0.265	2.4	8	NACA0021

Similarly, Fig. 6 and 7 demonstrates both results in the present study (i.e. DMST and CFD at λ = 2.5) are agreed each other except some bet of delay was observed on the CFD side. In general, it is logical to say the present numerical results well agreed with Sandia 2 m wind tunnel result [25], considering multiple loss factors and the present design parametric advantages i.e. airfoil type, VP-blade design, and 2D effect.

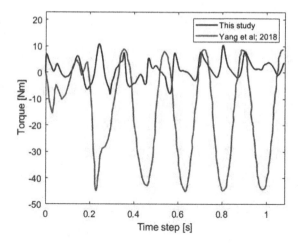

Fig. 6. A turbine torques comparisons.

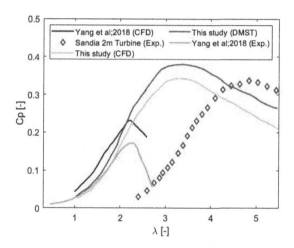

Fig. 7. Power coefficients comparisons.

4 Results and Discussions

4.1 Effect of Airfoil and Reynolds Number

Reynolds number (Re) plays a significant role in the performance of VAWT. The lower Re suffers turbine performance slope degradations and which leads the turbine unable to self-start. Hence, the turbine Reynolds number effect on the lift generation was done for five different airfoils presented in Fig. 8. At the same instant of chord (c) length, the performance comparison of airfoils was done within Reynolds number range 2.5×10^5

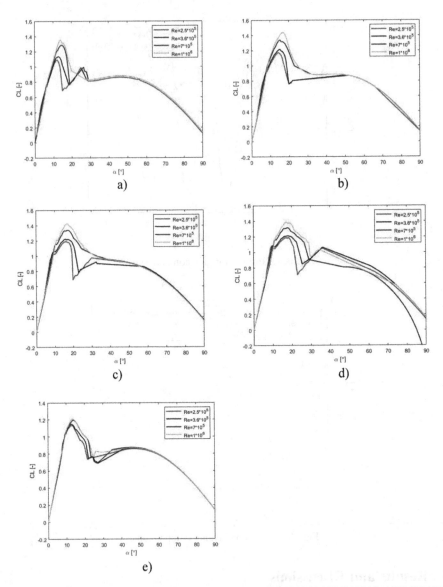

Fig. 8. Reynolds numbers affect different airfoils. a) NACA0012 b) NACA0015 c) NACA0018 d) NACA0021 e) S1046

to 1×10^6. The result shows that CL was increasing with Reynolds number until stall angle of attack. It demonstrated; all NACA-series airfoils are highly sensitive to Re values, and these are agreed with the result presented in [4]. While the lift coefficient of the S1046 airfoil is no longer disturbed with the change in operating Reynolds number because S1046 airfoil profile crossover NACA-series airfoils at the same camber scale.

According to Fig. 8 NACA0015 is the best performance at a high Reynolds number (Re $\geq 7 \times 10^5$) since it has a higher lift coefficient (CL). However, the detached flow has occurred at a low angle of attack (α) and it can be confirmed that S1046 airfoils offer a higher lift coefficient (CL) at a low Reynolds number ($2.5 \times 10^5 \leq$ Re 3.6×10^5). This shows S1046 airfoil significantly suppressed the flow separation at low AoA and augments the turbine performance.

4.2   Turbine Loading Conditions

Figure 9 comprises the simulation tangential force coefficient of the examined rotor with the design parameters presented in Table 1, from $-90°$ to $270°$ azimuth angles at an approximate TSR between 1.285 and 5.4. disregarding the dynamic stall effect, the results are agreed with the previously studied VAWT loading conditions [25, 37]. The maximum tangential force coefficients in the upwind and downwind sides of the present study were obtained at $-10°$ and $170°$ azimuth angles respectively. The instantaneous tangential force coefficients corresponding to upwind and downwind sides in the previous studies occurred at $10°$ and $210°$ azimuth angles respectively [25, 37]. However, deviations have occurred on both sides of the rotor. This is since the airfoil profile used in the study affects blade instantaneous loadings. Generally, the simulation gives suitable results at different combinations of TSR and pitch angles.

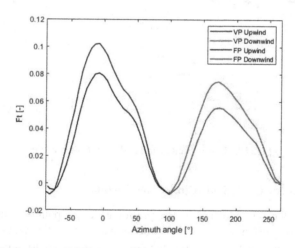

Fig. 9. Tangential Force coefficient at different azimuth positions.

4.3   The Turbine Self-starting

Figure 10 demonstrates the performance of the turbine with emphasis was computed by the proposed implementations under the range of $-5°$ to $5°$ pitch angle (β). The minimum simulated self-starting power coefficient (0.1691) was obtained at low TSR ($\lambda = 2.0769$) when the blades are fixed at a $3°$ pitch angle. This is approximated to the conventional performance of small-scale vertical axis wind turbines (i.e. $C_P = 0.17$). The maximum performance ($C_P = 0.45$) was determined at $\lambda = 3$ and $3°$ of β. But a small increment in β (approximately $3°$) reveals a significant increment in the C_P up to the limit of VAWT performance, I.Paraschivoiu (64% V∞) [25]. Hence, C_P is significantly dependent on the blade pitch angle (β). Similar effects of blade pitch angles on VAWT performance are presented in [37] which are in agreement with the current findings.

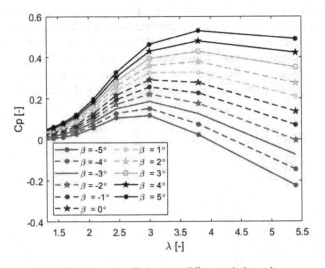

Fig. 10. Power coefficients at different pitch angles.

4.4   The Moment Coefficient (Cm) of the Turbine

Table 3 shows the optimum parametric presiding design point's obtained from the DMST model for CFD simulations. The process starts setting the rotational velocity of the turbine (ω) and then calculating the time step required to rotate one degree, Eq. (25), taking into account the relation between radians and degrees. This implies that for the whole range of TSR values from which we want to obtain the turbine performance, the time step must be changed accordingly. Figure 11 demonstrates the performance comparisons of VAWT with fixed and variable blade pitch angles which are obtained from CFD simulations. As was expected, the highest turbine performance was obtained when the blade is configured at a positive pitch angle. In the case of fixed pitch ($\beta = 0°$), the minimum and maximum C_m at DP3 were -0.071 and 0.0703 respectively. Under a similar simulation parameter (i.e. DP3), when the blade pitch angle varied to 3° (see Fig. 11c), the minimum and maximum rotor performance rose to −0.0409 and 0.15714 respectively.

$$\Delta t_{1^o} = \frac{1}{\omega(rps) \times 360}$$

(25)

Table 3. Rotor speed with a corresponding time steps.

Design point (DPs)	Rotor speed (rad/s)	Time step sizes (s)	TSR [-]
DP1	7.2	0.000385802469	1
DP2	14.4	0.000771604938	2
DP3	21.6	0.001157407407	3

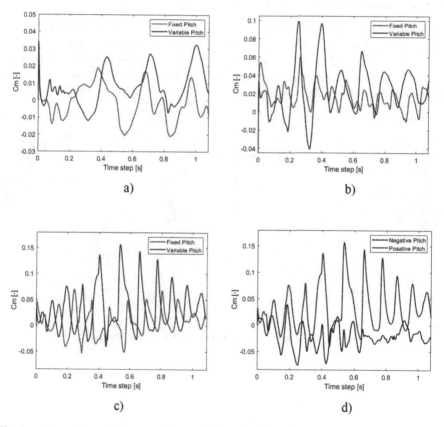

a)

b)

c)

d)

Fig. 11. Moment coefficients at different TSR. a) λ = 1 b) λ = 2 c) λ = 3 d) positive pitch (λ = 3) and negative pitch (λ = −3)

This shows that the turbine blade with a 3° pitch angle offered the maximum moment coefficient (Cm = 0.16) which is 37.2% higher than the turbine at zero pitch angle (Cm = 0.07). This shows blade pitching at a larger positive angle decelerates the turbine flow separation which occurred at low AoA and it enables the turbine to self-start. Next, the use of negative pitch angle (β = −3°) of the turbine blade was investigated. As can be seen in Fig. 11d, the rotor performance with inward (negative) and outward (positive) pitch angles are computed. It can be shown that blades with a positive pitch angle of 3° afforded a better performance improvement at every time step. This shows that the H-Darrieus rotor with positive blade pitch angle plays a significant role in the performance alleviation than negative pitch once. In addition to that, the rotor performance was depending upon its TSR. It indicates the turbine performance was slightly increased with TSR. Even though the performance was lower at TSR (λ = 1) (Fig. 11a), VP-rotor provides early starting at the initial time step.

4.5   Pressure Distributions of the Turbine Blades

Unsteady pressure and velocity contours have been plotted to understand the flow physics of the H-Darrieus wind turbine at two different pitch angles (i.e. 0° and 3°). Also, Fig. 12 and 13 demonstrate the velocity and pressure contours of the H-Darrieus rotors in the two different blade configurations. In the case of the FP rotor, the global pressure contour was at the range of (2.264 × 10)^2 to −(9.168 × 10)^2 Pa (Pa).

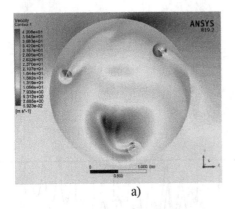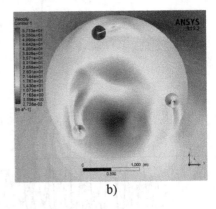

a)   b)

Fig. 12. Velocity contours. a) Fixed pitch b) Variable pitch

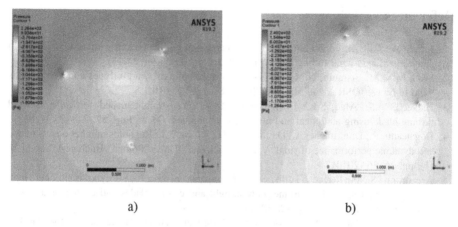

a)   b)

Fig. 13. Pressure contour. a) Fixed pitch b) Variable pitch

5 Conclusion

The current study reveals the performance analysis of straight blade H-Darrieus VAWT using DMST and CFD models. The important aspects of these studies include airfoil profile, optimum rotor design points, and blade pitch angles with TSR. Additionally, 2D unsteady flow with the same airfoil was also analyzed using CFD. All these results are analyzed to make a clear performance comparison between FP and VP H-Darrieus VAWT and the result was validated with numerical and wind tunnel experimental studies. The following conclusions are drawn:

- S1046 airfoil provides a higher lift-drag ratio than the other symmetrical NACA-sires airfoils used in this study. This is because the thickness of the S1046 airfoil reduces flow separation and its performance is no longer disturbed with the change in operating Reynolds number.
- Instantaneous aerodynamic loads (tangential force coefficient) acting on the upwind side of the rotor is higher than the downwind side once. This is because of the free-stream wind velocity reduced by upstream and downstream induction factors consecutively.
- The minimum performance (CP = 0.1691) requirements to enabling the rotor for self-starting at low TSR was obtained at the outward blade pitch angle ($\beta = 3°$). While at the same aerodynamic conditions but with blades in inward pitch angle ($\beta = -3°$) the corresponding rotor performance becomes too low. Hence, positive pitch angles exhibited superior performance than negative blade pitch angles.
- From the flow physics of the rotor, it has been seen that the greater pressure difference across VP-blades meaning enhanced aerodynamic performance of this rotor.

The present study has shown that small-scale symmetrical S1046 airfoil straight blade H-Darrieus rotor with VP configuration possess higher power coefficient and moment coefficients than FP blade. Once the present design will be scaled up or modified with a 3D-CFD model then future researchers can compare their findings with this work.

References

1. Johari, M., Jalil, M., Mohd Shariff, M.: Comparison of horizontal axis wind turbine (HAWT) and vertical axis wind turbine (VAWT). Int. J. Eng. Technol. **7**(4.13), 74–80 (2018)
2. Saad, M.M.M., Asmuin, N.: Comparison of horizontal axis wind turbines and vertical axis wind turbines. IOSR J. Eng. (IOSRJEN) **4**(08), 27–30 (2014)
3. Hameed, M.S., Afaq, S.K.: Design and analysis of a straight bladed vertical axis wind turbine blade using analytical and numerical techniques. Ocean Eng. **57**, 248–255 (2013)
4. Bogateanu, R., Dumitrache, A., Dumitrescu, H., Stoica, C.I.: Reynolds number effects on the aerodynamic performance of small VAWTs. Sci. Bull. Univ. "Politeh" Bucharest, Ser. D **76** (1), pp. 25–36 (2014)
5. Armstrong, S., Fiedler, A., Tullis, S.: Flow separation on a high Reynolds number, high solidity vertical axis wind turbine with straight and canted blades and canted blades with fences. Renew. Energy **41**, 13–22 (2012)
6. Hashem, I., Mohamed, M.: Aerodynamic performance enhancements of H-rotor Darrieus wind turbine. Energy **142**, 531–545 (2018)
7. Islam, M., Fartaj, A., Carriveau, R.: Analysis of the design parameters related to a fixed-pitch straight-bladed vertical axis wind turbine. Wind Eng. **32**(5), 491–507 (2008)
8. Kirke, B., Lazauskas, L.: Limitations of fixed pitch Darrieus hydrokinetic turbines and the challenge of variable pitch. Renew. Energy **36**(3), 893–897 (2011)
9. Kirke, B., Lazauskas, L.: Enhancing the performance of vertical axis wind turbine using a simple variable pitch system. Wind Eng. **15**(4), 187–195 (1991)
10. Paraschivoiu, I., Trifu, O., Saeed, F.: H-Darrieus wind turbine with blade pitch control. Int. J. Rotating Mach. **2009** (2009). https://doi.org/10.1155/2009/505343
11. Shuqin, L.: Magnetic suspension and self-pitch for vertical-axis wind turbines. Fundam. Adv. Top. Wind Power, 233–248 (2011). https://doi.org/10.5772/22598
12. Hwang, I.S., Min, S.Y., Jeong, I.O., Lee, Y.H., Kim, S.J.: Efficiency improvement of a new vertical axis wind turbine by individual active control of blade motion. In: Smart Structures and Materials 2006: Smart Structures and Integrated Systems, vol. 6173, p. 617311. International Society for Optics and Photonics (2006)
13. Paraschivoiu, I.: Double-multiple streamtube model for studying vertical-axis wind turbines. J. Propul. Power **4**(4), 370–377 (1988)
14. Ayati, A.A., Steiros, K., Miller, M.A., Duvvuri, S., Hultmark, M.: A double-multiple streamtube model for vertical axis wind turbines of arbitrary rotor loading. Wind Energy Sci. **4**(4), 653–662 (2019)
15. Manwell, J.F., McGowan, J.G., Rogers, A.L.: Wind Energy Explained: Theory, Design and Application. Wiley (2010)
16. Zhao, Z., et al.: Study on variable pitch strategy in H-type wind turbine considering effect of small angle of attack. J. Renew. Sustain. Energy **9**(5), 053302 (2017)
17. Zhao, Z., et al.: Variable pitch approach for performance improving of straight-bladed VAWT at rated tip speed ratio. Appl. Sci. **8**(6), 957 (2018)
18. Mohamed, M., Ali, A., Hafiz, A.: CFD analysis for H-rotor Darrieus turbine as a low speed wind energy converter. Eng. Sci. Technol. Int. J. **18**(1), 1–13 (2015)
19. Ghasemian, M., Ashrafi, Z.N., Sedaghat, A.: A review on computational fluid dynamic simulation techniques for Darrieus vertical axis wind turbines. Energy Convers. Manage. **149**, 87–100 (2017)
20. Li, Q.A., Maeda, T., Kamada, Y., Hiromori, Y., Nakai, A., Kasuya, T.: Study on stall behavior of a straight-bladed vertical axis wind turbine with numerical and experimental investigations. J. Wind Eng. Ind. Aerodyn. **164**, 1–12 (2017)

21. Castelli, M.R., De Betta, S., Benini, E.: Effect of blade number on a straight-bladed vertical-axis Darreius wind turbine. World Acad. Sci. Eng. Technol. **61**, 305–311 (2012)
22. Beri, H., Yao, Y.: Double multiple streamtube model and numerical analysis of vertical axis wind turbine. Energy Power Eng. **3**(03), 262 (2011)
23. Saber, E., Afify, R., Elgamal, H.: Performance of SB-VAWT using a modified double multiple streamtube model. Alex. Eng. J. **57**(4), 3099–3110 (2018)
24. Paraschivoiu, I.: Double-multiple streamtube model for Darrieus in turbines (1981)
25. Paraschivoiu, I.: Wind Turbine Design: with Emphasis on Darrieus Concept. Presses Inter Polytechnique (2002)
26. Mohammed, A.A., Ouakad, H.M., Sahin, A.Z., Bahaidarah, H.: Vertical axis wind turbine aerodynamics: summary and review of momentum models. J. Energy Resour. Technol. **141** (5), 050801 (2019)
27. Du, L., Ingram, G., Dominy, R.G.: Experimental study of the effects of turbine solidity, blade profile, pitch angle, surface roughness, and aspect ratio on the H-Darrieus wind turbine self-starting and overall performance. Energy Sci. Eng. **7**(6), 2421–2436 (2019)
28. Balduzzi, F., Bianchini, A., Maleci, R., Ferrara, G., Ferrari, L.: Critical issues in the CFD simulation of Darrieus wind turbines. Renew. Energy **85**, 419–435 (2016)
29. Alqurashi, F., Mohamed, M.: Aerodynamic forces affecting the H-Rotor Darrieus wind turbine. Modell. Simul. Eng. **2020** (2020)
30. Nguyen, M.T., Balduzzi, F., Bianchini, A., Ferrara, G., Goude, A.: Evaluation of the unsteady aerodynamic forces acting on a vertical-axis turbine by means of numerical simulations and open site experiments. J. Wind Eng. Ind. Aerodyn. **198**, 104093 (2020)
31. Wang, Y., Shen, S., Li, G., Huang, D., Zheng, Z.: Investigation on aerodynamic performance of vertical axis wind turbine with different series airfoil shapes. Renew. Energy **126**, 801–818 (2018)
32. Mazarbhuiya, H.M.S.M., Biswas, A., Sharma, K.K.: Low wind speed aerodynamics of asymmetric blade H-Darrieus wind turbine-its desired blade pitch for performance improvement in the built environment. J. Braz. Soc. Mech. Sci. Eng. **42**(6), 1–16 (2020). https://doi.org/10.1007/s40430-020-02408-0
33. Menter, F.R., Langtry, R.B., Likki, S., Suzen, Y., Huang, P., Völker, S.: A correlation-based transition model using local variables—part I: model formulation (2006)
34. Castelli, M.R., Dal Monte, A., Quaresimin, M., Benini, E.: Numerical evaluation of aerodynamic and inertial contributions to Darrieus wind turbine blade deformation. Renew. Energy **51**, 101–112 (2013)
35. Kavade, R.K., Ghanegaonkar, P.M.: Performance evaluation of small-scale vertical axis wind turbine by optimized best position blade pitching at different tip speed ratios. J. Inst. Eng. (India) Ser. C **100**(6), 1005–1014 (2019)
36. Yang, Y., Guo, Z., Song, Q., Zhang, Y., Li, Q.A.: Effect of blade pitch angle on the aerodynamic characteristics of a straight-bladed vertical axis wind turbine based on experiments and simulations. Energies **11**(6), 1514 (2018)
37. Vitale, A.J., Genchi, S.A., Rossi, A.P., Guillermo, E.D., di Prátula, H.R.: Aerodynamic performance of straight-bladed vertical axis wind turbines: a practical open source implementation. Int. J. Renew. Energy Res. (IJRER) **8**(2), 1025–1037 (2018)

Author Index

Printed in the United States
by Baker & Taylor Publisher Services